Zeppelin!

Zeppelin!

A BATTLE FOR AIR SUPREMACY IN WORLD WAR I

RAYMOND LAURENCE RIMELL

© Raymond Laurence Rimell, 1984

First published in Great Britain in 1984
by Conway Maritime Press Ltd, 24 Bride Lane,
Fleet Street, London EC4Y 8DR

ISBN 0 85177 239 0

Design and layout by Linewrights Ltd,
Chipping Ongar, Essex

Typesetting by Witwell Ltd, Liverpool

Printed and bound in Great Britain by
The Thetford Press Ltd, Thetford, Norfolk

*To all those whose names appear
throughout the following pages,
this book is humbly dedicated*

Frontispiece: William Leefe Robinson, 1895–1918

Contents

Foreword   7
Preface   8
Acknowledgements   9

I   THE COMBATANTS
1   The Strange Arena   12
2   'The Terror Weapon of the Skies'   18
3   The Raids   30
4   The Defences   54

II   COURAGE AND SELF-SACRIFICE
5   LZ37, 7 June 1915   62
6   Of Flaming Bullets and Other Things...   75
7   SL11, 3 September 1916   84
8   L32/L33 ('The Great Double Event'), 24 September 1916   117
9   L31, 2 October 1916   139
10   L34/L21, 27/28 November 1916   152
11   L22, 14 May 1917   165
12   L43, 14 June 1917   171
13   L48, 17 June 1917   177
14   L23, 21 August 1917   193
15   Carrying the Fight   197
16   L70, 5 August 1918   206
17   L53, 11 August 1918   217
18   Zeppelin Swansong   227

APPENDICES
I   German Airships Destroyed by Aircraft in World War I   234
II   Home Defence Squadrons up to 1916   235
III   Technical Data: The Airships   235
IV   Technical Data: The Aircraft   236
V   The Roll of Honour: British and Canadian Pilots   238
VI   The Roll of Honour: German Airship Crews   238
VII   Camouflage and Markings   240
Notes   242
Bibliography   251
Index   253

Foreword

Air Marshal Sir Frederick B Sowrey KCB CBE AFC

It was probably inevitable that I should be interested in Zeppelins, being born between the two wars, and brought up by those who had not only seen them in the sky but also fought against them. With so many reminders close at hand, particularly amongst my own family, they tended to be very personal and it was only with wider reading that the Zeppelin raids could be seen in their true perspective.

Ray Rimell's masterful description of the saga of the Zeppelin enables this to be done, and this book will remain the definitive authority for the future. The story unfolds with the broad sweep of policy and describes the raids themselves together with details of the combatants. It is a story of many parts, particularly remarkable for being the first opportunity for the strategic use of air power, although limited by the capability of equipment and the experience of those involved. One can only admire the technical ingenuity used to overcome the immense problems in the first complete war in the air and to recognise that, in spite of the advanced engineering involved, both offence and defence were literally working in the dark on the frontiers of existing knowledge. For the first time, the civil population of Britain was in the front line and ran the same risks as those in uniform. Civilians were the participants and together with those involved on the ground with the defences of Britain – the anti-aircraft gunners and searchlight crews, the mechanics of the Royal Flying Corps and Royal Naval Air Service, those in the air defence organisation, the police, wardens and firemen – ran into millions. Those who actually fought one another at close quarters in the air in full view of this vast audience seldom reached three figures in any particular action and had the popular appeal of few against many.

It is natural with the perspective of time that we should now be more concerned with the combatants as individual people and the overall achievements of the German Army and Naval Zeppelin campaign against this country. Although the actual damage inflicted on military targets in Britain was not all that great, the depressing effect on civilian morale was considerable, particularly as there seemed to be no answer to the Zeppelins' ability to raid Britain with near impunity for almost two years. This book meticulously weaves these threads together as seen from both sides in the struggle, and it makes enthralling reading.

The swing of advantage for offence or defence ebbs and flows as organisation is improved and technical innovations forged in the crucible of war. The major turning point was barely one month in the late summer of 1916 when, by extraordinary coincidence, three pilots from the same flight of the same squadron shot down three raiders in flames within sight and sound of the previously dispirited population of London. The result was electric – the Zeppelin was no longer invulnerable.

The death in action of *Korvettenkäpitan* Peter Strasser, Leader of Airships, in one of his beloved ships virtually ended the Zeppelin as an offensive weapon of war. If his vision had been tempered with greater flexibility, if he had listened more to his subordinates, if meteorology had been more precise, equipment more reliable, navigation and bombing more accurate, and advantage taken of the high altitude 'Height-Climbers' to operate by day above the range of the defences, the outcome might have been different. But this is pure speculation – the facts are that the men involved on both sides did their considerable best in an entirely new dimension of war to the full extent of human courage and resilience.

One last word. The book brings out the inescapable truth that there are no victors amongst the people in war. One nation's victory in any battle is another's tragic loss. This should help to strengthen our resolve to deter future wars – rather than having to fight them. In this way we can continue in an uneasy peace to salute those on both sides in the earlier days of the century who flew so confidently into the unknown.

Frederick Sowrey

Preface

Very few people ever go there now. Just a handful of relatives, interested local historians and perhaps one or two senior citizens who may have known him in their youth. Flowers are placed on the grave regularly by the staff of a heavily patronised nearby restaurant which bears his name over its broad entrance. Every year when Armistice Day comes around, extra wreaths and bouquets are sent from those who still revere the last resting place of a famous airman. He lies in a small weed-strewn cemetery at Harrow Weald, just a few miles from the author's study, and over the many years since his death history has served him ill.

I make no apology for the extended biography of Captain William Leefe Robinson VC that appears in this book. Being the first to bring down a raiding airship single-handed over English soil, his achievement marked the turning point of a most remarkable story. For the destruction of *SL11* over Cuffley in September 1916 forms the key chapter to this overall history of the aeroplane-versus-airship campaign of World War I. Yet it would be unfair to make this chronicle concern itself with just one man, for there were several other individuals who destroyed airships in mid-air. Some of them, like Warneford VC and Culley, are familiar names, while others, such as Pyott and Watkins, have enjoyed scant attention hitherto. My self-imposed task has been to describe in detail the actions of courage, perseverance and self-sacrifice performed by these pioneer members of the Royal Flying Corps, Royal Naval Air Service and Royal Air Force and their opposite numbers in the German Army and Naval Airship Divisions. Further, in order to give the reader a more general picture, several chapters detail the evolution of purpose-made armaments and the aircraft, equipment and materials at the disposal of both combatants.

During my many years of research, the main intention was to present a truly pictorial account of the events described, with particular emphasis on relevant photographs; only with the generosity of my publishers and the kind assistance freely given by individuals the world over has this been possible, and the result is a unique collection of archival material. It should be stressed that a high percentage of the photographs which appear throughout the following pages do so for the first time since World War I and are in themselves of significant historical interest as 'The Great War' slips ever deeper into our past.

As to those many individuals without whose help this book would have been impossible to create, readers will find them fully listed elsewhere, but I take a further opportunity to express special thanks to Douglas Hill Robinson. A world authority on the Zeppelin, Dr Robinson has generously supplied valued material from his extensive files and photographic collections together with constant encouragement and friendly advice. To *Herr* Kurt Puzicha, of the *Marine-Luftschiffer-Kameradschaft* in Hamburg, I also extend my grateful thanks for continual help with regard to the German side of the story.

The 'giant killers' have all gone now. I was extremely privileged to have met and talked with three of them, and to a man they were modest, quietly spoken and while enthusiastically answering all my questions took great pains to play down their part: as far as they were concerned, of course, it was just another job. It is for them and their German counterparts that I have written this book, and I sincerely hope that the reader will pause to consider the courage and skill of those protagonists who fought what must rank as the strangest battles in the whole history of aerial combat. Hopefully the memory of their deeds will linger on, serving as an example for future generations to aspire to whatever the years ahead have in store.

R L Rimell

Acknowledgements

Although this book is the result of single-handed research, with all the hazards which that entails, it could never have been completed to the author's satisfaction without the unstinting assistance and encouragement freely given by scores of correspondents and institutions the world over. For reasons of space it has been quite impossible to list each and every individual who has assisted the author, and of necessity the list below must remain incomplete. To them – all of them – I owe a great debt of gratitude and I now take this opportunity to thank those concerned for all their valuable contributions and helpful advice.

Undoubtedly the most enjoyable hours of research were spent interviewing ex-servicemen, and it is to my deep regret that not one of the three 'giant killers' with whom I talked have lived to see their deeds recounted in these pages. Thus special thanks and appreciation of some never-to-be-forgotten hours go to the late Captain G W R Fane DSO, the late Squadron Leader F D Holder OBE MC JP DL, and the late Captain B A Smart DSO.

To the following relatives of gallant airmen who supplied not only many anecdotes and letters but also their cherished photo albums, I am indebted: Mr Peter Cadbury; Mrs Marguerite Culley; Mrs Phyllis Fane; Lt Cdr Robert Leckie; Capt I V Pyott's son-in-law Mr D McKenzie; Capt W L Robinson's nieces Mrs Rose David and Mrs R G Libin; Lady Saundby; Miss Mary Sowrey; Air Marshal Sir Frederick B Sowrey KCB CBE AFC; Capt S R Stammers' sister Mrs Vera Tate; Major D Tempest; Mr H R Tempest; Mr N E Tempest; Sub-Lt R A J Warneford's sister Mrs Jeanne Dodington and stepbrother Group Capt M P C Corkery AFC RAF (ret); and, last but by no means least, *Frau* Hertha Mathy, wife of *L31*'s respected commander.

I must also express deep appreciation to the following individuals who gave up so much of their time on my behalf: Mr Peter Amesbury, who provided sorely needed photographs and material on German airship commanders; Messrs J R Barfoot, J Bennett and Chaz Bowyer; Mrs D Buck; Mr F Cheeseman; Major E N Clifton; Messrs J Colinson and P G Cooksley; Miss R E Coombs of the Imperial War Museum; Mary Delahunty; the late Capt J Edgecumbe; Mrs Mary Gibson; Sir Victor Goddard KCB CBE MA; Messrs B Gray, H E Hervey and E Hildesheim; Mr A H Vernon Hillier of the Fleet Air Arm Museum; Mr I D Huntley; Mrs Joy Jones; Mrs D Lambert, Messrs R S Larby and P S Leaman; Mr G W Lees, headmaster (ret) of St Bees School; Mr G S Leslie; Rev C K Macadam of Stonyhurst College; Mr C V McCann of the Imperial War Museum; Mrs W Millar; Messrs R Morgan, R G Moulton, and E A Munday; Mr R W Raby of the Civic Centre, Harrow; Group Capt W S O Randle CBE AFC DFM of the RAF Museum; Mrs Sue Vincent; local colleague Mr Colin Rust, for constant help with the Robinson story; Mrs K Rimell; Mr V Sheppard; Mrs E Smith; Messrs G E Smith and I Stair, the late Mr F W Thompson and the late Mr D Wheaton; Messrs H Woodman and P Woollacott; various members of Cross and Cockade (GB and USA), The Society of World War One Aero Historians; and the ever-willing staff of The British Newspaper Library, the Canadian Air Force Archives, The Cater Museum, the Essex Records Office, the Fleet Air Arm Museum, the General Register Office of Harrow Civic Centre, the Hertsmere UDC, the Imperial War Museum, the Ministry of Defence, the Patents Office, the Pinner Library, the POW 1914/18 Dining Club, the Public Records Office, the Royal Air Force Museum, The Shuttleworth Collection and the Ulster Historical Foundation. Acknowledgements are also due to the editors of local newspapers and periodicals in Essex, Hertfordshire, Humberside, Kent, London, Middlesex, Norfolk, Suffolk and Surrey who published my appeals for information, and to the hundreds of senior citizens in those areas who responded as a result.

I am grateful to the following institutes, newspapers and publishers for permission to use extracts and illustrations from relevant documents and works: the *Barnet Press*; William Blackwood and Sons Ltd; Geoffrey Bles; The Bodley Head; BBC Television; the Cambridge University Press; Cross and Cockade (USA); the *Daily Express*; the *Daily Mail*; the *Daily Mirror*, the *East Anglian Daily Times*; the Essex Records Office; Evans Brothers Ltd; Faber and Faber Ltd; Gale and Polden Ltd; the *Harrow Observer*; the Imperial War Museum; William Kimber and Co Ltd; Model and Allied Publications Ltd; John Murray; the Oxford University Press; the Public Records Office; *Punch*; the Royal Air Force Museum; *The Stonyhurst Magazine*; and *The Times*. Extracts from 'Pilots' Reports Relating to Destruction of Zeppelins' and 'CB1265: German Rigid

Airships' (Crown Copyright) are reproduced by kind permission of the Controller, Her Majesty's Stationery Office, London.

Finally, gratitude is expressed to my parents, Mr and Mrs L W W Rimell, for their forbearance; to Mr J M Bruce ISO MA FRHistS FRAeS and to Dr Douglas H Robinson for checking through the completed manuscript; to Roger Chesneau for much helpful advice; to Jek Mistry for line drawing work; to Ms Brenda Norrish for photographic assistance; to Keith Thomas BSc for German and French translations; and especially to Mrs Julie Stilwell, who competently tackled the daunting task of typing the manuscript.

Such help as I have received in no way relieves my responsibility in presenting an accurate account: obviously there are still gaps that need to be filled and I would stress that any errors, either of omission or of fact, are entirely of my own making. Further, although much use was made of official records, the text does not necessarily reflect official opinion. In closing, the author invites additional information and corrections on all aspects if they originate from reliable sources in order that this history be recorded with the accuracy it deserves.

R L Rimell

PART ONE
THE COMBATANTS

CHAPTER 1

The Strange Arena

> *'... Then Lieutenant Brandon got over one of the Zeppelins. He dropped several bombs, which did not appear to have any effect, but making a swift dive downwards, he dropped three more bombs and believes he smashed the back of the Zeppelin ...'*
>
> The Daily Telegraph, Monday 3 April 1916

Location: Hage, Germany
Time: Dawn

As the early morning March sun slowly breaks over the landing field, four hundred and sixty-eight members of the station ground troop are already at work. Towering above the mist-enshrouded scene are four giant structures: hangars, each measuring over 600ft in length and almost 112ft in width. Even now their doors are slowly being dragged open, and soon the sounds of deep-throated motors will be heard echoing around their cavernous interiors. Petrol, water and highly inflammable hydrogen gas are being piped into menacing shadowy forms beyond the doorways. Heavy wooden barrows loaded with strange pear-shaped bombs are busily being ferried to and fro.

At 11.00hrs, 33-year-old *Kapitänleutnant* Joachim Breithaupt discusses the weather prospects with his subordinates. The general consensus of opinion is that conditions for a bombing mission are ideal – the raid is 'on'. Strident blasts of whistles and klaxons following this decision rudely shatter the comparative peace of the surroundings. At the sounds, the ground troop is put on immediate standby as four groups of heavily garbed naval officers make their way to the imposing sheds beyond them.

Breithaupt climbs into the forward control car of his command, and his eyes meet those of the watch officer. The commander receives the welcome news that nearly everything is ready, but there is a slight delay whilst awaiting last-minute reports of atmospheric conditions.

L15 was built at Löwenthal and took to the air for the first time on 9 September 1915. The Zeppelin is shown landing at Nordholz. *Nora* and *Norbert* sheds loom in the background and the landing party is already on the field.
F Moch

These eventually arrive from the dark yellow tethered kite balloons, invisible *Drachen* lost to view high above the field.

On the shouted command 'Airships – march!', the mysterious denizens of the 91ft tall sheds are gingerly walked out one at a time. Scores of men firmly grip trailing handling ropes and metal grab-rails on aluminium engine cars. Very soon, the ominous grey shapes take on more tangible form and gradually the blunt noses of Germany's 'aerial cruisers' are revealed. On the bows of one, the legend 'L15' has been marked in stark black characters. The naval Zeppelin *L15*, builder's number LZ48, is a 'p' type ship built at Löwenthal and took to the air for the first time six months previously.[1] The vessel is enormous. Just over 536ft long and with a diameter of 61ft, the airship contains a gas volume of 1,126,400 cu ft and is pushed along at 59mph by four Maybach 4M HSLu engines. The greyish look of the undoped outer cover serves to emphasise the elephantine appearance of this sinister machine.

In the forward control car there are few creature comforts. Instrumentation and navigational equipment are spartan and utilitarian – an altimeter, thermometer, airspeed indicator and a liquid compass that all too often freezes up at high altitude. Radio equipment, though powerful, is unreliable, and the deafening roar and fumes from the adjacent engine add to the unease of the crew.

Manoeuvring the Zeppelins out and clear of their sheds is a delicate operation: even a slight crosswind at this juncture will be sufficient to smash the lightly constructed leviathans into the hangar sides. A trellis-work of duralumin girders braced with taut steel cables that encloses the gas cells, the petrol and the oil tanks, the water, the bombs, the machine guns, the ammunition and the crew needs careful handling, especially when just one unlucky spark could turn an entire ship into a vast funeral pyre.

However, there are no such mishaps, and once withdrawn from their hangars the Zeppelins are prepared for take-off by their crews. Sudden flashes of sparks and puffs of smoke from the long exhaust stubs of the engine cars precede the sound of motors coughing into life as the ships slowly begin to ascend. Heading for the coast, Breithaupt steers low over the Friesian Islands. The mist is still heavy but as the Zeppelins climb to 2000ft the weather becomes clearer and the airships, now seven in number, begin to form up. Later, at 17.30hrs, two vessels, *L9* and *L11*, turn back after developing mechanical defects over the Dutch islands near Vlieland.

In *L9* the 'defect' is serious: a bracing cable on the forward control car has parted and has been carried into the propeller arc. With the engine continuing to run, the cable inexorably winds itself around the propeller shaft, buckling supporting struts and pulling the car towards the hull. Before finally shattering, the 17ft wooden propeller tears into the overhead gangway and severs a number of girders, part of the central catwalk, armoured radio cables and control wires for ballast sacks and elevators. A section of splintered blade tears through a gas cell and, now alarmingly nose-heavy, the Zeppelin nearly pitches into the sea. Only rapid action by the crew, stopping all engines and dropping forward ballast, saves the situation.

Temporary repairs are effected as the Zeppelin limps back to Nordholz, leaving its companions to continue towards their objective. Hours pass and occasionally crew members of *L15* spot one or other of their consorts in the clouds and wave cheerfully. Eventually the ships draw near to the coast and several go their separate ways. The last rays of the sun vanish over the distant horizon as Breithaupt orders the drop of more water ballast. *L15* rises slowly to 5000ft and the bombs hanging vertically in their racks amidships are fused and prepared.

The commander awaits nightfall, then in company with *Kapitänleutnant* Heinrich Mathy in *L13* crosses the English coast at Dunwich and steers a course via Ipswich, Colchester and Danbury, flying at 7200ft. Cursory fire from 6pdr guns at Thames Haven, Kynochstown and Pitsea herald the airships' arrival, and a searchlight beam or two probe hesitantly amongst the clouds. These are rapidly left astern; further inland there is only darkness and silence, and Breithaupt is obliged to drop parachute flares to fix his ship's position. This has to be done on more than one occasion and is cause for anxiety, for the flares illuminate the night sky brilliantly and although vital for the navigator they serve as a bearing for British defences ranged below. The night is warmer than expected, and in spite of dropping all remaining water ballast Breithaupt cannot get his ship up to a safe enough attack altitude. Flying dynamically at 8500ft, and alone, *L15* steers towards the clearly visible winding ribbon that is the River Thames and on to the target area. At 21.30hrs the Zeppelin lies north-east of the capital of England.

Location: London
Time: Evening

London in 1916, and for the first time the very heart of the British Empire lies open to direct attack by an enemy. Now a war is being brought literally to the doorsteps of civilians. Decades of comparative peace, complacency, advancement and security – legacies of the Victorian and Edwardian eras – leave Londoners ill-suited to adapting to modern warfare. The heavy surge of patriotic enthusiasm so popular in 1914 has quickly evaporated after the realisation that the war would not be 'over by Christmas'.

Wartime is bringing many changes. Nightclubs have increased in popularity as the more traditional 'pubs' begin to lose their patrons – new regulation hours for serving alcohol are obviously making their mark. Even different social classes are beginning to mix as the sharing of common experiences cuts swathes through long-cherished etiquette. Newspapers become smaller, train services are being restricted, people are dressing more economically. Even

Kapitänleutnant Joachim Breithaupt (right), commander of *L15*, whose successful career in the German Naval Airship Division came to a dramatic end on 31 March 1916 when *L15* was brought down in the Thames Estuary. Breithaupt was repatriated after the war. He is seen with *Kapitänleutnant* Franz Stabbert, killed on 20 October 1917 when *L44* was shot down by AA fire at St Clement, France.
Archiv: Marine-Luftschiffer-Kameradschaft

more astonishing, suburban housewives are seen scrubbing their own doorsteps as smart, well-to-do businessmen carry home their spouses' shopping. Whisky is becoming more expensive – and weaker – while the postal service is even slower than usual.

On this particular Friday evening, daily problems are mainly forgotten and life carries on as normally as the circumstances permit. Nevertheless, many nervous pairs of eyes frequently glance upwards towards the stars. Recent Zeppelin raids are a matter of great concern: scores of men, women and children killed and mutilated, property destroyed, social lives ruined. Worst of all, there seems to be no defence against these 'Hun' raiders, these German airmen whom the newspapers and the public are not slow to dub 'baby killers' and 'barbarians'. The British home defence forces, as yet unblooded, come in for a great deal of angry criticism. Much of this is directed at the young men of the Royal Flying Corps and, indeed, three weeks previously, after a raider had successfully bombed Hull and left for home unscathed, frustrated civilians stoned an RFC tender and mobbed and hurled abuse at a young flying officer.

Perhaps serving as a welcome distraction from such horrors, the theatres and music halls, though now subject to 'amusement tax', are doing great business. Tonight patrons can see Moya Mannering in the hugely popular *Peg o' My Heart* at the Globe or Charles Hawtrey and Gladys Cooper in *Please Help Emily* at the Playhouse. The cinemas also thrive and a great many are showing official war films daily. At the Pavilion, Marble Arch, they are packing them in with the stirring *Britain Prepared*, which is billed as a 'cinematic survey of His Majesty's Naval and Military Forces'.

The newspapers, too, are full of war news, heavily censored of course although few readers are aware of the fact and avidly digest the latest reports of Allied victories. Letters to the *Daily Mail* cover a wide variety of topics, several guaranteed to spark off controversy. A Mr James of Bristol is concerned about the loss of a registered letter and the Post Office's reluctance to accept responsibility, and William Woodward FRIBA requests architects to exclude all articles of 'German and Austrian origin' from their buildings. In a few weeks' time it will be the anniversary of the terrible *Lusitania* tragedy, and J Landfear Lucas of Surrey, in an open letter to the Bishop of London, requests the setting up of a suitable memorial to the 'blood-lust of a Christian State'. In *The Daily Telegraph* there is a reward offered for anyone who finds a lost Pomeranian dog, 'white with a green harness and bells', and there are appeals for donations to the Ladies' Emergency Committee of the Navy League. All gentlemen staying in London are invited to lodge at Sutherland House in fashionable Norfolk Square, Hyde Park; terms are reasonable, from 30s per week and 5s per day, and the guests are promised freedom from the 'unrest of larger hotels'. For those requiring transport, a large pantechnicon is being offered for sale, 'Well bottom, light running, screw brake, perfect condition throughout, nearly new. Price 55 guineas complete'. The well-established British School of Motoring is advertising for women to become 'motor drivers' and will also instruct them in the gentle arts of 'mechanism and running repairs'. Travellers to Australia can voyage by P&O Line twin-screw steamers. The *Orsova*, 12,036 tons, leaves London on 5 May and arrives in Naples just ten days later. On a sadder note, the death is recorded of Lieutenant Gerald I Mortimer of the Royal Fusiliers; only son of Mr and Mrs Frederick Kerr of 80 Palace Gardens Terrace, the 22-year-old temporary captain has been killed in action just three days previously.

One of the day's main news stories is of the continuing strikes hitting the country's war industry. Over the last few days, 30,000 jute workers at Dundee, 20,000 Glasgow munitions workers and 15,000 Liverpool dockers have all downed tools. The men are unhappy with the long hours, poor working conditions, loss of privileges, rehousing into lesser dwellings, and their feeling of working just to line the pockets of their employers. Ben Tillett, the 'Dictator of Tower Hill', writes in the *Daily Mail* about the 'tragedy of the Clyde'. Whilst considering the disruption at the docks as having 'elements of betrayal', he goes on to state that 'long hours and overtime have been the rule and not the exception. Body and brain alike have been fatigued. Weariness due to physical strain, temper due to the greyness and monotony of their lives, have made them fit subjects for the promptings of revolt...'

But as evening passes into night, all today's papers are momentarily forgotten; so is drinking, dancing and the cinema. Policemen are riding round the streets blowing whistles and bearing placards advising civilians to 'take cover'. Anti-aircraft guns begin to bark while searchlight beams probe the heavens. The 'Bloody Zepps' have returned.

In the control car of *L15*, Breithaupt and his fellow-officers take on an eerie aspect as the searchlight beams flash around the windows, illuminating their faces. Guns below are now flinging shells towards them from all directions. Some burst uncomfortably close. The watch officer lays prone, observing the ground through field glasses, while gunners on the exposed upper platform keep a sharp lookout for hostile aircraft. Any observations will be passed through the speaking tube directly to the control car. Diligence is soon to be rewarded.

Second Lieutenant Claude Alward Ridley, flying a BE2c biplane from Joyce Green, attacks *L15* but loses the ship in the darkness. British gunners on the ground are more fortunate. An NCO in charge of the Perry Street searchlight is astonished when he receives the order to uncover the lamp. By pure chance the powerful beam immediately envelops the bows of Breithaupt's ship. Thus caught, the Zeppelin is fired on by the 3in gun at Brent and then held in the beams of five more searchlights. Instantly, guns at Abbey Wood, Erith, Plumstead Common, Plumstead Marsh, Purfleet and Southern Outfall engage the enemy.

Location: North Woolwich
Time: 21.40hrs

Lieutenant Smith, Sergeant G H Cooper and seven gunners of the Regular Royal Artillery are on standby to repel any invaders. Twenty-seven guns are ranged around London but tonight, 31 March, just seven fire upon the airships, and even then some will only discharge a few rounds at extreme range. The British 3in gun used by the gun teams is designed to take shells consisting of an 18pdr case and a 13pdr projectile. Each shell weighs just over 12lb and can be hurled to a vertical range of 18,000ft at a velocity of 2500ft per second. The rate of fire is 15 rounds per minute, the gun can traverse through 360°, and the elevation reaches 90°. For the time being at least it seems the ideal weapon for use against Zeppelins.

The Woolwich gun team observe their comrades' fall of shot, which tonight is extremely accurate. Over Wennington Marshes, *L15* receives two hits almost simultaneously in the stern, and the immediate loss of gas from ripped cells causes the Zeppelin's bows to rise almost vertically. Breithaupt rapidly weighs up the situation. Too busy to feel really scared, he takes stock and quickly realises that the airship's steering gear has been seriously damaged. The crew manage to regain control of their stricken craft, and to avoid more attention from the British gunners Breithaupt steers north over Rainham. At 21.43hrs the Zeppelin drops 20 explosives and 24 incendiary bombs which fall harmlessly on open fields. Flying now at 8000ft, *L15* is crossing the Rainham-Wennington road two minutes later when the Purfleet gun manages to strike the final crippling blow. Three gas cells amidships are shattered and, sinking gradually, *L15* staggers off towards the north-east. By some miracle the highly volatile hydrogen does not ignite, but the ordeal is far from over.

Location: Hainault Farm, Essex
Time: 21.35hrs

Second Lieutenant Albert de Bathe Brandon of the Royal Flying Corps straps himself to the wicker seat in the cramped open cockpit of a small fabric-covered biplane. The aircraft, a BE2c, powered by a fairly reliable 90hp air-cooled engine, spans 37ft and measures 27ft in length. A converted two-seater reconnaissance machine, the aircraft has become a makeshift night-fighter thrown into combat against the Zeppelins. Already obsolete on the Western Front and hopelessly outclassed by Fokker *Eindeckers* with their forward-firing machine guns, the stable BE is nevertheless ideally suited to its new role. Its slow landing speed is a great asset for pilots unaccustomed to the comparatively new perils of night flying. Home defence pilots also have access to a weird array of unlikely armaments.[2] These have included rudimentary rockets and, now, explosive darts and incendiary bombs. They are generally ineffectual, and in the majority of cases they prove more dangerous to RFC pilots than to the marauding airships they are trying to destroy.

Once airborne, the pilot circles the airfield, with its row of runway flares slowly fading from view as he laboriously climbs to 6000ft. It is a time-consuming process. Eventually Brandon observes a Zeppelin high above to starboard and held in the grip of several searchlights. Five minutes grind past and the Zeppelin manages to shake off the beams. Undaunted, Brandon doggedly heads for the area where he last observed the airship, a good 2000ft beyond.

West of Brentwood, *L15* is still sinking due to loss of gas, and at 21.45hrs Brandon overhauls and manages to get above the ship, a rare opportunity for home defence airmen. When he is 300ft above his quarry, Brandon leans over the leather-padded coaming of the cockpit and hurls out a batch of explosive Ranken darts. A few minutes later he hears three mild blasts followed by several others, but is unsure whether the airship has been struck or whether desperate German gunners are firing on him.

The question is soon answered, for after circling the Zeppelin's bows and flying alongside the ship Brandon is greeted by spirited machine-gun fire from Breithaupt's crew — an extremely hazardous affair considering the hydrogen escaping from the ripped gas cells around them. Prudently the RFC pilot extinguishes his machine's wingtip lights and turns again to line up the slow aircraft with the ponderous Zeppelin now passing rapidly 500ft below. Closing the throttle, Brandon glides towards the airship, pointing the nose of his BE2c to the rear of *L15*. Reaching down for incendiary darts with his right hand and holding the wooden control column with his left, the pilot attempts to place the darts into their dropping tube and is astonished to find that he has almost passed the Zeppelin. Dumping the darts hastily in his lap, Brandon flings another batch over the side. They all appear to fall wide of their target.

Such is the strange arena for two of the most unlikely protagonists in the history of warfare: the enormous lighter-than-air Zeppelin unevenly matched against the diminutive wire-braced aeroplane — a pair of early flying machines, each only a handful of years from the beginning of powered flight, thrown together in a cat-and-mouse combat in the darkness a mile and a half above London. And it is a deadly game.

Opening up the throttle, Brandon turns his machine in order to pursue the airship once more, switching on his lights as he does so. Now at 8000ft, he looks in vain for the Zeppelin, but the clouds have been kind to Breithaupt.

Brandon, still slowly descending, has now lost all sight of *L15*, and at 6000ft all he can see below him are the tell-tale lines of winking flares. Brandon makes for the airfield (which turns out to be South Farningham) and eventually lands at 23.10hrs. Inspection of the BE reveals a broken wingtip skid and Holt flare, the results of a heavy landing; more alarming are the three bullet holes in the starboard aileron, port tailplane and starboard elevator. The Zeppelin gunners' aim has been good.

Location: Zeppelin *L15*
Time: 22.00hrs

In *L15*, *Kapitänleutnant* Breithaupt and his crew, alone in the darkness, take stock of their serious predicament. With four shattered gas cells, there is a slim chance that the Zeppelin can just make Belgium. But the ship is extremely nose-heavy and the crew resort to dumping the rest of the bomb load and most of the precious fuel. Two machine guns are unbolted from their mountings and pitched over the side. These are soon followed by motor covers and spare parts in a desperate attempt to lighten the ship. Many of these hastily discarded remnants are later recovered from fields around Stock, South Hanningfield and Woodham Ferrers. Yet the efforts of Breithaupt's crew are to no avail. The commander of *L15* has already sent out brief distress signals, and after transmitting the final message, 'Need immediate assistance between River Thames and Ostend',[3] the radio set itself is also dumped unceremoniously out of the window. Soon afterwards Breithaupt picks up the River Crouch and, following the left bank, passes over Althorne at 22.25hrs and then moves on to Burnham and Southminster. He circles twice over Foulness and tests the ship's rudders but realises that the crippled *L15* can never reach the Belgian coast. The commander is now resigned to the loss of his vessel and hopes that he can pull off a soft landing in the sea, save the crew and founder the airship, thus denying the latter's secrets to the enemy. With this in mind Breithaupt orders nearly all the crew members up into the ship, leaving just two helmsmen with him in the control car.

Now only 1000ft above the waves, the crew await the end with nervous anticipation. Suddenly and without warning, *L15*'s framework at rings 7 and 11 collapses under the strain and the ship plunges towards the Thames Estuary a mile from the Kentish Knock lightship. Except for the roar of the rushing wind there is no sound as the ship falls seawards until it finally strikes the water at about 23.15hrs. Breithaupt is violently flung to the floor of the control car, which is already completely submerged; semi-conscious, he can feel his body being 'tossed around like a cork by the masses of water'[4] which roar in. Together with one of the helmsman, who loses all his teeth in the crash, Breithaupt manages to reach the surface and is eventually hauled by his comrades to the upper part of the Zeppelin's bows. The other helmsman is less fortunate: young Albrecht is the one fatality from *L15*'s crew. With no signs of the ship sinking, the seventeen surviving crew members crouch together on top of the envelope and survey the damage. Only the bows and stern are visible, the smashed middle section of *L15* being lost to view beneath the waves.

Second Lieutenant Albert de Bathe Brandon, a native New Zealander, learnt to fly at Hendon at his own expense, qualifying on 17 October 1915. Brandon played a major role in the actions against *L15* and *L33*, gaining a DSO for his part in the destruction of the latter.
Author's Collection

Royal Navy motor launches position themselves over the remains of *L15* on 2 April 1916. The tail portion, with most of its control surfaces intact, eventually sank along with the rest of the wreckage a few miles south of South Knock Buoy.
Sir Victor Goddard

An unusual view of the wrecked *L15* which reveals the translucent appearance of the fabric covering over the duralumin framework. On the control surfaces, the wire trailing edge adopted a 'scalloped' effect as the shrinking dope pulled in the fabric.
Sir Victor Goddard

On 28 May 1916 British paddle-boats towed the crumpled remains of *L15* on to Margate Sands, there to dry out at low water and afford access to naval Intelligence officers. This pile of tangled girders yielded one gondola, two propellers, several instruments, and the body of helmsman Albrecht, which the Navy buried following a short service. In June, the wreckage that remained was left to disappear under the shifting sands of Margate.
Sir Victor Goddard

An hour later, several armed trawlers surround the wreck and the commander of the *Olivine*, Lieutenant W R Mackintosh RN, rescues the Germans, who slash all the Zeppelin's gas cells before they leave. The trawlermen next transfer the crew to the destroyer HMS *Vulture*, whose captain demands that Breithaupt and his crew strip and board in groups of three. Other destroyers now on the scene attempt to tow *L15* to shore, but the framework collapses and the remains finally sink off Westgate.[5] Later in the morning *Vulture* lands her prisoners at Chatham, where inquisitive locals gather at the quayside to get their first glimpse of the 'baby killers'. A coal barge worker later gives his eyewitness account to a news reporter:

Me and my mates were busy unloading coal at about eight o'clock this morning, when we saw a torpedo boat destroyer come along and laid 18 men [*sic*]. We saw they were Germans. The chief officer was a youngish-looking chap, but very tall.[6]

Breithaupt and his men are quickly placed into separate cells at the Naval barracks and then, after much protest from the Germans, their uniforms are returned. Members of the Press are later allowed into the cells, and the London correspondent of the *New York Herald* secures a fascinating interview with *L15*'s commander:

He [Breithaupt] seized the opportunity presented by my visit to insist that the Zeppelins did not seek the slaughter of

Oberleutnant Otto Kühne of *L15* is escorted to Chatham Barracks following his capture. When he realised a photographer was at hand, Kühne turned his head away.
E E Maynard

Sergeant George Cooper's gold medallion, a much coveted and unique award presented to every officer and man on duty with London's anti-aircraft units on the night of 31 March 1 April 1916.
Author

non-combatants and women and children, saying that the object of the raids was to serve military purposes.

Breithaupt expressed incredulity when told that the latest efforts of the raiders had failed to damage any military establishments, that the houses destroyed were solely those of civilians and that the majority of lives lost were those of non-combatants.

'I am sure that the Zeppelins have effected damage to military establishments and munitions factories,' he said, but he could not give any specific information to corroborate his assertion, which is emphatically denied by the War Office and the Admiralty.

The Zeppelin Commander and his assistant, *Ober-Leutnant* Kuehne [*sic*] both speak English fluently, having many English and American aquaintances. They both declared that they at all times knew the position of their ship, and were able to identify the towns over which they were flying but when asked, 'Could you distinguish particular buildings, say churches like St Paul's or a structure like the Houses of Parliament?' each replied, 'I cannot answer that question'.

Asked point blank if they had dropped bombs during the latest raid, each officer again took refuge in the statement 'That also is a question which I cannot answer'. Both officers looked to be in the pink of condition. Their prison consists of two pleasant rooms in the barracks, where they are attended by their own servant and served with the same food as that supplied to British officers. Each acknowledged that the treatment was excellent. They are allowed daily open air exercises.

I also talked with half a dozen of the members of the Zeppelin crew, some of whom had been sailors and engineers on the Hamburg-America and North German Lloyd steamships, so they are familiar with New York and Hoboken. All of them denied any knowledge of bomb dropping. They were quite united in the statement, which apparently had been drilled into them, and declared that owing to heavy clouds, they were unable to see anything beneath them.[7]

Later the crew face more serious and rigorous interrogation by Major Trench RM of Admiralty Intelligence, and then the officers are transferred to Donington Hall in Berkshire. With the exception of executive officer Otto Kühne, repatriated in 1917, the crew of *L15* see out the war in captivity.[8]

Aftermath

At last the British home defences have been rewarded with success – albeit in unspectacular fashion. Indeed, the first that Londoners know of *L15*'s fate is when they read confused reports in newspapers over the next few days. Initial jubilation is tempered by the casualty list as a result of the raid. Breithaupt's comrades have accounted for 43 civilians killed and another 66 injured. Nevertheless, one 'symbol of frightfulness' has been destroyed and the sorely-tried RFC and searchlight and gun crews based around London have been vindicated at last.

For the anti-aircraft gunners there is an unexpected bonus in the form of gold medallions awarded to each officer and man in action that night. Several months previously, the Lord Mayor of London, Sir Charles Wakefield, had offered £500 for the first victors over a German Zeppelin. Now the money is to be turned into 353 medals. A little larger than a florin, the award is to be struck by Messrs Mappin and Webb; not designed to be worn, it nevertheless commemorates a unique victory and all those in receipt of it feel justly proud. Sergeant G H Cooper of the North Woolwich battery is one of them, although a gunner in his unit decides to put the medallion to a more practical use. An exchange at the Woolwich Pawn Shop leaves him £2 richer, but his delight is short-lived. Lieutenant Smith, the battery commander, discovers the deed and retrieves the medallion, and ultimately the £2, by stopping 1s per week from the gunner's pay.[9]

Following the destruction of *L15*, the officers and the men of C Flight, 39 Home Defence Squadron, at Hainault Farm have been heartened by the efforts of Second Lieutenant Brandon. His encounter with the Zeppelin and his use of the unreliable explosive darts have been warmly received, and although the results were inconclusive much valuable experience has been gained. Over the coming months the British defences will slowly begin to get the measure of Count Zeppelin's nocturnal raiders. Let battle commence . . .

CHAPTER 2

'The Terror Weapon of the Skies'

*'Zeppelin, flieg,
Hilf uns im Krieg,
Fliege nach England,
England wird abgebrannt,
Zeppelin, flieg!'*

Dr Adolf Saager, *'Zeppelin'*, 1916

While the turbulent history of the rigid airship is a fascinating one, it has no real place in this book. The trials and tribulations faced and overcome by Count Ferdinand von Zeppelin and his contemporaries have been more than ably recorded hitherto by specialist historians.[1] Nevertheless, in order that subsequent chapters can be viewed in their proper perspective, it is desirable that some attempt be made to describe in detail the complex construction and operation of the world's first strategic heavy bombers.

There were ten 'r' type Zeppelins constructed during 1916, of which *L33* (builder's number LZ36) was the fourth. The series continued in production, albeit extensively modified, until the end of World War I and can be considered fairly typical of the period which takes up the major proportion of this narrative. *L33* was constructed by *Luftschiffbau Zeppelin GmbH* at Factory Shed 1, Friedrichshafen, and its maiden flight took place on 30 August 1916. Commissioned on 2 September, the career of this particular Zeppelin was cut dramatically short on its first raid on England. Barely a month after completion, *L33* was attacked by aircraft and crippled by gunfire, and force-landed at Little Wigborough in Essex.

The Zeppelin struck the ground heavily but virtually intact, and recognising the value of the gift that they had unwillingly presented to the enemy, *Kapitänleutnant* Aloys Böcker and his crew fired the airship with pistol flares. Thanks to the accuracy of British defences, the riddled gas cells were almost drained and the resulting fire did little more than burn off the outer fabric covering. The British were delighted. Admiralty draughtsmen descended on the wreck, the twisted remains affording a unique opportunity of examining one of the much-vaunted 'Super Zeppelins' at close quarters. One positive result of their findings was CB1265 and 1265A (plans), generally accurate and comprehensive technical volumes which contained over 100 illustrations and exhaustive data on wartime German rigid airships and their operation.

General Construction
The typical Zeppelin frame was composed of aluminium and/or duralumin girders of various sections and thicknesses making up a number of polygonal transverse rings with radial and chord bracing cables of hard-drawn steel, the whole held together by a series of longitudinal girders. Between each of the main rings were situated the individual gas cells which filled almost the entire space when inflated to their maximum capacity. Externally the structure was covered in cotton fabric usually protected by coats of dope that also tautened the envelope. To the rear of the ship lay the flying and control surfaces, invariably cruciform in appearance, and below the hull, slung along the centreline and flanks, were gondolas carrying powerplants.

Main structure
Prior to the 'r' type class, Zeppelin hulls had featured a long cylindrical section amidships which, though doubtless speeding production, was aerodynamically inefficient. With the 'Thirties', the overall shape was considerably cleaned up, and there were fewer transverse rings of constant diameter. Paul Jaray, the Zeppelin company's chief aerodynamicist, desired an even fuller streamlined shape, yet he was overruled by his colleagues who argued that parallel sections generally afforded greater longitudinal stability and offered advantages in construction.

L33 carried 19 gas cells which were separated by the main rings (the largest spanning 78ft 6in across), firmly braced and installed at 10m intervals. These transverse rings were numbered by the factory in terms of distance in metres from the sternpost which was designated ring 0; from there the next was ring 10, then 20, and so on right up to 170 where the remaining nose rings were spaced at 8m intervals as 178 and 186. Most of the in-flight stresses were taken by the 13-sided main rings, although there were an additional 19 unbraced intermediate rings installed centrally between them. All the rings were constructed on the floor of the ring shed and built up from triangular-section girders. Once assembled these rings were carried manually into the main shed, then suspended from its roof at their predetermined distances. The vast 644ft 9in hull was formed by the addition of 13 main longitudinals lettered from top to bottom, 'A' being the top backbone girder and 'M' and 'M (starboard)' being the bottom keel girders. The longitudinals were of triangular section yet in isosceles form, with 'the longest axis in the plane of the load',[2] which constituted the main longitudinal strength of the vessel.

The upper central girder and the two lower girders which formed the base of the keel were each a double structure of 'W' section. These longitudinal girders by the very nature of their position remained the most heavily loaded of all members and consequently needed to be the strongest; additionally, the upper four port and starboard longitudinals were of heavier section and supported with thicker bracing and channels in order to cope with extra pressure that occurred near the tops of the gas cells. The remaining 12 sides of the main rings from number 20 up to 170 inclusive were stiffened up considerably by a simple truss fitted with a kingpost that pointed outwards and carried an intermediate longitudinal girder. Again these were triangular in section, although on a smaller scale, and contributed little to the overall strength of the structure. Their installation served to reduce drastically the tension on the outer covering which may well have fluttered over large unsupported areas. As a result these extra longitudinals served to give the long hull a 25-sided polygonal appearance once it was enclosed by the outer covering. These intermediate longitudinals weighed only 0.8lb per foot and when a 17ft section was tested in compression as a strut, it stood up to a load of 10,000lb before collapsing. The girders were certainly strong, and the lightness of the structure always surprises the uninitiated. A 3ft section of 'double-latticed' girder from L33 in the author's possession weighs a bare 25oz and is impossible to twist by hand.

Wiring

The internal bracing of the framework with its 'cat's-cradle' of solid, hard-drawn steel wires contributed greatly to the overall rigidity. In L33 and other vessels in the 'r' type series, an axial cable – the *Zentralverspannung* – was used for the first time in a Zeppelin.[3] Each complete gas cell contained a 10m segment which was attached by both ends to the central fittings of the adjacent main rings, the radial ring bracing also being attached to the central fittings.

Such an arrangement served to reduce considerably the various loads which were imparted to the framework should unequal pressure occur between adjacent gas cells. The diagonal bracing of the rectangular panels formed by the rings and longitudinals was provided by 15 hard-drawn steel cables; these were the shear wires, intended to distribute the heavy loads of the central keel of the ship on to the adjacent main frames.

The diameter of the cables varied from 2 to 3 mm and their ends were turned back on themselves, served with wire and soldered. Turnbuckles were not used and cables of carbon steel were cold galvanised; breaking strain tests carried out on the two main types of cable found in L33 ranged from 3750 to 10,000lb.

Flying and control surfaces

Each of the massive tail fins had their inner edges formed by one of the longitudinals, with outer edges being formed by the apex of a triangular-section girder. The vertical and horizontal fins were rigidly wire-braced both internally and externally, the latter tending to mar the otherwise clean streamlining of the hull.

Each of the rudders and elevators was controlled by two cables that ran along the lower part of the keel from the aft position to the control positions in the gondolas. The pairs of cables for the lower rudder and port elevator were painted at intervals in black and red and ran along the port side, while those opposite for upper rudder and starboard elevator were blue and green. Fairleads at each transverse ring supported the control cables, which were surprisingly flexible and boasted a hemp core and a breaking strain of 3750lb.

The keel

Structurally speaking, the keel of L33 was basically a long triangular girder frame which ran between main rings 0 and 170. It consisted of two lower girders, a catwalk support girder between these, and a top apex girder. An additional pair of box girders situated just 31in below the top of the keel supported the bombs, fuel tanks and water ballast bags amidships; this structure also supported a catwalk which measured less than 1ft wide and was constructed of plywood. Available headroom was as much as 6ft 3in amidships but reduced gradually to 4ft 6in at ring 40. Although the roof and floor were covered with cotton fabric, the catwalk sides were left open – there were no guard rails. Should an unfortunate crewman slip and be unable to save himself, he would have doubtless plunged down through the outer covering to his death.[4]

The keel, despite what one normally associates with the term, did not contribute greatly to the overall rigidity of the hull, rather it provided local strength where it was most needed. Stress points supported by the keel included gondola strut attachments, mooring points and the handling rope connections. A landing rope 410ft long together with a pair of shorter ones (249ft) were to be found coiled on hatches in the ship's nose. During landing, these hatches could be opened from the control gondola, then the ropes would be dropped and the bows of the Zeppelin gently hauled down by the ground crew. There were additional short ropes attached along the keel towards the tail.

The gas cells

L33 carried a total of 19 gas cells. Traditionally these were formed by layers of gold beaters' skin (the impermeable outer membrane of cattle caecum) which was affixed to cotton fabric with liberal amounts of glue. Each animal's skin 'grew' into its neighbour and measured roughly 39in by 6in, and a large cell required anything up to 50,000 of them. The complication of producing these high-quality cells, the skilled shingling together of the skins and the carefully controlled handling in the slaughter houses resulted in enormous expense. To fit out L33 in 1916 would have left little change out of £38,000.

The cells were thus designed to fit over the keel space and were laced to the apex girder itself. No support for the gas cells was required in the top of the ship, for the lift of the hydrogen caused the cells to press firmly against their supporting wiring and ramie cord netting. Particular attention was paid to bind rubberized tape around cable ends to avoid any tearing of the cells.[5] During inflation, handling lines attached to patches in the upper sections of the cells guided them into place at the top of the ship.

One of L33's control surfaces reveals its complex inner wire bracing. In common with all flying surfaces the section was absolutely flat and the trailing edges were formed by cable.
Flight L33/6

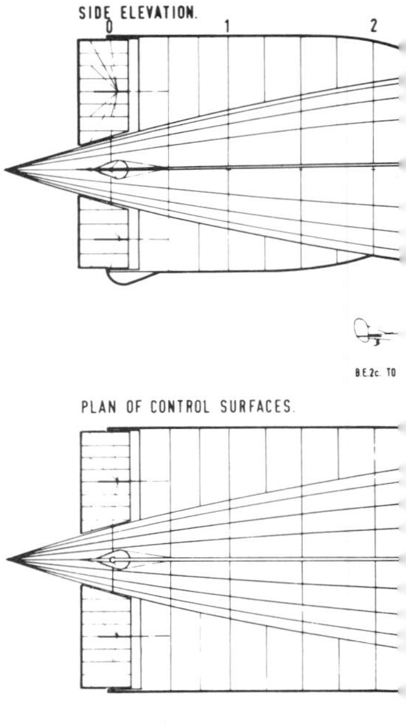

Thanks to the axial cable fitted to these ships, tears were often a problem with the gas cells. The cable passed through each of the cells and shear cables passed diagonally through ten of the largest cells from the upper girder to the keel. As a result, chafing often occurred, and the cells could be torn by cables if not carefully installed. Under interrogation one of the sailmakers from *L33* claimed that 'Rents less than four feet long and triangular tears and patches up to 18 inches or two feet can be repaired during flight. The repair is carried out simply by gathering up the slack of the gas bag round the hole and tying it off. Small punctures appear to be repaired by sticking on a patch of rubbered fabric by means of rubber solution. The larger holes, after being tied off, can be patched in a similar way'.[6]

Two types of gas valves were found on *L33*. There was an automatic valve in the bottom of every gas cell whilst some others had hand-operated manoeuvring valves actuated from the control gondola. Cells situated over the gondolas would not carry such valves and the positions of both types varied, being placed on either side without any apparent order about 38in from the ends of the cells to which they were attached. As far as *L33* was concerned, the automatic valves amidships were pre-set to blow at 22mm pressure whilst those further aft were set at 14mm.

Manoeuvring valves were fitted to cells 2, 5, 6, 7, 8, 11, 12, 14, and 15, their bodies being held to the adjacent structure by duralumin lugs.[7] Unlike many previous ships, *L33* was fitted with ventilation shafts which led from the catwalk. There were five of these, and they exited from the upper hull at rings 50, 90, 110, 130 and 150. Small wooden cowls covered the vents to some degree, the rear faces being open, and served to 'keep out the weather and induce a draught when the ship is in motion'.[8]

Water ballast sacks
There were 14 ballast bags in *L33*, arranged along the keel, all of which could be partially emptied from the control gondola by means of toggles. Made of rubberized cloth and containing 2200lb of water mixed with glycerin as an anti-

'p' Type Zeppelin L10
Manufactured by *Luftschiffbau Zeppelin GmbH*
Designed under E H L Dürr
Powerplants: Four 210hp Maybach 6-cylinder C-X
Main constructional material: Duralumin
Overall length: 536ft 5in (163.5m)
Max diameter: 61ft 4in (18.7m)
Main frame spacing: 33ft (10m)
Number of longitudinals: 19
Speed: 55mph (88.49km/h)
Cruising range: 1336 miles (2150km)
Operational ceiling: 12,800ft (3900m)
Crew number: 19 (on 3 September 1915)
Average bomb load: 2 tons
Volume: 1,126,400 cu ft (31,877m^3)
Drawings by Ian Stair

freeze, the bags had their outer sides marked with level lines, and the maximum weight of permitted ballast was clearly indicated:

Each water ballast bag consists of an inner and an outer bag. The inner bag is of parallel two-ply cotton fabric weighing 430 gms per square metre. The joints are stuck, with an overlap of 25 cms; and covered on the inside with strips 25 cms wide, of rubbered fabric, stuck on.[9]

Discharge pipes from aluminium tube were streamlined where they projected through the outer covering, and the valve-operating wires that led to the gondola passed first through the tops of each bag, then to sheaves located on supporting girders and thence met up with the toggles.

In order that the ship could be made lighter at short notice, in case of an emergency when taking off or landing, additional water ballast was carried in smaller bags of 550lb capacity situated fore and aft. Eight of these, universally dubbed 'breeches' (their shape suggested half a pair of trousers), were installed, and when the appropriate toggles were pulled they drained immediately – often to the general discomfort of ground crew personnel directly beneath!

Petrol tanks
Positions for 54 petrol tanks were provided in *L33*, although according to the authors of CB1625 'the number of tanks carried in a raid to England was usually about 30'.[10] Each of the duralumin drum-like 'slip tanks' contained '440 pounds' of fuel, although the total capacity was more in the region of 64gal. All these tanks were supported by wire cables attached to a slip-release bolt located on the girder above them. On withdrawal of the bolt the 'slip tank' could be allowed to fall straight through the outer covering if further ballast were dropped. In the keel areas directly above each engine gondola position were 148gal gravity tanks permanently fixed. The mechanics in the engine gondolas replenished these tanks as necessary by hand-pumping fuel from the 'slip tanks'. *L33* carried eight gravity tanks, in addition to the oil and water tanks above each engine position, fitted to crutches.

Bomb stowage
On its last raid *L33* carried four 660lb bombs, 40 weighing 128lb apiece, and 60 incendiary 'bombs' of 25lb each,

Some indication of a Zeppelin's intricate construction can be appreciated by this view of *L65* taken at Löwenthal in the spring of 1918 as the ship neared completion. Looking sternwards, the gas cells have yet to be installed, and, on either side, the stippled edges where the black dope terminates can be clearly seen through the outer covering. The triangular keel runs down the centre of the vessel, and the hooped climbing shaft with ladder in foreground leading to the top of the hull is noteworthy.
Luftschiffbau Zeppelin

'The Terror Weapon of the Skies'

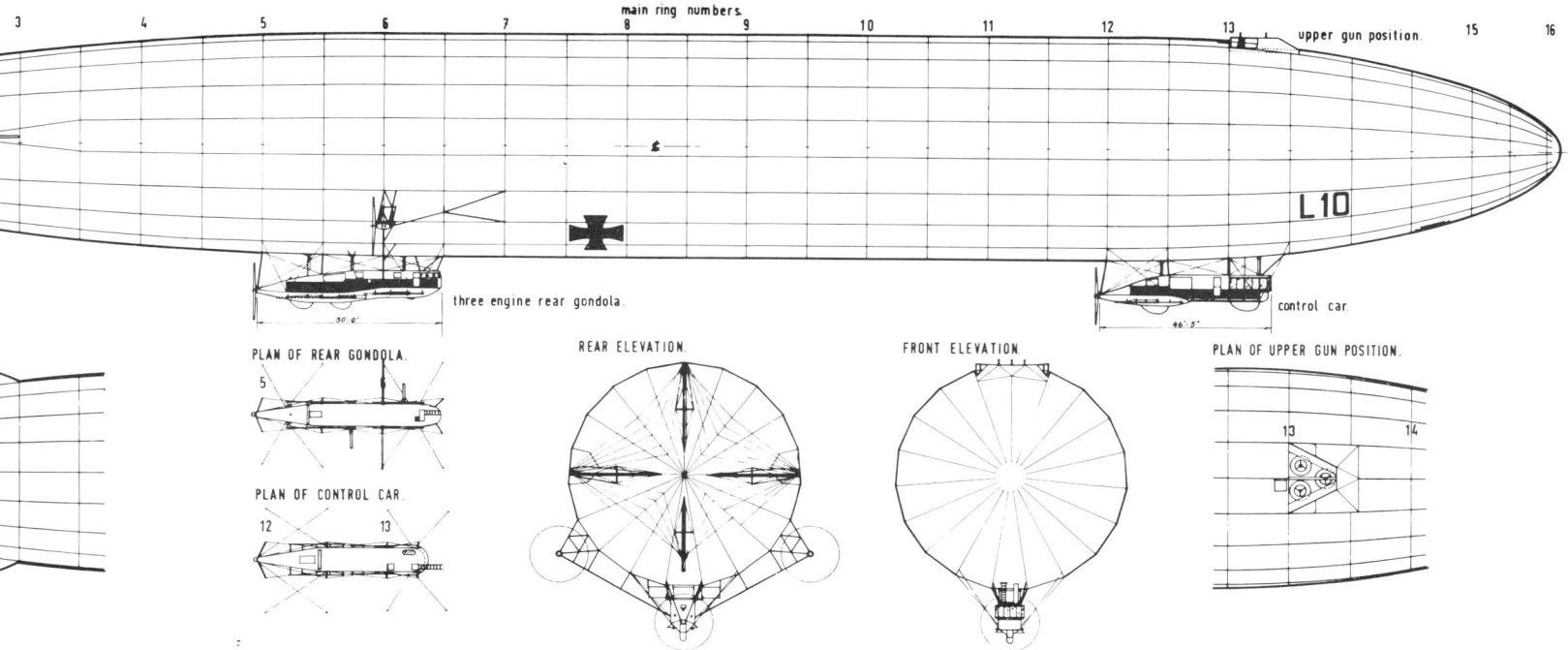

although the total load could attain almost five tons. The bombs were suspended vertically from racks amidships and under each bomb position was

> ... an opening in the outer cover above which is placed a horizontal shutter three feet two inches by seven feet three inches composed of an aluminium frame with fabric covering. At the ends of the shutter, rollers are fitted running in grooves on the frames enabling the shutter to slide freely in a transverse direction.
>
> Before dropping the bombs the shutter is moved outboard into a position clear of the opening in the outer cover, the operating wires for this purpose being worked from the control car, or locally, as desired.[11]

The release hooks for the larger bombs were attached to the main keel box girders, but smaller bombs of less than 220lb were suspended from short girders sited lower down. As a precaution against jamming, guide plates were installed at the ends of the keel uprights in each bomb position and the bombs themselves suspended as close to the shutter as possible for minimum passage through the ship. Various styles and weights of bombs were carried.

The outer covering
The frame of the ship was covered entirely in a light cotton fabric of constant weight and strength. On *L33* and most other ships the natural fabric was printed with a characteristic pattern of horizontal lines which gave the cloth an overall greyish appearance at a slight distance. The pigment used was actually ultramarine – a dark blue – and according to the prisoners of *L33* intended for protective purposes. The fabric used for covering upper portions of the gondolas was found to be of several thicknesses and finished with a dope that contained a grey pigment. A piece of such fabric from *L32* in the author's possession appears as a bluish grey close to the Methuen colour reference 21D2;[12] the fabric itself is off-white beneath the pigmented layer.

Cellulose acetate dope was used as a final finish over the outer envelope, this being colourless on the majority of 'r' type ships and earlier vessels; the upper regions of the envelope were initially left untreated to allow the emission of hydrogen. The covering was applied in a circular fashion around each section of the hull and firmly laced together with strong, three-ply cotton rope through eyelets, plenty of stitching and fabric strips. On later Zeppelins the covering was applied longitudinally using 65ft by 130ft sections.

Crew Stations
Gun platforms
On the upper hull were situated two gun platforms for defence against hostile aircraft. The main platform at the bows was located just forward of ring 160, and its floor, of corrugated duralumin sheet 0.32in thick, supported three sturdy tripods. The weapons were Maxim-Nordenfelt machine guns, standard German Army patterns of 8mm calibre. Ammunition belts 22ft long held 250 cartridges, weighed 40lb each and were stowed in duralumin boxes, two per gun. The rounds were a mixture of armour-piercing and explosive shell, the latter being supplied in the ratio of ten to one. Additionally the guns were swathed in heavy cloth jackets when not in use to prevent their cooling water freezing solid.

In order to reach the platform, crewmen climbed an access shaft which was constructed of channel rings 16in apart and

Typical bombs carried by naval Zeppelins. In order of weight these are 660lb, 220lb, 110lb, two 22lb explosives, and a pair of incendiaries to left and right of the cart. The men are gripping bomb fuses, and in front of the 660lb explosive bomb stands a parachute flare; the latter, made of thin sheet iron, carried an 8ft 6in diameter black gingham parachute inside the nose cap.
Archiv: Marine-Luftschiffer-Kameradschaft

Zeppelin!

just over 2ft square. Once outside on the platform, which boasted strong rails and a folding canvas wind fairing, communication to the control car some 60ft below could be made via a voicepipe with a separate whistle, or via two gongs worked by cables.

Aft of the upper rudder, near the extreme tail of the ship, another gun platform was installed. This was constructed of 0.2in thick plywood covered with cotton fabric on top. The machine gun was mounted on the central girder just beyond the rear of the platform, giving a wide firing arc. No more than two crew members were permitted in this position at any one time, and a placard to that effect was mounted in the cockpit. Access was gained by a small sloping ladder, the foot of which rested upon a plywood platform just behind ring 0 and level with the catwalk which terminated at this station. The gunner kept in contact with the control gondola by telegraph, which was often disconnected as crews considered it a fire hazard. Operationally, in fact, the platform guns were used with the utmost caution.[13] If the ship's cells had been rent by shrapnel or if the ship was rising with full gas cells, escaping hydrogen hissed upwards, forcing the gunners to hold their fire against attacking aircraft:

> I was forbidden to fire my machine gun on the platform just when and where I pleased. I had first to report to the control car, so that the men down there could prevent the ship from rising up into the mantle of inflammable gases while I was firing.[14]

In view of the small targets afforded by attacking aircraft, and since most raids were nocturnal, it is hardly surprising that a Zeppelin's defensive guns were generally ineffectual.

The control gondola
The forward gondola was rigidly fixed below the centreline of the Zeppelin some 72ft from the extreme nose. It contained the controls for rudders, elevators, gas cell valves and water ballast, the bomb release switchboard and bomb sights, the engine telegraphs, the trail and handling-rope release, the voicepipe and bells to the forward gun platform, crew space and bomb positions, a telephone to the aft gun platform, a wireless transmitter cabinet and a small space to man the machine guns. Immediately behind the control gondola was the forward engine car containing one Maybach HSLu 6-cylinder motor driving a large propeller through a spur reduction gear. Both cars had identical dimensions: aft was the control gondola, forward the engine car, the 2–3in gap between them faired by a laced fabric strip. Two facing doors on each gondola provided access from one to the other. Externally the two gondolas formed an impression of a single long car but the fact that they were separated, however slightly, reduced air resistance, and the vibration of the engine was not transmitted to the WT gear in the control gondola. Both gondolas were completely covered in: the lower portions of the cars were clad in duralumin of several thicknesses to enable them to float on water and the upper regions were covered in light canvas over the girder framework. The addition of wooden battens fitted between the frames gave further support to the fabric. Windows were celluloid, and wood or steel tube grab-rails ran along the lower sides for ground handling.

The nose of the gondola was surrounded with Triplex and celluloid panes, and a projecting shelf permitted a downward view. It was over two windows at the front that the bomb sight was situated. The sight, manufactured by Carl Zeiss of Jena, was at the disposal of the executive or bombing officer, and an adjacent switchboard operated the electrical bomb releases.

Floor space in the gondola was at a premium, and a typical

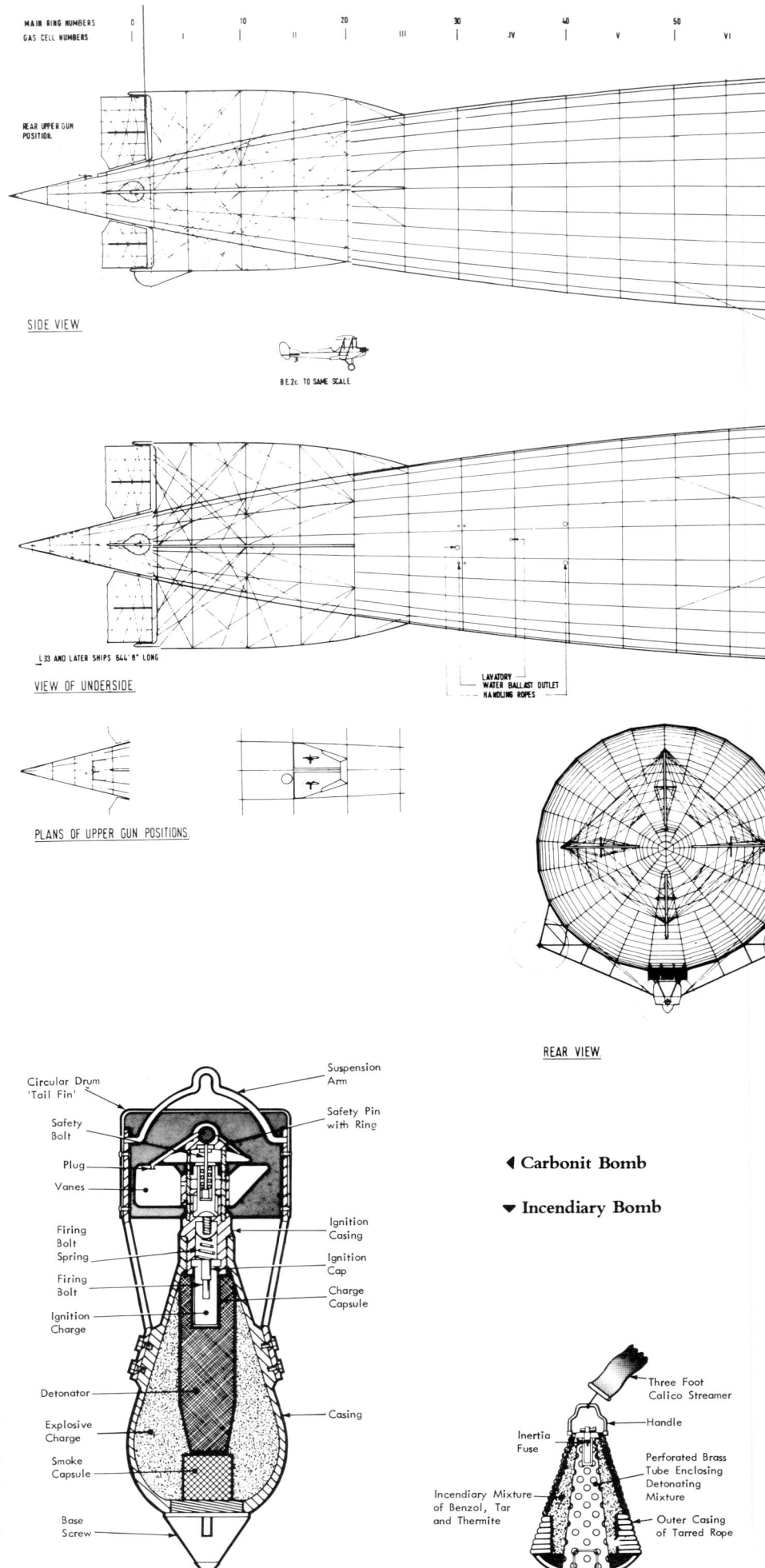

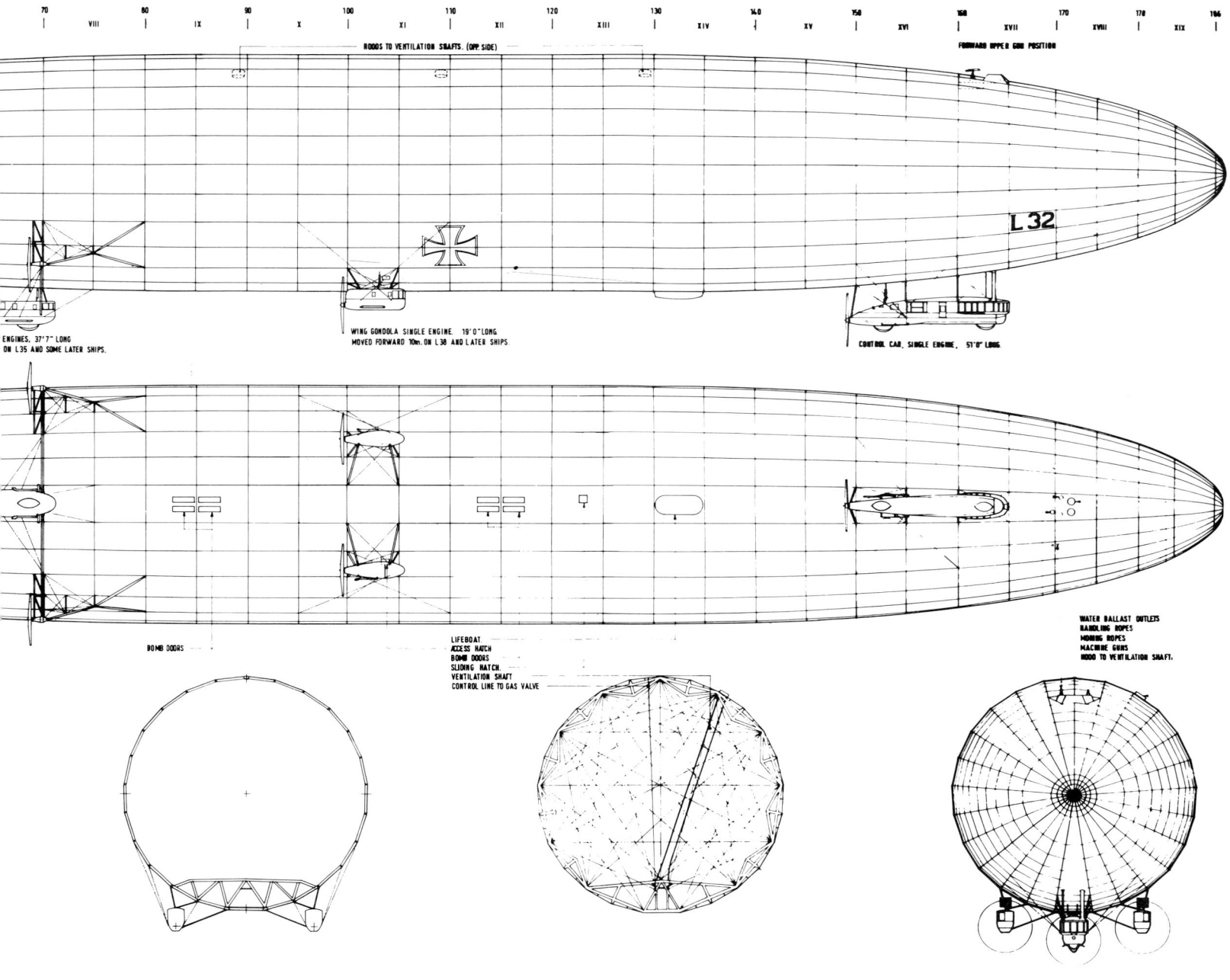

SECTION AT 105. (GAS CELL XI)   SECTION AT 110   FRONT VIEW

disposition of the crew and their functions was as follows. The rudder man was stationed well forward, where there was a small aluminium spoked wheel and a magnetic compass. The standard naval gyrocompasses were too heavy for use in Zeppelins and so a liquid type was chosen, but despite the addition of alcohol the liquid frequently froze, severely handicapping accurate navigation. On the port side of the control gondola stood the elevator man, handling the wheel which operated the elevators. Instruments for which he was responsible included the altimeter, an aneroid instrument (more correctly a barometer) that measured air pressure and was graduated to record height in metres. Like most of the other instruments, the altimeter was unreliable, for changes in barometric pressure following take-off could produce inaccurate readings requiring a radio check to correct them. The elevator man also had to check the inclinometer, which indicated the pitch of the ship, and the rate of climb indicator or statascope, which stated the rate of ascent and descent in metres per second.[15] If this were not enough there were the air and gas thermometers which were vital in determining the lift of the Zeppelin. If he were given an order so to do, the busy elevator man could also work the toggles which released water ballast, the fore and aft breeches and the manoeuvring valve handles. All of these, when connected to a common 'wheel', could be operated together and so make the ship heavy throughout its length.

The commander of the Zeppelin possessed a small chart table which was situated directly behind (*ie* abaft) the elevator man's position. From here the commander could fairly easily communicate with the engineers via telegraphs and with the upper gun platforms via the speaking tubes.[16] The executive officer was always close at hand to operate the bomb sight or more usually to station himself in the wireless transmitter cabin immediately aft in the gondola, where he coded and decoded radio messages. This cabin, heavily soundproofed with a snugly fitting door, and with a light disconnect switch and a lack of ventilation, was the warmest and therefore the most coveted station of the entire vessel. Towards the rear of the car was the so-called 'officers' lounge' with two large windows either side. Rather like the waist positions of the World War II B-17 Flying Fortress, behind each window was a machine gun.

'r' Type Zeppelin *L32*
Manufactured by *Luftschiffbau Zeppelin GmbH*
Designed under E H L Dürr
Powerplants: Six 240hp Maybach 6-cylinder HSLu
Main constructional material: Duralumin
Overall length: 649ft 11in (196.9m)
Max diameter: 78ft 5in (23.7m)
Main frame spacing: 33ft (10m)
Number of longitudinals: 25
Speed: 62.6mph (100.72km/h)
Cruising range: 2300 miles (3700km)
Operational ceiling: 17,700ft (5400m)
Crew number: 22 (on 24 August 1916)
Average bomb load: 4-5 tons
Volume: 1,949,600 cu ft (55,174m^3)
Drawings by Ian Stair

Zeppelin!

For naval Zeppelins the guns would be the heavy water-cooled 7.62mm Maxims which were usually among the first items to be jettisoned if the ship ran into difficulties.

In the separate engine gondola two mechanics tended the 240hp Maybach which drove the 17ft diameter wooden propeller. Made to fine cabinet-makers' standards, the six geared-down propellers each consisted of eight laminations of West African and Honduras mahogany, the whole unit being covered with a veneer of walnut to serve as weatherproofing. Leading and trailing edge sheathing was made from brass.

Access to the forward gondolas from the hull was via small hatches 2ft 6in square in both outer cover and gondola roof; a wooden ladder separated the two. There was one door on the starboard gondola side for use when the airship was on the ground, and entry to the engine compartment was made by climbing steps fitted up one side and stepping through an opening in the canvas covering.

Wing gondolas
Slung between main ring 100 and intermediate ring XI (heavily reinforced with a cantilever girder) were two midships wing gondolas each containing another Maybach and just enough space for the mechanics. They could reach the engines by gangways leading from the main catwalk and had provision for machine guns, although these were rarely carried.

Rear engine gondola
The rear gondola of *L33* was made shorter than in previous Zeppelins by virtue of the fact that two of the three Maybachs were installed side by side rather than in tandem. On both main gondolas landing buffers were fitted to the undersides. The buffers were shaped like small coracles, constructed from a framework of strong cane bound with cord, covered with canvas and protected by short lengths of rope sewn on. The bumper was secured to the gondolas by strong leather straps threaded through castings riveted to the duralumin. Two air-inflated bags made up from singly-ply rubberized fabric were inside each 'coracle'.

Despite the revised arrangement of the rear gondola Maybachs, the aerodynamically inefficient side brackets used in previous designs were retained, much to the detriment of the ship's performance

> ...because of the simple reversing gear which had been incorporated into the side propeller drive since the earliest days of the Zeppelin airship. Though the need to make the propellers of the small side gondolas reversible had been recognised, the development of the new gear drive, according to Dr Arnstein of the Zeppelin Company, required more time than the design and development of a new engine.[17]

The side plating of the rear gondola was carried higher than the others so that the greater rigidity required could be more easily achieved. A back-up control system was installed, together with a shelf situated forward which carried a steering wheel, a compass and an additional elevator control wheel on the port side. A pair of machine guns was also fitted, one per side window of the gondola, the latter usually manned by six mechanics.[18]

Above each of the engine gondolas were large, drag-producing, air-cooled radiators, and above the propellers, inside the outer cover, were ice shields. These plywood frames, backed by light girders, prevented lumps of ice from being slung off the outer cover into the rotating propellers and thence piercing the gas cells. In later ships the shields were made of canvas supported by cables: they were frequently shredded.

The crew
Life aboard the Zeppelins was hardly one of luxury or comfort. The complement of *L33* numbered 22 and comprised the commander, executive officer and warrant quartermaster acting as a navigator, a warrant engineer and a sailmaker (who all remained on duty throughout the flight), and two rudder men, two elevator men, two radio operators and two mechanics for each of the six engines. The ratings were usually divided up into two watches, and those 'off duty' took their ease by standing lookout behind the machine guns.

Intense bitter cold was perhaps the most serious of handicaps, and the temperature in the control gondola was invariably below freezing point. The mechanics tending the engines were only slightly better off, for the advantage of warmer surroundings was reduced by the constant throb of the Maybachs and the inhalation of noxious exhaust, petrol and oil fumes. Generally crewmen wore fur-lined jackets, trousers, gauntlets, boots and helmets to keep out the bitter cold; even layers of newspaper were used to line the coveralls. Yet all this was insufficient. Rope-soled boots as opposed to standard issue were worn in order to prevent possible sparks when clambering around the aluminium frame of the ship, and felt overshoes were often worn to cover the boots. Internal warmth was somewhat more effective, for in-flight meals were fairly nutritious:

> We got sausages, good butter, thermos flasks containing an extra brew of coffee, plenty of bread, chocolate and 50 grams of rum or brandy per man...

Cutting away at *L33*'s wreckage eventually enabled Commander C I R Campbell's men to separate one of the midships engine gondolas – the bow is to the left of the picture. In the foreground lies one of the radiators.
Flight L33/25

The fabric-covered roof of one of *L33*'s midships gondolas; the remains of a (presumably) celluloid window can be seen inside the car. Midships gondolas were mounted on rings 100 and 105 in this Zeppelin class.
By courtesy of E A Munday

We had several peculiar and very practical kinds of tinned foods, which might be described as chemical and gastronomical miracles. These were tins containing hashes and stew which were heated up by a certain chemical process as soon as you opened them. We were not allowed to cook anything on board on account of the danger from inflammable gas.[19]

Those crew members off duty would often relax, or attempt to, in hammocks slung from one of the box girders along the keel. Between rings 130 and 135 a floor of plywood measuring 6ft 8in wide served as a 'lounge area' for the crew, and an adjacent ballast bag contained drinking water. At the forward end of the crew space could be found a cleat and fairlead intended to hold a sling for a small lifeboat. Some ships had provision for a second boat on top of the hull, and this can clearly be seen in photographs of L31. These boats were to be used in the event of a forced landing on water and stemmed from the tragic L19 incident in which an entire German crew was left to drown with its ship by an indecisive British trawler captain.[20] Nevertheless the lifeboats were considered so much deadweight by most crews and were not carried by L33.

One final refinement of the 'r' type Zeppelin was the light, stamped aluminium flush toilet situated on intermediate ring IV. Self-control was required of any control gondola crewman wishing to relieve himself, for he faced a long swaying walk of over 800ft to reach the 'heads' and then return. 'Relief tubes' in gondolas and keel permitted urination at or near the crew members' positions and the two men in the gun platforms usually christened the outer cover which was often rotted by such practice.

'Flieg, Zeppelin, Flieg'

L33, like all other rigid airships built before and since, was nothing more than a large powered balloon supported in the air by a force which equalled the weight of the air displaced by the gas cells minus the weight of the hydrogen inside them. At that time the builders reckoned that if standard atmospheric conditions existed, 'barometer 760mm; relative humidity 60 per cent, and air and gas temperatures 0 degrees Centigrade, a cubic metre of hydrogen of specific gravity 0.1 would lift a load of 1.16 kg; or 72 pounds per 1000 cubic feet.'[21] Using this yardstick, L33, with its gas volume totalling 1,949,600 cu ft, would possess a gross lift of 141,200lb. However, from this figure one must subtract the overall weight of the frame, gas cells, gondolas, powerplants and covering, which in L33 totalled 75,300lb. The difference made up the useful lift which included the crew, ballast, fuel, bombs and machine guns.

Nevertheless the lift under other than standard conditions was variable, temperature changes, humidity and barometric pressure being responsible, together with air mixing into the gas and thereby increasing its weight. Warmer air temperatures or lower barometric pressures meant that the weight of displaced air was reduced and the lift of the Zeppelin correspondingly so; when the opposite of these two conditions prevailed then the lift was greater. When the gas in the cells was 'superheated', usually by the heat of the sun, it was less dense than normal, and thus lift was increased. Late at night the opposite occurred, and 'supercooling' reduced the lift.

Zeppelins were housed in giant sheds at their various airship bases. The sheds, invariably code-named, were each designed to accommodate one or two ships and featured huge sliding doors at either end. A fully loaded Zeppelin when ready to leave the ground was first 'ballasted up' in the hangar, and sandbags holding the ship down were then released. If the ship failed to rise, the commander compensated by dropping sufficient ballast for the ship to gain equilibrium and gently float. In such conditions it was theoretically possible to raise or lower the vessel, all 645ft of it, with one finger. At this juncture the executive officer jumped out of the control gondola to direct the 300 members of the ground crew who walked the Zeppelin out of its hangar. To compensate for the officer's weight in the airship, a rating of the same weight took his place in the gondola, and at the shouted order 'Airship – march!' the giant was gingerly hauled out on to the field. The Germans used only one ground handling aid for their airships – a trolley; this accessory was initiated by Dr Hugo Eckener as early as 1911. On the floor of the hangars and running out past the doors for 500yds or so were docking rails. On these ran hand-worked wheeled trucks, to which the Zeppelin was secured fore and aft by tackles, in order to prevent crosswinds from smashing the light framework against the shed doors while the ship was being extracted. Even so, accidents could, and did, happen, and the results could put the ship out of action for some considerable time.[22]

Once the Zeppelin was out into the field and clear of the hangar doors it was almost ready to go. At take-off the gas cells were invariably full, and as the engines started up and 500lb of water dropped, the ship would be made gradually lighter and begin to rise. In view of the fact that barometric pressure was reduced as altitude increased, the gas expanded and 'at a certain relative pressure'[23] the automatic

One of the L33's six 240hp Maybach HSLu engines seen here in one of the midship gondolas. The British Rigid Airship No 9 was actually fitted with one of the Maybachs salvaged from L33's rear gondola.
Flight L33/27

Inside the officers' *Kasino* (mess) at Ahlhorn. *The Times* newspaper placard refers to Schütze's raid of 5/6 March 1916, and presumably came in through one of the neutral countries.
R Frey, by courtesy of P Amesbury

Zeppelin officers usually enjoyed comfortable quarters and dining areas: many commanders lived nearby the bases with their wives and children – a unique privilege. This is at Nordholz.
P Amesbury

valves blew off, releasing sufficient hydrogen to equalise the pressure. Of course, further water ballast could be released in order for the ship to rise, or if the Zeppelin were 'heavy' due to hydrogen loss or to a rain-, snow- or hail-laden envelope. After a flight, when fuel was depleted and superheating had occurred, the ship was 'light' and the commander compensated by operating the manual gas cell valves to release further hydrogen. Degrees of lightness or heaviness could be controlled another way, this time using the dynamic lift derived from the power of the engines and flying the Zeppelin at an angle. Often a heavy ship could sustain altitude by the lift generated in flying nose-up, and conversely hydrogen could be saved by flying nose-down with a 'light' ship in order to gain negative dynamic lift. There were, however, traps for the unwary, and stalling was a likely prospect if the 'angle of attack' attitude in either plane was too great.

Flying a Zeppelin was not an easy task and relatively few men ever mastered the art entirely. Accidents were common. The term 'airship' is no idle one: the Zeppelins were literally ships of the air and shared with their sea-going brethren the problems of navigation, of operation and of always being at the mercy of the elements. Zeppelin commanders had their parallel in sailing clipper captains; indeed, before transfer to the Airship Division most reserve officers of the Imperial Navy were merchant mariners and had experience of deep-water sailing. Such experiences stood them in good stead when they were faced with controlling the operation of a rigid airship.[24]

Hardly a flight took place where some kind of emergency did not materialise. Engine failures were commonplace, either because the motors were unreliable or because at high altitude they simply failed and then froze solid. The ever-attentive mechanics could ill afford to relax their vigil and were constantly tinkering; in extreme cases even complete engine cylinders could be changed.

Structural failure was rare, but the outer covering often split and had to be quickly repaired to prevent air reaching the gas cells. Leaks, whether by wire cable chafing, bullets or shrapnel, were the responsibility of the sailmaker who faced a terrifying one-handed climb amongst the lofty frames, his free hand clutching fabric patches, dope can and brush. Sudden and extreme loss of gas was more serious, and if a midships cell emptied, severe overloading of the adjacent bay would occur. Hydrogen loss fore and aft could affect the trim considerably, and whenever this happened the engines were shut down and an attempt was made to retrim the ship. This usually meant ordering all available men to the high end first, then as a last resort physically humping all loose heavy items and pumping ballast and fuel uphill, as it were, in order to balance the ship. Sometimes the angle, whether up or down, was so acute that even these measures were not enough, and the outcome was then usually fatal.

Jammed control cables were just as deadly, and if the elevators were stuck in the 'down' position, the engines not stopped and ballast not dropped forward, the ship would dive into the ground. Fire was the extreme hazard and sparks from the engines a frequent possibility. More than one ship was lost on account of a gondola fire, and a bolt of lightning could have the same horrific effect if the ship was valving hydrogen. Invariably the crews faced a fiery death as the ship fell out of the sky; usually they jumped.

Accurate navigation in the wartime Zeppelins was almost non-existent and many commanders relied on dead reckoning or mere guesswork, which contributed largely to the overall ineffectiveness of the airship raids. Some naval commanders used a marine sextant to read the stars at morning or evening twilight. Old habits died hard, but perfect conditions needed to exist if such sights were to be taken. Even radio signals transmitted and received by the Zeppelin crews were often wildly inaccurate and were invariably picked up by the British even before the raiders reached the coast.

In *L33* there were two transmitting radios in the control gondola, a standard 1kW *Telefunken* set, the other a 40–50W apparatus. As for the wireless transmitter receiver, its circuit was divided and reception was either by crystal only or a combination of crystal and valve amplifiers. The former comprised a loosely coupled circuit, a secondary variable condenser, a silicon crystal and low-resistance telephones which were used in conjunction with a transformer.

The aerial wire, all 117ft of it, extended from the porcelain insulator in the wireless cabin. At the end of the aerial were two cables which formed a three-wire tail over 270ft in length. Various lead weights were attached so that the ship's motion would spread them out like a fan and they would not touch. A metal hand-driven drum was used to wind the aerial in, this was always done during a thunderstorm, so transmission and reception became impossible in these conditions. All of the foregoing apparatus was installed in a duralumin 'desk' (more correctly a crude cupboard) measuring roughly 5ft 6in long,

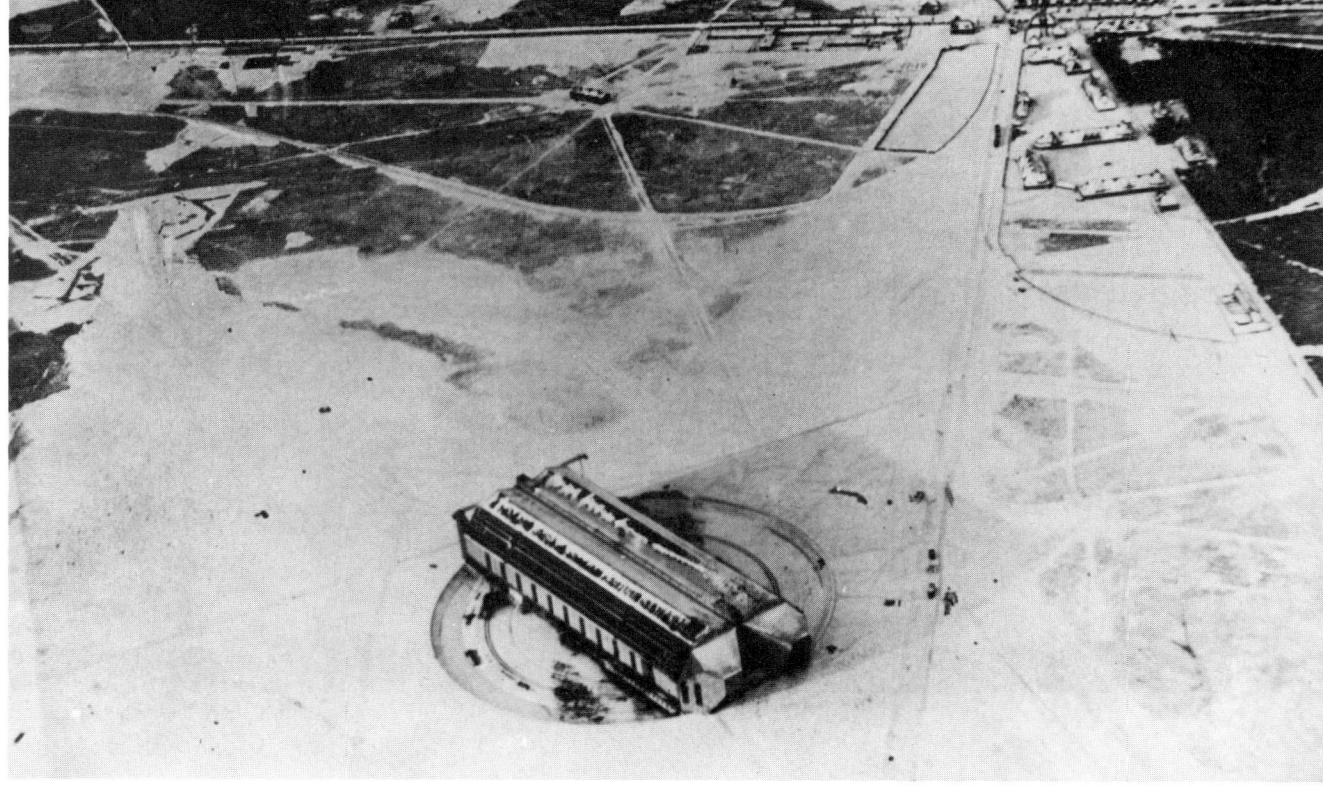

The famous revolving shed (*Drehhalle*) at Nordholz, seen here in the winter of 1917–18. Initially named *Hertha* and then changed to *Nobel*, the shed weighed 4000 tons and originally measured just over 597ft in length. Between December 1916 and May 1917 the shed was lengthened another 55ft by the addition of angular sections which officers dubbed *Busen* (breasts).
Archiv: Marine-Luftschiffer-Kameradschaft

just over 2ft in height and 1ft 8in in width. However, commanders relied somewhat too heavily on radios: in 1916 the curious phenomena of 'night effect' and 'aeroplane effect' went altogether unrealised, and positions were often off the mark by as much as 50 miles. Thus poor navigation was common, and in most cases a commander's experience, coupled with a fair degree of luck, often meant the difference between continuing an attack on England or returning to base unblooded.

As we have seen, space in the control gondola was restricted, and most of the various instruments were crude by present day standards. One of the notable exceptions was the Zeiss bomb sight, which could also double as a drift indicator if the operator was sufficiently conversant with its use. It was a complex instrument and demanded skill to use. The executive officer had first to obtain the ship's altitude from the altimeter and set it on the sight; he then produced a stop-watch and measured the ship's ground speed by timing the passage of an object between two fine 'cross hairs' roughly equating to an interval of 300m at ground level. Three compensating curves allowed the sight to be adjusted for the varying weights of bomb, including 110 and 220pdrs. At night the unit was illuminated by a small electric lamp which shone through a ruby glass, resulting in the sighting lines standing out against the dark background.

Once the Zeppelin was over the target, or what the crew imagined to be the target, the bombs could be released together, singly, or in salvos. Bombs were suspended by cables from a hook-shaped tumbler pivoted between two side plates with its opposite end shaped in the form of a transverse knife-edge. Behind this were two arms, also pivoted, which formed a catch, the upper ends being joined by a cross bar which engaged the upper end of the tumbler when cocked and its hooked end joined by another cross bar that engaged a 'bent' in the horizontal trigger. The right-hand side of the catch boasted a small arm which bore

Nobel's running track was laid in a flat-floored depression around 10ft in depth and 700ft in diameter. The floors of the double shed lay flush with the ground so that the Zeppelins could be run in and out with ease. The turning mechanism at the rear of the shed, and revolving with it, was powered by electricity, and just one lever set the entire building in motion and could stop it to within a millimetre of the position required – this being indicated on a dial by a needle showing the wind direction. The costs, both financial and in terms of precious materials, were so high that the Germans never built a second one, even though the *Drehhalle* remained the most practical method of berthing large rigids.
Bertha Dietrich, by courtesy of P Amesbury

Zeppelin!

A Naval airship, believed to be either *L45* or *L47*, over the Zeppelin building works at Staaken, near Berlin. Between the two large airship hangars is a purpose-built shed where the hull rings were constructed. The cameraman is stationed on the starboard side of the control gondola looking aft. The clumsy rear outrigger brackets seen here were discarded on later 'cleaned-up' Zeppelin designs.
Luftschiffbau Zeppelin

against a cylinder containing a quantity of mercury. The tops of the side plates were flanged outwards above the trigger and on the flanges a solenoid was attached. An armature situated behind the solenoid could also pivot, and its lower end was mortised to hold the tail of the trigger. Another pivoted bracket was screwed to the forward end of the solenoid and this tripped the mercury-filled cylinder.

To cock this complex unit, the catch was rotated until the rear cross bar engaged with the rear of the tumbler. The trigger tripped the cross bar in the hooked end of the catch and the tail of the trigger slipped into the mortice of the armature. When the electric current was passed, from the switches in the gondola, it attracted the armature head, the tail of the trigger was freed from the mortice, the catch swung clear of the rotating tumbler and instantly the bomb cleared the rack.

If the gear remained cocked, the mercury-filled cylinder rested horizontally on the arm of the catch. The mercury served to complete the lamp circuit and indicated that the bomb still hung on the rack. Once it was released the catch arm dropped, allowing the cylinder spring to depress it, the circuit was broken and the corresponding lamp on the switchboard went out, indicating that the bomb was on its way. There were two switchboards in *L33*, each fitted with six main switches, five being push-button and the other a lever. Additionally there were 25 single switches in two

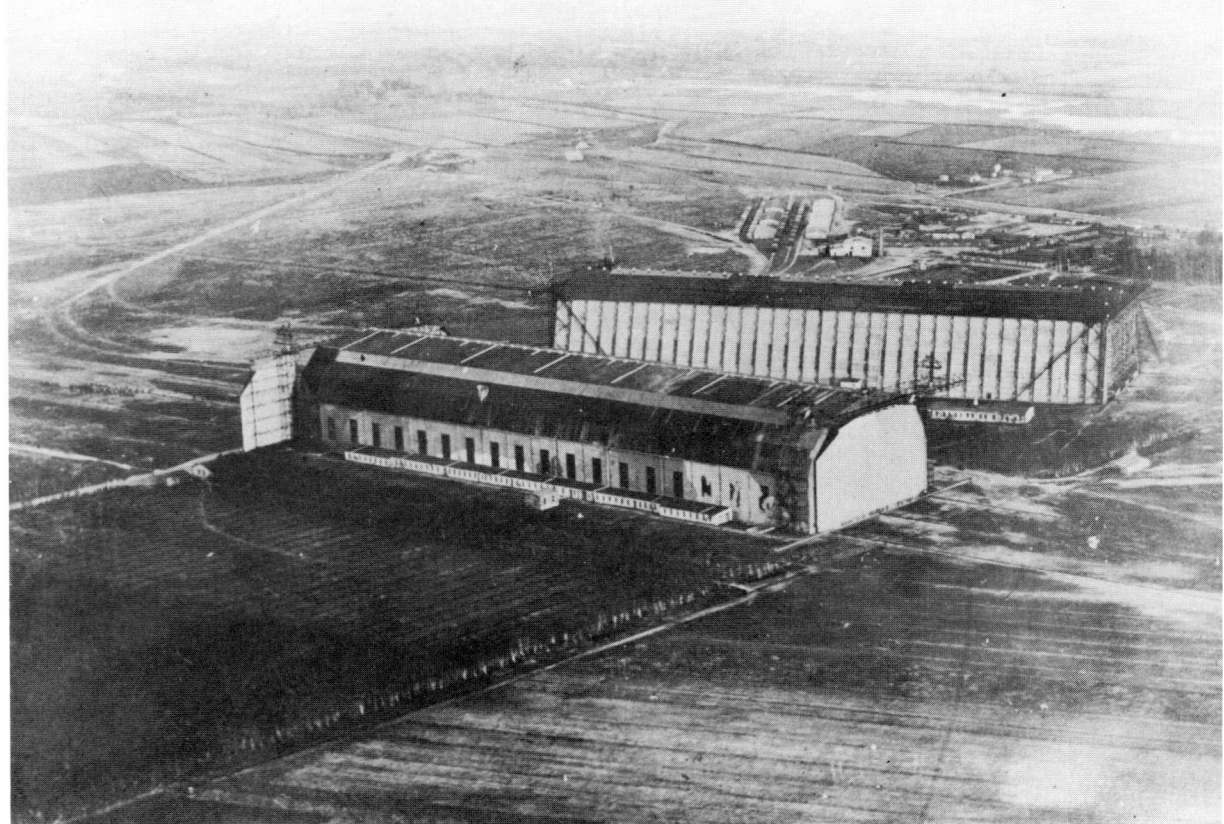

The naval airship base at Wittmundhaven which was taken over from the Army during April 1917. In the foreground is the *Wünsch* double shed, with another, code-named *Wille*, beyond it. It was customary for shed names to start with the initial, and often the second, letter of the station's location.
Archiv: Marine-Luftschiffer-Kameradschaft

rows at the top of each board, numerically identified by digits above the upper row. Of these switches (both sides), 24 were connected to a fuse in the solenoid circuit which operated the release gear and the twenty-fifth (central) switch controlled the lighting of the lamp which illuminated the board. The various main switches controlled the number of bombs dropped, closed the indicator lamp circuit, operated a voltmeter and measured the resistance of the solenoid circuit.

Even if the Zeppelin and its crew had evaded British searchlights, eluded anti-aircraft batteries, avoided attacking aeroplanes and safely completed the return flight there was still another major obstacle to overcome – landing. The commander's aim was gently to drop his ship into the waiting hands of the ground crew with the vessel being neither heavy nor light and having no forward speed. If the ship had a tendency to rise, hydrogen was released to bring it into equilibrium. Because the manoeuvring valves were prone to stick open and the cells to which they were attached could run empty in a short time, it was the doctrine in the Naval Airship Division to make the Zeppelin heavy by ascending over pressure height, gas then escaping from automatic valves in the keel. These could be checked by the sailmaker, and although if one failed to close properly no hydrogen would be lost, air might very easily be admitted.

If the ship returned heavy and with empty ballast bags, then every removable object would be ditched: ammunition boxes, fire extinguishers, tools, spare engine parts, machine guns and even the radio would follow each other out of the gondola windows. In an emergency, lift could be increased through adiabatic heating of the gas, which was effected by a fast dive from altitude. As a result the gas would be compressed, heated thereby by several degrees, and the lift thus increased.

As a final resort, a well-trained ground crew could grab the gondola hand-rails and gently ease the ship to the ground and thence back to the safety of its shed. After a thorough examination of the ship had been made, essential repairs undertaken and the vessel secured, fresh hydrogen was piped in. Gas cylinders were never brought into hangars because of the danger of fire and so were stacked outside and connected up with pipes, valves and manifolds. At the larger bases the cylinders were buried in the ground to protect them against air attack, and tunnels gave access to valves and gauges at their ends. Each cylinder contained 100m^3 of hydrogen at 100 atmospheres pressure and from them permanent piping led to the sheds and ran underneath the floors, where cloth filling sleeves were spaced at intervals.

The hydrogen itself, the lightest gas known, was often manufactured on the Zeppelin bases themselves. Produced by the Messerschmitt-patented method of passing steam over hot iron, the gas was highly inflammable and, if contaminated by from 6 to 90 per cent of air, highly explosive. Particular care was therefore taken to keep the gas as pure as possible.[25] Between flights the cells were fully inflated, but under slight positive pressure, which reduced the possibility of air mixing with the gas. If the daily routine checks discovered that the gas had become contaminated, the cell was immediately emptied and refilled.

The actual filling of the ships was a most hazardous operation and rigid safety precautions were imposed. Armed soldiers guarded the hangared ships night and day, and prior to inflation of the cells the filling valves and hoses were rigorously checked for signs of leakage. After all these checks, the repairs, refuelling and filling, it would be at least 24 hours before the Zeppelin was ready to embark on another raid on England.

CHAPTER 3

The Raids

'...In London one of the strangest sights resulting from the raids was provided by the rush of people to the cover of the Underground railways. For many nights following the attack on the capital on the 23rd/24th of September 1916, many thousands of people flocked to the tube railways without waiting for any warning...'

H A Jones, 1923

As early as 1898 an agreement, the Hague Declaration, was drawn up in order to prevent belligerent countries from launching projectiles or explosives from balloons or other kinds of aerial vessels.[1] This restriction remained valid until 1907 when it came up for renewal, but from representatives of 44 countries only 27 saw fit to add their names to the new agreement. Of the powers involved in the European war, a mere four gave their support: Belgium, Great Britain, Portugal and the United States of America. Germany declined. In the long term the agreement automatically became null and void at the start of hostilities in August 1914 because of a proviso which had stated that restrictions would be lifted if, in the event of war between the contracting powers, one country was supported by any one of those that had decided against signing the treaty.

Prologue
One outcome of the 1907 Hague Conference was the Land War Convention, of which Article 25 was the only existing international rule (prior to the outbreak of war) that specifically referred to air bombardment. It simply forbade the world powers from bombing undefended areas by 'any means whatsoever' and this was deliberately phrased to imply attack from the air. But it was not made clear exactly what constituted an undefended area, and so Article 2 of the Naval Convention attempted to clarify the situation:

> Military works, military or naval establishments, depots of arms or war material, workshops or plant which could be utilized for the needs of a hostile fleet or army, and ships of war in the harbour are not included in this prohibition... A naval commander may destroy them with artillery, after a summons followed by a reasonable interval of time, if all other means are impossible, and when the local authorities have not themselves destroyed them within the time fixed.[2]

All this would have been fine for surface vessels, but if applied too literally regarding aerial bombers certain problems seemed insurmountable. The Conference really failed to pin down precisely what were, and what were not, legitimate targets for aerial bombardment, although those of a military nature were liable to attack.

During the same year as the second conference, the British Government became more than a little concerned over the development of Count Zeppelin's airships. The Anglo-German 'arms race' was at its peak during this period and there were fears that the Teutonic Zeppelins would add marine reconnaissance and even bombing to their list of capabilities. A year later the Government formed a special committee, chaired by Lord Esher, to enquire into the possible dangers to which Great Britain could be subjected by the advance of aircraft technology. In a report dated January 1909 there was one clause that had particular significance:

> The evidence before the committee tends to show that the full practicalities of airships and the dangers to which we might be exposed by their use can only be ascertained definitely by building them ourselves. This was the original reason for constructing submarines, and in their case the policy since has been completely vindicated.[3]

The result was the Royal Navy's first rigid airship, officially His Majesty's Airship No 1 but unofficially known as the *Mayfly*, a somewhat pessimistic label yet strangely prophetic. On 22 September 1911 the pale yellow and silver giant was carefully withdrawn from its shed at the Cavendish Dock, Barrow, and promptly broke its back. Almost certainly a structural weakness had caused the disaster. As a result of earlier, quite drastic modifications to enable the grossly overweight airship to rise, many components were scrapped, including an all-important keel between the mahogany-planked engine cars. Thus the *Mayfly*'s overall rigidity was impaired and a tragedy inevitable. The court of enquiry which followed dismissed the airship as structurally weak, the Admiralty concurred, and despite protestations from those more enlightened individuals concerned with the project no more British rigids were to be built until 1916.[4] When war came Germany was the only world power to boast a large number of rigid airships at her disposal.

In peacetime the Zeppelins had safely carried hundreds of passengers, remained airborne for over 24 hours, covered distances of up to 900 miles and maintained high altitudes, and they were the centre of much exaggeration, mystique and sensationalism – perhaps even a little fear. Before the war many impressionable people in Great Britain reported seeing Zeppelins drifting along the coast, and rumours of

Stirring 1914 propaganda art by the French artist R Delville parodies 'frightfulness' and is typical of the period. The Zeppelin was the H-bomb of its day, an awesome Sword of Damocles to be held over the cowering heads of Germany's enemies.
By courtesy of S G English

"WE TWO":—THE WAR LORD AND HIS ALLY.
Drawing by R. Delville, a young French Artist.

German spies were rife; in September 1914 came the disturbing news that an airship was skulking in the hills of Cumberland by day and venturing over Westmorland by night. The Royal Flying Corps treated the rumours seriously enough to despatch Second Lieutenant Benjamin C Hucks in a Blériot monoplane to seek out the ghostly invader. The pilot made several patrols over the area, but apart from the glorious scenery saw nothing else to excite his interest. There was no Zeppelin, and of course there never had been.

Nevertheless the threat of bombardment by Zeppelin was a real one and not to be taken lightly; nor was it, for certain measures were instituted to repel likely attacks as some of the German airships *were* observed on several isolated occasions during the early months of the war lying off the coast, although none appears to have ventured any further. The expected 'terror raids' never materialised, and in fact the first bombs to fall on British soil came not from a Zeppelin at all but from an aeroplane.

Late in December the German Naval Air Service installed a naval aircraft squadron at Flanders, the machines taking part in combats on the Yser before being transferred to Mariakerke, whence they made the first sorties over Great Britain. On the 21st of the month, *Leutnant* von Prondzynsk from this unit flew high above Dover and dropped a brace of small bombs. They fell harmlessly in the sea near the Admiralty Pier, taking everybody completely by surprise, and the pilot returned to his base unchallenged. Exactly the same style of attack took place three days later, but this time the pilot's aim was slightly better. One bomb, the very first to fall on British soil, exploded in the grounds of Dover Castle and broke a few windows. An RNAS machine took off in pursuit but the German soon disappeared out to sea and the British pilot returned without making contact.

On Christmas Day, at 12.35hrs, a lone Albatros seaplane came in over Sheerness and, evading the anti-aircraft guns, flew up the Thames and reached Erith. This time three RNAS aircraft from the Isle of Grain and Eastchurch engaged the enemy, but the German pilot shook off his attackers and, taking advantage of superior speed, turned homewards via Shornmead Fort. As if to add injury to insult the Germans dropped two bombs near the Cliffe Station on the way and returned unscathed to Mariakerke.

Such desultory attacks were interesting diversions but with many civilians a gnawing apprehension set in. What had happened to the Zepps? Why were the Germans holding back? How long would it be before they brought their 'aerial cruisers' over Britain? Much the same questions were being voiced by German civilians, many of whom had been enraged at Britain's declaration of war on their country and had clamoured loudly for retribution ever since. Had any of the uninformed peoples of the two major powers been privy to the actual reasons for such uncharacteristic reluctance to press home an advantage, few would have believed it.

In September, the combined staffs of the German Army and the Naval Airship Divisions had discussed the bombing of England, but there were several problems to overcome before this could be achieved. One was that there were simply not enough airships to spare, and it was agreed that raids on the 'brutal huckster nation' would have to wait, at least until the large number of ships then being built were completed and had entered service, something which would not transpire for several months at least. Secondly, both *Kaiser* Wilhelm and Chancellor Theodor von Bethman-Hollweg were hesitant to sanction the bombing of London, despite *Konteradmiral* Paul Behncke's arguments to the contrary. The 'Supreme War Lord' felt some obligation for the safety of his royal cousins, King George V and Queen Mary, and further, was reluctant to allow his eager airship crews to damage any of London's historical buildings.

But eventually, after much political wrangling within the German General Staff, demands, counter-demands, inter-service rivalry, clashes of personalities, and a reluctance to offend the Emperor, things came to a head. On 7 January 1915 the Chief of the Naval Staff, Admiral Hugo von Pohl,

Zeppelin!

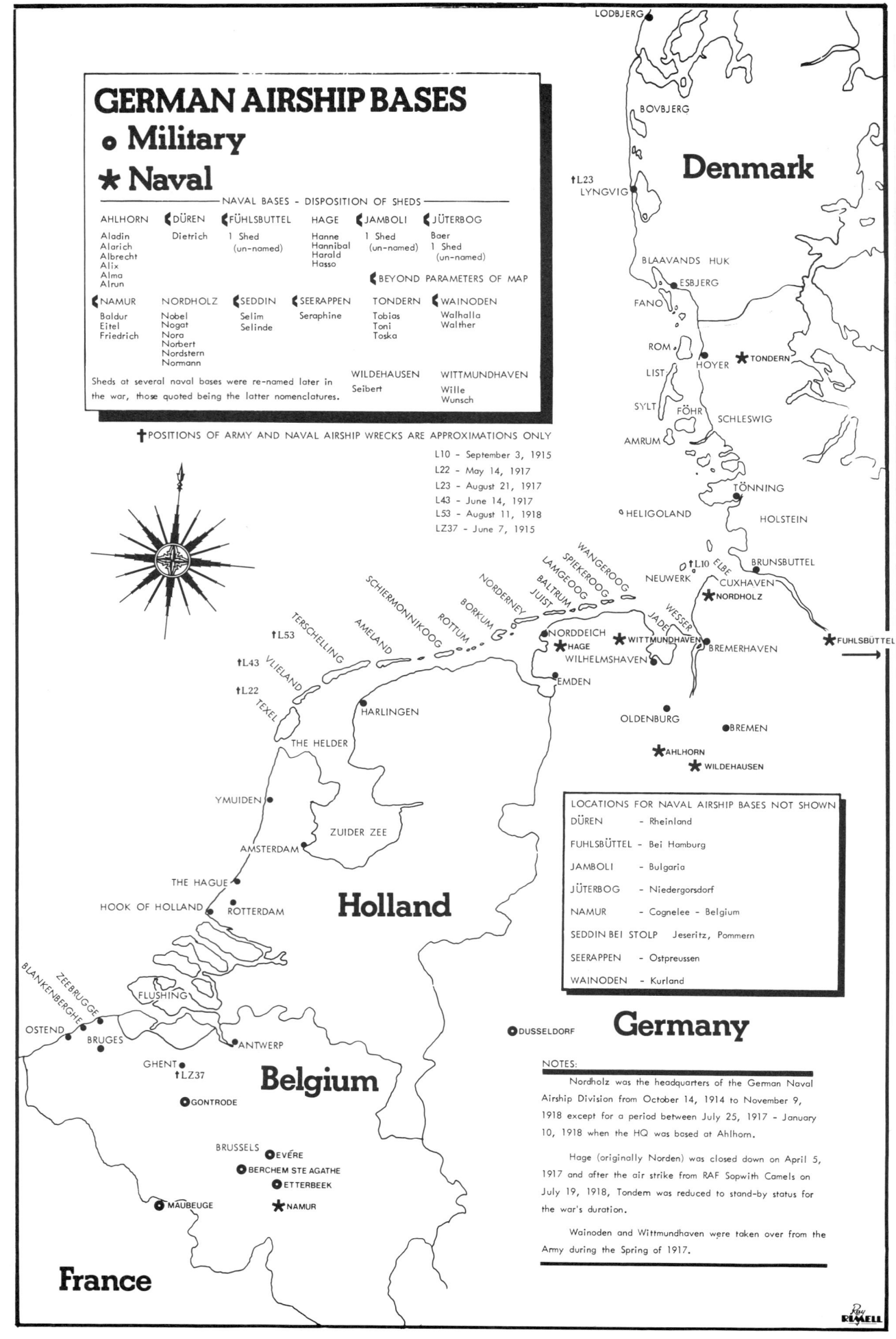

A *Punch* cartoon published in November 1914 reflects early British opinion. As the months immediately following the outbreak of war did not bring the expected air raids, the Zeppelin threat seemed less real as far as the civilian population was concerned. *Punch*

FOREWARNED.

Zeppelin (as "*The Fat Boy*"). "'I WANTS TO MAKE YOUR FLESH CREEP.'"
John Bull. "RIGHT-O!"

summoned his courage and demanded an audience with the *Kaiser*. Frequent badgering by his subordinates finally persuaded him to lay arguments before the 'All Highest' in a last effort to obtain sanction for airship attacks on the British Isles. The agenda stressed that only military buildings should be attacked – civilian homes were to be avoided if at all possible. It further eschewed any co-operation with the Army Airship Division, this being considered impracticable and likely to postpone the navy's planned offensive.

After the meeting, von Pohl came away fairly satisfied, and the telegraph he wired to the Commander-in-Chief of the High Seas Fleet three days later brought the news everyone wanted to hear:

Kapitänleutnant Freiherr Treusch von Buttlar Brandenfels took part in the 19 January raid, but when *L6* suffered a crankshaft failure the airship, with Strasser aboard, was forced to return to Nordholz. Von Buttlar was the only prewar German Naval Airship Division officer still flying at the Armistice, and the only airship commander to be honoured with Germany's highest award, the *Ordre pour le Mérite*, the so-called 'Blue Max'. Von Buttlar's book *Zeppelins over England*, published in 1931, gives a fascinating and highly coloured account of his personal experiences throughout the war. *Archiv: Marine-Luftschiffer-Kameradschaft*

The Raids

Air attacks on England approved by Supreme War Lord. Targets not to be attacked in London, but rather docks and military establishments in the Lower Thames and on the English coast.[5]

The wait was over at last.

The Raids of 1915
January 19/20: L3, L4, L6

After an abortive attempt on 13 January when severe weather forced four naval airships to abandon a planned attack, *Korvettenkapitän* Peter Strasser's crews had their second chance just five days later. *L3*, commanded by *Kapitänleutnant* Hans Fritz, and *L4* (*Kapitänleutnant* Magnus Graf von Platen Hallermund) ascended from Fuhlsbüttel at around 10.00hrs with orders to bomb military establishments on the River Humber. *L6*, under the command of *Oberleutnant zur See* Horst Freiherr Treusch von Buttlar Brandenfels from Nordholz, had taken off over two hours earlier in order to lead the attack on the Thames area. *L6* carried fuel for 33 hours' flying, ten 110pdr explosives and 12 incendiary bombs – and Peter Strasser. It would become practice for the Chief to participate in at least one raid per month so that he could experience at first hand the performances of both his ships and his subordinates. Luck was against Strasser on this particular occasion, for *L6* suffered a crankshaft failure five hours into the mission. Reluctantly, and after much consultation with von Buttlar, Strasser ordered the airship to return to Nordholz.

L3 and *L4* pressed on despite worsening weather conditions, and eventually *L3*, steering a course for the coast of Norfolk, made its landfall at 19.50hrs – the very first Zeppelin over England. Conditions in the forward open control car, with the Germans frozen to the marrow and unsure of their exact whereabouts, were not conducive to precision bombing, and Fritz had a parachute flare dropped to fix his position. Under the floating glare Fritz made out the village of Haisborough and the Winterton lighthouse; thus orientated, he set a course for Great Yarmouth. Having reached the town at 20.20hrs, he dropped another flare, which served to draw spirited response from a gun battery. Flying at 5000ft because of the rain-laden envelope, Fritz unleashed six 110pdrs and seven incendiaries as *L3* crossed the port.

One of many fascinated witnesses to the first raid on England was 17-year-old R Nouchton, a member of First Troop, Great Yarmouth Boy Scouts, on watch that night:

> As the war was on, we undertook to do some wartime duties, therefore I was on duty at the aerodrome on the South Denes, Great Yarmouth. The Zeppelin passed over and dropped five bombs – one exploded at the back of St Peter's Church killing one man, a bootmaker, [and] destroying his house and workshop.[6]

One bomb fell 50yds from a drill hall packed with National Reserve men, and although they were unharmed and the building undamaged, adjacent property was not so fortunate. In the same block as the bootmaker's house was J E Pestell's premises, which proudly proclaimed the owner as a master builder and undertaker on its walls. Fritz left the building blazing and in the morning it was a ruined shell, the interior completely gutted and the roof gone.

As Fritz continued on his course, other bombs fell near Trinity Wharf, the gasworks and the racecourse in a ten-minute attack, after which the Zeppelin headed out to sea. All credit must be given to the commander for having located and correctly identified his target with only flares to guide him amidst appalling weather conditions. Freezing rain and fog continued to bedevil *L3* on its trip back to

33

Zeppelin!

Among the casualties of *L3*'s bombs on Great Yarmouth was J E Pestell's premises in Lancaster Road. Five missiles struck this block, one narrowly missing a drill hall filled with National Reservists.
Author's Collection

Fuhlsbüttel, which it reached at 08.40hrs. Fritz and his crew had been airborne for 22 hours 15 minutes.

L4 made landfall at 20.30hrs over Bacton. Passing Cromer and unsure of his exact whereabouts, von Platen bombed the small village of Sheringham. The airship crew were having difficulty in plotting an exact course in the fog and were flying quite low in order to obtain bearings. Just how low can be gauged from the account of Lilian Bellamy, a volunteer canteen worker in Sheringham:

> [In] a thick fog a Zeppelin presumably lost its way and hovered very low over the main street of Sheringham. We all rushed out of the canteen to look at it and could see the faces of the men inside looking down at us. [Later] a Zepp dropped a dud bomb on a workman's cottage near us; it fell through the house, broke up the staircase and buried itself in the ground, leaving the baby alive and well in its cot upstairs and the parents eating their supper downstairs.[7]

Having provided the residents of Sheringham with a disturbing and eerie spectacle, von Platen went on to bomb Snettisham, mistaking it for Sandringham, and then unknowingly flew over the Royal House itself and on to King's Lynn, attracted by the town's lights. The commander later reported being fired on by artillery units in the 'big city' below, and had promptly bombed it. Seven explosives and six incendiaries tumbled from *L4*'s racks and destroyed several small houses, killing a woman and a small boy. Having thus accomplished his mission, von Platen went due east via Norwich and later radioed that he had successfully bombarded several fortified positions 'between the Tyne and Humber'.

April 14/15: L9

After two abortive attempts by *Kapitänleutnant* Helmut Beelitz in *L8* to raid the British Isles single-handed, once from Düsseldorf on 26 February and then on 4 March from Gontrode in Belgium, no further naval raids were mounted until the morning of 14 April, when *L9* left the base at Hage. This Zeppelin, under the command of *Kapitänleutnant* Heinrich Mathy, had orders to reconnoitre to the west beyond Terschelling and return before nightfall. Nevertheless *L9* was carrying bombs, and after flying near the English coast unobserved Mathy obtained permission for a raid if conditions were suitable. In fact the weather was untypically clement, and so the commander pressed on for Tyneside, although he actually crossed the coast at Blyth, a good nine miles further north.

As it turned out, the raid was a light one: several small mining villages north of the Tyne bore the brunt of Mathy's bombs, but a scorched barn roof was the only real damage

On 14 April 1915 Heinrich Mathy made a lone assault on the Tyne, reaching Wallsend where bombs from *L9* caused minor damage and injured two civilians. *L9* (builder's number LZ36) was built in the Friedrichshafen Ring Shed and made its maiden flight on 8 March 1915. It was commanded initially by Mathy, but Loewe, Martin Dietrich, Prölss, Stelling, Kraushaar, Ganzel, Hollender and Gayer all took their turn as commanders. *L9* served as a training ship for a brief period in September 1916, but its career ended on the 16th of that month when the Zeppelin burned itself out in the Fuhlsbüttel shed, the result of an inflation fire in *L6*. There were no casualties.
F Moch

caused. *L9* eventually reached Wallsend and its remaining bombs damaged a house and injured two civilians; 21.00hrs saw the ship over the coast south of the Tyne and setting a course homeward without being intercepted by the two RNAS aircraft that had taken off from Cramlington.

Mathy's single-handed foray only served to emphasise the ineffectual results of attacks by 'dead reckoning', even though this much-respected commander was confident that he had bombed important shipbuilding and industrial areas. His subsequent report, in fact, sufficiently encouraged Strasser himself to lead another raid the following day.

April 15/16: L5, L6, L7
Strasser's intended target was the Humber area, yet none of the commanders was able to report with absolute certainty exactly which towns they had bombed. *L5*, commanded by *Kapitänleutnant der Reserve* Aloys Böcker, led the attack, opening the raid with bombs on Henham Hall and Southwold. The next target was Lowestoft, which Böcker bombed from an altitude of just over 5000ft, causing extensive damage to a lumber yard there.[8]

Von Buttlar, in *L6*, was at the same altitude as Böcker when he bombed Maldon and Heybridge, damaging a house and injuring a young girl. At such low level *L6* became a natural target for rifle and gunfire and, indeed, von Buttlar turned back with cells 11 and 13 leaking rapidly from several rents and bullet holes. Flight Commander C W P Ireland, in an RNAS seaplane from Great Yarmouth, failed to locate the raider despite a 45-minute search.

Strasser, aboard *L7*, did not even manage to make landfall as strong headwinds brought the ship to a virtual standstill, and at 01.30hrs the commander, *Oberleutnant zur See* Werner Peterson, headed back for the Dutch coast. British official records show *L7* crossing the Norfolk coast and then following a line to Great Yarmouth, where the ship went out to sea at 02.35hrs having dropped no bombs on land. To most naval crewmen it seemed that whenever Strasser elected to join them on a raid something would invariably go wrong, and their Chief came to be regarded as something of a 'Jonah'.

April 29/30: LZ38
The first Army ship to attack England was *LZ38*, commanded by *Hauptmann* Erich Linnarz, the raid serving as a prelude to several spectacular onslaughts by this Zeppelin and its captain. From his base at Brussels-Evère, Linnarz eventually crossed the English coast over Felixstowe and flew on to Bury St Edmunds via Ipswich, unleashing 26 bombs in the process. Over Bury St Edmunds *LZ38* hovered for at least ten minutes whilst three high explosives and 40 incendiary bombs whistled down to destroy four houses. Linnarz then proceeded to follow the coastline and went out over Orfordness at 01.50hrs, then moved back over Aldeburgh a little later before finally leaving English shores altogether. There were no casualties, and aside from a total of six wrecked houses little material damage was caused by the 66 incendiary and ten HE bombs dropped. Yet this was just the beginning.

May 10/11: LZ38
The next target for Linnarz was Southend, which he reached at 02.45hrs, announcing his arrival by dropping an incendiary bomb that fell near the moored prison hulk SS *Royal Edward*. *LZ38* then passed over Southend itself, dropping several bombs, before following the Thames as far as Canvey Island, where fierce anti-aircraft fire from Cliffe resulted in a direct hit and turned the commander back. Returning to Southend, Linnarz dropped his remaining bombs over the town, causing considerable damage in the process.

One of several townspeople who gave their personal accounts of the raid to *Southend Standard* reporters the next day was motor engineer R D Boyce;

> About three o'clock I was aroused from my sleep by the sound of an explosion. I got up, put my head out of the window, and heard the noise of an engine. I woke my brother up, and we went downstairs and stood in the roadway. My brother saw a Zeppelin overhead. He saw it quite distinctly, and it was at a great height. We heard the noise of the engines, and why I know it was a Zeppelin was because the engines were running quite slowly. They were running as slowly as can the engine of an ordinary car. Suddenly the engines were shut off and everything was quiet. There were only two policemen out in the road, and when the engines stopped they said, 'All right; they have sheered off'. The engines were quite quiet for a quarter of an hour, then we heard them again.[9]

Between 100 and 120 explosive and incendiary bombs were estimated to have struck Southend that night,

Published in 1917, this dramatic scene from an original colour painting by Felix Schwormstadt portrays the interior of *LZ38*'s control car and can be considered typical for most 'p' and 'r' class Zeppelins. Left to right: executive officer with binoculars: elevator man with elevator control wheel (altimeter in front of him); statascope, with ballast and manoeuvring valve pulls overhead; rudder man at the bow (bomb sight to his right is much simplified); commanding officer (closely resembling Linnarz) holding speaking tube to the bomb 'room' in keel and with engine telegraphs above him; and a *Maschinist* descending the ladder from the keel.
Leipziger Illustrirte Zeitung

Zeppelin!

destroying Flaxman's timber yard and several shops. One woman was killed and two men injured as a result of this, the most effective raid so far in the campaign. The following day a small piece of cardboard was found on Canvey Island, presumably dropped by one of LZ38's crewmen resentful of the Cliffe gunners' reception. The scribbled message, in blue pencil, read 'You English! We have come, and will come again soon – Kill or cure – German!'[10] And come again they did, just one week later.

May 17/18: LZ38
At 01.40hrs on the 17th, Linnarz flew over Margate to Ramsgate by way of Thanet. Twenty bombs were dropped on Ramsgate, where the Bull and George hotel was struck and two people killed with another injured. Linnarz came under rifle fire soon afterwards and went out to sea, returning via Dover where searchlights held LZ38, the first Zeppelin to be thus illuminated over England. Unaware of this distinction, Linnarz became the target for anti-aircraft gunners and, making a hasty retreat, the commander jettisoned his remaining bombs, which fell at Oxney. It was at that moment that Flight Sub-Lieutenant R H Mulock of the RNAS, flying a converted Avro 504C, intercepted LZ38.[11] Armed with two grenades and a brace of incendiary bombs, Mulock had no chance of attacking the Zeppelin, which having been lightened by the release of its remaining bombs rose rapidly out of range. The RNAS pilot pursued his quarry as far as the West Hinder lightship although was unable to engage it. Linnarz hovered over the Goodwin Sands, but engine malfunctions and the approaching light of dawn compelled him to return to Evère.

May 26/27: LZ38
Southend experienced its second attack by Linnarz on the 26th; the commander was thought to have been exploring the area in order to find the easiest route to London for future attacks. At 22.30hrs LZ38 made landfall over Clacton and then passed on to Southminster where alert gunners opened fire, causing Linnarz to turn south for Burnham-on-Crouch. Passing over Shoeburyness, LZ38 was engaged by 3in naval gunfire there before reaching Southend, where 70 bombs were dropped. No great damage was done, although there were three fatalities and three seriously injured civilians.

LZ38 proceeded next to the north-west and, passing over Shoeburyness, once more came under attack by the 3in gun; then, at Burnham, a company of the 2nd/8th Battalion the Essex Regiment opened fire. Shortly before midnight Linnarz reached the north of the River Blackwater where his ship turned out to sea. During the attack five RNAS machines had taken off, yet all had failed to make contact and two suffered serious landing accidents.

May 31/June 1: LZ38
The residents of Margate were the first to witness the next attack by Linnarz, his ship arriving offshore at 21.42hrs where it was greeted by spirited machine-gun fire. Following the coastline, Linnarz made his landfall at Shoeburyness, cautiously giving the Cliffe naval guns a wide berth. When he eventually reached London, via Great Wakering, Billericay and Brentwood, Linnarz started to release his bombs over the city.

The dubious honour of being the first London house to be struck by an aerial bomb went to 16 Alkham Road on the outskirts of Hackney. The owner, Albert Henry Lovell, together with his wife, their children and two women visitors, escaped unscathed from the blazing upper rooms. A single incendiary tore through the roof and gutted the front bedroom and one back room. Further missiles struck houses in Stoke Newington. Some failed to explode and there were no casualties until one bomb struck 33 Cowper Road.

On the first floor lived Mr and Mrs Samuel Leggatt, who were on the point of retiring for the night when one of Linnarz's incendiaries ripped through an empty room above them and into their own premises. Instantly the floor was ablaze, and while Mrs Leggatt ran out into the street screaming for assistance her husband dragged four of his children from their blazing bedroom. All of them – May aged 11, George aged 10, Nellie aged 7, and Dorothy, 5 – suffered severe burns, and having reached the safety of the street Samuel Leggatt remembered that the young daughter of Rose Clark, who occupied the rooms above his own, was still up there. Despite the intensity of the fire he dashed back upstairs and succeeded in rescuing the toddler.

It was whilst neighbour Bernard Holland was helping Leggatt and his children to the Metropolitan Hospital in Kingsland Road that the distraught Mrs Leggatt missed her three-year-old daughter Elsie, although a neighbour assured the mother that she had seen the infant rescued and carried out into Shakespeare Road. Alas the facts were sadly different, for the hapless infant had taken the full force of the bomb which had struck the stove adjacent to her cot; the pathetic remains were discovered under the debris at 04.00hrs by Police Constable 755 Churchill. Even worse was to come, for May Leggatt died in hospital some days later as a result of her injuries.

The house at 187 Balls Pond Road received more of Linnarz's bombs, but the occupants escaped unharmed from the blazing upper storeys. As the fire broke out, Thomas Sharping, having rescued his daughters, went to the rear of the house and hurled a brick through the window of his lodgers' apartments. There came no reply from 49-year-old Henry Thomas Good or his wife Caroline, and having hurled another brick and again receiving a negative response Sharping assumed that the couple were out for the evening.

Inside the rear engine gondola of LZ38, looking forward. The cramped interior reveals an engine telegraph suspended from the roof, a radiator, and a drive shaft to the starboard propeller seen through the window. In the foreground three mechanics work on the 210hp Maybach C-X engine, and a gunner armed with a DWM 7.9mm Parabellum machine gun keeps a sharp lookout for British aircraft. Felix Schwormstadt's dramatic painting vividly conveys the uncomfortable conditions in which the crew had to operate.
Leipziger Illustrirte Zeitung

'The First England Crew': *Hauptmann* Erich Linnarz, spirited commander of LZ38, and his crew pose outside the airship shed at Evère on the morning after the first raid on London, 31 May 1915. The attack, though largely ineffective, resulted in the British Admiralty imposing strict censorship on newspaper accounts of air raids, thus denying airship commanders an opportunity to pinpoint their frequent navigational errors.
D H Robinson

36

As flames devoured the house, the couple's son arrived on the scene and expressed the gravest doubts that his parents were elsewhere. The hour was long past their usual bedtime and to him it seemed that they may still be trapped inside – yet there had been absolutely no sign of the couple.

By the morning the fire had been brought under control and a policeman placed a ladder outside the Good's upper window, climbed up and peered in. The scene which confronted him chilled him to the marrow:

> Mr and Mrs Good were kneeling beside the bed. They were unclothed, save of that of a band of cloth encircled Mr Good's arm, suggesting that a woollen jersey had been burnt from him. His right arm was about his wife's waist. A big tuft of hair was gripped firmly in Mrs Good's hand.
>
> Were the victims asleep when the crash came, and stumbled, confused and half dazed in a room of which they had temporarily lost their bearings? Did the friendly missiles coming through the window suggest a hostile attack from the very direction in which escape was still possible? Or did the fumes, spreading swiftly from the burning staircase, overtake them too soon, and the woman in her agony and terror, faced by the resistless [sic] advance of those terrible flames, sink in prayer at the bedside, to be joined by her husband?[12]

We will probably never know the answer to these questions, for it died in that burnt-out room with its scorched victims kneeling at the bedside in a horrific last embrace. The bodies were later examined by Dr Barlow, a Divisional Surgeon, who had them removed to the Hackney Mortuary for the inquest.

What Linnarz might have felt had he seen the results of his bombs on these civilian families will never be known. Way up in the night sky, the scene that drifted below the control car windows took on a very different aspect:

> One by one, every 30 seconds, the bombs moaned and burst. Flames sprung up like serpents goaded to attack. Taking one of the biggest fires, I was able by it to estimate my speed and my drift. Beside me my second-in-command carefully watched the result of every bomb and made rapid calculations at the navigation chart.[13]

At 23.15hrs, *LZ38* was over the Stepney area, where Linnarz dropped further bombs. These fell on Bishopsgate Goods Station, on the High Street, Shoreditch, damaging the roof of the Empire Music Hall; in the churchyard in the High Street, Whitechapel; and on Adler Street. Here a large boot warehouse was burnt out and a synagogue in Commercial Road was damaged, as, too, were Walker's Whisky Distillery and Summer's Stables.

Returning from Greenberg's Picture Palace were 30-year-old Leah Leahmann and 10-year-old Samuel Reuben, who passed together into Christian Street, St Georges, just as another bomb whistled down. A constable witnessed 'a blinding sheaf of flame', and when the smoke had cleared 12 people were lying in a shattered street. There was glass everywhere and the moans of the injured underlined the horror of the scene. The policeman rushed over to find the Reuben boy fatally injured having been 'disembowelled and otherwise mutilated.'[14]

Miss Leahmann had sustained a compound fracture at the base of her skull and a laceration of the right breast. She was quickly conveyed to the nearest hospital, where she died at 05.00hrs. Three doctors administered on-the-spot treatment to several other casualties before they were admitted to the nearby London Hospital.

Miss Sylvia Pankhurst was busily writing at her desk on the evening that Linnarz chose to 'come again'. Having forsaken politics for welfare work, she soon gained first-hand experience of the effect that the Zeppelin raiders were having on the ordinary civilian:

> The huge reports smote the ear, shattering, deafening, and the roar of falling masonry ... An air raid! Mrs Payne was on my threshold, her face ineffably tender. 'Miss Pankhurst, come down to us!' Half smiling, she reached out her arms to me.
>
> I went to her from my little table in the corner. She clung to me, trembling. The angry grinding still pulsated above us. Again that terrific burst of noise; those awful bangs, the roar of the falling buildings, the rattle of shrapnel on the roof close above our heads.[15]

When *LZ38* finally withdrew from English shores over the River Crouch, helped on its way by gunfire from Burnham and Southminster, it had left more than a ton of bombs in its wake. The casualties amounted to seven killed and 35 injured with the damage to property valued at over £18,000, whilst over the city not one of London's guns had engaged the Zeppelin.

Nine defence aircraft were sent up to intercept the raider as it had made its way to the capital, yet none came close to intercepting, let alone engaging, *LZ38*. Blériot pilot Flight Lieutenant A W Robertson, from Rochford, seems to have been the only pilot to observe the ship, but engine failure resulted in a forced landing at Leigh. Robertson was uninjured, but RNAS pilot Flight Lieutenant D M Barnes was killed when his two-seater Sopwith crashed whilst landing at Hatfield. The observer, Flight Sub-Lieutenant Ben Travers, was lucky to escape with only minor injuries.[16]

The result of this raid had a profound effect on Londoners. But far from being cowed, there was a feeling of bitterness and resentment. To German-born citizens and shopkeepers in the city, the following months would be harrowing, as they bore the brunt of wild rumour and personal persecution:

> In the centre of the turmoil men dragged a big, stout man, stumbling and resisting in their grasp, his clothes whitened by flour, his mouth dripping blood. They rushed him on. New throngs closed around him.
>
> From another direction arose more shouting. A woman's scream. The tail of the crowd dashed off towards the sound. Crowds raced to it from all directions ...
>
> A woman was in the midst of a struggling mob; her blouse half-torn off, her fair hair fallen, her face contorted with pain and terror, blood running down her bare white arm. A big, drunken man flung her to the ground. She was lost to sight ... 'Oh my God! Oh! They are kicking her!' a woman screamed.[17]

June 4/5: L10, SL3

The fact that an Army ship had been the first to bomb London rankled with the Navy and they were not long in pressing home their own attacks. There were only two ships involved, *L10*, commanded by *Kapitänleutnant* Klaus Hirsch, and the less efficient wooden-framed Schütte Lanz *SL3*, commanded by *Kapitänleutnant* Fritz Boemack. During the afternoon, Hirsch flew beyond the Dutch coast to avoid detection and reached the mouth of the Thames at 22.15hrs. Believing he was over Harwich, Hirsch dumped bombs over stretches of water, but the town itself was actually Gravesend. Twenty-one assorted bombs injured half a dozen civilians and destroyed the Yacht Club premises which were being used as a military hospital.

SL3 made landfall at 23.30hrs south of Flamborough Head; Boemack planned to attack Hull, although strong headwinds forced him to abandon this idea. Making little progress, with the light of dawn not far away, Boemack prudently turned for home, dropping three bombs as he did so. The bombs exploded harmlessly in a field and *SL3* returned to Nordholz with its remaining bombs still aboard. During the morning William Morgan, one of many local residents, went to view the damage:

The ill-fated *L10*, seen here at Friedrichshafen in May 1915. With the builder's number LZ40, *L10* was built at Friedrichshafen's Factory Shed 1 and made its first flight on 13 May 1915. Commanded initially by *Kapitänleutnant* Klaus Hirsch, who took over the ship on 17 May, *L10* was the second of the improved 'p' type, 1 million cu ft Zeppelins and the first naval ship to bomb London. On 3 September 1915 *L10* was struck by lightning and fell in flames off Neuwerk Island, killing all 19 members of its crew. *Luftschiffbau Zeppelin*

Fortunately this was not very great and the thing which impressed me the most was the vast number of like-minded sightseers crowding into the small riverside town. It was a solid mass of people slowly edging past the destroyed and damaged houses and never to be forgotten were their expressions of horror and anger at the wantonness of it.[18]

Four RFC and four RNAS aeroplanes were sent up during the raid, but none of them made contact with either of the raiding airships. *L10*, having steered an erratic course, finally went out to sea over Saxmundham, the commander happy to have bombed 'Harwich' so successfully:

[The bombs] all exploded and all caused fires in the town; moreover, judging by an especially violent explosion, one of the hits must have been on some gasworks or an oil tank. In many places fires broke out which were visible for a long time.[19]

June 6/7: LZ37, LZ38, LZ39; L9
It was mere coincidence that ships from both the Navy and the Army undertook the 6 June raid simultaneously, and it was a raid that would be a memorable one for a variety of reasons. Commanding *L9* was Heinrich Mathy, who elected to visit Hull after overcoming thick mist before getting his bearings. Parachute flares illuminated the docks at 23.50hrs as Mathy began his attack, dropping ten explosive and 50 incendiary bombs, the city's only defence being the 4in guns of the cruiser *Adventure* in the repair dock at Earl's yard. The damage caused by *L9*'s bombs was extensive – in fact the greatest inflicted by the raiders so far – and it cost the English taxpayer well over £44,000. Some of this was caused by the riots that resulted after Mathy's visit, when furious civilians mobbed and ransacked all German shops and non-Britishers of the city in a repetition of the ugly scenes that had occurred in London some days previously.

Although Mathy enjoyed a fair measure of success on this particular raid, the Army ships had a very hard time of it by comparison. *LZ38* turned back to Evère almost at once with serious engine trouble, whilst *LZ37* and *LZ39* met heavy fog and were unable to reach England. On their way back, both ships were attacked by RNAS machines and Flight Sub-Lieutenant R A J Warneford sent down *LZ37* a tumbling blazing wreck. Meanwhile Flight Lieutenants J P Wilson and J S Mills attacked the airship base at Evère.[20] As a result one Zeppelin and its shed were completely destroyed. The Zeppelin was Linnarz's – the 'luck' of *LZ38* had run out at last.

June 15/16: L10, L11
From Nordholz two Zeppelins arose on 15 June with orders to attack the Tyne, but von Buttlar in the newly commissioned *L11* was forced to return with a broken crankshaft. Hirsch in *L10* pressed on and arrived within sight of the English coast in broad daylight, cruised offshore until nightfall and then crossed the coast at Blyth around 23.25hrs.

Convinced he was over the well-lit city of Sunderland, Hirsch began to drop bombs which actually fell on Wallsend. Most of them struck the Marine Engineering Works, resulting in severe damage to the tune of £30,000; others fell on Palmer's Works at Jarrow and wreaked havoc on an engine construction plant, killing 17 and injuring 72. Further explosives struck Cookson's Antimony Works and Pochin's Chemical Works, and several houses at Willington, where a constable was killed, were also hit. The remaining bombs were distributed over collieries in South Shields, before *L10* finally passed out to sea. From the standpoint of pure military damage, this was the most successful raid to date, helped by the well-illuminated towns and the lack of searchlights or defences. The conditions could hardly have been better. Hirsch in fact took everyone completely by surprise and the only retaliatory fire came from the old cruiser HMS *Brilliant* moored on the Tyne.

On this occasion a commander was using radio bearings for the first time over England and yet the results were inconclusive; very many more stations would obviously be needed. Strasser was warned by *L10*'s commander that June and July nights were really too short for safety and thus raiding ships ran the risk of interception by English airmen. The advice was heeded for once and there were no further raids for nearly two months.

August 9/10; L9, L10, L11, L12, L13
Admiral Bachman, having delivered a petition to the Kaiser on 20 July, managed to obtain permission for the unrestricted bombing of London with the proviso that 'monuments like St Paul's Cathedral and the Tower will be spared as far as possible'.[21] The Navy hardly needed telling twice.

Mathy's 'lucky ship'. Built at Friedrichshafen's Factory Shed 1 and given builder's number LZ45, *L13* was commissioned on 25 July 1915 two days after its maiden flight. In a comparatively long career *L13* was variously commanded by Mathy, Prölss, Eichler, Schwonder and Flemming. On 29/30 April 1917, it was decommissioned at Hage and on 11 December the dismantling of the airship began. *L13* made a total of 159 flights, participated in 17 raids and made 45 scouting flights.
Luftschiffbau Zeppelin

Strasser, himself aboard *L10*, assembled a fleet of five airships over Borkum on the 9th and at 13.50hrs the Zeppelins turned west in formation. *L9*, commanded by *Kapitänleutnant* Odo Loewe, detached from the squadron and struck out alone for the Humber an hour later, approaching Flamborough Head at 20.15hrs where two RNAS machines arose to pursue the raider. Prudently Loewe went out to sea and tried again further down the coast; another aeroplane was observed, and the commander once more steered his ship away from possible danger. A broken rudder cable added to Loewe's discomfort, and *L9* circled aimlessly for a while as repairs were effected. When order was finally restored *L9* made its landfall over Aldbrough and steered erratically on to Goole, which the confused Loewe mistook for Hull. The town's position was given away by dimmed street lamps reflecting wet pavements and roads; taking advantage of this, Loewe commenced his bomb run. Forty-two assorted bombs killed 16 civilians, injured 11, destroyed several houses and damaged two warehouses before *L9* crossed Selby, dropping three incendiaries on a Hotham field and then leaving the English coast. Loewe was the only commander to reach his planned objective that night: for the others it was a frustrating experience, none of them even coming within sight of London.

Mathy, in *L13*, turned back near the English coast with engine trouble and heavy rain overloading the envelope, 120 bombs having to be dropped in order to lighten the ship. *L10*, also bedevilled by the worsening weather conditions, dropped 12 bombs over the Eastchurch naval aerodrome on the Isle of Sheppey. The acting commander, *Oberleutnant zur See der Reserve* Friedrich Wenke, was convinced he was over eastern London, an idea reinforced by a parachute flare which revealed part of the Thames. The bombs did no damage apart from breaking a few windows, yet they fell a bare 600yds from the aircraft sheds at Eastchurch where RNAS aircraft and personnel had a narrow escape.

Von Buttlar, in *L11*, made landfall over Lowestoft at 22.18hrs, dropping seven HE and four incendiary bombs which killed a woman and injured seven people. His ship was engaged by 6pdr naval guns, and so close came the shells that von Buttlar broke off, dumping further bombs in the sea which were mistaken for water flares by the British. Peterson, in *L12*, arrived over Westgate at 22.48hrs and followed a line to pass Margate, Ramsgate and Deal before finally reaching Dover harbour nearly two hours later. Peterson was sure that the cluster of lights beneath belonged to Harwich and, forsaking any idea of bombing London, dropped 92 explosives and incendiaries of which only three fell on land, injuring three civilians and causing little damage. The Dover 3in naval guns opened up on *L12* and several rounds struck the rear of the ship. Observers on the ground saw the Zeppelin 'shudder' as it disappeared behind a 'smoke screen' which was actually the water ballast being released as *L12* clawed for safer heights. Nevertheless the Dover guns had found their mark, for several cells were pierced and, despite the crew jettisoning all loose equipment, the loss of gas was too great for the ship to remain airborne. At 02.40hrs *L12* struck the waters of the English Channel with the tail surfaces and rear gondolas gradually settling under the waves. The crew could only sit out the night and hope for some form of rescue when dawn broke. As daylight came a surface vessel was seen approaching over the horizon and materialised into a German torpedo-boat. Its commander took *L12* in tow and just before noon the crippled airship was brought alongside the quay at Ostend.

The 2nd Wing of the RNAS based at Dunkirk soon learnt of Peterson's plight and three aircraft were despatched even before *L12* reached port. Flight Commander J R W Smyth-Pigott flying a BE2c was the first to locate the Zeppelin, and dropped two 20lb Hales bombs – both of which missed. Undaunted, Smyth-Pigott tried again:

[The] Zeppelin was surrounded by four TBDs which opened heavy machine gun fire as well as anti-aircraft batteries from shore. Pilot then dropped six grenades, apparently without further result. Next observations, however, showed the Zeppelin's back was broken. Machine was hit twice, one in the propeller and one in the fuselage. Returned 9.30am.

9.35am Flight Lieut. Johnston on a Henry Farman proceeded to Ostend for the purpose of continuing the bombardment but did not return.[22]

Flight Lieutenant D K Johnston was killed when his aircraft was shot down, but the RNAS had not yet finished with *L12*, for at 09.45hrs Flight Sub-Lieutenant Besson in a Bristol Scout took off into rain-laden low cloud:

Reaching Ostend at a height of 1000 feet, Besson climbed another 500 feet before releasing four bombs which all missed their huge target. A second attempt with 12 grenades at 2000 feet was also inconclusive and although the Zeppelin appeared to be badly crushed aft, no other damage was observed. Spirited anti-aircraft fire badgered the naval pilot during the entire attack and he broke off, returning to Dunkirk at 10.45 hours.[23]

In all, five more pilots made the trip out to the port in order to destroy *L12* lying helpless at the quayside. Between 09.55hrs and 12.35hrs bomb runs were made by Flight Lieutenant Bettingham in a Bristol Scout, Flight Sub-Lieutenant Buss in an Avro, Flight Commander Robinson in a Nieuport Scout and Flight Sub-Lieutenant Frank Besson making his second attempt, this time in a Nieuport. All were unsuccessful:

> Zeppelin was observed to have the rear half in the water and the remainder was covered by the smoke of a big oil flare burning alongside. When over the target [Besson] dropped four 10lb bombs but could not see the effect. Proceeding to Zeebrugge, he dropped from a similar height (1200 feet) two 10lb bombs on the anti-aircraft guns on the west side of the town.[24]

Heavy gunfire from shore batteries shook off the RNAS pilots, several machines being struck, and they finally gave up. After all the excitement had died down Peterson had the two gondolas detached from *L12* and brought on to the quayside, but later, when a large crane attempted to swing the bows of *L12* on to the pier, the airship exploded and burned itself out. The submerged after section was unharmed and yielded up part of the covering, framework and gas cells virtually intact.

August 12/13: L9, L10, L11, L13

Despite the disasters of the previous raid, Strasser remained undaunted and during the afternoon of the 12th four Zeppelins were despatched. A loose propeller shaft on *L9* forced Loewe to make a premature return and the aptly numbered *L13* suffered a breakdown on the port engine thus compelling Mathy to turn back.

Wenke, in *L10*, managed to reach the English coast despite fierce headwinds and appeared over Lowestoft at 21.25hrs. Realising that a raid on London was out of the question, the commander correctly identified Woodbridge, Ipswich and Harwich, dropping bombs on each. Woodbridge suffered 24 HE and incendiary bombs which killed seven and injured six civilians and damaged or destroyed 69 houses and a church. Machine-gun fire from the 2nd/3rd London Infantry Brigade greeted *L10* at Woodbridge and also Rushmere, but no hits were scored and Wenke cruised on to Harwich, where all his remaining bombs fell on Parkstone, injuring 17 civilians and wrecking two houses. Four RNAS pilots had taken off from South Denes at Great Yarmouth, yet none encountered *L10*, which went out to sea over Aldeburgh.

Von Buttlar returned without dropping a single missile. The weather forced him to abandon the attack, and a ferocious electrical storm plagued *L11* during its return trip. The thunderstorm threatened the very safety of the Zeppelin which was tossed around like a cork by the terrifying forces of nature. *L11* was lucky to reach the base at Nordholz unscathed, and it disgorged a badly shaken crew at 06.37hrs.

August 17/18: L10, L11, L13, L14

The city of London was again the target for the raid of 17 August when in the afternoon four airships arose from Nordholz and Hage. *L13* was again dogged by mechanical failure and forced to return, and *L14* (Böcker) suffered malfunctions on two engines whilst over England. Böcker later claimed to have bombed Ipswich and Woodbridge but none of the 70 assorted bombs was traced on land and they presumably fell into the sea off Great Yarmouth.

Von Buttlar came in over Herne Bay Pier at 21.30hrs, thence on to Canterbury, Ashford (where 21 bombs were dropped) and Faversham, then Badlesmere (which received 41 bombs) and Sheldwich, *L11* finally going out to sea not far from her original landfall. In the two hours he spent meandering over Kent, von Buttlar met only erratic rifle fire from the 2nd Provisional Battalion by way of retaliation, and all his bombs fell harmlessly into open fields.

Wenke, however, did manage to reach London, the first of the naval commanders to do so. *L10* had made landfall over Orfordness and with uncanny navigation Wenke approached the capital from the north. His arrival went unnoticed until the inhabitants of Walthamstow and Leyton were rudely awakened by the fall of bombs.

Few civilians were abroad at this time, so casualties were light and the last bombs caused no great havoc. Wenke himself was convinced that he had attacked central London and yet he had only bombed the outskirts of the city. During the raid four home defence machines were sent up and as usual none made contact with the enemy. Worse still, an RNAS aircraft from Chelmsford crash-landed and, with several bombs still aboard, blew up, killing the pilot, Flight Sub-Lieutenant C D Morrison, although the observer, Sub-Lieutenant H H Square, scrambled out unhurt.

The career of *L10* came to an abrupt and premature end just over two weeks later when, under the command of Hirsch, it went over pressure height in a thunderstorm and was struck by lightning. The Zeppelin immediately

Seven civilians were killed and six injured as a result of Wenke's handiwork at Woodbridge. Here, three lucky survivors confer with military personnel on the morning following the raid; in the background is St Johns Church, also damaged by bombs.
M J Taylor

Commissioned on 10 August 1915, *L14* (builder's number LZ46) was constructed at Löwenthal and its commanders included Böcker, Manger and Dose. *L14* made a total of 42 scouting flights, participated in 17 raids, and between 5 April 1917 and 8 September 1918 served as an elementary training ship. On 23 June 1919 *L14* was deliberately wrecked in the *Nora* shed at Nordholz by airship crews. The vessel is seen here passing the famous *Drehhalle*.
F Moch

On 8 September 1915, *L9*, *L11*, *L13* and *L14* embarked on a raid over England, only Mathy's *L13* reaching London, where a 660lb bomb, the first such to be dropped, did considerable damage to buildings in Bartholomew Close. This is the scene the following day: the crater caused by the bomb at right is cordoned off, the street littered with debris. Like most adjacent buildings, the windows of The Universal Transport Co Ltd and Van Oppen and Co Ltd, Universal Carriers and Shipping Agents, were all shattered by the blast of Mathy's missile.
IWM LC21

exploded and fell blazing into 6ft of water near Neuwark Island. There were no survivors, and Hirsch's men were the first naval airship crew to be killed in the war.

September 7/8: LZ74, LZ77, SL2
The German Army now weighed in with a raid that took everyone completely by surprise: ascending from their sheds in Belgium, three ships steered directly for England, their target London. *Hauptmann* Alfred Horn, commanding *LZ77*, made landfall at Clacton-on-Sea and passed over Hatfield Broad Oak – which was as far as he got. For some reason *LZ77* turned tail and, unleashing seven bombs, left the coast via Lowestoft. Further bombs fell into the sea beyond the coastline and the only material damage that could be attributed to *LZ77* was a farmer's threshing machine. Two RNAS machines from Great Yarmouth failed to make contact with *LZ77*, which returned to Belgium unscathed.

LZ74, commanded by *Hauptmann* Fritz George, was the first ship to reach London, approaching the capital via the Lea Valley, yet unaccountably almost the entire bomb load fell on Cheshunt. A total of 18 HE and 27 incendiary bombs destroyed greenhouses and private dwellings, after which the Zeppelin came under fire from the naval guns at Waltham Abbey. Proceeding towards the city, George found himself in the unenviable position of being over the heart of London with only a single bomb left. This fell on the warehouse of Joseph Barber and Company, not far from Fenchurch Street. The resulting blaze was quickly doused and guns at Purfleet shelled *LZ74* as it finally turned for the coast, going out via Harwich.

Wobeser, in *SL2*, had a much more adventurous night. The commander commenced his attack by bombing the Millwall Docks, causing serious damage to adjacent dwellings in Gaverick Street and injuring nine civilians. Moored offshore were three sailing barges, the *Louise*, *John Evelyn* and *Hastaway*, and it was the second vessel which Wobeser's fifth bomb struck. The ship's master, Ernest Gladwell, and mate, Edward Bowles, were badly burned, and scrambled out of their shattered cabin with their clothes blazing and their faces blackened. Frederick Wright, master of the *Louise* moored alongside, gave them as much first aid assistance as possible while awaiting a motor launch to take them to shore. Both seamen were admitted to Poplar Hospital but succumbed to their injuries some days later.

SL2 next released a brace of bombs, one of which struck the foreign Cattle Market Building, the other a three-storeyed building in Hughes Fields, Deptford. This house, occupied by William Beechey and his family of five, possessed a tiny attic in which slept old Mrs Beechey and her eight-year-old grand-daughter. Their beds were less than 3ft apart and Wobeser's bomb, tearing through the roof tiles, passed between the incumbent sleepers leaving them unscathed. The bomb's progress, however, was halted by the floor below – where it exploded:

> In the records of the Coroner's office there is a touching disposition by Miss Teresa Beechey, a daughter of the family then living at Greenwich:
> 'I identify the body of my father, William James Beechey, aged 56; my mother Elizabeth Emma Frances Beechey, aged 47; the body [*sic*] of my brother and two sisters, William Beechey, aged 11, Margaret Beechey, aged 7, and Eleanor Beechey aged 3, all residing with my parents at 34 Hughes Fields.'[25]

Following a course to Woolwich, Wobeser's next bomb fell on South Eastern and Chatham Railway track and then close to the Royal Dockyard's main gates; although damage to property was great, no serious casualties were reported. The commander of *SL2* then returned to the Millwall and Deptford areas seemingly unmoved by fierce gunfire and the many searchlights surrounding the ship. Eleven bombs fell in a triangle formed by New Cross, New Cross Gate and South Bermondsey railway stations just after midnight. When Wobeser finally departed the scene of his final attack he left 14 civilians dead and ten injured in his wake.

September 8/9: L9, L11, L13, L14
Spurred on by the success of the Army's *SL2* the previous night, Strasser despatched four of his ships to raid England, and for Mathy the 'jinx' on *L13* finally ended with telling effect. Loewe, in *L9*, was instructed to attack the Benzol works at Skinningrove, north Yorkshire, and he appeared over the target at 21.35hrs; he was unsure of the exact whereabouts of the benzol factory, but his bombs fell on it nevertheless. The damage done was light, bombs either failing to explode or failing to hit the main storage tanks holding 45,000gal of fuel. Three RNAS pilots took off to intercept the raider, but *L9* left via Sandsend at 21.45hrs without any of the aerial combatants encountering one another.

L13 and *L14* came under fire from the trawlers *Conway* and *Manx Queen* lying off the Haisborough lightship and Böcker, thus persuaded to abandon an attack on London, instead bombed 'Norwich'. Actually 55 bombs fell on

Byland, Scarning and East Dereham, the last suffering 11 civilians killed or injured. Von Buttlar, in *L11*, turned back almost immediately to Nordholz with engine trouble, having been only an hour and five minutes in the air.

Mathy's *L13* was the only ship to reach London, making landfall near Wells-next-the-Sea, Norfolk, at around 19.35hrs. Mathy hovered offshore for about an hour, waiting for darkness, before coming in over King's Lynn. The night was exceptionally clear, and from Cambridge Mathy could plainly see the lights of London illuminating the southern horizon. At 22.40hrs the first of *L13*'s bombs fell in Upper Bedford Place, Queen's Square and Theobald's Road. Henry Coombs, an employee of the London Gas Light and Coke Company, was standing in Lamb's Conduit Passage close to The Dolphin public house. He was killed outright by Mathy's fifth bomb, which also wrecked the bar and ground floor of the pub; a clock in an inner room was stopped by the explosion at precisely 22.49hrs. The next, most devastating bomb fell on Lane's Buildings at the end of Portpool Lane, killing four children instantly. In a police station close by, a telegraphist was sending out news of the raid in morse, doubtless wondering who the then unnamed victims of Lane's Buildings were. Only later did it transpire that PC John Palmer had lost two of his own children in the fire.

Hanging in *L13*'s bomb racks was the first of a new large kind of missile – a 660lb explosive bomb – which Mathy dropped on Bartholomew Close a little after 23.00hrs. In the Close was a duty fire box which Charles Henley, a London fireman, was manning that evening. At first the night seemed quiet but later Henley heard 'an unusual sound like the whir-r-r of a heavy motor. It seemed to get nearer and was accompanied by the ominous thud of distant explosions.'[26]

The 'heavy motor' belonged to Mathy's *L13*, and as Henley warned two men leaving The Admiral Carter to run for it, he was knocked off his feet by a tremendous explosion:

> I heard children calling 'Fireman', from the windows of one of the buildings, he reported later. I could see fire everywhere in the close. At one place it was gas alight; in another was a building on fire... I saw many houses very much damaged and wrecked, also a big hole in the road near to the fire box.[27]

The two men leaving the pub, William Fenge and Frederick Saunders, were killed outright, and the blast shattered all the windows and walls of the buildings in the square. The resulting conflagration impressed Mathy greatly as he watched his 'fall of shot' from above. 'The explosive effect of the 300kg bomb must be very great, since a whole cluster of lights vanished in its crater.'[28]

When the giant bomb exploded, 13-year-old Violet Buckthorpe was spending the evening at her parent's home at the Bartholomew Dairy in the company of her grandmother. The youngster dashed upstairs, grabbed two-year-old sister Marjorie from her cot and brought her out into the street. The stairs were rocking and several missing altogether but the sisters made it safely and Violet ran to the nearest hospital. The girl was streaming with blood and a shard of glass was later removed from her ear. Violet's act of bravery was rewarded with a gold watch and a £30 educational grant.

But it was the warehouses north of St Paul's that bore the full brunt of Mathy's attack, with huge fires in Wood Street, Silver Street, Addle Street and Aldermanbury. Despite valiant efforts by the crews of 22 fire appliances, many buildings and their valuable contents went up in flames. All 26 anti-aircraft guns in the London area were firing at *L13*, which was only flying at 9000ft. Few came close to the ship but Mathy, suitably impressed by the heat of the reception, rose to 11,200ft on a zig-zag course as 20 searchlights groped blindly for the Zeppelin.

The last of Mathy's bombs were aimed at Liverpool Street Station, one falling on railways lines and ripping up a few yards of track, the other three falling close to the terminal. An omnibus negotiating the bend into Blomfield Street took one bomb fair and square and another bus in Norton Folgate was similarly struck. In Sun Street Passage, a constable seeking shelter was buried by falling masonry. In just a few seconds, Mathy's parting shot had increased the night's death toll to 22.

From the ground *L13*'s progress over the city appeared almost leisurely and there was general dissatisfaction with the poor performance of the defences. Three RNAS pilots had taken off from Great Yarmouth during the raid and one, Flight Sub-Lieutenant Gerald William Hilliard, was killed landing at Bacton, when his bombs exploded. None of the airmen engaged the enemy, indeed all were back on the ground before Mathy went out over Great Yarmouth heading for Hage, which he reached at 08.10hrs.

This attack by *L13* was to be the most effective of any raid by any aircraft or airship on the British Isles during the entire war: Mathy had caused damage to the tune of £534,387, of which £530,787 was the result of the great fires in the city alone.

The next day a resident of Barnet found a parachute attached to a small bag in which was a scraped ham bone with the German red, white and black tricolour painted around its shank. On one side was a crude drawing of a Zeppelin dropping a bomb on the head of an elderly figure annotated as 'Edwart Grey' saying 'Was fang ich, armer Teufel, an?' ('What shall I, poor devil, do?'). On the reverse side was another inscription: 'Zum Andenken an das ausgehungerte Deutschland' ('A memento from starved-out Germany'). The British newspapers stated that the bone also bore the legend 'from commander and officers'. Mathy himself was severely rebuked by the *Kaiser* for this action and yet it was probably a member of his crew who dropped the message.

September 11/12: LZ77

Hauptmann Horn, in *LZ77*, made his single-handed attack arriving south of the Blackwater at 23.15hrs and making a direct course for London. Over Epping Forest *LZ77* met heavy fog, and Horn, under the impression he was over the city, dropped all his 60 bombs on the RFA camp near North Weald Bassett. The safety 'pins' had not been withdrawn from the HE bombs and all failed to explode. There was no damage nor any casualties as a result of the attack.

September 12/13: LZ74

The following night the Army tried again with a single ship, *LZ74* commanded by *Hauptmann* George, in more or less a carbon-copy of the previous night's raid. Thick fog severely hampered the airship commander who, confused by machine-gun fire from the Eastern Mobile Section, dropped 27 bombs on them thinking he was over Southend. Actually small villages between Colchester and Woodbridge were the targets, and although there was damage to fences and windows there were no casualties. On both nights RNAS machines took off, but the pilots failed to locate the ship.

September 13/14: L11, L13, L14

Severe weather hampered the next raid by the Navy and thunderstorms forced von Buttlar (*L11*) and Böcker (*L14*) to abandon the mission, but Mathy pressed on. At 23.10hrs he reached Orfordness on the Suffolk coast which he correctly identified. Almost an hour later, the Harwich guns opened up on *L13*, one shell striking gas cells and forcing Mathy to dump bombs in order to lighten his ship.

Compelled to return home with the Zeppelin in a critical condition, Mathy had a harrowing journey. Dumping thousands of pounds of fuel and oil, *L13* finally reached Hage at 04.20hrs where the ship made a heavy landing, resulting in damage that kept the Zeppelin out of commission for four days.

October 13/14: L11, L13, L14, L15, L16
The last raid of 1915 was particularly heavy, with 71 people killed, 128 injured, and thousands of pounds worth of damage caused. Five Zeppelins – *L11, L14* and *L15* from Nordholz, and *L13* and *L16* from Hage – flew in formation to their target above a thick overcast. Between 18.15 and 18.40hrs, Mathy (*L13*) led four of the ships over the coast near Winterton and Haisborough. *L11* made landfall almost exactly two hours later, and although von Buttlar made subsequent claims of bombing London, his 23 bombs actually fell on Coltishall, Great Hautbois and Horstead. Machine-gun fire from the Eastern Mobile Section persuaded the commander to penetrate inland no further, and *L11* turned back, being engaged by artillery fire from Mousehold Heath on its way out.

Over England for the first time was *Kapitänleutnant* Joachim Breithaupt, in *L15*, who on this night at least was to steal a little of Mathy's thunder. In fact Breithaupt was the first to reach London, drawing gunfire from the Broxbourne 13pdr on the way. The target was not difficult to find. The crew of *L15* could see the city easily as it was so well illuminated, and one later reported that the 'arcing' of trams leading into London was readily visible:

> Suddenly, from all sides, searchlights leapt out towards us, and as we flew over Tottenham [*sic*] a wild barrage from the anti-aircraft positions began. The shells burst at a good height right in our course. I therefore rose, after dropping three explosive bombs, and endeavoured to make an attack from another quarter.[29]

Having aimed four bombs at the 'Tottenham' gun, Breithaupt stayed his hand until well over the heart of London. The next batch of bombs was unleashed as *L15* was passing over Trafalgar Square: spreading out, they caused great explosions in the near vicinity of 'Theatre Land' – Drury Lane. The first missile struck the rear of The Lyceum, shattering a skylight and distributing shards of glass over the auditorium. The performance of *Between Two Women* was abruptly terminated amidst much consternation within the audience. One male patron hurried down a staircase to the outer door, leaving his wife behind in her seat as the gunfire started. No sooner had he dashed out into the street when shrapnel from an anti-aircraft shell killed him on the spot.

Meanwhile a second bomb had gouged a large hole in the centre of Wellington Street, rupturing a gas main and igniting the stream of gas that issued as a result. This bomb exploded between The Bell public house and the offices of the *Morning Post*. The street was crowded, and when the survivors gathered their wits, they found 38 people lying on the road and pavements, 17 of them dead. The scene was littered with millions of glass fragments from shattered windows, one woman was blown to pieces and another was cut in two by a falling sheet of glass. An old orange-seller had been standing by the entrance of The Lyceum: she too was dead. In The Bell ten people had been killed, including a barmaid, and a horribly injured corpse was discovered at the entrance, his dead hands still curled round a sandwich and a pint glass. Such was the greatest toll of any single bomb dropped up to that date.

Breithaupt's third missile fell in York Street and the fourth just outside the Strand Theatre where Fred Terry and Julia Nielson were performing in *The Scarlet Pimpernel*. The actors managed to quieten a restless audience alarmed by the explosion and the orchestra struck up several lively numbers. It had the desired effect and relative calm was restored. The next missile fell close to the Waldorf Hotel, the sixth landed at the foot of Kingsway, and two more severely damaged the temporary Aldwych headquarters of the Belgian Relief Fund. It was fortunate that five theatres

When Breithaupt bombed London's 'Theatreland' on 13 October 1915, one of his missiles struck London General Omnibus LE9347 outside the Waldorf Hotel. The driver, conductor and two passengers were killed outright and the bus was left shattered and blazing. The vehicle was later recovered and towed back to the LGOC's depot.
IWM Q70238

in the vicinity narrowly escaped destruction. At The Gaiety, then recently re-opened, George Grossmith, James Blakely and the Gaiety Company were in the successful comedy *Tonight's the Night*. James Wickham, an 18-year-old call-boy at the theatre, left the premises at 21.00hrs to post some urgent letters, and in company with a page boy he reached the nearest pillar box, in Catherine Street. On the way, Wickham halted momentarily to light a cigarette, carefully shielding the match in accordance with the imposed lighting restrictions:

> There was the sudden crackle of anti-aircraft gunfire, and simultaneously a dreadful sound that London knew only too well – a sound like no other on earth. It was the mournful wail created by the velocity of a descending bomb.
>
> In the one brief terrible moment before the impact I instinctively knew it was coming directly where we stood. I was not wrong. It exploded three yards from where we were standing. It flung me against the wall next to the pit entrance to the Strand Theatre. It sucked me back again. It dashed me to the ground. Masonry fell. Glass rained. I felt unhurt; only dazed. Yet I had 22 lumps of shrapnel embedded in me. They carried me downstairs into the bar of the Strand Theatre. I asked for Billy, but he had been blown to pieces. I could hear screams in the street outside. The dull vibrant thud of more bombs.
>
> Others were brought in and laid beside me. Some were moaning, some calling for missing friends and relatives. Someone rushed in and said a London General omnibus had been blown to bits in Aldwych opposite the Waldorf.[30]

The bus stood shattered and scorched outside the famous hotel, the driver, conductor and two passengers, one a constable, having been killed instantly. The theatres were used as temporary dressing stations, the killed and wounded being transported on improvised 'stretchers' hastily made up from theatre notice-boards.

As Breithaupt continued on his way, further bombs rained down on the Royal Courts of Justice up to Gray's Inn Road and Holborn, causing considerable damage. One incendiary bomb which gutted the Robing Room at Gray's Inn was subsequently salvaged and preserved in the Bencher's own law library. It was fortunate indeed that the Inn had its own fire brigade which prevented the flames from spreading further.

After Mathy's effective attack in September, the British Admiralty had secured a mobile 75mm gun from France. In charge of the weapon on this night was Lieutenant-Commander W Rawlinson, who had set it up in the Honourable Artillery Company ground at Finsbury. When Breithaupt's *L15* sailed majestically into view through a myriad searchlight beams, the gun opened up. The first shot missed, the gun crew rapidly reloaded for another attempt, and then a limitation of the gun was realised. It would not elevate further than 83° and Rawlinson and his men watched helplessly as, brightly illuminated, *L15* passed into the 'dead circle' of the gun. As the ship sailed on, so the angle decreased and a second shot was fired which burst close to the Zeppelin but did it no harm. British aircraft were also in the air:

> As we were about over Leyton, a new and murderous fire began from a direction in which we had not expected it. At the same time through the rays of the searchlights, a number of British aircraft appeared on both sides, and were simultaneously reported to be overhead by the lookout man on top of the ship.[31]

Five RFC machines had taken off from the makeshift home defence fields at Hainault Farm, Joyce Green and Suttons Farm. Although the commander of *L15* claimed to have seen four aircraft, only one British pilot spotted *L15*. Eighteen-year-old Lieutenant John Slessor, in a BE2c armed with Ranken explosive darts, was left standing by the Zeppelin, which simply stuck its nose upwards and kept climbing until safely out of range.[32]

After Rawlinson's second shell had exploded close to *L15*, the commander had dumped his remaining bombs and water ballast and quickly disappeared into the mist. The final missile fell in Cable Street, killing a horse and extensively damaging some commercial buildings.

Mathy reached the River Thames at 21.30hrs and followed the river to reach Hampton in order to attack the waterworks. Being misled by the curves of the Thames, Mathy then set a course along the River Wey, and at 23.30hrs the first of *L13*'s bombs fell upon Shalford, where several houses were damaged. Thinking he had bombed Hampton, the commander passed over Bromley and then moved on to Woolwich Arsenal, which received a 660pdr amongst the rest of *L13*'s bombs. Four men in the Woolwich Barracks were killed, and in the Arsenal itself nine succumbed. Material damage, however, was slight.

In *L14*, Böcker made landfall over Norwich in consort with the other airships before steering inland. Via Colchester, the Isle of Sheppey and Kent, Böcker reached Shorncliffe at 21.15hrs. The commander apparently mistook the Channel for the Thames, and bombs fell on Otterspool Army Camp, killing 15 soldiers and injuring 11. Böcker, assuming he had bombed the Woolwich Arsenal, then headed north-west and eventually found himself over Croydon at 23.20hrs. Here *L14* dumped 18 bombs which wrecked several private houses, nine civilians being killed and 15 injured as a result.

Werner Peterson, in command of *L16*, had seen Breithaupt's ship lit up by London's searchlights and, taking advantage of the gunners' attention to his companion, struck out for Hertford which he mistook for Stratford and East Ham. Altogether 48 incendiary and explosive bombs killed nine people and injured 15, as well as destroying ten buildings and causing negligible damage to a further 141.

The 13 October raid was one of the most effective of the war: its total of people killed and injured was to remain the highest figure in terms of raiders involved and bombs dropped throughout the entire conflict. The Zeppelin commanders were nevertheless impressed by the improved defences evident on the last raid of 1915. The guns, searchlights and aeroplanes were still to score a real success, yet their efforts were sufficient for Strasser's men to proceed with more caution in subsequent attacks.

The raids of 1915 killed 208 civilians and injured 432. Those under attack were more angry than humbled – angry that the Zeppelins bombed civilian targets and angry that they could do so practically unchallenged by the home forces. But there were no more squadron raids on London for over a year and the onset of winter reduced the activities of the airship divisions over England altogether.

The next time the Zeppelins came there was a different target.

The Raids of 1916

In the first week of 1916, Admiral von Pohl relinquished command of the High Seas Fleet to *Vizeadmiral* Reinhard Scheer. Pohl's successor showed policies which were warmly welcomed by Strasser, for Scheer desired to intensify campaigns against England with surface ship bombardment and increased Zeppelin raids on key cities. It was on 18 January that Strasser and Scheer held their first meeting, and from it there developed a mutual respect between both commanders as well as a grandiose scheme for bombing the whole of England. In order to issue simplified attack orders, the country was to be divided into three main areas: 'England South' to cover London and Great Yarmouth, 'England Middle' for Liverpool and the Humber and 'England North' for Edinburgh and the Tyne. Army airships were also to participate, in order that the maximum number of craft could embark on any one raid Thirteen days after the meeting, the new campaign began

January 31/February 1: L11, L13, L14, L15, L16, L17, L19, L20, L21

Towards midday, nine Zeppelins left their respective sheds at Hage, Nordholz and Tondern and later were all to report low, heavy fog as they made their way over the North Sea. Further problems occurred as the squadron neared the English coast, with rain clouds and snow icing up the airships' outer covers. In fact the severe weather and unreliable radio 'fixes' badly misled most of the commanders, several of whom made landfall much further south than planned, confusing subsequent navigation.

Bomb damage resulting from the first raid of 1916 on 31 January/1 February. Nine Zeppelins took part in this operation and the Strasser 'jinx' struck again, for although von Buttlar's *L11* got well inland, poor weather conditions forced a premature return to Nordholz.
IWM H043

The first Zeppelins to arrive were *L13* (Mathy) and *L21* (commanded by *Kapitänleutnant* Max Dietrich), both of which crossed the Norfolk coast near Mundesley at 16.50hrs. Steering a course that took him south of Nottingham and thence to Derby, Mathy eventually reached Stoke-on-Trent, upon which he dropped six bombs. The missiles found their mark on Fenton Colliery where a few windows were broken but no other damage resulted. Mathy dropped parachute flares to determine his position but they only revealed fog, and when he called for wireless bearings these only led him to believe he had bombed Manchester. Flying blindly on, 'blast furnaces' were seen through a gap in the clouds below, and Mathy dropped the remainder of his HE bombs together with 60 incendiaries. Several missiles fell close to the Frodingham Iron and Steel Works at Scunthorpe and blazing furnaces could easily be observed. At the nearby Redbourne Iron Works, which were closed down at the time, other bombs found their mark, killing two workmen but doing little damage to the plant itself. In the town, four private houses were destroyed, with one man killed and a further seven civilians injured; Mathy quit the scene just before midnight. Dietrich and *L21* soon outpaced Mathy and, passing Nottingham and north of Derby, turned south-west towards Wolverhampton and Birmingham. At this time Dietrich was convinced that he was over the west coast, and when he next observed the lights of two large towns he commenced the attack. What the commander took to be Liverpool and Birkenhead was actually the towns of Lower Bradley, Tipton, Wednesbury and Walsall, where 27 HE and 21 incendiaries fell in quick succession. There was minimal damage to property save a few wrecked houses, but the death toll was heavy: 33 were killed, including the Mayoress of Walsall, and 20 people suffered injuries of varying degrees of severity.

At this juncture Dietrich headed back to the coast, releasing the last of his incendiaries on the way over Islip Furnaces, Thrapston, at 21.15hrs. All six missiles failed to strike their target, falling instead on open fields. Confident that Manchester had received his parting shot, Dietrich pressed on, leaving the coast over Lowestoft at 23.35hrs.

Three airships developed engine trouble and had to make hasty alterations to their plans as a result. Peterson, in *L16*, abandoned his attack on Liverpool, thanks to a burnt-out bearing in the control car engine and an aft motor malfunction. On two engines and with a dangerous ice-laden envelope, Peterson decided to bomb Great Yarmouth instead, and at 19.20hrs aimed two tons of HE and incendiaries on that town. Actually he was way off the mark. British records place *L16* making its landfall near Hunstanton at 18.10hrs and then meandering over Norfolk for the next three hours until the Zeppelin finally left English shores at Lowestoft. Most of Peterson's bombs must have fallen out to sea as the only traceable missiles were a couple of HE bombs at Swaffham, and one of those failed to detonate.

Kapitänleutnant Herbert Ehrlich, in *L17*, suffered engine breakdowns for most of the way over, and despite the endeavours of the mechanics the troubles could not be cured. At 18.40hrs *L17* made landfall over Sheringham in Norfolk and soon after was caught in a searchlight from the RNAS airfield at Holt. Believing himself to be over Immingham, the commander ordered the release of the bomb load, and 40 missiles fell on Bayfield and one on nearby Letheringsett. Most fell harmlessly in open fields, a barn and a house being the only casualties. Ehrlich went out to sea via Great Yarmouth at 20.30hrs.

L20 was unable to climb above 6500ft with ice and snow forming on its hull, the forward engine out of action and the starboard motor running badly, *Kapitänleutnant* Franz Stabbert coming in over the Wash at 19.00hrs. Steering westward, Stabbert observed the lights of a town which turned out to be Loughborough, and pressed home his attack oblivious of the fact that he had passed over blacked-out Leicester. Ten people killed, 12 injured and several damaged buildings were attributed to four bombs that fell on Loughborough at 20.05hrs. The next targets were Bennersley and Trowley, where seven bombs struck a cattle shed and a trackside signal box, then Ilkeston, where the Stanton Iron Works at Hallam Fields received 15 explosives. Various buildings were extensively damaged and four casualties resulted, two of them fatal. *L20* then made its main attack on Burton-upon-Trent, which was undarkened, and here over a dozen incendiaries were sent down. The unfortunate town was attacked by three of the raiders that night and the casualties numbered 70 injured and 15 killed. Eventually, *L20* turned back for Tondern, passing out over Cromer just before midnight.

Strasser's reputation as a 'Jonah' was further substantiated on this first raid of 1916, for *L11* was fated to return without dropping a single bomb. Even before the Zeppelin reached England, it was loaded up with over two tons of ice and rain, and was unable to reach 6700ft. Mist and fog badly hampered von Buttlar, and despite tantalising glimpses of

Control and forward engine car of *L20*. Despite appearances there are actually two separate gondolas although the gap is concealed with fabric. Such a configuration reduced engine noise and vibration in the forward car and wireless cabin.
F Moch

targets through momentary breaks in the murk, the commander, having consulted with his superior, reluctantly decided to abort. The Zeppelin steered a course for Nordholz, arriving there at 09.50hrs after being airborne for just over 22 hours.

Böcker in the trustworthy *L14* came in north of Holkham at 18.15hrs and heralded his arrival by dropping a single incendiary on Wisbech, and then an HE near Knipton. The low fog obliterated the ground and Böcker flew on, searching vainly for Liverpool. British records place *L14* over Shrewsbury at 22.05hrs, and from there the Zeppelin flew eastwards, the light of furnaces at Ashby Woulds revealing a likely target. Bombs fell harmlessly there and then upon Overseal and Swadlincote, again without causing any damage. Turning back, Böcker believed that he bombed blast furnaces and factory premises in Nottingham, but in fact 4150lb of bombs fell on Derby. Nine HEs struck the Midland Railway works, damaging the engine sheds, killing three men and injuring two more, whilst three further bombs fell on the Metalite Lamp Works, inflicting a great deal of damage yet causing no casualties. The remaining bombs were ineffectual although an old woman died of shock. Leaving Derby at last, Böcker sailed out over the Lincolnshire coast a little after 02.10hrs.

The course of Breithaupt's *L15* confused British authorities, who credited this airship with having bombed the Fens north-east of Cambridge and then flying on to Lincolnshire. Breithaupt's subsequent report bears little relation to such actions, for he stated that Liverpool and Birkenhead were his targets. However, it seems likely that the Fen-raider was *L16* and that *L15* was the second airship to bomb Burton-on-Trent, as 25 bombs fell there at about 21.45hrs.

Breithaupt's return journey to Hage was not without incident. On the way over, two of *L15*'s motors were out of action for a couple of hours and on the homeward leg the magnetic compass was found to be in error by 90°. Radio bearings from the station at Bruges proved unreliable, and the rudder man was forced to navigate by the stars. The crew of *L15* were fortunate indeed that clearing weather enabled this to be done; not so fortunate, however, were the crew of *L19*, who were destined never to return – and in circumstances that remain controversial to this day.

Commanding *L19* was Loewe, who was determined to reach Liverpool despite being plagued by recent problems with his ship's motors. *L19* apparently came inland near Sheringham at 18.20hrs and made its way to Burton-on-Trent where Loewe became the third commander to attack that unfortunate town. *L19* then went on to the Birmingham suburbs more or less in the wake of *L21*, with bombs falling on Wednesbury, Dudley, Tipton and Walsall. No additional casualties resulted, and of 17 bombs aimed at Dudley only one fell on the town. Ground observers noted *L19* steering eastwards, and eventually at 05.25hrs the ship went out across Winterton, having experienced engine trouble during the nine hours it was over England. Earlier, at 02.53hrs, Loewe radioed for bearings, and then at 04.37hrs he despatched his attack report in which he claimed to have bombed 'several big factories in Sheffield'. No further signals were received that day after a final bearing at 05.41hrs gave *L19*'s position to the Haisborough lightship. The Germans became worried. Later in the day three destroyer flotillas 'coaled up' to institute a search, but as they were leaving port at 15.05hrs Nordholz received a signal from *L19*. The message revealed that three of the Zeppelin's engines had broken down and the radio was malfunctioning. Bearings were plotted, positions were radioed to *L19* and the destroyers recalled.

No further news was forthcoming, and at midnight destroyers were sent out again but failed to locate the airship. During the morning of 2 February, one destroyer picked up an aluminium fuel tank containing ten gallons of petrol. The tank was found some 12 miles north of Borkum and it was from *L19*.

Later that day, the Germans learnt that Loewe's Zeppelin had been observed flying low over Ameland during the afternoon of 1 February. Dutch sentries opened fire on the airship and claimed several hits before the mist swallowed up the target. The British had also spotted the ship earlier off Cromer, and as day dawned the Harwich Force of light cruisers and destroyers was despatched; however, the ships failed to locate *L19* and were recalled at 16.50hrs. Subsequent events indicate that *L19*, crippled by the Dutch gunfire and with no motive power, was ultimately driven down into the North Sea by loss of gas and strong winds. Loewe's ship fell about 100 miles from the English coast and the first task was to lighten it by cutting away the gondolas. Some of the crew rigged a rudimentary shelter on top of the envelope, where they clung tenaciously hoping for rescue.

At 06.00hrs on 2 February the crew were excited at the arrival of a fishing trawler, and Loewe hailed the vessel, requesting that his men be taken aboard. The British captain of the *King Stephen* weighed up the situation. There were only eight members of his crew, as opposed to 16 Germans, and thus there was a strong possibility that his men would be overpowered. The trawler captain was also fishing in a prohibited area, and bringing in the Zeppelin crew could have fixed his position and consequently put him in hot water with the authorities. The skipper made up his mind, and, ignoring the pleas of the Zeppelin crew, turned away in order to find a patrol vessel that could more easily accommodate them. In the event, he failed to find another ship, and sailed into Grimsby the next day where he was at last able to make a report. By then it was too late. In the time left before the Zeppelin foundered several crew members despatched final messages in bottles, which were recovered in subsequent months.[33]

Not unnaturally, reports about the trawler skipper's actions caused a great deal of unrest, but German newspapers saved their vitriol for the Bishop of London, who publicly approved of the captain leaving the 'baby killers' to their fate. It is difficult and perhaps unwise to apportion blame so long after the event, but surviving airshipmen in Germany still angrily hold the trawler master responsible for a callous act. It is doubtful whether the freezing and exhausted Zeppelin crew could have overpowered the English sailors even had they desired so to do. But of course the *King Stephen*'s captain could not know this for certain. We have to accept that he made an attempt to locate assistance elsewhere rather than make a deliberate decision to let the Germans drown. But whatever the motives, it was a tragic incident and one that few members of the German Naval Airship Division ever forgot or forgave.

The British defences were shaken by the raid, and stricter measures were developed during following months. The Zeppelins had carried out their respective missions virtually unchallenged, gunfire was desultory, and the 20 aircraft which took off at various times all failed to find any of the airships. In fact the British pilots had a bad night. Eight aircraft were damaged in landing accidents and Majors L da C Penn Gaskell and E F Unwin of the RFC died of injuries after crashing on take-off.

March 5/6: L11, L13, L14

'Attack England North, chief target Firth of Forth' were the orders for 5 March, but all three airships were forced to abandon the plan when unexpected weather conditions brought snow squalls and freshening winds. Instead, the Midlands were selected as the secondary target, and *Korvettenkäpitan* Viktor Schütze in *L11* made landfall over Tunstall at 21.45hrs. The Zeppelin battled through snow and hail showers until it reached the outskirts of Hull, where another airship could be seen unloading its bombs upon the undefended city. Schütze held position for 20 minutes at around 4000ft against gale force winds whilst 3600lb of bombs rained down. The first missile struck the river close to Earle's Shipyard and resulted in the collapse of a steamer on the stocks the next day; a further 20 bombs destroyed houses, severed water mains, ignited the Mariner's Almhouses and damaged many other buildings. To Schütze peering from the control gondola the bombing looked most dramatic:

> One hit had a specially far reaching effect; radiating round the burst more and more houses collapsed and finally showed up, in the snow covered harbour area, as a black and gigantic hole. A similar bigger dark patch in the neighbourhood seemed to be due to the raid of *L14*...With binoculars it was possible to see people running hither and thither in the glare of the fires.[34]

Having finished with Hull, *L11* ploughed over Killingholme, was greeted by anti-aircraft fire, responded with four bombs, and sheered off towards the coast which it crossed at 01.40hrs. *L14*, whose attack on Hull had preceded that of *L11*, came in over Flamborough Head at around 22.30hrs and eventually dropped a brace of explosives on Beverley. Böcker picked up the Humber, which showed up clearly against the snow-covered fields, and followed the river into Hull; 21 incendiary and HE bombs fell on the city, houses in the vicinity of the docks faring the worst. Strong north winds prevented Böcker from making a second attack, and *L11* turned for Grimsby, where it came under shellfire from guns at Killingholme. Grimsby itself was hidden by cloud and, dropping a further seven bombs, Böcker went out over Tunstall.

Mathy, in *L13*, had a terrifying journey across the North Sea, a burnt-out crankshaft bearing forcing him to shut down the starboard engine and heavy falls of snow necessitating the release of 1300lb of fuel to compensate. Mathy eventually crossed the Lincolnshire coast at 21.14hrs and flew on to Lincoln itself and then Newark, over which he circled before making off to the south-east. Owing to his problem of power loss and weight, Mathy dropped a large number of bombs to lighten his ship. These did no damage, falling on fields in Sproxton and Thistleton; the detonations could be heard in Norwich, well over 80 miles away. At 12.30hrs *L13* was over the Thames Estuary, where gunfire from Shoeburyness and Sheerness opened up on the Zeppelin as it hovered almost stationary with bows to wind. With such an easy target held in the searchlight beams one can imagine the frustration of the gun crews as their meagre 6pdr guns failed to reach the target. *L13* then passed out over Kent via Deal, fighting against squalls all the way.

March 31/April 1: L9, L11, L13, L14, L15, L16, L22; LZ88, LZ90, LZ93

Towards noon, seven Zeppelins rose with orders to attack London, and this time Strasser forbade the sending of the usual take-off messages in order not to alert British radio operators. *L9* and *L11* soon turned back north-west of Terschelling, but the remaining five pressed on to their objective. In *L22*, engine trouble forced *Käpitanleutnant* Martin Dietrich to abandon London and attack the Humber. The commander reached Mablethorpe at 01.00hrs and then turned north; half an hour later 26 bombs fell on Humberstone but only damaged a farmhouse. The next missiles were far more effective, with six HEs falling on Cleethorpes: a chapel was destroyed and 29 soldiers of the 3rd Manchesters billeted there were killed and 53 injured. Dietrich left the coast at Spurn Head, accompanied by gunfire from a paddle minesweeper moored in the mouth of the Humber.

Mathy made landfall at 20.00hrs over Aldeburgh, and as the temperature proved too warm to reach a safe altitude for an attack on London he decided to gain height by dropping some bombs on Stowmarket first. At 20.45hrs Mathy was over the town, but a parachute flare failed to illuminate the New Explosive Works, his intended target. As his lights floated slowly down alert gunners in the area opened up and Mathy responded by hurling down a dozen bombs which did no more than shatter a few windows. *L13* then proceeded to Haughley, but turned back for Stowmarket shortly afterwards and made a second attempt on the Explosive Works. Once again he was engaged by the 6pdr guns there and this time the Zeppelin was hit.

Two gas cells had been struck and, having signalled the fact to Strasser, Mathy gave up any idea of further action. Dumping his last 33 bombs on Wangford and the Covehithe aerodrome, he went out to sea north of Southwold. Having dropped these remaining missiles, the Zeppelin rapidly rose and made off towards Hage, arriving there safely at 02.30hrs.

Breithaupt, in *L15*, came in with Mathy and made course for London via Ipswich and Chelmsford. At 21.30hrs *L15* was flying dynamically at 8500ft and north-east of the well-darkened capital. Nevertheless, the searchlight and gun teams were fully awake, as were many civilians in and around the suburbs of London to whom the lone attacker was readily visible.

Bill Morgan had an uninterrupted view right over into Essex from his home near the centre of Dartford in Kent. The raids on London provided an exciting nocturnal spectacle for the youngster, situated as he was over 150ft above the Thames. To the west could be seen Shooters Hill on the outskirts of the capital and on a clear day the old Crystal Palace buildings were visible. But on the night of 31 March something much more exciting held his attention:

> The airship was coned by several searchlights, including our local one, over the village of Bean, about two miles to the east

Few fighting positions could be as hazardous as the upper gun platforms of the Zeppelins. Another of Felix Schwormstadt's paintings shows two members of *LZ38*'s crew gallantly fending off British fighter aircraft. As befits an Army ship, the gun is a Parabellum; naval airships were usually armed with 8mm Maxims.
Leipziger Illustrirte Zeitung

of us and a mile to the south of Watling Street. It was so near it looked enormous and very menacing. All the local guns, including those on Dartford Brent, ¾ mile to our west, were firing at it at a very fast rate with that sequence with which we had become so familiar. First the bright white flash, followed at once by a hollow-sounding staccato double bang and then the high pitched whine of the passing shell on its way to the target. The Dartford Brent battery of two AA guns was firing on a line parallel to Watling Street, on which we lived, and at such a high elevation, that from our windows we could follow the passage of its shells, by their rear tracer lights, until they exploded with a red pin point flash and a cracking kind of bang.

For a time it was very hectic with many red flashes around the airship which must have had a hot time to be comfortable for it seemed to suddenly go up like a lift and disappeared into the darkness above. This was Zeppelin L15 which at about that time was also attacked in the air by Second Lieutenant C A Ridley, who was flying from the nearby Joyce Green aerodrome, then a home defence station. He fired a few rounds at it before he lost it but I have no recollection of hearing the pop-pop-pop of machine-gun fire and imagine it was drowned by the racket of the AA guns.

L15 was attacked again later and this time hit by the Purfleet Gun which was sited three miles to the north of us and just over the Thames on the Essex side from Joyce Green aerodrome on the Kent side.

Second Lieutenant A de B Brandon also sighted it and shot at it, causing more damage, which was extensive enough to prevent it getting back to its base and it came down in the sea off our coast.[35]

The two remaining Zeppelin commanders later claimed to have attacked London, but British records show otherwise. Peterson, in *L16*, remained convinced that he had bombed the Hornsea district, and yet his bombs were traced at Bury St Edmunds where 37 houses were damaged, with seven civilians killed and five injured. Having accomplished this feat, *L16* went out to sea, dropping a single bomb over Lowestoft which damaged a tramcar shed.

Böcker and Strasser, in *L14*, bombarded Sudbury, which they mistook for Cambridge factories. The 27 HE and incendiary bombs killed five and injured one, and damaged private houses, whilst further bombs at Braintree resulted in 11 casualties, four being fatalities. *L14* left the Essex town and moved thence west of Brentwood, where Böcker turned back for Sudbury and then south to the Thames Estuary. The remaining bombs fell on Blackmore, Doddinghurst, Springfield, Stanford-le-Hope and Thames Haven, where oil tanks narrowly escaped destruction. Although a brace of incendiaries struck two tanks of the Asiatic Oil Company, they were dry and a holocaust was avoided. *L14* finally went out to sea over Dunwich, its last bombs causing no casualties.

Earlier in the day the Army had despatched *LZ88*, *LZ90* and *LZ93* to attack England, and *LZ90*'s commander later claimed to have bombed Norwich, although no missiles were ever traced. The remaining ships apparently turned back with their bomb load intact, weather conditions being decidedly unfavourable.

April 1/2: L11, L17
Although London was to be the target for the next raid, the inclement weather decreed otherwise and the two airship commanders, Ehrlich and Schutze, received radio messages to divert to the Midlands. As dusk approached, Ehrlich, in *L17*, appeared over Flamborough Head and cruised around for an hour waiting for darkness. Just as he deemed it safe to move inland, the propeller shaft of the rear engine broke and the Zeppelin was brought to a stop. Repairs were carried out, the entire bomb load being jettisoned in the sea in order to provide extra buoyancy. The subsequent reports could be heard at Tunstall over 26 miles away as *L17* turned for home.

L11 had better luck and crossed the coast at Seaham around 23.00hrs before dropping the first of its bombs on Eppleton Colliery near Houghton-le-Spring. More bombs struck Hetton Downs, Philadelphia, Sunderland, Port Clarence, Middlesbrough, Brotton and the River Tees. One eyewitness to the bombing of Sunderland was H D Raine, who observed *L11* passing over the town:

> Bombs dropped in the Hylton Road, Millfield and Deptford areas and then near the Wearmouth Colliery. The airship continued with a bomb on the Wheatsheaf junction where tramcar No 10 was destroyed, killing a good number of people. Further bombs dropped in the Rober area, and in Victor Street my mother's cousin, a 12-year-old boy named Glasgow, was killed. As it was April Fool's Day the raid was referred to as the day the Germans made a fool of us.[36]

A great deal of damage was done to Sunderland shops, and *L11* left 22 dead, 25 seriously injured and 103 slightly injured civilians in its wake. The 6in gun at Fulwell Quarry fired a single shell at the Zeppelin, which missed, and four RNAS pilots who took off failed to make contact. *L11* landed safely at Nordholz around 09.00hrs the following day.

April 2/3: L13, L14, L16, L22; LZ88, LZ90
Three hours after *L11* had returned from its successful raid on Sunderland, four Naval Zeppelins took off for the Firth of Forth. Mathy, in *L13*, turned back at an early stage with engine trouble, but the remaining airships carried on. *L22* was the first to cross the coast at Berwick-on-Tweed, and Martin Dietrich dropped most of his bombs on Berwick fields, believing he had attacked a Newcastle factory. The Zeppelin moved back out to sea but came in again at Edinburgh just as Böcker in *L14* commenced his attack on that city. Dietrich's contribution was a mere three HE bombs which managed to shatter a few windows.

Böcker had shaken off gunfire from destroyers as he moved inland via St Abbs Head before fixing his position by the lights of Leith and Edinburgh. On the town Böcker dropped 9 HE and 11 incendiary bombs which killed a man and a child and wrecked three houses. A major tragedy was the destruction of Messrs Innes and Grieve's whisky bond warehouse: it went up in flames, the total loss of building and contents being valued at £44,000. The warehouse, like several other premises destroyed that night, was not even insured against aerial attack, indicative perhaps of a general feeling that still failed to take the German raiders seriously.

Edinburgh was the next target for Böcker, and 24 bombs killed 11 and injured 24 and damaged a fair amount of property including three hotels and Princes Street Station. Eventually, *L14* made off at 00.55hrs, meeting no opposition apart from desultory machine-gun fire from the southern slopes of Arthur's Seat.

Peterson, in *L16*, bombed Ponteland, and Broomhill, but none of the 41 missiles inflicted any harm, despite the commander's conviction that Tyneside factories had been damaged. Eleven of Peterson's bombs fell on the landing ground at Cramlington, attracted by the flares along the runway there. Two of the aircraft stationed on the field took off in pursuit but failed to overhaul the raider. One pilot had a lucky escape when his aircraft caught fire on landing, its bombs exploding on impact.

Two military Zeppelins, *LZ88* and *LZ90*, crossed the East Coast that night, having left bases in Belgium. *LZ90*, commanded by *Oberleutnant zur See der Reserve* Lehmann, soon came under heavy fire from guns at Waltham Abbey. As a result Lehmann unleashed all 90 bombs on what he thought was London, although the missiles actually damaged several houses in the vicinity of Woodridden Farm and Windmill Hill. *LZ90* shook off several searchlight beams and escaped out to sea via Clacton. *LZ88* made its landfall south of Orfordness, passing across Ipswich, and dropped 74 HE and incendiary bombs over Alderton, Hollesley and Ramsholt, where a few windows were broken. *Hauptmann* Falck had also planned to bomb London, but strong winds forced the ship off course and so he made for the Harwich area instead.

Several home defence aircraft had taken off to intercept the raiders, but although one Zeppelin was sighted, all failed to make interceptions. Whilst the airships carried out their respective attacks, naval squadrons sailed out from Rosyth to intercept them on their return but failed to see a single airship. Additionally, four Harwich destroyers left port at 04.30hrs to meet the Army Zeppelins, but by this time *LZ88* and *LZ90* were almost back in their sheds.

The forward engine/control car of *L20*, with its commander, *Kapitänleutnant* Franz Stabbert, at the windows. Note the Army officer at the doorway, the sandbags in foreground, and the characteristic 'rippling' of the celluloid windows. *M Dietrich/P Amesbury*

April 3/4: L11, L17
Two airships planned to attack London, but strong winds forced Ehrlich in *L17* to abandon the attempt, which left *L11* to make a solo effort. This Zeppelin made landfall at Sheringham soon after 01.30hrs but due to the late hour and poor visibility the commander, Schütze, was inclined to attack Lowestoft, Norwich and Great Yarmouth. Nevertheless, he was unable to locate any of these towns and went out to sea over Caister. Only four bombs, which *L11* had presumably dropped whilst searching for likely targets, were traced on land. Three groups of bombs were later heard falling in the sea just south of Caister, and *L11* returned without having caused any damage.

April 5/6: L11, L13, L16
Mathy's run of bad luck with *L13* continued when engine trouble forced him to abort during the next raid when he was halfway to his objective. Rain squalls diverted *L11* from its course to the Firth of Forth, and Schütze made landfall at Hornsea Mere instead. The Zeppelin approached Hull and came under immediate heavy gunfire: the town's defences had improved considerably since Schütze's last visit, and this violent reception was quite a shock. Dropping four bombs, *L11* beat a hasty retreat seawards and steered north towards Hartlepool after engine failure forced Schütze to change his mind about returning to Hull. Hartlepool was also abandoned when another motor failed, but as *L11* turned out to sea again Schütze observed the fires of an ironworks. These were at Skinningrove, upon which the commander promptly dropped 29 HE and incendiary bombs; six failed to explode and only the works laboratory was destroyed. Several nearby buildings were also damaged but there were no casualties and the gun crew at Skinningrove, with no searchlights to guide them, failed to fire even a single shot.

Peterson came in north of Hartlepool, passing over Bishop Auckland, and drifted on to Everwood where 23 bombs fell; Randolf Colliery was also struck. At Everwood, 15 cottages were wrecked and 70 more damaged, yet casualties remained slight and only one man and a child were killed. On the way back to the coast, *L16* bombed more collieries but failed to hit them, although there were four more casualties with another child being killed. Before Peterson and his crew reached their landing field they had to weather a whirlwind which threatened to engulf them. But as dawn came Peterson managed to descend lower into clearer weather, and *L16* proceeded homeward without further incident.

RFC machines were up from Beverley and Cramlington that night, and so too was an RNAS machine from Scarborough, yet none managed to find, let alone intercept, any of the Zeppelins. One of the pilots, Captain J Nichol, managed somehow to crash into a house and was killed outright. Surface vessels sent out from the Tyne and the Humber failed to spot anything, and the crew of the sloop *Poppy* were the only seamen to report a sighting, but they remained unable to do anything as one of the Zeppelins disappeared from view on its return to Germany.

April 24/25: L11, L13, L16, L17, L21, L23
All the airships taking part in the next raid crossed the coastline between Cromer and Southwold excepting *L17* (Ehrlich) which arrived later north of the Wash. Improved defences gave the raiders a healthy reception, yet only one airship was struck – Mathy's *L13*, on this occasion under the command of *Kapitänleutnant der Reserve* Eduard Prölss. Shell splinters struck the forward gondola, but the damage was not serious and Prölss carried on, only to meet with strong south-westerly winds. Such conditions forced all the airship

commanders to abandon any idea of reaching London, and instead they opted to attack alternative targets. But even these plans were thwarted by fog and rain, resulting in Zeppelins aimlessly cruising about dropping their bombs at random.

Peterson, in *L16*, threw out a bundle of German newspapers tied to a parachute which fell at Kimberley, and then bombed Newmarket after having been fired at by machine gunners there. Nineteen bombs demolished five houses and damaged 100 others, one civilian was injured and the champion racehorse Coup de Main killed in its Bury Road stable. Peterson dropped two more bombs on the outskirts of the town and five over Honingham on his return to the coast, which he crossed near Mundesley at 01.35hrs.

The raid was more or less a washout, and many of the raiders returned with most of their bomb load intact. British records trace 49 bombs on Honing Hill and Dilham from *L11*, 10 on Old Newton and Witton from *L21*, 18 on Bacton, Caister and Ridlington from *L23* and 4 on Alford and Anderby from *L17*.

All the Zeppelins succeeded in avoiding both searchlights and defending aeroplanes, and although a few RNAS pilots managed to take off, none made contact, as Flight Sub-Lieutenant Stanley Kemball reported:

> At 11.15pm a message from Yarmouth was brought to me ordering me to go up at once, and at the same time the telephone operator informed me that a Zeppelin was overhead, steering south-east, the first information I received of it being in the immediate vicinity.
>
> The men immediately turned out, and after warming up my engine I proceeded into the air at 11.22pm, steering south-east, and continued on this course for about 30 minutes, when I turned north, after observing bombs being dropped, which appeared to be in the direction of Lowestoft.
>
> After patrolling for 1 hour 35 minutes, I landed at 12.57am having seen nothing of the hostile airship. I reported same to Yarmouth.
>
> The station continued to stand by until 2.45am, when we resumed normal conditions; having received a message from Yarmouth to this effect, machine was returned to its shed.[37]

Reports from other pilots that night, including Flight Sub-Lieutenants F Reeves and G W R Fane, were in a similar vein. Bombs were heard, and sometimes the engines of the raiders themselves, but all went out unobserved by pilots of the RNAS.

The only serious casualty of the raid was at Dilham, where the bombs from *L11* caused a woman to die of shock; material damage, however, was restricted to several buildings and a few shattered windows. The last Zeppelin to leave the country went out at 02.05hrs just as battlecruisers of the German High Seas Fleet were preparing to bombard Lowestoft and Great Yarmouth.

April 25/26: LZ87, LZ88, LZ93, LZ97
Favourable weather persuaded the Army to rejoin the campaign, and five Zeppelins came in completely unexpectedly. One turned back before even reaching the coast, and *LZ87* was thwarted by spirited fire from gunners at Walmer. The only bombs attributed to this airship were a stick of eight that narrowly missed the steamer *Argus* moored in Deal harbour. *LZ87* made no further attempt to attack England, and made off soon afterwards.

LZ88 passed over Canterbury via Whitstable and dropped nine incendiaries on Preston, all of which exploded harmlessly in open fields. Thirteen bombs rained down upon Sarre and the Chislet Marshes, and a further 15 failed to strike any target at all; the commander finally went out to sea over Minnis Bay. *LZ93* bombed the Harwich area and its cargo did no damage either, two duds falling close to Government House and an incendiary between two naval dormitories in a training barracks. There were no casualties.

In *LZ97* the redoubtable Linnarz arrived over the River Blackwater at around 20.00hrs and directly made for London: 47 incendiaries fell in a line between Fyfield and Ongar, the commander having mistaken the River Roding for the Thames. Linnarz next turned south-west over Dog Kennel Hill, where the gun stationed there opened fire at 23.08hrs without striking its target. *LZ97* next dropped a dozen high explosives on Barkingside, damaging several houses, and then moved on towards Ilford, dropping a bomb over Newbury Park on the way. Over Seven Kings, anti-aircraft fire and home defence aeroplanes forced Linnarz to beat a hasty retreat.

Eight RFC pilots had taken off during the raid, three from Hounslow, three from Suttons Farm and two from Hainault. Only two BE2cs attacked *LZ97* that night, Lieutenant W L Robinson managing to loose off several rounds at the Zeppelin. However, the range was too great, and with the airship 2000ft away the defender's bullets fell far short of the target. Captain A T Harris up from Hounslow was also unable to get any closer than Robinson, but as his Lewis gun jammed it made little difference. Shaken, Linnarz made off eastwards, having successfully eluded London's searchlights.

April 26/27: LZ93
LZ93, commanded by *Hauptmann* Wilhelm Schramm, made a single-handed attack the following night, arriving over the Kent coast near Kingsdown. Three bombs were traced as having fallen to sea off Deal, and gunners stationed there loosed off several rounds at the raider. Schramm steered northwards over Kent and finally went out east of Margate without having dropped any bombs on land.

May 2/3: L11, L13, L14, L16, L17, L20, L21, L23; LZ98
With orders to attack Rosyth and the Forth Bridge, eight naval Zeppelins sailed from their bases and crossed the North Sea in consort. Still 100 miles from their target, the Zeppelins met with severe winds, which forced all but the commanders of *L14* and *L20* to select alternative cities in the Midlands area. Schütze, in *L11*, came in over the Northumberland coast at Holy Island, having been fired upon by patrol vessels east of St Abbs Head. Only two bombs were traced from *L11*, and Schütze, failing to find objectives beneath the snow squalls, went out over Amble with his bomb load virtually intact.

Kapitänleutnant Otto von Schubert, in *L23*, dropped an incendiary on Danby High Moor whilst cruising over Yorkshire, and succeeded in setting the heather alight. Then 11 bombs were aimed at the lights of Skinningrove Iron Works, where a storehouse and a few other buildings were damaged. *L23* came under fire as searchlight beams held the ship over Brotton, but Schubert lost them and, passing over Easington, where six of his bombs wrecked a house and injured a child, he left English shores with most of his bombs still aboard.

The heather on Danby High Moor was still burning merrily as Peterson arrived. Observing the conflagration below and convinced it represented blazing railway buildings, *L16*'s commander dumped a large number of bombs on the waste lands. The result, however, was merely to increase the flames and terrorise the local rabbit population. *L16* then dropped ten bombs on Lealholm and Moorsholm, where a farm building was damaged, before commencing its homeward journey.

Ehrlich, in *L17*, came in over Saltburn and headed for

One of the best Zeppelin pictures of the war: in the control car of *L24* is a relaxed *Kapitänleutnant* Robert Koch. Koch took part in several raids on England, and on 8/9 August he bombed Hull with conclusive results, leaving 21 killed and injured as *L24* sailed over the town releasing a salvo of 44 bombs. He was killed on 17 March 1917 when *L39* was destroyed over Compiègne, France, by AA fire.
M Dietrich/P Amesbury

Skinningrove, dropping 13 HE and four incendiary bombs on Carlin How, demolishing six houses and damaging several others. He then turned over the Yorkshire Moors and, like Peterson, became attracted by the blazing heather; he dumped a number of bombs there before going out at Whitby. Prölss, in *L13*, was another commander who managed to bomb the moor, having already abandoned an attack on Leeds because of navigational problems; two bombs which fell at Fridaythorpe and Seamer were also attributed to *L13*. Max Dietrich arrived to the north of Scarborough and headed for York, having dropped 18 bombs on Dringhouses where a few windows were smashed and two wounded soldiers were the only casualties. Reaching York at 22.40hrs, *L21* spent ten minutes over the city, 16 bombs destroying 18 houses, damaging many others, killing nine people and injuring 27. Dietrich departed, convinced he had bombed Middlesbrough and Stockton.

In *L14*, Böcker appeared at 23.30hrs over the Tay Estuary where the lights of fishing vessels misled him into thinking that he was looking down on warships moored in the Firth of Forth. He aimed five bombs at the lights, several falling in a field near Arbroath. Confused, Böcker failed to locate any further suitable targets and aborted, turning back over the coast with his remaining bombs still in their racks.

The commander of *L20*, *Kapitänleutnant* Franz Stabbert, made landfall over Redcastle and struck off towards Forfarshire. Snow and fog forced Stabbert to make repeated radio calls for bearings, and just after midnight *L20* was over Loch Ness. Steering south and then east, Stabbert made his way to the coast, bombing Craig Castle which was undarkened.[38] The building was damaged as a result, but no casualties were reported, and *L20*, dropping eight bombs on open fields, went out near Peterhead at 02.40hrs. *L20* never made it back to Tondern. At around 10.00hrs Stabbert made a forced landing in a fjord near Stavanger in Norway, the ship was wrecked, six crewmen were repatriated and ten of them, Stabbert included, were interned.[39]

Lehmann in *LZ98*, had planned to bomb Manchester, but unfavourable weather conditions forced the commander to abandon any thoughts of an attack.

July 28/29: L11, L13, L16, L17, L24, L31
With Mathy in one of the latest airships, the second of the 'Super Zeppelins', nine dirigibles left their bases in Northern Germany during the afternoon of the 28th. Four turned back and the remainder failed to penetrate very far inland, being hampered by fog and thick ground mist. Prölss, in *L13*, came in over North Somercotes at 00.37hrs and steered for Lincoln, where two bombs were dropped on nearby Fiskerton. *L13* was east of Newark sometime later and bombs were dropped on villages in the vicinity. Prölss went over the Wash, and as a parting shot hurled down one last bomb which reportedly fell into the sea off Cromer.

L31 flew over Lowestoft and failed to drop any bombs, *L11* attacked Cromer where the missiles did no more than kill a cow, and *L16* bombed Hunstanton, again with inconclusive results. *L17* and *L24* meandered over the Humber, bombs falling on Killingholme, Immingham and East Halton, where another cow was the only casualty.

July 31/August 1: L11, L13, L14, L16, L17, L21, L22, L23, L30, L31
The next raid was equally abortive, thanks once again to severe weather conditions which served to force the commanders of *L21* and *L30* to make premature returns. Eight Zeppelins crossed the coast, *L16* bombing

Lincolnshire and Nottingham and *L11*, *L13*, *L14*, *L17*, *L22* and *L23* attacking Norfolk, Suffolk and Ely. Mathy in the new *L31*, flying at 13,000ft, attacked Ramsgate and Sandwich, although he believed that London was the recipient of his bombs. Most of the raider's missiles exploded harmlessly in the sea and only 103 were traced inland. Damage was slight and no casualties were reported.

August 2/3: L11, L13, L16, L17, L21, L31
L21, commanded by *Hauptmann* August Stelling, came in over Wells-next-the-Sea at 23.55hrs, flying directly to Thetford, where airfield Money flares caused the Zeppelin commander to drop five HE bombs. *L13*, *L16* and *L17* attacked Norfolk and Suffolk roughly in the wake of *L21*, but none reached as far, most of their bombs falling on villages, damaging houses and killing a few cows. *L17* was one of two Zeppelins which cruised close to Norwich, and guns there engaged the airship at extreme range with the result that *L17* sheered off with several cells riddled by 127 rents.

Schütze attempted to bomb Harwich, cruising over the town for 20 minutes despite heavy groundfire. *L11* dropped 13 bombs, but only one fell close to Harwich; a boy was injured at Kirton, and other missiles on that village damaged a few private cottages.

Mathy, in *L31*, passed inland over Deal at 01.00hrs. Poor visibility hampered the commander, whose bombs fell in the sea off Dover and not on London as he believed, coastal guns keeping him at bay. None of *L31*'s missiles was traced on land, and eventually Mathy headed out to sea; several RNAS aircraft took off to intercept the raiders, with inconclusive results. When Stelling bombed Thetford he was soon tackled by a BE2c from Great Yarmouth, flown by Flight Lieutenant Edward Laston Pulling, who engaged his quarry over Burgh Castle. The pilot, flying underneath the Zeppelin, emptied a drum of Lewis gun ammunition into the hull with no apparent result and in the time it took him to clip on a fresh drum, *L21* had disappeared behind convenient banks of mist.

Another pilot from Great Yarmouth was Flight Lieutenant Christopher John Galpin, who pursued a Zeppelin out to sea but was forced to ditch when his petrol ran out at 20.45hrs. Landing close to a Belgian ship, the SS *Albertville*, he was picked up and his aircraft retrieved without mishap. There were quite a few other defending aeroplanes abroad during this raid. Earlier, as the raiders approached the coast, they were met by the aircraft carrier *Vindex*, the cruiser *Conquest* and several destroyers. The Zeppelins easily outpaced the ships, but Flight Lieutenant Charles Teverill Freeman, flying Bristol Scout 8953 from *Vindex*, attacked *L17* for some time. The results were, however, inconclusive and, like Galpin, Freeman had to ditch but was later picked up by another Belgian vessel, the SS *Anvers* from Antwerp, which later docked at the Hook of Holland. After several days' internment, Freeman was eventually released as a 'shipwrecked mariner'.[40]

August 8/9: L11, L13, L14, L16, L17, L21, L22, L23, L24, L30, L31
Out of 11 Zeppelins that left their sheds for the next raid, only nine managed to reach English shores, most of them coming in between Berwick and the Humber. *L11*, *L13*, *L21*, *L22*, *L30* and *L31* bombed coastal towns between Tynemouth and Whitby, a total of 76 bombs being traced from these Zeppelins. Most of the missiles exploded harmlessly in the sea, and for all their efforts the Germans only managed to wreck a house and an office. Five civilians were injured at Whitley Bay, and the gun there claimed to have hit one of the raiders.

In *L14*, *Hauptmann* Kuno Manger made landfall south of Berwick and circled inland, where eight bombs fell in open fields, then went out again over Alnmouth. The results of *L24*'s bombing were more conclusive; *Kapitänleutnant* Robert Koch hurled 44 bombs down on Hull and these killed ten people and injured 11, with several shops and houses destroyed. Mist prevented the city defences from loosing more than eight rounds from anti-aircraft guns.

L16 dropped 35 bombs on several small villages south of the Wash, but did little damage and the commander turned back out to sea. Two of his consorts never even came inland. *L17* was attacked off Whitby by the armed trawler *Itonian*, Erhlich responding by dumping his entire bomb load over the vessel and a fishing fleet moored off the Tyne. All the vessels emerged unscathed and *L17* sheered off. The *Itonian* also fired upon *L23* when that ship was cruising over Scarborough. Spirited fire from the trawler was successful in driving off the Zeppelin, which returned to base with its bomb racks fully laden. *L21* came under fire from the yacht *Miranda II* lying off Skinningrove as the commander dropped three bombs above the vessel which all missed – just. One exploded a mere 400yds short of its target.

Defending aeroplanes found the mist too thick for safe take-offs but at Redcar, where it was clearer, Flight Lieutenant Bruno Philip Henry de Roeper managed to intercept one of the raiders over Saltburn. The pilot chased the Zeppelin out to sea, but with its superior speed the airship soon outdistanced him and mist covered its escape 20 miles out from the coast.

August 23/24: LZ97
Linnarz made another of his 'lone wolf' attacks on England which more or less acted as a weak curtain-raiser for Strasser's next onslaught the following evening. The Army commander, flying in *LZ97*, dropped 34 bombs in open fields near Trimley, Walton and Old Felixstowe, but did so completely undetected by the defences. Linnarz returned to Belgium unscathed, and although his ship's engines could be heard by Royal Navy destroyers the Zeppelin was never once observed.

August 24/25: L11, L13, L14, L16, L17, L21, L23, L24, L30, L31, L32; SL8, SL9
Strasser himself was aboard *L32* when 13 airships left their bases with orders to 'attack England South.' Forewarned by radio signals, the light cruisers *Conquest*, *Carysfort* and *Canterbury* sailed from Harwich, together with several destroyers, to lay in wait for the raiders. Six commanders later reported being fired upon as they came in, *L13* taking a direct hit from *Conquest* in cell 8 which ran empty. Dumping bombs and some fuel, Prölss sent out a distress signal and returned to Hage with cell 9 having lost half its contents.

Strong winds at sea persuaded five commanders to turn back, dumping most of their bomb load. *L23*, dangerously overladen with rain, jettisoned 1300lb of petrol as well as all bombs before returning to its base.

In fact only four Zeppelins went inland, including the experienced Mathy, who followed the Thames right into London. The first Zeppelin over the capital since October of 1915 caught the defences by surprise. Using mist to conceal his approach, Mathy dropped his first bombs on Millwall then quickly followed these up with further missiles on Deptford, Greenwich, Blackheath, Eltham and Plumstead. A total of eight incendiary and 35 HE bombs fell on these areas, killing nine and injuring 40.

Due to the low mist, London's searchlights failed to locate Mathy until his bombs fell on Eltham at 01.35hrs. Lights from Erith held the Zeppelin, and gun batteries were not slow in rising to the occasion: 120 rounds were aimed at

Mathy's *L31*, the second of the 'Super Zeppelins', commissioned on 14 July 1916. Built at Lowenthal, *L31* is seen here being walked towards the *Normann* shed at Nordholz. Behind the upper gun platform at the top of the bows and below the hull just forward of the midships gondolas are two canvas lifeboats. After the tragedy of *L19* these lifeboats were carried on several naval Zeppelins for a while but as far as is known were never actually used and were ultimately discarded. In the foreground, striding purposefully towards the shed, is *Fregattenkäpitan* Peter Strasser himself, revered chief of the German Naval Airship Division. *L31*'s maiden raid took place on 28/29 July 1916 when Mathy flew over Lowestoft but failed to drop any bombs. *L31* took part in eight raids, the last being on 2 October 1916 when the Zeppelin was shot down in flames. Mathy and his 18 comrades perished.
Frau Hertha Mathy

L31, which turned for Rainham, finally going out east of Shoeburyness.

L16 almost reached Ipswich, but her commander had to be content with dropping 20 bombs between Woodbridge and Bealings. None of them caused any damage. Frankenberg, in *L21*, unloaded most of his bombs in the sea before coming in over Frinton. The only missiles traced on land from this airship fell at Great Oakley and Pewit Island, where the buildings owned by the Explosive and Chemical Products Company narrowly escaped destruction.

Peterson made landfall over Folkestone at around 01.00hrs and dropped most of his bombs in the sea off Dover and Deal. Guns at these towns gave Peterson a hot reception, and *L32* was attacked by an RFC pilot, Captain J W Woodhouse from 50 HDS, who pursued the Zeppelin as it turned away from the English coast. Momentarily losing the ship in clouds, he refused to give up the chase and was rewarded by relocating his elusive enemy. One drum of Lewis gun ammunition disappeared into the underside of *L32*'s hull with no effect. Whilst Woodhouse was clipping on a new drum the airship vanished into the clouds.

The Army ships fared even worse that night. *SL8* suffered an engine breakdown at sea and turned back for Nordholz, and *SL9* flew at 9000ft through heavy cloud and claimed to have bombed a city after the commander had observed lights below him. Neither this airship nor its bombs were traced over land by the British authorities.

Several ships, their hulls overladen with rain, made heavy landings on their return, and some were out of commission for several days whilst repairs were effected. Even Mathy's *L31* suffered damage and had to have its after gondola entirely replaced after a landing accident; it did not fly again until 21 September.[41] All in all the Germans had very little cause to be complacent after this largely abortive raid.

The next raid took place on 2 September, when 16 airships set out to attack London in the biggest raid yet mounted by both airship services. Never before had so many raiders set out for England, but this time the tables would be turned, for one RFC pilot, his gun armed with a new kind of bullet, was to put in serious question the viability of airships as strategic combat weapons.

CHAPTER 4

The Defences

'...It was evident that the machine gun was the only thing likely to meet with success and although a satisfactory mounting for firing upwards was designed, no night sights or incendiary ammunition were available. The former however was designed at Hounslow in June but the latter was not available until about July when the Brock bullet made its appearance...'

Air Commodore T C R Higgins, 1920

'What are you going to do about these airship raids?' This question, posed by British Secretary of War, Lord Earl Kitchener, reflected the serious inadequacy of air defence during 1915. On the receiving end of Kitchener's demand was Sir David Henderson, Director General of Military Aeronautics, whose reply that responsibility rested with the RNAS failed to impress his superior: 'I do not care who has the responsibility, if there are any more Zeppelin raids and the Royal Flying Corps do not interfere with them, I shall hold you responsible.'[1]

At this juncture Sir David wisely withdrew, having been given a seemingly impossible directive. With daily requests from the expanding RFC squadrons in France for more aircraft and pilots, there were simply none to spare for home defence. Nevertheless 'K's orders had to be carried out, and the Director General's immediate priority was drastically to reshape his command into an effective Zeppelin deterrent. It was not going to be easy.

A Question of Responsibility
In 1910 the possibility of aerial bombardment had been discussed by an Admiralty conference which had drawn up preliminary proposals for air defence. With remarkable foresight it was concluded that both aircraft and 'high-angle fire' guns would be best suited to repel airship attack.

The Royal Flying Corps officially came into being on 13 May 1912 and comprised two Wings, one military, the other naval. The latter was established at Eastchurch on the Thames Estuary, with the Military Wing at Farnborough. From the start the Naval Wing evolved rapidly, thanks to the efforts of Captain Murray Sueter, its first director, and the First Lord, Winston Churchill.

In August the Army Council endeavoured to divide the responsibility for air defence between the Wings and proposed a breakdown of three classes. The first included machines used for 'fleet purposes', the Army being adamant that such aircraft were not available for coastal defence. This condition also applied in Class Two, where aircraft were primarily to be employed in conjunction with Coast Defence Flotillas. The final class embraced aircraft operating with both fixed and mobile land defences, the Army further stipulating that Class Three come under the complete control of the Military Wing, the Naval Wing maintaining the others. These proposals were accepted by the Admiralty, although a proviso was added that the third class should 'include all aircraft employed to protect magazines and storage tanks.'[2]

Despite their proposals, the War Office failed to carry out the organisation of Class Three, although the Royal Navy was not slow to establish several seaplane stations along the East Coast. By November 1913 most of these new stations were fully operational and the disposition of both arms redefined:

The War Office to be responsible for our aerial supremacy in the British Isles, or in any land operations in which the Army are concerned.

The Admiralty to be responsible for all aerial services of the Fleet.

In order to avoid duplication and overlapping it was agreed that in cases where the naval seaplane stations are close to points of naval importance vulnerable to aerial attack, the Naval Wing should undertake the responsibility for the aerial defence of naval property.[3]

In July 1914 the Naval Wing of the RFC came under the control of the Admiralty to become the Royal Naval Air Service; just 28 days later came orders that patrol duties were to be considered secondary to repelling hostile aircraft should the latter appear. Prior to hostilities, however, the War Office challenged the Admiralty and demanded sole responsibility for air defence including coastal areas; further, the General Staff of the Army requested that naval pilots co-operate with the RFC in carrying out these measures. The only problem was that the War Office did not have sufficient resources to meet its own demands. Churchill was quick to grasp the situation as war came:

The War Office claimed on behalf of the RFC complete and sole responsibility for the aerial defence of Great Britain. But owing to the difficulties of getting money, they were unable to make any provision for this responsibility, every aeroplane they had being earmarked for the Expeditionary Force.[4]

By August the RNAS boasted some 50 fully operational machines, but the Army could only muster a third of this number. Lord Kitchener realised that it would be some time before the War Office could fulfil its intentions and, having received government sanction, arranged with Churchill that the immediate defence of the country be passed to the Admiralty. This took place on 3 September 1914, the Army agreeing to lend support with guns and available aircraft where possible.

RNAS aircraft, poorly armed with a limited assortment of grenades, patrolled the coast between the Humber and Thames areas. The Wash was thought to be a possible landfall for Zeppelins and was guarded accordingly, but the expected raids did not materialise for many months.

Progress with effective anti-aircraft gun defence was slow by comparison. By August only 30 high-angle guns had been installed, 25 of these 1pdr pom-poms of dubious efficiency. The balance included one 4in gun at Portsmouth and two 3in guns at Chattenden and Lodge Hill, with a 3in apiece at Purfleet and Waltham Abbey. Though the gunners were to play a major role in the defence of England their part in the Zeppelin campaign falls outside the parameters of this story, but is only just to record here that the guns and searchlight teams gave valuable support to the RFC and RNAS pilots whose tireless efforts were eventually to bear fruit.

During 1914 the RNAS opened the offensive, two daring raids being made on the Zeppelin bases along the north German coast. One Zeppelin was destroyed and another damaged, with hangars and other buildings gutted. Such actions caused the Germans to press for concerted attacks on England before any more airships were destroyed on the ground. But it was not until 9 January 1915 that the *Kaiser* finally sanctioned the Zeppelin bombing offensive.

On 4 September the Third Sea Lord, Rear Admiral Tudor, advised Churchill that many additional guns would soon be available, and plans for London's own defence included an extra 24 guns and 36 searchlights. Churchill, however, did not entirely agree with these proposals:

> There can be no question of defending London by artillery against aerial attack. It is quite impossible to cover so vast an area, and if London why not every other city?...Searchlights should, however, be provided without delay.[5]

September 5 saw the first meeting of a special committee instigated by Churchill and chaired by Tudor. Those present included Rear-Admiral Morgan Singer, Director of Naval Operations; Colonel Louis Charles, Assistant Director of Fortifications at the War Office; and Murray Sueter. They drew up a detailed scheme for London's defence, marking the area from Buckingham Palace to Charing Cross as the central defensive position supported by searchlights and guns; further, a ring of airfields was to be established ten miles from the centre of this area. A complete system of telephone communications was set up between the Admiralty and the various batteries and air stations. As no naval personnel were available to operate the searchlights, the Police Commissioner, Sir Edward Henry, detailed 120 Special Constables for this vital task.

Other measures included the formation on 9 October of the Anti-Aircraft Corps of the Royal Naval Volunteer Reserve, bringing in part-time voluntary help to man both guns and searchlights. Their numbers were increased throughout the city and special lookout posts were established, connected to a central control by telephone. Lighting restrictions were also imposed for the first time, on 17 September. In order to confuse airship navigators the lights of London were to be reduced in a specific manner:

> In long easily-recognised thoroughfares such as the Mile End Road and the Victoria Embankment, and on bridges, the uniformity of the lighting was to be broken up. The London parks, which would appear to an air observer as tell-tale patches of dark, were to be given a number of lights to bring them into conformity with their surroundings.[6]

A typical warning poster published by HMSO and distributed throughout the country during 1915, giving sound advice to the civilian population.
Author's Collection

By this time a flight of RNAS aircraft had been despatched to Hendon and emergency landing grounds set up in Battersea Park, Kensington Gardens, Regents Park and the grounds of Buckingham Palace. More permanent airfields were to be established at Hainault Farm and Woodford Green in Essex, whilst small numbers of RFC aircraft were stationed at Brooklands and Farnborough to meet any Zeppelins approaching London. The lighting restrictions were well in force by December, and even the coastal towns and the Midlands began to take London's lead, reducing street, tram, railway and advertising lighting, while gun defences were being steadily increased.

Following further discussions, the War Office eventually became responsible for protecting almost every key town and military installation, the Army virtually taking full control of the anti-aircraft defence of the country outside London. By Christmas 1914 anti-aircraft corps had formed in Dover and Sheffield, while police telephone communications had been set up in Berkshire, Cambridge, Hampshire, Huntingdon, Norfolk, Northampton, Oxford and Suffolk.

The 'Christmas Day Raid' by a lone German seaplane led to the Government redirecting three 3in guns to bear along expected airship routes from the north with additional RNAS aircraft set aside for extra defence. Eastchurch was to receive four aircraft on permanent standby, with four each at Dover, Hendon and Joyce Green and three apiece at Felixstowe, Killingholme and Great Yarmouth. Seaplanes were stationed at the latter fields and at Dover, Clacton, the Isle of Grain and Westgate. Landing fields also appeared at Chelmsford, Chingford, Maidstone and Ramsgate in order that defending aircraft could form the widest possible screen to meet airships crossing the North Sea.

As a result of the first Zeppelin raids in January 1915, Sueter proposed the rapid formation of a mobilised anti-aircraft force. Churchill readily agreed, and the Eastern Mobile Section was soon organised to cover the whole East Anglian area. The new unit was equipped with high-angle machine guns, 1pdr pom-poms and searchlights mounted on trucks. It was never intended to pursue Zeppelins, rather to move up the guns into the best position on receipt of an attack warning. While such guns, with their limited range, were generally ineffective, their very presence did much to restore public confidence.

In the first half of 1915 the War Office increased the gun defences of coastal ports and strategic areas, placing emphasis on the towns concerned with the production of war materials. London's defences were also improved following the successful raid by Linnarz on 31 May. In June and July more guns were installed to bring the total of 3in guns in and around London to eight.

In April, Lord Fisher, the First Sea Lord, had called for a squadron of light cruisers mounting anti-aircraft guns to be moored on the Humber. Churchill accepted this suggestion but added a refinement of his own – submarines. Also fitted with guns, these were stationed in the Heligoland Bight and its approaches. So it was that in June the Sixth Light Cruiser Squadron was formed, with RNAS seaplanes allocated to certain cruisers and trawlers to extend their range by being lowered into the water should a Zeppelin be sighted.

Another gap in the defences was revealed following the successful attack on Tyneside by Hirsch in *L10*. The fact that the 5 June raid met with little opposition incurred the wrath of local civilians, and immediate steps were taken to remedy the situation. But the War Office objected to the Admiralty plan of transferring twelve 6in guns from warships to railway rolling stock: the East Coast was *their* responsibility, and the guns should be handed over to them. Surprisingly the Navy agreed, stipulating that the guns be manned by artillery crew. As it turned out, it was many months before the conversion was complete, and even then tests revealed that the range of the guns was insufficient.

Additional landing grounds were established by the RNAS to support the increased Tyneside defences at Hornsea, Redcar and Scarborough, with further fields being set up at 15–20-mile intervals between the Tyne and Humber. The machines then available included a mixed assortment of Blériot monoplanes, Caudrons and BE2cs. All had shortcomings, and night flying itself was then regarded as extremely hazardous. Accidents were frequent:

> The Admiralty view, therefore, was that as airship attacks were made after dark, counter attacks by the existing types of aeroplane were uncertain and precarious and could not be looked upon as offering any security.[7]

The First Lord was now Arthur Balfour (Churchill having left the Admiralty in May), who had little knowledge of aerial warfare and even less enthusiasm. In addition the RNAS, heavily committed in other areas, was hard put to provide further pilots and machines for defence, and so the Admiralty strove to pass the responsibility back to the Army, the formal request for the transfer being made on 18 June. A preliminary meeting between the two arms was inconclusive, the War Office accepting the proposal in principle but reminding the Admiralty that they did not have the materials to carry it out. Meanwhile the Zeppelins came again, twice to London, while a few brave RFC and RNAS pilots groped blindly around trying to make contact with the raiders. In July representatives from both arms met again, but the Army was unwilling to go further than promise to assume control by 1916, providing no other demands on its stretched resources were made.

The highly destructive raid upon London by Mathy on 8 September incensed public opinion, and the combined defences bore the brunt of much bitter criticism. It was felt by many that London's defence should fall under the jurisdiction of one officer and one only. On 12 September this was put into effect by the temporary appointment of Admiral Sir Percy Scott, a gunnery specialist of wide experience. This officer had sufficient vision to lay great store in the aeroplane for defence, and held the view that it should play a much more important role. It was certainly a case of a 'new broom sweeping clean', for little time passed before Scott wrote to Churchill threatening to resign unless he were given a free hand to obtain just what he wanted.

Opening Moves

First to go were the six pom-poms. These had limited range and fired shells that exploded on impact: they were unlikely to hit a Zeppelin, and in fact many civilians had been injured by shrapnel. Next Sir Percy demanded 104 new guns and 50 searchlights; he had already despatched Lieutenant-Commander W Rawlinson to Paris in order that an example of the new French 75mm anti-aircraft gun could be procured. In this he was successful, and the mobile gun became the nucleus of the London Mobile Section formed under Rawlinson in October.

Next, the expansion and restructuring of the aeroplane defence had to be considered, and following a meeting on 16 September an additional four airfields, 24 pilots and 40 aircraft were requested. A study of the Paris air defences had proved how difficult it was for pilots to locate raiders at night, and with this in mind the Director of the Air Services, Rear-Admiral Vaughn-Lee, was reluctant to increase the number of airfields; instead, existing fields were to be improved and a rigorous programme of night-

Many Zeppelin postcards were in a light-hearted vein. This 1916 published number is typical.
Author's Collection

"I say you two, come out of that cellar. The Airship's been gone ever so long!"

flying training instigated. These proposals were agreed by 28 September when the Admiralty suddenly affirmed that overseas units had first claim on trained pilots – which meant, more or less, the effective cessation of night flying.

The RFC had meanwhile mounted an experimental scheme along the north-east edge of the capital. Reconnaissance parties had located two suitable pieces of farmland that could be turned into temporary landing grounds. One, occupying 90 acres, was Suttons Farm in Essex, two miles from Hornchurch. Owned by Mr Tom Crawford, it was an irregular section of stubble in well-drained country, partially obstructed by sheep netting and six haystacks. It looked promising. The other field, smaller at 60 acres, belonged to Hainault Farm, was owned by Mr W Poulter and lay alongside the road to Chadwell Heath, four miles from Romford. The fields were requisitioned from their owners and designated Temporary Landing Grounds II and III.

At the beginning of October the War Office and Admiralty devised an experimental defence scheme which provided cordons of ground observers in telephone contact with home defence headquarters. Additionally, a number of 13pdr mobile and anti-aircraft guns, plus extra searchlights, were ringed around the north-eastern outskirts of the capital. Aircraft were also to be brought up during the period of the experiment, which was to last from 4 to 12 October inclusive.

Lieutenant-Colonel W G Salmond, Officer Commanding the Fifth Wing, was ordered to provide seven BE2cs and their pilots while SE4a 5610 was provided by the Sixth Wing and despatched to Joyce Green along with one BE2c. The other six went in pairs to Hainault Farm, Northolt and Suttons Farm. During Sunday 3 October two large RE5 hangars, having earlier been collected from Romford Station, were erected at Suttons Farm and acted as welcome landmarks for Second Lieutenant H MacD O'Malley flying in from 23 Squadron at Gosport. A couple of bomb racks, eight 20lb bombs, a landing T and a supply of aviation fuel in tins made up the equipment they found on their arrival.[8] The pilots were to be billeted in Tom Crawford's farmhouse after a telephone had been installed in the building.

At each of the landing grounds, it was ordered, a pilot was to be on standby every night. If raiders were seen approaching London, the War Office telephoned each field and gave the hour at which the aircraft was to take off. Sufficient lead time had been calculated for the slow-climbing BE2c to reach 8000ft in order to intercept a Zeppelin. If the pilot failed to make contact he was to land after 90 minutes, and in the event of bad weather the War Office was to be informed before the pilot stood down. Searchlights were to be placed near Becontree Heath and near Chigwell Row, while two additional lights were considered for Buckhurst Hill and Upminster:

> If no airship approaches, at the expiration of 1½ hours from the time the flight starts, these searchlights will be turned on to the nearest landing ground for about a minute to indicate its position.[9]

Later a chain of observers was placed to the north-east of the landing grounds to send up rockets if a Zeppelin were seen passing overhead. These rockets were to be of different colours to denote the direction the Zeppelin was taking, the colours to be notified to each pilot.

Within two days the aircraft had been delivered, pilots and groundcrew billeted, equipment installed, telephones connected and flight tests made. On 2 October Lieutenant Jenkins from 14 Squadron and Second Lieutenant Yates of 23 flew into Suttons Farm to relieve O'Malley. Later that day Second Lieutenant John Slessor, also of 23 Squadron, was ordered to collect a new BE2c from the Daimler works at Coventry and report to Suttons Farm. On arrival he relieved Jenkins, who flew the few miles to Hainault Farm and brought the flight there to full strength. The experimental air defence scheme had been extended a few days in the hope that a raid would be forthcoming and the new measures put into operation.

That same evening Slessor was at the telephone when reports came in of an impending Zeppelin attack, but it was not until around 19.30hrs that he received orders to take off. The facilities at Suttons Farm were, to say the least, rudimentary. The flare path was formed by rows of petrol cans, their lids removed and crammed with a mix of petrol, paraffin and cotton waste. They were laid out in the shape of an L, with the shorter arm at the upwind end of the field. The length of the flare path was about 300yds, and the airfield itself was only 500yds square.

Pilots carried a Very pistol and on preparation to land would fire a green light when in the circuit. If the flare path were clear, the ground crew also fired a green flare before the pilot brought his aircraft down. No machine guns were installed in the BE2c, the idea at that time being to attack the Zeppelins from above with 20lb Hales bombs or batches of Ranken explosive darts.

As we have seen, the 13 October raid was successful from the German point of view, only Slessor intercepting one of the raiders and inconclusively at that. Civilian casualties were high, and once London had recovered there were further bitter demonstrations and speeches attacking the Government for its failure to protect the capital. To all those living under the bomb it seemed that the air defence of their country left a great deal to be desired: it simply was not working. However, a respite in the Zeppelin attacks due to the waxing moon and the onset of winter weather gave the Admiralty and War Office another breathing space to thrash out the problems and pin down the time for a transfer of responsibility.

By 26 October, the aeroplane defence of London had ceased to exist; the fields remained War Office property but the aircraft and men had returned to their units and thence to France. At Suttons Farm sheep returned to graze on their old field but found scant pickings on the now oil-

At the outbreak of war the threat of airship attack was taken seriously enough for air raid precautions to be made. Here sandbags and deflective netting protect the Royal Family at Buckingham Palace.
IWM MH3957

Zeppelin!

Punch cartoon published on 25 August 1915, presumably in direct reference to the ineffective raids of that month and the subsequent destruction of both L12 and L10
Punch

THE ACHIEVEMENT.
Count Zeppelin. "STANDS LONDON WHERE IT DID, MY CHILD?"
The Child. "YES, FATHER; MISSED IT AGAIN."
Count Zeppelin. "THEN YOU HAD NO SUCCESS?"
The Child. "OH, YES, FATHER; I'VE GOT HOME AGAIN."

soaked ground. Still the Army and Naval authorities could not reach a firm decision. A week passed before the Admiralty announced that while originally it had considered aircraft vital for London's defence it had modified its opinion in the light of recent raids. Then another conference was arranged, and despite the absence of Kitchener, overseas in the Dardanelles, it was agreed that the RFC be responsible for *all* inland air defence whilst the RNAS supplied cover over the sea. Slowly the Army gained control of London's guns and searchlights, while in December two BE2cs with experienced night-flying pilots were despatched to each of ten airfields on permanent standby. The fields were Chingford, Croydon, Hainault Farm, Hendon, Hounslow (the headquarters), Joyce Green, Northolt, South Farningham, Suttons Farm and Wimbledon Common. As before, each field was maintained by six mechanics and a Royal Engineer party in charge of a searchlight. The pilots, provided by various units training for overseas duty, took shifts and were in constant telephone contact with the War Office.

Kitchener's reaction to these events on his return to England came as a shock to his subordinates. Reviewing the new proposals during January 1916 he reasoned that the urgent requirements for Corps expansion in France would preclude the establishment of a dozen permanent home defence units. Since the introduction on the Western Front of the Fokker *Eindecker*s with their interrupter gear, RFC losses were mounting daily. As a result, on 10 January Kitchener had the Army reverse their decision: Army gunners already manning the guns and searchlights would remain at their posts but come under Admiralty jurisdiction. Not surprisingly the Navy was incensed, and while they were insisting that the Army meet their previously agreed arrangements, the 'Bloody Zepps' came again. The raid on the Midlands with nine Zeppelins, while not inflicting much damage, did serve to underline yet again the ragged holes in the defences.

The Defences Build Up

Despite the conflicts between the two services, the War Office took one major step following the Midlands raid. They appointed Major T C R Higgins, the Officer Commanding 19 Reserve Squadron at Hounslow, to take control of all RFC airfields around London and organise his own unit for the defence of the city. He was an ideal choice.

Born on 21 July 1890 at Turvey, Bedfordshire, Higgins had begun his military career as a naval cadet when aged 17 and later served with the King's Own Royal Regiment, and then, in the Boer War, with the King's Own and Mounted Infantry. On 16 May 1911 he obtained Aero Club Certificate 88 at Hendon, and when war was declared went with the BEF to France. Wounded on 26 August, he returned to England and, when fully recovered, joined the RFC. First he was sent to Shoreham in May 1915, obtaining his 'wings' at Dover two months later, and then he joined 7 Squadron as a Flying Officer in September. After various postings he finally came to Hounslow as Squadron Commander of 19 Training Squadron:

> I could not give much attention to the pupils and had to concentrate on finding out how to fit up machines for night flying and night fighting and to find out which of the numerous and heterogeneous gadgets supplied were useful and which were not.[10]

On 10 February the War Committee met again and finally they made up their minds. The Admiralty undertook to deal with all hostiles attempting to reach England and to co-operate with the Fleet and patrol the coastal areas. The Army responsibility was clearly defined:

> All defence arrangements on land to be undertaken by the Army, which will also provide the aeroplanes required to work with the Home Defence troops and to protect garrisons and vulnerable areas and the Flying Stations required to enable their aircraft to undertake these duties.[11]

Six days later the responsibility for London's defence was passed to Field Marshal Lord French, Commander-in-Chief Home Forces. Later the entire country's defence came under his command. Under the initial scheme of this new command a number of aircraft were to be permanently based near each defence 'area or garrison port', with additional machines in advance of those areas for mobile defence. Unfortunately the organisation of special home defence units could not evolve immediately owing to the acute shortage of personnel and equipment. One solution was to despatch three BE2c aircraft each to training squadrons in the key areas of Doncaster, Dover, Norwich and Thetford; a further six were sent to reinforce 5 Reserve Squadron in the defence of Birmingham and Coventry. All these moves had been completed by 1 March. For the Leeds and Hull areas, 37 Squadron was moved to Branham Moor from Bristol, and 34 Squadron from Castle Bromwich went to Beverley (in due course, for initially 47 Squadron had been stationed there). The senior officer of each squadron was solely responsible for ordering his pilots aloft on receipt of an air raid warning. The aircraft from each station made successive patrols at heights between 8000 and 10,000ft above their own landing grounds, a normal patrol lasting two hours. A second aircraft was sent up after 90 minutes to ensure continuity.

In March 1916 Vaughn-Lee had put forward proposals to 'deter hostile airships from raiding England.'[12] The proposals were divided into two distinct operations, first to encounter Zeppelins before they reached the coast and secondly to meet them on the way out should the first stage be unsuccessful.

The operation called for six armed trawlers each carrying

a Sopwith Baby seaplane to be in a specified positon during a likely raid night some 90 minutes before dusk. At this juncture the Baby would be flown off to patrol until dark. The aircraft were to be 'armed with Ranken darts and to carry a plentiful supply of Very's [sic] lights for use in the event of a breakdown after dark.'[13] If this failed, the second operation was set in motion. Seaplane carriers (HMS *Engadine* and HMS *Vindex* were specified) would proceed to previously arranged positions and would arrive by daylight when the Sopwiths were sent up to patrol:

> As soon as the machines are clear of the ships, the ships themselves will proceed at full speed for Harbour, while the patrolling line of machines is so worked to cover the whole area of the line and some considerable distance north and south of it.[14]

Despite the urgent requirements in France, December 1915 had seen ten out of 70 new squadrons being held back and officially designated Home Defence Squadrons. For easier handling in the London area, all RFC units there were grouped together on March 25, thenceforth being known as the 18th Wing. All the units involved, still called Reserve Squadrons, came under the command of Lieutenant-Colonel F V Holt, recently returned from France. Eventually these particular detachments, hitherto under the control of 19 Reserve Squadron, became 39 Home Defence Squadron, on 15 April 1916. The newly formed unit would have its base at Hounslow where a flight of six machines was sent along, with Higgins appointed overall commander. During May and June two further flights of six aeroplanes each were flown to Hainault Farm and Suttons Farm.

In June the War Office began to realise that the idea of combining anti-Zeppelin patrols and night-flying training was not working. Both men and machines were suffering from constant flying and so on the 25th a Home Defence Wing was formed and training duties were removed from the home defence squadrons. Under the command of Holt and with its headquarters at Adastral House, the Wing comprised 39 and 33 Squadrons at Bramham Moor, 36 at Cramlington, 38 formed at Castle Bromwich, 50 at Dover and 51 Squadron at Norwich. Six searchlights were installed at each home defence unit. One of the improvements instigated by Major Higgins concerned the rudimentary flarepaths, and the Money flare was introduced. This was composed of asbestos packed into a wire cage which in turn was soaked in a bucket of paraffin and placed at regular intervals either side of the 'runway' – which was usually little more than a cinder track. Money flares burned off only 1.2gal of paraffin every hour and blazed quite brightly and steadily through ground mist and fog. Additionally, Lyons searchlight sets or oxy-acetylene sets were used to further illuminate the landing grounds.

Away from the stations, extra searchlights were placed along patrol lines covered by the aircraft, their crews being in telephone communication with the squadron commanders. Defence units had certain views about their duties and many offered interesting suggestions for improvements:

> The most wonderful of any of the creeds was that forbidding the exposure of a searchlight beam until the enemy airship was detected by the naked eye...[15]

When Zeppelins were reported, two aircraft from each flight took off to patrol their specified areas with orders to go as high as possible. Squadrons south of Melton Mowbray received general orders from GHQ Home Forces via the officers commanding the Home Defence Wing. Units at fields from Lincoln to the Forth were in communication with area Warning Controllers and Squadron Commanders, receiving information from them before ordering pilots aloft.

Another result of the shift of responsibility was the total revision of intelligence and warning organisations, both playing a major role in defence. When Rear-Admiral Sir Reginald Hall became the Director of Intelligence in November 1914 he found that a select band of cryptographers under the direction of Sir Alfred Ewing was already hard at work intercepting German Navy wireless messages. Hall, born on 28 June 1870 at Britford, Wiltshire, was to become a legendary figure in the little-told story of intelligence operations in World War I. Room 40, Old Building, at the Admiralty was where Hall's men were to receive and decode vital transmissions and then advise British forces accordingly. The code-breakers were able to decipher messages from the very beginning of the war when a copy of the *Handelsschiffsverkehrsbuch* – a code used between German naval and merchant ships – arrived from Australia where it had been captured from a merchantman. There was an even greater stroke of fortune to come.

On August 20 the German light cruiser *Magdeburg* was destroyed by Russian warships in the Baltic. Recovered from the wreck was a copy of the German Signal Book, which arrived at Room 40 in October and was soon put to good use. Fleet Paymaster Rotter, the chief German expert of the Division, was given the book, and in a short while he had produced a workable key.

Direction-finding stations set up throughout the country made it possible for bearings to be taken on German Navy transmissions from warships and Zeppelins and thus pinpoint their positions. Naval airship call-signs were invariably of two letters and changed three times during the year, while Army ships used three letters taken from their commanders' surnames. Hall's men soon learnt how to anticipate a raid on England. In the event that airships be brought down over enemy territory, the secret Naval signal book was left behind and only the *Handelsschiffsverkehrsbuch*, already known by the Germans to be compromised, was carried: thus the signal 'Only HVB on board' invariably meant a raid on England. The naval airship radio operators were surprisingly talkative, giving course changes and requests for bearings, and the commanders themselves, incredibly, often carried secret code-books and documents on their persons. Hall had organised a flying squad on standby to rush to fallen Zeppelins and search the wreckage and bodies for signal books, and on at least one occasion the squad returned to the Admiralty with valuable documents.

After the raid on the Midlands in January 1916 the public became even more agitated, and wild reports ensued of massed Zeppelins flying over towns where in fact there were no Zeppelins at all. Such hysteria caused a serious disruption of vital services and could not be tolerated. Lord French quickly devised means to provide a proper warning scheme which would help to prevent 'Phantom Zeppelin' scares, and it became the task of Lieutenant-Colonel Philip

Landing Lights
Initially, landing lights to guide pilots to their airfields consisted of acetylene flares directed towards the corners of the sheds. Petrol flares, in buckets, were stationed on the field in the form of an 'L' and a searchlight used along the 'path' for additional illumination. The pilot would fire a red Very light to signify he was about to land and also that he required flares to be lit.

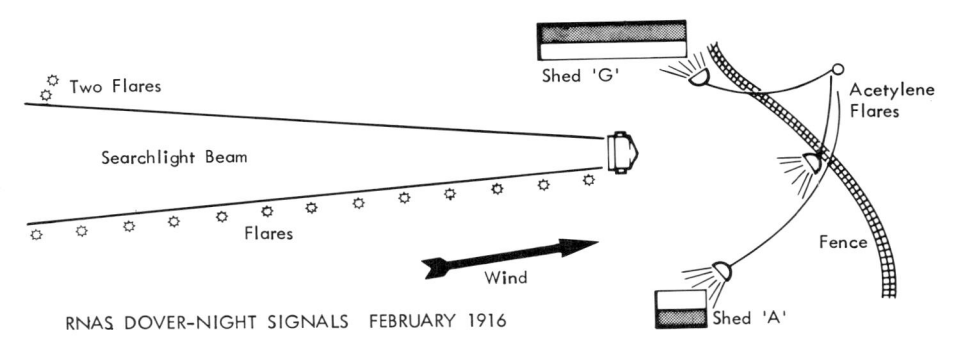

RNAS DOVER–NIGHT SIGNALS FEBRUARY 1916

Maud to set up a new system based mainly on telephone communication. England, Wales and part of Scotland were divided up into eight warning controls, each under a controller who represented GHQ Home Forces and responsible for passing on information and issuing warnings. Each area was sub-divided into numbered warning districts about 35 miles square in area:

> Assuming the average speed of the enemy airships to be 60mph the passage across each district would thus take about half an hour. Districts in the path of the Zeppelin could be warned in succession and, with a few exceptions, need only put their final precautions into effect when the danger was near. In other words work could go on to the last moment consistent with safety.[16]

The Warning Controller relied on the extensive cordons of observer posts to inform him of the raiders' movements. These observers passed their information to the Controller, who was in touch with GHQ Home Forces, Home Defence Squadrons, anti-aircraft stations and each adjacent Warning Controller.

To avoid possible confusion of identification, each airship being 'followed' was given a temporary code-name to which all units referred while the raider was over England. Girls' christian names like Annie, Jane and Mary were reserved for naval ships, while military airships were labelled in the male gender, Tom, Dick or Harry.

Once the Warning Controller had been advised of the whereabouts of raiders he telephoned the local GPO exchange manager, who would in turn contact individual subscribers on his 'warning list'. These lists were divided so that priority could be given to firms and military authorities who were required to take preliminary precautions:

> Everyone on the warning lists had, under penalties imposed by the Defence of the Realm Regulations, to answer a warning call at any time of the night, within 15 seconds. If no answer came in this time, the telephone operator passed to the next name on the list, but when he had gone through the list, he again called those who had not answered. The persons or firms who failed to answer were prosecuted, but those required to take air-raid action were fully alive to the importance of the efficient working of the system.[17]

There were four distinct, laid-down warnings issued by the controllers, and these were to alter little throughout the war:

i) Field Marshal's Warning Only
This was passed to persons or authorities on the 'Special Warning Lists' and, so far as possible, was issued to reach them when the enemy aircraft were still about 50 or 60 miles distant from the nearest boundary of the district. On receipt of this message, preliminary precautions were taken.

ii) Field Marshal's Warning: Take Air Raid Action
This was communicated to all persons on the warning lists and was timed to reach them when the enemy aircraft were 15 to 20 miles from the district boundary. At once, on receipt of this message, all final pre-arranged precautions were taken.

iii) Field Marshal's Order: Resume Normal Conditions
This was issued generally when immediate danger of attack on a district had passed. It was a signal to revert to the conditions which were obtained before the issue of message (ii).

iv) Field Marshal's Order: All Clear
This indicated that all emergency precautions might be withdrawn.[18]

Similar orders were issued by the military in coastal areas where attacks might materialise suddenly and give little time to inform the Warning Controller. The police could also issue such warnings if the GPO system failed or if Zeppelins attacked a town where no previous warnings had been issued.

It took many raids before it became certain that a warning could effectively clear the streets. Initially, civilians flocked outdoors to gaze at this new spectacle of bursting shells and sweeping searchlights:

> Those who set their faces against a general public warning argued that it would have the effect of attracting into the streets people who might otherwise remain indoors.[19]

In provincial towns where this had occurred, public warning systems had been abandoned, although a few others retained them. In October 1915, Hull's Chief Constable had stated that he would not have introduced a warning buzzer had he foreseen the effects it produced:

> When it sounds great numbers of people leave their houses and troop out with their children into the country and in some cases stay there for hours in the fields...Sick people, old people, others who cannot leave their houses, and many of the better classes, who prefer to stay at home are always greatly upset on 'Buzzer' nights.[20]

Nevertheless, a system of public warning was established by March 1916 where local conditions required it. Three months later, churches, theatres and other places of worship and amusement were placed on the warning list, although the orders were not compulsory.

One other factor which worried the Home Office was the control of sounds that might attract Zeppelins. In December 1915 Chief Constables had been advised that the use of church and clock bells be discontinued between sunset and sunrise, especially in coastal areas. March 1916 saw a new regulation which prohibited the ringing of bells or striking of clocks 'audible at such a distance as to be capable of serving as a guide for hostile aircraft' within areas in which a Lights Order was in force.

PART TWO
COURAGE AND SELF-SACRIFICE

CHAPTER 5

LZ37, 7 June 1915

'...Little Patrick Corkery, Lieutenant Warneford's half-brother, who is aged only four, cannot understand the tragedy which has fallen on the family. "Will God mind Rex and bring him back to us, Mummy?" he plaintively inquired of his mother as he came running up to her this morning.

'She turned her head, and looked out on the bright sunlight which steeped the garden. "Perhaps He may, dear", she answered quietly...'

Daily Express, Saturday 19 June 1915

It was almost dark as the long slow march began. All traffic outside the railway station was brought to a halt as 18 members of the Royal Naval Division drew the gun carriage and its wreath-showered coffin on to the streets. Soldiers stood stiffly to attention. Crowds had gathered, quiet and respectful. Flanking the cortege were two RNAS Flight Sub-Lieutenants, a further detachment from the Royal Naval Division bringing up the rear. Several hundred people separated from the crowd to join the procession as it wound through Buckingham Palace Road, Pimlico Road, the Chelsea Embankment and into the Fulham Road.

By the time that the imposing iron gates of Brompton Cemetery had been reached, the scores of men, women and children accompanying the gun carriage joined hundreds more that had been silently waiting outside for over an hour. As the longest day of the year made way for darkness, the gates swung open to allow the funeral procession through, and after they were closed the large crowd, denied access, slowly began to disperse.

'Wild Hawk'
Reginald Alexander John Warneford was born on 15 October 1891 at Cooch Behar in India. His father, Reginald William Henry, was chief engineer on the railway being built there, and in earlier years had served in both the Oudh Volunteers and the Northern Bengal Mounted Rifles. Reginald had married pretty Alexandra Campbell on 3 September 1890 after a long romance which the girl's father had done much to discourage. Only when Warneford's new post had gained him a large bungalow and a veritable fortune did Captain Campbell DSO consent to his daughter's marriage.

'Rex' was the couple's first child and over the next few years Alexandra bore four daughters, Gladys, Jeanne, Dorothy and Violet. But all was not well between her and Reginald: the marriage had been a mistake. While her husband worked on his beloved railway, Alexandra and her children spent protracted periods at the Campbell home in Darjeeling. She also stayed at Simla on several occasions, where 'Rex' had his first taste of education at a kindergarten. More often than not, however, the boy was left behind with his father, and the pair became utterly devoted to each other, a devotion that Alexandra and her family grew to resent.

By 1899 it was all over: Alexandra and her daughters packed themselves off to Darjeeling without 'Rex', who was nowhere to be found. Several days passed, then Alexandra's father and brother visited the Cooch Behar bungalow, forcibly taking a protesting young Warneford back to his mother. To the boy's father this whirlwind succession of events came as a severe shock, from which he never recovered. Turning to the bottle for solace he literally drank himself to death; a year later he was found unconscious in a Bombay Street and rushed to hospital, where he died soon afterwards. The tragic loss of his father had a deep effect on Warneford and he openly rebelled against his mother's Irish admirer, Captain Martin Percy Corkery RAMC, whom she subsequently married. Eventually the friction between the boy and his stepfather was so intolerable that it became clear that both of them could not share the same house. As a result of a family conference Warneford found himself packed off to England for his education, and who better suited (it was thought) to care for the boy than his grandfather, Rev Tom Lewis Warneford?

Once in England at the peaceful Satley Rectory, Warneford soon settled in, warming quickly to the elderly parson and his young family. When the boy had turned 12 years of age it was time to commence his education, and Grandfather Warneford had the ideal academy in mind, the King Edward VI School in Stratford-upon-Avon, run by his old friend, Rev Cornwall Robertson. With the exception of mathematics, Warneford did not particularly shine in the academic subjects, nor did he appear to enjoy games greatly, but he readily took to practical subjects such as carpentry and light engineering. Edgar Cranmer, a dayboy at KES during the few years Warneford was there, remembers 'a boy of spirit' always in hot water for some kind of mischief and constantly being punished by his housemaster Mr Williams.[1]

During 1904 Thomas Warneford became seriously ill, was forced to leave the rectory, and went to live with his daughter Maude Nightingale and her husband. The couple's Ealing household was decidedly cramped with the new intake; indeed, the old parson's wife and baby Katherine were obliged to seek lodgings nearby. Warneford hated it; his aunt and uncle did little to make him feel at home and, with his grandfather dying, they sent the boy back to India, apprenticed to the British India Steam Navigation Company. On 11 January 1905 Warneford worked his passage to Calcutta on the SS *Somali*, a small liner of the Peninsular and Oriental Steam Navigation Company.

On 16 July that same year the old parson died at the Nightingale's home; he was buried at Brompton Cemetery in London. The sad news reached Warneford just before Christmas and, although this was expected, the boy felt the loss very deeply. For another eight years he served on some 14 vessels and learnt much of the world and its ways, first as an unpaid apprentice and eventually working up to Fourth Officer by January 1911. Although he enjoyed the life, managing to put the sadness of his earlier years behind him, he nevertheless became bored with liners, and when *Somali* docked at San Francisco on 21 December 1913 he sought, and found, an alternative. She was the *Mina Brea*, an oil tanker owned by the London and Pacific Petroleum Co Ltd, and Warneford joined the crew as First Officer. When the ship arrived in England Warneford found himself with three weeks' leave and sought out the mother he had not seen for 11 years. He found the Corkery household at Woolwich, and there followed a strained and awkward reunion with 'Pretty Mama', Dorothy, Violet and two young stepbrothers, Patrick Courtenay and Terence Reginald.[2] The meeting was a short one; Reginald felt apart from them and left before his stepfather returned. They never saw him again.

On his return to the *Mina Brea*, Warneford was promoted to First Officer and it was during the return voyage to San Francisco that he learnt of the war with Germany. On 19 September the ship ran aground off Chile, necessitating extensive and lengthy repairs. Warneford was despatched to England, reporting personally to the ship's owners and appraising them of the situation, after which he lost little time in leaving the merchant service in order to join up along with thousands of others. His first application was to the Royal Navy, and having been turned down because of insufficient background training Warneford resigned himself to an Army life. On 17 January 1915 he joined the Second Sportsman's Battalion, and having passed his entrance examinations and been kitted out was posted to Grey Towers, a less than imposing mansion near Hornchurch in Essex that was used as a training camp. In the weeks that followed it became clear to Warneford that service with this unit was nothing more than 'a sort of Boy Scouts' jamboree for old gentlemen'.[3] Attached to the Royal Fusiliers, the Battalions, as their name implied, were formed entirely of sportsmen from all walks of life and whose ages ranged between 19 and 45. It was all lectures, route marches and moves from one dismal camp to another, and not surprisingly Warneford applied for a transfer – to the Royal Naval Air Service.

On 10 February 1915 he was accepted as a probationary pilot, passed all the required medical and entrance examinations, and was despatched to the civilian flying school at Hendon; 15 days later he gained Royal Aero Club Certificate 1098, having had an able instructor in Flight Lieutenant Warren Merriam. A notable pre-war airman, Merriam regarded his pupil as a natural pilot but did not approve of the extreme over-confidence that Warneford exhibited, a trait which did little to endear him either to fellow trainees or to the school's CO, Squadron Commander Sitwell. A disciplinarian of the old school, Sitwell did not consider Warneford as officer material at all, an opinion somewhat reinforced when Warneford managed to write off two training machines by landing one on top of another. But Merriam realised Warneford's potential and saved the situation when Commander 'Crasher' Groves, Officer Commanding Naval Air Stations, paid a chance visit to Hendon. Taking Warneford aside, Merriam told him to 'give the show of his young life'.[4] Groves was much impressed with the spirited performance of the pilot in the Bristol biplane and remarked that he would 'either do big things or kill himself'.[5] Before the year was out, Warneford had done both.

During his initial period of training Warneford often stayed at an apartment house in Russell Square and formed a friendly relationship with the landlady Mrs Robinson and her three-year-old daughter Doris:

The young 'Rex' Warneford relaxes at Stratford-upon-Avon, where he was educated for a short period at King Edward VI School. Warneford usually preferred his own company, showed little enthusiasm for sports, and excelled at all the practical subjects in the curriculum.
By courtesy of the Fleet Air Arm Museum

Warneford, in the uniform of an RNAS Flight Sub-Lieutenant, poses in front of a Maurice Farman MF11 trainer at Hendon in 1915.
King Edward VI School

Even when Lieutenant Warneford had to live at the Hendon Headquarters, he made a point of coming here once or sometimes twice a week.

His first question when once he had set foot inside the door was always 'Where's Doris?' and he would never come without bringing her a present of some kind. Sometimes it would be a doll or a picture book, sometimes chocolate or fruit...[6]

Having completed his course at Hendon, Warneford went on to further training with the Central Flying School at Upavon in Wiltshire, whence he was posted to 2 Squadron RNAS at Eastchurch on the Isle of Sheppey. In charge of the station was Squadron Commander E L Gerrard, who also found Warneford to be an excellent flyer, which more than made up for the undisciplined behaviour that many of his fellows had found so intolerable. Warneford's reputation preceded him to his new posting but did not appear to bother him – rather, he took a savage delight in living up to it:

> As he paused in the doorway of the long wooden hut which served as the Officers' Mess, all eyes were turned towards him. Rex strode into the middle of the room, pulled out his revolver, twirled it round in his hand cowboy fashion and said, in the deep South American drawl which he liked to affect, 'Hi suckers! What about this?' Then he fired six shots up into the roof. Nobody moved or spoke. Rex replaced his gun in its holster, turned on his heel and left the Mess. As soon as the door closed behind him all hell broke loose.[7]

But it was Warneford's flying ability that made the biggest impression on Gerrard, who was largely instrumental in arranging for the unpredictable youngster's posting to a unit overseas. On 7 May Warneford set off to join 1 Squadron RNAS, based at Dunkirk under Wing Commander Arthur M Longmore. The unit had been formed at Fort Grange, Gosport, on 14 October 1914, and by January of the following year had moved to Dover, where all training has been completed by February. That month the squadron found itself at Dunkirk, where the RNAS undertook specific duties. These included preventing Zeppelins and aircraft operating from their Belgian bases against England, attacking U-boats in the vicinity and reporting their movements, co-operating with naval monitors of the Dover Patrol, obtaining information on enemy shipping movements, and developing aerial photography and wireless communication from aircraft under active service conditions.[8]

At St Pol, which adjoined Dunkirk, the RNAS had established a depot and aerodrome under Commander Charles Rumney Samson in order to carry out their various offensive duties, before leaving for England and thence to the Dardanelles. Longmore and his squadron soon settled in at St Pol, although accommodation at the airfield was limited while Samson's men remained there. It was the cross-channel steamer *Empress* that saved the situation: moored alongside the jetty at Dunkirk, it served as a most comfortable billet for officers and men alike.

Warneford flew into St Pol on 7 May and, after a textbook landing, reported to Longmore's office. The Squadron CO lost no time putting his new pilot in the picture, telling him that despite Warneford's 'unsavoury reputation' he would be judged solely on what he did in the squadron rather than on his past record at Eastchurch. That night, true to form, Warneford drove one of the unit's Talbot tenders into a ditch and damaged it further when returning to camp. Patiently, Longmore gave him one more chance, but warned that if he offended again he would be posted elsewhere.[9]

The following day Warneford and one of Longmore's more experienced observers, John H D'Albiac (the unit's resident musician), left in a squadron Voisin to carry out a reconnaissance flight. Heading up the coast at a height of 4000ft, the slow pusher biplane was heavily shelled as it passed over Ostend. Disregarding D'Albiac's frantic signals to fly beyond range, Warneford held doggedly to his course, the aircraft running a veritable gauntlet towards Zeebrugge.

When two and a half hours had elapsed and there was still no sign of the Voisin, Longmore presumed that the aircraft, running out of fuel, had been compelled to make a forced landing. But eventually, to everyone's relief, the biplane appeared, and once down was found to have only a few pints left in the fuel tank. Warneford's shaken observer, on reporting to his CO, pleaded never to be sent up again with 'this madman'.[10] An incredulous Longmore learnt how Warneford had pursued a German machine all the way back to its Ostend aerodrome, often at rooftop height, firing all the while with his rifle.

Leading Mechanic G E Meddis, a singularly brave individual, volunteered to fly with Warneford, and together they carried out many aggressive sorties over enemy lines. The 'madman' simply attacked anything and everything. If a patrol proved uneventful, Warneford was apt to liven things up, as he did on one occasion by 'buzzing' a church used by the squadron's ground crew as a billet:

> How he missed it I shall never know. He headed straight into it, then yanked the Voisin, complaining in every joint, into a steep left handed bank. The chaps inside, hearing the roar of our engine, rushed out. They told me afterwards that we were not 20 feet above them. As our undercarriage slithered past the side of the church, Rex leaned out the cockpit and waved. They just yelled and shook their fists at us...[12]

Flight Commander A W Bigsworth and Avro 504B 1009 in which he attacked *LZ39* on 17 May 1915. Six other pilots of No 1 Wing RNAS also took part in the action. The Avro's fuselage fabric is saturated with oil, and students of markings should note the absence of the white inner rings on the roundels.
R G Gray, by courtesy of D Furze

LZ37, 7 June 1915

Following the destruction of *LZ37* and the rapid announcement of the VC, life for Warneford was never quite the same again. Temporarily taken off active duty, he was sent to Paris where the *Croix de Guerre* was awarded to him. Warneford always referred to his victory in modest terms, insisting that what he did anyone else could have done in similar circumstances, dismissing the feat as 'just routine'. Later he confided his deep regret in having brought the Zeppelin down over a convent.
By courtesy of the Fleet Air Arm Museum

On 17 May Warneford had his first brush with a Zeppelin when he and other pilots were ordered to patrol the coast as far as Zeebrugge and attack any airships they might encounter. At 03.20hrs Warneford and Meddis left the ground in a Nieuport and even as they cleared the airfield a Zeppelin was seen out at sea flying towards Ostend. In all, seven machines were sent up to attack it.

Flight Sub-Lieutenant Kilner had been first away, and on his return from Zeebrugge sighted *LZ39* at a height he estimated to be 8000ft, but with a faulty engine was unable to engage the enemy. Warneford, however, managed to close with the giant dirigible over Ostend and Meddis let fly at 1000ft range. His .45 rifle was loaded with new incendiary bullets, but he only managed to loose off five before the Zeppelin climbed away. The first rounds were seen to hit the nose of *LZ39*, but most of them 'did not flame', and the final shot, although seen to strike the airship amidships, had no obvious effect. *LZ39*, rising all the while, easily left Warneford behind, the weight of observer, Lewis gun, rifle, ammunition and hand grenades severely curtailing the Nieuport's performance. Over Zeebrugge Warneford spotted a U-boat and a small steamer clearing the harbour and heading north-west. It probably came as no surprise to Meddis when Warneford dived on the submarine and within 2000ft had hurled all the hand grenades at it. The U-boat was apparently unharmed by the attack, and Warneford returned to Dunkirk.

Flight Commander A W Bigsworth in Avro 504B 1009 continued to shadow *LZ39* and eventually managed to overtake it 10,000ft over Ostend. Having passed 200ft above the Zeppelin's back and dropped four 20lb Hales bombs, Bigsworth noticed black smoke being emitted from the tail of the Zeppelin which he fancied was a result of his attack. In spite of his proximity to the airship, anti-aircraft fire was so intense that he was quite unable to distinguish between bomb and shell bursts, and so he turned seawards to avoid the barrage.

Squadron Commander Spenser D A Grey, flying a Nieuport, reached a height of 9800ft, and when abreast of *LZ39* as she began to rise decided to attack the rear gondola. At a range of 100ft he was subjected to heavy machine-gun fire from the German crew:

> The gondolas seemed to be about 300 feet apart – no machine guns were mounted on top of the fuselage [*sic*]. There did not appear to be any aluminium casing. The colour of the fabric was muddy and of a neutral tint. The propellers were only turning from 300 to 400 revolutions. [I] was at a height of 9000 feet when close to her, but she very rapidly climbed around to 15,000 to 20,000 feet immediately after the attack and headed for the SE.[13]

The other aircraft failed to engage *LZ39*, which was last seen at around 05.00hrs making for Ghent.[14] Thus ended one of the first close-quarter aeroplane-versus-airship combats, which answered many questions and posed several others about how such encounters should be dealt with in the future. Longmore called a conference among his senior officers immediately after the action, and submitted their findings in the official report sent to the Air Department Director, Murray Sueter. The findings, some of which were quite erroneous, revealed:

A) The necessity of employing fast single-seater machines with a very fast climb.

B) Once having obtained a position above the airship no great difficulty appears to prevent a successful attack with a bomb, the target being extremely large.

C) The general impression of the officers of my Squadron and myself is that Flaming Bullets will not be effective and that it is necessary to properly tear the envelope and effect a good escape of gas before it can be set alight to.

D) For this reason, for the time being it has been decided to use a group of different types of bombs on each machine. One group, for instance, to consist of a 10lb Hales bomb, a Zeppelin Bomb and perhaps a Petrol Bomb, or Fusée Arrows.[15]

Warneford was given charge of a single-seater aeroplane following his attack on *LZ39*. It was a Morane Saulnier L, a French-built parasol monoplane and one of the first to be fitted with metal deflector plates on the airscrew; the true synchronised machine gun had yet to be properly developed. The plates, simple metal V-shaped wedges, would protect the airscrew from being shattered by every one out of the ten bullets that spat from the Lewis gun mounted in front of the pilot's cockpit. Warneford's fitters also bolted a rack to the machine's undercarriage, this to carry six 20lb Hales bombs which could be released via toggle and wire from a sight lever mounted on the starboard side of the fuselage.

Longmore gave his impetuous pilot a 'roving commission', and Warneford spent much of his time over the lines attacking enemy observation aircraft and balloons. He rarely returned without some kind of combat damage to his aircraft, and so constantly was it under repair that Longmore obtained 3253, a replacement machine without a machine gun, for use when the other was *hors de combat*.[16]

The next opportunity to combat Zeppelins came on the evening of 6 June when Longmore received a message from the Admiralty that three airships were on their way back to Belgium following an abortive attack on England. Longmore sent off Warneford and Rose in their Moranes to intercept the raiders over Ghent, and Wilson and Mills in their big weight-carrying Farmans to bomb the Zeppelin shed at Evère, near Brussels. He hoped by this arrangement to either catch one or more of the Zeppelins in the air or set them alight after they had returned to their bases.[17]

As Wilson and Mills cleared the aerodrome two Moranes were being bombed up at Furnes, a Belgian airfield 15 miles away and used by certain RNAS pilots as an advanced landing ground. Warneford boarded 3253 and strapped himself in, and at 01.00hrs both he and Rose took off into the mist. Warneford soon lost sight of his companion, who became disorientated and with instrument lights failing made a forced-landing near Cassel, flipping the Morane over on its back. Rose scrambled out unhurt. Warneford continued his patrol and was nearing Dixmude when to the north, beyond Ostend, he saw it: there was no mistaking the pencil-like shape of a Zeppelin.

Zeppelin!

The commander of *LZ37*, *Oberleutnant* Otto von der Haegen, seen here in the control gondola of Zeppelin Ersatz *EZ1* (fourth along from the left). Von der Haegen, born at Creuzthal on 23 May 1887, took over *LZ37* from its Potsdam builders on 28 February 1915; the subsequent trip to Cologne nearly ended in disaster, adverse weather conditions and engine malfunctions occuring during the flight.
Archiv: Marine-Luftschiffer-Kameradschaft

◀ *Army Zeppelin LZ37* ▶ photographed at Cologne before moving on to Etterbeek where it was based when lost. *LZ37*, an 'm' type Zeppelin, had a gas volume of 794,500 cu ft, measured 518ft 2in long and was powered by three Maybach CX engines delivering 630hp to provide a maximum speed of 50.9mph. Both gondolas were of the open type with the four propellers mounted on outriggers. The keel was externally mounted and widened at the centre to accommodate a small cabin that housed the wireless and bomb racks. Above the nose was a gun platform with mounts for two or three Parabellum machine guns. Despite Warneford's combat report, *LZ37* was indeed armed, and the platform is readily obvious in these photographs. Of incidental interest is the so-called 'Maltese Cross' insignia painted amidships, which is plain on the starboard side but outlined in white on the port.
Elias/Miller, by courtesy of D H Robinson

66

Zeppelin *LZ37*

Three days after Warneford had gained his Royal Aero Club Certificate, *Obersteuermann* Alfred Mühler was at his post in the forward gondola of Zeppelin *LZ37* expectantly awaiting the news that the ship was ready for command. That day *Oberleutnant* Otto von der Haegen took over the Army's latest ship from its builders at Potsdam after a trial flight had proven successful, and the stern ensign was hoisted for the first official flight. For Mühler, at the control wheel, it was a proud moment:

> At our destination we had to make several landing approaches, owing to severe wind gusts. After the ground crew had secured our ship with ropes, our commanding officer left the ship to report our landing to the Air Chief of Staff. The weather at ground level was the worst imaginable, the gusts now gaining strength. Just as the First Officer was giving orders intended to relieve the ground crew a great gust of wind hit us. With elemental force it snatched the front end of the ship high into the air hurling both officers, the flight engineer and the assistant engine operator out of the gondola. Immediately afterwards the ship was torn out of the grip of the rear ground crew... The ship was free and, with no engines running, the storm took us to a height of 2000 metres in less than ten minutes.
>
> Two courageous members of the ground crew still clung grimly to the ropes: comrade [Hermann] Kirchner and I finally managed to pull these two involuntary acrobats into the gondola.[18]

LZ37 was still rising, but encountered less violent gusts as Mühler assumed command and tried to restore the vessel's equilibrium by ditching machine guns to compensate for the two extra passengers who had so narrowly cheated death. The nose of *LZ37* was slanted downwards, but insufficiently so, and Mühler tried every trick in the book to check the unruly airship while he vainly opened, closed and reopened the gas valves and *LZ37*'s mechanics attempted to repair the two damaged rear engines which eventually they succeeded in doing. A relieved Mühler turned the Zeppelin towards the landing ground:

> No sooner had I got over my first feeling of excitement, and lined the ship up for a classic approach to the airfield and a fine landing, when – I could hardly believe my own ears – both rear engines stopped! Once more we swung sideways and climbed rapidly. In a flash my hopes vanished like butter in the sun. Thank God this test of nerves did not last long – after a short silence the two rear engines thundered into life at full power.
>
> I steered downwards, and we descended from 1500 metres, to 1000, to 800, 600 down to 200, until finally, recovering well, I cried 'Half Speed' with my breast full of courage and we came into a successful landing.[19]

Shaken, Mühler was greeted by a relieved von der Haegen who praised the helmsman for his actions and ability, passing the comment that with such a crew he 'could safely travel to Hell'. In the light of subsequent events these words were chillingly prophetic.

Repairs to *LZ37* were soon completed, and subsequently the ship flew to its base at the Brussels-Etterbeek landing ground. Mühler was on watch during the evening of Sunday 6 June when the telephone rang; picking up the receiver he was given attack orders, and within a short while both *LZ37* and *LZ39* were prepared for take-off and, once airborne, headed for the coast. Mühler later recounted the dramatic events of that night:

> After quite a long flight we slipped out of sight of the enemy. The lights which shone up to us now and then through gaps in the cloud appeared to be our target. Ackermann prepared the LZ37's bombs. The commanding officer gave me a few practical tips, and then came the signal that the bombs were away. I noticed from the controls that the ship felt much

Zeppelin!

The ill-fated crew of the Army Zeppelin *LZ37* pose proudly for the cameraman. Only *Steuermann* Alfred Mühler (second from left) survived the destruction of the ship by Warneford on the night of 7 June 1917.
Archiv: Marine-Luftschiffer-Kameradschaft

The tangled wreckage of *LZ37* lying in the courtyard of the Convent of St Elisabeth, Ghent. It took a fortnight for the wreckage to be cleared away by the military, the remains of von der Haegen's ship being transported by teams of horse-drawn wagons. One of the nuns recalled the scene of 7 June as the blazing Zeppelin drifted towards the convent: '...We were terribly afraid that it would fall on us. It came nearer and nearer. The sound of its burning was terrible. There were screams, and pieces of metal began to fall all around. Our big bell began to ring its warning for fire. Sisters and the refugees came running out ...'
By courtesy of the Fleet Air Arm Museum

lighter. Naturally night time aiming is much more difficult, so we turned from our target and flew around the bomb drop zone in great circles. The effect must have been great. 'That was Dover', *Leutnant* Ackermann called to me.[20]

Taking account of the westerly wind our course was now due south to take us on the short journey to Calais, lying to the east. It was our commanding officer's intention to approach Calais as quickly as possible. Not far from Calais, we stopped the engines and allowed the west wind to drive us to our target. The surprise element was successful, and our bombs were released on the designated targets. We now flew out at top speed over the water in a north-easterly direction, to avoid being attacked from the coast. The searchlights from the warships, now at action stations, could be seen on the thin covering of cloud beneath us. The anti-airship shells produced bursts of mid-air explosions here and there around us. To the right of us lay Dunkirk. The French and English had stationed three defensive squadrons there, and also eight anti-airship guns. We steered towards Ostend, with its flashing lights. Then we flew on a general course for Brussels. A weak redness was beginning to show in the morning sky. Through the grey vapours the first outlines of Ghent could be seen in the distance.

We could already pick out houses and trees under us, and we began to feel safe again. Now and then we would look back at the glowing fires in the dark distance, started by our bomb attack.[21]

At 01.50hrs Warneford's approach to *LZ37* was met by vigorous gunfire from the Zeppelin's crew and he wisely flew out of range and began to climb away for another attack. *LZ37* turned to port, and as the Morane dived on its huge target a second time, the German gunners retaliated with vigour. With the Zeppelin rising all the while, Warneford made off westwards in order that the commander of the ship would think the pilot had given up the attack. As the Morane wheeled away the machine-gun fire ceased, and Warneford took up a safer station well behind his quarry.

At 02.15hrs *LZ37* was nearing Ghent, and at last began to descend in preparation for a landing. Here was Warneford's only chance, and he was not slow to seize it. Ten minutes later he was at 11,000ft and above the airship, when he switched off the engine of his aircraft 'to descend on top of him'.[22] At a height of 7000ft Warneford pulled the bomb release handle as he began a run in along the back of the Zeppelin. When the sixth and last bomb cleared the rack there came a tremendous explosion as *LZ37* was almost ripped in two. The savage eruption which tore through the doomed airship in seconds sent Warneford and his tiny aircraft reeling, the pilot fighting to gain control. In the forward gondola of *LZ37* the scene was horrific:

I rushed from the wheel to the gondola door; I was overcome by terror. What had happened? A crackling, rattling sound, otherwise there was dead silence in the gondola.

The commanding officer was slumped over the side; the first officer lay over the chart table; the [others] had fallen to the floor of the gondola. Nobody moved. Were they unconscious? I just stood there. What had happened? A shudder of horror. A quick glance at the rear gondola brought a new terror. Almighty God! The ship was on fire!

I was heading straight for my death. 'I don't want to be burned alive!' a voice inside me cried. Thoughts rushed through my mind in a mad storm: my whole life, my wife, my parents, my brothers and sisters – I saw them all around me reading my obituary. Good God, the thoughts that crowd into the brain in those few seconds! Slowly I too sank to the floor. Glowing, smouldering pieces of fabric from the ship's covering fell on my face and neck, and on my comrades. I felt another thunderous crashing and shuddering. The airship had broken up. I lost consciousness.

An impact brought me round again. I was still alive. Had I dreamed it all? Or had a miracle happened? How had I got here? Was I still falling?

No. I was on a bed, and a nun was standing by me. I stared at her wide-eyed. Above us were the flames crackling loudly, and a beam fell in. How could I escape? I ran as best as I could, this way and that – there was no way out! Was I to burn here, after surviving the very greatest danger? Where was that nun? Why did she leave me alone? Parts of the ceiling were caving in, bringing large sections of the wall with them.

There was a light coming through a gap! Was it a way out? No, the ship's skeleton lay just outside. I hurled myself against it with all my force, but sprang back. I tensed my muscles. In desperation I made a jump through the distorted half open door. The waist clasps of my leather coat caught on something, but the force of my leap tore them out. I landed outside amid the burning wreckage of the ship, and dashed through the glowing, smouldering remains.[23]

The burning skeleton of *LZ37* fell across the convent of St Elizabeth in the Mont St Amand district of Ghent, killing two nuns and a man. Another man broke both legs when he fell headlong from a second-storey window in an attempt to save a child. Some of the Zeppelin's dead and dying crew members were lying in the wreckage and a number of the convent's nuns going out to attend to them were prevented from doing so by German police and soldiers who had quickly arrived on the scene. One eyewitness to Warneford's destruction of the airship was Max Börgemann:

I saw the crash of the LZ37 from the beginning to its terrible end. I could not get to the scene quickly. I shuddered at each incendiary projectile, but the enemy pilot aimed so well that one cell after another exploded until the Zeppelin collapsed in the middle. It was around the hour of dawn. It was terrible to watch the pilot come round again and again to destroy the mortally wounded giant and its crew.[24]

Alfred Mühler was an extremely lucky man. They found him in the convent garden lying semi-conscious by a stone wall, the dying von der Haegen and Ackerman close by. A civilian doctor attended to Mühler, removing many metal splinters from his elbow, but the painful dressing of his burns was the worst part of the helmsman's ordeals. Mühler spent six weeks in a military hospital and learnt how he had been given up for dead, a grave dug for him next to his comrades being filled in afterwards when he was known to have survived. Visiting the Ghent cemetery was a miserable experience for the helmsman who next made his way towards the actual site of the disaster:

> The ship, its back broken in the air, lay as a tangled mass of scrap iron, its nose and tail downwards, over the convent. The front gondola's engine must have come free in the crash, plunging on to the side wing of the convent and penetrating the roof and ceiling of the single-storey building. The convent's inhabitants must have been surprised and terror-stricken by the ship's impact in the middle of their night's sleep. I took away a melted lump of metal from the ship's wreckage as a souvenir.[25]

But there was little opportunity for other relic-hunters. The German police, who had arrived so promptly on the scene after the crash, closed off all surrounding streets and ordered civilians to remain in their houses. One of the nuns tried to take a snapshot of the wreckage but a guard took her camera, only to return it later without the film. Over the following fortnight the scorched remains of LZ37 were carted away on wagons and scrapped.

Although Warneford had managed to regain control of the Morane after the airship's destruction he was unable to restart his engine and at 02.40hrs, 35 miles behind enemy lines, was obliged to land, coming down on the side of a small hill. Owing to the mist and constant changes of direction, he had little idea of his exact whereabouts, and he did not relish the thought of being taken prisoner.

An inspection of the Morane revealed a broken connection between the gravity and pressure tanks. Warneford's flair for mechanics stood him in good stead, for he had fixed the break within a quarter of an hour. On completion of the repair he heard the sounds of German cavalry searching the woods close by; he was both surprised and relieved when they rode away, but capture was inevitable if he could not get the Morane off. Later, safely back at Dunkirk, he explained how he managed to get airborne single-handed:

> I religiously doped every one of the cylinders with petrol, by filling an empty Very cartridge cap and dropping it on the cylinder heads. Then I swung the prop. Another problem cropped up, for without another chap I could not keep the engine running long enough for me to get back into the cockpit – I was pretty desperate by then. I pulled and pushed and bounced her along until I got her nose pointing downhill which was luckily pretty steep. Then I swung the prop. I kept on hauling and pushing her – she started to move slowly at first and then as she gathered speed and I knew she wouldn't stop I made a leap for the cockpit just as the Boche charged out of the wood firing their carbines in my direction.[26]

After this quite astonishing feat Warneford flew on through mist and fog, dropping to ground level on several occasions in an attempt to get his bearings. As his engine, starved of fuel, began to 'splutter and give up', Warneford caught sight of the sea and made a bumpy landing on the

Inside the Evère shed, 8 June 1915. The forward control and engine gondola of LZ38 lie crushed beneath the collapsed structure. Note the hinged door towards the rear of the car. Despite the fiery devastation there were few casualties as a result of the RNAS airmen's attack.
D H Robinson

The burnt-out shed at Evère with the remains of LZ38 inside on the morning of 8 June 1915, following Mills and Wilson's attack hours previously. As a consequence of both LZ37 and LZ38's destruction, the surviving LZ39 and ZXII were rapidly transferred to the Russian front, the vulnerable sheds of Brussels being used only for emergencies or brief periods of hangarage.
D H Robinson

RNAS 'giant killers' at St Pol. From left to right, Sub-Lieutenant R S Mills, Squadron Commander A W Bigsworth, Lieutenant J P Wilson and Sub-Lieutenant R A J Warneford relax during an off-duty period. Between them these airmen destroyed two Zeppelins and damaged a third within the space of a month.
IWM Q69479

beach at Cap Gris Nez to an unexpected greeting. As the Morane rolled to a stop he noticed French troops running towards him, their rifles at the ready, and despite Warneford's protestations and the RNAS cockades on the aeroplane's fuselage, he was marched, hands held high, to their commanding officer. The French were extremely suspicious, but Warneford eventually persuaded their English-speaking captain to phone his aerodrome for verification. When Warneford's identity was confirmed the *poilus* plied him with cognac and salutations whilst the tanks of the Morane were replenished.

It was 10.30hrs when an exhausted Warneford finally landed at St Pol, where after a short report to Longmore he was taken to the *Empress*. He rolled into his bunk and slept for fully eight hours.

Longmore's men had quite a successful night, for both Mills and Wilson had reached the airship shed at Evère and wreaked considerable havoc. Flight Lieutenant J P Wilson, in Henry Farman 3998, had arrived over Evère at 02.05hrs and commenced his attack on the huge shed 15 minutes later. His first bomb fell just beyond the south-east corner of the hangar, his second and third also seemingly falling short of their target:

I then steered away to the north-westward, circling round Brussels, and afterwards steering a south-westerly course. On looking at the shed it appeared that a large column of black smoke was above the shed, but no flames were observed.

On reaching Itterveek [*sic*] or thereabouts to the SW of Brussels, I was at a height of 7000 feet, when a very bright star shell, or rocket, came up quite close to me and remained in the air for 10 to 15 seconds and then died out.[27]

Wilson later became lost in thick mist, but at 05.15hrs he sighted the ground through a gap and he made a safe landing in a field near Montrevill. Flight Sub-Lieutenant J S Mills had taken off at 00.45hrs and arrived over the target a good ten minutes behind Wilson. He too noted the flashing signal lamps which his colleague had earlier answered in order to perplex the enemy, and then both searchlights and gunfire were aimed at the Farman:

I then decided to get more height, and, reaching 5000 feet, I got on a line heading about NW, and going straight for the shed, dropped all my bombs, 12 in number, one after the other, when I thought I was in position, which was about 2.40am.[28]

Glancing back over his shoulder, Mills saw the huge shed burning furiously, flames and black smoke belching from its roof. Only later did he learn that inside was London's first raider, *LZ38*, which just a few hours earlier had returned to base following the abortive attack on England.

Dodging heavy anti-aircraft fire, Mills made for home, steering the whole way by compass, and, at a loss as to his actual position, he dropped from 7000 to 1200ft, hoping to locate a clear patch. After nearly pitching into the sea, the result of a miscalculated dive, he turned south, picked up the coastline and landed on the beach of Le Clipon at 04.45hrs. Mills clambered out of the Farman's nacelle, eventually located a telephone and rang Longmore to inform him that he was down safely.[29]

Newspapers the world over soon leapt on the airmen's actions, which were already front-page news in London on the Tuesday morning following the dramatic destruction of

Warneford and his famous Morane Saulnier L3253 at Dunkirk. The bomb rack is fitted between the undercarriage legs, and forward of the fuselage roundel is the 'sight lever' bomb release manufactured by Stanley of London.
J M Bruce/G S Leslie Collection

the two Zeppelins. After a hero's welcome at St Pol, Warneford had gone into Longmore's office where he was handed a very special telegram from Buckingham Palace:

> I most heartily congratulate you upon your splendid achievement of yesterday in which you single-handed destroyed an enemy Zeppelin. I have much pleasure in conferring upon you the Victoria Cross for this gallant act.
> George RI.[30]

Warneford was stunned and Longmore had orders to keep the new air hero out of trouble 'as long as his value as propaganda was fully exploited and until he had returned from London.'[31] Warneford had no desire to go to London, nor face the attention of an adoring population, but there seemed no way out. From then on, and for the remaining few days left to him, it never really let up. Grounded and frustrated, Warneford learnt later that the French wanted him in Paris so that they could confer the Knights Cross of the Legion of Honour upon him. There he would attend various functions and celebrations, after which he was to collect a new machine for the squadron and bring it back to St Pol.

Flight Lieutenant Michael S Marsden was detailed to keep an eye on Warneford during his stay in the French capital. It was Longmore's idea: he doubtless feared that if left to his own devices Warneford might well try and slip off somewhere. Marsden met Warneford at Villacoublay and, following a civic reception and celebration dinner, the two airmen travelled by taxi to Paris, where they booked into the Ritz Hotel. Everything had been prepared for their visit, and after another reception Marsden had quite a job to dissuade the reluctant hero from immediately leaving the capital.

On 12 June both officers went to the Ministère de la Marine where *Monsieur* Alexandre Millerand, the French Minister of War, proudly pinned his own Chevalier of the Legion of Honour on Warneford's tunic. As the minister kissed the pilot on both cheeks in the time-honoured tradition, he expressed his pride in wearing the medal destined for the VC hero. Lunches, engagements and invitations followed, and during their rounds the airmen made the aquaintance of France's first aviatrix, the beautiful Baroness Raymonde de Laroche, who was obviously quite taken with Warneford. On one occasion he dined at her house in the Rue St Honore, and to Marsden it seemed that his friend was actually in love for the first time in his life. During the final few days of his visit Warneford had little time to himself: wherever he went hordes greeted him, and on more than one occasion he was unable to walk the streets of the city without an escort of *gendarmes*.

During the evening of 16 June, the Baroness, Warneford and Marsden were at a large restaurant enjoying a final celebration before they all went their separate ways the next morning. Marsden would later recall a rather disturbing scene that took place after most of the other guests had left the table:

> I looked up, sensing that someone wished to give us a message. It was the cigarette girl. She was standing just behind Rex, and in her tray was a bunch of red roses, full-blown and wilting from the heat of the room. 'Pour vous, Monsieur,' she said holding them out to Rex. He stood up and took them from her, and as he held them their crimson petals began to fall, one by one, over the cross of the Legion of Honour on the breast of his tunic. As they fell the girl burst into tears, ashamed that her gift was composed of faded flowers. Stammering her regret in broken English she said: 'I brought them to wish you happiness when you go back to England.' Taking her hand Rex replied: 'Mademoiselle, thank you for your flowers, but they will be for my grave, for I shall not reach England. I will not live to see England again.'[32]

When morning came it was back to duty again for there was the acceptance flight in the Henry Farman that afternoon at Buc aerodrome. But it was to be a little more complicated than that, for Warneford was obliged to give one more interview, to an American newspaper reporter whose request for such and a short flight over Paris had been granted that morning by the French authorities. Warneford was not over-enthusiastic about the idea, but for Henry Beech Needham it was a real scoop.

Needham hailed from Wyncote in Pennsylvania, USA, and was a freelance reporter but had served on the editorial

This photograph, first published in L'Illustration, *shows the pathetic remains of Henry Farman F27 in which Warneford and American journalist Henry Beach Needham were killed on 17 June 1915. In the foreground a cushion from one of the seats lies outside the nacelle, the Canton-Unné engine is seen to the left of the picture, and beyond is the rudder bearing the constructor's number HF18. Even now the exact cause of the tragedy remains a mystery; several solutions have been put forward, including sabotage, excess of alcohol or foolhardiness.*
By courtesy of the Fleet Air Arm Museum

Aircraft 3253 was subsequently exhibited in the UK following Warneford's death, but research has failed to discover its ultimate fate. At the end of the war 3253, along with many other wartime aircraft, was taken to the Crystal Palace and it was known to be there as late as 1922 as part of the Air Ministry Collection. Doubtless it ended up on the scrapheap along with many other machines.
Aeromodeller

staff of the *New York Evening Post* for several years before becoming assistant managing editor of *McClure's Magazine* before moving to the staff of *The World's Work*. He counted at least two Presidents amongst his personal friends, and in 1908 Roosevelt had personally appointed him as special commissioner to investigate labour and housing conditions in the Panama Canal Zone. Since the outbreak of hostilities Needham had travelled through Germany, Switzerland and England, interviewing many notables including Lloyd George and Joffre.

At midday Warneford dined with Needham in Paris, and it is thought that the interview (which was never published) took place over lunch. After settling plans for the afternoon they parted, and Warneford returned to the Ritz in order to collect a new aquaintance, one Lieutenant Robert Francis Fitzgibbon RN, who had been spending leave at the Ritz in company with his wife Georgette. All three drove to the RNAS headquarters in Paris, picked up Needham and then went to Buc, Warneford having offered the Farman's spare seat to Fitzgibbon for the test.

Once at the airfield Warneford prepared for the flight. The squadron's latest acquisition was a Henry Farman F27 pusher biplane. It featured a steel tube airframe, a shorter nacelle than previous variants, equal-span wings, and a simplified four-wheeled undercarriage without skids: it looked for all the world like a flying pram. Being newly delivered, the aircraft was devoid of any markings, with the exception of the constructor's number, HF18, painted in black on the rudder. The test flight was over within five minutes and as Fitzgibbon clambered down, Needham took his place. Neither the newspaperman nor Warneford strapped themselves in.

Even as the biplane taxied out into the field, a large Hispano Suiza limousine arrived at the gates of the aerodrome and Baroness de Laroche stepped out. Had Warneford's disturbing presentiment the previous night prompted her to try and prevent the flight? If that was indeed the reason for her appearance it was now too late – the Farman was already airborne. At 2000ft the biplane banked as it approached the airfield, spectators saw the turn followed by an unexpected spin – deliberate or not will never be known – which ended in a steep dive and a sharp pull out. It was then that the tail assembly and the supporting booms parted company with a terrific crash that could be heard over the noise of the machine's engine. The flailing booms struck the propeller, and as it shattered into splinters the dismembered aircraft began to roll. The watchers looked on horrified as, turning over, the stricken aircraft pitched out both its hapless occupants 700ft above the ground, Warneford, Needham and the Farman falling in a green cornfield. Everyone rushed forward. They found that Needham had been killed outright, one of his hands still tightly clutching part of the wicker seat; Warneford lay some distance away, quite still. Gingerly they turned him over: unconscious and barely breathing, he was obviously terribly injured. The Legion of Honour had been partially driven through his tunic deep into his side.

The airfield ambulance bore Warneford to the British Military Hospital in the Versailles Trianon Palace Hotel, followed by a shaken Baroness in her chauffeur-driven car.[33] Marsden, having learnt of the tragedy on his return to the Ritz, reached the hospital just as the two vehicles drew up. Both he and the Baroness looked down upon the prostrate form lying on the stretcher; less than 24 hours ago they had been together dining in style, and now Marsden was doubtful if his friend even knew they were there:

> As we stood helplessly looking, he gave a little sigh and opened his eyes. For less than a second he looked straight at me, almost as though he was going to make a sign that he knew us. Then his head turned away and before the orderlies had wheeled him out of our sight he died.[34]

To many the cause of the tragedy was a complete mystery. Press stories attributed the crash to sabotage, to the result of a wild party held the previous night, to a fault in the aircraft, to reckless flying. None of these could really be considered seriously:

> At the official enquiry it was suggested that Lieutenant Warneford was coming in to land too high. To lose height he dived the machine too steeply and pulled up too hard. Under the strain the right wing went back and broke. With the propeller smashed by part of the tail, and the engine still running, it was impossible to prevent disaster.[35]

With Warneford's reputation as a first rate flyer, it seemed inconceivable that he should have died in such a manner, and even today the real cause of the tragedy remains something of an open question. Newspapers that had spread the news of Warneford's deed a fortnight earlier splashed his picture all over their front pages again. The special fund to which *Daily Express* readers had subscribed following the destruction of *LZ37*, to provide the airman with some kind of presentation (a silver statuette had been suggested), would now be used for a memorial.

On 18 June Warneford's body was laid out in the mortuary of the Versailles hospital alongside that of Needham, and the coffins were draped with a large Union Flag and the

The scene at Brompton Cemetery's chapel on the afternoon of 22 June 1916. A guard of honour stands to attention while Warneford's coffin is loaded reverently on to a naval gun carriage by members of the Royal Naval Division.
By courtesy of the Fleet Air Arm Museum

Warneford's mother, sisters and other relatives comfort themselves as the 50-strong naval firing party prepares to loose off a volley.
By courtesy of the Fleet Air Arm Museum

Stars and Stripes respectively. Dozens of roses and other flowers had been placed around the two coffins by nurses and hospital staff, two soldiers standing guard being relieved at regular intervals. One of the most impressive floral tributes had been jointly presented by the Governor of the Army of Paris, French officers attached to the RFC, and wounded British soldiers. It took the form of a giant aeroplane with a floral Victoria Cross on one wing, a large *Légion d'Honneur* on the other, a tricolour adorning the tail and at the extreme nose an 'engine' of white roses. A card was attached, and it bore a simple inscription:

Honoured by the King, admired by the Empire, but mourned by all.

Throughout the day large knots of people passed through the chapel in order to pay their last respects, and while Needham's coffin was to be sent to the USA it had been intended to inter Warneford in the hospital grounds following a short service in the chapel. Such plans came as something of a shock, and the English Press were quick to point out that Warneford deserved nothing less than a public funeral in England. It was reported that French authorities consented to alter their arrangements in deference to the wishes of Warneford's mother who would be unable to reach Versailles for her son's funeral.

Meanwhile the tributes poured in . Henry Deutsch de la Meurthe, president of the Aero Club of France:

France mingles her tears with England's mourning for a son of the allied nations. Alas, that a life risked on the aerial battlefield should be sacrificed so lightly! It is the irony of fate.

Louis Blériot, first man to fly the Channel:

Lieutenant Warneford was a hero; a true son of Britain. His death leaves a gap in the ranks of the brave airmen of the allied nations.

For Robert Morane, aircraft designer, Warneford's death was particularly sad:

When the workmen of our factory learnt that he was to be decorated with the Legion of Honour, they opened a subscription to present him with a diamond cross. Although we cannot now give it to him, the cross will be purchased and offered to his mother.

Earlier Mrs Corkery had been sent scores of congratulatory letters and telegrams following her son's dramatic fight with *LZ37*. She found that she was unable to answer them all, there were so many:

I should like to convey my thanks through your newspaper to the numerous people who have written to me to congratulate me on my son, Flight Sub-Lieutenant Warneford's great achievement in bringing down the Zeppelin, and on his getting the VC, and the Legion of Honour. I find it impossible to answer all the letters personally which I receive from his many admirers and must ask them to kindly accept this acknowledgement.[36]

She was still receiving them after the heartbreaking telegram from the Admiralty was delivered to her home at Runfold near Aldershot. But not every correspondent wished her well: the day prior to learning of her son's death an unsigned letter arrived. It merely stated, 'God's curse on you all'; the envelope bore a Kensington postmark. Mrs Corkery was convinced a pro-German woman was responsible for this missive and another which arrived on 19 June expressing surprise that any mother could be 'aethiestic [*sic*] at the fact of her son being a murderer.'[37]

But most of the letters now contained messages of sympathy and condolence; Warneford's mother was especially proud to receive a personal telegram from the King and Queen who expressed their deep regret at the death of her son.

On Monday 21 June Warneford's coffin was taken from the Versailles Military Hospital and driven to the St Lazare railway station in Paris quite unannounced, the only escort being eight members of the RNAS under Flight Lieutenant Thurston. As the guard was about to close the van bearing the coffin, an English woman obtained permission to pray beside it – her son was a pilot on active service at the front. On the train's arrival at Dieppe, the plain varnished coffin was carefully hoisted aboard a cross-channel steamer and placed between decks on the port side, a forest of flowers grouped around it. The eight men from Buc and M Jellerol of the French Army Air Service accompanied the coffin on its sad voyage.

Ten members of the RNAS from Dover received the coffin after the steamer had docked at Folkestone, and only when the last passenger had disembarked was the coffin hoisted on to the pier. As the steamer's flags were struck to half-mast, the airmen shouldered the flag-draped casket and carried it to a waiting Victoria-bound train. During the late evening the train arrived at the station, where a large crowd had already gathered, and there it was met by Captain Corkery and two of Warneford's sisters. Slowly the coffin was transferred to a gun carriage and borne through London's streets and into Brompton Cemetery, there to lay in the annexe of the chapel overnight.

Early during the following day dense crowds had gathered round the cemetery, police and military presence being very necessary to control them. Before the iron gates had swung shut, many thousands had been admitted and taken up silent station around the chapel, in the white-stoned arcades and along the avenue leading to the fern- and laurel-lined graveside.

At 16.00hrs the service began, conducted by two chaplains of the Royal Naval Division, Rev Hugh Stallard and Rev G H Hewitt. The congregation had been limited to Mrs Corkery, other members of the family, officers of the Admiralty, RNAS, RFC and Royal Naval Division, and C G Greenhill of the Royal Aero Club. At 16.10hrs the chapel bell tolled as eight members of the Royal Naval Division raised the coffin shoulder high to the gun carriage which bore it to the grave. The following morning *The Times* reported the solemn scene at Brompton:

> The avenue along which the carriage passed was lined by men of the Armoured Car Section and the Royal Naval Division. More officers and men of the Division walked behind the coffin carrying wreaths. Before the grave a firing party of 50 men stood with arms reversed and bowed heads.
>
> The concluding prayers were quietly read, and the coffin was lowered into the grave. Then a sharp command brought the firing party to attention. Three volleys rang out, the bugles sounding the last post, and the men of the Naval Divison with bayonets fixed presented arms, while the mourners and the crowd, bareheaded, stood for a few moments in reverent silence. Thousands of people afterwards passed slowly by the grave and looked at the coffin before it was covered.[38]

Slowly the crowd dispersed, and only when the last of them had left was the grave quietly filled; nearby was another, that of old Thomas Warneford, the kindly grandfather to whom young Reginald had been so close. A few weeks later the *Daily Express* erected their impressive memorial designed by Flynn Jenkins RBS, and on 11 July it was unveiled by Lord Derby during a special ceremony at the graveside which was attended by large crowds. Mrs Corkery eventually was to receive her son's Victoria Cross direct from the Admiralty, and a letter came with it:

> Their lordships deeply deplore the sad occurrence which has prevented your son from being personally invested with this decoration by His Majesty, and they desire to record their high appreciation of the singular service rendered by him and their sense of the great loss sustained by the death of this intrepid young officer, following as it did so shortly after the brilliant achievement which will always be associated with his name.[39]

In the Warneford Chapel in Highworth Church, Wiltshire, there is a memorial tablet, subscribed to by members of the family throughout the world, which on 21 August 1917 was unveiled by Maude Nightingale and duly dedicated by Rev H L Warneford.[40] At Hackney in 1918 the London County Council renamed Gotha Street and Victoria Street in honour of the dead airman, and in Harrow, which has its own claim to an 'airship VC' there is a 'Warneford Road'.

On 7 November 1979 the Fleet Air Arm Museum opened a permanent 'Warneford VC' exhibition in their new extension at RNAS Yeovilton in Somerset, a lasting tribute to Reginald Alexander John Warneford, the first airman to bring down an airship in aerial combat. But there would be others, and one in particular whose brief career paralleled in several respects that of the tragic young man whose body lies in the large cemetery at Brompton.

The *Daily Express* memorial over the grave of Sub-Lieutenant Reginald Alexander John Warneford VC as it appears today in London's Brompton Cemetery. *Author*

CHAPTER 6

Of Flaming Bullets and Other Things...

> *'...I stated in this report that my armament consisted solely of a Lewis gun and drums of explosive bullets, as I had discarded the remainder, standardised by the war office, owing to its cumbersome nature, which greatly diminished the climbing efficiency of the aeroplane. For this I was severely hauled over the coals, in fact I had dared to destroy a Zeppelin without Le Prieur rockets...'*
>
> Major Wulstan Joseph Tempest, 15 August 1920

When Warneford and Meddis grappled inconclusively with *LZ39* in May, 'flaming bullets' had been used for the first time against an airship. The few rounds that did find their target failed, it was assumed, because German airships used inert gas between cells and outer covering. Actually Meddis' bullets failed because insufficient air was able to mix with the hydrogen and thus ignition of the incendiary charge was averted. Later experiments led to aircraft being armed with machine guns carrying a mixture of armour-piercing, explosive, incendiary and tracer bullets. But while these were being developed, home defence pilots were forced to rely on a variety of unlikely armaments which to modern eyes must seem as antiquated as David's slingshot against Goliath.

BE2c – Night-Fighter Supreme

Of the many aircraft hastily modified and thrown into battle against Zeppelins, the most effective was to be the Royal Aircraft Factory BE2c. The very first example of this type had flown during the summer of 1914 and was a result of untiring research by a talented designer. Edward Teshmaker Busk was determined to produce an inherently stable machine that could safely be flown 'hands off': in the BE2c he succeeded admirably.

Considerable production orders were placed, nearly 24 contractors being responsible for the eventual 1308 BE2c and BE2d aircraft that were delivered to the RFC. Since many of these contractors had never built aircraft before, production problems were commonplace, and as a result the aircraft was late getting into service; indeed, it was not until 15 April 1915 that 8 Squadron, the first to be fully equipped with the BE2c, went to war.

Once in service it was soon realised that the aircraft fulfilled all expectations, proving to be a far superior reconnaissance platform than any other type preceding it; but these very qualities proved its undoing. In the latter half of 1915, when the stars of German air aces like Boelcke and Immelmann were in their ascendancy, BE2cs were shot down with alarming frequency. No match for the nimble Fokker *Eindecker* with its synchronised machine gun firing through the airscrew, the BEs were unable to outfly their enemy and too slow to outrun him. Even worse, the rule of placing the pilot in the rear seat was still enforced.[1]

But despite the charges of criminal negligence brought against RFC High Command by Noel Pemberton Billing MP, and despite crippling losses, the BE2c was ordered in even greater numbers. Many were still in service on the Western Front by early 1917 when the German Army Air Service all but cleared the RFC from the skies during 'Bloody April'. But if the machine was rapidly outclassed in France, it still had an important role to play as a home defence night-fighter. The machine's slow speed and easy handling made night-flying considerably less hazardous, and its inherent stability provided a steady platform from which to unleash a wide variety of anti-Zeppelin devices. By early 1916 those aircraft issued to home defence units had been suitably modified 'in the field' in order to fulfil their new role.

Although the BE2c was constructed following the usual practice of the time, it was not particularly simple to manufacture, another reason that held up production. Its wooden fuselage was a basic wire-braced box girder made in two sections that joined together aft of the cockpit. Mainplanes 37ft in span were built up from wooden spars, ribs and riblets, while the fin and rudder were constructed of steel tube. The two-bay wings were liberally braced, as was the tail unit, by Rafwires, flying and landing bracing rods of streamlined section which served to reduce drag. Each complete airframe, less engine, armament and instruments, cost the British taxpayer £1072 10s by 1916 values.

The standard powerplant for the aircraft was the air-cooled RAF (Royal Aircraft Factory) 1a, delivering 90hp, the eight cylinders arranged in 'V' formation, four to a side, and exposed to the elements. Exhaust pipes varied in length and configuration, but home defence BEs, in common with most, featured twin vertical stacks running up in front of the centre section and carrying the fumes over the wing. The engine turned a large four-bladed wooden airscrew which was usually built up from seven laminations of mahogany and bound at the tips with fabric.

The undercarriage was simply two steel-tube 'Vs' faired with wood which separated a pair of steel-tube spreader bars with the axle between them; 44ft of ⅜in rubber shock cord bound the axle to each 'V' strut to provide rudimentary springing for the wire-spoked wheels. The aircraft

A BE2c converted to the night-fighter role for home defence use. This is 4112, in which Lieutenant Frederick Sowrey (seated in the cockpit) destroyed *L32* on 23 September 1916. The front cockpit has been faired over, lamps appear above each lower wingtip and beneath the tailplane, and Holt flares are attached beneath the wing lamps. An upward-firing Lewis gun is mounted in front of the pilot, and rocket tube attachment lugs are visible on outboard interplane struts.
Photographed at Suttons Farm, Hornchurch, in 1916, 4112 is half way through having its upper surfaces doped in PC10 Khaki brown.
N E Tempest

was covered entirely with fabric, laced and stitched to the framework and then treated with several coats of clear dope. Plywood decking around the cockpits was usually varnished, and metal components either remained untouched or were doped in a medium grey.

Home defence BE2c machines were invariably flown as single seat 'fighters', and experience soon showed that the slightly increased performance was offset by air suction, a result of the vacant front cockpit. Consequently these were faired over with an aluminium cover, secured by straps, to overcome the problem. Instrumentation for the pilot included an inclinometer, a revolution counter, an altimeter, an airspeed indicator and a centrally mounted compass fitted to a cut-out in the cockpit decking underneath the large curved windscreen. Engine on/off switches were large brass affairs and mounted outside the cockpit, usually on the port side; internally, a pressure pump was fixed to the starboard side and a rudimentary throttle to port. A wooden control column and rudder bar carried the cables via control horns to ailerons, elevators and rudder, the cables often doubled as insurance against severance. On a basket-weave seat, the pilot sat swathed in protective leathers, his face smeared with grease to combat the cold, and secured with a wide safety strap around his midriff. There was no oxygen equipment, no radio, no cockpit heating and no parachute.

For anti-Zeppelin patrols the BE2c could be armed with either four rack-mounted high explosive bombs or one box containing 24 explosive darts, Le Prieur rockets carried on the outer interplane struts and/or an upward-firing Lewis machine gun with three to five drums of mixed ammunition; small lamps were mounted on the instrument panel and readings were daubed with 'radium'. Identification lamps were fitted to each wingtip, and below them, on special brackets, were landing flares. These were the brainchild of a retired Lieutenant-Colonel, one Harold Edward Sherwin Holt, and were to become standard equipment for all night-flying aeroplanes. Manufactured by the Yorkshire Steel Co Ltd, the patented device consisted of a metal bracket secured to the leading edge of each lower wing. At the end was a metal clamp holding the flare made from a magnesium compound and invariably in cylindrical form. An igniter was fitted to the base of the flare, the suspension bracket carrying terminals that led wires to a battery and two brass buttons in the cockpit. Thus

equipped, the pilot could light them singly or together as necessary, the flare lasting about one minute.[2]

The Experimenters

Before moving on to discuss the development of successful anti-Zeppelin ordnance, some mention must be made of the several, often wild alternatives put forward by non-combatants and servicemen in the early years of the war. In August 1914 a Frenchman, Grivolas, proposed an interesting scheme whereby an aeroplane trailed a mine at the end of a 400m cable.[3] Once above a Zeppelin our intrepid aerial fisherman would try and bump one of the triggers against the airship hull and send the whole lot to perdition. This exciting suggestion was not taken up, even when Major C F G Low of the Army Ordnance Department later explained it all in a two-page memo. Major-General G F Ellison from Horse Guards Parade tersely dismissed the scheme in a one-line note as 'a matter for the experts',[4] and nothing more was heard of the trailing mine.

During 1915 various aircraft designers came up with curious prototypes designed specifically to combat airships. Harris Booth, of the Admiralty Air Department, was responsible for the AD Scout and later the Blackburn Triplane. Both were ungainly looking machines, both carried a 'bathtub' nacelle at least 10ft above ground level, and both were of doubtful efficacy. Each would have been armed with a single Lewis gun, but performance was considered less than satisfactory and the aircraft was abandoned.

The Port Victoria PV2 was a small, nippy floatplane designed at the Experimental Depot at Port Victoria on the Isle of Grain and nominated to carry the American Davis gun, but by the time the PV2 was successfully flown the cumbersome Davis had been abandoned. An unwieldly weapon to say the least, its excessive length was due to its recoilless design. The gun fired a compensating charge along a rear-facing barrel simultaneously with the ejection of a 2pdr shell from the forward barrel. Various machines were experimentally fitted with the device, but few were specifically designed to carry it. An exception was the unlikely Robey Peters Davis Gun Carrier. Wings spanning over 54ft carried a pulpit either side of the fuselage in which a Davis and gunner were to be installed. The aircraft was developed late in the war; only one machine was built, and on its second flight attempt it completed half a circuit of the

Of Flaming Bullets and Other Things...

◀ The Holt Landing Light Bracket 369, Mark A.
The clamp (A) was designed to hold the bracket to the wing trailing edge of pusher aircraft or the leading edge of tractor machines. In the wing undersurface. In the event, the clamp was useless and could not be affixed to the BE2c 'owing to the leading edge of the plane being tapered, whilst the jaws of the bracket are parallel'. Thus reported Major F F Waldron, Commander of 1 Reserve Squadron, on 3 February 1916. Modifications were made and the brackets were subsequently affixed directly under the outer front interplane struts on the forward spars. Two terminals (B) were installed from which to run the electric leads, and the clamp (C) was fitted with a thumb-screw to hold the flare.
PRO Air 1/814

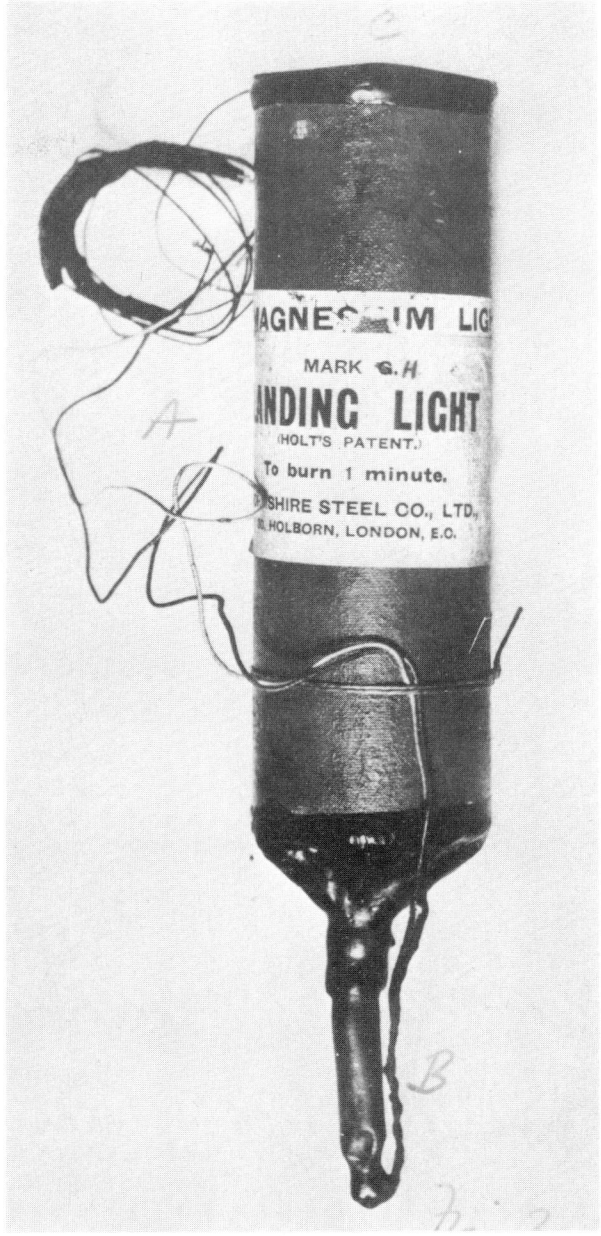

Wing Tip Flare Mark H ▶
The flare, which burnt for 60 seconds, consisted of a wire lead (A) that entered the light at (B), which contained an electric fuse with a 1-second delay. Wire leads were connected to terminal (B) shown on the previous illustration, and the upper portion was inserted into, and held by, the thumb-screw clamp on the bracket.
PRO Air 1/814

aerodrome and then crashed rather appropriately on a mental hospital. The pilot esaped unhurt but the 'RRF 25 Mk II' burned itself out: nobody bothered to build another.

Prior to his election as MP for East Hertfordshire on 10 March 1916, Pemberton Billing had written a book, *Air War: How to Wage It*, and designed several quite extraordinary aircraft. In his book, 'PB' defined his conception of an anti-airship aeroplane. He envisaged an 80mph machine, with a minimum speed of 35mph, being able to reach 10,000ft in 20 minutes, having an endurance of 12 hours, and including dual controls and a searchlight. It says a lot for the man's character and determination that most of these ideals were realised – via the PB29, which crashed – in the incredible Supermarine Night Hawk. Spanning 60ft, this revolutionary quadruplane boasted a rest 'bunk', a glazed cabin, positions for a Davis gun and two Lewis guns, and a searchlight mounted on gimbals in the nose. Power for the light came from a 5hp AEC flat twin driving a generator, one of the first installations of its kind.[5] Underpowered with two 100hp Anzani radials, the Night Hawk's duration with a ton of fuel was about 18 hours.[6] Test flights were successful, but the aeroplane was not adopted probably because, by 1916, standard machines had been successful in dealing with the airships.

A Holt wingtip flare attached to BE2c 2693 (W L Robinson's machine) photographed at Eastchurch in June 1916. The aircraft lacks underwing roundels, but the fabric in the region of the roundels appears darker. This contrast could be the result of overpainting or of the application of silvered black silk cloth: the latter was often used with Holt flares, the cloth acting to reflect the lights and 'brilliantly light up the ground', to quote CFS report 138 dated 9 September 1915 on 'Landing Lights for Use in Night Flying'.
J M Bruce/G S Leslie Collection

77

Zeppelin!

The AD Scout, Harris Booth's design to meet a 1915 Admiralty requirement for an anti-airship fighter. The RNAS officer at right seems to be expressing a somewhat violent opinion about the machine's dubious qualities! Despite reports to the contrary, it seems unlikely that the 'Sparrow' could have carried the 2pdr Davis gun, a standard 0.303 Lewis machine gun being quoted in official reports of the Scout's armament. Only four machines were built this is 1536.
J M Bruce/G S Leslie Collection

The Royal Aircraft Factory's NE1 was yet another night-fighter design. Six prototypes were built, and this is believed to be the third aircraft (B3973), at the Experimental Station, Orfordness, during 1917. Flare brackets are visible under lower wings and what appears to be a Crayford rocket gun is mounted on the nose of the nacelle. The three six-pointed designs are personal markings.
Aeromodeller

Robey-Peters Davis Gun Carrier
The amazing Robey-Peters Davis Gun Carrier, of which only one was completed. It was designed to carry a Davis gun and its operator in a special 'pulpit' mounted under both upper mainplanes either side of the fuselage, but the aircraft was not developed. On its second flight the prototype crashed and burnt itself out, the pilot managing to escape from the unconventionally placed cockpit.

Supermarine PB31E
The Supermarine PB31E, the so-called 'Nighthawk', was armed with a 1½pdr Davis gun and two Lewis machine guns, and was designed to lie in wait for any passing Zeppelin. Performance figures for the sole aircraft built (1388) fell below the manufacturer's estimates and the type was not proceeded with. Despite its disappointing attributes, the 'Nighthawk' did include such refinements as an enclosed – and heated – cabin, and a nose-mounted searchlight powered by a generator in the form of a 5hp ABC 2-cylinder engine.

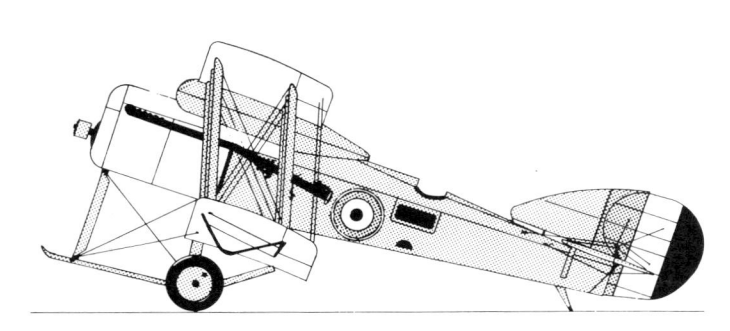

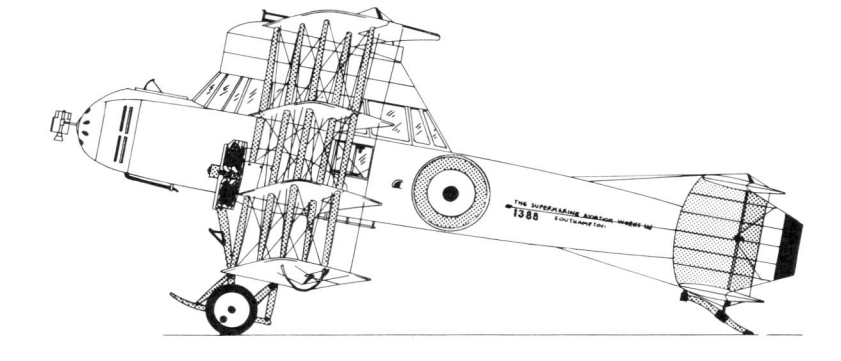

Of Flaming Bullets and Other Things...

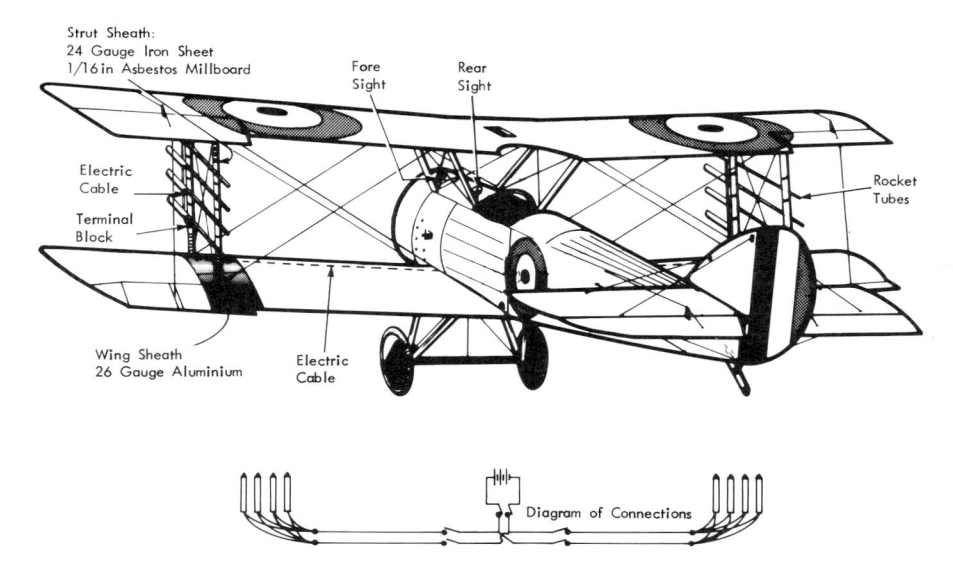

Le Prieur Rocket System
As fitted to a Sopwith Pup.

low service ceiling of 17,500ft, the NE1 never could have reached the airships it was designed to repel, and these deficiencies led to its abandonment. A similar fate also befell the Vickers FB25, of which only one was built. It too was to be armed with the Crayford Rocket gun, but after several flight tests it finally crashed at Martlesham Heath during 1917. The official report dismissed the type as wholly unsatisfactory for night-flying duties.

During October 1915 other defence schemes were abroad. Proposals were put forward by Wing Commander N Usborne in a memo on anti-Zeppelin defence. One of the plans was to establish kite balloons around London, each carrying a Davis gun. At the approach of a Zeppelin the balloons would be released, and those closest to the raider would blast away at it. An improvement on this was to substitute an aeroplane for the basket. Once at 12,000ft the balloon would 'slip' the aircraft, which was then free to attack the airship. A third scheme involved kite balloons moored at 12,000ft with a car and armed crew lying in wait. Although a few experiments were carried out, the plans were considered too costly as well as impracticable, and consequently were not proceeded with.[8]

Predating the guided missile by several decades was a scheme for an aerial torpedo. This device consisted of a model airship envelope with suitable planes and controls attached to an explosive charge that was to be released from the ground, 'allowed to *vol plane* upwards' and be directed by a wireless transmitter. According to Major Usborne, such a device had been successfully tested, and he concluded that if the 'proposed mechanism whereby the torpedo listens to the enemy and attacks it' became successful, it would seem the ideal deterrent.[9]

Several home defence units experimented for a time with French Le Prieur rockets, which were launched from tubes mounted on the outboard interplane struts. Matching the traditional firework rocket in appearance, these electrically triggered missiles were used to good effect in France against kite balloons, but there is no record of them ever having been used in anger against Zeppelins. Most RFC units, whilst having official orders to carry the rockets, regarded them as so much dead weight and refused to have anything more to do with them. The RNAS was similarly unimpressed, as an ex-pilot of that service has admitted:

> The trouble with those rockets was that they only had a range of about 50 yards and if you were to destroy a Zeppelin

Then there was the Parnall Scout. Designed in 1916 by A Camden Pratt, it was variously (and unofficially) known as the 'Zeppelin Chaser', 'Zepp Strafer' or 'Night Flyer'. Only one, N505, was built, powered by a 260hp Sunbeam Maori, but some question remains as to whether it was ever flown. Armament was to have been a single Lewis gun mounted in the cockpit and firing upwards at 45°. The latter was of considerable importance, since tests had revealed that bullets fired by a Lewis at this angle, from an aircraft flying at 100mph, maintained an unwavering course of 800yds. Home defence BE2cs had their guns similarly mounted.[7] In any event, stress calculations at Upavon revealed unacceptably low safety factors. The aeroplane, thus condemned, was returned to Parnall and Sons who reportedly broke it up and put a match to the remains, along with works drawings and other design data.

Two pusher aircraft of the same category were the Vickers FB25 and the NE1 of the Royal Aircraft Factory, both having been the result of utilising designs and components from earlier aircraft built by their respective companies. The Nightflying Experimental 1 first flew on 8 September 1917, and while successive trials were not very encouraging at least six prototypes were built. Armament was to have been two Lewis guns or a Vickers Crayford Rocket gun, provision for searchlights also being made on at least one example. With its poor climbing performance and

Parnall Scout
The Parnall Scout, N505, as designed by A Camden Pratt, was (unofficially) variously known at the 'Zeppelin Chaser', 'Zepp Strafer' or 'Night Flyer'. In the event it did nothing to live up to any of these evocative titles – indeed it remains doubtful if it ever flew at all. The armament was a single Lewis machine gun firing upwards at 45° from the cockpit. Condemned as unsafe, the Scout was returned to its Bristol-based manufacturer who eventually scrapped it.

Vickers FB25
The Vickers FB25 was a development of the FB23 and built as a two-seat night-fighter intended to carry a searchlight and one Vickers Crayford rocket gun. In May 1917, the sole example built went to Martlesham Heath for official trials. The subsequent report was not encouraging: 'The machine was extremely slack on all controls even with the engine on, but with it off it became very dangerous, the controls having practically no effect. The machine was almost unmanageable in a wind over 20mph, and it was owing to this that the machine crashed on test...'

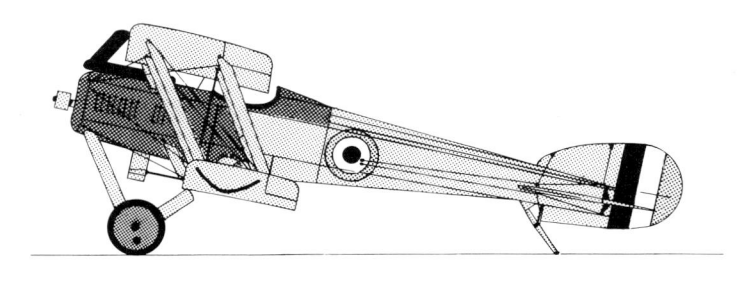

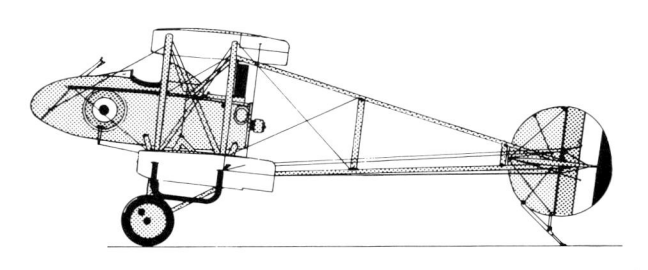

79

Zeppelin!

The RAF Fiery Grapnel Mk II. The various parts annotated on this contemporary photograph are as follows:
2 Lowering gear with 250 feet of No 12 Bowden cable
8 Wire loop
11 Brake locking screw
12 Guide studs
15 Brake lever
19 Safety fan
20 Striker
21 Igniter arms
22 Shackle
23 Safety 'V' pin
24 Safety block
26A, 26B Slip catch (slipped by a light pull on a connecting wire fastened to axle of winding drum)
27 Slip catch cable
28 Shock absorber (connecting grapnel to axle of winding drum)
30 Wire supporting grapnel to aircraft
PRO Air 1/863

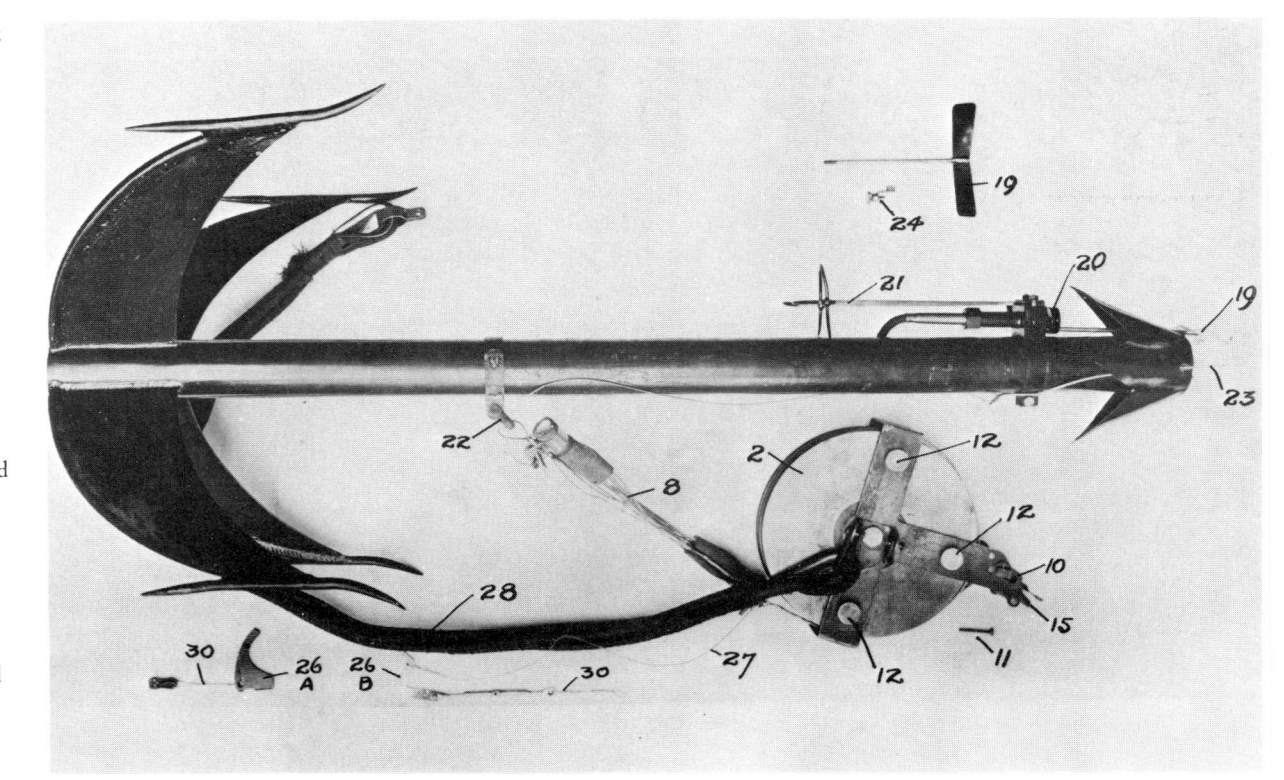

you had to get so damned close to ensure hitting it you might as well not have had rockets at all and rammed the thing because you couldn't have gotten out of the way. They were terribly unreliable too, they were inaccurate in flight and would go all over the bloody show when you pressed the trigger.[10]

Lieutenant Le Prieur's system for mounting the rockets on to the aircraft was fairly simple. Firing tubes of 1in diameter were mounted to the outboard struts, set at an angle of 17°, or 15° if the Lighter Brock Immediate Rockets were to be installed. Struts supporting the tubes were sheathed with 24 gauge iron sheet and $\frac{1}{16}$in asbestos millboard carried some 6in beyond the upper and lower tube fixtures. Additional protection took the form of 26 gauge aluminium sheet fixed over the upper surface of the lower wing, extending a foot either side of the strut mountings. To arm the aircraft, the rocket sticks were lightly greased and inserted into their tubes. Electric leads from the rockets were securely fastened to the tubes about 4in behind each rocket; the rest of the circuit was then led down the strut and connected to the terminals at its base. In order to 'aim' the rockets, pilots were provided with both fore and hind sights. The former consisted of a ring placed at a convenient distance from the hind sight and set low enough to obtain a good all round view of the target. The ring size was designed to cover the diameter of a Zeppelin at a 200yd range. Pilots were instructed always to aim at the leading half of the Zeppelin to allow for the combined speeds of both aircraft.[11]

Of the devices designed but never adopted for anti-Zeppelin work, the most dramatic was unquestionably the Fiery Grapnel. Almost medieval in appearance, the weapon consisted of four barbed flukes mounted at one end of a tube which carried a 'firework'. This was touched off by a standard .303 cartridge containing the cap only, 'fired by a striker [and] actuated by a spring as in a rifle.'[12]

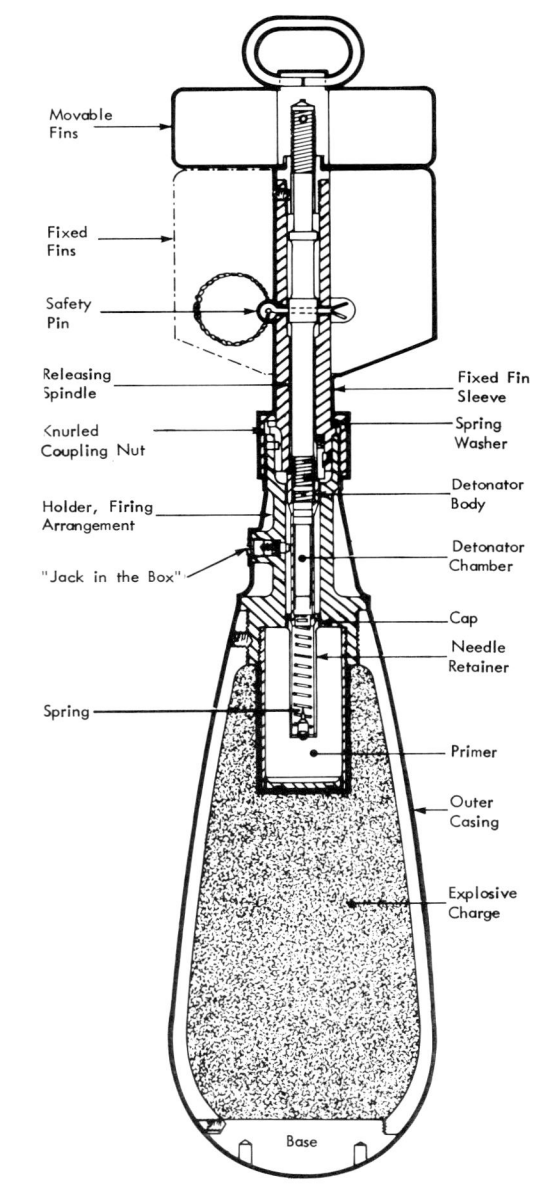

Two grapnels were to be installed between the undercarriage legs of the aircraft, connected together by a steel cable. If the first grapnel managed to strike a Zeppelin, the impact freed the second by shearing a 'weak link',[13] and one or both would tear through the fabric, the wicked-looking barbs protecting the igniter. The striker was activated by the mere pressure of the fabric on a pair of arms 'spread out on each side of the point',[14] and lit the firework which shot a tongue of flame from both ends of the tube followed by a shower of sparks. Burning for 60 seconds, the firework would ignite hydrogen released through the ruptured gas cells, the result of the grapnel flukes. The Royal Aircraft Factory was charged to produce 12 of these fearsome weapons for trials during April 1916. An apprentice centre lathe turner recalls having hastily to manufacture the grapnels during a night shift:

> There were only three lathes with a throw of over four feet and taking it in turns, we had to bolt these [grapnel] heads back on wooden blocks and, with long boring bars, machine and screw cut the centre to take the eight foot three inch body tube. To me it was one of the most frightening jobs I have ever done. We wrapped the barbs in rags and waste and could not rotate them very fast but, working from a distance of about six feet and not daring to bend forward for a close inspection, it proved a nervy job.[15]

In experiments on balloons with BE2 aircraft at Upavon, pilots found the grapnels difficult to deploy, and 'greatly underestimated' the height above the target on the initial attempt. Perhaps for such reasons the RAF Fiery Grapnel Mk II was never used in anger, and none was issued to the RFC.

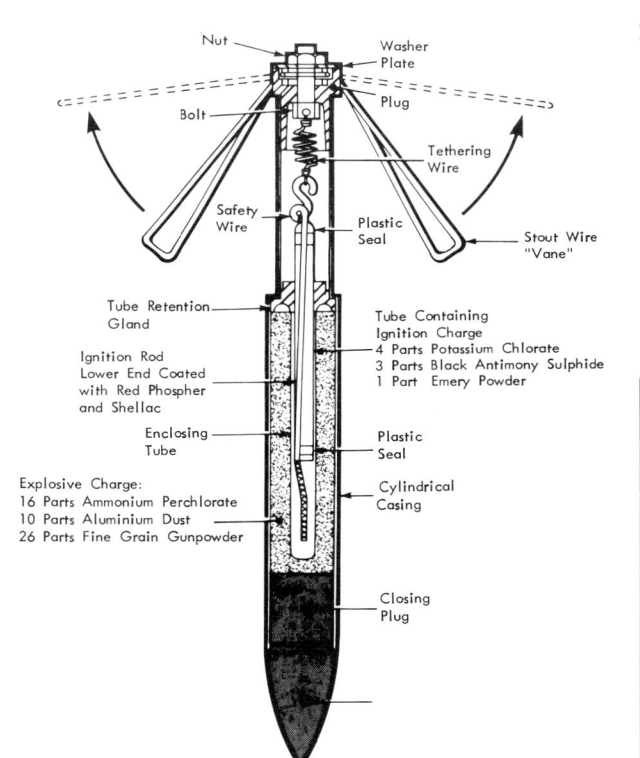

Other weapons very much in vogue during the early war years were Flechettes, mild steel darts which, while varying in detail design, were each 5in long and $\frac{5}{16}$in diameter. Slung under aircraft in boxes, they could be released in batches of up to 200, and it was claimed that a single dart when dropped from 4000ft would pass through both man and horse. Many thousands were produced at Farnborough, at Altrincham and in France. There were two distinct styles: at Farnborough the steel noses had a length of brass tube pressed into place to serve as a rudimentary tail; other designs were entirely steel, two-thirds of the body being fluted, leaving the tail in cross section.[16]

Bombs available at the time were comparatively small, 10 and 20lb Hales incendiaries being standard equipment. These were improved versions of missiles first designed in 1913 by Frederick Marten Hale and Thomas Cooper, both engineers. In its most common form the Hales bomb consisted of a steel casing and base, with a suspension lug for heavier versions. To the casing was attached a cylindrical holder and a 'firing arrangement' which contained a needle holder, then a sleeve with three fixed vanes, topped with a spindle mounting four rotating vanes. As the bomb fell the lower vanes fed air to those above and revolved them together with the release spindle, which gradually unwound from the detonator body until it held the spring just off the firing needle. The tail kept the bomb nose-downwards, and on impact the detonator overcame the spring's resistance, forcing the cap on to the needle, firing the detonator and exploding the bomb. But the missiles had to be carefully treated, and accidents could happen:

> At that time [1915] we were armed with a 12-bore double-barrelled shotgun with chainshot in one and an incendiary shell in the other. Additionally you had a 10lb bomb on your lap – there was no rack. What happened on one occasion was that a pilot crashed on the aerodrome and broke the neck of the bomb which was touched off, blowing everything to smithereens.[17]

Then Engineer Lieutenant-Commander Francis Ranken's explosive dart was issued as official equipment to anti-

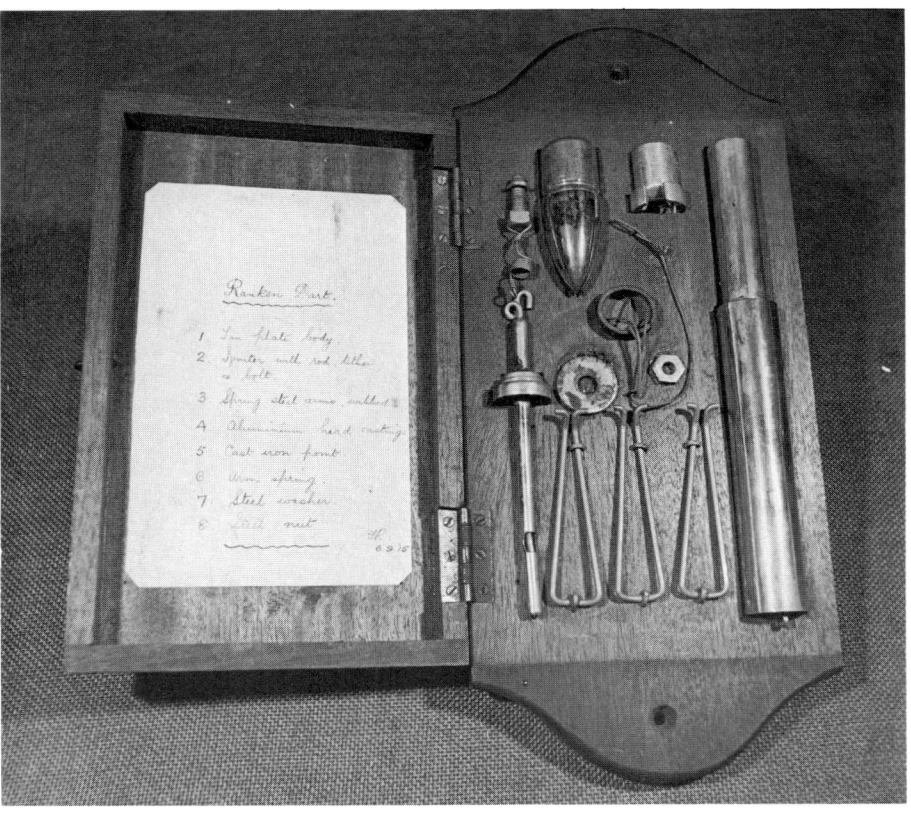

Ranken Dart

RANKEN EXPLOSIVE DART

Hales Bomb

The original Ranken Dart in a special presentation case made by its inventor, Francis Ranken, on 6 August 1915. This valuable relic has been donated to the Fleet Air Arm Museum by the Ranken family.
By courtesy of the Fleet Air Arm Museum

Zeppelin!

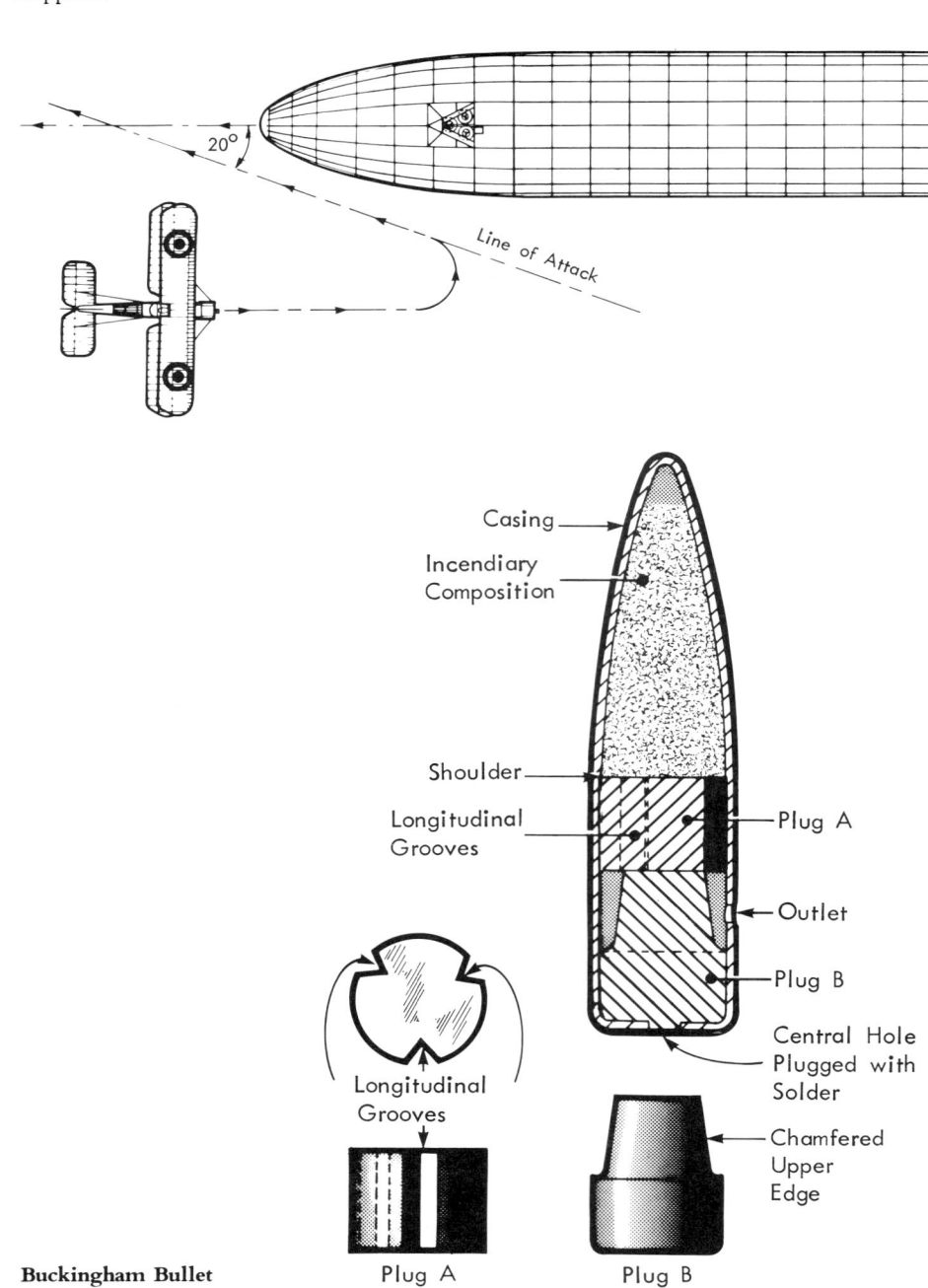

Zeppelin units in the UK and used operationally on several occasions. It consisted of a tinplate tube 9in long, with a cast iron point at one end with an aluminium head and three spring arms topped by a cap at the other. The arms were kept closed in storage by means of the cap, either tin or rubber, which acted as a buffer when the dart was in its dropping box. A cavity in the dart's centre contained an ignition tube through which passed a friction bar coated with phosphor at one end. The top of the bar was tethered by a 7in wire to the head with the spring arms attached. If the pilot managed to get above the Zeppelin, he pulled the release handle of the dropper box, releasing the darts in batches of three.

On leaving the tubes (which were always well greased), the arms sprung outwards serving as a grapnel, and once striking the airship the body of the dart entered the fabric. The tether wire then pulled the igniter, and resultant friction between the phosphor and ignition tube caused a flash which touched off the charge when the dart had penetrated about 18in. The tail, filled with coarse black powder, caused a shower of sparks which flamed the air and hydrogen mix blown through the burst fabric. It seemed foolproof enough in theory.

The dropping boxes, containing 24 tubes, were made of tin for home use, and while batches of three darts could be released all 24 could be dropped in one salvo. Boxes were fitted to the floor of the aircraft at an angle of 40° and inclined rearwards. On the BE2c it was placed between the crossed wires under the pilot's seat; if two boxes were carried they could be installed on either side. In both cases the tubes protruded 6in below the fuselage and were often 'streamlined' with a section of tinplate. They were used mainly by the RNAS but were not thought highly of by most pilots, the phosphor often being affected by damp.[18]

Incendiary Bullets

Subsequent events proved that the most effective weapon against Zeppelins was the standard American-designed .303 Lewis machine gun armed with a mixture of incendiary, tracer and explosive bullets. On the BE2c the Lewis was usually fixed to a Strange Mounting, installed immediately in front of the pilot; it could be fired upwards at about 45° and was operated by a Bowden cable attached to the trigger. Early experiments with tracer bullets had not been very encouraging, but in 1916 the Ministry of Munitions took over part of the Aerators Company and their experimental factory. In June 1915 trials of a new tracing composition of one part magnesium to eight parts of barium peroxide were found satisfactory, and after extensive tests at the Musketry School in Hythe, the bullet was approved for immediate issue to the RFC in July 1916. From its configuration and place of origin it was universally dubbed 'Sparklet' but later officially designated SPK Mk VIIT.

James Francis Buckingham, an experienced chemist, was the proprietor of a small engineering works in Coventry dealing in the manufacture of engines and motor cars. In 1914 Buckingham had foreseen the value of incendiary ammunition for use against airships and decided to sketch out some preliminary ideas for a new kind of bullet. After a series of experiments he elected to use phosphor as a basis for such and took out his first patent on 25 January 1915. Three months later he proudly demonstrated his .45 bullet before RNAS officers. Following the successful destruction of test balloons at a range of 400yds, he was encouraged by the Admiralty to improve the projectile. The result was a .303 version for use in machine guns, and on 23 October the Admiralty were suitably impressed to place a firm contract for production, later increased by RNAS demand.

On 27 April, the first contract from the Ministry of Munitions on behalf of the RFC was placed. The next stage was to develop and improve the bullets even further, Buckingham modifying the shape to match Mk VII rounds and to ensure uniformity for mass production. On 24 June the tireless inventor patented his Mk VII bullet, which was used without modification for the duration of World War I.

Buckingham's bullet consisted essentially of a cupro-nickel 'envelope' which contained the phosphor compos-

Ranken Dart Deployment.
In a memorandum dated 14 April 1916, temporary instructions were issued to instruct pilots in the use of the Ranken Dart: 'The best height from which to attack is between 150 to 750 feet and preferably about the middle of this range. If the aeroplane attempts to attack by flying exactly in the same direction as the Zeppelin, there is considerable chance of the whole of the dart shower falling either on the port or starboard side of the target. For this reason it will probably be found best to fly at a slight angle, such as 20°, to the centreline of the Zeppelin, so that the flight path crosses it obliquely. If this be done, and the dart shower started with an interval of rather less than one second between each set of three darts, a considerable space will be covered, and there will be a good chance of hitting the Zeppelin, providing the pilot begins to turn the handle of the dart box well before the point at which he will cross the path of the Zeppelin.

'In order to remain under machine gun fire as short a time as possible, pilots are recommended to approach the Zeppelin from ahead, if possible, then turn to a course within 20°–45° of that of the Zeppelin, and cross her course well ahead of her nose.

'The darts take about 4 seconds to reach a distance of 200 feet below the aeroplane, 6 seconds for a depth of 500 feet, and 8 seconds for a depth of 880 feet. If the attack is at 500 feet, the time of fall is 6 seconds, and if the Zeppelin is travelling at 60 mph, it will travel its own length while the dart is falling. It is for this reason that the dart shower must be aimed well ahead of the nose of the Zeppelin.'

ition with two lead plugs inserted, the first serrated and the second acting as a base plug. This was tapered at one end, forming an annular cavity and lining up with the side hole in the envelope, which was sealed with a fusible alloy that melted on firing, the base of the bullet being spun over and soldered. On firing, the phosphor ran down the serrations in the first lead pellet into the annular space formed around the front of the second, whence it was ejected through the hole in the envelope, igniting on contact with air. In both this form and a flat-nosed version to punch bigger holes in balloon fabric, the Buckingham was used in large numbers by France and the USA. Over 26 million rounds were manufactured during the war.[19]

In 1915 the bogus inert gas theory had induced Commander Frederick Arthur Brock, in charge of the Intelligence Section of the Air Department of the Admiralty, to experiment with a bullet that would explode between gas cells and outer covering. He developed the design in his own time and at his own expense, trials in October 1915 proving highly successful when the bullet was fired from a Lewis gun at short range. Later modifications increased the range to 800yds, and in May the following year an order for half a million Brock bullets was placed with Messrs C T Brock and Co Ltd of Sutton. Actually they only filled the casings, complete cartridges with special bullets being supplied to them from elsewhere. Despite manufacturing problems, the order was completed by December, after which there were no more, since the bullets were superseded early in 1917 in the RFC. The RNAS however, used the Brock until the close of hostilities.[20]

John Pomeroy, an Australian engineer, submitted his design for an explosive bullet to the War Office in August 1914, but, receiving scant encouragement, returned home. Following several trials in America, he returned to England in June 1915 and tried the War Office once again but without success. Nevertheless, by December someone in the Munitions Inventions Department took up Pomeroy's idea and carried out a series of trials; in May an order for half a million rounds was placed. Whilst the bullet was being developed, the RFC expressed keen interest and asked for large supplies for their squadrons, but problems arose. During mass production it was found that premature explosions were occurring because the composition was 'nipped' between the core and envelope. A copper tube or 'warhead' was inserted to cover the joint and the composition inside, thus curing the trouble. Trials undertaken in July gave satisfactory results, and the Pomeroy bullet, officially the PSA, was generally approved during the following month. Towards the end of 1916 the design was improved to render it more sensitive, and the PSA Mk II bullet was accepted in February 1917, superseding the original issue. Only the RFC used the Pomeroy for home defence use, supplies always exceeding requirements. 'Sparklet', Buckingham, Brock or Pomeroy were rarely, if ever, used singly, but mixed in several combinations they proved deadly. The days of the 'invulnerable' Zeppelin were numbered.

CHAPTER 7

SL11, 3 September 1916

*'And Robinson brought it down,
In a field near Enfield Town,
He was right there to meet it,
And he made short work to beat it,
And it came down,
And it came down,
In a field near Enfield Town'.*

Popular schoolboy song, 1916

As dawn broke on the morning of Saturday 2 September 1916, residents of London awoke to grey skies, a drizzle having already set in. Throughout the day, life in the wartime capital continued as normally as conditions allowed, and towards evening music halls and theatres offered welcome distractions. At The Globe, Moya Mannering and A E Matthews in the long running *Peg O' My Heart* enjoyed a full house, and *Chu Chin Chow* at His Majesty's was likewise heavily patronised; few bothered to sit through official War Office reels at the Scala – nobody needed reminding of the Somme when Zeppelins brought war literally to the doorstep. To date, England's defences had enjoyed scant success, and to a nation used to the immunity of being 'an island race', presiding over a huge sprawling empire and protected by a powerful navy, the fact that German airships could, and did, bomb towns and cities with impunity was a difficult pill to swallow. The public grew more restless and bitter towards the handling of the home defence forces; to war-weary civilians it seemed that nothing could thwart the Zeppelins. Yet in the early hours of 3 September a young officer of the Royal Flying Corps changed all that.

Early Years

The story really begins in India, where at Pollibetta, South Coorg, during the late 1800s, coffee planter Horace Robinson ran the Kaima Betta estate. Born on 10 November 1851, Horace could boast a family lineage that had distinctly nautical connections: his father William Braham had until his retirement in 1877 been Chief Naval Constructor at the Royal Navy dockyard at Portsmouth, and William's father and grandfather, Abrahams both, had served with distinction in the Navy during the eighteenth and early nineteenth centuries.

Horace Robinson's first wife, Alice Holding, tragically died within a year of their marriage, and four years passed before Robinson took another bride. She was 30-year-old Elizabeth Eshe Leefe, and at Penge on 19 September 1883 she gave birth to the couple's first child, Ernest.[1] Soon afterwards, the Robinsons went out to India, where they were to make their home in Pollibetta. In subsequent years Elizabeth bore a further six children, Katherine, Grace, Irene, Ruth, Harold (who was born in England at the Boscombe house of the children's guardian, Lady Alabaster) and finally William, born in the family's bungalow on the

Horace Robinson stands in front of his bungalow on the Kaima Betta estate, Pollibetta, South Coorg, where his son William was born in 1895. In the foreground sits 'Billy' himself. This photograph was taken around the turn of the century.
Mrs R G Libin

84

One of the earliest photographs of the younger Robinson brothers: William (left) and Harold flank their sister Ruth.
Mrs R G Libin

Dragon School football team 1903–04. William Leefe Robinson stands in the back row, third from the left.
Mrs R G Libin

throughout his short life it was this sense of humour that endeared 'Billy' to all those who came into contact with him, and many decades later, remains their best memory of him. And the youngest Robinson had compassionate qualities too, for one story handed down through family generations recalls the time he accidentally chopped a worm in half whilst playing with a spade and how he was inconsolable for several days afterwards.

William enjoyed all types of sport, academic subjects somewhat less so, and his early letters home reveal honest admission to his initial scholastic shortcomings:

> It was so good of you both to have written. I do so like to have every little detail about Coorg. I often think of the jolly times we had together. I and Harold are in the first form; I find the lessons a little hard, but Harold can do them alright and is third to the top of the form.
> Both of us are in the Cadet Corps and we go to parade every Saturday. I find it is not all play by any means.[3]

Towards the end of 1907, both William and Harold had sailed for England, where they completed their education. During September 1909 they enrolled at St Bees School on the coast of Cumberland, a long-established and well-respected academy that would later boast no fewer than three recipients of the Victoria Cross amongst its roster of 'old boys'.[4] Wherever he went William won friends easily; St Bees was no exception, and in addition to later becoming a more than useful member of the First XV he was subsequently appointed prefect and then sergeant in the school's Officer Training Corps. During the five years the Robinson brothers spent at St Bees, they usually boarded locally with the Burnett family of Richmond Crescent, while holiday periods often found them with the Davidsons of Knoll Road, Wandsworth, or at Keswick staying with a Mrs Wise:

> We arrived at Keswick station about 4.15 when we took a cab and drove up here. This is quite a large house, a mile out of Keswick, with a glorious view of the surrounding country which consists of velvety green fields and a glittering lake of diamonds, surrounded by lofty wooded mountains, whose snow-tipped summits sparkle in the sunlight... I have a beautifully snug bedroom commanding a lovely view and a nice cosy sitting room in which we have all meals brought.[5]

Like any young teenage boys, the Robinson brothers enjoyed life to the full, and William for one had an eye for a pretty face:

> There are *so* many that I like, yes I love in a *small* way, that I really can't tell you which is best; they are all best. Harold is right when he says he is not a ladies' – or a girls' – man, a rather shy boy. I daresay he likes them but is rather reserved in their company.
> I suppose Harold has told you all about our Keswick trip. I had a *fine* time taking one of the chap's sisters, Ruby Jenkinson by name, about. She is deuced pretty. Then there was Ethel Waters, Doris Iredale and Dorothy Wise there as well. By jove! Some of the chaps were envious! And one of them snapped me with Ruby.[6]

In 1912 during late August and early September the boys enjoyed a memorable holiday in Kurland, Russia, staying at Berghof, an imposing mansion owned by the Baroness von der Recke. It appears that the two families had become acquainted in India years previously, and as a result the Baroness had invited Katherine to stay with them in Russia for a period, acting as a tutor of English and pianoforte to their family and friends. Irene went there in June and later, when Grace joined her brothers and sisters, a good time was apparently had by all:

Kaima Betta estate on 14 July 1895. All the children adopted their mother's maiden name for their second christian name but rarely, if ever, referred to it other than by initial.

During 1901 Harold and William commenced their education in England, enrolling as dayboys at Dragon School, Oxford, for a year, and by 1903 returning to India with their mother. The inseparable brothers resumed their studies at the Bishop Cotton School in Bangalore, and on at least one occasion were given additional tutelage by neighbours:

> Billy was always the favourite as he was always full of mischief which delighted us. He was always up to jokes and at lessons asking our governess the most awkward questions, especially scripture! He and his brother Harold were up to pranks in every way. We four girls found it most amusing but our governess threatened to leave so the family of Robinsons had to go![2]

William's penchant for fun and practical jokes exhibited at this early stage never diminished as he grew older:

Zeppelin!

Saturday morning Baroness, Kitty, Harold and I all drove over to Count Pahlen's to stay the day; we arrived at their house at about 12.30 and strolled round with the young Count. After dinner we listened to their beautiful gramophone and to the Pahlen boy's music mistress who of course plays the piano beautifully. Then we, the younger members of the community, the two young Countesses, the Count, Harold and I went and ragged about in the hay loft, from whence we emerged like scarecrows, after about half an hour, to play tennis.

Just as we were beginning a fresh set, we caught sight of a carriage coming along the main road; it being just about the time that Grace would pass that place – the Pahlens, I should have told you, being on the road to Berghof from the station at Autz. I rushed to view the carriage and, as luck would have it, it was G. So of course she came in and rested a while at the house; the poor girl thought she had at *last* arrived at 'Berghof' and when told it was only a little over halfway, her face fell a good few inches. However, after the Pahlens had kindly refreshed her with a cup of tea, we all started on our way 'home'. Kitty got into G's carriage and Madam, Harold and I led the way in Baroness Recke's carriage.[7]

Irene stayed on in Russia with Kitty until April 1913, and the boys would keep up a steady stream of correspondence at regular intervals. The holiday had been 'a huge success', and the Baroness had shown great affection for the brothers, seeing them to the boat when they sailed for England. As Harold wrote later:

There were six passengers in all, counting ourselves, two old men (commoners) and two young girls about 14 or 17. The latter was very reticent, but Billy as usual started sending out feelers in her direction and wormed his way into talking to her. I knew they were *rather* pally but I discovered afterwards that while I read in the cabin in the afternoon they used to hold clandestine meetings on the deck and I believe Billy actually gained her handkerchief and address before he left. He also took some 24 photos out of 25 of her in that Jicko camera. She rejoices in the name of Muriel Hogg. There's something too piggish about it to please me. Catch Billy for taking every opportunity.[8]

On their return to St Bees, both William and Harold found that their slightly extended holiday in Russia had set them back in their studies, William at least finding his end-of-term examination marks hardly encouraging. Both Kitty and Grace, the latter by then a nurse, spent Christmas 1912 in England, the boys and their sisters taking time out to visit cinemas, teashops, theatres and skating rinks. They even managed to take in the Alabasters:

We arrived at Bournemouth at about 2 o'clock, when we took [the] train to Boscombe Arcade. It was delightful trying to remember all the old places. I was surprised that I remembered as much as I did considering I was about 4 or 5 years old when I left. I remembered the old arcade I think best of all, although it was changed a bit.[9]

William wrote to his mother again on 23 January 1913 and seemed to have developed a very clear picture of what the future should hold for him. He outlined in detail a planned holiday in France with Kitty, his desire to leave school in April 1914, seeking a private tutor to complete his education, and his intention to join the armed services:

I feel sure I will pass into the Royal Engineers; if I do, well and good, if not I think the best plan for me to do is to again try Sandhurst and get, if I can, into the Indian Army, then, if I don't find the Indian climate agrees with me, I could either get into the English Army or if luck smiled upon me and I made a few influential friends I would go... into the Egyptian Army. It's aiming high I know, but then it is better to aim at the bull than the outer circle: I may at least get an inner...[10]

For the Robinson family the year 1913 was one of change: two of the girls had married, Grace to her cousin Arthur Limnell Robinson, the son of Dr Mark Robinson whose Geraldine Lodge in East Hill, Wandsworth, was frequented by the boys whilst they were staying with the Davidsons. Grace and her husband later went to live in West Africa, where Arthur had a job as a mining engineer and where Grace subsequently contracted malaria.

Irene returned to India in the autumn of 1913 and Ruth, who had remained there, married John W Irwin in October, the couple travelling to England but returning to their 'Jumboor' Coffee Estate in North Coorg during the latter months of 1914. As for Harold, he too had returned to India by late 1913 in order to manage a tea estate; William succeeded his elder brother as head of Eaglesfield House at St Bees and on 14 August, 1914 partly realised his ambitions by entering Sandhurst. Among the cadets that 'crammed' with the youngest Robinson was C S Cay, who many years later recalled those happy days with affection:

Leefe was the most compatible friend among many I've met before and after. His cheerful personality brought out the best in me and I can honestly say the short time at the RMC, in spite of the physical and mental cramming, was the happiest of my long life, largely due to his endearing influence.[11]

Berghof, summer 1912. In the back row (left to right) are Harold, Daisy Pahlen, 'Billy' and Nickie Pahlen; seated (at left) is Baroness von der Recke, next to her Baroness Lille draws a bead on the photographer, whilst on her left sit Frau von Stizk and May Recke.
Mrs R G Libin

Towards the end of his final term at St Bees, Robinson entered the school OTC and attained the rank of Sergeant. Here, while on manoeuvres at Mytchett, Kent, in 1913, he joins his comrades in a welcome break.
Mrs R G Libin

On 14 August 1914 Robinson entered the Royal Military College at Sandhurst. He is seen here on manoeuvres with B Company practising the gentle art of knotting. The original photograph was taken in October 1914 by a Captain Paterson.
Mrs R G Libin

It was an opinion shared by many who came into contact with Robinson throughout his life. Several have testified to a quiet, almost shy demeanour, yet in contrast he was an ardent exponent of the practical joke. On one occasion his sense of fun dropped both him and Cay into hot water:

> TEWTs, or Tactical Exercises Without Troops, were a frequent part of our curriculum. One hot day our platoon was going on bicycles to the rendezvous and passing a Pub, with Leefe and I at the rear, we saw some Dragoons' horses tethered outside. Leefe suggested we let our tyres down, borrow a couple of 'nags' and go for a cross-country ride to reconnoitre the 'enemy' position. After an exhilarating gallop we returned to the pub to find a couple of irate Dragoons vowing vengeance. We got reported to our Company Commander, but as Leefe pointed out, quoting the military slogan 'Time spent on reconnaissance is seldom wasted', we got off with a few extra fatigues. When it was pointed out as odd that both our bikes got punctured at the same time, Leefe replied that as I always followed in his footsteps, I must have gone over the same nail that punctured his tyre![12]

It appears that Robinson was not slow to seize an opportunity and act promptly upon his own initiative, important qualities which would stand him in good stead during years to come. He also appeared to have held 'authority' in slight contempt, and rarely passed up a chance to deflate those he considered pompous or conceited. An example of this involved a cadet in Robinson's Company who was generally disliked by his comrades. Following standard military drill practice, cadets' places in the platoon were changed daily, and before long it was the turn of the Company's most unpopular member to be on the right of the line. In practice this entailed his stepping smartly forward on the command 'Fix bayonets!' and performing this action for the others to follow. The embarrassment of this hapless individual is best imagined as he struggled in vain with a bayonet that refused to be drawn from its scabbard. No matter how hard he tried, the obstinate blade remained firmly in place, and, red-faced, the cadet stepped back into line amidst much subdued mirth. The rest of the Company were not slow to discover that the perpetrator of this crime was a certain Cadet Robinson who a few hours previously had discovered a novel application for a tin of Seccotine adhesive. In similar vein:

> Each day's roll call was in alphabetical order roared by our Staff Sergeant. Near my name came that of Cadet Douglas who also had a title. Each morning we got sick of the repeated: 'Cadet Cay – Present!', 'Cadet Lord Douglas of Hawick & Tibbers – Present!' that one day a very loud voice shouted 'Serve him right!' from the rear rank. We all sniggered and Leefe got a few extra parades, but the blasted title vanished from future roll calls.[13]

Robinson's five-month sojourn at the Royal Military College ended with him gaining a welcome commission. On 16 December 1914 he was gazetted to the Worcester Regiment and posted to the Fifth Militia Battalion, then a training unit based at Tregantle, near Antony in Cornwall, where it was destined to remain until 1916. Thus Robinson's desire for an early chance of action was thwarted, and the young second lieutenant soon became frustrated and put in applications for transfer:

> The latest news is that I have sent in my name for the West African job. The only drawback is the climate. I'm told subs get £25 a month besides all kinds of allowances and at any rate the fighting out there is far more lively and sporting than in France – at least in this stagnant period. But although they want officers out in W Africa, I'm afraid I won't get it as I'm too young, one really ought to be over 21 years of age, and a full Lieutenant.
>
> This war *is* sickening, the other day I heard of the death of a great friend of mine at school – Hawkesworth by name – he was one of the best of fellows. And there are several awfully nice Sandhurst men I know who have met the same fate – yet I'm longing to get out somehow – I want to be *doing* something.[14]

Occasional trips to Plymouth relieved the monotony, and whenever Ruth and her husband John came over from the latter's sister's house in Seaton, William made the most of it:

> We had lunch at the Royal Hotel and went to a matinée afterwards, *Business as Usual* review. It was very good and I enjoyed it thoroughly. We had tea at a restaurant and afterwards did a little shopping. Ruth bought an awfully nice dressing case thing for Harold's twenty-first birthday. I think I will send the old boy my photo and a note just to show I've not forgotten him. Thank the Lord he's not out in France.[15]

Into the Flying Corps

Although Robinson's application to enter the Army in Africa was unsuccessful, he was more fortunate in another direction: on 29 March 1915 he entered the Royal Flying Corps, posted overseas as an observer with 4 Squadron at St Omer, the unit equipped with BE2cs under the command of Major C A H Longcroft. Robinson and his fellow-observers were responsible for ranging British artillery on German positions; a tricky task, it involved them in making a tracing

Convalescence: Robinson recovering from his arm wound sustained by a 'shrapnel bullet' whilst he was engaged on reconnaissance over Lille on 7 May 1915. Soon afterwards Robinson applied for pilot training.
Sir Frederick Sowrey/RAF Museum

Robinson seated in an early production BE2c prior to a flight 'somewhere in England', c1915.
Mrs R G Libin

A corner of Suttons Farm early in 1916. B Flight's three BE2c aircraft are under canvas, the wooden airscrews protected by purpose-designed covers (which accounts for the 'clipped' appearance of their tips).
Sir Frederick Sowrey/RAF Museum

showing the exact position of each target and the last three shots fired at them. If the target turned out to be a gun battery the tracing was to show the number of guns and the direction in which they were facing. Robinson participated in many such patrols over the lines during April, and also spent much of his time in the squadron office, having been appointed officer in charge of aerial photography. In a letter to his mother he confessed to having been glad that his transfer had been successful:

No of course I didn't join the Corps for the extra pay – although of course it's very nice getting it – I was quite well off in my regiment and am not a penny in debt.
I get a full observer's pay now having been made 'efficient' about a week ago, up until then I was getting 10/6 with allowances; now I get 7/6 (regimental pay) plus 5/– (efficient observer's pay) plus fuel, light and field allowance which comes to about 4/– or 5/–.
So you see my total pay per day comes to about 17/–. Of course we are *much* better off than those poor trenchites – do they get excellent food and always a comfortable bed with clean sheets? Ye Gods no, I wouldn't swap my position with anyone.[16]

It was at about 04.50hrs on Saturday 8 May and whilst over Lille that Robinson was wounded by shrapnel from a closely bursting anti-aircraft shell. He felt a blow in his right forearm and initially dismissed it as a bruise, signalling to his pilot to continue the reconnaissance. After a while his arm became stiff, and when he noticed that his maps were smeared with blood the flight was cut short and the BE2c returned to the aerodrome. Robinson was swiftly admitted to 7 Stationary Hospital, where a shrapnel bullet and a fragment of shell were quickly removed before he was despatched to Boulogne, there to be told he was sailing back to England with one month's leave:

We got into a bit of bother over Lille the other day but my pilot was simply wonderful and had us out of trouble in no time. I'm afraid I was of no use to him as I was feeling a little Hors D Combat [sic], as you might say, but anyway all's well that ends well. Tell John I hope to have another drive of the car in the near future and before you go to India, as I shall be coming back to England for more training as soon as I can break out of here. I am going to be a pilot – there's nothing like driving oneself about.[17]

Once back in England and having enjoyed a brief spell of convalescence, Robinson was first posted to South Farnborough, where he reported for duty on 29 June to commence flying instruction, making his first flight the following day. Robinson went solo on 18 July, and just ten days later, flying a Maurice Farman, he qualified for Royal Aero Club Certificate 1475 after a mere 230 minutes of tuition. Saturday 14 August saw Robinson arriving at Upavon in Wiltshire to join the Central Flying School for a course of advanced instruction.

Robinson's log book, currently in the possession of the RAF Museum, yields a fascinating insight into his early flying experiences and, coupled with personal correspondence, creates a vivid impression of his life at the CFS. On 18 August 1915 at 11.25hrs, flying BE8 693, he made a 20-minute flight, reaching an altitude over the aerodrome of 1200ft. In the 'Remarks' column of his log book, Robinson laconically reported his first solo at Upavon as simply being 'bad'.

Robinson's BE2c 2693 (at Eastchurch on 6 June 1916, prior to joining the strength of B Flight, 39 HDS, at Suttons Farm) shows the Lewis gun and Strange Mounting to advantage. Note the collapsible windscreen, in the 'down' position.
J M Bruce/G S Leslie Collection

Robinson flew a variety of types at the CFS including BE8s, BE8As, and Martinsyde S1 single-seaters 2448 and 4240. The latter machines did not enjoy the same pleasant flying characteristics as contemporary Sopwith and Bristol types, yet Robinson appears to have experienced no problems with them. On 20 September, two days after he had been appointed Flying Officer and seconded following the gaining of his 'wings' on the 15th, Robinson joined the strength of 19 Squadron at Castle Bromwich near Birmingham, under the command of Captain (later Major) R M Rodwell. On 11 November Robinson wrote a long letter to his mother:

> I have delivered and brought machines to and from Farnborough, Northolt (Harrow) and various other places and between times I manage to have a peep at 'Town' and my various friends there. Whenever I do, I have a simply *ripping* time. I landed for lunch near Banbury the other day – you are immediately surrounded by people offering you cars, lunch, tea, bed and the Lord knows what not. Of course, if you are wise you generally pick out the grounds of a country house or large villa of some kind to land in. My last landing was at Kenilworth. I had a passenger with me and we had the time of our lives. Talk about autograph books and cameras. By gad, I was positively sick of seeing and signing my own signature.

> When I swore I would not sign another book one girl caught hold of my machine and said she would not leave go until I signed. So after much amusing argument I told her to give me the book whereupon I placed my filthy hand, writing 'The mark of an aviator, W L Robinson' over the top of the handmark – my hand was all dirty with the oil of the engine.[18]

On 7 December Robinson had to transfer observer Lieutenant Payne over to Gosport, but BE2c 2107 only got as far as Oxford when wind, rain and fog compelled the pilot to land at Port Meadow. The airmen stayed overnight at the nearby Mitre Hotel:

> Next morning the sky was perfect – and we decided to go on our way via Farnborough where we would fill up our petrol and oil tanks.
>
> I flew fairly high, touching nearly 9000 feet. As luck would have it my engine began missing; I knew exactly what the matter was but could not remedy it in the air. The poor observer, a fellow who had only been in an aeroplane about once before in his life, grew quite nervous; he kept on passing back notes to me: 'The front part of the machine is vibrating horribly' – 'What is the matter with the engine?' – 'Will she hold out 'till we get to Farnborough?' etc. I laughed like anything at him, made a long nose and put my tongue out at him for reply (you can't hear each other speak of course). Once or twice I held up my hands to show I wasn't holding anything – I thought the poor man would have a fit. Anybody who knew the least little bit about flying would know we were as safe as a rock.[19]

On 24 December 1915 Robinson arrived at Joyce Green aerodrome, the home of 10 Reserve Squadron, having been 'loaned' by his unit to the London defence. At noon the same day he took off in BE2c 4147, and after a 20-minute flight arrived over the landing ground at South Farningham, near Dartford, Kent. Robinson had already made many night flights at Castle Bromwich and was quite familiar with the risks and difficulties that went with them. In the brief period the airmen were at Farningham they were comfortably billeted in the nearby Lion Hotel:

> ...Here I am 18 miles east of the city and five miles out of Dartford, tucked away with another pilot, some mechanics and two aeroplanes for the purpose of 'Strafing Zepps', when they next come this way.
>
> The other pilot (who by the way was with me learning to fly at Farnborough) and myself are living in this sweet little country hotel, all on our own – we are awfully comfortable here and the job is really a very slack one. We are chosen for it because we are supposed to be able to fly by night, an accomplishment which not every pilot can boast of I may state.

There are only 20 aeroplanes on the London defence, but we are absolutely the first to receive the enemy should they come over. Now for heaven's sake don't get nervous mother, the job is quite safe if one has plenty of confidence.[20]

Robinson only remained at South Farningham until 12 January 1916, having been recalled by his commanding officer to Castle Bromwich. The next day he was despatched to Newcastle, there to fly one of the first Armstrong Whitworth FK3s, with the 120hp Austro Daimler engine, to CFS Upavon, a distance of about 350 miles. As bad weather delayed the trip for four days, Robinson and his companion, Captain Williamson, found plenty of time on their hands, but killed much of it touring the Armstrong Whitworth works at Gosforth as well as a local heavy gun factory. Eventually, on Wednesday 16 January, the airmen were ready to start on their journey. It turned out to be a protracted flight, fog and mist obliging Robinson to land and put up at Bilborough, near York, and then Chesterfield, some 12 miles from Sheffield:

We stayed at this place two days and two nights and were entertained by the people belonging to a hospital nearby although we actually slept and had breakfast at the Station Hotel. The second night we took the matron and awfully charming young and pretty girl doctor to Sheffield where we 'did' supper and a ripping theatre.

On the Saturday morning following, we left, after writing our names in autograph albums, imposing our beaming visages to the camera and bidding tender farewells – arriving at Birmingham about an hour later.

I wanted to see a friend in Birmingham on Sunday, so we didn't go to the CFS until the Wednesday. We did the journey from Birmingham to Salisbury Plain in about an hour and a half which isn't so bad considering I went via Oxford, where I landed at Port Meadow and thereby amused a number of subalterns in training there.

I came back to Birmingham the same night (Monday) but as I went straight to my billet I heard nothing about the Zepp raid till the next morning. I then went off on the London Zepp Strafing job at Croydon – and the next day (Wednesday) was shunted off here – one of the outer circle of London defence stations.[21]

'Here' was Suttons Farm in Hornchurch, where Robinson arrived on 2 February, the landing ground having come under the overall control of Major T C R Higgins commanding the newly formed 19 Reserve Squadron at Hounslow. On 4 February Robinson made his first flight from Suttons Farm, taking aloft BE2c 4110 to test the incidence of its tail unit. The pilots were only supposed to fly their aircraft twice a week if there were no raids, 'just to see if they are working alright'.[22] It was mainly routine, and Robinson often took the opportunity to indulge in a few mild aerobatics to relieve the boredom:

Today being a lovely day I went up, mucked about a bit, looped the loop four times and came down. Now don't for heaven's sake get nervous when I tell you I loop the loop – it's the easiest and safest thing to do in the world in the machines you have got.[23]

On 25 March 1916 the 18th Wing was formed under Lieutenant-Colonel F V Holt to encompass all the air defence detachments in the London area. Previously administered by 19RS, these detachments officially became 39 Home Defence Squadron on 15 April, with its headquarters at Hounslow under Major Higgins. On 13 June Major W C H Mansfield took over command of the unit for a short period, and two flights each of six BE2c aircraft were stationed at Suttons Farm and Hainault Farm in Essex. C Flight at Hainault came under the command of Brandon, and Robinson would eventually take over control of B Flight at Suttons which comprised Lieutenants C C G Brock, C C Durston, P R Mallinson, F Sowrey and W J Tempest. On 26 July the command of the squadron passed to Major A H Morton, and soon afterwards A Flight, under Captain L S Ross at Hounslow, switched to North Weald Bassett, the headquarters being moved to Salway Lodge at Woodford Green.

At Suttons Farm, wooden hangars of a permanent nature were built to replace the temporary canvas RE5s. Living accommodation, converted from aircraft transport crates, and proper workshop facilities began to spring up on the farmland, whilst Thomas Crawford and his son Tom continued to work what was left of their 385-acre farm. Their land formed part of the Manor of Suttons, and the farmhouse was built on the plot where the ancient manor house had stood in days of yore. The latter had been acquired, along with the Manor of Hornchurch Hall, by William of Wykeham in 1392 from the Monks of St Bernard and presented by him to St Mary de Winton College, Oxford. Truly a historic site by any standards, Suttons Farm was strategically well placed for the defence of London, and from there three pilots would ultimately vindicate the defences after months of frustration.

Under Robinson, who was no strict disciplinarian, the officers and men of B Flight enjoyed a fairly relaxed atmosphere. He was greatly respected by all those who came into contact with him, as his sister Ruth was later to record:

He had a remarkable gift for managing men, especially bad characters, and he endeared himself to all who served him. He was never out of temper or depressed, and wherever he was he diffused an air of confidence and hope. He managed to get the best out of everybody and won a general affection because he himself gave out so much of it.[24]

Amongst Robinson's closest companions were Second Lieutenant Frederick Sowrey and Captain Robert Sidney Stammers, whose young sister Vera accompanied her brother's fiancée on frequent visits to Suttons Farm. Vera remembers that all the pre-flight briefings were around a card table just inside one of the hangars, and that visitors to the station were numerous:

Weekend after weekend, there was never any thought of stopping people going. My sister-in-law went every weekend and took her knitting with her. All the mechanics would be coming and going and there was Muriel, Muskin as she was then, sitting passively knitting.[25]

During the early months of 1916 the home defence airmen were slowly gaining valuable experience of night-flying, and a marked drop in the number of accidents proved their newly found proficiency. On 31 January, 15 aircraft had left the ground to combat the raiders: of these, 11 had crashed on landing and three pilots were killed. Four months had elapsed since that fateful occurrence, and now the airmen were able to take off and land without mishap.

On 25 February the war had struck its first blow at the Robinson family. Grace's husband Arthur, a second lieutenant in the Eighth Battalion of the Northamptonshire Regiment, died of wounds received on the Western Front and was buried at Lepugnoy's military cemetery. A short while afterwards, from his lodgings at The Haylands in Hornchurch, Robinson wrote to his bereaved sister:

My darling girl I wish I had sufficient power of expression to comfort you in the minutest degree. He is a loss – a greater loss than I can express – to all who knew him, but my dear girl

SL11, 3 September 1916

These two remarkable photos are unique in that they clearly show the cockpit appointments of a typical 1916 BE2c night-fighter, but of even greater historical importance is the fact that the aircraft is 2693, as flown by 'Billy' Robinson when he shot down *SL11* over Cuffley. The left-hand picture reveals a number of interesting items in the cockpit. These include a small placard that reads
 'Red: Landing
  Green: Forced Land
  White: Ground OK, Land
  Red: Obstruction',
which indicates the laid-down system for air-to-ground communication using coloured flares fired from a Very pistol which pilots invariably carried in these aircraft. Below the placard is a rack for three Lewis gun drums (a map is folded into the centre recess) and beneath this, slightly to the right, are the two brass buttons which operated the Holt wingtip flares. The right-hand picture shows three big brass switches on the starboard cockpit side, together with a mass of wiring, which related to the night-flying equipment and which probably activated the wingtip and tail navigation lights. Other points on interest include the central rack for 12 signal cartridges to the left of the compass, and the forward cockpit with its fittings for the cover plate (not present here) which reduced air suction. Another oft-unappreciated feature of this aircraft is the collapsible windscreen with its fabric covered sides which could be laid down flat in order that the Lewis gun could be lowered further without fear of cracking the screen.
J M Bruce/G S Leslie Collection

one is bound to gain some consolation in knowing that one of the finest men on God's earth has met with the finest ends that man can possibly hope for.

Yet even worse was to follow, for in April came the shocking news of Harold's death in Mesopotamia. Serving as a Second Lieutenant with the 101st Grenadiers of the Indian Army, Harold had been taking part in the ill-fated attempt to relieve General Townsend's beleaguered force at Kut-el-Amara. The divisions attempting to break through the Turkish positions were thwarted at every turn, and British casualties were heavy – among them Harold, who on 10 April, succumbed to wounds received in action.

Close Encounter
When Linnarz, in *LZ97*, made his solo assault on London during the night of 25 April, he had come under attack by two pilots of 39 HDS, giving Robinson his first crack at one of the raiders. Linnarz, having mistaken the River Roding for the Thames, had bombed Fyfield and Ongar on his way in, and at 23.08hrs came under fire from the Dog Kennel Hill gun. The improved defences had been an unwelcome surprise for Linnarz as myriad searchlights stabbed the night sky. *LZ97*'s executive officer, *Oberleutnant* Lampel, later recorded his version of the events:

> We are out of the dazzling rays and once more in the depths of night. But it is no longer pitch dark. The countless beams of searchlights fill the sky with a vivid light. They have lost us – strike, as it were, wildly past us, catch us once again, go on over us; one remains still, the others hunt around, crossing it or searching along it for the objective, while we steer in quite a different direction.
> The mad frolic continues for hours on end.
> We lose all idea of the passage of time as we fly on, every half-minute releasing another bomb. Every explosion is observed, and its position pinpricked on the map.[27]

At 23.00hrs one of *LZ97*'s bombs fell in Forest Road, Barkingside, near Fairlop railway station, where the missile made a 5ft crater and damaged seven adjacent cottages owned by the Great Eastern Railway.

> In Nos 1 to 6, occupied by Mrs Slade, widow, Mr Carrington, signalman, PC 546 'J' Saunders, Mr Peake, platelayer, Mr Wright, platelayer, and Mr Arundel, clerk, respectively, the front doors were blown in, and all the front windows smashed. Several windows were also broken in the Railway Station, and the gas main in the roadway was damaged, resulting in an escape of gas, which was immediately attended by the workmen of the Ilford Gas Co, who were called by Police.[28]

Nine more bombs fell over the area, mostly in fields: damage sustained was slight and there were no casualties. *LZ97* was next seen over Chadwell Heath, where it was caught by searchlights, and then, apparently circling, over Seven Kings railway station, where the airship was engaged by home defence airmen.

Major Higgins sent eight of his pilots aloft that night, Lieutenants 'Bobby' Holme, M S Stewart and George H Birley from Hounslow, Second Lieutenants C T Black and Brandon from Hainault Farm, and, from Suttons, Captain Arthur Travers Harris, with Lieutenants Powell and Robinson:

> At about 10.45am on the night of 25th inst, I received orders to patrol at 5000 feet. This I did and kept at 5000 feet for a few minutes, then decided to climb. When just over 7000 feet, I noticed a great number of searchlights pointing in a northerly direction; turning round I saw the Zeppelin. I at once turned and climbed in its direction. When just over 8000 feet, I was in a fairly good position to use my machine gun; this I did, firing immediately under the ship. The firing must have had little or no effect, for the Zeppelin must have been a good 2000 feet above me, if not more (by this time I was about 8000 feet).
> At about 11.20 (by the machine watch which is some minutes fast) I distinctly saw a bright flash in the front part of the forward gondola of the Zeppelin – I thought it rather prolonged for the burst of a shell.
> I fired at the Zeppelin three times (each time almost immediately below it): the machine gun jammed five times, and I only got off about twenty rounds. When the Zeppelin made off in a ENE direction, I followed for some minutes, but lost sight of it.
> I saw no more of the Zeppelin, and landed at about 1.15. Five sets of flares were visible at my greatest height (11,000 feet) although Hainault Farm was badly laid out, there being far too many lights, and I could make out no distinct 'L'. The whole countryside, I thought, was very much more lighted up than it had been on previous raid occasions. The river could easily be traced from lights on its banks.
> I noticed signalling about five miles NE of Suttons Farm – it appeared to be five fast flashes, then a pause, followed by another five flashes.[29]

All the pilots criticised the flare layout at Hainault, and most of them reported the disturbing news that somebody appeared to be signalling to the raider. The then commander of B Flight, Arthur Harris:

> I distinctly saw signalling in and around London; the first I noticed being a white light giving five dots intermittently about four to five miles due south of Hainault flares. I noticed three giving the same type of signal on south bank of river somewhere – I estimated about Woolwich. At a point between Leyton and East and West Ham – where the Zeppelin was first caught by the searchlights – a very brilliant green light flashed intermittently for about 20 secs to half a minute. I noticed the Zeppelin immediately turned in the direction of this light, and steered a course over it, which would have taken it straight over Woolwich. Before reaching the river, however, it turned due east, and it was shortly after this that I attacked it. I have not the least doubt that these lights were signals; they could not possibly have been mistaken for anything else.[30]

Whoever or whatever was responsible for the signals, and whether any action was ever taken over the matter, has gone unrecorded, but the supportive claims by all the pilots could not have been ignored. Harris was the only other pilot to attack Linnarz, but gun jams forced him to abandon the action. He also reported that his machine was climbing sluggishly: 'I had the utmost difficulty in getting my machine up to 13,000 feet, the last 4500 taking a great time...'[31]

So Linnarz made good his escape, but he had to run the gauntlet of gun batteries as he went out, and for the crew of *LZ97* a few more frights were in store. Between Bruges and Ghent the airship was attacked by two RNAS machines, and Lampel was quick to man one of the guns in the control gondola:

> I watch their approach, but they are flying too high. I cannot bring my gun to bear unless we get above them. Aloft, on the platform, the machine gun is chattering. A stream of flaming bullets flickers past us – too short.
> Again and again at frequent intervals there are bursts of fire overhead. We know them of old! The commander orders a climb; they can't cope with us at that. They are of course, faster than we are, but we can beat them at climbing. The

SL11, 3 September 1916

distance between us increases and they are left behind. Suddenly there is another burst of machine-gun fire. The enemy has managed to overtake us, and is attacking us from below. We must not allow them to get above us at any price, because then they will be in a position to dive.

We climb higher and higher. The gas blows off madly amid the rattle of the machine guns. A minute later, the blazing bullets are flashing past again. Again too short. All at once one of the aeroplanes turns and goes down in a side-slip. It is suddenly surrounded by fleecy puffs. We are close to the Dutch frontier. Nevertheless the machine goes on down and must therefore be damaged, probably by bullets in the engine.

The other aeroplane does not like the look of things. He has, perhaps, expended all his ammunition; at any rate he sheers off and disappears.[32]

Eventually, after a flight lasting almost 12 hours, Linnarz and the crew of *LZ97* made a safe landing, counting themselves fortunate to have survived London's improved defences.

So ended the Zeppelin raid of 25/26 April, and Major Higgins duly submitted his pilots' patrol reports to 18th Wing headquarters in Albermarle Street, together with a covering note:

All the pilots agree that the Acetylene Flares at Hainault Farm are very confusing to land by. They also report that they saw extensive signalling to the Zeppelins from the ground.

The direct line telephone to the War Office was hit by a Zeppelin bomb and cut. It is now repaired and in working order again.

Hainault Farm reports that bombs were dropped by the Zeppelins all around their Aerodrome at a distance of one mile.[33]

Robinson had suffered the frustration of failure at his inconclusive grappling with *LZ97*, and vowed that on the next occasion it would be 'either the Zepp or I'.[34] When that next occasion came it would be the 'Zepp'.

September 2, 1916
Despite the poor weather conditions that prevailed over England and much of war-torn Europe on the second day of September, the Germans were preparing their biggest airship raid of the war. For the first time ever, Army and Naval Airship Divisions joined forces for the attack. From noon until 15.30hrs, no fewer than a dozen naval ships left their North Sea bases: *L11, L13, L14, L16, L17, L21, L22, L23, L24, L30, L32* and *SL8*; in support, the Army weighed in with *LZ90, LZ97, LZ98* and the newly-commissioned *SL11*.

Schramm stands in front of *LZ39* following its forced landing at Kovno, Russia, on 18 December 1915. Anti-aircraft fire was responsible for the Zeppelin's demise and its commander suffered an injury to his right hand in the process.
Archiv: Marine-Luftschiffer-Kameradschaft

Even before the first of the raiders had reached England, home defence units were already at full alert, having the benefit of previously intercepted radio messages via Admiral Hall's Room 40 in Whitehall. Not far from Bacton, Rawlinson's mobile gun section prepared to meet the raiders; nearby lay the coastguard station which maintained a telephone link to the Haisborough lightship anchored some eight miles out to sea. The airship commanders regularly used the vessel as a landmark on their way in, and this raid was no exception.

At 23.50hrs Rawlinson heard five loud reports, some ten miles south of his position and undoubtedly from a confused Koch in *L24*. For the next 35 minutes more bombs fell on land and airship motors were heard, but the raiders passed over unseen, the low cloud effectively screening them from view. Rawlinson tried his two searchlights as one of the airships flew over his position, but the beams merely bounced off the clouds, and no attempt was made to fire upon the invisible raider as the dull throb of Maybach motors receded towards the south-west.

At 23.05hrs the latest news from Horse Guards was transmitted to the little wooden hut standing in the grounds of Suttons Farm which acted as a rudimentary mess. The

Wilhelm Schramm, seated third from left, and *SL10* personnel. In the back row (left to right) are *Obermaschinist* Migefroren, *Obersteuermann* Scholz, *Obermaschinists* Mather, Stahl, Linkhart and Schuster. Seated next to Schramm are *Leutnant* Grafstrop, von Wobeser, and, far right, *Fahnrich* Matharst. *Fahnrich* was not only a naval term for midshipman but was also used by the Army to denote an Ensign, *ie* the lowest officer grade.
P Amesbury Collection

Zeppelin!

hut was filled with the members of B Flight seated around their treasured gramophone and enjoying selections from *The Bing Boys*. It was during a rendering of 'Another Little Drink Won't Do Us Any Harm!' that the shrill of the telephone cut across the strains of the music. Following a brief exchange, the orderly officer turned towards the pilots, informing them to 'Take Air Raid Action!'

That night it was Robinson's 'trick' to patrol the air space between Suttons Farm and Joyce Green, with A and C Flight pilots covering their allotted sectors in order to scour as wide an area as possible. In accordance with usual practice, the pilots left the ground at 60-second intervals; following Robinson were Ross in BE12 6484 from North Weald Bassett and Brandon in BE2c 2090 from Hainault Farm.

It was foggy and still damp when they wheeled 2693 from the hangar, and as usual Robinson personally supervised the pre-flight checks before seating himself in the cramped confines of the rear cockpit. The fog was slowly thickening, but the pilot was convinced that it would be clearer higher up. As he went through the usual cockpit drill, Money flares were already being lit on both sides of the cinder runway.

The aircraft was guided on to the field by ground crew, a man stationed at each wingtip, and at Robinson's signal they released the BE, which bumped hesitantly down the flarepath, making a safe take-off into the mist, into the night and into history.

SL11

Wilhelm Emil Eugen Schramm was one of three children born to electrical engineer Otto Carl and his wife Josena Hopmeister. The elder Schramm became a director of the Siemens electrical firm and for a while was that firm's London representative, living at Old Charlton, Kent, where Wilhelm was born on 11 December 1885. His father's untimely death in 1900 resulted in the teenage Wilhelm returning to Germany, there to embark upon a military career.

Towards the latter months of 1905 Schramm entered the Second Railway Regiment and soon rose from Officer Cadet to Lieutenant. Another five years passed before he went into the Prussian Army Airship Battalion, and when the Second Battalion was formed in 1912 Schramm went along with it to Königsberg.

One of his first flights took place in the Army Parseval PIII, in which he made a seven-hour trip from Tegel to his home base, covering a distance of over 340 miles. Later he was elevated to the rank of *Oberleutnant* and returned to Tegel as Adjutant of the unit. Just prior to 1914, Schramm had served on the Zeppelins *Z1* and *Z11*, and subsequently as First Officer on board the *SL2*, commanded by the redoubtable *Hauptmann* von Wobeser. It was in *SL2* that Schramm took part in his first raid over London, when on 7 September 1915 the old wooden-hulled ship, in company with *LZ74*, *LZ77* and *LZ79*, made a daring attack. Of the four, only *SL2* was successful, managing to drop bombs on houses in the dock areas of Deptford, Greenwich, Millwall and Woolwich.

In December Schramm took up his first command, the elderly *ZXII*, and later, when commanding *LZ39*, he made several successful sorties over the Eastern Front. It was not until 23 February that Schramm was able to take charge of a more modern ship, and in this, *LZ93*, he made a few raids upon the English and French coasts. June saw *LZ93* despatched to Dresden for additional sections to be added, and Schramm, together with his crew, went to Leipzig to take over their new ship, *SL11*. After initial flight tests were successfully completed the ship went on to Spich on 12 August 1916 to prepare for the new offensive against

Hauptmann Wilhelm Schramm photographed during 1916 when in command of Zeppelin *LZ93*.
P Amesbury

The only authenticated photo of Schütte Lanz *SL11*, shown here flying over Hamelin in August 1916. The photograph was taken by Schramm's elder brother Otto.
Mrs Scheller-Niemeyer, by courtesy of P Amesbury

London. There came an abortive attempt on 31 August, which was thwarted by adverse weather conditions – but Schramm had not long to wait before the next raid was scheduled.

On 2 September the weather could have been better. The air was extremely turbulent at high altitude, there was a keen wind blowing in from the south-west and west-south-west, and on nearing the English coast a few ships iced up. As a result several failed to reach their target. *L17* got as far inland as Norfolk but, experiencing engine trouble, the commander decided it would be prudent to abandon his attack. So too did the commander of *LZ97*, who was forced to reverse direction owing to some really heavy rain squalls.

Out of the trio of remaining Army Zeppelins, *LZ98* was

SL11, 3 September 1916

Schütte Lanz *SL13* at Wittmundhaven. 20 October 1916. Built at Leipzig. *SL13* came off the stocks right after *SL11* and can be considered identical in almost every aspect to Schramm's ill-starred command. Of interest here is the upper machine gun platform and the hoods which cover the tops of the gas shafts. Each of the latter served two cells alternating up to the top on both port and starboard sides. Most exited at longitudinal 9, although the three forward ones exited lower at 7 in order to lead the hydrogen away from the gun platform. (The gunners were not allowed to fire their guns if the ship was climbing and valving gas.) Externally the wooden-hulled Schütte Lanz airships can be quickly distinguished from Zeppelins in that the forward control gondola and engine gondola were distinctly separate.
G Blasweiler, by courtesy of D H Robinson

Catching the control car of *SL13* as it comes in to land at Wittmundhaven. The windows with their characteristic 'ripples' are clearly seen, as, also noteworthy, is the projecting glazed forward 'shelf' which afforded an excellent downward view for the bomb sight operator.
G Blasweiler, by courtesy of D H Robinson

the first ship to reach London, crossing the coast over Dungeness just after midnight; over Tilbury the ship, under the command of Ernst Lehmann, came into intense AA fire from the Dartford and Tilbury guns. As a consequence Lehmann, thinking he was over the London Docks, dropped his entire load of bombs. By 01.15hrs the ship was considerably lightened, rising to 13,000ft and steering north-east. One of three defending aircraft from 39 HDS attacked the Zeppelin unsuccessfully, having sacrificed precious speed to retain height, but Robinson could do little to prevent *LZ98* slipping through his clutches and the Zeppelin commander taking advantage of cloud cover to make good his escape.

LZ90 had earlier shut down its motors at 23.00hrs and lowered its sub-cloud car, which broke free, taking with it some 5000ft of cable, to fall near Manningtree in Essex. Minutes later the Zeppelin crew ditched the winch, and subsequent examination by British experts revealed hapless attempts by the Germans to arrest the car's progress, probably by jamming an iron bar into the gear teeth. Reports were confused as to whether the sub-cloud car was occupied, although no evidence has ever been found to suggest that it had been.[35]

Wilhelm Schramm's *SL11* flew over the River Crouch at 10.40hrs, the ship turning to follow a wide circle in order that London could be approached from the North. Having flown over Chelmsford and Colchester, the ship turned west to pass over Saffron Walden, and in an attempt to

One of the finest photographs ever taken from a wartime airship. This evocative view of *SL13* is from the rear of the control gondola looking aft. Of note are the bomb shutters running down the hull centreline, the 'wire' ladder to starboard, and the retractable radiators on the engine gondolas.
G Blasweiler, by courtesy of D H Robinson

obtain his bearings the commander ploughed on over Royston, then Hitchin, before eventually reaching the outskirts of the capital where surprised residents heard the heavy drone of motors at about 01.00hrs.

Over London Colney, Schramm had six HE and incendiary bombs released in order to gain extra buoyancy and, thus lightened, *SL11* climbed steadily beyond the range of London's guns. The airship's bombs fell harmlessly on wheat fields in the vicinity of Bell Lane and St Albans Road, South Mimms. A further eight then struck the Market Gardens at Bulls Cross, causing small craters amongst lettuce and potato fields. The owner, a Mr Hollington, was fortunate that his house was not struck, the building being narrowly missed by one of the missiles.

At 01.45hrs another HE and four incendiaries tumbled from *SL11*'s racks, this time finding a target: one incendiary fell on out-buildings at the Glasgow Stud Farm in Clayhill, Enfield, a large stable being gutted as a result. Although William Elliott Groom and several of his stable lads saved five of the terrified animals, three valuable race horses belonging to Sir Hedworth Meux were burnt to death. Much hay, straw and equipment was also destroyed, and it was some time before the Enfield Fire Brigade brought the blaze under control.

At 02.00hrs another HE bomb fell on Osbourne Road in Little Heath, Potters Bar, just outside 'Kerdistone', occupied by a Miss Bishop; a 30ft crater was the result of a blast, which also ruptured a water main and damaged the roofs of two nearby houses. Continuing its leisurely course over the capital, *SL11* dropped more incendiaries over Edmonton, none of which caused any damage, and at 02.10hrs, directly over Alexandra Palace, the airship was finally held by the Finsbury and Victoria Park searchlights. The Finsbury gunners opened the engagement, and soon dozens of shells were speeding towards their target. So spirited was the gunfire that it forced Schramm to turn over Tottenham and avoid the violent barrage.

Two minutes later the airship dropped 24 HE and three incendiary bombs over an area bounded by Ponders End, Enfield Highway and Walthamstow. Fortunately there were no casualties, but the roadway and a water main was badly damaged in the High Street, Ponders End, as were 63 dwellings, with various tram and telephone wires brought down. Fourteen houses in Enfield Highway and several greenhouses belonging to Smith's Nurseries in Hertford Road also suffered damage, as did three houses in Turkey Street which were struck. No casualties were reported, and even as this last batch of bombs found their mark, three aircraft coming from the south-east dived on *SL11*. The pilots of these machines were all from 39 Home Defence Squadron: Second Lieutenant J I Mackay, in BE2c 2574, had left North Weald Bassett at 01.08hrs and Second Lieutenant B H Hunt (BE2c 2727) 14 minutes later from Hainault Farm. The third aircraft was 2693 and it got there first.

Having failed to relocate *LZ98* amongst the clouds, Robinson had wasted 15 valuable minutes fruitlessly searching and had reluctantly been forced to give up. Flying on in the hope that the many searchlights would indicate which directions other airships might take, he eventually observed one of the raiders illuminated by the flashes of exploding shells. Despite an intense barrage the British pilot dived straight for the airship, which was being twisted and turned in an effort to evade the grip of the searchlights and the gunfire. Seizing his chance, Schramm took refuge in a cloud bank and steered *SL11* out of view. The gunfire below ceased momentarily, and searchlight beams swung around vainly trying to illuminate the vessel. Awakened by all the noise and flash of guns, hundreds of excited Londoners who had turned out of their beds and into the streets breathed their disappointment.

Robinson's aircraft was rocking in the blast of renewed shellfire as he dived below the blunt nose of *SL11* with the intention of raking its underside. Flying along the entire length of the dirigible he emptied one whole drum of incendiary ammunition without apparent effect and turned away to prepare for a second attempt. Clipping on another drum, he dived at the airship, and once more fired into the vast flanks of his adversary. Again the bullets appeared to have no effect, and like some great aerial whale *SL11* floated on, seemingly invulnerable. There was no retaliatory fire from the airship's gondolas and it therefore remains doubtful that the crew were even aware of the aeroplane. Indeed, Robinson was to remark later 'that she might have been the Flying Dutchman for all the signs of life I saw.'[36]

Making one final effort Robinson attacked the airship a

SL11, 3 September 1916

third time, and positioning his aircraft behind and below *SL11*'s massive elevators and rudders he concentrated the entire contents of his last drum into a single area.

A dull pink-stained glow deep inside the airship was the prelude to fiery disaster which was about to engulf *Hauptmann* Wilhelm Schramm and the 15 members of his crew. In a matter of seconds the entire tail assembly of the Schütte Lanz was ablaze with flames towering over 100ft high that shot up in front of the elated Robinson. Roaring and spitting, the blazing hull of the doomed raider illuminated the night sky and ground below over a 60-mile radius. Observers at Reigate 35 miles away saw the awful glow, as did the residents of Cambridge and the surrounding Home Counties. It was 02.30hrs. Most of the searchlights blinked out, their beams no longer required since there was a new and terrible light in the heavens.

Schramm's ship was seen as a ball of fire which expanded and exploded with a terrific flash, bathing the whole of the capital with its brilliance. This was the moment that so many Londoners had waited to see for so long, and they made the most of it. Complete pandemonium broke out as people rushed out on the streets. Singing, clapping and cheering seemed to go on and on echoing over the rooftops. Many groups patriotically launched into 'God Save the King', while children and women danced in the streets. Railway engine whistles and factory hooters added to the cacophony of delirium. Excited parents held toddlers up to the windows to witness the event, and for many it would be a lasting impression even over 60 years later. Just no one could tear his eyes from the blazing hulk as it hung

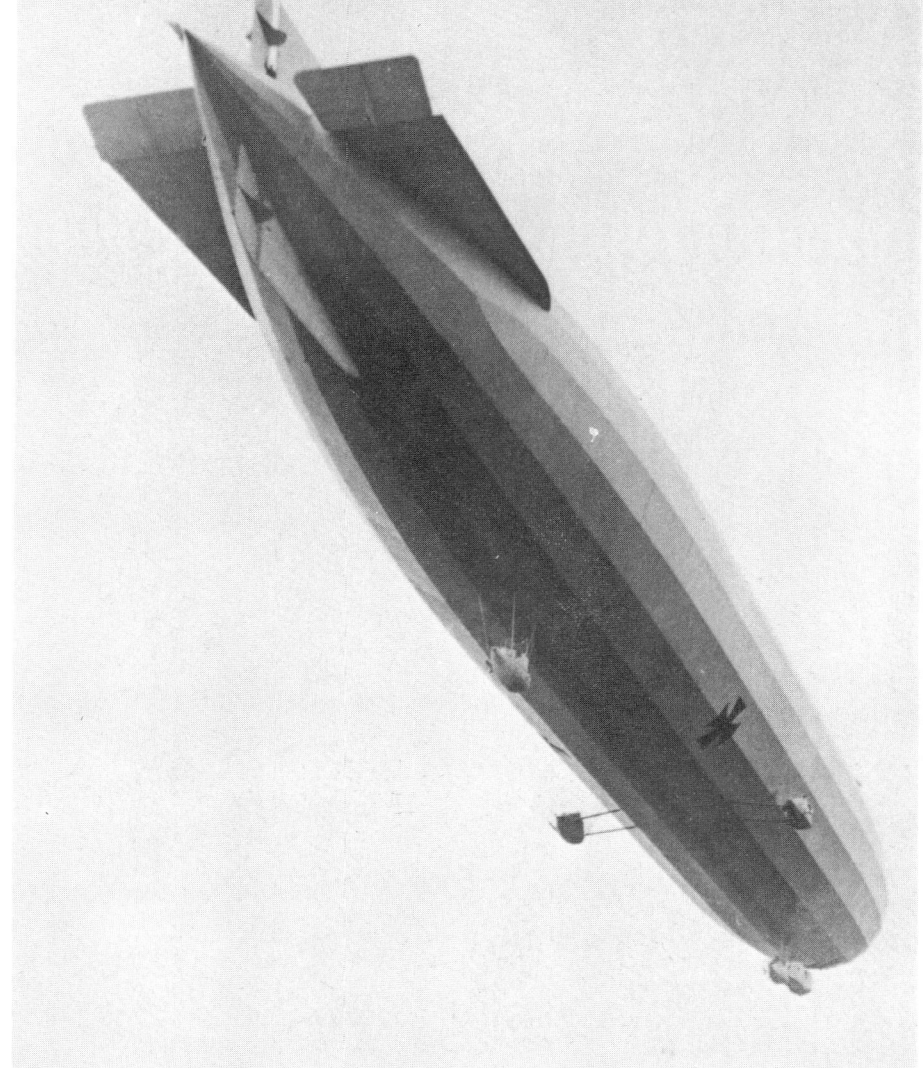

SL13 seen here during its transfer flight from Leipzig to Hannover on 19 October 1916. In all, ten 'e' type Schütte Lanz airships were built, at sheds in Leipzig, Rheinau and Zeesen. Each was powered by four Maybach HSLu engines delivering a total of 960hp, and a top speed of just over 60mph could be attained.
G Blasweiler, by courtesy of D H Robinson

SL13 berthed in the Wittmundhaven shed, 1916. This ship made seven flights from this station, including the delivery flight, and was transferred to Wildeshausen on 17 November for repairs. On 26 January 1917 a civilian crew flew *SL13* back to the building works at Leipzig, where the vessel was destroyed on 8 February. The weight of heavy snow was too much for the Leipzig shed roof: it collapsed and *SL13* caught fire. Repeated failures of the wooden girders, and even glued joints, were not uncommon in Schütte Lanz airships and one of several reasons why the Navy disliked them so much. Strasser termed their supporters as 'glue potters' and once said of the ships 'Experience has thoroughly demonstrated that wood is an unsuitable material for airship construction, because it weakens and breaks with even a moderate degree of humidity...'
G Blasweiler, by courtesy of D H Robinson

The remains of SL11 burn fiercely at Cuffley on the morning of 3 September 1916 as livestock flee in panic. St Andrew's Church (left) is accurately portrayed, indicating that F Matania's contemporary painting was more carefully researched than others which were circulated at the time.
By courtesy of S G English

RFC personnel bundle up miles of wire cable, virtually all that remained of SL11's wooden-framed structure, prior to loading it on trucks. In the background stands the original St Andrew's Church that was built in 1910 and demolished in 1966. It narrowly missed premature destruction as the blazing airship struck the open fields close by.
Sir Frederick Sowrey

motionless, for several seconds, 11,500ft up, before finally sinking nose-down in a shallow dive. An acrid smell of burnt fabric and wood was reported to have remained in the air long after the awesome wreck had vanished from view. Among thousands of excited eyewitnesses was ten-year-old Henry Tuttle, living with his family in Barnsbury Road, Islington, over a boot repairer's shop:

> We opened the front door and there it was: it was a fantastic sight like a big silver cigar and it [seemed] to be going very slow by this time. A lot of people came out of their houses and then all of a sudden flames started to come from the Zeppelin and then it broke in half and was one mass of flames. It was an incredible sight: people were cheering, dancing, singing and somebody started playing the bagpipes. This went on well into the night. The Italian in our house was walking in the centre of the road shouting at the sky in Italian and waving a big boot knife.
> All the children (and I was one of them) marched up and down with him, cheering like merry hell. What a sight, which I shall never forget. We were told afterwards, at school, that the 'Zepp' was shot down by Lt Robinson RFC.[37]

Lieutenant Robinson RFC had barely enough time to manoeuvre his machine away from the rapidly descending Schütte Lanz which threatened to engulf the very engineer of its destruction. Shaken but naturally exuberant, Robinson watched the burning ship fall away earthwards and then pulled the Very pistol from its holster and fired off cartridge and parachute flares. The thousands below, seeing the little red and green twinkling stars, guessed their origin, and renewed cheering broke out. But what of Robinson's personal reactions as the stricken airship slid out of the sky? History can count itself fortunate that in a letter to his mother some weeks later he recorded them for posterity:

> When the colossal thing actually burst into flames, of course it was a *glorious* sight – wonderful! It literally lit up all the sky around and me as well of course. I saw my machine as in the firelight and sat still half-dazed staring at the wonderful sight before me, not realising to the least degree the wonderful thing that had happened!
> My feelings, *can* I describe my feelings? I hardly know how I felt as I watched the huge mass gradually turn on end – as it seemed to me – [and] slowly sink, one glowing blazing mass. I gradually realised what I had done and grew wild with excitement. When I had cooled down a bit, I did what I don't think many people would think I would do, and that was thanked God with all my heart, you darling old mother and father, I'm not what is popularly known as a religious person but on an occasion such as this one must realise a little how one does trust in providence. I felt an overpowering feeling of thankfulness, so it was strange that I should pause and think for a moment after the first 'blast' of excitement, as it were, was over and thank from the bottom of my heart that supreme power that rules and guides our destinies.[38]

The home defence units of the RFC had sent up ten pilots altogether but, Robinson apart, their efforts went unrewarded. Only three squadrons were involved, and the first to go into action was 33 HDS which covered the Humber area. Captain R C L (Bobby) Holme of A Flight attempted a take-off from the Beverley aerodrome at 12.55hrs. To his chagrin, he crashed getting off and his aircraft, BE2c 2661, was wrecked, although Holme escaped without a scratch.

The two pilots who had followed Robinson, having taken off safely, failed to engage the enemy. Ross patrolled the area between his aerodrome and Hainault Farm for just under two hours but saw no sign of the raiders. On his return to North Weald Bassett he made a forced landing and wrote off his aircraft, clambering out unhurt. Brandon reached a height of 9900ft and after an uneventful 2½-hour flight returned to Hainault.

Engine failure forced Frederick Sowrey to abandon his patrol 13 minutes after leaving Suttons Farm, when at a height of 2500ft the RAF motor cut out and Sowrey was obliged to return to the aerodrome.

Mackay had taken off at 01.08hrs from North Weald Bassett, a minute behind Sowrey, with instructions to patrol from the airfield to the river at Joyce Green, and at 8000ft he headed towards exploding anti-aircraft shells, tell-tale signs that a Zeppelin was abroad. The pilot saw nothing until he turned back for Joyce Green, when while climbing steadily to 10,000ft he observed an airship some way off and held by the searchlights. For 25 minutes he flew in the direction of *SL11* and was less than a mile away when Robinson's bullets found their mark. As the ship was evidently doomed, Mackay abandoned his plans to attack and headed back for Joyce Green, but before long another airship was illuminated just north-east of Hainault Farm. A 15-minute chase was terminated when the Zeppelin sheered off into cloud, and Mackay resumed his patrol for a while longer before finally landing at 04.10hrs.

Hunt, too, was robbed of a share of the kill. This pilot had left the ground at 01.22hrs to patrol the area from Joyce Green to South Farningham, and around 02.10hrs was at

10,000ft, closing rapidly with *SL11*. He was 200yds from the dirigible when it exploded in his face, and in the glare Hunt observed *L16* some 1000ft below. Although momentarily dazzled, he gave chase to the naval ship, but was forced to abandon his attack when Erich Sommerfeldt's Zeppelin vanished from view as the blazing *SL11* tumbled away. After pursuing another airship without being able to overhaul it, Hunt returned to Hainault, landing at 03.44hrs.

The three aircraft of B Flight, 50 HDS, left their airfield at Dover around 23.30hrs. Captain Woodhouse, in BE2c 4588, patrolled for two hours between Dover and the North Foreland, finally reaching a height of 9000ft. He saw nothing of the raiding airships and landed at Manston. Second Lieutenant Fraser patrolled the same area at a height of 6000ft without incident, and returned to the aerodrome having been airborne for just under two hours. Captain John Sowrey in BE2c 2711 met with the same problems as his brother and, forced to break off the patrol due to engine failure, returned to Dover almost immediately.

The dramatic destruction of *SL11* had quite an effect on residents of London and the Home Counties; one of them was 13-year-old Walter Ash:

> I saw the 'Zepp' floating along for some distance, flames shooting out from the middle of the ship, and then pieces of fire kept dropping off. The 'Zepp' kept on course over Potters Bar, gradually losing height until it seemed to suddenly break in half and fall to the ground and out of sight. People were out in the street by then, all excited and wondering where it had fallen.[39]

Twelve-year-old W J Clark nearly missed all the excitement:

> Now the Zeppelin was standing still. All was so very quiet as though all London was praying. Suddenly the Zeppelin changed to a massive flame which turned into a much smaller sausage-like flame rapidly falling head first to earth. I heard no explosion. The next day, the HAC announced that the remains of the Zeppelin would be on show at their training ground in two days time.[40]

A young ten-year-old girl had other impressions, and her mixture of elation and horror was one shared by many others as she stood at her bedroom window with her mother and saw

> ...what had been a beautiful silver cigar passing across the sky a moment before becoming a raging inferno. As it floated downwards in a mass of flames it seemed as though it would fall on top of us here at Hampstead. Everyone rushed out onto the street cheering but I only remember that I wept for the poor men, enemies though they were, who met such a terrible fate.[41]

Twenty miles away, over Tring, Werner Peterson and his crew witnessed the destruction of the Army ship, and the commander of *L32* wasted no time in having his ship turned about and making off eastwards, his remaining bombs being jettisoned over Ware. *L32*'s war diary, retrieved when Peterson's luck ran out a few weeks later, laconically recorded the destruction of *SL11*:

> [I saw] a great fire which shone out with a reddish yellow light and lit up the surroundings within a large radius and then fell to the ground slowly. We could see the conflagration on the ground up to the limit of the range of visibility. The burning object was one of our own airships which had been shot down.[42]

Earlier, at 22.03hrs, *L32* had met unexpected snow squalls over Cromer and thin layers of ice had begun to form on the envelope. The additional weight became so serious that Peterson was forced to compensate by dropping several bombs and trim the ship out.

Over to the south-west, Kurt Frankenberg's *L21* was hovering over Hitchin. This ship never reached London either, owing to freshening winds, and so bombed Norwich instead, *L21* dropping its entire bomb load on Sandringham as a result of being fired upon by alert gunners there. Frankenberg had an eventful and protracted return flight to Nordholz, and with engine and generator failures plaguing the crew most of the way back the ship finally landed at the base, having been in the air for over 21 hours. Manger, in *L14*, dropped most of his ship's bombs on Haughley as he turned back for Germany via Bacton.

Strong headwinds were certainly a problem for many of the raiders that night. *SL8*, commanded by *Kapitänleutnant* Guido Wolff, was turned back by them, its bomb load scattered over Norfolk. *L11* had an eventful night, sustaining slight damage by shrapnel from well-aimed shells. The commander, Schütze, was able to observe other ships over the capital from a distance of 50 miles, and *L11*'s war diary described the death-throes of Schramm's ship as an 'enormous flame over London, slowly sinking below cloud horizon, gradually diminishing'.[43]

The other remaining ships of the fleet also made abortive attempts to reach and bomb the city. In *L30*, von Buttlar only flew as far as Lowestoft although he later claimed to have reached London. His bombs were released over the small village of Bungay and the airship turned back for the coast soon afterwards. Another commander who had lost his bearings was Koch, who believed he had steered *L24* over Norwich and Great Yarmouth. Attracted to the rows of Money flares at Bacton airfield, the Zeppelin's bombs fell harmlessly on nearby Mundesley.

Freezing conditions were responsible for turning back Wilhelm Ganzel in *L23*, and an engine failure resulted in Martin Dietrich aborting his planned attack. Confused by conflicting radio bearings, Dietrich was convinced he had bombed the south bank of the Humber river, but with the hull beginning to ice up *L22* turned back, crossing the coast at 23.20hrs. It was at this point that the Zeppelin was reportedly attacked by a home defence aircraft, with crewmen stationed on *L22*'s upper platform finding their guns jamming with the cold and unable to return the fire. Doubtless they and the rest of the airship's crew were relieved as *L22* took refuge in convenient clouds, thus effectively eluding the British pilot.

L13 was blown north and bombed East Retford, nearly 30 miles from Nottingham, the intended target. Eduard Prölss was attracted by railway lights and the ship's explosives struck a gasholder, causing a great deal of damage from the ensuing blaze.

So ended the largest airship attack ever made on the British Isles during the war and the only time the Navy and Army joined forces. Between them the 16 airships had carried 32 tons of bombs, only 17 tons of which were eventually traced on land. The total weight of bombs which fell within the London area added up to 4559lb, but the resultant damage was negligible. Four civilians were killed and 12 injured, and the damage to property amounted to just over £21,000. The Germans fared much worse by comparison, for not only had they lost a valuable and highly trained airship crew, but the destruction of one airship amounted to a total loss of nearly £93,750. To the crews of the raiding fleet, the most vivid memory they carried back to Germany was that of the blazing *SL11* sinking slowly earthwards and finally vanishing from their horrified gaze.

The remains of Schramm, his crew and his last command eventually came to rest in a shower of sparks at the

Hertfordshire village of Cuffley, striking a beet field in Castle Farm. Just narrowly missed by the falling wreckage was McMullen's Plough Inn and the tiny corrugated church of St Andrew. The remains of *SL11* burned for two hours.

At Rose Cottage, a few hundred yards away, young A J Gogh, his father and the rest of the family had run out towards the railway station, their house lying near to the embankment:

> At first we did not dream it was the 'Zepp' on fire, but some form of fire bomb as it got closer, for it was right above us. We could hear the crackling like burning wood, also a roaring noise as it was falling. We were so terrified we did not know which way to run.
>
> It did not seem very long in coming down, and just as we thought it was coming on us a gust of wind blew it across the fields to where it fell. There were very few houses in Cuffley at that time and within a short space of time, people began to flock out to see it.
>
> My father, who had gone up to see where it had fallen, came back to say he could not get very near because of the heat, and it appeared to be a tangled mass of wire.[44]

The police were the first to arrive on the scene, in the shape of Special Constable Moore from Potters Bar, who was soon joined by Acting Sergeant 770N Jesse White of the Metropolitan Police stationed at Cheshunt, some three miles away. At 03.00hrs White, in the company of Constables Leakey and Green, was amongst the first to discover the pathetic remains of the airship's crew. The sergeant located three burning bodies by one of the huge wooden propellers all pinned down by a mass of wire. The constables commandeered some buckets and water was thrown over the corpses before they were gingerly extricated. The first had his legs burnt away with both arms off to the elbows, and the policemen dragged the awful remains to one side. Of the three bodies, only one was readily identifiable as being that of a human being.

There was a lot of other debris strewn over the wreckage – purses, a few watches, and personal effects, all charred – but hardly a particle of clothing was left on any of the crew. One of the bodies was discovered with a hand still clutching the remains of a control wheel. It was assumed that this would be the airship's commander and the body was laid aside from the rest. Eventually, when all 16 bodies were recovered and brought together, a large tarpaulin was placed over them away from curious eyes – a just precaution, for even before dawn thousands were making their way to 'The Place Where It Fell'.

As for Robinson, he had landed safely at Suttons Farm at 02.45hrs, with little petrol and oil left in his machine's tanks, after a most exciting three and a half hours. L A Aves lived just two miles from the aerodrome, and together with his pals had 'got friendly' with the crew manning one of the most powerful searchlights in the area. Based at Harrow Drive in Hornchurch, the searchlight was subsequently moved to a field behind the aerodrome in case of sabotage. Young Aves witnessed the return of the victorious pilot:

> During a pause we heard an aeroplane engine. Looking up, we could see a solitary moving light approaching. Behind us the aerodrome lights went on and only then did we realise he was one of ours.
>
> Later the story went around that the aircraft landed with only half a pint of petrol left. Undoubtedly a 'tall one', but after a long patrol Lt Robinson had little juice left. Before returning to bed one was conscious of sustained movement, a dull distant noise. Already bicycles, motorbikes, possibly a few cars, were on their way to view the wreckage.[45]

Even before 2693 had rolled to a halt it was immediately surrounded as the station's personnel ran up from every direction and clamoured for details:

> I was greeted with 'Was it you, Robin?', etc, etc. 'Yes, I've strafed the beggar this time', I said, whereupon the whole flight set up a yell and carried me out of my machine to the office – cheering like mad.[46]

It was probably just as well that the exhausted pilot was borne shoulder-high in triumph for, frozen stiff and suffering from cramp, it remains doubtful whether he could have walked from his aircraft unaided. Once in the comparative comfort of the office he yearned for sleep, but a telephone message from Lieutenant-Colonel Holt at Adastral House prevented that. Congratulations from Holt were followed by a demand for a full report on the action. Robinson dutifully scribbled out the whirlwind events of the previous few hours as quickly as he could despite constant interruptions from flight members offering their congratulations. When a reporter entered the hut and asked him what had been the night's most difficult task, Robinson had answered wryly 'To write this bloomin' report'.[47]

Yet write it he did, and when the task was completed Robinson was finally able to collapse on his bed for well-earned slumber. Later in the morning Sowrey shook his friend to disgruntled consciousness and, despite pleading that he be allowed to lie in, Robinson was bundled into a tender with other flight members for the 20-mile drive to Cuffley. By the time the Suttons Farm contingent arrived, the scene was already one of chaos.

'Zepp Sunday'

All that later visitors to Cuffley could see was a huge tangle of wire being rolled up and loaded on to waiting lorries. Burnt pieces of wood and cotton fabric were strewn everywhere, and the four Maybach engines lay smashed in various parts of the field: deeply imbedded into the soft damp earth, each was scorched black, and in the crankcase of one somebody found a jagged hole plugged with cotton waste, which seemed to indicate that there had been time for quick shrapnel repairs before Robinson's fatal rounds had struck.

Even during the very early hours, thousands of curious people were streaming to the quiet Hertfordshire hamlet. The narrow lane bordering the field was soon choked with cars, omnibuses, traps, donkey carts and farm waggons. In the weak morning sun, the northern roads could be seen glimmering with the dimmed headlamps of hundreds of cars and as many bicycles in their wake. All forms of public transport had been besieged by scores of Londoners all determined to make their pilgrimage to the spot.

A violent thunderstorm, a typical English summer diversion, broke during the morning, and before long the field became a quagmire. Visitors may have been dampened but their enthusiasm was not. As trains returned 1000 people to London, another 1000 came out to Cuffley. It was a scene repeated continually for the next few days.

Despite military guards placed around the wreckage, sneak souveniring continued unabated, although the smouldering remains yielded little potential for large relics. Initially the soldiers were tolerant, but they soon became rather impatient with the morbid curiosity of several visitors. When a man attempted to lift up a corner of the tarpaulin covering the crew, he was roughly kicked aside by a disgusted soldier. When one of the more persistent women begged for a remnant of *SL11* she received a less violent rebuke from one long-suffering corporal who, straight-faced, invited her to give him her address so that he could 'send the Zeppelin round'.[48]

Several interesting artifacts were to be found in the

wreckage: a thermos flask, a ceremonial sword, a bible, a revolver, three Iron Crosses, a gold cross, and a clock which had stopped at 03.10hrs. Later the clock and one of the medals were presented to Robinson, whose initial appearance at Cuffley that morning caused much excitement when word got around that he was the one responsible for bringing down the raider. Cheering loudly, the crowd surrounded the embarrassed officer, who was valiantly shielded by his fellows. Scores of smiling people fought for a handshake, whilst others waved scraps of paper clamouring for autographs.

A J Gogh spent an eventful morning 'darting in and out of the wreckage to find bits and pieces' and receiving a 'few coppers from people who wanted souvenirs'. The wreckage was not at all that he had expected, for

> ... unlike other Zepps this one contained what seemed to be wire ribbing [sic] and I found pieces of brackets on wood of what seemed to be alloy.
>
> At the corner of the field stood a little church made of corrugated iron. The bodies, all badly charred, 16 of them, [were] laid on all the doors that could be found. They took our lavatory and shed doors to lay the bodies on until the coffins were ready.[49]

Later on in the afternoon, Robinson returned to Cuffley, but with vivid memories of the earlier hysteria still fresh in his mind wisely donned civilian clothes. Nonetheless many of the people who had cheered him in the morning were still there and had little difficulty in recognising him again. Amongst the admiring throng was 15-year-old Albert Hatt, who managed to sell quite a few relics to eager visitors although not all his scraps of wood and metal originated in Germany! The boy was most impressed by the scene, especially when young girls threw flowers over the embarrassed hero. There seemed to be literally thousands of people there, but Albert managed to get close enough to the 'Zepp Strafer' for a few words: 'See what a mess you've made' he said, and Robinson 'just laughed'.[50]

The scores of visitors who had walked many miles that morning to reach Cuffley found themselves unable to get return trains in the evening. Resignedly they faced a long stride to Barnet, a good seven miles away. But by then many were utterly exhausted, especially young girls who, having donned light clothing for a 'summer afternoon's expedition', had made no allowances for torrential rain.

Cars lay abandoned at the roadside for lack of petrol by drivers who had miscalculated the distance, and there were many heartfelt pleas for cans of fuel. Every available telephone in the district was besieged by desperate individuals phoning for taxis to come out from London and pick them up. Despite such problems, the lunacy went on for days. In just 48 hours 10,000 people came by specially appointed trains that bore the magic word 'Cuffley' on their forward buffers. Indeed, so heavy was the extra rail traffic that King's Cross Station despatched two 'expert ticket collectors' to help out perplexed staff at the tiny Hertfordshire station.

There were further scenes of despair on Monday morning. Wearied travellers dragged their way home, whilst yet more arrived only to find 'The Place Where It Fell' a complete shambles. Only small insignificant fragments from the airship remained, which even so soldiers and police continued to gather. But new visitors received a greater shock. The Plough, the only inn, had its doors finally bolted and barred, with a curt note pinned up which bore the awful news that there was 'nothing to open with'. The landlord, a Mr William, had he only realised sooner, could have made a tidy sum out of extra drink and food, for even before breakfast time the previous day the 'pub' had been completely cleaned out and hundreds were left hammering on the door in vain.

The remains of *SL11*'s crew had been temporarily interred inside St Andrews, which itself had so narrowly escaped fiery destruction, and were a natural target for the inquisitive. Young Dorothy Stead peered through the small keyhole of the chapel door and saw the 16 wooden coffins resting on their makeshift wooden stands. She was shocked by the sight of several policemen 'playing ball' with their helmets over the airship crew and obviously enjoying the game.[51]

At 17.00hrs an inquest was held for the *SL11* crew in the bar parlour of The Plough. Conducting these unprecedented proceedings was the South Hertfordshire coroner, Dr Lovell Drage, who received several testimonies from police and RFC representatives. The first witness was Captain Rene de Sarigny of the First Eastern Rifles, South African (attached RFC), who was a member of 39 HDS and whose statement gave a unique account of events:

There were few recognisable remains after the wreck of SL11 had burnt itself out, only the control car and the engines being left relatively intact. Here, local policemen gather up portions of one of the engine gondolas during the afternoon of 3 September.
Mrs R G Libin

'Zepp Sunday': even by the early hours of 3 September 1916 the long pilgrimage had begun. Literally thousands would make their way to Cuffley, the tiny Hertfordshire village where the blazing ruins of SL11 fell. By rail, car, cycle and foot they came, eager for any wayward scrap of wreckage that might have been overlooked.
By courtesy of C Rust

The Plough, Cuffley, as it was in 1916; behind it fell the blazing wreckage of SL11 on the morning of 3 September. After the war the 'pub' was rebuilt and in 1955 new gardens laid out on its grounds were named after William Leefe Robinson.
Cheshunt Library

The Commanding Officer, three men and myself then came out here [Cuffley] in the Squadron car. It took us about 50 minutes and we arrived about 03.15hrs, September 3. We saw the burning wreckage of a Zeppelin [sic] in a field at the back of the Plough PH. Some police arrived and threw buckets of water on the flames. The commanding officer then went away and left me in charge of the wreckage. When it got sufficiently light, we picked out the bodies of the airmen, there were 16 and we covered them over. There were no identity discs on the bodies and there were no means of identification. There was a Commander's coat with a badge and crown, but there was no name on it. Some personal articles were found among the debris...everything including the bodies was much burnt and charred.[52]

After hearing Sergeant White's statement of his involvement in removing the grisly remains, Dr Drage addressed the court:

You have heard the evidence, gentlemen, that they were Germans employed on the Zeppelin airship. The exact cause of their death it is impossible to ascertain, but there is no reason to doubt that those men lost their lives while on a raiding expedition to this country and further that they lost their lives by being attacked by soldiers using anti-aircraft guns.[53]

Here the foreman of the jury interrupted, suggesting that the airship was probably brought down by an aeroplane. Dr Drage countered by saying that there was no evidence to support this claim. Then Captain Morton spoke up: 'There is no doubt about it – there was an interval of three to four minutes before the Zeppelin came down, when there were no guns fired.' 'Then the gunfire had no effect?' queried Dr Drage. In answer a juryman confirmed Captain Morton's statement, and the coroner, having acquainted himself with those new facts, asked if there were any objections to record that the airship was brought down by an aircraft. There were none, and it was further suggested that the name of the pilot responsible be mentioned. Further discussion between de Sarigny, Morton and Dr Drage centred around the manner in which the final verdict was to be phrased. The coroner pledged that there was little danger of the jury returning a verdict of murder – a remark which caused some amusement. As a result a rather naively worded verdict was finally announced:

16 unknown German airmen were found dead in a wrecked German Zeppelin ship [sic] in a field near Plough Inn, Cuffley.

The Zeppelin was brought down by the fire of a British aeroplane manned by a pilot, Lieutenant Robinson, Royal Flying Corps.

The cause of their death was injuries, the result of the destruction of the Zeppelin, the same 16 Germans at the time of their death were male persons, airmen in the service of the German Government.[54]

Having dealt with the court of enquiry, the next problem was to dispose of the bodies in a proper manner. The War Office instructed GHQ Home Forces that the crew were to be given a military funeral in accordance with the 'international code' and that the RFC were to take charge of the affair. When Dr Drage was informed of these plans he was reported to have said, 'Their burial is no matter for me; I only give the certificate.'[55]

The Superintendent from Enfield's division of the Metropolitan Police anticipated that such a burial would create problems, and stated so:

It is reported that the burial will take place at Cheshunt (6th), but we have no instructions to that effect. It is desirable that [the] police be told of the time and route in order that arrangements be made to control the crowds.[56]

Wednesday 6 September was the day of the funeral, which took place not at Cheshunt but at the Potters Bar cemetery in Mutton Lane. A large communal grave measuring 25ft long and 7ft across was made, with a separate plot reserved. The graves had been dug by two women and a man. Shortly before 14.00hrs, two WD lorries, one towing a trailer, arrived at St Andrews. A few minutes later 20 RFC men entered the church whilst others lined the path from the gate to the lorries. The coffins, made of Japanese Ash, were then borne out, only one of which carried any form of identification. The casket carrying the 'commander' bore a brass plate which read:

An unknown German officer, killed while commanding Zeppelin L21 [sic], 3rd Sept 1916.[57]

This coffin did not travel with the others but was placed separately in a small RFC tender and covered with a black sheet as a mark of respect.

A dozen coffins were placed in one lorry in two stacks of six and the other three loaded on to the trailer. Thus laden, the cortège made its way to the Mutton Lane cemetery. The funeral attracted a great many people to Potters Bar but, understandably, there was little sympathy for the wretched crew of *SL11* and the planned military funeral was not well received by the great majority of civilians. Feelings ran high and the flames of discontent were fanned by another inquest which had been carried out on the same day as that held in The Plough. This inquest took place at Essendon, just a few miles from Cuffley, which had been the unlucky target for Eric Sommerfeldt's *L16*. When that Zeppelin's bombs were falling, two frightened sisters had dashed out of their cottage into the garden and were immediately cut down.

Their father, the village blacksmith, had been first on the scene and found both his daughters with horrifying injuries. Shrapnel had struck 26-year-old Frances Mary Louis Bamford, killing her instantly, and 12-year-old Eleanor Grace had received a dozen wounds on her left side, her leg so severely shattered it had to be amputated. Despite the efforts of the local doctor, the unfortunate youngster succumbed to her injuries the following morning.

The RFC buries the crew of *SL11* on 8 September 1916. The official ceremony caused a mild furore amongst many members of the public: that a military-style funeral was accorded the 'baby killers' seemed blatant hypocrisy. At the cemetery gates a woman even hurled some eggs at the coffins as they were brought in.
Sir Frederick Sowrey

The funeral of the sisters took place on 6 September as the crew of *SL11* were being interred at Potters Bar. The whole population of Essendon turned out to pay its last respects to the innocent victims, and people wept openly as the four-wheeled trailers carried the flower-decked coffins through the entrance of St Mary the Virgin. The service had to be conducted in the western portion of the church, the chancel having been badly damaged by *L16*'s bombs. It was poignant scenes like this which incensed public attitudes, and there were many protests over the military-style funeral for the Germans. Letters pages in newspapers bore witness to many people's bitterness; columnists had a field day. The vicar of Potters Bar, Rev E Preston, had actually been threatened with a riot and received many telegrams and letters from people protesting against the Christian burial of the 'German murderers'.

The funeral cortège arrived at Mutton Lane around 14.50hrs amidst large crowds, but admission to the cemetery was restricted to servicemen and parishioners only. Several men bared their heads as the procession wound slowly past and many women, taking advantage of the clement weather, were wearing light summer dresses. Generally the crowds were silent, few showing any expression of feelings.

Over 300 special constables and officers under Commander Gollin were charged with crowd control, the men being spread throughout the route and especially around Mutton Lane, the south end of the Great North Road and the cemetery entrance, where most onlookers gathered. St John's Ambulance men from Walthamstow were also in attendance and rendered first aid to at least eight people suffering from slight accidents and fainting. After the coffins had been lowered into position, the service commenced. The first was conducted over the separate casket by the officiating Rev M Hancock CF and Rev Preston. The service was an abbreviated version of that usually presented by the Anglican Church and was repeated over the remaining coffins. To close the somewhat incongruous proceedings, buglers of the Grenadier Guards sounded 'The Last Post' at 15.10hrs.

Only at the gates to the cemetery had there been an incident. The spectacle of the black-draped coffins being taken from the lorries by RFC officers was too much for 40-year-old Ellena Farrington. Hurling several stale eggs, one of which struck one of the coffins on the lorry and stained the pall, she was promptly arrested by Police Sergeant 112 Thomas Ogden and on 13 September was brought before the Barnet Petty Sessions:

> Counsel addressing the Bench said the best answer to the charge was the fact that no breach of the peace occurred. The eggs were thrown and the crowd made no attempt to stop the lady. In fact the attitude of the crowds was one of sympathy. Mrs Farrington was the mother of three children. She was herself the victim of two of the Zeppelin raids last year. She was a witness of the two raids and upon one occasion was within 25 yards of where bombs burst. As a result of the raids she lay on a bed of sickness for some days and she was now a permanent sufferer from neuritis and but a wreck of her former self. Her children, before the attacks perfectly healthy, were now bundles of nerves...[58]

The Bench retired to consider their verdict, having heard Mrs Farrington's testimony along with those of her barrister, Mr J D Cassels, and Sergeant Ogden. Returning to the courtroom, the chairman, Sir Samuel Boulton, was of the opinion that a technical offence had been committed and fined Mrs Farrington five shillings whilst sympathising with the woman's feelings.

Following the burial of *SL11*'s crew, protests from various quarters continued to be expressed, and the editorial of *The*

One of many souvenir postcards issued following 'Zepp Sunday' was this somewhat macabre offering. *SL11* remained identified at 'L21' on the memorial at Cuffley until the late 1960s, when a local historian persuaded those concerned to have it corrected.
Author's Collection

'The man behind the gun': perhaps the most popular of all the postcard designs that enjoyed such healthy sales in the late summer months of 1916.
Author's Collection

Zeppelin!

Barnet Press for 9 September was particularly vitriolic:

> So we buried with military honours the baked Huns brought down at Cuffley. Military honours for murderers and a Christian burial service! What hypocrisy. Within seven miles from where we are writing... we have seen a village church and vicarage wrecked by Zeppelin bombs, cottages razed to the ground, amongst the ruins of which was found the body of a poor woman, while a girl, still living but with a leg torn off, was rescued in agony that ended in death. And the authors of such atrocities are given Christian burial and military honours! In such circumstances the Burial Service becomes a travesty and the 'honours' are a reproach.[59]

Such stirring and dramatic tub-thumping could be expected to bring forth strong reactions and almost universal acceptance, yet not everybody agreed with the editor's remarks. Sergeant H Tinsley of the 43rd Company, RDC, responded with a lengthy missive which *The Barnet Press* carried the following week. Tinsley took exception to several points and in particular the reference to hypocrisy, defending the airship crew who were, after all, only obeying orders:

> They were not given full military honours, but it was an English and a Christian act that gave them part, and I fail to see how the 'Christian burial service' can be termed 'hypocrisy'. Had we dug a hole in the field at Cuffley and put them in without coffins or a burial service, how much better should we have been or felt? Would it have stopped future raids, and should we have felt that we had done our duty as English? I think not.[60]

Whilst accepting this critique, the editor remained unmoved, but newspapers were more concerned with the young man responsible for the airship's destruction. Following the Germans' burial, an official despatch was issued by Lord French:

> Our experts hope to be able to reconstruct certain portions of the framework. The large amount of wood employed in the framework is startling and would seem to point to a shortage of aluminium in Germany.
>
> It is hoped that any persons who have picked up fragments of the wrecked airship will report them to General Headquarters, Home Forces, the Horse Guards, Whitehall without delay. If of no value in the reconstruction of the airship they will be returned to their owners. It should be remembered that the retention of such articles constitutes a contravention of the Defence of the Realm Regulations, Section 35B.[61]

Of course the War Office realised *SL11* for what it was. Construction of the German Schütte Lanz dirigibles was hardly a great secret, but to the lay public Lord French's communiqué was the icing on the cake.

Lieutenant-Colonel Holt issued the following summary from Adastral House that accompanied Robinson's own combat report:

> Herewith report by Lieutenant W L Robinson of his attack against the hostile airship this morning; a full 'operations summary' will be forwarded as soon as the other reports have been received.
>
> Six pilots were sent up around London and others in Kent and Yorkshire. There were no casualties to pilots, two machines were wrecked. Operations were interfered with by fog in some districts.
>
> Lieutenant Robinson has done good night work against Zeppelins during previous raids. It is very important that the successful method of attack remains secret, and instructions have therefore been issued that the public are to be told that the attack was made by incendiary bombs from above.[62]

The following day, Major-General W Shaw, on Lord French's behalf, memoed Lieutenant-General Henderson, commander of the Royal Flying Corps:

> The Field Marshal Commanding-in-Chief has seen the attached reports, and will be glad to know if you have any recommendation to make with regard to any reward which you may consider the Officer concerned may be deserving of. He will be glad of an early reply.[63]

Henderson was not slow in replying:

> I recommend Lieut W L Robinson for the Victoria Cross, for the most conspicuous gallantry displayed in this successful attack.[64]

From then on Robinson was to receive nationwide acclaim. Of the 19 airmen to gain the VC during the war, none, with the possible exception of Captain Albert Ball, was to receive as much public adulation.

Reluctant Hero

That an airship had been destroyed at last resulted in almost hysterical relief, which guaranteed the end of anonymity for William Leefe Robinson. He was showered with gifts, congratulatory letters and presentations which poured in from all over the country – indeed, at one stage the volume of mail arriving at Suttons Farm became so great that several officers were detailed to help answer it all.

On 5 September came the official announcement of the Victoria Cross for Robinson's achievement, its promulgation barely 48 hours after the action. It was one of the quickest bestowals in the medal's history, and the newspapers were full of it. Robinson's delicately handsome face smiled out from innumerable postcards, serviettes, matchbox lids, even biscuit tins. Babies, flowers and hats were named after him, poems and prose dedicated to his victory, at least five artists offered to paint his portrait for the Royal Academy, and wherever young Robinson went he was mobbed.

On 9 September a large eager crowd milled around Windsor's railway station. They had been gathering since the small hours awaiting the arrival of the 12.43 train which, it was rumoured, would bring a certain young man to be presented with the VC at the hands of his monarch. No fewer than six royal carriages, drawn by pairs of greys,

The scene outside Windsor Castle following Robinson's investiture with the Victoria Cross on 9 September. It was some time before the modest young airman could be driven off to the comparative peace of a nearby hotel.
Sir Frederick Sowrey

SL11, 3 September 1916

Robinson seated in BE2c 2693 at Suttons Farm. The airmen display the tattered centresection of the upper wing damaged by Robinson's own gun during his attack on *SL11*. Aircraft 2693 carried a natural clear doped finish, with the forward fuselage, part of the starboard lower wing and the wheel discs doped PC10 khaki.
Sir Frederick Sowrey

Robinson is roundly cheered by Suttons Farm personnel, their sentiments expressed many times over by a grateful public. The wooden aircraft hangars are also seen in the background of this picture postcard.
Author's Collection

One for the squadron album. Posing in front of 2693 are Second Lieutenants C C Durston and F Sowrey, Robinson, Captain R S Stammers and Second Lieutenant W J Tempest.
Sir Frederick Sowrey/RAF Museum

Zeppelin!

Durston, Sowrey, Robinson and Stammers pose with 2693; part of the serial number is just visible on the fin. This particular aircraft was built by Ruston, Proctor and Co Ltd of Lincoln.
Sir Frederick Sowrey

were lined up waiting for a number of other military officers due for decoration. The wait was in vain for, when the train finally puffed into the station, of William Leefe Robinson there was no sign. Despite frantic enquiries, the mystery remained unsolved, and eventually a most disappointed reception gave up and thronged out of the station. The six carriages had by this time already arrived at the castle, where King George V received and decorated the officers presented to him.

While all this was taking place Kitty Robinson, having previously arranged to meet her brother, was also at a loss to know his whereabouts. It was not until 15.25hrs that Windsor was finally rewarded with Robinson's arrival at the stationmaster's house behind the wheel of a borrowed car. His own vehicle was left stranded at Runneymede three miles away, having suffered an untimely breakdown.

The castle was quickly telephoned and the delay explained as Robinson 'in a fearful fright', was at last driven to his destination. After a hearty lunch in the state dining room, the airman was finally received by his sovereign. Following the investiture, the King plied Robinson with a variety of questions then went on to discuss general aviation topics, showing off some aerial photographs of the German lines and expressing the opinion that allied airmen 'were infinitely superior to those of the enemy'. After quizzing Robinson about his family the King introduced him to the Queen, Princess Mary and Prince Albert, the Queen in particular expressing more than a little interest in the pilot's attack on 'L21'.

After this ordeal, Robinson had to face another. The waiting crowds outside the castle surrounded the car in which he was a passenger, shouting and yelling their affectionate encouragement and gratitude. Eventually Robinson arrived at the White Hart Hotel, where he was met by his sister and another large crowd which cheered wildly as he was driven up. Such scenes were to be repeated many times and would prove an embarrassment to the modest airman who insisted that he was only doing his job. It was typical of Robinson that before leaving the castle to face the crowds he had carefully hidden the leather-cased bronze cross in the inside pocket of his tunic.

Whilst Robinson's VC award met with universal approval from the civilian population, there is some evidence to suggest that it was not quite so well received by a few fellow RFC officers. Such comments, though rarely voiced, often came through in personal correspondence:

> It is rather amusing to see that old Boelcke is taking to flying again. I should like to shoot him down, though I suppose one isn't much good if you don't get a Zepp down these days. Poor old Robinson must regret having performed at all. His life isn't worth living. All the risk that I can see he took was coming down again, though of course as a feat it was magnificent. I would rather attack one of those gas bags than a couple of fighting Huns any day...[65]

But it wasn't only the VC that Robinson gained as a result

Robinson and Sowrey aboard the Prince Henry Vauxhall that the 'Zepp Strafer' purchased out of the large amount of money he received from several wealthy patriots. The car's fate is not known, but the late Captain R S Stammers believed it was auctioned off to an Essex farmer in later years.
Sir Frederick Sowrey/RAF Museum

106

of his victory; there was also over £4000 in 'prize money', since considerable cash awards had been offered some months previously by several notable and wealthy patriots for the first airman to bring down an airship over England:

> I went up to Newcastle for a day and was entertained by the Lord Mayor who gave a dinner in my honour when I was presented with a cheque for £2000 by Col Cowen of Newcastle. They wanted to make the whole thing a grand public function but HQ wouldn't let them, for which I was very thankful.[66]

Colonel Joseph Cowen, proprietor of the *Newcastle Daily Chronicle* had 'never dispursed money with so much goodwill before', an opinion doubtless shared by his fellow benefactors: £1000 came from Lord Michelham, senior partner of the banking firm of Herbert Stern; £500 was presented by William Bow of Bow, McLachlin and Company, a shipbuilding concern in Paisley; another £500 came from L A Oldfield Esq; and Messrs G Wigley and J Ball parted with £100 apiece. Such awards were frowned upon in official circles, and a regulation was swiftly passed to prevent the recurrence of similar gestures.

The constant attention of well-wishers obliged Robinson to don mufti whenever he was off duty, although this did little to prevent recognition. When dining at the Piccadilly Grill, a London restaurant he had hitherto frequently patronised, he found it uncomfortable to be the centre of attraction and was unable to relax quite as readily as he had done on previous occasions:

> I am recognised wherever I go about Town now, whether in uniform or mufti. The city police salute me, the waiters, hall porters and pages of hotels and restaurants bow and scrape, visitors turn round and stare – oh, it's *too* thick![67]

Trips to music halls and theatres had the same results. Robinson would share the rapturous attention of the audience with the stars of the show. As one of his contemporaries remarked:

> He was every girl's epitome of the chocolate-box hero and so good looking. The whole house rose and cheered when once he entered a box at the Gaiety.[68]

Life was never quite the same at Suttons Farm after the destruction of *SL11*, even before Sowrey and Tempest repeated their flight commander's feat. The little aerodrome was frequently besieged by visitors, some of whom were more welcome than others:

> They had a lot of the actresses down from Town. There was Madge Saunders, and Heather Thatcher, an up and coming young actress; Leslie Henson was always down there; George Grossmith was a frequent visitor. Madge Saunders was at the time married to Leslie Henson and they used to go down a lot but Madge used to 'slip' her husband a few times and go down there on her own![69]

Another visitor to Suttons was singer Alice Delysia, who had 'an absolute passion for Robinson' although he apparently showed scant interest in her or any other of the theatre girls that turned up at the aerodrome. As Stammers' younger sister Vera recalled:

> He wasn't a man who went after women, he did *not* go after these actresses. My brother was the 'rogue' of the place, there wasn't an actress in London he didn't know. Alice Delysia fell very heavily for him and my sister-in-law would be knitting while they went off round the back of the sheds...[70]

On 16 September Robinson was preparing for a night patrol in BE2c 2693 which nearly ended in tragedy. Charles Perfect and a few colleagues were 'waiting to witness the

'Something untoward'. On 16 September 1916, Robinson's night patrol came to an abrupt end when 2693 crashed into a hedge on take-off and immediately burst into flames. The pilot was lucky to escape unscathed.
Sir Frederick Sowrey

The serial number of the wrecked BE2c tends to confirm this aircraft as the machine Robinson flew against Schramm's Schütte Lanz. The tail unit was one of the few recognisable remnants left after the fire.
Sir Frederick Sowrey/RAF Museum

Robinson at Suttons Farm with Captain Robert Sidney Stammers and the latter's fiancée, Muriel. The BE2c behind them has rocket rails mounted on the outer interplane struts.
Mrs R G Libin

Zeppelin!

Sowrey, Robinson and Stammers read through telegrams and letters from admirers. These came through to Suttons Farm thick and fast when the airmen brought down their airships.
Sir Frederick Sowrey/RAF Museum

ascent, but instead, we suddenly saw a bright light in the aerodrome and concluded that something untoward had happened.'71

Robinson's machine had struck a hedge just after leaving the ground, the tail tipped and the BE2c nosed into the ground, bursting into flames. Fortunately the pilot was uninjured and, clambering out of the cockpit, he ran from danger as quickly as possible:

> In the burning machine were a number of explosive darts, and Robinson's warning shouts kept officers and mechanics clear of the danger. In a few minutes the machine went up in one large explosion. All that survived of the aeroplane that destroyed the Cuffley airship was a heap of smouldering wood, wire and fabric.72

One reason why Robinson seemed to avoid the attention of so many female admirers may have been his romance with Mrs Joan Whipple, to whom he announced his engagement shortly after his investiture at Windsor. History has not recorded the exact circumstances, but it seems likely they were introduced via mutual friends living in the Harrow Weald and Stanmore areas of Middlesex.

Joan Uppleby Stapylton-Smith was widowed on 24 November, 1914 when her husband, Captain Herbert Connell Whipple of the Devonshire Regiment, had died of wounds received in France. During 1916 Joan was working in a Surrey post office yet was a frequent visitor to Harrow Weald House where lived her friend Violet Grinling. Both girls had some years previously attended a finishing school at nearby Bentley Priory in Stanmore, and had struck up a friendship with another local girl, Nancie Vera Nicholson, of Tile House, Harrow Weald. Nancie was engaged to Captain Edward Noel Clifton, who was on the strength of 39 Home Defence Squadron, and Violet frequently exchanged correspondence with Sowrey. Her letters frequently offered invitations for the Suttons Farm officers to join the girls for games of tennis, tea parties and trips to London theatres. Clifton and Nancie were subsequently married on Wednesday 8 November, 1916 at St Paul's in Knightsbridge, and the wedding was well attended. RFC officers were there in force. Five days prior to the ceremony the bride-to-be wrote a short note to Sowrey, having secured his services as usher:

> Please be at St Pauls at 1.45 as some of the guests are sure to arrive early and don't forget Bride's people to the left Bridegroom's to the right of the aisle.73

Robinson was 'rested' from active flying for a period, yet his precise movements between the end of 1916 up until March the following year remain something of a mystery. It would be typical of the man that any protracted period of inactivity would be intolerable, and he pestered the War Office for a posting overseas. On 13 October his appointment to Flight Commander, and Temporary Captain whilst so employed, was officially announced, back-dated to 1 September. A few weeks later, Lieutenant (later Captain) Tryggve Gran, 39 HDS official chronicler, visited Suttons Farm with Lieutenant Colonel Holt:74

> ...Before long Col Holt, Robinson and myself were sitting in front of a wonderful fire enjoying a good long drink. The conversation concerned flying, and especially it was the conditions in the north of England which were discussed. The zone of barrage from London to Edinburgh should still more be strengthened and it seemed that Colonel Holt wished

Robinson enjoys an off-duty period and relaxes with a stroll in the gardens of Harrow Weald House in Stanmore. His companions are Violet Grinling and her second brother Geoffrey.
Sir Frederick Sowrey/RAF Museum

A leafy lane in Hornchurch is the backdrop for this informal portrait of Robinson.
D Whetton

This charming 1916 postcard was one of many designs offering humorous aspects of the airship campaign and doing much to raise morale amongst civilians.
Author's Collection

Aircraft 2092 was another Suttons Farm BE2c that Robinson flew but it was not the machine he matched against *SL11* on the morning of 3 September. This aircraft is doped overall in PC10, and the sheet metal cover over the front cockpit is readily apparent. The photograph is doubly interesting as it shows the temporary RE5 canvas hangars at Suttons Farm giving way to permanent wooden structures, one of which can be seen under construction at far right.
Sir Frederick Sowrey/RAF Museum

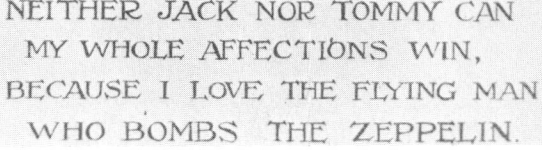

'...Because I love the flying man who bombs the Zeppelin'. Robinson poses with his fiancée Joan Whipple after the announcement of their engagement in 1916. Some time after the war Joan married Colonel J G Brockbank CBE DSO; she died at Muddiford in 1968.
Sir Frederick Sowrey/RAF Museum

Robinson preparing for a flight in a BE2e with a passenger aboard, date and locale not known. Of note are the rearward firing Lewis gun mount at right and, beneath the pilot's cockpit, the camera mounting rails.
Sir Frederick Sowrey/RAF Museum

Robinson to take a command in the north. This idea, however, did not seem to fall in with the young Captain's taste. When the car half an hour later on passed the door with the Colonel, Robinson exclaimed 'He thinks London is too jolly near my station, well I am going to volunteer for France at once.'[75]

Eventually Robinson's wish was granted, and on 9 February 1917 he was posted to Rendcombe in Gloucestershire, there to join the strength of 48 Squadron working up for operations overseas.

Return to France

No 48 Squadron was formed at Netheravon on 15 April, 1916 under Major L Parker, the intention being to equip the unit with the BE12 for service in France; however, these aircraft went instead to 21 Squadron, replacing that unit's RE7s, and thus 48 never took delivery of their machines. The squadron moved to a training brigade at Rendcombe in June 1916, and later became the first to be equipped with the Bristol F2a Fighter. Frank Barnwell's superb creation, the 'Biff', was a powerful and purposeful-looking two-seater biplane which once its potential had been fully realised proved to be one of the finest aircraft of the war, continuing in RAF service well into the 1930s. Its operational début, however, was an embarrassing and tragic disaster.

From the outset there were delays in getting the aircraft to Rendcombe, production problems with the Constantinesco synchronising gear for the forward-firing Vickers gun creating havoc with works schedules. On 16 January Captain J M Bentley of the DADAE sent a brief enquiry to Captain G Drydale of Adastral House in London:

> In view of the fact that the subsequent machines are being delivered to Filton aerodrome minus interrupter gears, and that these machines are required for the equipment of 48 Squadron, can it be said please if any arrangements have been made to fit these machines with interrupter gear, and if not, when machines will be available so fitted.[76]

The reply was not long in coming:

> From now onwards all machines will have the bracket and large gear wheel fitted at Brislington works and the interrupter gear will be fitted by the squadron when they are ready – the machines now at the aerodrome will have the bracket and gear wheel fitted there before going to the squadron.[77]

Problems were also encountered because of an initial shortage of metal workers at the British and Colonial Aeroplane Works, but extra labour helped to alleviate production delays and at last the full complement of Bristols for 48 Squadron was ready for action. The unit flew out to France on 18 March 1917 to take up quarters at Bertangles, and four days later Major General Hugh Trenchard, commanding the RFC in the field, sent a memo to the War Office:

> I would like to point out that No 48 Squadron arrived out here with 18 machines intact all on the same day before noon.
> This is the first Squadron to arrive out here like this and it was undoubtedly due to the excellent arrangements made and to the training of the squadron.[78]

The squadron moved to La Bellevue in April as the pilots and observers 'worked up' on their aircraft, only to encounter serious problems with the newly issued Lewis and Vickers guns. A pilot who joined the unit in 1918 recalled the situation:

> One of the early problems that was put to Leefe Robinson was the trouble the crews were having with the guns jamming up at height through, it was thought, the freezing up of the [lubricating] oil.
> The story we were told six or nine months later was that when the Gunnery Officer consulted Leefe Robinson as to what should be done, he replied that 'If the guns are freezing up through the freezing of the oil, stop oiling the guns and therefore there will be nothing to freeze'.[79]

Flight Commander Robinson's orders were carried out, and on 5 April he led a flight of six Bristols for the squadron's first operational sortie over enemy lines.

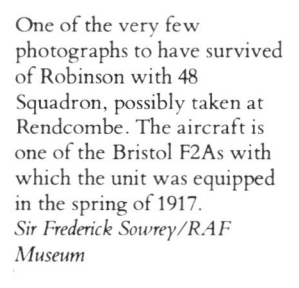

One of the very few photographs to have survived of Robinson with 48 Squadron, possibly taken at Rendcombe. The aircraft is one of the Bristol F2As with which the unit was equipped in the spring of 1917.
Sir Frederick Sowrey/RAF Museum

Sergeant Sebastian Festner of *Jagdstaffel 11* and his Albatros DIII. It was Festner who shot down Robinson and Warburton on 5 April 1917, condemning them to imprisonment for the war's duration.
D Whetton

Robinson's aircraft was A3337 and his observer for the offensive patrol was Lieutenant Edward Darien Warburton. Skilled pilot that he was, Robinson had had no practical experience of flying over the Western Front since the early part of 1916. The first few months of 1917 were vastly different, for the German *Jagdstaffeln*, with their speedy twin-gun Albatros fighters, were taking a heavy toll of British reconnaissance machines; fighter tactics were being evolved at a heavy price.

Allan Machin Wilkinson had seen plenty of active service during 1915 and 1916 when flying DH2s with 24 Squadron, and was a flight commander with 48 Squadron in 1917. He confirmed that Robinson was advised not to take the flight over at the low altitude of 4000ft:

> Robinson favoured the tight formation as he felt it gave a better chance for overall protection for other members of the flight. This method might have been successful if Robinson had been flying the FE2b and if they had not the misfortune to meet the aircraft of *Jagdstaffel* 11. Once Robinson's flight had been broken up, unless the Bristol had been used in an offensive role, which it wasn't, it could only be a matter of time before the experience of the German pilots overcame the group.
>
> Robinson did not appreciate the fact that the Bristol could be used as an offensive weapon by the pilot, and that it was not necessary to provide one another with protection. We were not bothered about Robinson's VC, only that he seemed to dislike any opinion other than his own in matters [of] which, I might say, he had no experience.

The five-strong *Kette* of Albatros DIII fighters led by *Leutnant* Manfred Freiherr von Richthofen tore into the British aircraft as they were beginning to turn back, having completed their patrol over Douai. In the resultant mêlée, which lasted barely ten minutes, four of the Bristols had been brought down and, of the pair that escaped, one was severely damaged. The British crews stood little chance against their more experienced opponents and were further hampered by their troublesome armament. Almost immediately the guns ceased to function, but not due to freezing this time: with the lack of lubrication they simply seized up. The result was inevitable, and the airmen of 48 succumbed without firing a shot.

It was von Richthofen who accounted for two of the Bristols. His first victim was A3340, which was the rearmost machine in the formation, and after being raked with accurate bursts from the attacking Albatros, Second Lieutenant Arthur Norman Leckler managed to make a forced landing behind the lines at Lembras. In the process both Leckler and his observer, Second Lieutenant H D K George, were badly injured, yet the pilot managed to set fire to the Bristol with his Very pistol. George later died of his wounds at the Douai POW hospital.

Overtaking the remaining aircraft, von Richthofen took a little longer to despatch A3343, which, having also crashed behind the lines, was set alight by its crew, Lieutenant A T Adams and a wounded Lieutenant D J Stewart. Within minutes they were captured by German soldiers, and later von Richthofen summarily dismissed the new Bristols:

> After the attack, which was similar to a cavalry charge, the enemy squadron lay demolished on the ground. Not a single one of us was even wounded. The opposition went down on our side of the lines.[81]

Robinson was attacked by *Vizefeldwebel* Sebastian Festner flying Albatros DIII 2023/16. A3337 was brought down near Mericourt with its Rolls-Royce Falcon engine shot out of action by the German pilot. It was Festner's fourth accredited victory. The remaining Bristol (A3320) was shot down by *Leutnant* George Simon, and both Lieutenant H A Cooper and Second Lieutenant A Boldison were captured.

First reports of the action gave the impression that Robinson had been killed, but a letter to Joan Whipple written later that day confirmed that he was safe and had been captured along with other surviving members of his flight. They had been taken to Karlsruhe, there to await transfer to a prisoner-of-war camp. From then until the end of the war Robinson suffered imprisonment in a succession of camps, the first being at Freiburg-in-Breisgau.

In Durance Vile

Whatever state Robinson's spirits were in after his capture, they were tragically lowered on 20 July when a letter from Joan broke the news that his sister Grace had died in London of malaria. Robinson wrote to his parents:

> I can't tell you what a terrible shock it was – we understood each other so well, I might have done so much more for her. I might have been a far more dutiful brother. And what gives me such pain is thinking you dear ones will have to hear this so many miles from most of your children. How I wish I was with you and that I could try and bring you some comfort in my own poor way... Joan comes first in one way, you two darlings come first in another. I firmly believe that sorrow does not come into our lives and go without leaving some good behind, this extra bond of love and sympathy may not be the only good this intense sorrow has left.
>
> After Arthur's death last year the dear girl was never quite happy – but pray God she has perfect happiness now and for that let us all be glad to sacrifice our own feelings...
>
> I am wonderfully well here at present and we have a very good time on the whole. We have formed a debating society and have arranged for debates to be held every Tuesday evening. We went to the swimming baths as usual yesterday morning and for a glorious walk afterwards. After climbing a hill we had a lovely view of Freiburg and the surrounding

country, which is very beautiful about these parts. I must close now darlings – you know you have the deepest sympathy from your ever loving son.[82]

Almost from the moment he arrived at Freiburg, Robinson was determined to escape. During August, together with three companions, he made an attempt via a tunnel laboriously dug under the walls; the plan came to nothing. Later Robinson teamed up with Second Lieutenant Arthur A Baerlin of 16 Squadron.[83] The two officers had been planning an escape for days and were on standby each night awaiting their chance. Somehow the German guards uncovered the plot and both Robinson and Baerlin were sentenced to be court-martialled for attempting to bribe the sergeant of the guard. It later transpired that Flipsen, a camp interpreter of Swiss-German extraction, had arranged to smuggle the two airmen out of camp with the aid of more experienced escapees and for such services was to be paid a considerable amount of money. When Robinson and Baerlin were arrested the situation did little to aid other officers' attempts to get away.

Nevertheless on 14 September a group of officers, Robinson among them, made an abortive attempt. The following night another was made, this time in the company of several other officers, and their plans were laid carefully. A small courtyard used by sentries could be entered through a door in a corridor directly opposite the commandant's office, the path from the door leading to another in the outer wall and separated from the rest of the yard by a barbed wire fence. Robinson's scheme was simple enough and involved the picking of the two door locks, thereby gaining access to the street beyond. It was of course impossible to cross between the doors unseen by the German guards and so Robinson had arranged that his orderly hang washing on the barbed wire fence. Since the officers' orderlies had ready access daily to the yard, it was easy on the week prior to the escape for the amount of washing to be increased until an effective screen resulted. Robinson's orderly, a one-time locksmith, had agreed to pick the two locks but at the first attempt his nerves failed him. However, after much cajoling, he reluctantly agreed to try again the next night.

After roll call on 15 September the would-be escapers took their belongings into Robinson's room and at 21.30hrs donned civilian attire, converted clothes from orderlies' uniforms. Eventually Robinson, with three companions and Second Lieutenants Hamilton E Hervey and Robert R Macintosh, were fully prepared, but at the last moment Robinson's orderly let them down again.[84] The airmen pleaded without success until Macintosh volunteered to accompany the man while he picked the locks, and at last he conceded to persuasion:

> After about half an hour 'Mac' returned fuming. Our orderly had successfully picked the lock of the passage door, but had absolutely refused to set foot outside it, and, to save further argument had decamped to his own quarters. In spite of our disappointment, we could not but realise his position. If successful he had little enough to gain, whereas discovery would probably led to a spell in the dreaded salt mines, a far worse punishment than would fall to our lot. There was nothing for it but to give up all idea of getting away that night, so once more we concealed our kit and went to bed, cursing our luck.[85]

The airmen were not slow to seize another chance, and next morning Hervey and Macintosh, watching a German work party in the camp's woodhouse, hit upon the ideal scheme. If they could get into the shed using the firewood as a screen, a hole could be dug through the wall and access

In captivity: Robinson poses with an unidentified officer in this official photograph taken by Oskar Brauer of Frankfurt. Robinson made several escape attempts during his imprisonment, all ending in recapture. At Holzminden he was allegedly persecuted by the camp's commandant, Karl Niemeyer.
Mrs R G Libin

gained to a known staircase that led to an attic from which windows of two wings would afford an exit. Alternatively an entrance into the camp church could be made and from there it would be easy to force open a window and the airmen gain freedom that way. Within two days the plan was put into operation, and despite minor setbacks and several nail-biting situations the group gained access to the church and at last managed to escape from a small window via a series of carefully planned moves. Finally sliding down a rope, the airmen stole away in stockinged feet under the noses of the guards and off into the night. Later, in company

The last known photograph ever taken of Captain William Leefe Robinson, some time after his repatriation in December 1918. Victim of influenza, Robinson died at the Clifton's house in Stanmore on 31 December.
Mrs R G Libin

with Second Lieutenant C M Reece[86] of 43 Squadron, Robinson and Baerlin passed through a small town during their second night of freedom and it was there that they noticed two posters announcing the breakout and giving full descriptions of the escapees. Later the trio came across an imposing hotel on the shores of a large lake. Tired and ravenous, they hid in the shadow of the dining-room windows and enviously watched the festivities taking place inside. They eventually arrived within four miles of their objective, Stuhlingen, before an alert sentry challenged and recaptured them. On their return to Freiburg they were able to confirm just how heavily guarded that particular section of the border had been.

Eventually all the escapers were caught and Hervey, whilst at Lorach awaiting to be transported back to Freiburg, noted with some amusement how, even in Germany, the name of Robinson was well known:

> Before being taken to our new quarters, we obtained permission to have a shave, haircut and general clean up. Accordingly, escorted by our guard, we repaired to the local barber's shop.
>
> The barber seemed very much interested in our adventures, and in the course of conversation asked which one of us was Robinson. This question gave us the first definite information that the latter had succeeded us out of the camp, and 'Mac', for a joke, claimed ownership of the name.
>
> It was amusing to note the rapidity with which this false news was spread around, and every now and then a head bobbed round the saloon door to gaze with awe at the famous 'Zeppelin Strafer'. During my term of captivity, I did a fair amount of travelling about Germany with Robinson, and learnt that his name was as familiar to the German people as it was to those of his own country; wherever we went, the news of his coming preceded him, and, although he was regarded with awe rather than with anger, his fame was often most inconvenient. He was considered a desperate character and guarded accordingly.[87]

On 5 October 1917 the court-martial of Baerlin and Robinson took place at Freiburg. The court consisted of *Oberst Leutnant* Rummel, *Kriegsgerichtsrat* Dr Walter, Dr Simons, von Bothmer and *Hauptmann* Luppe. Witnesses included *Unteroffiziere* Hackenjors, Kuntze, Hagen and Finter, in addition to British orderlies Coulter and MacGregor. The airmen's defence was conducted by *Rechtsanwalt* Dr Metzger, and a soldier acted as interpreter. Hackenjors was the principle witness:

> He was on duty at the *Offizier-Gefangenenlager* at Freiburg and had in his possession the keys of several doors, including that of the main door. One morning at the beginning of August, Lieutenant Baerlin said to him with a smile: 'For £200 you will give me the key', and Captain Robinson said in the same manner 'I will give you 6000 marks.' Hackenjors took this for a joke, but on August 12 he discovered a hole in the wall between the room in which all kinds of sports material was stored and the sacristy of the church. As Hackenjors was of the opinion that Baerlin had the key of this room, as he had once given him this key, he came to the conclusion that it was no longer a joke, but that Baerlin really did mean to attempt to escape. He therefore reported the matter immediately to the commandant, informing him at the same time of Captain Robinson's remark. On September 22, these two officers with four others made an attempt to escape, and succeeded in reaching the Swiss frontier where they were captured.[88]

Naturally enough both RFC officers denied the charges, and Dr Metzger defended them as vigorously as he could. First he submitted that there was no absolute proof of a bribe, and he proposed that Hackenjors might have misunderstood what was said to him:

> Secondly he pointed out that if the accused seriously contemplated bribery, they would have done this in a much cleverer manner, especially taking into consideration the fact that Baerlin is an avocate by profession. Thirdly he argued that the accused would not have been satisfied with just one attempt to bribe the *Unteroffizier* but would have made other attempts, but as they had not done so, he could scarcely believe that they had ever made the offer with which they were charged. Fourthly he contended that the key would not have been of any use to them, as they could not in an attempt to escape leave the building by the main door because this led them directly into the arms of the main guard. In conclusion he respectfully begged to disagree with the statement that there were no mitigating circumstances which could be taken into consideration, inasmuch as he could well understand British officers in prison in Germany making an attempt to regain their freedom.[89]

The court then adjourned, yet the verdict had probably been decided even before the proceedings began, and Baerlin and Robinson received three and one month's imprisonment respectively. In the latter's case it was solitary confinement in the dreaded fortress at Zorndorf, which to the casual onlooker was nothing more than a large, grass-covered mound, the summit of which rose a few feet above ground level. Flickering arc lamps shone down upon

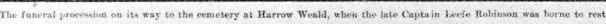

How the *Daily Mirror* recorded the passing of 'London's Zeppelin VC'. Among the pallbearers that shouldered the flag-draped coffin were Majors Sowrey and Clifton, two of Robinson's closest friends. Sowrey was 'very cut up' over his friend's untimely death.
Daily Mirror

Zeppelin!

Scores of these memorial cards and others were distributed amongst the many mourners that attended the funeral on 1 January 1919 at Harrow Weald. Even in death the souvenir trade followed Robinson VC.
Author's Collection

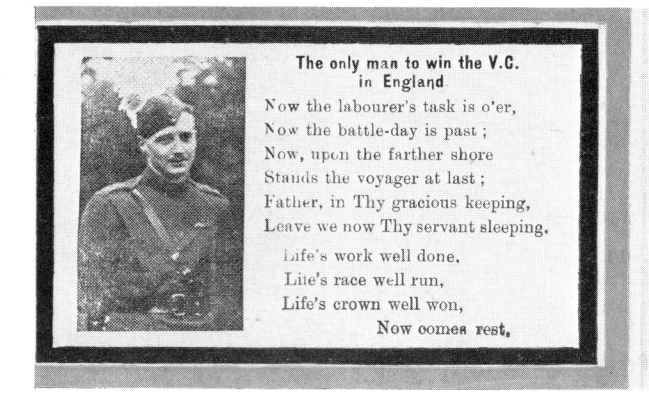

The only man to win the V.C. in England

Now the labourer's task is o'er,
Now the battle-day is past;
Now, upon the farther shore
Stands the voyager at last;
Father, in Thy gracious keeping,
Leave we now Thy servant sleeping.

Life's work well done,
Life's race well run,
Life's crown well won,
Now comes rest.

In Sacred Memory of Capt. Leefe ROBINSON, V.C.
the first Airman who brought down a Zeppelin at Cuffley in Sept. 1916.
who died on Tuesday December 31st, 1918.
at Stanmore, Near Harrow.
He was a prisoner in Germany and returned Dec. 14.
May his soul rest in peace.
Interred Friday Jan. 3rd, at 2.30 at Wealdstone Cemetery Near Harrow

the 'roof' of this fortress and 'starkly silhouetted the sentries against the skyline'.

On 2 May Robinson and several companions were on the move again, this time to Clausthal's POW camp in the Harz mountains. On the train speeding them to their destination, another escape attempt was put into operation. It was decided that Macintosh and Robinson would jump the train. The two officers sat in one corner next to the carriage door with an armed sentry next to them. Opposite, another guarded Hervey who, according to plan, would ask this guard to escort him to the lavatory.

The prisoners had been playing cards on a suitcase, and this was to be left on the floor between Macintosh and his sentry. Once Hervey and his guard had left, it was hoped that surprise and the suitcase to impede the guard's progress would be sufficient for one or both officers to open the door and jump clear. The plan was put into execution just after the train was pulling out of a wayside station. Hervey and his unsuspecting guard were halfway down the corridor when they heard a door slam and the shouts of the sentry. On their return to the compartment Hervey saw the sorry spectacle of a dejected Robinson at the business end of a carbine; of 'Mac' there was no sign. They had both nearly got away with it, for the sentry had indeed tripped over the case, but he had recovered himself in time to prevent Robinson from reaching the opposite door. The train was halted and a lengthy search ensued, but Macintosh had got clean away in the darkness.

Once at Clausthal Robinson found himself under the jurisdiction of camp commandant Heinrich Niemeyer, one of twin brothers whose harsh treatment of allied POWs under their charge became notorious. In July Robinson was transferred to Holzminden by Niemeyer, who handed him over to brother Karl. The Clausthal camp officer had taken a dislike to the British pilot the instant he arrived and was quick to be rid of him.

Captain W S Stephenson of 73 Squadron was at Holzminden in 1918 and planned an escape with Robinson.[90] They were subsequently recaptured, and not for the first time each was thrown into solitary confinement; for Robinson, an apparent sufferer of claustrophobia, such punishment can best be imagined. Although the treatment meted out to Robinson by Karl Niemeyer has often been exaggerated, there is little doubt that the camp commandant made life for the airman as uncomfortable as possible. The mail that came in via the Red Cross must have been a welcome distraction:

> Our thoughts are constantly with you and we would appreciate real news from yourself. Trusting you are keeping well and fit. It was so strange, we thought we heard your voice calling three times outside the diningroom window to Mr Weightman. The next day we heard you were not in England...
>
> Won't it be lovely when the war's over? All our loved ones home again. Captain Sowrey wrote to us this week – he still adores and loves you. His letters are full of 'dear Robin'. If you were here you should have junket and bananas this hot weather. Major Tempest called on Thursday and is coming this week to see Mr Weightman. I tease him about 'Tootsie' and Scotch magnetos. Do you remember those little times? The garden is looking lovely and the roses perfect...Mrs Crook often asks of you, also a number of friends in Hornchurch.
>
> Our dear old Bruce died and we buried him in the hayfield. He was a faithful creature! The cat is still here! You remember her. At least Sowrey does! Didn't he lead her a life!
>
> Did I tell you in my last letter, poor Brown was killed in an accident near the Grey Towers. He was made corporal of the mess and was a most faithful and devoted servant to you...[91]

Robinson's fellow prisoners became incensed at the harsh treatment he received, as inmate Ronald Adam of 73 Squadron could attest:

> The Boche harried and badgered and bullied him in every way possible. He wasn't in any way *physically* ill-treated but they were always having special roll calls for him, waking him up at night to see if he was still there etc. All this must have bothered him a great deal.[92]

The British adjutant at Holzminden was H G Durnford of the RFA, and he provided further evidence of Robinson's persecution. Officers suspected of being involved in escape preparations were not kindly looked upon and soon found themselves bundled unceremoniously into the ground floor cells of 'A' *Kaserne*:

At 15.30hrs on 9 June 1921 a memorial to Captain William Leefe Robinson VC was unveiled at Cuffley close to the spot where *SL11* fell to earth. The monument was erected following the raising of subscriptions by *Daily Express* readers, the site being presented by Mrs J M S Kidston of nearby Nyn Park, Northaw. The unveiling was undertaken by the Secretary of State for Air, the Right Honourable F E Guest CBE DSO MP, and the dedication made by the RAF's Chaplain-in-Chief, the Rev H D L Viener CBE MA.
Mrs R G Libin

114

[The] flies and staleness of the atmosphere were correspondingly oppressive... These particular rooms used to be visited two or three times in a night by a *Feldwebel* with an electric torch, which he used to flash on the occupant of each bed in turn, thereby effectively waking everybody up.

Here I myself lay... and here also lay Leefe Robinson VC whose gallant spirit Niemeyer with subtle cruelty had endeavoured for months past to break... The handling to which Leefe Robinson was subjected was so outrageous that it was communicated to the home authorities in a concealed report (in the hollow of a tennis racket handle) via an exchange party. Robinson had come from Freiburg in Baden where he had made an attempt with several others to escape. 'The English Richthofen' – as Niemeyer with coarse urbanity called him to his face – was at once singled out as the victim of a malevolent scheme of repression. He was placed in the most uncomfortable room in the camp, whereas his rank entitled him to the privilege of a small room; he was caused to answer to a special *appel* two or three times a day; and he was forbidden under any pretext to enter *Kaserne* B.

On the occasion of a visit from some inspecting General, and on the pretext of all the rooms having to be cleaned up and ready for inspection by 9 o'clock *appel*, Robinson's room was entered by a *Feldwebel* and sentries at 7.45 and Robinson himself was forcibly pulled out of bed and the table next to the bed upset on the floor. Two hours later, Niemeyer was introducing 'the English Richthofen' to the august visitor with a profusion of deaginous compliments, and four hours later Robinson was in the cells for having disobeyed camp orders.[93]

Not surprisingly, such experiences had their effect on Robinson, and when the Armistice was declared in November 1918 he was not in the best of health. For a few days prior to boarding the boat back to England he stayed in Denmark. During the war that country was not the industrial one it is today and in those agricultural days suffered no lack of food, unlike Germany. Danish citizens learned that Allied officers had a tough time in the POW camps, and were asked by the Red Cross to contribute gift parcels. One citizen, a notable prewar pilot, specified that the recipient of his parcels should be an airman. In due course he received a letter of gratitude from Robinson, and when the airman was repatriated via Denmark he received an invitation from his benefactor. The 'committee in charge of arrangements' would not permit this, and Robinson was booked into the Terminus Hotel opposite Copenhagen's main railway station. Nevertheless his Danish friend stood him a dinner:

> He was not much for wet wares, but enjoyed the rich Danish food and particularly succumbed to whipped cream. I told him that I did not begrudge him any amount he could enjoy and stand. However I warned him that he had better go a bit easy after the lean diet that his stomach had to endure for so long.
>
> It was a very sick Leefe Robinson and a sad sight I met when calling for him the next morning to take him for the sights of the town. He was in bed and groaning, his head swollen, and his skin very red. I quickly called a doctor and for the rest of his four day stay in Copenhagen, poor Leefe was permitted to consume nothing but water wherein potatoes had been boiled.[94]

'Now Comes Rest'

Robinson arrived at Leith on 14 December with two months' leave at his disposal. He spent his last Christmas with the Cliftons at their Lavender Cottage in Gordon Avenue, Harrow Weald. At least two independent eye-witnesses can remember his return, recalling that his back was bent over and that he needed a walking stick to aid him.

Robinson's future was unsure as far as he was concerned, for Harold's death had put paid to their cherished plans of a tea plantation in India. Fate cruelly had the answer for it was not long after arriving at Harrow Weald that Robinson contracted influenza and was confined to bed. A deadly pandemic swept the entire globe at that time, nature providing her own postscript to the wholesale slaughter of millions. In England alone over 150,000 died, among them Robinson who, his health having rapidly deteriorated, finally succumbed on 31 December. Joan and the Cliftons were at the bedside as he died.

The local coroner, W S Darby, recorded a verdict of cardiac failure brought on by influenza as the cause of death, and soon afterwards both Joan and Baroness Heyking[95] prevailed upon the British Government to arrest Niemeyer whom they held personally responsible for the tragedy. They wanted the camp officer brought to trial and were not slow in publicly voicing their accusations:

> During the delirium which preceded his last moments, Captain Robinson was haunted by the vision of the arch-brute. He imagined that Niemeyer and sentries with fixed bayonets were standing by his deathbed. Several times he called out to be protected from the fiend.[96]

Joan, in an interview with a newspaper reporter, was convinced that the British public would share her fury at the way her fiancé had been treated:

> The attack of virulent influenza was not the real cause of his death. He was murdered by Niemeyer who employed every instrument of cruelty against him...
>
> As another instance of cruelty, [Robinson] was placed in solitary confinement with no light, fuel or even as much as a cigarette. Sentries dogged his footsteps. They jeered and scoffed at him. They outraged him in every possible fashion.[97]

Kitty was equally bitter. Following his return to England her brother made no mention of his treatment in Holzminden; apparently the whole story came out in his

The memorial as it stands today. Only comparatively recently was the erroneous reference to 'L21' corrected. *Author*

delirium. Kitty claimed it was the periods of solitary confinement that killed him, guards had stolen his parole [sic] and cigarettes, and in three months Robinson had received only two parcels. But it wasn't merely the airman's relatives who sought revenge. At least one former prisoner remained in Europe after the war in the hope of finding the Niemeyer twins but they simply vanished. Some reports would indicate that Karl had committed suicide, but even to this day the fate of the despised brothers remains something of a mystery.[98]

Robinson's funeral took place during the afternoon of Friday 3 January 1919 at Harrow Weald. It was a full military affair and attracted many hundreds of mourners. There had been suggestions that the late airman should be interred at Cuffley, but under pressure from his many friends in the area Harrow Weald was considered more appropriate.

The routes from Wealdstone and Stanmore were thronged by a continuous stream of people, and the narrow lanes leading by Brockhurst Corner to All Saints Church were packed a dozen deep on both sides. Proceedings were delayed for some time after the appointed hour, as in the distance could be heard the drone of powerful aero engines. A sea of faces turned skywards as a flight of aircraft came into view led by Brigadier Higgins. Almost simultaneously with their arrival was another sound even closer to hand. The muffled peal of bells rang out from the church tower as the biplanes soared overhead. One detached itself from the formation and circled Lavender Cottage. Flying low over Gordon Avenue, the pilot dropped a giant wreath of laurels which with remarkable accuracy fell in front of the house. It was picked up by one of the mourners, who placed it reverently on the coffin inside.

Strains of a Funeral March were then heard, for the crowds the wait was over, and before long the cortège came into view. Leading the procession was local policeman, Sergeant Albert Sands, clearing crowds from the path, while 50yds behind walked the Central Band of the RAF. Following in their wake was a motor lorry towing an Air Force trailer bearing the coffin; draped with the Union Flag and a profusion of flowers, it was an impressive sight. The late captain's fellow-officers walked on either side, and then came contingents of RAF men from Hounslow and Northolt.

As the sombre procession neared the church to the sounds of Chopin's *Marche Funèbre* it was met by the local choir and vicar, Rev H van Cooten, and Chaplain to the RAF, Rev Basil Phillips. The coffin was shouldered by Majors Frederick Sowrey and Clifton and Captains Wilkens, Hamming, Selwyn and Evans into the church for the service which was conducted by the RAF Chaplain. Following this, six bell ringers chimed out 720 'Grandsire Doubles' fully muffled as the coffin was borne to the tiny Harrow Weald cemetery. The grave had been dug in the furthest corner, the nearest point to 'where he had spent many happy hours' and after prayers in which hundreds joined members of the family and RAF personnel, Sergeant Major Murrell, chief RAF trumpeter, sounded 'The Last Post' to close the ceremony.

The number of wreaths placed around the headstone was breathtaking; indeed, there were so many that a separate carriage was required to bring them to the cemetery. Kitty's contribution was a large cross of lilies, azaleas and violets; equally impressive floral tributes came from the Cliftons, the Grinlings and St Bees, Robinson's old school. Around the grave a stone border was later positioned on which a mason had inscribed a poignant epitaph:

> He was the first airman to attack a Zeppelin at night. After a most daring single-handed fight he brought down L21 [sic] a flaming wreck on the 3rd of September 1916. Thus he led the way against the German Zeppelin peril threatening England.[99]

But to the mourners at Harrow Weald on the first January day of peace for five years, the most impressive tribute of all was the enormous cross of orchids that had lain upon the flag-draped coffin throughout the ceremony. Taking premier position on the grave, the cross, almost 4ft in height, dwarfed most of the other floral contributions, and attached to its centre was a small white card. It bore only a single word: 'Joan'.

The grave at Harrow Weald upon which flowers are regularly placed by staff of the Leefe Robinson restaurant situated on the opposite side of the Uxbridge Road which flanks the tiny cemetery. Every Armistice Day St Bees School sends a wreath. *Author*

CHAPTER 8

L32/L33 ('The Great Double Event'), 24 September 1916

'... According to a South Essex correspondent the only casualty caused by 35 bombs was one rabbit which the village policeman has arrested as a trophy...'

Daily Sketch, 25 September 1916

Barely 20 days had passed after 'Zepp Sunday' before Strasser despatched 12 airships to 'Attack in the south, if possible with cloud cover, London. Middle permitted if wind veers to the right.'[1] Eight older airships, L13, L14, L16, L17, L21, L22, L23 and L24, made their approach to England via the North Sea, only to meet freshening southwest winds and virtually no cloud. Consequently they raided the Midlands as instructed, with varying degrees of success. The rest of the force included four of the new 'Thirties', the so-called 'Super Zeppelins', each commanded by one of the Navy's most distinguished and experienced officers: von Buttlar in L30, Mathy in L31, Peterson in L32 and Böcker in L33. As senior officer of the group, Mathy led this part of the force via Belgium in order to make an approach windward of London.

Of all the ships over the Midlands, L17 penetrated the furthest and was responsible for a fair amount of damage and 20 civilian casualties, three being fatalities. At 00.10hrs somewhere above the outskirts of Lincoln, this ship's commander, *Kapitänleutnant* Herman Kraushaar, was looking southwards. From his vantage point in the control car he observed a bright light in the distance. Even as he watched, the light expanded momentarily, contracted, then sank slowly to earth, finally being lost from view, swallowed up in the low ground mist...

The Germans Deliver an Airship

Saturday 23 September had dawned dull and cold to begin like any other autumn day in wartime London, and in the days following the destruction of SL11 citizens went about their daily business in a new mood. The gnawing apprehension that had been felt in preceding weeks was already beginning to diminish, replaced instead by a feeling of anticipation. As afternoon turned into evening, the theatres and cinemas, the ale houses and the clubs were beginning to fill, but the handful of Admiralty codebreakers in Whitehall's Room 40 were engaged in more serious pursuits.[2]

Rear-Admiral Hall and his élite staff, important cogs in a well-oiled machine, had become more than adept at decoding Zeppelin radio call-signs. The *Handelsschiffsverkehrsbuch* and *Magdeburg* signal code books proved invaluable assets to the Intelligence cryptographers, but in August 1916, when the Germans replaced *Magdeburg*, the British were severely handicapped. Nevertheless, on this particular evening, certain carefully worded radio messages had been received, messages which to the experienced staff of Room 40 were unmistakable: Zeppelins had left their bases in Germany. Once the reports were confirmed, GHQ Home Forces lost little time in secretly alerting the searchlight and gun divisions as well as the home defence airfields scattered around the outskirts of the city.

Von Buttlar in L30 claimed to have been the first to attack the capital, approaching via the south bank of the Thames and dropping bombs on east London at 21.35hrs. The commander proceeded no further but steered a return course, dumping the rest of his bombs on what he believed to be Gravesend. British records do not substantiate von Buttlar's report, and confusion still exists as to the exact whereabouts of L30 during the raid.

It was Böcker who was actually the first to reach London, in the newly commissioned L33. Arriving via the North Foreland out from the Belgian coast, he eventually located the Thames Estuary and steered a course along its length. Gunners aboard British destroyers stationed in the Edinburgh Deep were alerted by the drone of Maybach engines and opened fire on L33 at 21.12hrs. Land-based guns soon took up the challenge, and before long a considerable barrage surrounded the airship. Despite this vigorous reception, Böcker resolutely held his course, and 28 minutes later crossed over the River Crouch and thence towards the city.

The approach of L33 was an unpleasant surprise for the inner ground defences, and Böcker heralded his arrival by dropping a brace of parachute flares, one over the southern part of Brentwood at 22.35hrs and the other over Chadwell Heath 20 minutes later. This second flare caused something of a furore among the local searchlight crew, who were uncleared for action at the time, and although the Zeppelin's engines were clearly audible its hull was momentarily rendered invisible beyond the glaring brilliance of the magnesium. In anticipation of stronger fire nearer London, Böcker had water released from L33's ballast bags, and the ship clawed for altitude. Despite such precautionary measures, the searchlights and guns soon relocated the ship, and once more it was bracketed by exploding shells.

117

Zeppelin!

Kapitänleutnant der Reserve Aloys Böcker (second from left, front row) was born on 12 May 1879, entered the German Navy during October 1896 and later joined the German Naval Airship Division, where he would command *L5* (the crew of which are seen here), *L14* and *L33*. To Böcker's left sits Kurt Frankenberg, *L5*'s executive officer, subsequently killed when commanding *L21*. After interrogation by Major Trench of the German Section of British Naval Intelligence following *L33*'s forced landing on 24 September 1916, Böcker and his crew were sent to the Stobs POW camp in Scotland. The commander was eventually exchanged for a British prisoner in the early part of 1918 and by June that year was back at Nordholz as director of airship training and flying his old *L14* again. One of the exchange conditions, of course, had been that Böcker would not return to combat service. He died in Cologne during 1940.
Archiv: Marine-Luftschiffer-Kameradschaft

L33 landing at Nordholz. Built at Friedrichshafen's Factory Shed 1, *L33* made its first flight on 30 August 1916 and was commissioned on 2 September. Fourth of the 'r' type series, *L33* was, at 644ft 8in, 4ft 9in shorter than the first three in the class, and this standard length was retained until the introduction of the 'w' type initiated by *L57*.
F Moch

Between 23.00 and 23.40hrs, the first bombs tumbled from *L33*'s racks: two 300kg, eight 100kg, thirty-two 50kg bombs and twenty incendiaries caused extensive damage in the Bromley-by-Bow, Bow and Stratford areas. Incendiaries wreaked havoc on the Homelight Oil Company's depot in Old Ford Road and the timber yard of Messrs Lusty and Sons, a respected packing case manufacturer of Bell Road, St Leonards Street. The resulting conflagrations were two of the fiercest that the Metropolitan Fire Brigade had to control throughout the entire period of airship raids. In the oil depot, over 100 empty oil barrels were set alight, and at one stage it was feared that the flames would engulf reserve tanks and a nearby gasholder. At the Lusty timber yard it only took three incendiaries to reduce over 43,000 cu ft of timber to smouldering ashes.

Although only 26 of *L33*'s bombs were later accounted for by the British authorities, Böcker's bombing was certainly effective. A further explosive bomb flattened a row of small tenements in St Leonards Street, killing six civilians and injuring a dozen more. Yet another struck The Black Swan which stood at the junction of the main Bow Road and Bromley High Road and that, too, was completely destroyed. The landlord, his wife and infant daughter were miraculously rescued unharmed, but four of their patrons were not so fortunate, and firemen later recovered their bodies from the ruins.

The British defences eventually sorted themselves out, and before long 30 searchlights swept the heavens like giant fingers, several holding *L33* which from the ground resembled a 'tiny white pencil of light'. The guns soon found the range and once again a stiff barrage erupted around the ship. It was a relatively balmy night for the time of year; at 13,000ft it was just at freezing point, but to Böcker and his crew it must have seemed very warm indeed. Somewhere over Bromley one artillery shell burst inside *L33*'s hull just behind the control gondola. It completely destroyed cell 14, fractured main ring 120 and severed the axial cable, shrapnel shredding four adjacent gas cells and riddling several others. Escaping hydrogen hissed out into the freezing atmosphere but incredibly failed to ignite. Even so, the ship was mortally wounded.

Böcker ordered the helmsman to steer the stricken Zeppelin seawards as the ship lost precious height at the alarming rate of 800ft every minute. The descent could not be checked despite dumping the last of the water ballast, which appeared as a 'smoke screen' to the Kelvedon Hatch searchlight crew. As the ship continued to fall, the sailmakers were joined by other crew members as they clambered precariously around the lofty girders of the hull. In total darkness they attempted to repair the numerous punctures with only flashlights to guide them. Cans of toxic cellulose dope and stiff-haired brushes, tearing wind, bitter cold, escaping gas – it was a situation fraught with hazards. At one point the sailmaker, overcome by fumes, nearly lost his grip on the duralumin frames, but once recovered he continued his herculean efforts alongside his comrades. British defences, however, had not yet finished with *L33*.

Over Chelmsford a home defence aircraft of 39 HDS from Hainault Farm attacked Böcker's ship for nearly 20 minutes, and although a great many of the Pomeroy and Brock bullets struck several fuel tanks, the Zeppelin stubbornly refused to catch fire. The aeroplane, BE2c 4544, was piloted by Brandon, who already had some experience of Zeppelin fighting:

Brandon gained the DSO for his part in the destruction of *L33*, and he is seen here leaving Buckingham Palace after his investiture.
D Whetton

> I left Hainault at 11.33pm on the 23rd instant with orders to patrol between Hainault and Suttons Farm. At 12.12 I saw a Zeppelin in the searchlights some distance away and made for it. Very shortly after this it escaped from the searchlights and I lost it, but I continued on and picked it up again. I went on climbing and managed with some difficulty to keep it in view, as there were no searchlights on it and my automatic pump had failed and I had to work the cockpit handle of the Lewis gun. After putting on a drum of ammunition I came up behind the Zeppelin and on raising the gun jerked it out of the mounting, the gun and the yoke falling across the nacelle. I managed to replace the gun but in the meantime had passed under and past the Zepp. I turned and passed along it again, but from the bow, but we passed each other too quickly for me to aim. On turning I came up from behind and fixed a drum of ammunition. The Brock ammunition seemed to be bursting all along it but the Zepp did not catch fire. I was using Brock, Pomeroy and Sparklet. I turned again and put on a fresh drum and came up from behind and fired again. The gun jammed after about nine rounds. I now decided to get above the Zepp and went on climbing but there was a large bank of grey cloud all around the horizon and it was impossible to see the Zepp against it, after I had got level with the Zepp. I first saw the Zepp at 12.13 and lost it at 12.33. I continued to patrol in various directions owing to having lost my bearings. I was at about 10,200 when attacking the Zepp and I should say the Zepp was about 1000 to 1200 feet higher.[3]

Brandon's frustration is not difficult to imagine. Having already been robbed of victory when he encountered Breithaupt's *L15* in March, again he was denied a conclusive result. Later, interrogation of the *L33* crew disclosed that the majority of them were unaware of Brandon's presence, which is hardly surprising considering their preoccupation in trying to keep the Zeppelin airborne. Only the gunners high up on the upper machine gun platform caught sight of British pilot during his attack, yet they dared not open fire for fear of igniting the escaping hydrogen which hissed upwards around them from the shattered cells.

Zeppelin!

An aerial view of *L33* as it lies across the Little Wigborough road; New Hall Cottages and the farms are evident. The rows of white objects at lower right are the Bell tents in which Commander Campbell's men were quartered during their long investigation.
Sir Frederick Sowrey

This contemporary artist's impression depicts the 'arrest' of Böcker and the crew of *L33*. The likeness of Special Constable Edgar Nicholas is exact and obviously based upon one of the several newspaper photographs which appeared after the event.
By courtesy of H A Snowling

Böcker eventually managed to lose the British pilot and steered the ship towards the coast. In a desperate attempt to keep *L33* in the air, he flew the Zeppelin with its nose so high that most of the crew had to clutch the nearest girder to avoid falling aft. Hurriedly, *L33*'s officers began to jettison all loose fittings in a desperate attempt to lighten their vessel. The course taken by the Zeppelin over the Essex countryside was later traced from certain artifacts recovered during subsequent days. Spare parts, two aluminium cartridge cases and a leather machine-gun jacket fell at Broomfield, whilst a few miles further on at Boreham a complete machine gun hit the ground. At 00.30hrs the radio man transmitted the last message, 'Need help mouth of Thames, L33', before the set was broken up and the remnants flung over the side. Fifty-five minutes later the crippled Zeppelin was staggering between Witham and Maldon, and at 01.00hrs the grounds of Monkton's House at Wickham Bishops received one machine gun, a third and fourth falling on Gate House Farm, Tiptree. Five minutes later, *L33* was nearing Tolleshunt Major and now very close to the ground. Böcker realised that he could not possibly reach the coast, let alone the base at Nordholz, with his ship in such a dangerous sinking condition. The Zeppelin, tail-down and at an altitude of only 500ft, finally dropped and heavily struck an open field at 01.20hrs. A wind gust picked up the ship slightly, only to carry it 100yds further on where it fell across a lane between Little Wigborough and Peldon, three miles east of Mersea. When the ship struck the earth for the last time there was a small explosion and the control gondola was practically demolished. Böcker and his 20-man crew managed to jump clear, virtually unscathed except for one man who cracked some ribs in a heavy fall.

Whilst Böcker's reports were often extravagant, his own version of the loss of *L33* set down some months later tends to equate with British records:

> Near the British coast we were fired on heavily by destroyers with incendiary ammunition. We turned off to the south, but were once more heavily fired on by four destroyers which stood to the south of us. By climbing to 3500 metres we were hidden by a thick layer of cloud from the sight of the enemy and once more steered for the coast, which we crossed somewhat to the north of the Thames' mouth. Towards 23.00 hours four bombs were dropped on the hangars of a large air station, and all the lights there were extinguished. Since it was a clear starlit night over London the searchlights in the suburbs promptly picked us up. The SW wind at our altitude of 4000 metres and temperature of 0°C had considerably increased. The gunfire from all sides was so extraordinarily heavy, more so than I had ever experienced. Between 00.15 and 00.40 hours starting at Tower Bridge, two bombs of 300, eight of 100, 32 of 50 and 20 incendiaries were dropped over the big warehouses along the Thames and over the City. Several enormous fires and the collapse of large groups of houses were observed. While the bombs were still being dropped, L33 received her first hit abaft the forward engine gondola, the shell exploding inside the ship and splinters damaged four cells. Because of the gas streaming out the top of the ship, the machine-gunners on top of the ship could not be used to drive off several planes which fired on the ship, from a considerable distance. Also several cells in the stern of the ship suffered large tears from shell splinters, which were stopped as well as possible [*sic*]. Aircraft machine-gun fire pierced some of the fuel tanks so that fuel flowed out in the gangway.
>
> Due to loss of gas the ship fell 1000 metres in four minutes, and I realised the ship could not be saved, so I had dropped overboard all fuel and oil except for a one hour supply, machine guns and ammunition, spare parts and equipment, and finally the entire wireless apparatus. The ship, which could only be kept up dynamically, was flying at such an angle that it was difficult to hold on: she could no longer be steered and drove away with the wind. I hoped to get the ship to the coast where she could be sunk, but I did not succeed. Suddenly we were forced straight down by a gust from a height of 150 metres. The ship landed hard and was carried a further 100 metres.[4]

The bows of *L33* lay across Knapps Field and 25yds from New Hall Farm, while the stern rested in part of the five-acre Glebe Field. The midships section had collapsed and its starboard side was another 25yds from New Hall Cottages, whose awakened occupants were peering apprehensively from the windows. Understandably they were quite unnerved by the arrival of a monstrous Zeppelin on their doorstep, and the sound of Anglo-Saxon expletives emanating from the German crew only served to add a further touch of incongruity to the scene.[5]

The small explosion which heralded the arrival of *L33* had done little damage except burn off most of the cotton covering. There was little hydrogen left in the Zeppelin and so the risk of a huge conflagration was slight. Nevertheless, Böcker decided to attempt to fire the ship and complete its destruction, but because of the chance of an explosion he and several members of the crew crossed over to New Hall Cottages to warn its occupants. The cottages were shared by two farm labourers. In the left-hand side lived Thomas Lewis and family and in the right Frederick Choat, both workers from New Hall Farm. Not one of them responded to the Germans' repeated hammerings at the doors and windows; instead the families took shelter in their back rooms and stayed there. Finally Böcker gave up and he returned to *L33*, gathered the ship's secret documents and the crew's papers together, flung them into the control car and fired a signal flare into the spilled petrol in the gangway. Instantly the Zeppelin caught fire, flames towered high in the air, and machine-gun ammunition ignited in the heat with a frightening clatter. Three mild explosions of oxy-hydrogen from the leaky cells knocked most of the Germans flat and the nearby cottages, built from weatherboard on brick foundations, were shifted two inches off square as a result. The subsequent blaze caused little other damage apart from scorching paint from the walls, blowing out the front windows and, reportedly, singeing the back of a terrier which was in an outside kennel.

One of the labourers in New Hall Cottages later gave newspaper reporters his version of what occurred when the Zeppelin crew knocked on his front door:

> I never answered, and I heard the commander cursing. He said something about the 'damned house!' I don't know what else he said, but I put my wife and children in a back room and made myself scarce too.[6]

As the Zeppelin burned, its exposed framework glowing with the heat, Böcker called his men to attention and in a body they struck off up the lane past New Hall Farm to the Peldon Road. As they marched, they emptied their service revolvers into the night sky and tossed the weapons into the hedgerows. The Germans turned right towards Peldon and it was at 'Kidhearts Corner' that they marched straight into the path of a bicycle ridden by Special Constable Edgar Nicholas.

Despite the overwhelming odds confronting him, Nicholas pulled up, dismounted and barred the path of the advancing Germans. He trained his flashlight on Böcker who stood apart from the others, and enquired as to whether a Zeppelin had come down. The commander of *L33* responded by asking, in perfect English, how many miles it was to Colchester. When the surprised policeman replied 'About six', Böcker politely thanked him, and in his subsequent report Nicholas stated that he 'at once recognised [a] foreign accent':

> The men proceeded towards Peldon Village; I followed walking with the rear men one of whom spoke in broken English. I asked this man if he was hit by gunfire; he answered, 'Zeppelin explode, we crew prisoners of war'. Later he remarked, 'What people think of war?' I replied, 'I hardly know.' He said, 'Did I think [the war] nearly over?' I replied, 'It's over for you anyway.' He answered, 'Good, good,' offering me his hand to shake which I did. After this he gave me his lifesaving vest and a screwhammer which latter he informed me in good English was his revolver; with regard to his vest, he said, 'Schwim, Schwim' [*sic*] extending his arms in a swimming fashion and added, 'Souvenir. Commander speak English, I learn English at school.'
>
> Opposite Peldon Hall Lower Barn Gate I was joined by Special Constable Taylor and Sergeant Edwards ECC (on leave staying at Wigborough). We all continued towards Peldon Post Office where we were met by PC Smith, stationed at Peldon, who then took charge of the men.[7]

Police Sergeant E A Edwards, who together with PC354 Charles Smith and seven constables escorted the crew of *L33* to Mersea Strood where a military escort took over.
A E J Edwards

It was then that Constable PC 354 Charles Smith of the Colchester Division formally arrested the crew of *L33*. In 1976, when the author interviewed him, 94-year-old Charles Smith remembered with absolute clarity the events of that morning. His recollections, 60 years on, differed very little from the official police report he made on 25 September 1916:

> I beg to report about 1am on Sunday, the 24th Sept, 1916, a Zeppelin passed over Peldon flying very low travelling in a south-west course and appeared to be suffering with engine trouble. About 1.20am I last saw of her [*sic*] and almost immediately she burst into flames and there was a terrific

Sergeant Charles Smith of the Essex County Constabulary: a photograph taken after the *L33* incident. It was Smith who refused Böcker's request to use a telephone.
C Smith

One of *L33*'s crew in captivity. This is the executive officer, *Leutnant zur See* Ernst Wilhelm Schirlitz, who later reached the rank of *Vize-Admiral*. Schirlitz, born on 7 September 1893, died in Kiel on 27 November 1978, and was a member of the MLK. *By courtesy of E A Munday*

explosion. I rang up Intelligence and informed them of the fact. While waiting to get on to Headquarters, Sergeant Edwards, who was on leave from Hatfield Broad Oak, came into the Post Office with the Commander of the Zeppelin.[8]

Edwards informed PC Smith that the Zeppelin crew were standing in the road outside and asked what he was going to do with them. Recovering from his surprise, Smith decided that the only thing to do was hand the Germans over to a military escort, and it was at that point that Böcker asked Smith if he could use the telephone.

There have been many versions of Böcker's request recorded over the years; few are accurate, most being based, apparently, on contemporary newspaper accounts. Charles Smith's version holds true, and other official police reports of the time only serve to confirm his original statement. On 30 September, the brigadier-general of the Southern Army despatched a note to Captain Unett of the Essex County Constabulary questioning the validity of the reports. Unett's reply set the record straight once and for all that there was

...no truth in the report that the Captain of the German Airship recently brought down at Little Wigborough asked to be allowed to telephone to a friend in London who would let his wife know he was safe. What appears to have happened is that the Captain asked the Constable if he might telephone but not saying where or to whom. I presume that the officer wanted to telephone to the military authorities.[9]

In any event, the constable flatly refused and asked the German to proceed with the Specials until he and his crew could be handed over to the military authorities. Böcker consented. Smith and Edwards went out of the post office with the Zeppelin commander, and together with seven other constables the party struck off up the road. With Smith at the head and the constables forming a rough circle around the Germans, they followed the route to Mersea, stopping when they encountered four soldiers. As there was no officer amongst them, Smith refused to hand his prisoners over and continued the journey, to reach the Mersea Strood a good mile and a half further on. Smith reported

There I met Colonel Oevee and said to him, 'I have the crew of the wrecked Zeppelin here, Sir'. He said, 'How many have you?' I said, 'I don't know Sir, but with your permission I will count them.' Which I did and found there were 21 all told. I was assisted with [*sic*] Special Constables Fairhead, Clement Hyam, Charles King, Elijah Traylor, Joseph May, Horace Charles Meade, Harry Bead, and Edgar Nicholas. I have since made enquiries and find that the Zeppelin landed quite safe near New Hall Cottages, Little Wigborough. It appears after the Zeppelin landed, the crew knocked at the doors of the cottages close by and they were heard to say, 'The wind lays right' and then they fired her.[10]

The policemen were quite relieved when they finally handed over their charges to the armed soldiers, who then escorted the Germans to the church house at West Mersea. They arrived there at about 04.00hrs, and resentment was expressed by local villagers as the crew prepared to spend the rest of the night in the relative comfort of the church house. The vicar, Rev C Pierreport Edwards MC, appeased his parishioners by suggesting they should raise the Union Flag and join him in 'God Save the King' as the crew filed in through the front door. The vicar subsequently gave tea to his unexpected 'guests', only Böcker refusing to partake of it, and the injured crewman slept in a bed specially made up for him.

Very soon a large crowd had gathered outside the church house, and many of them stayed on until later in the day, when the Germans were eventually driven off to the detention barracks at Colchester to face interrogation by the military authorities. The injured man was placed in the Detention Ward of Colchester Hospital, and then the crew of *L33* were subjected to 14 days of questioning by the German Section of British Naval Intelligence. The head of this unique service was Major Trench of the Royal Marines, whose background knowledge of Zeppelins and their operations seemed little short of phenomenal. Böcker initially declined to answer any of the various questions put to him, and later he related that the major finally resorted to threats. On one occasion, Trench showed the German photographs of dead civilians as a result of Böcker's raid on Hull the previous March when he had commanded *L14*. 'These are your heroic deeds in Hull; you don't drop bombs on military targets but murder defenceless women and children,' stormed Trench, and then he actually threatened Böcker with a civil trial for murder. In another instance, Trench showed the commander plans of the latest Zeppelins, complete with correct designations, and claimed he had even spent a day at Friedrichshafen quite recently. Böcker, for his part, gave very little away, and at a later stage even managed to smuggle back reports of the interrogations to Germany.[11]

The crew of *L33* remained prisoners of war for the duration, at the Stobbs POW Camp in Scotland, but at least one member, *Maschinistenmaat* Adolf Schultz, was freed under a prisoner exchange scheme at the end of 1916.[12] Böcker himself was exchanged two years later for a British officer, with the standard proviso that he should no longer serve in combat. June 1918 saw Böcker back in command of his beloved *L14* and he finished his war as a Director of Training at Nordholz. But the story of *L33*'s forced landing does not end here, for there were other events which took place on that dramatic morning in Essex and deserve to be recorded.

A local boy, 13-year-old George Rout, had been in bed when the Germans marched past prior to their encounter with Constable Nicholas:

> I was upstairs that night with asthma. When my father came down he got a two-gallon bottle of wine out and started swigging it into him. He said, 'If they come over here they're not going to have this...' My mother kept saying, 'The old Germans are coming up the road, I can hear them talking. They'll burn the whole place down.' After they blew it up you could see to read a newspaper indoors. My father got his back up against the door and that's when he did get the wind-up a bit. He said, 'If we go, we all go together.' And I was almost ready to go because my asthma near killed me... 21 of them walked past – and that was a big relief, when they did...[13]

Not far away, in Great Wigborough, a baby daughter was born to Mr and Mrs Clark at about the same time *L33* was set alight. Mr Clark, chairman of the court at Witham, was amused when the doctor who delivered the infant suggested she be called Zeppelina to mark the event.

In the graveyard of Little Wigborough's church, a mere 600yds from where *L33* fell to earth, there stands a gravestone recording the death of Alfred John Wright, who died on 13 November 1916 aged 45 years. Mr Wright, a cripple, was a seed grower and owned Grove Farm just a few yards up the road from George Rout. When Wright and his brother-in-law saw the Zeppelin burning, they hurried over to the spot where they saw the crew standing in the road. Not knowing if the Germans were armed, they returned to the farm, where Alfred set out for West Mersea on his motorcycle to warn the military authorities. On the way he collided with a car in the darkness and smashed his leg.

Dr J H Salter of Tolleshunt D'Arcy was very much a man to whom the term 'local character' applied with a vengeance. Sportsman, hunter, medical practitioner, and with a wide range of earthy expletives at his disposal, he was a popular and respected figure. He also kept a detailed diary of his life and recorded his own version of these events in Little Wigborough:

> I was just going to settle down again for the night, when my night bell rang and a midwifery case turned up at Wigborough close to the Zeppelin wreck. I got my partner Dr Spinks to take it, but before the man left the door, a motor from Mersea drew up and wished me to go at once to see young Wright of Little Wigborough, who in motorcycling after military and police at the fall of the Zeppelin, collided with a motor car and got smashed up. I was soon into my clothes and off with splints, bandages etc. Reaching Little Wigborough I found great excitement. The Zeppelin had come down within a few yards of New Hall buildings without doing them any damage and lay there, a huge wreck like a Crystal Palace without its glass.
>
> I found my patient with a badly smashed leg – immediate removal being necessary. I rigged up my car for him and took him to Colchester Hospital. We had adventures on the way. In the narrow road below Wigborough Church we encountered military lorries full of soldiers and there was no room to pass.
>
> They wanted us to turn but I insisted on their doing so, held my ground and got my way. I told them there was no special need for them at the Zeppelin wreck – it was down and useless and the crew had been taken prisoners...[14]

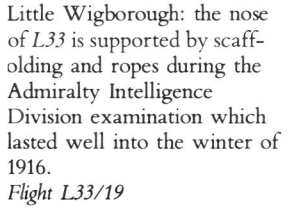

Little Wigborough: the nose of *L33* is supported by scaffolding and ropes during the Admiralty Intelligence Division examination which lasted well into the winter of 1916.
Flight L33/19

Zeppelin!

Alfred Wright and Dr Salter finally made their way to Colchester; the injured seed grower was admitted and his leg subsequently amputated. Two months later he was dead.[15]

The following morning was a busy one for the military. As early as 04.00hrs there were 450 men guarding the wreck from the 2nd/9th Manchester Regiment and 66th Division Cyclists. Realising the great value in the burnt-out (but virtually intact) Zeppelin, they placed a stiff cordon around it, sightseers and souvenir hunters being kept away until the more important components had been studied by the experts. Later, Admiralty draughtsmen, headed by Commander C I R Campbell, of the Royal Corps of Naval Constructors, arrived to take measurements and photographs. Camped out in Bell tents, they were to stay with the wreck until late December.

For Constable Charles Smith, 24 September was memorable for another occasion. With unprecedented expediency he was promoted to sergeant and awarded the highly coveted six-pointed Essex Constabulary Merit badge. In subsequent days people handed him various relics from *L33* which were jettisoned by the crew as it staggered over the Essex fields. Articles such as Bosch magnetos, clocks, tool boxes, revolvers – even Böcker's muffs – were received and dutifully handed over to Captain Duncan of the Royal Engineers who was temporarily installed at Witham House. Smith himself was to find, behind a hedgerow that bordered the Little Wigborough to Peldon road, torn remnants of pocket books that Böcker's crew had discarded. He was given several rewards for the items he found and gave over.

Not everyone was quite so conscientious. Staying at Keston's Farm, Great Wigborough, were three sisters whose uncles recovered several items, including a heavy brass instrument casing found during the early hours of the morning. Later in the day, soldiers rode around with megaphones ordering anyone who possessed items of the Zeppelin to hand them over to the military. Instead the uncles wrapped their valuable prizes in a tarpaulin and submerged them in the Farm's horse pond, where they went undetected.[16]

There were, however, penalties for hoarders if caught. The retention of relics constituted a contravention of the Defence of the Realm Regulations, Section 35B, and several prosecutions and fines were meted out to souvenir hunters. Indeed, the two labourers from New Hall Cottages were visited by police and several instruments and portions of framework from *L33* were found in their possession. As a result both were charged and each formed the subject of lengthy reports before they were taken to court. Some months later, on 31 March 1917, Police Superintendent N Cowell of the Colchester Division reported, 'that at the Lexden and Winstree Petty Sessions, the summons against Thomas Lewis in the Regulation 35B was dismissed: the Justices were of the opinion that he acted in ignorance. Choat has been cautioned as requested.'[17]

Captain Unett, the Chief Constable of Essex, was one of several officers surprised at the court's verdict. Indeed, on 8 April 1917 he wrote to the Intelligence Officer of the Southern Army (HD) in Brentwood:

> My superintendent reports that he is quite unable to form an opinion as to why the case was dismissed by the justices. The facts were put before them fully and it was suggested strongly to them that defendant's explanation as to where and when he (Lewis) found the gauge was not a feasible one having regard to its clean condition and further that there had been crowds of people both Military and civilians looking about at the spot where it was said to have been found.[18]

The wreck of *L33* attracted a great number of sightseers who tramped unconcernedly over valuable crops in order to view the stricken raider. Charles Hutley owned a farm at Great Wigborough, and to preserve what was left of his eight-acre harvest he cut down a hedge and fashioned rudimentary steps and a pathway which led away from the crops; in addition, he charged visitors twopence a head. This went on every day for more than a week, the farmer donating the eventual amount of £79 4s 10d to the Red Cross and other deserving war charities. But what of the sight that confronted the scores of fascinated visitors to the remote hamlet? A Reuter's correspondent later helped to describe the scene:

> After a motor drive of several miles through narrow winding leaf-strewn and rain-sodden lanes, the car slowed down while an officer appeared in the middle of the road and scrutinised our passes. Then we saw that at intervals along the road were sentries with fixed bayonets, and a little beyond, wire entanglements blocked the approach to all side tracks. Looking across the flat green fields one observed in the distance what at first looked like the ribs of a stranded whale silhouetted against the grey sky. Proceeding slowly and

Lord French visits Mrs Lewis of New Hall Cottages, Little Wigborough. When Böcker and his men hammered at the cottage to warn its occupants of their intention to set L33 afire, they received no response. The family's fear can be imagined.
By courtesy of E A Munday

Mrs Lewis and her family. All had a lucky escape as L33 grounded only yards from their front gate. The cottage still stands today.
By courtesy of E A Munday

skidding round corners in the muddy lanes we came upon many troops, and more sentries, while another officer examined passes. Presently was brought up [sic] in the garden of a small cottage, and looking up saw for the first time in detail the gigantic form of one of Germany's latest specimens of frightfulness.

We had, of course, all seen photographs of the fallen Zeppelin, but no camera picture can ever convey an adequate idea of the monster that was lying helpless, but to all intents and purposes intact, in these Essex fields. One thing struck the whole of our party – namely surprise at the huge dimensions of the airship, and a sense of wonder that it could possibly have come down in the condition in which it is to be found today.

Although bent and twisted, the trellis aluminium frame shows quite clearly the general lines of the ship. It lies across the road, each half resting in fields. The road itself is blocked by a tangle of metal and wire-work. One neutral journalist said the mass looked like the glassless roof of Olympia, after being dented by a huge hammer, while another penetrating into the interior of the frame, said that the view was much the same as that obtained in regarding the Crystal Palace from the floor. To others it seemed like standing in the centre of a huge aluminium liner and looking up from the keel plate to the deck.

What impressed everyone, next to the dimensions of the airship, was the extraordinary lightness of the structure, and we were surprised to find that a length of the trellis framework of 10 or 12 feet could be raised and held quite easily with the little finger.

Within reasonable limits, officers guarding the machine were quite ready to answer any questions put to them. [The Zeppelin] is fitted with 60 bomb droppers, right forward is to be seen the captain's cabin, with three control wheels, while in close proximity is the wireless room, enclosed in a casing of cotton wool to ensure as much silence as possible.

Lying on one side of the Zeppelin itself was a small cane or basket coracle, the use of which is not quite clear. It may have been intended for use in the case of descent on the water or for lowering men for the purposes of observation.[19]

Because of the guards placed around the wreck, the nearest that later visitors got to *L33* was 200yds, but this did little to prevent the steady stream of curious civilians arriving during the following weeks. Over a quarter of a million people were later claimed to have made their way to Little Wigborough. All of this became an unusual distraction for the locals. George Rout's sister lived at Tiptree, and as 'she was in service there and got a new bicycle she started to come over to see. Well, she got part of the way here and left the bicycle, she couldn't ride, there were so many people on the road.'[20] Another young girl remembered 'cycling from Tiptree after it came down and [getting] quite near to the ruins. We had to leave our cycles some distance away and tramp over ploughed fields.'[21]

Among several notable visitors to Little Wigborough were Lieutenant W O Bentley, the distinguished engine designer, and William Leefe Robinson, who surprisingly was not even allowed in the immediate vicinity of the wreck. The remains of Böcker's penultimate wartime command were eventually broken up piecemeal, brought through Heybridge and packed off in railway wagons leaving Maldon station. The ultimate fate of the bulk of *L33* is unknown, although various components do still exist in several museums and private collections.

As a result of the Admiralty draughtsmen's findings, the British Cabinet subsequently ordered production of two copies of *L33*, these being numbered, with startling originality, *R33* and *R34*. The former ship was completed in

Lord French and staff officers examine the starboard midships engine gondola of *L33*. At the extreme left can be seen one of the cylindrical petrol tanks.
By courtesy of E A Munday

Commander C I R Campbell of the Royal Corps of Naval Constructors stands upon part of the wooden covered 'catwalk' of *L33* at Little Wigborough.
Flight L33/4

Army and naval officers examine the wrecked upper gun platforms of *L33*; a buckled tripod mount can be seen and one of the 8mm Maxims is in the immediate foreground.
By courtesy of E A Munday

Zeppelin!

1919 and later used for a large amount of experimental work, including hook-up trials with a De Havilland Humming Bird and a pair of Gloster Grebe single-seat fighters. *R33* was eventually broken up in 1928 as an economy measure, and today the control car can be seen in the Royal Air Force Museum, giving some impression as to the degree of comfort, or rather lack of it, enjoyed by wartime airship crews.

Sixty-eight years on, the small lane leading to Copt Hall Farm, New Hall Cottages, and the surrounding farmland remain basically unaltered from the appearance they presented in 1916. In the village church at the end of the lane there is a framed record of the event and a large portion of framework is fixed on the 'Tower Arch' to remind visitors of the village's involvement in 'The Great War'.

Thus ends the dramatic and almost farcical story of *L33*, but by no means does it close the table of events for 23 and 24 September 1916, for what of the other 'Thirties'? Mathy and Peterson, in consort, had made their landfall at Dungeness at 21.45hrs, where *L32* circled the area presumably due to engine trouble. Mathy, however, had decided to press on for London.

Unable to reach a safe enough attack height, *L31*'s commander hurled 1280lb of bombs at the Dungeness lighthouse to lighten his ship. On the approach to London, several parachute flares were dropped, and over Croydon at 23.10hrs they blinded anti-aircraft gunners, enabling *L31* to pass over unseen. The ship's bombing run commenced over Brixton and Streatham, where many houses were badly hit. One of the bombs struck a tramcar close to Streatham Hill station, resulting in the death of the driver, conductor and three passengers. In all, another nine people were killed and 33 injured in the attack.

At 23.15hrs Mathy observed *L33* and the result of Böcker's bombing way over to the east. The smoke from these fires, Mathy was later to attest, screened his ship from the gunners. *L31* dropped the last of its bombs over Lea Bridge Road and Leyton, the ship's commander taking advantage of mist to get clear of the city unscathed.

Altogether Mathy dropped almost 9000lb of explosives and eventually left the British Isles via Great Yarmouth. Nevertheless, he had lingered long enough to witness a terrible tragedy.

Peterson Falls

It was around 23.00hrs when the young commander of *L32* steered his ship in the general direction of London, but somehow he wandered off course and headed eastwards. An hour later the Zeppelin approached the River Thames, and 12 miles from the very centre of the capital came into clear air and was almost at once held in the grip of several searchlight beams. The anti-aircraft gunners soon opened fire, and at least one gun crew claimed two hits. At 23.10hrs Peterson dumped the remainder of his bombs and turned to avoid the heavy barrage.

At Suttons Farm, the orderly officer had been constantly keeping the duty pilots in touch with the raiders' movements. In one corner of the Flight Office a leather-coated figure was slumbering in a deck chair awaiting his turn for patrol. When the call eventually came through, the pilot, aroused from sleep, gathered up his gauntlets, goggles, helmet and flashlight, ran out of the hut and was soon being strapped into BE2c 4112. Not very long after the aircraft had taken off into the darkness, 'the familiar whistle of a falling bomb was heard'.[22] It came from *L33*; Böcker, attracted by the Money flares, was drifting overhead, and four bombs fell on and around the airfield.

William Leefe Robinson VC was standing in front of the aircraft sheds when the first bomb struck, and he lost no time in ordering nearby officers and men to lie flat. This bomb and a second narrowly missed the farmhouse, following a line towards the sheds. A third struck the ground behind the hangars and the fourth should, according to the law of averages, have struck the shed sheltering Robinson and members of his flight. Unaccountably the bomb fell 100yds beyond, much to everyone's relief, and 'Robinson's remark that it was much safer in the air on such occasions was cordially agreed with by all the pilots'.[23]

In the meantime the pilot who had taken off earlier had laboriously managed to reach 9000ft, and, skirting the Thames, he lay in wait for the raiders as they returned from their attacks on the city. He observed one Zeppelin a few miles away caught in searchlights, and, opening the throttle, he flew towards it.

Lieutenant Frederick Sowrey had been in the air for almost two hours with the flashlight on a strap around his neck to illuminate the dashboard from time to time. He made his way over to a Zeppelin hovering over Tilbury which twice vanished from view as it shook free of the searchlights. Before long the airship was held again, and Sowrey eventually got into firing range as the airship, bereft of its bomb load, began to rise. Peterson's *L32* was by then quite visible in the searchlight beams, although gunfire from below had momentarily ceased.

L33 lies across Glebe Field and Knapps Field; twenty-five yards beyond are New Hall Cottages. When Alfred Wright's funeral took place some weeks later, the wreckage had to be cut away to allow the cortège to pass.
By courtesy of E A Munday

Little Wigborough today. The author holds a section of double-latticed girder from *L33* close to the exact spot where the Zeppelin crashed in 1916. In the background can be seen New Hall Cottages; extensions have been added but little else has changed since that eventful September night.
M B Delahunty

Peterson, whose father was Major Werner Peterson of Charlottenburg, entered the German Navy on 1 April 1906 and by 1913 was a junior officer on the destroyer *V191* of the 1st Division of the 1st Destroyer Flotilla. Peterson married during the war and his wife Else bore him a daughter who was subsequently educated in England.
Archiv: Marine-Luftschiffer-Kameradschaft

Throttling back, Sowrey manoeuvred his small biplane beneath the monster and saw clearly the six revolving propellers glinting from time to time as the ship was twisted and turned in a vain attempt to shake off the lights. Now flying beneath the huge, swaying tail surfaces, he gripped the Lewis gun, and into the vast hull above him emptied an entire drum along the length of the ship. Brandon, still airborne and 2000ft away, saw the tracers glowing in the dark, and later reported seeing the Zeppelin being 'hosed with a stream of fire.'[24]

The first drum appeared to have little effect other than to make the Zeppelin 'wriggle considerably and change its course'[25] and draw some heavy return fire from machine guns in the main gondolas. Sowrey flung the empty drum over the cockpit, fixed on the second and tried again. He had to turn his aircraft about in order to catch up with the airship, and having done so approached the target once more. His second attempt was as inconclusive as the first, which to the British pilot was 'rather disheartening'. Possibly recalling Robinson's mode of attack, Sowrey concentrated the third drum in one area. Brock, Pomeroy and tracer rounds struck the centre of Peterson's ship and found their mark, several riddling petrol tanks. This time Sowrey was rewarded with the awesome spectacle of a deep rosy glow within the heart of the airship that made the vessel look like a 'huge Chinese Lantern'. Seconds later *L32* was rocked with explosions that ripped through cells, past the stark tracery of girders, and through into the night, tearing the outer skin asunder in their terrifying progress. Flames devoured the cotton covering with incredible speed as the doomed vessel hung momentarily before it slid earthwards for the last time, tipping vertically in its death-throes. Blazing gondolas, petrol tanks and white hot girders detached themselves and hissed downwards, each leaving fiery trails in their wake.

Sowrey only just managed to avoid the blazing hulk as it bore down on him and then fell past, roaring furiously. His gaze followed it all the way down until it finally neared the ground in a river of fiery orange which turned into a lake of vivid green on impact.

Londoners shouted and cheered as 40 tons of burning Zeppelin cascaded slowly to earth. For young Leslie Goddard, living in Shenfield, the events of that night were left indelibly on his memory:

Being so close to London, there were anti-aircraft defences in our neighbourhood. There was a gun on the Common, whilst there was a powerful searchlight in a big field which bordered on the main railway line between Shenfield and Brentwood. The searchlight was midway between the gun and the house in which we were living.

It wasn't long before I saw that our local searchlight had picked up the Zeppelin which was clearly making its way westwards towards London. It looked like a long silver cigar. As soon as he knew his whereabouts had been discovered, the commander began to manoeuvre his craft to get out of the searchlight's beam. I saw the Zeppelin go up and come down; gain height and lose it. But the engineers working the searchlight held onto him.

L32 at Nordholz, 1916, being held by its ground crew. Under the bows, the circular fittings that cover the rope handling tubs have been dropped to allow the lines to be caught by the station ground troop. A lifeboat is also seen beyond the control gondola.
F Moch

Zeppelin!

One of the few surviving photographs of Peterson's *L32* is this one showing the 'Super Zeppelin' landing at Nordholz during 1916. *L32* was built in the Friedrichshafen Factory Shed 11 and made its first flight on 6 August 1916. During a short career *L32* only made a dozen flights – the thirteenth was its last.
F Moch

After some little time, I saw another object in the searchlight's beam. Nor was it long before I identified it as an aeroplane, presumably one of our own which had for some months been stationed at Hornchurch. The murmur of the voices of our neighbours along the road confirmed my conviction. It was an aeroplane and an English one. The whole atmosphere, both inside the house and outside became electric.

The aeroplane was approaching the Zeppelin head on; it was flying from west to east. We all watched fascinated. Then we saw the pilot of the aircraft drop Very lights – apparently to indicate to the gunners on Shenfield Common that he was going to attack and would like them to stop firing.

Then things happened with bewildering speed. The searchlight was still on the Zeppelin despite all the latter's manoeuvring. Flt Lt [*sic*] Sowrey flew straight towards the Zeppelin and fired what must have been tracer bullets into it. Immediately the front of the Zeppelin went up in the most appalling blaze. The searchlight was switched off; there was clearly no further need for it.

The light from the blazing Zeppelin was colossal; it was beyond imagination or description. We had been watching from a very privileged position as remarkable an encounter we could have wished. It was an aerial David overcoming his Goliath. As the blaze enveloped the countryside, everything suddenly became very quiet. We were all stunned. Then one heard the babble of voices; it seemed that everyone in Shenfield was watching this macabre spectacle. And probably they were. As people gradually realised the magnitude and significance of all they witnessed, a long cheer went up which appeared louder and more prolonged because of the silence which had preceded it.

As we continued to gaze upwards at the crumbling blazing monster, we could clearly see the airship's crew climbing on to the railings of the gondolas and jumping to their deaths; clearly they preferred to meet their end that way than by being roasted alive. My mother turned to go back to her bed and as she slowly crossed the room, I remember her saying, 'Oh Les, they are all someone's sons'. I think that remark of hers remains my chief recollection of that astonishing experience.[26]

Another witness of that astonishing experience was 12-year-old I D Jarvis, whose diary entry dated 1 October 1916 briefly describes the event as *L32* fell at Billericay:

[It was] about three miles from our home. I watched it caught in the searchlights, and saw an aeroplane above it apparently giving the signal for the guns to cease fire. It then dropped what looked like a little red light which in a moment set fire to the airship [*sic*]. There was a great stillness when the guns stopped firing, but this was soon broken by the sound of the roaring flames and the engines of the doomed ship which still seemed to be running.

As it began to fall, the countryside miles around was lit up by the flames, and the stillness was further broken by the sound of cheering from people all around our village as they watched this spectacle.[27]

A well-qualified witness to the successful attack by Frederick Sowrey was 'Billy' Robinson who, having recovered from his narrow escape together with other members of B Flight, could clearly see the drama being enacted 10,000ft above his head. Caught up in the excitement, Robinson shouted directions to the attacking pilot whose tracer rounds were just visible:

'Good shot! Good shot! Give her another burst! Steady you've got her now!' As Peterson's ship exploded Robinson's elation knew no bounds and he literally danced for joy and hit everybody within range in the middle of the back with disconcerting vigour.[28]

RFC pilots and Army officers gaze upon the wreckage of *L32* at Great Burstead on the morning of 24 September 1916. In the foreground lies a shattered propeller and its gear casing.
By courtesy of E A Munday

Sowrey's Aero Club Certificate 2838, dated 23 April 1916. On the reverse of the right hand page in six languages: 'The Civil, Naval and Military Authorities, including the Police, are respectfully requested to aid and assist the holder of this certificate'.
Sowrey Family

L32/L33, 24 September 1916

The blazing wreckage of *L32* finally struck the ground at Snail's Hall Farm, South Green, near Billericay, where it stripped the branches of several trees in the process. The ship burned for 45 minutes and there were no survivors. Two of the enormous elevating planes and rudders were discovered intact and unscorched in a wood half a mile away, and a wooden propeller complete with gear case turned up three miles from the farm. Wreckage had spilled over a wide area and yielded sightseers and souvenir hunters masses of fragments for weeks afterwards. Admiral Hall's men were amongst the first to arrive on the scene, and were fortunate to find charred documents and a usable secret signal book in the control gondola. With this invaluable piece of data they quietly left the scene without a word.[29]

The entries in the *L32*'s war diary for that raid record the ship as having lifted off from Ahlhorn in 'partially overcast and squally' conditions. After steering a course via Aachen, Brussels and Zeebrugge, Peterson had headed towards Dover at around 21.50hrs. The log ends with the writer recording, 'Sighted English coast near Folkestone, flew parallel with coast line. Crossed coast near Dungeness.'[30]

When Lieutenant Sowrey finally landed at Suttons Farm at around 01.45hrs, he showed a great deal of concern as to where the airship had fallen. He greatly feared that the wreckage might have struck houses and killed more civilians, yet he had to curb his natural impatience. There was still the report to be made out for Captain Morton which was done hurriedly amidst much hearty congratulation from fellow officers. After the almost traditional mug of cocoa, Sowrey was bundled into Robinson's waiting Vauxhall and off into the night. Even as the car left the field, locals ran out with their own messages of goodwill, as C T Perfect recorded not long afterwards:

> Presently Captain Robinson's car came tearing up the lane filled with officers from the aerodrome, amongst them being the hero of the night, Lieutenant Frederick Sowrey. With him were Captain Stammers, Captain Bowers and Lieutenant C C Durston. They were on the way to visit the ruins of the burning Zeppelin lying at Billericay, and after receiving our heartiest congratulations, the car proceeded on its triumphant way, followed by Lieuts Mallinson and Brock on motorcycles. It was then that we knew that the whole village was astir, for shouts rent the air until the car, ablaze with lights, passed away into the countryside.[31]

Sowrey

The hero of the night was born in Gloucester on 25 August 1893, his father John being the Deputy Chief Inspector of the Inland Revenue and living at that time at Yeoveney Lodge, Staines. John Sowrey had married Susan Chambers in 1889 and theirs was a large family of three girls, Cissy, Mary and Joan, and three boys, William, John and Frederick. The children were brought up by parents who were Victorian in every sense of the word: sport did not play a large part in the Sowrey household, study and learning took precedence, and discipline was rigidly enforced.

During 1890 the family moved to Kingston-upon-Thames to live with John's sister Jenny, who often used to take the children for walks in Bushey Park. On one occasion Mary Sowrey recalls her brother 'Freddie' almost coming to grief at the horns of a large and belligerent deer and being saved only by the timely intervention of his umbrella-brandishing aunt who succeeded in driving the animal off. From an early age Frederick became the natural ringleader of his brothers and sisters, blessed with an ability to turn his hand to almost anything, a quality which could prove beneficial to other members of the family:

An engaging Sowrey family scene taken in the late 1890s: (left to right) mother Susan, children Freddie and William, John Senior's sister Jenny, John, and Cissy (who was to die at an early age). Kate, the children's nanny, is to the right of the picture.
Miss M Sowrey

A formal portrait of 'Freddie' Sowrey in the uniform of the Royal Fusiliers taken by Knowles of Worthing. Sowrey's army career was brief: wounded in the Battle of Loos, he spent several months in hospital, applying for transfer to the RFC on his release.
Miss M Sowrey

Zeppelin!

A formal studio portrait of Lieutenant Frederick Sowrey, following his DSO award, taken by the well-respected Swaines of New Bond Street.
Miss M Sowrey

The sheds at Suttons Farm, late September 1916. The tail of Sowrey's 4112 is just visible in the entrance of the first hangar.
Sir Frederick Sowrey/RAF Museum

I can remember him standing watching a cobbler working in a shop window and saying how easy it looked. Before long he had bought out of his pocket money (we earned it by gardening) leather, a very sharp knife, and other necessary things including a little anvil. He used to repair our shoes and of course he was always paid. We all had our duties. John used to keep the schoolroom in order and repaired books whilst Bill looked after the bicycles and mended the punctures.[32]

Another move took the Sowreys to Colliers Wood, and after initial education at home, undertaken by their father, all three boys eventually won open scholarships to King's College School near Wimbledon Common. Frederick joined the academy during the autumn term of 1906 and left in the spring of 1912. In the six years he was there, the young Sowrey proved to be an adept pupil, gaining two leaving scholarships (tenable at a university) and eventually taking an intermediate BSc degree. He was not a games player, but he did enjoy active membership of the school's Scientific Society, which had closely followed the rapid development of aeronautics in prewar years. Whilst at King's College, Frederick also used to sneak off to Bisley, where he learnt to become a superb shot, and one year his team managed to win the coveted Ashburton Shield.

John Sowrey had great ambitions for his three sons. Especially he wanted them to enter the Indian Civil Service, and Frederick was in the last stages of a graduate course that would enable him to fulfil his father's wishes when world events took a hand. Caught up in the patriotic fervour of August 1914, Frederick Sowrey and his brothers, like thousands of other young men fresh from the colleges, promptly enlisted into the armed services. Commisioned into the Royal Fusiliers, it was not long before 'Freddie' was in action on the Western Front.

During the fierce Battle of Loos that lasted from 25

Tempest, Bowers, Sowrey, Durston and BE2c 4112 at Suttons Farm. In the end hangar can be seen a row of Crossley tenders, standard equipment for many RFC units.
Sir Frederick Sowrey/RAF Museum

September to the first week of November, Frederick had the misfortune to be wounded and was subsequently invalided home. He was to spend three months under medical care, and on leaving hospital decided he would follow in his brothers' footsteps and applied for a transfer to the Royal Flying Corps. Sowrey's initial posting was to Reading on 8 January 1916, for a course of instruction, and three months later he was with 12 Reserve Squadron at Thetford for further tuition. On 23 April, Frederick qualified for Royal Aero Club Certificate 2838, on 3 May arrived at 19 Reserve Squadron at Hounslow for a night-flying course, then on 17 June was posted to Suttons Farm, there to join the strength of B Flight, 39 HDS.

Sowrey's natural flying ability and above-average intelligence quickly resulted in Major Higgins making him assistant to the unit's adjutant, Captain James Annsley. Sowrey got on famously with his fellow flight members, and in particular formed a close friendship with Robinson and Stammers. The latter's sister Vera, then an impressionable 14-year-old schoolgirl, remembered Sowrey with affection:

He was nice, he was cosy, he was fun. He had a tremendous sense of humour; he and my brother got on terribly well with each other and did all sorts of mad things. They often used to leave Tempest in charge and go tearing up to London's West End in Robinson's car, usually ending up at the Café Royal.[33]

Sowrey was a popular member of the unit and earned the greatest respect from fellow-airmen and friends alike:

Fred Sowrey, whom most of us call 'Butt', though why I couldn't tell you, was always frightfully keen on motor machinery. So it was no surprise to any of us when he recovered from the wound he received at Loos, to know that he had put in for transfer to the Flying Corps...

It was not long before he showed that he was really a pretty cool customer in the air. I have seen him more than once circle round his own home at Staines just skimming past the tall trees that surround it, come down plump into a cornfield and hop out to run up to the house for a cup of tea.[34]

Following Robinson's destruction of *SL11* life at Suttons Farm changed dramatically, and the little band of airmen were thrust into the limelight, the targets of a host of admirers and well-wishers. The papers were full of it for days and prompted Mrs Sowrey to write a letter to her youngest son:

You must have lived in a whirl of excitement during the last few days. We know practically nothing of what had happened until we saw your dear old face (I mean head) in the *Daily Mail* this morning, and then we sent up to Staines for all the papers – why, you are everywhere.

Come and tell us all that happened and Queenie wants you to send Lieutenant Robinson's autograph. What a lucky bounder he is, but please don't try to do the same thing. It's far too risky.[35]

For once Frederick disobeyed his mother and by repeating Robinson's feat found himself the cynosure of all eyes. Again, in came telegrams, tributes and letters, mainly from young girls inviting the latest 'Zepp Strafer' to tea parties or begging for locks of hair, photos and autographs. But not only did the victor enjoy congratulatory messages. Sowrey Senior was the recipient of similar tidings, especially when Frederick's DSO award was announced on 4 October:

I notice in the paper that your son, Second Lieutenant

Sowrey was a popular character with officers and men alike. Like Robinson, he had a keen sense of humour, and the two had become firm friends since their first meeting while serving with 19 Reserve Squadron at Hounslow.
Miss M Sowrey

Sowrey, has accomplished a very noble action on a recent occasion when we were visited by an incubus which we are well rid of. It is very pleasant reading to note that His Majesty has recognised this noble action by the DSO. Such men as these who risk their lives day after day protecting property and innocent lives deserve the greatest appreciation and thanks that any patriotic Englishman can give.[36]

Following the furore caused by Robinson's receipt of prize money, and despite appeals made on his behalf, no prize-money was forthcoming to Sowrey and Lord Michelham was prevented from making his intended contribution, much to that distinguished patriot's deep regret. Other groups of individuals that had promised monetary awards were similarly disappointed, and many of Sowrey's friends expressed incredulity at the official standpoint. Among them was Violet Grinling, who regularly corresponded with 'Freddie', the two having become acquainted during the Suttons Farm airmen's visits to Harrow Weald House. Violet's brother Jimmy often used to write to his sister's friend from Moretons, one of Harrow School's boarding houses. Young Grinling did not seem to care much for his surroundings:

> You simply must come up and see me at this Godforsaken spot. If you can tear yourself from your receptions and dinners with the Great King. I wonder if you will ever be sober again? I've just had the police in my room complaining that I show too much light. You might strafe a few more Zepps will you? and then I can show as much light as I want.[37]

Another of Freddie's acquaintances was the actress Madge Saunders, and on one occasion Sowrey and Robinson saw an ideal opportunity to 'put the wind up' Stammers, whose fiancée was as usual spending the weekend at Suttons. As Vera recalls:

> Robinson took my brother to one side and said, 'Madge Saunders is here, how are you going to get rid of Muriel?' Sowrey said he'd tell her that they were on the alert, that she must get off the air station, and offered to drive her to the train, which he did. After they had left Robinson burst out laughing, admitting that Madge had never been there at all. That's just the sort of joke they would play; my poor brother was in a terrible state![38]

It was typical that the airmen wasted little time in driving over to Billericay in the early hours of 24 September to view the results of Sowrey's handiwork. When they arrived on the scene and bundled out of Robinson's Vauxhall the area was already swarming with sightseers, despite the early hour. Special constables and men of the Irish Guards were posted around the smouldering remains of *L32*, and there was a heated exchange with an obdurate general who refused the RFC contingent access to the wreck. At length he reluctantly allowed Sowrey to pass through the cordon and only then because the latter convinced the Army officer just who *was* responsible for the airship's destruction!

One of the first officials to arrive on the scene was Inspector Allen Ellis of the Essex County Constabulary, who was on duty in the High Street, Billericay, when Sowrey torched *L32*. He bicycled the few miles to South Green and arrived a bare ten minutes after the ship had fallen. There were already several local men in the vicinity, but Ellis ordered them back for their own safety. Soon the group were joined by special constables from Billericay and Little and Great Burstead, who formed a rough cordon around the blazing wreckage, endeavouring with difficulty to keep the growing crowd at a respectable distance. About an hour later the Billericay Fire Brigade arrived, closely followed by constables from Hutton and Brentwood who ably reinforced the cordon around the Zeppelin. Once they got the pumps working, the firemen played their hoses over the wreckage and finally the blaze was brought under control.

Inspector Ellis was called over to examine a body lying in a meadow adjoining the lane and a good 30yds from the main bulk of the tangled white-hot girders. A preliminary check revealed no evidence of life, and Ellis searched the German only to find a pocket book which he later handed over to an Intelligence Officer of the Southern Army. Placing a 'special' in charge of the remains, he crossed over to another body. There was little that could be done as this one was still burning too, and later, like the first, it was removed. The grisly task was repeated several times up to and beyond the arrival of General Burn Murdoch and the officers of the Second Mounted Division, who subsequently took charge. All 22 bodies were eventually placed together, having been searched for papers:

> During the time the bodies were lying in the open, after being brought to my notice, they were in charge of Special Constables and had anyone made an attempt to search them I

am sure it would have been brought to my notice by the Special Constables of whom Supt Magor was in charge.

When I searched the body of the Commander of the Zeppelin, I found he was wearing a long silk sleeve waistcoat, and from the time I searched him the Military were placed in charge of the body.[39]

The Medical Officer in charge, Headquarters Southern Army Home Defence, was Major H Myddleton-Gavey of the RAMC. To him fell the unpleasant task of examining what was left of Peterson and his crew:

I beg to report that in accordance with instructions, I visited the vicinity of Billericay this morning and examined 22 of the bodies of the crew of the Zeppelin brought down there, and report as follows.

With the exception of three, the 22 bodies were all very much burned, in many cases the clothing of them consisted only of a few charred remnants, several had their hands and feet burned off, nearly all had broken limbs. The burning in most cases appeared to be after death but in a few instances it was evidently before this happened.[40]

Conflict at the Crash Site

A little later the Army took over, and during the next few hours the bodies of the crew were laid out in the 'High Barn' which stood at the top of Jacksons Lane on Snail's Hall Farm and very close to the wreck. The barn, a large wooden affair, was variously referred to as the 'Black' or 'Dead Man's Barn', but history does not record whether this was connected with the *L32* incident or because a 17-year-old youth once hanged himself inside.[41] One of the soldiers claims being told to prop the bodies up so that photographs could be taken of them by officials from the War Office. These were to be dropped over German territory to 'show the kind of deaths to which they were sending their airmen.'[42] Such ill-considered 'propaganda' was not unique to those times, and the feelings of any German unfortunate enough to have seen such photographs can be imagined.

Around midday, Inspector Ellis entered the barn along with an Army officer and the Essex Coroner, C E Lewis. At once, Ellis noticed that the body of the 'commander' had been tampered with for 'all the front of the silk vest had been cut or torn away and was missing and the buttons had

Sowrey and his mechanics pose with 4112 at Suttons Farm, September 1916; this is the machine in which he destroyed *L32*. The forward portion of the fuselage and wing upper surfaces have been doped with PC10 khaki for camouflage purposes. The characteristic rippling of the fuselage fabric covering is evident; the centre-section struts are wrapped with fabric for additional strength. *National Museums of Canada*

Zeppelin!

Robinson and Sowrey, in 'mufti', pose with young Geoffrey Grinling in the gardens of Harrow Weald House in late 1916.
Sir Frederick Sowrey/RAF Museum

All 22 members of *L32*'s crew died with their ship and at least one of them had a premonition of disaster. The night before the raid one of Peterson's men confided: 'Death will come so quickly that there will be no time for deliberation or even for instinctive action'.
By courtesy of E A Munday

all been taken from the coat'.[43] He was later told that some Irish Guards had been seen searching one of the bodies and PC 186 Sparkes had intervened when he saw a Guardsman remove an Iron Cross.

Independent witnesses were sought, and Mrs Clara Eales of the High Street, Billericay, later made a formal statement:

> At about 1.10am on Sunday the 24th of September 1916 I saw a Zeppelin fall at Great Burstead. I at once went to the spot arriving there about 1.30am. After I had been there about five minutes I saw a dead body of one of the crew lying in a ditch against the gate leading from the meadow into the field where the Zeppelin was lying. I saw a Soldier stooping down over the body and was apparently searching the clothing, he asked some girls if they would like a button, I believe he gave three girls a button each. I heard the Soldier say, 'He has got some money I can feel it.' I do not know whether he took any money as at that time the body slipped further into the ditch. I got a bit nervous and walked away. While searching the body the Soldier said, 'Don't make a row or somebody will hear us.' The Soldier hit his coat pockets and said 'I have got my pockets full.' I do not know the Soldier or to what Regiment he belonged.[44]

One of the many Royal Flying Corps officers present informed Ellis that he came upon 23 Guardsmen searching one of the Germans. Once they realised his presence they ran off, but when the officer challenged them they halted and were immediately placed under arrest. The whole sordid state of affairs was getting a little out of hand.

Several soldiers later told the special constables to 'clear off' as they were no longer required at the site, an instruction which not unnaturally incensed the Chief of the Essex Constabulary. Memos and accusations flew thick and fast: the Army claimed that the police had rifled the Germans' pockets, but the constables countered and insisted that several members of the Irish Guards were responsible.

Backed up by independent witnesses, the whole fracas went to court, and many statements by RFC, police and Army officers were recorded. An officer of the Irish Guards went on oath and presented his case:

> On night of 23rd-24th September, 1916, I saw a Zeppelin Airship attacked by an aeroplane (East) of Warley Barracks where I am quartered. The Airship burst into flame, and as it fell the 'Alarm' was sounded. Captain Walker, Adjutant, in pursuance of War Office orders, 11th September, 1916, started in the direction of the fallen Airship, by motor lorry, accompanied by a small party of 12 all ranks. Meanwhile the Battalion was falling in in the Barrack Square and about 1.45am, by order of my Commanding Officer, I marched towards Billericay with two Officers and 340 Other Ranks. The exact position of the Airship wreck was obtained from a despatch rider whom we met not far from Little Burstead. We arrived at our objective at about 3.40am, when I reported myself for duty to Major General Burn-Murdoch. He explained the situation and ordered me to form a cordon with a good area round the wreck and adjoining fields. This was done with the least possible delay and General Burn-Murdoch's order *viz*:– that no one whatsoever, save those bearing passes, were to be let through the cordon, was communicated to the Officers and Men, [and] a portion of the cordon, comprising one field bordering the road, was formed by the Royal Bucks Hussars, with whom I got in touch on

The shattered starboard midships gondola of *L32*. In the background, large crowds are held back at a respectful distance; thousands came and the roads leading to the site became jammed with sightseers. Several cockle stalls were set up and fragments of wreckage were bartered and sold; even pieces of the wooden gates bordering the field were hacked off by enthusiastic souvenir hunters.
By courtesy of E A Munday

both flanks. The night was still very dark and beyond clearing civilians off the field, it was impossible to do more than preserve the wreck and bodies within the cordon. When daylight came, the clearance became more thorough and an official, whom I took to be Chief of the Special Constabulary, asked me if I required them any longer and I told him the cordon was complete. Up to then, there appeared to be a thin line of Special Consts, odd soldiers and RFC men guarding the wreck. I was informed of three bodies lying within the cordon, two in the same field as the wreck and one in a ditch behind it. These bodies were guarded by men of the RFC who were subsequently relieved by sentries of the Irish Guards. The senior RFC Officer present, Captain Sarigny, walked about the neighbourhood of the ship with me and anything he suggested in the way of preserving it or pieces lying about, I had done. Hearing that some odd pieces were in a field beyond the cordon, I sent sentries into the field and warned off some civilians who were picking up odd pieces of aluminium from the ship. During the time I was walking round the cordon with Captain Sarigny, my drummer picked up, about 90 yards from the wreck, a copy book with black cover; he handed it to me, and I gave it over to Captain Sarigny. There was but little light at the time so our examination was brief but it afterwards turned out to be the ship's Log Book...

Not very long after, the Admiralty representatives, with duly accredited passes, arrived and the ship was then taken over by the Royal Navy. From that until the Irish Guards were relieved, I was under the direction of Captain Norris, RN, Senior Naval Officer. I supplied him with a fatigue party to get out three dead bodies under the wreckage and while this work was in progress, I superintended the operations. The fatigue party were working in my view and after considerable difficulty, got the bodies out of the rear gondolas and put them down by the hedge about 10 yards away. A 'dump' for collected articles had already been made at the same place and two sentries put over it. The bodies were partially charred and much of their clothing demolished [sic]. Everything found was shown by me to Captain Norris and deposited in the 'dump'. Among the articles I might mention, the control gear, bomb dropping switchboard, two pairs of glasses, or rather one and a half as the fire had taken effect on one pair, the tools of the rear engines and a cap, from which I believe I was the first to discover the identity of the ship, as it was marked in pencil inside 'K.R.A.V.S.' L32. Later we recovered various maps and charts all more or less burnt but every single article was produced to the Senior Naval Officer and then placed in the dump. The bodies were placed on hurdles and carried to the Mortuary Barn by stretcher bearers supplied by the Irish Guards. They were carried up in full view through the fields.

A reliable NCO accompanied each party and the bodies were placed in the barn under a guard of the Yeomanry Regiment on duty there. One of the NCOs informed me that he had to help the Yeomanry Sentries who were trying to keep the crowd back from the road wall of the barn. I cannot say for certain which of the bodies I noticed an Iron Cross ribbon on, but it struck me that it, only, would be worn as is the case now in the German Army. Later Captain Walker told me he had seen an Iron Cross removed from the body nearest the ship, by a policeman who immediately handed it to a Staff Officer. I cannot say anything about the bodies lying outside the wreckage except that they gave me the idea of having been searched, for in the case of the two in the airship field the clothes were open. With regard to the body in the ditch, it was face downwards and was as far as I could see, untouched. I assumed the torn clothes were due to passage through the branches and impact with the ground at a terrible rate. The Irish Guards collected and conveyed 18 corpses to the barn, and the remainder were taken by the RAMC [Royal Army Medical Corps] who came on the scene in the forenoon...[45]

Michael Macdonagh of *The Times* was despatched to Billericay later that Monday morning to secure his own impressions for that illustrious paper:

Vendors of mineral waters, fruit and cake, who put up stalls in the fields, did a roaring trade, as we say, for refreshment was not to be had elsewhere and the weather was oppressively hot. In the distance I could see the huge aluminium framework of the wrecked airship gleaming brightly in the sunshine. I came upon a woman standing at the garden gate of her cottage talking to a group who were eagerly listening to what she was saying: 'My husband and I are farmhands. We were awakened from our sleep by a terrible crashing noise, and getting up and dressing we went out to see what had happened. Then we saw the Zeppelin on the ground blazing.

The tail section of *L32* impaled itself on an oak tree, stripping the branches completely, while the bulk of the wreckage was strewn diagonally over the corner of a mangold field at Snail's Hall Farm at Great Burstead. This is a view looking aft, with the starboard outrigger gear housing and propeller at left.
By courtesy of E A Munday

Untouched by fire, one of *L32*'s control surfaces, its fabric intact, lies under military guard. Another was discovered in a wood half a mile away, and a further two and a half miles beyond that the other outrigger propeller and gear case were found.
By courtesy of E A Munday

Zeppelin!

The old High Barn at Great Burstead which served as a temporary mortuary for *L32*'s dead prior to their burial. Often called 'Black' or 'Dead Man's Barn' possibly because a 17-year-old youth hanged himself in there during the 1930s, the barn was believed by many locals to be haunted; some attested otherwise, since a local circus family once kept its elephants there, the animals often scaring courting couples who mistook the animals' trunks for ghostly waving 'arms'. Over the years the barn simply rotted away and the final remains were removed in early 1966, but the footings can still be seen.
Cater Museum, Billericay

Sowrey poses with 'Miss Frimley', date and location unknown. Sowrey's career in the RFC (and later the RAF) was, like those of his two brothers William and John, both long and distinguished. All three ended World War I with the rank of Major.
Sir Frederick Sowrey/RAF Museum

As we walked towards it we came upon the body of a dead man lying in the field. We looked at him by the light of the lantern, and guessed from his appearance that he must be one of the crew from the Zeppelin... I felt sorry to see the poor young fellow lying there...'

Soldiers with fixed bayonets surrounded the Zeppelin. What the crowds saw was an immense tangle of twisted metal, girders, machinery, extending across two fields separated by a hedgerow. The enormous length and spread of the airship astonished me. It was like the skeleton of a monstrous prehistoric reptile, the aluminium girders, corroded by fire, suggesting its bleak bones. A conspicuous object amid the wreckage was the bare trunk of what was a spreading oak tree, which was struck by the airship and stripped of its branches. It stood 30 or 40 feet high...

Men of the Flying Corps were sorting out the wreckage. Not less busy were the souvenir hunters. Men and women, boys and girls, in hundreds were industriously searching the potato and mangel crops and the pasture fields in a wide circle for remnants of the airship. It appears she drifted across the sky for miles a blazing mass, before she fell, scattering odds and ends of all kinds over the countryside. The farmer told me his lands early in the morning were strewn with patches of the envelope and pieces of the framework. These were picked up by the farmhands who made an honest penny by selling them as souvenirs.[46]

Another correspondent painted a more lurid picture:

[The ship] lay with her nose crumpled and bent out of shape, but the framework of girders and lattice was strong enough to hold together. All this twisted mass of metal fell its length on the ground. As she lay it did not seem that the fabric was burnt off the gaunt ribs until one noticed pieces of molten aluminium and brass in the debris.

One realised the cost of such a craft looking even at the wreck. Lying on the ground was a red leather cushion. This covered the seat of the engineman and the ghastly evidences still to be seen showed that he died at his post. One at least of the petrol tanks had burst in half, and the heat of the burning spirit had melted the broken edges until they looked like some fine fretted lace. The airship was built of aluminium girders, and some of the parts were almost massive, although of course, comparatively light. There were the remains of an air mattress and a blanket, perhaps the bed for one of the night shift when on duty.

Curious evidence of the crew's breakfast still remained. There were slices of bacon and hunks of brown greasy *Kriegsbrod* [*sic*] with delicately sliced potatoes. Even with the subsequent unanticipated cooking the breakfast was not done, so presumably the crew intended to have their meal when they got clear of the coast.[47]

The burial of Peterson and his crew of 21 took place with military honours on 27 September 1916. The church of Great Burstead stands in high ground beyond Billericay and its spire is a well-known landmark. Michael Macdonagh, one of several newspaper reporters allowed to attend the funeral, was impressed by the 'lovely agricultural landscape – an extensive and richly cultivated land set with jewels of villages framed by spreading elms.'[48]

One obvious blight on this tranquil rural scene was the scorched and battered wreck of *L32* lying a mile away and readily visible to those who made the trek to the funeral. The cortège proceeded slowly uphill from Snail's Hall Farm

Zeppelin 'aces' relax at the Hage airship base. Werner Peterson points to a map of England as Kurt Frankenberg, Martin Dietrich and Mathy look on. Former comrades regarded Peterson as a cheerful character always ready with a joke and held great respect for his ability as an airship handler – he never once made a bad landing.
Bertha Dietrich, by courtesy of P Amesbury

The L32 crew's first resting place was the cemetery of Great Burstead. In 1966 their remains were transferred to Cannock Chase.
D H Robinson

Herr Liebel, Vice President of the National Socialist War Victims Association and a member of the Reichstag, gives a familiar salute over the graves of Peterson and his men in 1936. Twenty-three German ex-servicemen attended a memorial ceremony to their fallen comrades, having spent a week at Maldon as guests of the local branch of the British Legion. Swastika-emblazoned flags were raised alongside British Legion standards; similar scenes were enacted at Potters Bar, but as Hitler began his rise to power, the memorial services were banned.
Mrs H Hamilton, by courtesy of R C Shelley

through the twisting narrow lanes until it reached the churchyard. An RFC motor lorry led the procession, loaded with 21 coffins covered with a black pall. One casket was carried separately on a trailer towed by a tender and followed the larger vehicle. Bringing up the rear was a staff car containing six officers and a detachment of men marching behind. The individual coffin bore the erroneous inscription 'Commander Brodruck. Killed on service, Sept 24, 1916'.

In one far corner of the churchyard a large communal pit had been dug for the crew, with a separate plot in front. The six RFC officers carried Brodruck's casket through the gates and the others followed, with four men to each of the other coffins. The service was a brief one, conducted by Rev Hermann Coldwell assisted by an Army chaplain, and it was closed by the Lord's Prayer. During the service the RFC officers stood to attention by the grave of the 'Commander', whilst the other ranks were lined up opposite around the larger plot. Local special constables were allowed to attend the proceedings, but members of the public had to be content with the view from nearby fields. Quite a few people had gathered, mainly women and young girls, who watched impassively as two buglers sounded 'The Last Post'. The vicar later told the writer from *The Times* that the local parishioners, intended to 'put up in the church a tablet cast from part of the remains of the Zeppelin, recording the fall of the airship'. Other fragments of *L32* were made into bracelets, charms and rings for sale in aid of the Red Cross.

The mass grave of the crew, in the shape of a T, had 22 headstones arranged around its periphery each with the crew member's name and rank painted on; for each man there was planted a single rose bush. In the years before World War II, ex-German servicemen visited the graves annually and held their own memorial. In 1936, on the twentieth anniversary, they came over with swastika-emblazoned flags and several gave the Nazi salute over their fallen comrades. One wonders what Peterson and his crew would have thought. In later years the condition of the headstones suffered under the elements, and the painted inscriptions faded away along with the rose bushes. In 1966, like other airship crews, the bodies were reinterred at Cannock Chase, where their sarcophagi can be seen today.

The loss of two 'Thirties', together with their experienced and much respected commanders, was a bitter blow for Strasser, and the results of the raid itself came nowhere near to offsetting the double disaster. It was 23.45hrs when Kraushaar in *L17* observed the tell-tale glow of blast furnaces in an industrial town that he mistakenly took to be Sheffield. Actually the fires were burning at Nottingham, which became the unfortunate recipient of 11 incendiary bombs and eight high explosives.[49] There, the Midland Railways freight station was severely damaged, and further havoc, albeit less serious, was wreaked on the Great Central Station and several yards of railway track. Thick mist in the Trent Valley area fortuitously concealed the Zeppelin as it bombed the town, and Kraushaar eventually went out over the Humber unchallenged. Further bombs from *L17* were heard to explode out to sea as the airship continued its homeward course, the awesome spectacle of Peterson's burning *L32* fresh in the minds of Kraushaar and his crew. *L17* eventually reached Tondern at 09.25hrs.

The remaining Zeppelins failed to reach their objectives altogether. *L21* was unable to climb any higher than 8000ft, and spirited fire from the anti-aircraft gun teams at Stowmarket served to hold off the airship, which dropped 36 bombs on several villages in Suffolk but failed to create any damage. *L14* made for Lincoln, where the raider was soon held by searchlights and then promptly engaged by the gun at Canwick. Suitably chastened, the commander of the Zeppelin wisely eschewed valour in lieu of discretion and, turning for the coast, unloaded 44 bombs. These fell harmlessly in open fields.

L31 approached Sleaford, its commander determined to bomb the town beneath, but vigorous anti-aircraft fire forced him to change his plans. The Zeppelin unloaded its bombs and made off for the coast. All the missiles fell on open fields and *L13* returned home safely, despite being attacked by an RNAS machine up from Cranwell.

Martin Dietrich in *L22*, misled by various radio bearings, attacked the port of Grimsby, but the bombs aimed at the town fell short and little damage was reported. *Kapitänleutnant* Ganzel, in *L23*, was close to Lincoln at 00.20hrs when he too witnessed the demise of Peterson's ship, 150 miles away. *L23* dropped most of its bombs in the sea off Cromer and Overstrand before commencing the return flight to Nordholz.

Despite the misty conditions, many home defence airmen were abroad that night, but although several encountered and attacked the raiders only Sowrey was rewarded with success. RNAS pilots ascended from Bacton, Covehithe, Eastchurch, Westgate and Great Yarmouth, and at least two naval pilots reported having attacked Zeppelins over Suffolk. The men of 39 HDS were not the only Royal Flying Corps pilots aloft that night either, with several patrols from 33 HDS at Beverley and 50 HDS at Thetford being made.

The redoubtable Mathy was fortunate to escape the patrolling aircraft that were desperately trying to locate *L31* as it passed over the countryside towards the coast. Once again the mist in the Trent and Lea Valley regions hampered the defences. With London's searchlights out of action as a result, Mathy probably avoided fiery destruction from the defending flyers. Once more his luck and skill had served him well.

A total of 371 bombs had been dropped in the raid, resulting in the death of 40 civilians and injury to a further 120. Most of the bombs fell on the capital, where monetary damage amounted to £64,662. As for the Midlands, 118 bombs were later traced over Lincolnshire, material damage, aside from shattered windows, being confined to a church, a farm building and several telegraph wires.

In later months, as the defence units forced the Zeppelins to reduce the number of London raids and adopt other tactics, several Suttons Farm airmen left for other units. On 1 December Sowrey joined the strength of 37 HDS and went on to lead a distinguished career with the RFC and later the RAF throughout the remainder of the war, gaining the Military Cross whilst serving in France during the early months of 1917.[50] On 1 February the following year he took over command of 143 Squadron in England and on 19 May 1918 fought a night engagement in an SE5a, jointly attacking a raiding Gotha bomber together with a Bristol F2b of 141 Squadron crewed by Lieutenant E E Turner and Air Mechanic H B Barwise. The German bomber crashed, killing all but one of its crew.

In the postwar years Major Sowrey served at Halton, Uxbridge and Tangmere, reaching the rank of Group Captain and finally retiring from the RAF on 26 May 1940. However, three years later he was re-employed on 15 October as SE Command ATC Gliding officer, but he finally left the Air Force altogether at the end of the war, retiring with his wife and family to Sussex. He died on 21 October 1968 in Eastbourne, and was buried alongside his two brothers at Staines cemetery.

Only two aircraft flown successfully by their pilots against airships have survived. One of them is Culley's Camel, displayed in the Imperial War Museum; the other is BE2c 4112, but the UK-based enthusiast will need to make an Atlantic crossing to view it. The famous BE2c was acquired for Canada by Lieutenant-Colonel Arthur Doughty, Dominion archivist, as part of a number of war trophies, and arrived in Canada in June 1919, being initially exhibited during August at the Canadian National Exhibition in Toronto and eventually winding up as a prized exhibit in the Canadian War Museum in Ottawa.

The aircraft was loaned to the RCAF on 17 November 1959 for the purpose of being exhibited during the Air Force's 50th anniversary, and was in very poor condition when it arrived. The RCAF completely refurbished the machine, obtaining a new engine from England and making up various parts that were missing. In 1962 the original airscrew was donated to the War Museum by the Air Ministry at the suggestion of Wing Commander F B Sowrey.[51]

As originally displayed, 4112 was painted in black and PC10, with simple white rings in the usual roundel positions, the restoration team faithfully following the original finish of the aircraft as it appeared in 1919. Such a scheme was used as night-fighter camouflage for the latter war years, in distinct contrast to the finish worn by 4112 when Frederick Sowrey matched it against a 'Super Zeppelin' over six decades ago.[52]

The loss of *L32* and *L33* on that fateful night proved to be a turning point in the naval airship offensive against England, and even Strasser began to appreciate that his cherished dream of Zeppelin supremacy would probably never be realised and certainly no longer affect the morale of the English civilian as deeply as he had once expected. But for the Leader of Airships and his subordinates, a far greater tragedy was to come, a tragedy instigated yet again by one of the small band of pilots who made up B Flight, 39 HDS, RFC.

In the centre of this photo lies the hedgerow on Snail's Hall Farm where L32 fell to earth as it can be seen today. The old mangold field is beyond the line of trees.
Author

A famous BE2c. This is 4112 in all-black finish as displayed for many years at Ottawa's Canadian War Museum. Just before this book went to press came the welcome news that the aircraft is to be totally restored to its original 1916 appearance.
Canadian Forces Photo Unit PL 104900

CHAPTER 9

L31, 2 October 1916

'...During these days when you lay our little daughter down to sleep, a good angel will see you and will read what is in your heart, and he will hasten to guard my ship against the dangers which throng the air everywhere about her...'

Heinrich Mathy, to his wife, 25 September 1916

Strasser's reaction to the tragic loss of *L32*, *L33* and their highly trained crews was clearly revealed by orders regarding the next raid, which was scheduled for 25 September. Seven elderly Zeppelins were directed to attack the Midlands and two 'Thirties' authorised to head for London with the limitation that 'caution is ordered in case of clear weather'. Once more in command of *L31* was Heinrich Mathy, at 33 years of age the most experienced of Strasser's senior officers and undoubtedly one of the most daring and skilful. Revered by his comrades and respected by his enemies, Mathy was embarking on his penultimate flight to England.

Once airborne, Mathy steered for the Channel via the Rhineland and Belgium; eventually he was to realise that an attack on London would be impossible due to clear weather and thus sought an alternative. As far as Mathy was concerned the bombing of Portsmouth was a great success; mercifully he did not live long enough to realise the failure it actually was.[1]

Mathy
Heinrich Mathy was born on 4 April 1883 at Mannheim, the eldest child of Eduard Mathy, a bank director. A great uncle, Karl, had earlier played a major role in the 1848 revolution to end up as Prime Minister of Baden after the 1866 Prussian–Austrian war: other Mathys were Army officers, yet from an early age Heinrich resolved to enter the Navy. During the years up to 1900, when at 17 he realised his life-long ambition, Mathy had enjoyed a good education and developed a strong talent for sketching. The budding young artist whiled many an hour away drawing squadrons of battleships or members of the Karlsruhe Garrison mounted cavalry, the family having moved to this town during 1889; later they went to live at Strassburg in Elsass.

Mathy's initial naval postings were to armoured cruisers, his captain in the *Friedrich Karl* and *Gneisenau* being *Kapitän zur See* Franz von Hipper, later to command the battlecruisers at Jutland. After cruisers came destroyers, in which Mathy served for three years with distinction, but it was not too long before ships of the air caught the young officer's imagination. The 'great flight' of *LZ4* in August 1908 that ended in disaster at Echterdingen[2] nevertheless considerably impressed Mathy, for in one of his letters home he suggested how airships could be successfully employed as naval scouts and expressed his strong desire to command one.

Between 1912 and 1914 Mathy attended the *Marineakademie* in Kiel where, during summer terms, students were allowed to choose interesting assignments either with the Fleet or with heavy industry. Not surprisingly, Mathy elected to enter the MLA and commenced airship training, his log book recording early flights in both *L1* and *L2*.

Although Mathy was the senior surviving officer at Fuhlsbüttel on 9 September 1913, he was not senior enough to succeed *Korvettenkäpitan* Friedrich Metzing, accidentally killed in *L1*, as *Kommander* of the Naval Airship Division.

Mathy in the control car of *L13*. One of Strasser's most experienced and skilful officers, Mathy enjoyed a notable career with the German Naval Airship Division, having already served with distinction aboard destroyers and the armoured cruisers *Friedrich Karl* and *Gneisenau*.
Archiv: Marine-Luftschiffer-Kameradschaft

Zeppelin!

A honeymoon portrait of Heinrich and Hertha Mathy taken at Friedrichshafen in July 1915 by Major Wilcke. *Frau Hertha Mathy*

Instead the post went to 37-year-old Peter Strasser, a gunnery specialist serving at that time with the *Reichsmarineamt* of the Admiralty Department in Berlin. Such an appointment may have rankled with a lesser man, but Mathy instantly took to his new chief and there soon developed a very close professional relationship between the two men, quite devoid of envy. Strasser kept Mathy for special assignments, Heinrich becoming the first commanding officer of Hage before moving on to Ahlhorn where he was charged to establish that airship base. At the outbreak of hostilities in August 1914, Mathy found himself posted to the destroyer *S177* (later, as *T177*, mined and sunk in the Baltic) but by 9 January 1915 he had returned to his beloved airships, nominated as commander of *L9*.

Mathy's service with the Naval Airship Division proved to be exemplary, as a study of his part in the raids will testify. His uncanny accuracy in orientating himself by known landmarks and his persistence in pressing home attacks soon made him a legend in the service. Indeed the name of Mathy is still revered to this day among the ranks of the *Marine Luftschiffer Kameradschaft* in Hamburg, and Captain H A Jones, writing in the official air war history, nominated him 'the greatest airship commander of the war'.[3]

On 28 June 1915 Heinrich married Hertha Wichelhausen, and the couple spent their honeymoon in Friedrichshafen, whilst Mathy awaited completion of *L13*, before moving to their new home at Hage. It is rarely appreciated that the Zeppelin captains lived in comparative luxury close to the bases, together with their wives and children, whom they might leave one morning to be dead in England by the next. It was a unique situation, one that has no real parallel in that war; even at Rosyth, wives of Grand Fleet officers lived ashore and their husbands often slept on board ship.

The Mathys rented a substantial two-storey brick cottage which lay in the grounds of a large estate owned by the *Fürst von Knyphausen*. But besides accommodation for the *Herr Kapitänleutnant* and his wife, there were rooms for Mathy's batman, one Kuhlmann, who always donned uniform when he went out, and a personal maid for Hertha. Then there was Hertha's pet dachshund Hexe (Witch) who once accompanied her mistress on a short flight in *L13*!

When rain and fog made flying impossible, there were train excursions into Norden, and Mathy's wife, because she was so young, received special attention from the officers at the base – including Strasser himself. Invariably the duty officer would ring her up at night with the latest news when her husband's Zeppelin was out on a raid. Even after Mathy had given up his lucky *L13*, his wife stayed on in Hage; only on the last night of his life were the couple finally together in their Oldenburg apartment close to Ahlhorn.

On 29 April 1916 Hertha gave birth to a daughter, Gisela, to whom Mathy became a model father for the remaining few months of his life. After Peterson and *L32* were sent to fiery oblivion, Mathy must have realised that even his days were numbered. On 26 September, he wrote a letter to his wife:

> Peterson is dead, Böcker a prisoner, Hertha, the war is becoming a serious matter. We have both of us remembered this, and in our own good fortune have given heartfelt thanks for the blessed providence that has preserved Gisela's father to her. It is my earnest wish that you may be spared this most heavy sacrifice for the Fatherland and that I may remain with you to surround you with love as a garment...[4]

The day prior to penning these poignant words, Mathy was preparing for another attack on England. Strasser's 25 September raid comprised two distinct assaults, although

L31 prepares to land at Nordholz. The vessel was on its nineteenth raid when shot down in flames over Potters Bar on 2 October 1916. *Frau Hertha Mathy*

L31, 2 October 1916

L31 at Nordholz in 1916. This vessel took part in eight raids over England during a brief combat period that lasted just three months.
Frau Hertha Mathy

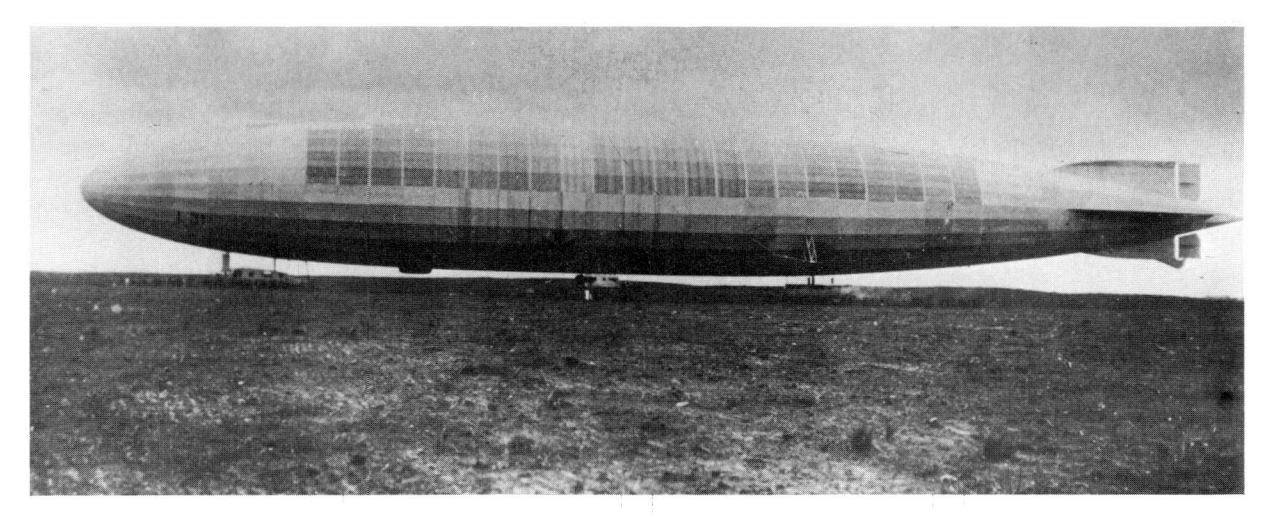

The control car of L31. Its much-respected commander, Heinrich Mathy, is silhouetted through the open windows.
Frau Hertha Mathy

Kapitänleutnant Wilhelm Ganzel took part in the 25 September raid but turned back three times from the Norfolk coast. He was later transferred to a light cruiser. Commander of L23 from 10 August 1916 to December that year, Ganzel participated in several raids on England.
R Frey, by courtesy of P Amesbury

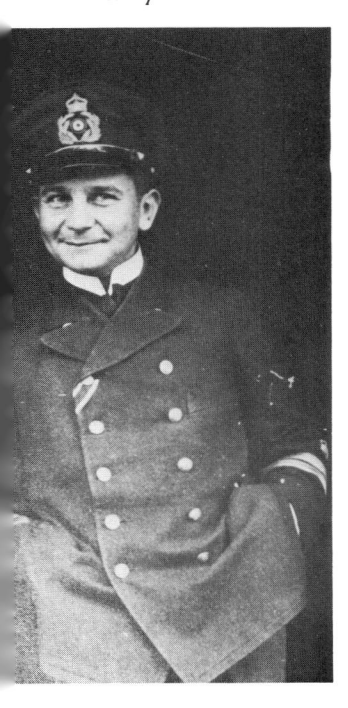

three of the Zeppelins aborted on nearing the English coast. In *L23*, Ganzel made three approaches to Norfolk's coastline, and on each occasion he turned back. Ganzel later explained away his actions as a result of recurring engine failure but in truth he was suffering from severe combat neurosis – such symptoms were barely appreciated in the early years of aerial warfare – and within two months the unfortunate commander of *L23* had been transferred to the light cruiser *Kolberg*.

Martin Dietrich in *L22* made accurate landfall over Mablethorpe around 21.40hrs and subsequently sailed over Sheffield, releasing 15 high explosives and an equal number of incendiaries. Only by sheer good fortune did the missiles fail to strike that town's armament factories, although one incendiary did start a small fire at a machine shop belonging to shipbuilders John Brown and Company. Other damage was restricted to small cottages in the vicinity, but by comparison casualties were heavy, with 28 dead and 19 injured. Fired upon by anti-aircraft gunners, *L22* passed over Sheffield unseen, and Dietrich left English shores, dropping his remaining bombs in the Humber off Immingham as a final gesture before going out.

Frankenberg (*L21*) came inland over Sutton-on-Sea at Lincoln, passing across the outskirts of Sheffield before reaching Todmorden, where the first bombs tumbled down. Bolton suffered the most: 13 people were killed there, and another 13 injured, but material damage was reported to be slight in the villages of Ewood Bridge, Holcombe, Holcombe Brook, Newchurch, Ramsbottom and Rawtenstall. A final bomb, which did not explode, fell near the grounds of Bolton Abbey as Frankenburg turned coastwards, firmly of the opinion that he had attacked Derby.

L14 managed to reach York but, thwarted by the Acomb gun, the Zeppelin's captain made a wide sweep and approached Leeds from the north. Nevertheless alert crews manning the searchlight and gun at Collingham soon picked up *L14*, which dropped its remaining 43 bombs, causing slight damage to property in the town and wrecking a house in York. No casualties were reported. Of the Midlands raiders it only remains to record that *L16* came inland undetected and meandered over Yorkshire for a couple of hours, only three of its bombs subsequently being accounted for by GHQ Home Forces.

Commanding *L30* was von Buttlar, who earlier had left Belgian shores at Blankenberghe around 19.20hrs and

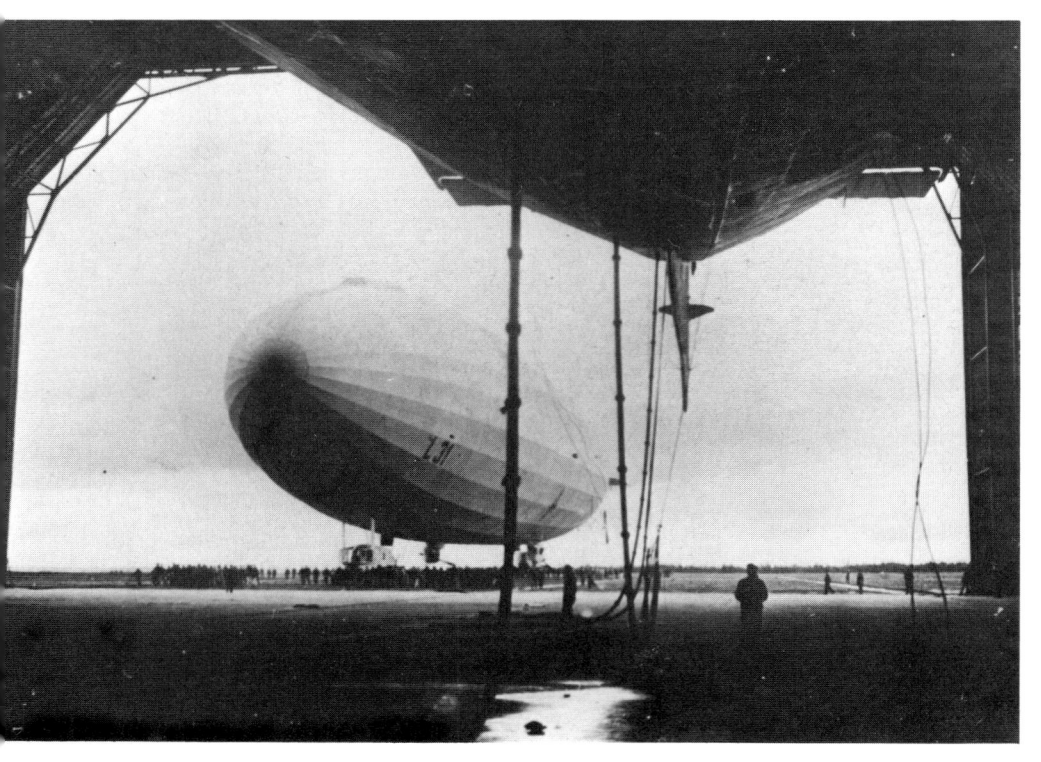

An evocative view of *L31* framed by the open doorway of the *Normann* shed at Nordholz. Above the cameraman looms the tail of *L30*, knotted handling ropes hanging from the hull. *Luftschiffbau Zeppelin*

L31 being walked towards the *Normann* shed at Nordholz in 1916 July. Two lifeboats can be seen. It should be noted that all hull numbers on Naval airships were prefixed with the letter 'L'; on Army vessels, 'LZ' was adopted. *Frau Hertha Mathy*

steered for the North Foreland. Conditions were extremely clear, with no protective cloud cover to conceal the approach of the raiders. Prudently von Buttlar chose to give London and its spiteful defences a wide berth, and later claimed to have bombed both Margate and Ramsgate. Yet no bombs were traced at either town, and even to this day von Buttlar's precise course over England that night has remained something of a mystery.

At 21.15hrs Heinrich Mathy was over Beachy Head, and 45 minutes later passed over Selsey Bill, where *L31* descended to 4000ft, Mathy ordering a parachute flare dropped to obtain a bearing. Thanks to the clear weather a London attack was impossible, and therefore Mathy approached Portsmouth at an altitude of 11,000ft. Here he was greeted by a spirited barrage from alert gunners, aided by many searchlights, which in the clear air were particularly blinding. Inexperience and several misfires hampered the British gunners, but *L31* was well beyond range in any case. Mathy hovered over his target for a full two minutes before releasing the Zeppelin's entire bomb load. Nevertheless, not one of the four 300kg, fifteen 100kg, or fifteen 58kg high explosive bombs, nor any of the thirty incendiaries, was ever traced on land, and they obviously fell offshore. Confident he had successfully pounded the town and dockyards, Mathy steered east, chased unsuccessfully by an RNAS aeroplane up from Calshot. At 00.15hrs Mathy left England over St Leonards, having earlier shut down his motors to obtain further radio bearings. Three bombs were heard to explode off Dover at 01.30hrs as *L31* commenced the homeward leg.

Weather precluded any further raids for the next few days, and the crew of *L31* had time to reflect on the dramatic events of the previous week. Several confided their secret fears, realising that it would only be a question of time before *L31* would succumb to the improved British defences. *Obersteuermannsmaat* Friedrich Peters confessed a recurring nightmare to fellow crew member Pitt Klein:

> Pitt, you know that I'm no coward; out in eastern Asia we made many hair-raising voyages through typhoons. But I dream constantly of falling Zeppelins. There is something in me that I can't describe. It's as if I saw a strange darkness before me into which I must go.[5]

The next raid was planned for the afternoon of 1 October, 11 Zeppelins rising from their bases only to encounter gusty conditions and deep cloud once over the German Bight. On nearing the English coast, the weather deteriorated even further, and most of the airships were blown south of their reckoned positions. The commanders of *L13*, *L22* and *L23* abandoned their attacks altogether, and *L30* came in and went out unobserved even though von Buttlar rashly claimed to have bombed the Humber area. In all, only seven of the raiders were destined to cross the coast: *L14*, *L16*, *L17*, *L21*, *L24*, *L31* and the newly-commissioned *L34* under Max Dietrich.

L14, *L16* and *L21* reportedly bombed Lincolnshire, where 58 bombs fell, killing several farm animals in the process. *L17* released a pair of bombs west of Norwich, and *L34* dropped 30 between Corby and Gretton, all of them falling harmlessly on open fields. These particular Zeppelins suffered a great deal from the vile weather: most iced up dangerously and were obliged to get rid of their bombs at random to lighten the load.

Koch in *L24* came inland west of Sheringham but, failing to fix a position in solid cloud, abandoned his original intention to reach Manchester and turned instead for the capital. Just before midnight, Koch approached London in time to witness a blazing Zeppelin 'north-east of the docks'; nevertheless, he held resolutely to his course, releasing several bombs over the 'districts of Stoke Newington and Hackney'.[6] Actually it was the night landing ground at Hitchin that collected 28 HE and 26 incendiary bombs, 'runway' flares being responsible for misleading *L24*'s commander. Koch's bombs killed a member of the Royal Defence Corps on duty, the sole casualty of this airship's attack, which ended as it went out over Lowestoft at 02.35hrs. Over the North Sea some time later, the tailshaft of *L24*'s forward propeller sheared. Insufficient ballast and a heavy rain-sodden envelope prevented Koch from slowing his ship down to remedy matters. The problem eventually solved itself when the windmilling propeller pulled out of the shaft and spiralled seawards.

Enter Mathy, who made landfall north of Lowestoft at 20.00hrs, determined to carry out Strasser's orders to attack the capital 'if possible according to weather conditions'. For 70 miles, Mathy, aggressive to the end, followed a compass course of 245° and eventually reached the tracks of the Great Eastern Railway at Chelmsford. At this juncture the Zeppelin's six Maybachs were throttled back and the ship slowed whilst radio bearings were made to check its position.

At 21.45hrs *L31* was illuminated momentarily by the Kelvedon Hatch searchlight, although Mathy successfully evaded it before veering to the north-west. Nearing the outskirts of Buntingford an hour later, he turned back once again, throttling the engines down as *L31* drifted with the wind to make a wide sweep south of Hertford and Ware. This manoeuvre took *L31* north of London where, with its engines opened up, the Zeppelin was greeted by a particularly intense barrage. Gunners at Newmans and Temple House came into action once their target had been illuminated, and at 23.27hrs the first three bursts from Newmans caused Mathy hastily to release several bombs and make off southwards:

> The shooting of both gun stations was very accurate, the tracers being clearly visible, but shell bursts were rare. Out of 50 rounds fired from Temple House gun only 20 bursts were visible to the Fire Observer. It is estimated that 75% of the rounds fired from Newmans failed to burst...The target finally went away due west following a zig-zag course. At about 23.45 Newmans ceased fire and at 23.50 Temple House reported the target out of range.[7]

Such a heavy curtain of fire changed Mathy's intentions to attack the capital, and he began to release *L31*'s bomb load in order to climb beyond the range of London's improved defences. Cheshunt was the unfortunate recipient of the Zeppelin's cargo, and at 11.40hrs a bomb struck the rear of 167 Turner's Hill, causing serious damage; a further 50 bombs were then dropped in a half-mile line. Five explosive bombs struck Walnut Tree Nursery, where all 40 greenhouses covering 6½ acres were completely destroyed; 11 bombs then struck the Cheshunt Recreation Ground, demolishing the pavilion.

In all, 347 homes in the area were damaged, four seriously, the rest suffering shattered windows, ceilings and doors. Casualties, on the other hand, were minimal. Catherine Bouette, sixteen, sustained a slight cut on her left hand from falling glass, and a bay pony owned by a Mr Groome, proprietor of The Spread Eagle public house, was cut on the legs by shrapnel. Later Mr Groome had it destroyed.[8]

Although considerably lightened as a result of jettisoning its bomb load, *L31* climbed but slowly, possibly because gunfire had damaged a few gas cells. Mathy was attempting to avoid not only the London gunners but also several aircraft which, attracted by the explosions of bombs, the shell bursts and the numerous swaying searchlights, were approaching fast. Just one of them, from 39 HDS's B Flight, managed to close with *L31*.

The young pilot of BE2c 4577 was over south-west London by 23.45hrs, flying at an altitude of over 14,000ft. Despite the heavy ground fog through which he had taken off and the bitter cold at extreme altitude, the pilot had occasion to reflect on the beauty of such a clear and starlit night. Looking towards the north-eastern area of the city, he noticed that all the searchlights in that quarter were concentrated in the form of an enormous pyramid. At the apex of the beams was a cigar-shaped object, which could only be a Zeppelin, heading straight for London:

> At first I drew near to my objective very rapidly (as I was on one side of London and it was on the other and both heading for the centre of the town) all the time I was having an extremely unpleasant time, as to get to the Zep I had to pass through a very inferno of bursting shells from the AA guns below.[9]

With the throttle fully opened the BE2c began to overhaul the Zeppelin, when without warning the machine's pressure pump failed, the pilot being obliged to retain pressure in the petrol tank by hand. Such an exercise at this height was extremely exhausting besides robbing the pilot of a free hand to operate the Lewis gun mounted in front of him.

London's barrage showed no signs of letting up, but the shells were a good three miles behind as the British aircraft closed with *L31*. The pilot dived at the still-rising airship, giving a tremendous shove on the pressure pump, changing hands and firing a long burst into the Zeppelin's hull. Passing underneath, he let fly with another burst, swung the machine around, and came in under the massive tail fins, pumping lead into her for all he was worth as he flew along the underside of the hull. Gunners in the gondolas vainly endeavoured to draw a bead on their attacker but the aircraft was too close and too fast for them to get any shots in.

Even as the British airman was firing he saw the Zeppelin 'go red inside like an enormous Chinese lantern',[10] and then a tongue of flame erupted from the bows. Doomed, the stricken Zeppelin reared up about 200ft as the sudden heat expanded the gas in its cells, hung momentarily, then slowly sank, threatening to take the British biplane with it. Pushing the control column forward, the BE2c pilot dived earthwards, the blazing wreckage of *L31* tearing down behind him. He threw the machine into a spin and barely managed to corkscrew out of the way as Mathy's last command crackled and spat past, 'roaring like a furnace'.[11]

Recovering control of the aircraft, the airman followed the burning wreck with his eyes as it struck the ground in a shower of sparks, after which he gave vent to his feelings by firing dozens of green Very lights. Reaction quickly set in: feeling sick and giddy, occasionally fainting, and then recovering, the pilot tried to obtain his bearings. Dropping down to 5000ft, he eventually picked out the flares of North Weald Bassett. Coming straight in he misjudged his height in the fog and crashed, wiping the undercarriage away and catching his head on the butt of the Lewis gun as the aircraft jolted to a standstill. Almost immediately he was hauled out bodily of the cockpit by his fellows and in triumph Lieutenant Wulstan Joseph Tempest was carried shoulder-high off the landing field, suffering from a slight cut and a severe headache.

The Fighting Tempests

Mathy's victor was born at Ackworth Grange, Pontefract, on 22 January 1891, second son of Wilfred Francis Tempest by his second wife Florence Helen, daughter of Vincent O'Rourke from Rathgar, County Down, Ireland.[12] Wilfred's first marriage to Mary Perry, of Bitham House, Warwickshire, ended when she died on 19 November 1885. Wilfred fathered eight children and Florence bore him another six. Apart from two sisters, Audrey and Monica, they were all boys, Ælred, Edmund, Wilfred and Wulstan. The second Mrs Tempest was a well-respected tennis player in the mid-1860s, earning laurels both with the famous Badsworth Hunt Lawn Tennis Club and during the Yorkshire tournaments in which she regularly competed.

Wilfred Senior was for a period the chairman of the Pontefract (West Riding) Bench, and his young sons revelled in tennis and cricket, such pursuits usually taking place in the extensive grounds of Ackworth Grange itself, which remains the country seat of the Tempests to this day. The boys also hunted with the Badsworth Hounds, the kennels being conveniently situated in a corner of the estate. Wulstan rode regularly with the York, Ansty and Bramham Moor hounds, and in his day gained an enviable reputation as one of the best riders in Yorkshire.

At the age of nine, Wulstan entered the long-established

Zeppelin!

'The Fighting Tempests'. Lieutenant Wulstan Joseph Tempest DSO with his brothers Major Wilfred Norman Tempest of the KOYLI (seated), killed the same day Wulstan's DSO announcement was made, Sergeant Ælred and, right, Lieutenant Edmund, who served throughout the war on the Western Front. *Stonyhurst School*

An early formal portrait of Second Lieutenant Wulstan Joseph Tempest in the uniform of the King's Own Yorkshire Light Infantry. Like Sowrey, Tempest was wounded in action in France, was sent home and subsequently applied for a transfer to the RFC. *Stonyhurst School*

Second Lieutenant Wulstan Joseph Tempest at Suttons Farm, 1916. On 22 May 1916 Tempest qualified for Royal Aero Club Certificate 2965 and following night-flying training joined the strength of 39 HD Squadron's B Flight at Suttons Farm. *Sir Frederick Sowrey/RAF Museum*

Stonyhurst College in Lancashire on 30 September 1900, joining the Elements. An aptitude for cricket and mathematics distinguished his school career, and he was a regular winner of class prizes. He entered the Navy class after his Figures year and subsequently left in 1905, and it was probably towards the end of this final term that he vowed 'never to go up in an aeroplane'.[13] One small step that ought to have helped change his mind was when brother Edmund began to design, construct and fly model aeroplanes, although at the time Wulstan appeared to evince little interest.[14]

During 1908 he embarked upon a naval career by spending three years on the training ship *Worcester*. Then came another change, to mining engineering, followed by a trip to South Africa with the idea of taking up sugar farming, but as Wulstan only remained for a few months this new venture was obviously none too successful.

While Heinrich Mathy was serving with some distinction in the German Navy, Wulstan and Edmund Tempest were working a section of land at Perdue, in Saskatchewan, Canada, having bought the plot during 1911. They were still busily farming three years later when war came, and, receiving the 'call' from elder brother Wilfred, already a captain in the King's Own Yorkshire Light Infantry, they returned to England, leaving their land in the care of a steward.

Once home, Wulstan found time for hunting with the Badsworth hounds, but the slim six-footer went unrecognised by many of his former associates and during one of the first meets received the 'cold shoulder' from several who took him for a stranger. Typically, Wulstan chose to ignore them, concerned only with the hunt and quite satisfied to enjoy his day keeping his place at the front of the field.

Tempest's military career began on 30 November 1914 with a temporary commission as a second lieutenant in the Sixth Battalion the KOYLI. May 1915 saw Wulstan taking part in the Second Battle of Ypres, where that town was held only after enormous sacrifices. Between the third week of April until the end of May, the British and Canadians lost nearly 6000 officers and men in bloody slaughter. Wulstan was one of hundreds wounded, and after a harrowing twenty-four hours buried in a dugout was invalided home. The results of this traumatic experience led to periodic rheumatic gout which left him somewhat lame; indeed, it was quite some time before he was again fit for military service.

In July of that year Wulstan rejoined the KOYLI but soon found himself transferred to a garrison battalion at Newcastle. During his front-line service he had seen much aerial activity, and the love of it grew on him to such an extent that he resolved that his future 'must be in the air',[15] so, following Edmund's lead, he was transferred to the General List for duty with the RFC on 17 June 1916. There followed a period of training, and he was subsequently posted to 39 HDS for home defence duties. Those who can

144

still remember him recall Wulstan as 'something of a loner' and being 'a little reserved', certainly in distinct contrast to the boisterous humour of Robinson and Sowrey; nevertheless, the trio became inseparable companions.[16]

Wulstan's father received news of his son's destruction of *L31* via a telegram which awaited him on his return home from a holiday in Ireland, but within 12 hours another telegram bore tragic news; Wilfred had been killed in the Battle of the Somme on 25 September.[17] It was of course a tremendous blow to the family and took the gloss off Wulstan's victory. Later, in quieter moments, Tempest Senior wrote to his wife describing his son's successful attack on the Zeppelin:

> He was away from the aerodrome the night of the raid having been told that no notice of a raid had come. A phone message came, a single word which was a warning. He got on his motorbike and drove like a lunatic to his aerodrome and was just starting his engine when the word came to go, consequently he was off at once. When he got up he saw some miles away a long silver thing lit up by searchlights and set off in chase. When he got about five miles from the Zepp he thinks, our Archies were sending shells all about him that were meant for the Zepp, showing what rotten shots they were, many burst below him. He was so afraid of losing pace if he went up higher that he went straight for the Zepp which tried to dodge him, and if I remember rightly, passed under her and shot with his Lewis gun from under her and thinks he pierced a petrol tank. However, he saw her begin to glow and managed to get on one side of her. Then she began to burst into flames and he was covered with sparks and feared his machine would take fire and for a bit he said it was like being in hell. Then he threw out green lights to let his comrades know he had succeeded and then he says he went mad. Stood up in his machine and shouted and yelled and started doing nose dives until he realised he must control his machine. When he got nearly down he began to faint but stuck to it till nearly down when he fainted off and came down with a crash and broke his undercarriage. The shock revived him and they pulled him out and then the whole squadron came out and thumped him on the back till it was sore and then they all seemed to have gone off their heads and I believe nearly wrecked their mess room.
>
> I asked him if the Zepp did not shoot at him and he said he never noticed she did, but one of his flight who could not get the height, said he saw it all, and she was blazing at him hammer and tongs.[18]

For bringing down *L31*, Tempest was awarded the DSO on October 13, 'in recognition of conspicuous gallantry and devotion to duty in connection with the destruction of an Enemy Airship.'[19] Promoted later to Captain, Wulstan was to take over command of 100 Squadron on 11 December 1917. This unit had been formed in England from squadrons of the Home Defence Wing and was the first night-bombing squadron to go overseas, mobilisation taking place at Farnborough in February 1917. Research has not discovered the exact date that Tempest joined 100 Squadron, but the unit history first places him taking part in a bombing raid on Douai's railway on the night of 29/30 April 1917.[20] Wulstan subsequently went on to fly many successful missions over German-occupied positions.

On 10 October 1917, Flight Commander Tempest was awarded the Military Cross, the citation being announced several months later in the *London Gazette*:

> For conspicuous gallantry and devotion to duty on many occasions. He has successfully bombed railway sidings and aerodromes, often in misty and cloudy weather, and at a low altitude, causing much damage to his objectives. On one occasion he descended to a very low altitude and dropped bombs on two moving trains, causing them both to be derailed. This officer has taken part in 34 night bombing raids.[21]

Wulstan left 100 Squadron on 16 June 1918, being succeeded by Major C G Burge and having attained the rank of Squadron Commander (Temporary Major) when the RAF was formed on 1 April. A year later saw Wulstan announcing his engagement to *Mlle* Camille Millicent Best, eldest daughter of *Madame* C M Best and the late J P Best of Brussels and Antwerp. The romance had apparently blossomed since the Armistice, dating from King Albert's state entry into the capital. Wulstan had flown the Prince of Wales to Brussels at that time and during his stay met the young woman to whom he became engaged. However, the couple never married, and in 1921 Wulstan retired from the RAF, retaining his Army rank of Major. Wartime injuries kept Tempest in and out of hospitals after his retirement, but they probably didn't bother him overmuch on 5 April 1923, when he married Ethel Fernandes, who later bore him a son, Norman Edmund.

During World War II, Wulstan commanded a battalion of the Home Guard and later a squadron of the Air Training Corps in Newbury. In 1958, the Tempests joined their married son who had emigrated to Grimsby in Canada and it was there, at the age of 75, that Wulstan Joseph Tempest died on 20 December 1966.[22]

Potters Bar

When *L31* began its death plunge, Londoners and those in outlying districts witnessed the demise of a 'baby killer' for the third time within a month; once again excited men, women and children swarmed out into flame-tinged streets to gaze in awe as the latest victim of the air defences fell slowly earthwards:

> At first we could hear gunfire and see shellbursts like little sparks in its vicinity but these stopped and she seemed to go slowly on unharmed. Soon after, quite suddenly, a pinkish spot appeared near the centre of the silver cylinder; it spread until the whole ship had taken on a fiery orange colour but for a short time no other change seemed apparent. Then the

Overleaf:
The tangled heap that represents the fore section of Mathy's *L31* piled up against an oak tree in Oakmere Farm, Potters Bar, on 2 October 1916. A gondola can be seen at the top of the twisted pile. Picket fences and guards keep the crowds at a respectful distance.
By courtesy of E A Munday

Sowrey and Tempest at Suttons Farm. The farmhouse stands at right and temporary quarters for the station personnel are to the left. The retreating figure is believed to be Robinson.
Sir Frederick Sowrey/RAF Museum

Zeppelin!

A Royal Navy truck takes away portions of *L31* as a drizzle falls over the crash site at Potters Bar. Amongst the tangled heap at right, portions of a gondola can be seen underneath what appears to be a frame for some of the bomb release shutters.
By courtesy of E A Munday

One of the crushed gondolas of *L31*. The wreckage of Mathy's ship fell to earth in two separate parts, the rear half strewn across several fields and the bows piled up against the large oak. Despite contemporary claims to the contrary, neither Mathy nor any member of his crew were found alive by those first on the scene.
By courtesy of E A Munday

L31, 2 October 1916

Army personnel attempt to drag wreckage away from the oak tree with ropes. Despite the presence of the military, many souvenir hunters managed to sneak off with fragments of duralumin.
By courtesy of E A Munday

A buckled fuel tank from *L31* bears the date 13 June 1916, a month prior to the vessel's first flight.
By courtesy of E A Munday

Among the many thousands who made the trek to Oakmere Farm to view the remains of *L31* were the entire band of the *Garde Republicaine*, at that time touring England to entertain wounded servicemen. The destruction of the third Zeppelin over England was an unexpected distraction from their concert duties.
By courtesy of E A Munday

whole began to fall, slowly at first then bending near the centre in an inverted 'V' and dropping, a blazing mass which broke into two molten blobs of fire, until it was hidden by intervening roofs.[23]

From his observation post at Alexandra Palace, Lieutenant Harry Carter of the Royal Defence Corps watched *L31* as it sailed across London, bracketed by exploding shells.

[The] gunfire ceased and a flame appeared in the petrol tank or gondola of the Zeppelin, the reflection from same shining brilliantly on the outer skin of the ballonette [sic] which subsequently caught fire and burnt slowly from rear to fore, crumpling in the middle, practically breaking in half and falling in two pieces to the earth.[24]

The blazing remains of *L31* fell in two distant heaps, the front portion around a large oak tree in Oakmere Park, Potters Bar, in a field owned by a Mrs Kemble. The wreckage completely stripped one side of the tree of all its branches and piled up around the trunk, the control gondola remaining on top of the ghastly heap. Several bodies lay around the wreckage, making obscene dents in the earth. Mathy and most of his crew had preferred a jump as the lesser of two evils. Several hundred feet away the rear half of *L31* was strewn over several fields. The two main heaps continued to burn for some time drawing on the fuel from split petrol tanks; even a steady drizzle that fell before dawn and the efforts of the local fire brigade had failed to extinguish the smouldering remains.

The owner of the field was farmer W Bird, who along with several labourers was among the first on the scene. Bird was quite relieved to discover that the Zeppelin had fallen beyond the farm outbuildings:

'Our Fallen Zeppelin Heroes'. A 1916 German postcard pays tribute to Peterson, Schramm and Mathy, killed over England on active service...
Cheshunt Library

...And the men responsible. Tempest (*L31*), Robinson (*SL11*) and Sowrey (*L32*) pictured at Suttons Farm in October 1916.
Author's Collection

I ran through the stable yard and down by a lane leading to some grass fields. In the corner of one of those were some large haystacks and I was afraid that they might be set on fire. When I reached the spot I found they were alright; but about 200 yards away the remains of the Zeppelin lay blazing furiously. I dared not go very near to it for two reasons: one was that the heat was very great and another was that ammunition of some kind was exploding at intervals. I afterwards discovered that this was machine-gun ammunition, a large quantity of which seems to have been carried, for some was found in boxes unexploded. I saw some dead bodies lying about. One appeared to be that of an officer, for I could see gold stripes on the arm of his coat. Another was wearing the Iron Cross.

I had a herd of valuable dairy cows in the field and these were very much alarmed at the blazing Zeppelin. They galloped round the field in terror, and one of them seemed determined to rush into the blazing mass. I had some difficulty in keeping her away and I was very glad when the fire brigade came on the scene and began to throw water on the ruins.[25]

Another local eyewitness was the young daughter of the vicar of Potters Bar. Rev E Preston was on duty that night in his spare-time capacity of special constable, and Miss Preston went out into the family's front garden to watch *L31* fall head-first in a blaze of fire:

The air was so hot that I felt I could hardly stay in the garden. After a time I went to the field where the Zeppelin lay, but the wreckage was too hot for me to get near it. The greater part of it lay crumpled up at one point by the trunk of a large tree, part of which had been smashed down.[26]

It didn't take long for the pilgrimage to start. Police, firemen and members of the Army and RFC were quickly on the scene in order to prevent any looting of the wreck. They found one German officer untouched by fire lying flat on his back embedded in the ground in one corner of the field. By the flickering light of the burning wreckage they fancied he still breathed; later, RFC officers pulled out the dead man's identity disc which bore a simple legend – 'Kaptlt Mathy. L31'.

Throughout the early hours of 2 October and the following few days the wreck of *L31* was visited by thousands, although a 'khaki cordon' prevented close access. Souvenir hunters were lucky to get away with anything other than small fragments, Army personnel relieving many civilians of their morbid 'treasures'. Recovery of the 19 bodies was undertaken quite quickly, and all of them were placed in an adjacent barn.

What with the persistent rain and the tramping of civilian and military feet, Mr Bird's field was rapidly turned into a quagmire. The enterprising farmer charged visitors a shilling per head to view the wreckage, a condition approved by the War Office so that he could obtain some recompense for the damage caused to his valuable farmland. The Red Cross had what was left of the takings.

Guarding the wreckage were two detachments of the HAC, one from the Horse Guards and one of Scots Guards, the soldiers having been brought down by omnibuses from their Tower and Wellington Barracks within an hour of *L31* striking the ground. Subsequent visitors to Potters Bar included the entire band of the *Garde Republicaine*, over from France to entertain English civilians and wounded troops, a veritable army of newspaper reporters, and Tempest himself, who forked out his shilling and went in.

Newspapers over the next few days were full of it: 'Another Zepp Destroyed Last Night'; 'The Fourth in a Month'; 'A Midnight Spectacle'; 'Germany Plunged into Depression' – the headline copywriters had a field day.

L31, 2 October 1916

They even provided their readers with precise directions on how to reach the battered wreck:

Visitors may reach the scene by train from Kings Cross to Potters Bar Station on the main line. On leaving the station, walk to the village, about a mile distant, and through the main street until the police station is reached. The wrecked Zeppelin lies in a field behind the police station.'[27]

One visitor who heeded the advice was young Clifford Cole, who arrived at Potters Bar station early on the Sunday morning:

I followed the crowd to the village and as I passed the police station at the junction of Great North Road and The Causeway I noticed one of the Zepp engines. [It] had apparently been brought from the scene of the crash which occurred in a field on the south side of The Causeway at the rear of the police station. I noticed particularly the depressions in the soft ground where some of the crew had fallen or jumped out, showing clearly the oustretched arms, body and legs. The crew, who perished, were buried in the cemetery on the south side of Mutton Lane.[28]

An inquest on Mathy and his crew took place at the Cottage Hospital, Potters Bar, on the afternoon of 4 October. Presiding was Dr Cohen, the Middlesex County Coroner, and members of the jury included Messrs Forbes (foreman), C H Belsey JP, H Joy, G Simcox and G Wychett. Only two witnesses were called, Sub-Divisional Inspector Lane from Y Division of the Enfield Constabulary, and Major Charles Lloyd of the Royal Garrison Artillery. Both were questioned by the coroner, who soon established that, contrary to rumour, not one of the crew had been found alive. The jury returned a verdict that the crew of the wrecked Zeppelin had been 'killed whilst travelling in a hostile aircraft which was brought down by the antiaircraft organisation.'[29] Dr Cohen concluded the proceedings by indicating that he would highly commend Lane and two police colleagues, Sergeant Croxon and Acting Sergeant Crack, for the 'admirable way in which they had discharged their duty after the Zeppelin had fallen'.

It only remained for the crew of *L31* to be buried, and once again the services of local undertaker Mr Edwin Birt were called upon to handle the arrangements. Thursday afternoon, 5 October, saw the coffins transported to Mutton Lane and buried alongside the victims of *SL11*. Care was taken to keep the time of the burial a secret, and as a result there were few civilian sightseers other than a handful of local residents. It was a military affair once again, Army officers bearing Mathy's coffin, with members of the RFC carrying those of the crew. An Army chaplain and Rev Preston officiated at the ceremony:

On Saturday 14 October 1916, special presentations were made in the NZ Camp at Grey Towers to Robinson and Sowrey in recognition of their successful attacks on the airships. Each airman was awarded a handsome silver cup; the inscriptions were similar: 'Presented by the residents of Hornchurch, Essex, as a token of admiration and gratitude to Lieutenant William Leefe Robinson VC, Worcestershire Regiment and Royal Flying Corps. Lieutenant Robinson with conspicuous bravery attacked and destroyed an enemy aeroplane under circumstances of great difficulty and danger during the night of September 2/3 1916.' Something like 3000 individual subscriptions had been raised for Robinson's cup, who following Sowrey's success wrote to W H Legg, Chairman of the Parish Council, suggesting that his comrade share the gift; when Tempest brought down *L31*, a third cup was purchased. Grey Towers, it will be remembered, was where 'Rex' Warneford had his first taste of service life.
Author's Collection

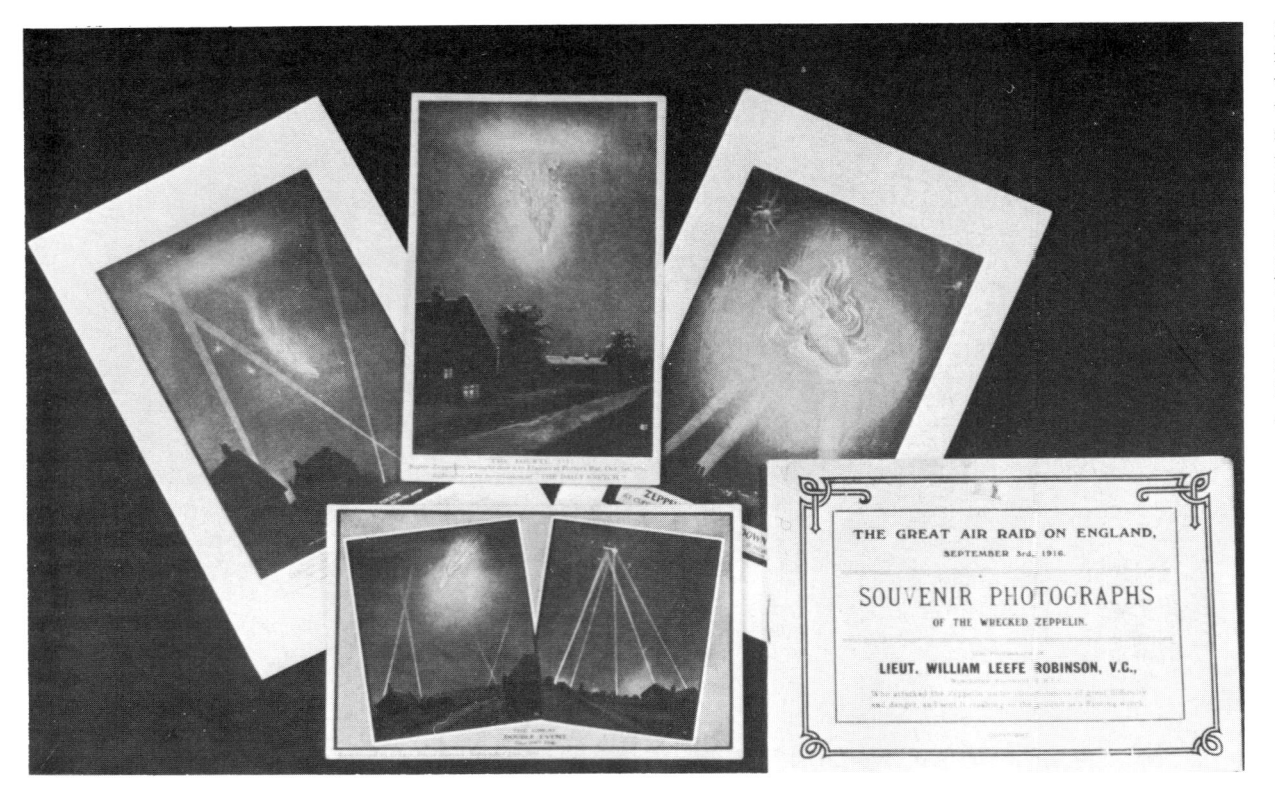

Following the destruction of four airships within four weeks, picture postcards were rapidly circulated and sold in their thousands; most were based on artists' impressions, and despite claims to the contrary by the publishers few showed 'real photos'. This souvenir booklet of the Cuffley airship was later recirculated, with additional material on *L31* and *L32* included.
Author's Collection

Forasmuch as it hath pleased Almighty God of His great mercy to take unto Himself the souls of these airmen here departed, we therefore commit their bodies to the ground... in the sure and certain hope of the Resurrection to eternal Life.[30]

'The Last Post' was sounded to close the affair, and there were no 'unseemly incidents' to mar the occasion. Mathy's remains were enclosed in a coffin of Japanese oak, covered by a black pall, and on the lid was a plate bearing a simple inscription: 'Commander Mathy. Died on Service. Oct 1 1916'.

So passed Strasser's most valuable airship commander, whose loss had a deep effect on his superior and all the men of the Naval Airship Division. As one petty officer later wrote:

There was only one airship commander with whom I ever flew that I would have trusted to find his way over England without making a bad mistake. That was Heinrich Mathy... It was the aeroplane firing the incendiary bullet that brought about his downfall and with him the life and soul of our airship service went out too.[31]

Strasser wrote to Mathy's young widow on 3 October and stressed the late commander's 'tireless energy' and his being a 'cheerful, helpful and true comrade and friend, high in the estimation of his superiors, his equals and his subordinates.'[32]

Over the following days at Potters Bar the police were still busy: having guarded the wreckage for a time and having attended the crew's funeral, there was still the problem of souvenir hunters to be considered. While many sightseers

Airship crew graves at the Mutton Lane cemetery, Potters Bar, photographed in the summer of 1937. *SL11*'s dead lie nearest the camera, with Mathy and his comrades beyond. In 1966 the remains were transferred to the German War Graves at Cannock Chase, Staffordshire.
D H Robinson

had snatched up small aluminium fragments without detection, several locals had acquired more impressive relics and a number of them were summoned for having failed to report their finds. The Barnet Petty Sessions held on Wednesday 19 October heard several cases.

Messrs Baggot, Casey, Longworth, Thain, Viola and Wilson had charges brought before them; all except Wilson pleaded guilty. Wilson was found with parts from one of the Maybach engines, Longworth and Viola with portions of lattice girder and Casey and Thain with sections of fabric, and Baggot had tripped over a piece of propeller and taken it away.

Chairman Alderman Pank DL decided that all the defendants would be treated the same way and ordered the men to pay costs of 40s per head. Pank submitted that the men were probably unaware of the gravity of their offences but warned that in future cases the Bench 'would take a very different view'.[33]

In the years after World War I annual remembrance services were held at Potters Bar for the crews of both wrecked airships. At the 1932 service there were 'interruptions' by a member of the Nazi party and the then vicar of Potters Bar, Rev Andrew Robinson, refused to conduct the 1933 service unless he had an assurance it would not serve as an excuse for another such demonstration. But although the conditions were agreed, 1933 was the last occasion that the ceremony was performed. The following year Rev Robinson declined to continue the service because of the Nazi attitude towards religion and the disturbing effects of Hitler's regime.

In 1966 both crews were removed to the German war graves at Cannock Chase. At Potters Bar little is left as a reminder of the exciting events of October 1916. For many years the 'Zeppelin Oak', scarred but still standing, was preserved as a memorial to the destruction of *L31*. In the 1930s a new housing estate was built on the old farmlands; the oak stood for several more years until it decayed to so dangerous a condition that it had to be chopped down.[34] Today the only reminder of that night long ago is the name of the road which passes close by the site of the old oak – Tempest Avenue.

The famous 'Zeppelin Oak' at Potters Bar, seen decaying in the summer of 1937. Despite pleas by historically minded locals, the rotting trunk was hacked down several years afterwards. More houses were built around the site subsequently and all traces of the tree have long since vanished.
D H Robinson

Tempest Avenue in Potters Bar. A few yards down this street to the right, between houses 9 and 11, is the exact spot where the 'Zeppelin Oak' once stood and where the bulk of Mathy's *L31* struck the ground.
Author

CHAPTER 10

L34/L21, 27/28 November 1916

'...At a North East Coast town yesterday a man was sent to gaol for 21 days for striking matches while a Zeppelin was overhead.
'The magistrate said the man had endangered the lives of thousands of people. Another man was fined £2 for a similar offence...'

Daily Sketch, 29 November 1916

Noon, 27 November 1916, and three officers of the German Naval Airship Division were seated around a dinner table in the *Kasino* at Nordholz. For Max Dietrich the occasion was one of much celebration for today was his 46th birthday. During previous days storms and gales had raged unabated, and Strasser's crews had given up any hope of any improvement when the comparative peace of the lunchtime scene was shattered. Strasser's adjutant burst in with welcome news: 'Gentlemen, orders to attack the industrial district of the English Midlands; splendid prospects; the first ship must be in the air by one o'clock at the latest!'

Cutlery and napkins fell to the tables as officers leapt to their feet and followed the adjutant through the doorway, Kurt Frankenberg pausing to shout back, 'Leave the birthday decorations, we'll celebrate tomorrow!' Hans-Werner Salzbrunn, executive officer of *L21*, was not so confident: 'I know we won't come back from this flight' was his portentous comment to *L22*'s Richard Frey.[1]

'Egbert'

When the definitive history of 'The Great War' comes to be written, Egbert Cadbury will surely occupy an unusual position as one of few airmen directly involved with the destruction of two German airships. Cadbury, heir to his father's chocolate empire, was born at Selly Oak, Birmingham, on 20 April 1893, the youngest son of an 11-strong Quaker family. He enjoyed a good education, first at Leighton Park School, Reading, then at Trinity College, Cambridge, where he took an honours degree in Economics.

When war broke out Cadbury lost little time in entering the Royal Navy, and as an able seaman joined the steam yacht *Zarefa* which was crewed mainly by Cambridge men. His next ship was the minesweeper *Sagitta*, on which he served for several months before making an application to join the RNAS.

It was on 1 June 1915 that Cadbury took to the air for the first time at Hendon aerodrome in Maurice Farman 109. He learnt the art rapidly, and within a fortnight flew solo after a mere three and a quarter hours' instruction:

> I started going alone yesterday for the first time, and then experienced really what flying was like – it was magnificent. Till one gets one's landings all right by oneself, one does 'straights', that is, one just flies from one corner of the field to the other, about three-quarters of a mile. This one does so as to learn how to get up and land. Having done this with an instructor till one makes fairly good landings, one does 'straights' by oneself, and from straights one goes to half circuits and from half circuits to circuits. When one gets to circuits and climbs about 800 feet, going round and round the aerodrome, then one really learns what great fun flying is. One has a feeling of such infinite security, till one suddenly gets into the backwash of another machine, and gets chucked about – with perfect safety so long as one keeps one's head. Then having done enough circuits you switch off the engine and dive to earth, with just the wind whistling through the rigging and no confounded roar from the engine.[2]

Cadbury went on to take his ticket, being granted Royal Aero Club Certificate 1343 on 19 June, and further weeks of instruction at Chingford followed, mainly on Farmans, Caudrons and Avros. As Cadbury explained in a letter to his mother, crashes by pupils were not uncommon:

> There has been a run of bad luck this week, at least 12 machines being put out of action! Six have been really bad smashes for the machines, but all the pilots have been flying again next day.[3]

By 10 July, Cadbury was pronounced ready for service and posted to the air station at Great Yarmouth, where he arrived on 27 July in Sopwith two-seater Scout 1056. There followed extensive training, bomb-dropping, night-flying and getting used to operating seaplanes, as well as flying many anti-Zeppelin patrols. Mostly the latter were just 'scares', which to Cadbury at least were worse than the real thing:

> Our actual sleeping quarters is [sic] about 1½ miles from the actual sheds and the Denes which we use as our aerodrome. On about five successive nights now, just as we were sitting down to dinner, a Zepp would be reported approaching the coast somewhere in our beat. Result – a general panic. All the pilots jump into cars and dash down to the sheds, closely followed by all the mechanics in lorries. As our way is right along the front several cars and two four-ton lorries loaded

with men hurtling down to the Air Station frighten the whole of Yarmouth.

On arriving down there our machines are put on the Denes and engines tested – perhaps some unlucky fellow is sent up to do a patrol, the night being as black as pitch. Then starts the most nerve-racking process I know. We all sit around the fire in the officer's quarters down there like so many doomed men. Suddenly, with a nerve-shattering roar the telephone rings and an officer is wanted immediately on the phone. Someone dashes to it, the rest sitting round in deathly silence trying to read the message by the look of the said officer's face. Then a tremendous sigh of relief when his face lights up and he announces that the Zepp is travelling north, east, south or west, anywhere but towards us. Or the other thing – sickening roar of engines, everyone getting hopelessly rattled and up go the machines, racing backward and forward along the coast, searching the sky or the depths beneath them for any signs of enemy activity.

Having stayed up for their appointed periods, the heavens above the aerodrome are suddenly lit by the firing of what is known as a Very's Light [sic] which is like a ball of fire and is fired from a pistol – the sign that the machine is about to come down. Almost instantaneous with the firing of the light the inky night is illuminated by the countless flares placed in two long lines, the length of the Denes, about 150 yards separating the lines of blazing petrol. There is a roar and a whistling of wind and a machine glides and bumps to earth between the two rows of fire, and almost before the machine comes to a standstill it is swallowed up in the night, the flares being doused with a surprising rapidity least [sic] a Zepp should be attracted to the spot by the glare.

On occasions when they do not actually come near we sit down there waiting and waiting sometimes till dawn breaks for the telephone to blurt out its unwelcome message. I only wish I could give some of those blighters who wrote to the papers asking what the RNAS is doing, and if machines are up at night in full force, one short trip at night. The feeling of absolute loneliness – no passenger being carried – is almost unbearable. Nothing to see save a thin gleam of silver where the waves break on the shore and give off a phosphorescent glint. If it were not for the compass it would be impossible to tell which was land and which sea. Then the awful descent knowing that there is enough TNT beneath one in one's bombs to blow up the Air Station. This mercifully, has been changed, as now all bombs are to be dropped into the sea before landing...[4]

On 20 February two German seaplanes bombed Lowestoft and Walmer: 25 bombs fell on these towns, killing one civilian and injuring another. Cadbury and Flight Lieutenant Chichester-Smith went up in pursuit. Both pilots suffered the ignominy of being fired upon by British anti-aircraft gunners as they pursued the seaplanes, which unfortunately vanished into clouds and got clean away. Another night patrol on 31 July saw Cadbury apparently getting to inconclusive grips with his first Zeppelin, although he was severely hampered by adverse weather conditions and a faulty pressure system:

I had to use the hand pump the whole time I was up, which proved very trying. I must have passed right over a Zeppelin as it was going back, but owing to the mist and darkness I could see nothing below me...

Several of our seaplanes attacked the Zepps breaking up their formations, and driving them off their course, so when they finally reached inland they had no idea of their position, and so unloaded all their bombs into fields. Although Yarmouth did very well indeed – the only unfortunate part seemed to be the colossal number of old ladies who died from heart failure when they heard the terrific explosions of the bombs...[5]

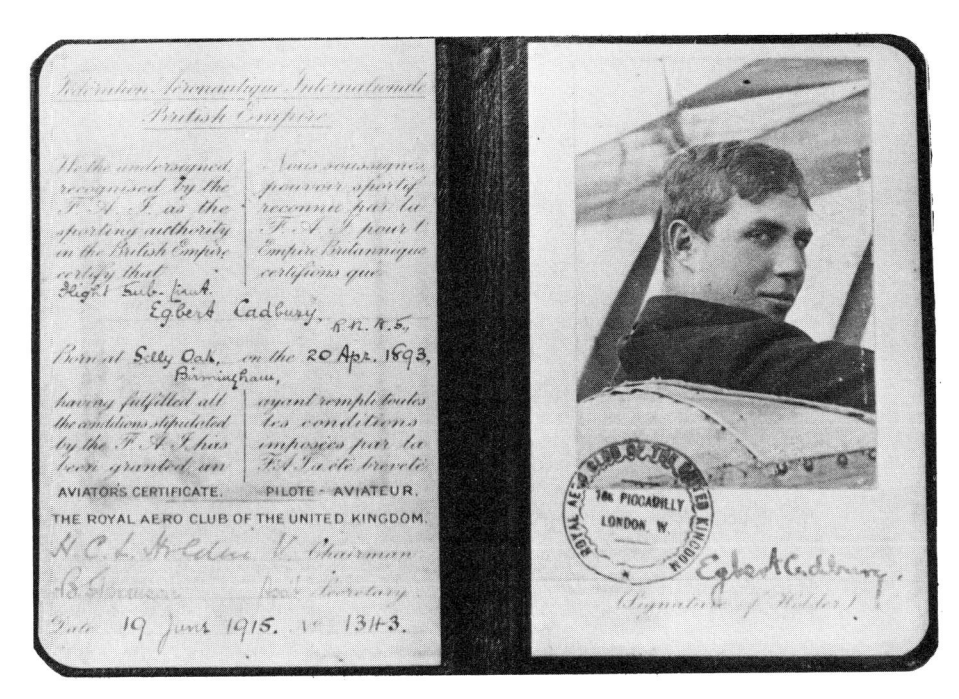

The same night that Robinson torched SL11, Great Yarmouth's pilots were aloft after the raiders. At 22.25hrs Cadbury left the ground in BE2c 8626 in pursuit of one airship which had been held by Lowestoft's searchlight. To his disgust he was unable to reach the Zeppelin before it made off into cloud and out of sight. Cadbury assessed the airship's height as 6000ft, and, whilst anti-aircraft fire was mostly ill-directed, he noted that at least two shells burst very close. After 85 minutes in the air he landed safely back at the air station.

September 23 saw Cadbury flying two night patrols in search of the raiders, and on his second his flying career almost came to an untimely end. Flying in a Sopwith Schneider, he was airborne for over 90 minutes without sighting anything and then prepared to land. Following a few aerobatics close to the sea, his goggles slipped across his eyes and before he could readjust them he had flown straight into the water:

I found myself upside down in about two feet of water. I unfortunately could not get my head clear; I was just wondering how many mouthfuls of beastly salt water I could swallow with impunity when, by a superhuman effort, I managed to clear my lungs, and just got my head clear. The crash occurred just opposite our quarters and only a few feet from the beach, so help was soon arriving. I managed to clear

Egbert Cadbury's Aero Club Certificate 1343, dated 19 June 1915. Cadbury enjoyed a successful career whilst stationed at Great Yarmouth during the war: not only was he responsible for bringing down L21, he also piloted a DH4 against L70, and his gunner, Major Robert Leckie, got in the fatal rounds. Cadbury was a popular character and a most efficient pilot who flew all types of aircraft except for the large flying boats.
Peter Cadbury

RNAS BE2c 8624, built by the Blackburn Aeroplane and Motor Co Ltd of Leeds. The next aircraft off the stocks was 8625 – the machine that Cadbury flew when he attacked L21.
G W R Fane

Zeppelin!

Kapitänleutnant der Reserve Max Dietrich (left), commander of *L34*, poses with his watch officer *Oberleutnant* Christian von Nathusius in 1916. Dietrich joined the Naval Reserve on 10 January 1893 and was promoted to *Kapitänleutnant der Reserve* on 11 October 1906.
P Amesbury

L34 being walked into the *Normann* shed at Nordholz, 1916. *L34* (builder's number LZ78) was built at Löwenthal, made its first flight on 22 September 1916 and was commissioned into service five days later.
D H Robinson

myself and get out, being greeted by a huge cheer from hundreds of people collected on the foreshore! Old men and maidens were wading up to their waists collecting souvenirs. I walked up to the mess, and having my head dressed turned in.

The only damage I sustained, apart from a few bruises on my legs, was a gash on my head and my nose split a bit! Both are all right now, and I hope to be flying again tomorrow or the next day – luckily it has not shaken me up at all and I feel perfectly capable of flying the same machine again – or rather a similar one – now immediately. There is nothing left of my machine...[6]

Cadbury was a burly and rather boisterous character, and following the accident wasted little time in getting back into the air. He jokingly remarked later that he was sure his size had saved him, 'for instead of the machine breaking me, I broke the machine'.[7]

Over the next few weeks no more Zeppelin raids were mounted, but Cadbury and his fellows continued their night patrols besides carrying out live bomb dropping and Le Prieur rocket testing. Cadbury also served on a Selection Committee, along with other officers, to interview prospective officers. The committee saw some 50 candidates but gave commissions to only 20 of them.[8]

On the night of 28 November the Zeppelins came again in force and the various home defence squadrons were put into action once more. At 17.03hrs Cadbury left Great Yarmouth in BE2c 8265, but within 12 minutes had landed at Burgh Castle with sparking plug trouble. On landing, Cadbury met 18-year-old Flight Sub-Lieutenant Gerard William Reginald Fane, to whom he gave latest reports of the Zeppelins' movements. Fane left the airfield at 16.35hrs and within two hours, replacement plugs having been installed, Cadbury also took off into the inky blackness of the night.

The Giant-Killers

In the weeks following the loss of Mathy and his crew no Zeppelins appeared over England, and during the next full moon period Strasser's ships were deployed on scouting missions with the German fleet. Days of storms followed, and then on Dietrich's birthday came orders for the next attack – which, as it turned out, would be the final onslaught of 1916. During the afternoon of 27 November, ten Zeppelins left their bases: *L13, L14, L16, L21, L22, L24, L30, L34, L35* and *L36*, the last two for their maiden raids on England. Ten minutes after take-off von Buttlar's *L30* suffered a burnt-out crank-bearing in the starboard after engine, and at 19.10hrs, when the starboard midship's Maybach failed altogether, he returned.

Once over the North Sea, all the ships encountered weak south-west to north-west winds flying through great banks of vapour, *L35* actually passing within 900yds of a waterspout. *L22*'s crew received a bad fright when *L36* loomed out of a cloud bank barely 600ft above their ship 'then disappeared again like a ghost'.[9]

As evening came the clouds vanished to reveal starkly the sea under a bright starlit sky, the northern horizon glowing with the Aurora Borealis. Such conditions worried the commanders a great deal, in particular Viktor Schütze of *L36*, who 'claimed he could still read his pocket watch in the control car.'[10] Even when this flickering light show had diminished, visibility remained excellent and, hampered by stiff headwinds, the Zeppelins made slow progress towards England in two groups. The captains of *L34, L35* and *L36*, with specific targets in mind, kept close consort heading for the Durham coast, followed by *L24* which struck out for Stockton-on-Tees. The second group headed further south to make landfall over Flamborough Head, but it was *L34*, heading the northern Zeppelins, that was first to come in, arriving over Black Halls Rocks at 22.30hrs. Dietrich headed inland over Castle Eden and before long was caught by the Hutton Henry searchlight. The commander responded by dropping 13 bombs, all of which fell wide of the light and caused no damage.

Max Konrad Johannes Dietrich was another of Strasser's

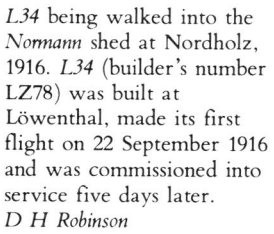

Dietrich and the crew of *L34*: 20 of them were aboard the airship when it was destroyed on 28 November 1916. One of the men had transferred from *L21* since he failed to get along with his comrades in that vessel; ironically, they also perished when *L21* was brought down on the same raid.
Archiv: Marine-Luftschiffer-Kameradschaft

Second Lieutenant Ian Vernon Pyott photographed here in the rank of Captain by Haines of Southampton Row. The ribbon above the RFC 'wings' dates this photograph as post-November 1916.
Mrs N F Pyott

most experienced and respected officers. Born on 27 November 1870 in Angermünde, a lakeside village on the west side of the River Oder, he was said to have come from a very old Brandenburg family. He joined the Naval Reserve on 10 January 1893, and four years later was captain of a sailing ship belonging to the well-known Hamburg travel firm of Laeisz'schen. On 17 April 1901 Dietrich entered service with the Norddeutscher Lloyd as instructor and captain of the *Herzogin Cecilie* in charge of officer cadets, was promoted to the rank of *Kapitänleutnant der Reserve* on 11 October 1906 and travelled the world many times without mishap. On 26 February 1909 Dietrich was commanding the *Sigmaringen* and on 19 May of the following year the steamer *Mainz*, in which Prince Henry of Prussia once travelled to Spitzbergen in the company of a certain Count von Zeppelin.

Dietrich's next ship, which he took over on 4 October, was the *Grosser Kurfürst*, and when war broke out he found himself in New York. As captain of the *Brandenburg*, Dietrich sailed from America and reached Germany where he was awarded the *Eiserne Kreuz* (Second Class) to celebrate his safe arrival. On 15 September of that same year, Dietrich joined the *Kaiserlichen Marine* and ultimately went on to serve as commander of Zeppelins *L7*, *L18* and *L21* before taking over *L34* on 27 September 1916.

After successfully eluding the Hutton Henry light, Dietrich prudently ventured inland no further and turned back, dropping 16 explosive bombs on West Hartlepool on his way out to sea:

> The first bomb fell on Ward Jackson Park – at one time a worded pavement marked the spot.
> Proceeding over the town, anti-aircraft fire ceased when one of our planes attacked it. Further bombs were dropped on Murray Street and adjacent side streets.
> The attack by the plane forced the Zeppelin to try and rise to escape and its last bombs were dropped on Lowthian Road and Hartlepool United's grandstand. My home in No 6 Lowthian Road received a direct hit. My mother and father were badly hurt and luckily my sister was unhurt and I only had slight injuries.
> I was able to scramble through the debris and see the broken burning Zeppelin slowly sink into the sea.[11]

Dietrich had made the fatal error of flying at only 9500ft

and was unable to escape from a determined young pilot at the controls of BE2c 2738 up from Seaton Carew. Second Lieutenant Ian Vernon Pyott from A Flight, 36 HDS, was on his second patrol of the evening, having earlier taken off at 22.22hrs with orders to cover an allotted area until 00.50hrs. He had been airborne for about an hour when he observed a Zeppelin over West Hartlepool, caught in the beam of Castle Eden's searchlight.

As Pyott closed with *L34*, the airship's crew doubtless had already observed the British aircraft because, showing its tail to the enemy, the Zeppelin slowly began to rise. Pyott pulled the Bowden cable of the Lewis gun trigger as he neared his quarry, to be met with return fire from *L34*'s upper platform. It seemed to Pyott that the German gunner's aim was deadly accurate as he felt 'hits and strikes on his body', none of which dissuaded him from pressing home the attack on the marauding leviathan ahead of him. Nonetheless, Pyott was beginning to feel despondent as the Zeppelin was rapidly outdistancing him, when suddenly the airship's hull 'became incandescent' and almost immediately grew into a terrifying holocaust.

Pyott momentarily lost control of the aircraft but quickly regained it, the pilot putting down his temporary lapse to loss of blood, for in feeling his face it seemed soaked. During his return to Seaton Carew he began to realise that he was uninjured after all and what he had taken for rounds from the airship were actually spent cartridges from his own gun and the blood was in fact perspiration: pure sweat from all the excitement, as he later told a fellow pilot, mixed with fright.[12]

Burning furiously, the wreckage of *L34* fell into the sea about 1800yds east of the Heugh lighthouse at the mouth of the River Tees. To excited inhabitants in West Hartlepool and adjacent towns the successful attack presented an enthralling spectacle. Schoolboy Stanley Thompson was awakened by his father and observed the action with utter fascination:

> In the light of the searchlights, a tiny silver fly-like object appeared in the sky flying in circles underneath the Zeppelin and climbing higher with each circuit, until eventually it was flying over the Zeppelin. Once it was overhead, it appeared to change its course and commenced flying lengthwise over the object.
>
> My father told me that it was one of our own aeroplanes which had been sent up to attack the Zeppelin in some way: it was at this time that everyone in the crowd watching became silent as they watched the spectacular drama taking place.
>
> And then it happened! The tiny aircraft appeared to be firing some incendiary devices [sic] at the envelope of the Zeppelin. A tiny lick of flame appeared at the end of the envelope and very quickly the flames spread until the whole structure was a blazing mass. It was then that the whole crowd of people watching gave one great cheer, which carried for miles in the cold night air...[13]

George Sedgewick, another local boy, saw *L34* as a 'huge cigar shaped object entirely in flames moving overhead very slowly'. If the spectacle of another flaming airship warmed the hearts of the civilians massing in the streets, it had quite the opposite effect on the ill-starred vessel's companions. Ehrlich, in *L35*, was above Seaham harbour, a bare eight miles away, when the latest tragedy occurred:

> After three to five minutes the ship became a brightly glowing ball of fire, held her altitude a moment then tipped to the vertical, burning over her whole length, and fell. Behind the ship and apparently separate from her there was a great red ball of burning gas streaming out of the ship.[14]

Not surprisingly, Ehrlich abandoned any thoughts of continuing the raid as *L35* turned for home, and *L24*, 15 miles out to sea with an engine breakdown, did the same. This ship's commander, *Oberleutnant zur See* Kurt Friemel, later reported that he had released bombs along the coast, but none was traced. Schütze, in *L36*, was bedevilled by engine malfunctions and was forced to forget his intended assault on Edinburgh. Dropping all its bombs and a large quantity of fuel as ballast, *L36* limped back across the North Sea, at one stage running on just two of its motors.

Hauptmann Manger, commanding *L14*, meandered over the East Riding of Yorkshire for an hour, managing to avoid the defences there, but on nearing Hull the guns located the Zeppelin and Manger wisely withdrew. Forty-four bombs rained down on Mappleton in response to fire from the mobile guns at Cowden, neither protagonist caused any damage, and, suffering engine trouble, *L14* turned for home.

L13 released 24 bombs over fields on Barnby Moor and went on to York, where the Zeppelin's arrival was greeted by heavy anti-aircraft fire. Its captain dropped his remaining pair of high explosive and 21 incendiary bombs over the eastern outskirts of the city. Several houses were damaged and two people were wounded in the wake of *L13* before it turned back for the coast.

Both Barnsley and Wakefield were visited by *L16*, although neither town was bombed; instead, this Zeppelin's 39 missiles were distributed over the West Riding of Yorkshire. No damage was reported, and on its homeward leg *L16* was engaged by the Acomb gun, which effectively kept the airship away from York. The remaining bombs from *L16* fell harmlessly over the East Riding as the airship went out south of Scarborough to a barrage of gunfire.

In *L22*, *Kapitänleutnant* Heinrich Hollender, on his first raid over England, observed the destruction of *L34* 70 miles away:

> The ship at first stayed on an even keel, then tipped up vertically and we saw the red-hot framework falling. L34 was flying at 11,800 to 12,000 feet and the fall lasted at least eight minutes.[15]

Shortly after witnessing this traumatic event, the crew of *L22* nearly came to grief themselves for, going out over the coast north of Flamborough Head, Hollender's ship came under heavy gunfire. Shrapnel tore gas cells in over 150 places and the Zeppelin became dangerously heavy as cells 5 and 12 rapidly drained. Much fuel was dumped and spare parts hurriedly jettisoned at *L22* assumed an alarming nose-up attitude. At a safe distance from English shores, Hollender brought the Zeppelin down to 2000ft in an effort to compress the hydrogen in the undamaged upper regions of the riddled gas cells. As dawn broke *L22* was still aloft, the warmth of the early morning sun beginning to expand the gas. Aware that his ship would never reach Nordholz, Hollender was obliged to head for the nearest airship base, and once over Hage he had dumped everything detachable from *L22*. Still three tons overweight, the ship fell heavily on the landing ground, most of the shock being taken by the rear gondola which struck a fence post. The force of the impact drove the stake into the ground as well as buckling the gondola support struts, the side propeller shafts and several girders. Yet within six days the Zeppelin had been repaired and was back in service.

The remaining raider was *L21*, commanded by 29-year-old Kurt Frankenberg who, having crossed the coast over Atwick at 21.20hrs, had met a lively reception from gun batteries at Barmston. Frankenberg swung away and made another approach further north, changing course several times in order to avoid RNAS aircraft in the vicinity.

L21 berthed inside the Normann double shed at Nordholz, 1916. Built at Löwenthal, this vessel first flew on 10 January 1916 and was initially commanded by Max Dietrich, then Stelling, before Frankenberg took it over on 15 August. L21 was on its thirteenth raid when shot down and had made a total of 70 flights.
Luftschiffbau Zeppelin

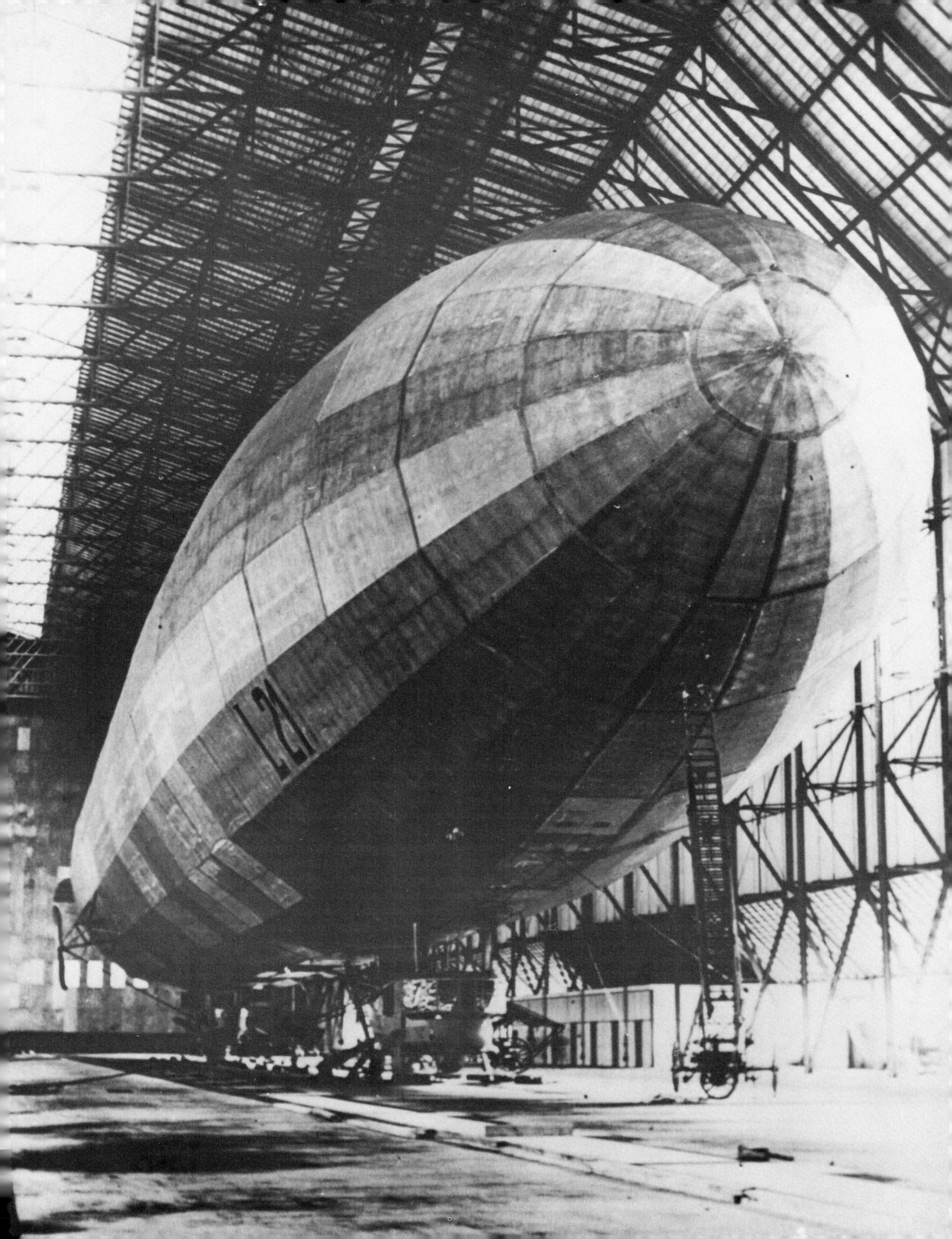
L 21

Zeppelin:

Eventually arriving inland, *L21* made straight for Leeds, where the Zeppelin was held off by the Brierlands gun ten miles east of the city at 23.34hrs.

Altering course southwards, Frankenberg dropped one high explosive bomb and a pair of incendiaries on Sharlston, which an hour earlier had suffered from a visit by *L16*. *L21* was next seen over a well blacked out Barnsley, and Frankenberg's salvo of bombs fell wide at Dodworth. He then moved on over the Peak District to Macclesfield, but the improved lighting orders were so effective that the commander was unsure of his exact whereabouts. Bombs fell on Goldenhill, Kidsgrove and Tunstall, before a glare of lights over to the west attracted Frankenberg who made off towards the new target to drop 16 HE bombs and seven incendiaries on Chesterton, the glare coming from ironstone-burning hearths there. Frankenberg's bombs caused scant damage beyond breaking a few windows. Four additional incendiaries falling on burning waste heaps in collieries between Fentham and Trentham had similarly ineffective results.

At around 00.30hrs *L21* steered away from Trentham, turning towards Great Yarmouth, but north of Peterborough the Zeppelin was met by defending aeroplanes. Two RNAS machines closed with Frankenberg, but although the mismatched adversaries swapped shots, *L21* eluded its attackers and eventually resumed an easterly course, only to be intercepted one final time by the RNAS:

> At 5.7am a report was received that a Zeppelin was over Swaffham at 4.40am and at Dereham at 5.3am.
> On receipt of this information I ordered two aeroplanes (one from Bacton and one from Holt) to ascend in the hope of intercepting her before she got over the coastline.[16]

One of the two pilots thus despatched by Commander A Ellison from the naval base at Lowestoft was Lieutenant W R Gaynor, who located *L21* over East Dereham, attracted by a light that the Zeppelin crew had carelessly shown. Just as Gaynor got within firing range his engine failed, and he helplessly watched as *L21* made good its escape. Frankenberg next appeared drifting slowly over Great Yarmouth, where he was fired upon, then he passed out towards Lowestoft where he was fired on again – Ellison had by now sent up other machines from Bacton, Burgh Castle and Great Yarmouth.

On landing safely back at Seaton Carew, Pyott, almost frostbitten from the intense cold, was borne shoulder-high from the cockpit of his aircraft by jubilant comrades. For Pyott, who was initially turned down by the RFC ten months previously 'owing to partial colour blindness', his victory over the raiding Zeppelin must have seemed vindication indeed.

'IVP'

Ian Vernon Pyott was born on 31 August 1895 in Dundee, Scotland. His father John Pyott and his Belfast-born mother had emigrated to South Africa during the 1880s, but the repercussions of the Boer War compelled the couple to return to Scotland for the birth of their first son. John was the managing director of Pyott Ltd, a company of flour millers at Port Elizabeth, having begun this long and successful business career in Scotland prior to emigration.

'IVP' began his education at the Grey Institute in Port Elizabeth and completed it in 1913 at George Watson's College in Edinburgh, training as an engineer. When war broke out Pyott endeavoured to join up but found himself an inch too short of the required height and, disappointed, returned to South Africa. His next step was to join the Port Elizabeth Volunteers and School Officers Training Corps, and he eventually obtained the rank of Machine Gunner. At the end of January 1916 he had left for England, and following medical examinations was commissioned into the Heavy Section of the Machine Gun Corps during March. Within a month, however, Pyott had applied for a transfer to both the RFC and the RNAS:

> I spoke yesterday to the Commander of the Naval Flying School at Hendon but he tells me there is no chance whatsoever of getting a commission in the RNAS until you have your flying certificate. A good many men enter the RNAS as mechanics and then by degrees get up and get their Certificate and subsequent promotion, so that either you will have to go in in that way or you will have to go to one of the flying schools (there is a Civilian's Flying School at Hendon, Hall's Flying School) and get your certificate and then go for your commission.[17]

Oberleutnant zur See Kurt Frankenberg, born at Marburg near Kassel on 30 April 1887, entered the Navy on 3 April 1907. Among his classmates were the future Admirals Schniewind and Lütjens, the latter killed in 1941 when the German battleship *Bismarck* was sunk by the Royal Navy. In 1913 Frankenberg was known to have been serving on the dreadnought *Kaiserin*.
Archiv: Marine-Luftschiffer-Kameradschaft.

Pyott, at Candas in 1917, takes time off for a little riding. Pyott joined 55 Squadron in March 1917 and in August of that year returned to England, joining a navigation and bomb-dropping school at Stonehenge.
Mrs N F Pyott

From the War Office, Pyott received a much briefer communication:

> As you are aware the waiting lists for candidates for the Flying Corps is an extremely long one but I will bear in mind your letter of April 1st when considering any opportunity that may occur for applying for your services.[18]

Finally the opportunity did occur, and on 3 June Pyott entered the RFC to commence theoretical training at Oxford. From there he was sent to Montrose and Edinburgh for initial flight training, undergoing lessons in such diverse types as the Maurice Farman MF7, Avro 504 and Martinsyde S1. Whilst in Edinburgh Pyott renewed friendships made several years earlier in Dundee before moving on to Catterick for a night-flying course. On 30 August Second Lieutenant Ian Vernon Pyott RFC joined the strength of 36 HDS's A Flight at Seaton Carew.

Following the destruction of *L34*, Pyott received many congratulatory telegrams from delighted English citizens, and in December the *London Gazette* made an important announcement:

> The King has appointed Temporary Second Lieutenant Ian Vernon Pyott, Royal Flying Corps, a Companion of the Distinguished Service Order in recognition of conspicuous gallantry and devotion to duty in connection with the destruction of an enemy airship.[19]

Pyott remained on home defence duties until 17 March 1917, when as captain he joined the strength of 55 Squadron in Candas, France, flying DH4s, but August saw him back in England at 1 School of Navigation and Bomb Dropping near Stonehenge, flying Handley Page 0/100 bombers. As a result of his training he joined 7 Squadron RNAS based at Dunkirk and took part in several night-bombing sorties, remaining with that unit until 9 November 1917. Pyott's final posting was to 27 Squadron RAF, where he flew DH9 bombers until a few months prior to the Armistice when he 'took sick and was hospitalised'. After the war Pyott returned to South Africa and was released from the RAF with effect from 12 January 1919.

On 20 July 1937 Pyott joined the South African Air Force as a captain in the General Reserve of Officers, a post that he held for many years. He started the Durban factory of Pyott (Natal) Ltd, and in 1946, with his wife Norah, returned to Port Elizabeth where a new plant was being planned. On the death of his brother Robert on 5 March 1964, 'IVP' became chairman of the biscuit company which is still enjoying healthy trading. On 23 July 1972, after a long illness, Ian Vernon Pyott died and was cremated at Port Elizabeth the following day.

Pyott's success in destroying *L34* on the night of 27 November was quickly followed up, for the second airship to fall victim to the defences was Frankenberg's, and this time it was the RNAS who were responsible:

> Aeroplanes were immediately despatched from Burgh Castle and Yarmouth, and as, by this time, dawn was breaking, they could clearly follow the course of the Zeppelin, which was then steering SSE from Yarmouth.
> Flight Lieutenant E Cadbury and Flight Sub-Lieutenant G W R Fane, from Burgh Castle, proceeded immediately after her, and Flight Sub-Lieutenant E L Pulling (who had ascended at 5am from Bacton Night Landing Ground), attracted by the sound of firing from the Anti-Aircraft guns at Great Yarmouth, proceeded south at full speed.[20]

It was Cadbury who commenced the attack on *L21*, getting under the ship and firing at a range of 700ft. To Fane, who was nearest the Zeppelin, the pilot behind him was just wasting ammunition, and he decided to get really close before bringing his gun to bear. As Cadbury continued to fire at the Zeppelin he came under spirited attack by the crew manning the gondola guns. Changing drums, Cadbury came in for a second attack, which proved as inconclusive as the first. In all, he would fire four complete drums into the Zeppelin, but before expending all his ammunition Fane attacked:

> As I came in the gunners started shooting at me, which had the most extraordinary effect of putting me into a towering rage. I flew in underneath the envelope and into the slipstream from the front engine which was some way away.[21]

But luck was not with young Fane, who only managed to loose off one round before his gun jammed, its oil having frozen. He pulled away to clear the jam and make way for the third pilot who took up the attack. It was Pulling who came level with the airship at 8000ft then passed underneath, firing as he did so. Pulling only managed to get two rounds off before his gun also jammed, and he turned starboard in order to avoid the heavy gunfire from the gondolas. As Fane, his gun useless, continued to climb fast with the intention of getting above the Zeppelin to bomb it, he noticed that its stern was alight:

> At the same moment the gunner who was in the cockpit on the top of the airship saw the flames, stopped firing at me; whether or not he had a parachute I don't know, but he ran straight over the nose of the ship just before she exploded and disappeared.
> The flames spread very quickly and with all the buoyancy remaining at the front end, it fell by the stern straight into the sea like a spent rocket leaving pieces of burning fabric in the sky.[22]

Fane's face and flying helmet were scorched and parts of his BE2c, 8421, were blistered by the flames of the dying airship, so close was he when the gas ignited. Pulling, in BE2c 8626, was to the south-east of the airship when it caught alight, and he noted that the German gunners kept up retaliatory fire even as the flames consumed the airship:

> I flew parallel to the Zeppelin for a short time a few hundred yards to the starboard of her, and watched her sink by the tail and dive into the sea. The flames spread with great rapidity.
> I was unable to discern any number on the airship as she was

In 1917 the London Chamber of Commerce, through the Imperial Air Fleet Committee, presented a DH4 for the Union of South Africa to Lieutenant-General J C Smuts. Pyott was put in charge of this presentation machine and is seen here with his observer, Lieutenant McKeever.
Mrs N F Pyott

between my machine and the light. As I dived under her I noticed her propellers working and also two black crosses, one on each side of her stern... after witnessing the fall of the Zeppelin I steered due West, hitting the coast about two miles North of Southwold. I steered due North to Yarmouth and landed there at 7.12am.[23]

L21 fell into the sea about nine miles to the east of Lowestoft, where Commodore Ellison had watched the whole affair from the pier. Another close witness was Flight Commander V Nicholl, who had left Great Yarmouth too late to participate in the action. After *L21* disappeared beneath the waves only a large oil slick remained to mark its final position. Excited civilians on the sea front at Great Yarmouth saw the destruction of the latest 'baby killer' as a huge glare which sank slowly and finally vanished into a bank of mist:

Down in the harbour the steamers blew great shrieks of triumph from their sirens and hooters, and I can tell you that for minutes the din was perfectly deafening. It fairly aroused the whole town, and those who were not already at the front very quickly joined the crowd, which was still dancing about and cheering in its excitement...

Once the glare from the burning Zeppelin died down nothing could be seen, and although many people climbed the cliffs and other prominent spots to get a better view in the rapidly growing daylight, the general mistiness blotted out everything from sight.

There was one amusing incident when a flock of seagulls, flying high above in the mist, was mistaken for the returning airmen. 'Here they are!' shouted many of the crowd, and many others had started to cheer when the blunder was discovered, and the shouts were lost in a great shriek of half-hysterical laughter.

Directly afterwards, however, the real 'birds' were seen winging their way rapidly to their station at the south of the town. They were given a tremendous reception, the great crowds cheering enthusiastically and waving hats and handkerchiefs. With one accord the great mass of people began to troop off in the direction of the air station, but they were not permitted to get near and had to content themselves with cheering again and again from a distance.[24]

Cadbury's bullets had undoubtedly been responsible for Frankenberg's destruction, for he was the only pilot to have attacked the Zeppelin from the stern, which was where the fire had started. He landed back at Great Yarmouth shortly before Pulling, who leapt out of the aircraft in a 'most frightfully excited condition' and rushed up to the CO yelling 'I got it! I got it! I got it!' As Cadbury was later to recall it seemed to him quite immaterial who had been responsible for the Zeppelin's destruction and modestly did not contest Pulling's claim.

In *The Yarmouth Independent* a few days later, the drama of the raid was recounted in great detail and the editorial waxed typically lyrical:

After the sinking of the *Lusitania*, Germans celebrated their achievement by holding [a] general holiday for rejoicing. I do not believe that such a thing would be possible in Britain, even if one could imagine Britishers being guilty of such a deed. We should like every Zepp that crosses our coast brought down, even though it entailed the roasting of the crew, but our immediate and instinctive exultation could never pass into 'mafficking'. The general British public could never be guilty of rejoicing in the drowning of German women and children nor does it gloat over the spectacle of Huns consumed by fire.[25]

For several days the names of the victorious pilots went unrecorded, and then in the first week of December the papers announced that three RNAS airmen were to be honoured by their monarch:

The King has been pleased to approve the award of the Distinguished Service Order to Flight Sub-Lieutenant Edward L Pulling RNAS, and of the Distinguished Service Cross to Flight Lieutenant Egbert Cadbury and Flight Sub-Lieutenant G W R Fane of the RNAS in recognition of their distinguished services on the occasion of the destruction of a Zeppelin airship off the Norfolk coast in early morning of Tuesday, November 28th 1916.[26]

Edward Laston Pulling was born in Sidcup, Kent, the son of George Perriam Pulling and his wife Adeline, formerly Laston, (hence the boy's second Christian name). The young Pulling was educated at St Anne's School, Redhill, a charitable foundation intended for children who had 'seen better days' and run by Rev W J Perry. As an 'old boy' remembers it, the highest proportion of pupils were sons and daughters of the clergy, and entry was very much dependent on a strict voting system. Pulling left the school during 1910 and worked as a government telegraphist in the Redhill post office prior to the outbreak of war.

On 21 August 1915 Pulling entered the RNAS as a cadet and went on to make his qualifying flight at Salisbury Plain. On 15 January 1916 his probationary commission as a Flight Sub-Lieutenant was confirmed, with effective seniority dating from 21 August 1915, and then on 31 December, less than a fortnight after his encounter with *L21*, came promotion to Flight Lieutenant.

During the 2 August raid Pulling, in BE2c 8418, had his first encounter with *L21*, then under the command of *Hauptmann* August Stelling. It was the result of an experiment that Commodore Ellison had instigated, a simple trick to lure Zeppelins into the path of Great Yarmouth's aeroplanes. Pulling left Burgh Castle and climbed to 7000ft, and then flares were lit on the landing ground to attract the enemy:

This ruse succeeded admirably and within five minutes of the ground being lit up a Zeppelin proceeded towards it with the obvious intention of bombing it, but the pilot observed the Zeppelin and engaged it before the Zeppelin could carry out its intentions and drove it off into the clouds.

This same ruse will, I am convinced, succeed in the future, and at least six Zeppelins passed inland within the limits of my area on the last raid and as they nearly always do come in somewhere along that area I consider it most necessary to further utilise this means of defence.[27]

Nevertheless *L21* escaped into clouds, and a frustrated Pulling, having emptied two drums at the airship, returned to Burgh Castle.

Pulling was in command of the landing ground at Burgh Castle during the early months of 1917, looking after 'doubtful pilots' who received extra tuition and training new airmen in the rigours of night-flying. As one contemporary recalls, Pulling was a quiet type and an exceptional night pilot – just the man to assist in teaching the new intake of RNAS home defence trainees.

On Friday 2 March tragedy struck. Flight Sub-Lieutenant John C Northrop flew to Burgh Castle, bringing in another airman for duty. On landing Northrop met Pulling and asked whether 'he would loop him'. Without hesitation Pulling agreed and the BE2c was soon airborne. At a height of 2000ft the pilot put the nose of his aircraft down to build up speed for the loop, pulled back on the stick, and as the BE was at the top of its manoeuvre the starboard lower wing gave way. The aircraft spun all the way down and crashed in the middle of the Denes aerodrome. To Cadbury the tragedy was not entirely unexpected:

L21 being walked into the revolving shed at Nordholz, 1916. The machine guns atop the hull are covered in heavy jackets to protect them from frost.
F Moch

Fane later commanded a unit of Camels at Burgh Castle and was aloft on the night of 5 August 1918 when Cadbury and Leckie brought down *L70*.
G W R Fane

We recovered their charred bodies half an hour later. So a gallant fellow met his untimely end through mere foolishness. I have told Pulling countless times not to loop his machine because it strained it unduly, and warned him that one day it would break in the air. The day before he looped at about 1500 feet, and when he landed I talked to him in no gentle terms and had his machine examined. But it was no use.[28]

On the following Monday Cadbury attended both men's funerals and was most impressed by the service held in the huge parish church: over 2000 were in attendance. Cadbury was also present at the official enquiry held into the tragedy:

Fortunately Pulling's machine had an extra amount of attention from expert carpenters during the last three weeks and especially the last two days, so no negligence could possibly be hinted at. This was a great thing for me, for I am directly reponsible for the general care, maintenance and fitness of all land machines on the Station. The Court found that the accident was due to a wire inside the lower right-hand plane (an internal drift wire to be exact) carrying away, due to progressive strain through looping with a passenger.[29]

Gerard William Reginald Fane, who also shared in the destruction of *L21*, was born in London on 7 August 1898, the second son of Sydney Algernon and Selina Violet (née Fitzwygram). At the age of 12 young Fane commenced his education at the Osborne Naval College but was invalided out following a severe bout of pneumonia. After this he entered Charterhouse, but 18 months later Fane, much against his father's desire, decided to leave, and he entered the RNAS on 22 July 1915. He learnt to fly at Eastchurch, taking his ticket after three and a half hours, and proudly held the station flight record there before being sent to Great Yarmouth. On 5 November he was commissioned as a Flight Sub-Lieutenant. Contemporaries remember him as an excellent aerobatic pilot, an experienced night-flyer and a chain-smoker; his youthful appearance, looking younger than his 18 years, earned Gerard the universal nickname of 'Boy Fane'. Several anti-Zeppelin patrols were already recorded in his logbook before the *L21* encounter, and Fane went on to undertake many more whilst at Great Yarmouth. In June 1917 he was aloft and saw *L48* shot down in flames over Suffolk, then on 12 December flew a DH4 in consort with Curtiss H12 8666 to Terschelling following reports of Zeppelin reconnaissance. It nearly ended in disaster, for the DH4 had to return with engine trouble and managed to land at Covehithe aerodrome with '15 feet to spare'.[30]

Fane was promoted to Captain when the RAF came into being on 1 April 1918, and later took charge of the air station at Burgh Castle:

> I had seven pilots, all of whom were particularly keen, and I set out to train them as well and as quickly as I could to the various patrols which had to be done daily. Owing to the distances out to sea which had to be covered, it was deemed advisable to go up in pairs, although the losses the station sustained through engine failure amounted to one only.[31]

Fane continued to serve with the RAF until 4 August 1921, testing aircraft at Martlesham Heath until he was grounded as unfit, with an enlarged heart due to high flying. He had by then flown some 38 different types of single-engined aircraft and five types of seaplane. During 1919 he had married Constance Rhoda Elizabeth Bacon of Raveningham Hall, Norfolk, and they had two sons.

Following his retirement from the RAF, Fane joined the firm of King and Shaxson, billbrokers, in which his father was already a partner, and he continued to work there as partner and sometime chairman up to his retirement in 1930.

Whilst working in the civilian world he still retained his love of aviation, was granted a Civil Air Licence in 1930 and continued to fly regularly; for the 1931 King's Cup Air Race he entered a machine which, piloted by Squadron Leader J M Robb, finished in sixth position. One of his greatest friends was Nick Comper, the aircraft designer, and Fane himself was no slouch when it came to originating ideas of a similar nature. He designed the Fane F1/40 two-seat observation aircraft which was developed from Comper's pre-World War II Scamp, a small pusher monoplane. Fane personally demonstrated his aircraft before assembled heads of staff at Croydon in 1941, although the aircraft was never adopted and was subsequently scrapped. Only one prototype had been built by the Fane Aircraft Company at Norbury and it was issued with the RAF serial T1788.

In 1953 Fane had a lung removed, and during his convalescence worked on plans he was perfecting for a new type of spindle which proved highly successful in the spinning trade. During 1969 Fane's first wife died, but within a year he had remarried and continued to enjoy his retirement to the full. Fane never lost his brilliant and inventive mind, nor his love for the countryside. An excellent shot and expert fisherman, he enjoyed both sports up to the time of his death in 1979, spending his final season shooting and fishing from a wheelchair.

There had been no survivors amongst either crews of *L34* and *L21*. Salvage operations took place the morning following the destruction of both Zeppelins, and most of the reclaimed wreckage came from *L34*, only a splintered propeller and fragments of framework being recovered from *L21*. The trawler *Active* spent several days over the wreck of *L34*, and several divers went down, but gales suspended operations.

Their haul included part of a midships gondola, a propeller bracket and strut, 50 fathoms of wire cable, a portion of propeller, a fuel tank and many feet of girder. On 15 December salvage was abandoned when a collier nearing the vicinity of the wreck was blown up by a mine. Others soon appeared and another, snagged in *Active*'s net, exploded and almost tore the trawler's hull open. All recovered wreckage was brought ashore at West Hartlepool and placed under military guard while the experts made drawings and took photographs:

> It is found that the wreckage is very brittle, presumably owing to [the] change in temperature due to sudden

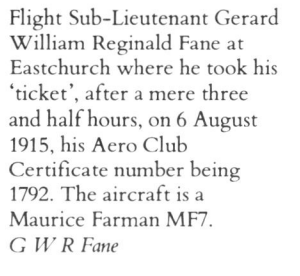

Flight Sub-Lieutenant Gerard William Reginald Fane at Eastchurch where he took his 'ticket', after a mere three and half hours, on 6 August 1915, his Aero Club Certificate number being 1792. The aircraft is a Maurice Farman MF7.
G W R Fane

L34/L21, 27/28 November 1916

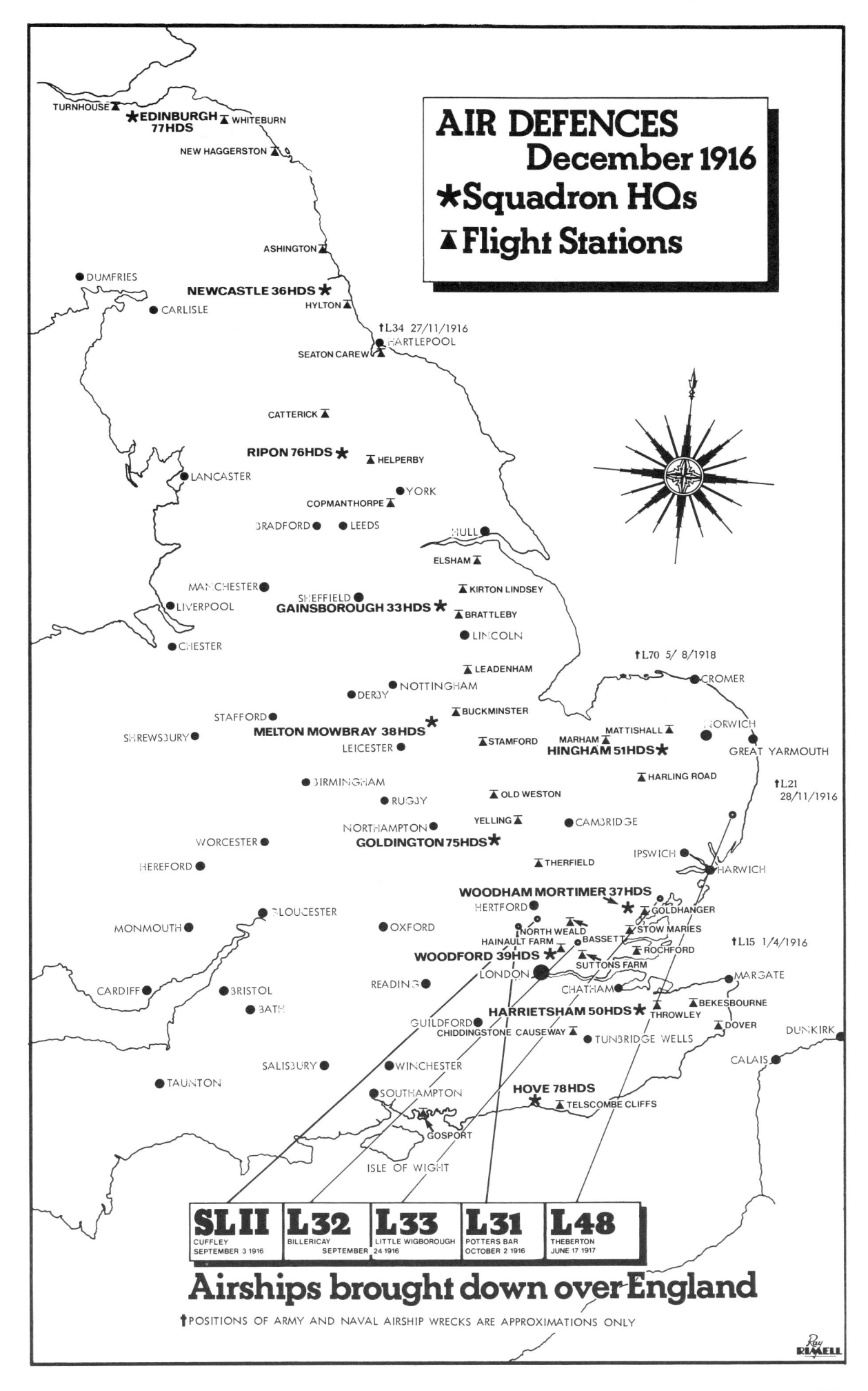

163

immersion while hot so that only small pieces are generally recovered by fishing. Divers have been working under great difficulty owing to the darkness of the water and trouble with wire.[32]

Eventually the salvage was abandoned, for little of use was found and it was not considered wise to risk the divers' lives any longer. What happened to the remains brought ashore is unknown, but following examination by the experts the wreckage may well have been dumped back into the sea.

During January five bodies in various degrees of decomposition were washed ashore at Seaton Carew, Redcar, South Gare and Hartlepool. At least two of them could be positively identified by identity tags and papers found in their clothing. They were subsequently buried at Seaton Carew and during 1966 were transferred to the German War Graves at Cannock Chase, Staffordshire. Intelligence staff searched diligently through the uniforms of those crew members who were found clothed and the contents of their pockets were carefully tagged and forwarded to GHQ Home Forces. All five bodies came from the *L34*, proved by a notebook which listed the doomed ship's maintenance party; no-one was ever recovered from *L21*.

With the loss of two Zeppelins in one night, 1916 ended in defeat as far as the German Naval Airship Division was concerned. Even Strasser had to concede that the defending British airmen had got the measure of his beloved Zeppelins. The year 1915 had seen the airships cause £815,000 worth of damage with the loss of just one ship. In 1916 there had been many more raids undertaken by many more ships, yet less damage was caused – £594,523 worth to be exact. Even worse, six airships, together with their highly-trained crews, had been lost, among them some of the Division's most experienced officers, and, for a while at least, Strasser sat back and took stock. Yet there would be no great reprieve for English civilians; the last raid of 1916 was quickly followed up by an event little-publicised at the time but one which served as a portent of what was to follow – an aeroplane bombed London in broad daylight.

Deck-Offizier Paul Brandt and *Leutnant* Walter Ilges were the observer and pilot respectively of an LVG CII which took off from Mariakerke early on the morning of 28 November with orders to bomb the Admiralty. Following railway lines from a height of 13,000ft, their LVG arrived over London at midday and due to a thick haze that hung over the city very few people reported actually seeing the 'Taube'. Six 20lb bombs were dropped in a stick across the West End, but damage was negligible: the baker's shop at 108 Brompton Road suffered a damaged chimney, a dairy office was wrecked, a roof was demolished at the back of 13 Saunders Square, glass was broken in Eccleston Square and the Victoria Palace suffered a wrecked dressing room. Nine civilians were injured:

> One lady who was within 50 yards of the spot where one bomb dropped was very surprised to hear the news when told an hour and a half afterwards. She said she thought it was a 'bus back-firing and so did not trouble to look round.'[33]

Questions were raised in the House of Commons as to whether the daylight raider was a captured British aircraft or a German one so disguised. Obviously nobody wanted to think that the Germans had sneaked in under the very noses of the defences. Yet surprise was on the raiders' side, and the LVG turned for home unmolested, only to force-land near Boulogne at 18.12hrs with engine trouble. Ilges and Brandt were captured by the French, and the only item salvaged from the wreck of their aircraft, which they fired, was a map of London. It had been a bold adventure indeed, and, despite the minimal damaged caused, paved the way for the aeroplane attacks made night and day during 1917 and 1918.

Comrades in arms. Cadbury (right) with Flight Sub-Lieutenant Edward Laston Pulling, who entered the service as a cadet on 21 August 1915, qualifying at Salisbury Plain for Aero Club Certificate 1936 on 22 October 1915. An exceptional night pilot, Pulling was tragically killed in March 1917 whilst stunting a BE2c which broke up in mid-air. Peter Cadbury

CHAPTER 11
L22, 14 May 1917

'...Galpin did not see the number of his adversary, but as she was falling in flames, Chief Petty Officer Whatling – who had seen it – scribbled the number on a signal pad and pushed it into the hands of the former, for the noise of the engines prevented speech...'

C F Snowden Gamble, 1928

On 5 May 1917, Curtiss H12 8666 arrived over the Great Yarmouth air station, piloted by Sub-Lieutenants Robert Leckie and H G Boswell and with Air Mechanic Rolls aboard. As it touched down on the water the big wooden-hulled flying boat presented an impressive and graceful spectacle. Spanning a massive 93ft, the biplane was powered by two Rolls-Royce Eagle engines which could pull it along comfortably at a speed of over 90mph. The H12 was able to carry an 860lb bomb load and a four-man crew which included a bow gunner manning two Lewis guns as well as another to the rear with a single gun: in this aircraft the RNAS had a formidable new weapon indeed. Hitherto, defence units had sat back and waited for the Zeppelins to appear within range, but the advent of the long-endurance flying boats heralded a new phase of the airship campaign. At long last the offensive could be carried right into the enemy's own waters.

A North Sea Air Station
During the autumn of 1912 it befell Lieutenant L'Estrange Malone and R F M Pearson of the Admiralty Works Department to locate a suitable site on the Norfolk coast where a new seaplane station could be established. Eventually they settled for an area on the South Denes at Great Yarmouth, although other nearby locations – the North Denes between Caister and Great Yarmouth, as well as the foreshore south of Gorleston – had been considered:

> The suggested site at Great Yarmouth had the advantages that the Corporation were prepared to lease the land on favourable terms at a low rental; that the 'South Denes' were suitable as a landing-ground for aeroplanes; that accommodation for some of the personnel could be found in the local Coastguard station; and that lodgings were easily obtainable in the town.[1]

It was the latter condition more than any other that really settled the matter, for the RNAS had simply no spare funds to build houses for its airmen, all available money being reserved for aircraft and the acquisition of suitable hangars. Great Yarmouth Corporation consented to rent out a five-acre area bounded by the Marine Parade, the beach and a point some 1000yds south of Nelson's Monument for £2 10s 0d per acre per annum. As it turned out, the Denes were not the most suitable of areas to choose for an operational aerodrome as they were extremely narrow, roughly 40yds wide and 80yds long. Eastwards lay the sea, to the south the harbour entrance, and to the west side the River Yare; to the north were situated large numbers of 'herring-pickling' plots and Nelson's Monument. North of that 144ft-high memorial was Great Yarmouth itself, and west of the Yare ran the steep hill covered with cottages that formed Gorleston village. The hill bordered the entire length of the Denes, and running down the centre of the aerodrome was a high ridge, the east side ideal for landing only when the wind blew either north or south. West of the ridge the ground sloped steeply towards the Yare and was covered with deep holes; if this were not enough, the aerodrome was encircled by a macadam road. For the uninitiated, Great Yarmouth's new aerodrome could be 'a difficult one to negotiate'.[2]

On 15 April the air station was officially commissioned under the command of Lieutenant Reginald Gregory who had previously served as squadron commander of the RFC Naval Wing at Felixstowe. Joining Gregory at Great Yarmouth were Lieutenants C L Courtney RN and T S Cresswell RMLI, along with five naval ratings. Having secured lodgings locally, the first task for the station personnel was to erect an RAF canvas hangar, and on 31 May Courtney flew in the first aircraft, Maurice Farman 69:

> The biplane which Lieutenant Courtney piloted to Yarmouth on Saturday morning is not one of the orthodox machines for naval aviation stations. Hydro-aeroplanes are the things, and two of these are expected to be completed for the Yarmouth station before the middle of August. The biplane, which is purely a land machine, will, however, serve a useful purpose, and, to quote the words of Lieutenant Courtney, 'It will be brought out for flying as often as possible, due regard always been [sic] paid to the weather'.[3]

By 4 August 1914 Great Yarmouth Air Station personnel had increased to eight officers and there were two warrant officers (including Squadron Commander Gregory) and 40 ratings, although still only a handful of machines – and unarmed at that. Nevertheless, within a week the first patrol was flown when three flights were made, and at least one pilot fancied he saw two German seaplanes flying along the coast. As it turned out he was mistaken, but as a precautionary measure DFW biplane 154, stationed at Immingham, was grounded, in case it was 'mistaken for the enemy, being of German type'.[4] It was an undramatic curtain-raiser by any standards, but as the war ground on, Great Yarmouth's air station grew into a formidable fighting unit and would play a considerable part in anti-Zeppelin operations. From 1916, much night-flying was undertaken, mainly in BE2cs, whose pilots were responsible for a large area stretching from Covehithe to Narborough, a distance covering some 100 miles of coastline. As we have seen, a fair number of these pilots did sterling service during airship raids, but with the advent of the flying boats in 1917 and more advanced land machines, the total of destroyed airships rose even further.

Invalided out of the Royal Navy in 1911 suffering from tuberculosis, Lieutenant John Cyril Porte was to play a major role in development of the flying boat. An ardent aviation enthusiast, he had learnt to fly at Rheims, gaining Aero Club Certificate 548 on 28 July 1911, and within a year was appointed technical director and designer of the British Deperdussin Company. This position brought him into contact with one Captain E C Bass who, on behalf of White and Thompson Ltd, had acquired the British rights for aircraft produced in the USA by the Curtiss Aeroplane Company, of Hammondsport, New York. October 1913 saw Glenn Curtiss flying one of his latest flying boats to Brighton, and Porte took the opportunity of grabbing the spare seat for a flight. Porte was so impressed by the machine's potential that he resigned as White and Thompson's test pilot and a year later had joined Curtiss in Hammondsport on Lake Keuka.

In the year that war broke out the Curtiss company had designed and built a flying boat appropriately named 'America'. Capable of long endurance, it was built to compete for the £1000 prize offered the previous year by the *Daily Mail* for the first transatlantic flight. The 'America' spanned 72ft, was powered by two 90hp Curtiss engines, and boasted an enclosed cabin for its two-man crew. Porte was to have participated in the attempt, but world events compelled him to return home and he lost little time in entering the RNAS, being given the rank of Squadron Commander in charge of RNAS Hendon.

At Porte's personal recommendation the RNAS purchased two 'Americas' and, given the British serials 950 and 951, the machines were eventually delivered to the air station at Felixstowe. Like Porte, the Admiralty were impressed by the aircraft, and following further trials 50 machines were ordered in March 1915. 100hp Anzanis replaced the original Curtiss OX-5 engines which were not powerful enough and, although American-built, these Curtiss H4s in the 3545–3594 serial range were assembled at the Felixstowe Air Station which by September was commanded by Porte.

Despite the change of engines, the Curtiss flying boats were still underpowered, the fault being levelled at poor hull design. Thus with official support Porte undertook a great deal of research and experimentation to evolve a thoroughly seaworthy and efficient hull. Ably assisted by Chief Technical Officer Lieutenant J D Rennie, Porte built four hulls altogether, but it was the fifth that seemed to meet all requirements and was fitted to 3580 for sea trials. The new design was a radical one in every sense, for the basic structure of the hull was similar to the then standard method of building landplane fuselages. Porte built a four-longeroned, slab-sided fuselage with vertical and horizontal spacers, cross-braced, to which were added longitudinal fins and a 'V' planing bottom of cedar and mahogany with a

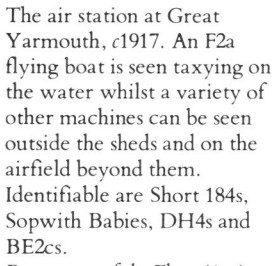

The air station at Great Yarmouth, *c*1917. An F2a flying boat is seen taxying on the water whilst a variety of other machines can be seen outside the sheds and on the airfield beyond them. Identifiable are Short 184s, Sopwith Babies, DH4s and BE2cs.
By courtesy of the Fleet Air Arm Museum

L22, 14 May 1917

Curtiss H12 8666 at Great Yarmouth early in its distinguished career. The uppersurface camouflage dope and national markings have yet to be applied.
By courtesy of F Cheeseman

layer of varnished linen sandwiched between the two. In its original form the new hull featured a single step below the rear wing spar position and, measuring 36ft 2in, carried more fully flared bows than previous versions. Aircraft 3580 was powered by two 150hp Hispano Suizas, and whilst initial tests were mainly encouraging, the machine revealed a tail-dragging tendency that made 'unsticking' difficult, so a second step was added and ultimately another between the first two. Thus did this final hull design prove satisfactory in every way: the flared bows prevented shipping of water, and both landing and take-off performance were exceptional. With the empennage and wings from the H4, the 'new' aircraft became the first Felixstowe F1, subsequent standard RNAS machines being fitted with 100hp Anzani radials.

Following the success of the F1, Porte then turned his not inconsiderable design talents towards experiments with larger hulls, and he soon began work on the first of the 50 Curtiss H12s delivered to the RNAS. Generally speaking, the H12 was a scaled-up version of the H4 and upon entering service was dubbed the 'Large America', with the earlier type distinguished as the 'Small America'. Early H12s were powered by 160hp Curtiss engines, but when Porte began his experiments on the type it was found that a loaded machine of 8700lb was unable even to leave the water. The first obvious step was to increase the power, and so 250hp Rolls Royce Eagle 2s were fitted, but again it was really the hull design at fault: it was structurally weak, and take-offs were difficult owing to insufficient buoyancy forward. It did not take a genius to work out that the F1 hull was superior to that of the H12, and so a version was built that could be suitably married to the wings and tail unit of a 'Large America'. The result of this was the Porte II hull, and the aircraft to which it was fitted, the Felixstowe F2, was

L22 at Nordholz while under the command of Martin Dietrich. This Zeppelin, built at Löwenthal, participated in 11 raids and made a total of 81 flights prior to its destruction. Mounted on the upper gun platform is the 'Bluff Cannon', a dummy weapon installed to warn off attacking aircraft.
F Moch

167

Zeppelin!

the first of a long line of successful 'F Boats' that performed magnificently right up to the Armistice and beyond. After designing further flying boats, notably the F5 and the Felixstowe Fury five-engined triplane, Wing Commander Porte joined the Gosport Aviation Co Ltd after the war in August 1919. Within three months he had succumbed to his illness at the early age of 36, his death hastened by sheer hard work, yet his influence was to remain until the end of the flying boat era.[5]

Despite their shortcomings, the Curtiss H12s used operationally by the RNAS during 1917 proved to be excellent fighting machines. Great Yarmouth was the first station to be equipped with the type, and 13 April saw Flight Sub-Lieutenant Leckie deliver 8660 from Felixstowe and, within a month, the second machine, 8666.[6]

Like Egbert Cadbury, Robert Leckie was to become a 'Zeppelin ace' and eventually ended his service career as Canada's Chief of Air Staff from 1944 to 1947. Born in Glasgow, Scotland, in April 1890, Leckie sailed to Canada in 1907, and the 17-year-old joined his uncle's firm of John Leckie Ltd, makers of fishing nets. For the next few years he resided in Toronto and toured Ontario, selling his uncle's nets to commercial fishermen working the Great Lakes and in Muskoka. He learnt to love the outdoor life and also became a member of the Rusholm Tennis Club, Leckie developing a determined passion for the game.

At the outbreak of war 'he reasoned that there was a place in it for men who knew how to fly', and the following year saw him at the Curtiss Flying School on Toronto Island learning to fly at his own expense.[7] On 6 December 1915 he was appointed Probationary Flight Sub-Lieutenant at RNAS Ottawa, and returned to England posted to Chingford on 10 January 1916 for further training. On 16 June his probationary commission was confirmed, with effective seniority dating from 6 December of the previous year. Three days after the confirmation, 'Bob' Leckie was posted to Felixstowe, then to Great Yarmouth on 4 September, having successfully completed training on the big boats. While Zeppelin raids were still considered a major threat, the use that the Germans made of their airships for reconnaissance was a constant thorn in the side of the British. To the chagrin of the Royal Navy, Strasser's ships continued to protect their own fleet's submarines and minesweepers as well as spotting British ships whenever they entered the German Bight. The Zeppelin captains showed their contempt of the limited range of British seaplanes and ineffectual 'aircraft carriers' by carrying out their work at 'comfortable' altitudes, on occasion boldly dropping as low as 200ft when spotting mines. It was a situation that could not be tolerated for much longer.

RNAS on the Offensive

The requirement was for more sophisticated aircraft, but the Admiralty's Intelligence Division also realised that their task would become even more vital. Zeppelin radio operators had learnt to forsake the tell-tale take-off signals when embarking on a raid but did not bother to conceal their movements when making reconnaissance flights. Indeed, they even radioed each course change, requests for bearings, sightings of enemy shipping and even local weather reports. Such a blatant disregard for radio silence was to prove extremely beneficial to Admiral Hall's men, as accurate fixes could be intercepted and quickly transmitted to coastal defence units. On 26 April 1917 a specially coded chart was issued, together with instructions that the first airship heard was to be labelled 'Annie', the second 'Betty' and so on, girls' names being used throughout.

During the morning of 14 May, following several days of bad weather that had precluded any reconnaissance flights, Strasser despatched L23 to patrol north, with L22 westwards. The Admiralty picked up the latter's take-off message and reasoned that the Zeppelin was probably heading for its routine patrol off Terschelling; they lost little time in alerting the nearest air station.

At 03.30hrs, in thick weather, 8666 left Great Yarmouth with 'Bob' Leckie at the controls, Flight Lieutenant Christopher John Galpin in command and navigating, Chief Petty Officer V F Whatling as wireless telegraphic observer and Air Mechanic O R Laycock acting as engineer. The H12 was fully armed: its three Lewis guns and ammunition drums were loaded with Brock, Buckingham and Pomeroy bullets, it carried four 100lb bombs, and in addition to the wireless equipment there were 40 extra gallons of petrol in cans.

On clearing the air station, Leckie steered a course for the Terschelling lightship, and at 04.15hrs Galpin relieved him at the control wheel. Eighty miles out from the Norfolk coast, 8666 ceased 'W/T communication to avoid discovery.'[8] Just over half an hour later, the flying boat crew sighted a Zeppelin 15 miles away and slowly began to close the gap. For 36-year-old *Kapitänleutnant* Ulrich Lehmann and 20 crewmen, violent death was but minutes away:

> At time of sighting Zeppelin, machine was being piloted by Flight Lieutenant Galpin. Before closing with the Zeppelin I released bombs and took control of Boat and Flight Lieutenant Galpin manned the guns. At time of attack the Zeppelin was about 4000ft and Boat 5000ft. When about half a mile astern of the Zeppelin Boat's engines were throttled down and machine held down until a speed of 90–95 knots was attained. When behind Zeppelin and 100–150 feet to Starboard of her machine was levelled out and normal flying speed made, ie 75 knots.[9]

It was at this moment that Galpin let fly with the twin Lewis guns in the bow cockpit, and at a range of barely 50yds put several shots into L22's starboard quarter. The port Lewis jammed after only a few rounds, and as the ammunition drum of the starboard gun emptied this too jammed. Galpin attempted to clear the stoppages as Leckie bought 8666 in a thunderous tight turn so that a second attack could be made. But Galpin's guns had already found their mark:

> As we began to turn I thought I saw a slight glow inside the

The top gun platform of L22. The pair of 8mm Maxims are protected by quilting to prevent their cooling water from freezing. Two 'attached' type parachutes lie on the outer cover; these were only installed for a brief period on Navy ships and were rarely, if ever, carried operationally. *F Moch*

envelope and 15 seconds later when she came in sight on our other side she was hanging tail down at an angle of 45 degrees with the lower half of her envelope thoroughly alight. Five or six seconds later the whole ship was a glowing mass and she fell vertically by the tail. CPO Whatling, observing from the after hatch, saw the number L22 painted under the nose before it was consumed. He also saw two of the crew jump out, one from the after gun position on the top of the tail fin [sic] and one from the after gondola. They had no parachutes.[10]

When the stricken Zeppelin was about 1000ft above the sea, the crew of 8666 noted four large columns of water which appeared in quick succession, 'either from bombs or engines becoming detached from the framework'. In less than a minute L22's fabric covering had completely burnt off, and the scorched skeleton plunged into the sea leaving a large area of black ash on the surface from which a long column of smoke wafted upwards.

Another airman on patrol that afternoon was Egbert Cadbury, flying Short 184 8066 from Great Yarmouth:

> In pursuance of your orders I left Yarmouth Roads at 3.45am GMT to patrol to a position 90 miles east of Yarmouth. Owing to the presence of thick fog banks and rain visibility was exceptionally poor. At approximately 5.10 GMT the weather cleared momentarily to the Eastward and I saw some 15 miles to the NE an object which I took to be an airship. I had just altered course to close with object when the fog came down again and I lost sight of everything. On emerging from the fog 15 to 20 minutes later I noticed a large black smoke cloud on my starboard beam. I went to investigate but could find no reason for the cloud, there being nothing in the vicinity save a trawler about seven miles away to the south east. I did not see the airship again and conclude that this cloud was caused by the burning of L22, my position at this time being approximately 4.30E, 53.20N, the Dutch Coast being dimly visible.[11]

As Galpin was later to explain in his three-page combat report, the Curtiss had at least 25kts of speed in hand as the engines were not opened right out during the encounter. This, combined with the element of surprise, gave him an 'incalculable advantage', although there were signs that at least some members of the Zeppelin crew were aware that they were under attack. On landing, an examination of 8666 revealed where a bullet had entered the starboard side of the hull and severed a switch wire (repaired en route to Great Yarmouth) and a second in the upper port mainplane which caused no vital damage. It was a satisfying victory since the boat crew had destroyed L22 not only on its maiden patrol into the Bight, but also undetected, and the Germans could only guess at the reason for the latest loss:

> No communication from L22 since report that she had risen. Thunderstorms in the west. It is possible that she has taken in her wireless mast and can send no message. In the late afternoon thick fog over the whole Bight, consequently not possible to have search made by seaplanes or surface craft. Seaplane No 859 noted an explosion and a cloud of smoke at 9.50am.
> 7.40pm – The leader of the airships reports that according to telephonic information from Borkum this observation is very probably connected with the loss of L22. A telegram arriving at night from the Admiralty confirms this statement. The probability is that on account of the thunderstorm L22 had to remain below the level where the gas would completely fill the cells, and was shot down by British warships.[12]

Following the disappearance of L22 into the sea, Galpin set a course for Great Yarmouth at 05.20hrs, and when 80 miles from his destination resumed wireless telegraphic communication. The return journey was made in almost continuous heavy rain, but eventually, at 07.50hrs, 8666 arrived safely over the air station. For their efforts the four crew members of the flying boat were decorated: on 22 June it was announced that Galpin had gained the DSO, Leckie the DSC and Whatling and Laycock a DSM apiece.

During the early months of 1917 two desultory airship raids were undertaken: the first, on 16/17 February, was by LZ107 which flew over Deal and Kingsdown after dropping a few bombs near Calais; the second, exactly one calendar month later, was made over Kent and Sussex, although the target was London. Naval Zeppelins L35, L39, L40, L41 and L42 took part in a largely abortive action which left no British casualties. On the homeward journey L39, commanded by Robert Koch, was brought down in flames over Compiègne by anti-aircraft fire and L35, buffeted by storms, was smashed against its hangar door at Dresden, necessitating a three-month repair. Although the 79 bombs traced on land caused only £163 worth of damage, GHQ Home Forces were not crowing – indeed, there was a considerable dissatisfaction that not one of the raiders had even been intercepted by any of the 16 RFC machines sent up during the raid. There was a good reason for the empty bag: Strasser's airship division had a new kind of Zeppelin specially built to operate above the ceiling of defending fighter aircraft. The first of the new 'Height Climbers' had arrived.[13]

On 23 May another London raid was attempted, and this time the force included L40, L42, L43, L44, L45 and L47. It proved to be an abortive attack, a combination of bad weather, mechanical malfunctions and the newly experienced and debilitating effects of 'altitude sickness' effectively reducing the mission to a débâcle. The homeward journey was little better for some of the crews, in particular that of L40 under Erich Sommerfeldt.

Curtiss H12 8666 had left Great Yarmouth at 03.15hrs during the morning of 24 May, piloted by Galpin and crewed by Leckie, Laycock and Whatling. Heading for Terschelling, the boat proceeded east for a quarter of an hour without sighting anything. As a result Galpin decided to abort the patrol since visibility was decreasing rapidly. It was at 05.38hrs that L40 made its appearance. The Zeppelin suddenly loomed out of the clouds at 1600ft, and on spotting the flying boat its crew dropped two white flares which the British did not answer as Galpin opened the throttle, released all bombs and climbed to intercept:

Running up the engines of 8666 at Great Yarmouth. Standing on the bow of the flying boat is Flight Lieutenant Christopher John Galpin; Flight Sub-Lieutenant Robert ('Bob') Leckie looks on from the cockpit. On 14 May Leckie flew against L22 and with Galpin manning the guns in 8666's bows succeeded in destroying the Zeppelin. *By courtesy of the Fleet Air Arm Museum*

A very famous flying boat, Curtiss H12 8666, photographed on delivery at Great Yarmouth in 1917. The advent of these heavily armed aircraft with their four-man crew and comparatively long endurance heralded a new phase of the anti-Zeppelin campaign. The defenders could now take the war into the enemy's own waters and combat was frequent.
By courtesy of the Oxford University Press

When he reached 3000 feet we had gained on him and were actually 300 yards astern. He threw out a smoke screen, under cover of which he gained the main bank of clouds; it was not feasible for us to attempt to follow him there. As he disappeared I fired half a tray of Brock, Pomeroy and tracer into him, but was unable to observe the effect.[14]

Several days later, on 5 June, the same protaganists met again when *L40*, flying the westerly patrol off Terschelling, was fired upon by 8666. Having exchanged white flares, Galpin and Leckie chased Sommerfeldt until 07.25hrs when the boat's crew opened up with the two guns at the bow and another two amidships. They kept this up for ten minutes, and although ten drums were expended the tracer ammunition seemed to have burnt itself out before reaching the target. With fuel and ammunition getting very low Galpin broke off the attack and once again the crew of *L40* were spared, yet Sommerfeldt failed to identify 8666 for the deadly weapon it really was. For the second time he was sure that the attack represented a harmless seaplane carrier operation:

> Plane is a biplane resembling Nieuport type, carries two black circles on planes as recognition mark. 9.48am in 081 ϵ, plane at 3200 metres under ship at 5300 metres. Three bombs of 10kg dropped. Plane turns off and steers for Terschelling.[15]

Flying boat 8666 returned to Great Yarmouth at 11.20hrs after a five-hour patrol and with 45 minutes flying time of fuel to spare. Twenty-five days later, exactly one year to the day from his first promotion to Flight Lieutenant, Christopher John Galpin was promoted to Flight Commander. The 24-year-old airman had been born on 13 July 1892 in Witham, Essex, and entered the RNAS as Flight Sub-Lieutenant on 30 March 1915, joining Great Yarmouth's air station during the following year. Galpin had close encounters with Zeppelins from an early stage in his career, having come to inconclusive grips with them on 2 August and 23 September 1916. Following the destruction of *L22*, Galpin, again with Leckie, attacked *L46* on 26 July 1917 and came close to destroying it. The Zeppelin, under the command of Heinrich Hollender, returned fire and, with its ability for rapid lift, soon left the flying boat beyond effective range. Galpin continued to serve with distinction at Great Yarmouth and was appointed Captain (Temporary Major) on the inauguration of the Royal Air Force on 1 April 1918. On 15 September the following year he was demobilised, and he subsequently worked as a civil servant at the Air Ministry. After World War II he retired with his wife to Brighton. As for Leckie, he was destined to join Egbert Cadbury in delivering the greatest blow of all to the German Naval Airship Division.[16]

CHAPTER 12

L43, 14 June 1917

'Zeppelin L43 was destroyed this morning by our Naval Forces in the North Sea. Soon after being attacked she burst into flames fore and aft, broke in two, and fell into the sea. No survivors were seen.'

The Times, 15 June 1917

Operation in Blockade area. With north winds towards Firth of Forth, observe especially traffic in Dogger bank area and western position of line Lindesnes–St Abbs Head, Farne Island. Particularly observe whether traffic heavy or light, single steamers or convoys. With southerly winds cover blockade area from Hoofden to 54 degrees as northern boundary. L48 proceeding in direction Christiansand–Firth of Forth, in case of south winds north of 55th parallel. Take off 10pm, report 9pm. Patrolling: L23, L42, L43.[1]

With these orders from Strasser issued during the evening of 13 June, five naval Zeppelins were to embark upon a fate-filled mission from which one was destined never to return.

Felixstowe

Basil Deacon Hobbs was born in Reading, England, on 20 December 1894,[2] but within six years he was in Ontario, Canada, growing up on the family farm at Sault Ste Marie and being initially educated at the Public and High School there. Hobbs later attended the High School, Cleveland, before entering a business and commercial course at Sault Ste Marie, and then joined the staff of ICS Electrical Engineering. His civilian occupation prior to the outbreak of war was a ten-month stint as an electrician in the Cleveland Illuminating Company. On 8 December 1915 Hobbs could be found at the Wright Flying School, Dayton, Ohio, commencing flying training, and 19 days later was accepted by the RNAS as Probationary Flight Sub-Lieutenant at Ottawa. On 3 January Hobbs was on passage to England, and on 24 January was posted to the Felixstowe Air Station for further flying instruction. It was then that his probationary period ended, and his commission was confirmed on 3 March.

Felixstowe Air Station was situated on the shores of Harwich harbour, opposite to Harwich and Shotley, and to the newcomer its size was impressive:

> It was enclosed on the three land sides by a high iron fence. As I passed the sentry box and entered by the main gate, the guardhouse occupied by the ancient marines was on my right, flanked by the kennel of Joe, a ferocious watch-dog who had a strong antipathy to anybody in civilian attire. Beside guarding the gate, Joe provided a steady income to the marines, for his puppies fetched good prices. On my left were the ship's office and garrage [sic]. I entered the former and reported my arrival to the First Lieutenant...
>
> Leaving the office of the First Lieutenant I stepped out on the quarter-deck. On the mast, on the far side of this gravelled expanse, rippling and snapping in the breeze, flew the white ensign.
>
> Crossing the quarter-deck and steering close to the bright and shining ship's bell, which I passed on my left, I found a path leading to the harbour. The left side of the path was the starting-point of an interminable row of huts for the men. Carrying on, after stumbling over a railway siding, and passing between two of the huge seaplane sheds, of which there were three sheds – 300 feet by 200 feet wide – I eventually arrived at the concrete area on the water front.
>
> Before each of the big sheds was a slipway. These were wide wooden gangways running out from the concrete into the harbour and sloping down into the water and were used for launching the flying-boats... Walking down the concrete to my left I finally came to the pre-war buildings of the Old Station. These buildings were used by Commander Porte for his experimental work.[3]

During his wartime service at Felixstowe, 'Billiken' Hobbs logged over 900 hours on a wide range of types including the Curtiss H8, H12 and H16 and Felixstowe F3 and F5. Not surprisingly he became an exceptional practitioner of the large flying boats, earning well-deserved respect from his crew:

> A good boat pilot is one who can handle his boat under any conditions, a mist flier, a stout and determined fellow; one who can navigate and trusts his own calculations; a tireless observer, who knows where and what to look for; a possessor of sea sense and seamanship; a man of physical stamina or nervous staying power; a man of quick and correct thought and action, but, at the same time, one who could endure monotony and wait for his opportunity.
>
> And Billiken, short, stocky, and with plenty of energy, possessed most of these characteristics, and others equally as valuable. He was modest, keen and never given to swell-headedness or boasting...[4]

Preparing one of the 'Large Americas' for anti-Zeppelin or submarine patrol was an exacting business. Usually the

Zeppelin!

Basil Deacon Hobbs learned to fly in 1915, gaining US Aero Certificate 365 on 2 December. Hobbs was awarded the DSO for his part in the destruction of *L43*, but as well as airship patrols he flew a great many sorties against U-boats.
Canadian Forces Photo RE64–2558

opening procedure involved some 20 ratings rolling the aircraft, perched on its large wooden beaching trolley, from the hangars on to the concrete area. Here the boat was chocked up with trestles under both bow and tail in order to prevent a nose stand when the engines were being run up. Two engineers would clamber up to each of the engines and start them by hand crank. After 15 minutes of slow running to warm the oil, both engines were opened out to full power, 'shaking the whole structure of the boat'. While all this was going on, the armourer's party had been installing the four Lewis guns and the four 110lb bombs under the wings, two either side of the hull. These bombs were fitted with delayed action fuses which detonated them a few seconds after striking the water or a German U-boat; when the former occurred the bombs would explode some 60 to 80ft below the surface. Once the flying boat had been armed, the crew were ready to climb aboard:

Billiken took his seat in a little padded armchair on the right-hand side of the control cockpit, a cockpit which ran across the full width of the boat some distance back from the nose. He was covered in by a transparent wheel-house so that he did not have to wear goggles, an important point in submarine hunting, as goggles interfere with efficient observation.[5]

Confronting the pilot on the varnished wooden instrument panel was a compass, an air speed indicator, an altimeter, a bubble cross-level which indicated if the boat was correctly balanced laterally, an inclinometer, oil pressure gauges and revolution counters; close by were engine switches, throttle control levers and, immediately in front, an 18in control wheel carried vertically upright on a wooden yoke. The second pilot took up a station on the port side of the cockpit and, if the enemy were sighted, he would dive forward into the bow to operate the machine guns or man the bomb sight and bomb levers as the situation demanded.

To starboard and immediately behind the pilot sat the wireless operator, who could both transmit and receive radio messages up to a range of 100 miles. He also coded and decoded signals, and the valuable code-books themselves had weighted covers so that in the event of capture they would immediately sink once cast overboard. An Aldis signalling lamp for communication with ships and aircraft was standard issue, as was a Red Cross box containing a tourniquet, first aid kit, sandwiches for immediate needs, emergency five-day rations and the vital carrier pigeons which on at least one occasion saved the lives of a ditched flying boat crew.[6]

Amidships was the engineer's station, surrounded by a maze of piping, numerous instruments and the main fuel tanks. The engineer's duties involved keeping a careful eye on the engines, ensuring that the water in the radiators did not boil and taking care of the petrol system. Two wind-driven pumps forced the fuel from the fuselage tanks up to a smaller gravity tank situated in the upper wing. Both engines were actually fed by the top tank, any surplus fuel that was drawn up running back to the main tanks. The engineer was able to regulate the flow so that the fuel was pumped and overflowed in such a manner that the fore and aft equilibrium of the aircraft was maintained. If one of the engines suffered a mechanical failure the engineer was often obliged to climb out on the wing and effect a repair in flight.

Curtiss H12 convert 8677 in which, in its original configuration, Hobbs and Dickey shared the destruction of *L43* on 14 June 1917. The aircraft was later shot down by the German seaplane 'ace' Friedrich Christiansen.
By courtesy of B Robertson

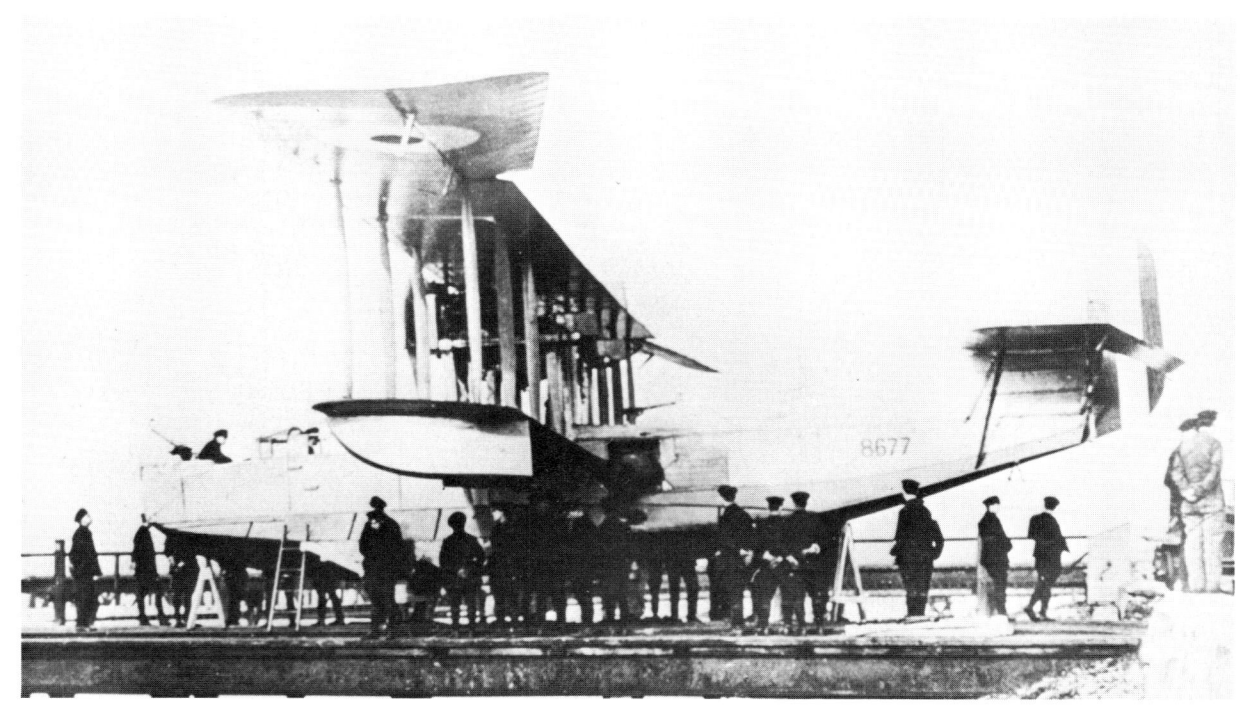

L43, 14 June 1917

Once the crew had settled into their respective stations, the working party attached a stout cable to the rear of the trolley, knocked away the wooden chocks and rolled the aircraft on to one of the slipways that sloped down to the water. Six waders in waterproof breeches riding up to their armpits and wearing weighted boots for a secure foothold guided the aircraft into the water, the working party easing the machine down by paying out the cable.[7] On entering the water, the heavy beaching trolley remained on the slipway and the flying boat floated free; under power the pilot taxied clear, out into the harbour and into wind, and then opened up the throttles:

> Driven by 700 tearing horsepower, the boat ran along the water with ever-increasing speed, a big white wave bursting into spray beneath her bow. As the speed increased, the boat was lifted on top of the water by her hydroplane step until she was skimming lightly over the surface. The air speed indicator was registering 35 knots. Then Hobbs pulled back the control wheel, and the boat leaped into the air, the air speed jumping to 60 knots. Climbing in a straight line until he was at 1000 feet, he turned the bow of the boat out to sea.[8]

One of Hobb's regular co-pilots was Irishman Robert Frederick Lea Dickey, born in Clarendon Street, Londonderry, on July 30 1895, his father Robert Henry Frederick Dickey being a professor in the Presbyterian College at that time. Dickey enlisted in the Royal Navy at the age of 23, as Petty Officer for the hostilities only, on 19 April 1915. Rated as First Class Airman in the RNAS on 15 September, he was discharged on appointment to a commission on 9 July 1916, and next day was granted a temporary commission as Flight Sub-Lieutenant on probation, this being confirmed on 14 February 1917, with seniority effective from 10 June the previous year. Like Hobbs, Dickey was well respected by his fellows:

> He was one of the best second pilots it is possible for any first pilot to desire. He was a good shot, a capable navigator, a fine observer, and always keen on going forward and loth to turn back. He always gave his first pilot the comfortable feeling of being absolutely trusted, and this is why I liked flying with him...[9]

Flying Boats Take On the Zeppelins

At around midnight on 13 June 1917, in accordance with orders from the Leader of Airships, *L46* and *L48* took off from Ahlhorn and Nordholz respectively to patrol the U-boat blockade area, while other Zeppelins left two hours later to cover minesweepers 40 miles north of Terschelling. At 05.36hrs *L43*'s crew radioed that they had arrived over the Terschelling Bank lightship and were commencing the patrol. Meanwhile British radio operators had already

RNAS officers adopt a candid pose for the photographer at Felixstowe. In the back row, left to right, are Flight Sub-Lieutenants J L Gordon, H Ilinan, F S McGill, Davis and 'Bob' Leckie. Seated are George F Hodson (who was drowned on 5 August 1918 on the night L70 was destroyed), Basil Hobbs and W E Robinson.
Canadian Forces Photo RMA 74–508

173

obtained a fix on two airships over the Bight, and when it was realised the first was heading westwards, orders were rapidly despatched to the coastal air stations.

At 05.15hrs Curtiss H12 8677 left Felixstowe crewed by Hobbs and Dickey, with wireless operator H M Davies and engineer A W Goody. At 07.30hrs the crew sighted the Dutch coastline at Vlieland and 'carried on various courses which brought us at 7.58am off Amieland [sic] where we changed course for Felixstowe';[10] 42 minutes later 8677 was off Vlieland again, flying at a height of 500ft, when a Zeppelin was observed five miles away to starboard and 1000ft above them, steering due north. Hobbs opened the throttles and climbed to the attack:

As we approached the Zeppelin we dived for her tail at about 100 knots. Her number L43 was observed on the tail and bow, also Maltese Cross in black circle. Midship gun opened fire with tracer ammunition and when about 100 feet above Sub-Lieut. Dickie [sic] opened fire with Brock and Pomeroy ammunition as the machine passed diagonally over the tail from starboard to port. After two bursts the Zeppelin burst into flames. Cutting off engines we turned sharply to starboard and passed over her again; she was by this time completely enveloped in flames and falling very fast. Three men were observed to fall out of her on her way down. Flames and black smoke were observed for some time after wreckage reached the water.[11]

Thus did the first of the new 'Height Climbers' fall to British defences.

Commanded by 36-year-old *Kapitänleutnant* Hermann Kraushaar, *L43* had been commissioned a mere three months before its untimely destruction; neither Kraushaar nor any member of his 23-man crew survived. Even as the blazing wreckage of the black-doped Zeppelin vanished beneath the waves, the crew of 8677 were applauding their victory:

Everybody crowded into the control cockpit. During the demonstration Billiken got the heavy boat into extraordinary positions.

Just in nice time for luncheon, at 15 minutes after 11 o'clock, having completed a flight of nearly 400 miles, Billiken brought '77 into the harbour, Dickey firing Very's lights [sic] and the handkerchiefs of the crew fluttering from the barrels of the machine guns.[12]

Once again the Germans were unaware of how an airship of theirs had been destroyed, and official British

Kapitänleutnant Hermann Kraushaar entered the German Navy on 7 April 1900, for a time a classmate of Mathy at the *Marineakademie* in Kiel during 1913. In the frame on his desk is a portrait of his English wife Mabel, who was rejected by her family and lived out her life in Kiel where she died in the early 1970s.
R Frey by courtesy of P Amesbury

announcements gave nothing away. Four days later an official telegram from Berlin made the following statement:

> Naval airship L43 is missing since Thursday last. According to English reports it was shot down in the North Sea by English naval forces.[13]

But to Heinrich Hollender in *L46* there seemed little doubt as to the manner of his comrade's destruction. At 07.18hrs *L46*, within sight of the Hook of Holland, steered northwards in order to scout towards the Humber area. Thirteen minutes earlier Galpin and Leckie in 8660 left Great Yarmouth with Leading Mechanic Thompson and Air Mechanic A Grant aboard, following orders to 'search the area 25 miles east of Southwold for hostile aircraft indicated by enemy W/T signals'.[14] At 08.15hrs, having turned north at the Noord Hinder lightship, 8660's crew observed a Zeppelin 15 miles to the east and at an estimated height of 10,500ft:

> She saw us ten minutes later, threw out her water ballast and went up to 15,000 feet, at the same time turning north-north-east and making off. By 8.45am we had reached a height of 12,500 feet immediately under the Zeppelin, and fired four trays of Brock, Pomeroy and Buckingham into her. I observed the bursts of tracer going well on to the target, but the incendiary must have burnt out by the time it reached her; it is quite possible she was hit by explosive bullets, but no immediate results took place; four tracers were seen to be fired at us.
>
> At 9.15am, after we had manoeuvred without effect for another half an hour endeavouring to get up to her, as she showed no signs of coming down, I decided to break off the fight without wasting further fuel and ammunition.[15]

The Zeppelin had escaped destruction, and its captain later reported on the encounter:

> The plane came out of a cloud bank at about 2500 metres and approached the ship very fast. I at once dropped all water except three 'breeches' and in seven minutes climbed to 5700 metres and ran off before the wind. As the plane was at about 3000 metres his speed fell very markedly. He got up to about 3500 metres, 4000 at the very most. Attempts to drive him off failed as the machine guns could not be depressed enough. Several attempts to get to one side of him were prevented by the plane keeping constantly right under the ship.[16]

Although Galpin and Leckie returned to Great Yarmouth unblooded they had caused Hollender to leave the patrol area a good six hours before the other Zeppelins were recalled at 15.37hrs. Understandably, Strasser and his comrades believed that Kraushaar and *L43* had fallen to the same aircraft that had attacked Hollender's ship. Subsequently, orders were given to the effect that all future patrols were to operate at an altitude of 13,000ft, a height that rendered the whole value of scouting null and void for it was quite impossible to detect submarines at such a level and neither could mines be spotted.

In the early morning of 26 July *L44*, *L45* and *L46* arose with orders to patrol over the German Bight. At 07.22hrs, after German radio signals had been intercepted, Galpin and Leckie in 8666 left Great Yarmouth and, having reached Texel, headed east. At 09.10hrs the crew spotted *L46* and immediately gave chase, catching up with the Zeppelin within 25 minutes:

> L46 appeared to be unaware of our presence, probably owing to the sun behind us, until we came within a mile of her. She then suddenly threw out ballast, at the same time putting her nose up to an angle of 15 to 20 degrees, and her

L43, second of the 'Height-Climbers', on a trial flight at Friedrichshafen in March 1917. *L43* made its maiden flight on 6 March 1917 and was based at Ahlhorn, usually berthed in either the *Alix* or the *Albrecht* shed. *Kapitänleutnant* Kraushaar took the ship over on March 15; two months later almost to the day, *L43* was shot down in flames over Vlieland.
Luftschiffbau Zeppelin

helm hard over. She did not stop climbing until she reached 14,000 feet, when she turned north-east and made off home. In this position we fired four trays of Brock, Pomeroy and Buckingham at her from 11,500 feet, which was our maximum attainable height, but without apparent effect.[17]

Once Hollender had released water ballast the flying boat had no chance of catching up and, collecting a few bullet holes from the Zeppelin's gunners, 8666 broke off the attack. On observing *L44* ten miles away, Galpin and Leckie gave chase but, warned by radio from Hollender's ship, *L44* threw out ballast and climbed to safety. Once again *L46* had cheated destruction by 8666, and the observation officer of the airship later gave his version of the action:

> The flying boat had reached the same height as us and was now only 1000 metres astern. Round about the ship we saw the small shots detonating, one of which would have been sufficient to bring about the destruction of the ship. Hollender said to me: 'I am only waiting for the report – "The ship is on fire"'. I can still see each single man in the gondola. There was not one who lost his head or was afraid, each one carried on with his duty down to the slightest detail, they would all have given their lives courageously for Emperor and Country.
>
> ... As for myself, there went through my mind in this moment of greatest danger the thought: 'And this is how good old Kraushaar must have died'. Then at last the ship righted herself and rose up again, swift as an arrow; it looked almost as if it was the flying boat falling headlong. We immediately opened a brisk machine-gun fire against our enemy and wirelessed to the fleet. Both these actions were actually risky during the swift ascent of the ship, since self-ignition might have occurred owing to the streaming out of the gas.[18]

Another encounter involving the flying boats and the Zeppelins, plus a DH4, took place over the Bight on 5 September,[19] but no more airships fell to naval defences, and nor would they until August 1918 when a land-based fighter was towed to the German coast on a special flying-off platform attached to a lighter.[20]

Basil Deacon Hobbs enjoyed a full career with the RNAS while based at Felixstowe. For the role he played in the destruction of *L43* he was awarded the DSC on 22 June 1917, and he was promoted to Temporary Lieutenant eight days later. Hobbs and Dickey flew a great many anti-submarine patrols, and on 28 September, in Curtiss H12 8676, they spotted the *UC6* cruising on the surface 30 miles south of the Noord Hinder. They dropped a brace of 230lb bombs on the submarine, which was sunk as a result of the action, 8676 coming under fire from three other U-boats and three destroyers in the vicinity.

On 1 January 1918 Hobbs was appointed Temporary Commander and on 22 March, was posted to the British Aviation Mission in Washington, attached to the US Army Air Service, acting in an advisory capacity on the employment of large flying boats. On 13 December Hobbs was back in England, and he took charge of 231 Squadron at Felixstowe on 26 February 1919. It was during that year that he married Helen Edith Thompson, and being transferred to the unemployed list on 3 December he finally relinquished his temporary RAF commission on 1 September 1921, retaining the rank of Major.

Hobbs entered the Canadian Air Force as a squadron leader at the Winnipeg Air Station on 26 May 1922, then the newly-formed RCAF at its headquarters in Ottawa on 1 April 1924, resigning his commission on 1 October of the following year. Hobbs had lost little time in obtaining his private pilot's licence (2 February 1920), and participated in the first Trans-Canadian flight that year prior to helping map Northern Canada by aerial survey. During World War II Hobbs re-entered the RCAF on 18 June 1940 at Trenton, commanding the air force stations at Dartmouth and Patricia Bay and serving with the latter until 11 July 1945; on 7 August he was finally released from the service. Eventually he retired to Montreal and died there on Sunday, 28 November 1965, the funeral service taking place the following Wednesday at the Church of St James the Apostle.

Squadron Leader Hobbs resigned his commission with the RCAF on 1 September 1925 but in June 1940 he re-entered the service at Trenton. He was in command of the Air Force station at Patricia Bay until July 1945, finally leaving the RCAF as a Group Captain. *Canadian Forces Photo RE 8514*

Robert Frederick Lea Dickey also gained the DSC for the *L43* action and was promoted to Flight Lieutenant on 1 October, 1917. There came another promotion, to Captain, on 1 April 1918, when the RFC and RNAS became the fledgeling Royal Air Force. On 4 June, Dickey took part in a combined operation out to the Haaks lightvessel with the intention of engaging enemy seaplanes. Led by Leckie in 12a N4295, the force consisted of F2a N4298 from Great Yarmouth, Curtiss H12 8689, and F2as N4302 and N4533 from Felixstowe. Dickey, in N4533, became the first casualty when a broken petrol feed pipe from one of the engines obliged him to land ten miles north of Terschelling Island. Leckie signalled his comrade to taxi the crippled flying boat into Dutch waters, beach it and set it afire. Five German Hansa Brandenburg seaplanes promptly arrived and began to attack Dickey's aircraft, although the combined efforts of the other boats drove them back. Reinforcements arrived in the shape of 14 German seaplanes, and a pitched battle ensued. N4302 was also compelled to land with a broken petrol pipe, and Captain John Hodson flew N4289 on one engine while the engineer repaired the other during the combat. Additionally Private Reid, engineer of N4302, affected a temporary repair, enabling Captain Barker to return to base with a damaged wing-tip float.[21] Six German seaplanes were brought down, but Dickey managed to get close to the shore, get his crew off and set his aircraft alight, thenceforth to face internment:

> While walking in a quiet street of a Dutch town just at dusk a huge German elbowed him into the roadway. He seized the coat-tails of the Hun and demanded an apology. The Hun swore in German – not a pretty exhibition.
>
> Dickey was small, but he carried a big stick, and when the stick came in contact with the skull of the German the latter fell senseless. Informing the police that a man had been found unconcious in the roadway, the little fire-eater obtained an ambulance and tenderly removed his fallen foe to hospital.[22]

After the Armistice Dickey continued to serve at Felixstowe until resigning his commission on 14 January 1925, subsequently, it is believed, returning to Eire.

CHAPTER 13
L48, 17 June 1917

> '...This afternoon in the blaze of the summer sun, thousands on foot and in every kind of vehicle visited the grisly relic. A Sunday school teacher marched the girls of her class to the place. Some 80ft of her nose-end is stuck aslant in the air, the framework gleaming in the sunshine, with scattered remnants of her covering fluttering in the breeze...'
>
> The Daily Mail, Monday 18 June 1917

Suddenly there was a terrible, continuous roaring smashing of metal as the stern struck the ground and the hull structure collapsed beneath me. I found myself on the ground with the breath half knocked out of me, the framework crashing down on top of me, fuel and oil tanks bursting on impact and their burning contents flowing towards me through the shattered wreckage. I was trapped in a tangle of red-hot girders, the heat roasting me alive through my heavy flying coat. If I had lost consciousness I would have burned to death. But I could still think and move, and with all my strength I forced some girders apart – I never felt the pain of my burned hands until later – and burst out of my prison. I fell full length on cool, wet grass.[1]

Machinist's Mate Heinrich Ellerkamm was an extremely lucky man, for whenever British defences turned Zeppelins into 2-million-cubic-foot fireballs it could hardly be expected that any members of the crew would survive the holocaust. Yet on a June morning in 1917 Ellerkamm and two of his comrades did just that.

The 'Height-Climbers'

The latter months of 1916 had convinced Strasser that his airships could anticipate grievous losses whenever they ventured over England; indeed, the German Fleet Command, appalled at the losses, debated whether further raids were justifiable, and may have vetoed them altogether were it not for Strasser fervently pleading the cause he personally considered far from lost. At a conference with Admiral Scheer, the Leader of Airships suggested that

> ...it was not upon the direct material damage that the value of the airship attacks depended, but rather on the general result of the German onslaught upon England's insularity otherwise undisturbed by war.[2]

Strasser went on to argue that continuation of airship raids would serve to tie down large numbers of men and equipment necessary for England's defence. It was a sound enough argument, as the British official air history was later to record:

> The threat of their raiding potentialities compelled us to set up at home a formidable organisation which diverted men,

guns, and aeroplanes from more important theatres of war. By the end of 1916 there were specifically retained in Great Britain for home anti-aircraft defence 17,341 officers and men. There were 12 Royal Flying Corps squadrons, comprising approximately 200 officers, 2000 men and 110 aeroplanes. The anti-aircraft guns and searchlights were served by 12,000 officers and men who would have found a ready place, with continuous work, in France or other war theatres.[3]

Thus airship raids, if only for their nuisance value, continued, mainly on the north of England and the Midlands, which lay beyond the effective range of Gotha and Staaken aircraft that took over the Zeppelin's role of London bombers. In fact the capital was only once more visited by airship, and then accidentally, yet Strasser remained convinced that he could still inflict mortal damage on the city, although the performance of his ships would have to be greatly improved if defending aircraft were to be avoided.

Initially the German Admiralty's Aviation Department mooted that an increase in speed would prove to be the ideal solution. This suggestion was based on a new, highly streamlined gondola design housing a pair of Maybach HSLus geared to a single propeller – certainly more efficient than the clumsy three-engine car and outrigger brackets of old. Luftschiffbau Zeppelin GmbH proposed two applications for the new gondola, Design 157 for a seven-engine, 682ft vessel of 2,090,000 cu ft capacity, and Design 160, 716ft long, with eight engines, and of 2,239,000 cu ft capacity. Calculated speeds for the projected ships were 65.5 and 67.5mph respectively, yet in the event the designs were never realised, owing to development delays in the twin-engine drive. But Strasser had an alternative in mind, in fact an entirely opposite course – that of high operational ceiling at the expense of speed.

On 17 January 1917 Strasser outlined his arguments in a letter to the Admiralty, and within ten days was attending a special conference chaired by Admiral Starke, head of the Dockyard Bureau, and accompanied by his own airship expert, one *Marine Schiffbaumeister* Engberding. As well as Strasser, who represented the 'Front', others present included Drs Dürr and Dörr, both designers with the

L40 is seen here in the *Albrecht* shed at Ahlhorn shortly after receiving its black camouflage dope. At left can be seen a stack of spare fuel tanks and at right one of the station's captive balloons used to mark the base in fog.
Archiv: Marine-Luftschiffer-Kameradschaft

Zeppelin Company. Many and varied were the arguments that were thrashed out, proposals and counter-proposals swayed back and forth, and statements were made and vehemently challenged, but the outcome was a positive one with the appointment of a special commission. This was to include Dürr, Dörr, two naval architects and the captain of a new airship to be built at Friedrichshafen which would incorporate certain innovations that included:

1. The substitution of the three-engined rear gondola and outrigger brackets with a twin-engine version mounting a single propeller.
2. A reduction in fuel capacity (range) from 36 hours to 30.
3. The removal of all defensive armament, including the upper gun platforms.
4. A reduction in the number of bomb release mechanisms by 50 per cent, to leave eight releases for 660lb bombs, 16 for 200pdrs and 60 for incendiaries.
5. A lightened hull structure.
6. A new, more compact control car.
7. The elimination of crews' quarters and comforts.

On his return to Nordholz, Strasser lost little time applying most of these innovations to the latest Zeppelins already in service, *L35*, *L36*, *L39* and *L40*.[4] At the beginning of February, these ships undertook short altitude test flights, the results of which were generally encouraging. No problems were encountered with the powerplants, although several men suffered slight dizziness and mild palpitations when unprecedented heights of between 17,100 and 17,700ft were attained.

It was on 28 February that Martin Dietrich commissioned *L42*, the very first Zeppelin constructed entirely to conference specifications. Externally the new airship differed little from the earlier 'Thirties' in either hull or gondola design, although the after engine of the rear car was not installed, but there was one noticeable change. In order to elude English defences even more effectively, a coat of black dope had been applied over the entire vessel except for the upper portion of the hull. Searchlight crews and ground observers were certainly going to encounter great difficulty finding the new high-flying Zeppelins, which in their sombre warpaint appeared even more sinister. On 10 March Dietrich took *L42*, with Strasser aboad, for an altitude test, and managed to attain 19,700ft. The Leader of Airships clambered through the Zeppelin at its ceiling and Dietrich's most lasting impression of that trip involved his superior painfully negotiating the control gondola ladder, gasping for breath in the rarefied air.

Over the ensuing months, performances improved even further as new ships were built. On 21 August was commissioned *L53*, which with its redesigned hull structure – the nine largest frames were spaced 15 metres apart rather than 10 – achieved a useful lift of over 89,500lb (67 per cent of the total), and reached 20,700ft on its maiden raid with ease. This airship, first of the 'v' type Zeppelins, while too fragile for full speed manouvring at low height, remained the standard version over the North Sea for nearly a year. The 'Height-Climbers', as the new Zeppelins became known, boasted other refinements, including a tightly doped outer cover to lower skin friction and a reduction of gold beaters' skin layers in the gas cells from three to two, later improved even further when silk was substituted for cotton fabric. During April 1917 Strasser had second thoughts in regard to defensive armament, as gun platforms were installed in *L43* and *L44* and development of the 20mm Becker cannon accelerated. With their 'Height-Climbers' the German Naval Airship Division rendered England's defences totally helpless: flying at altitudes between 16,000 and 20,000ft, the Zeppelins were well beyond the range of aircraft and guns. Yet this tactical advantage was marred by serious drawbacks which occurred as a result of operating at extreme altitude.

German weather forecasters at the Hamburg Observatory were quite unable to predict sub-stratospheric conditions accurately, and were thus powerless to warn commanders of impending gales in the upper regions. Navigation, too, was made more difficult, for at these unheard-of heights the ground below became indistinct and landmarks virtually invisible, whilst at night, hampered by cloud beneath and upper air currents, commanders were forced to rely solely on radio. This worked against them as well as for them, since English operators were able to listen in, pinpointing the Zeppelins' positions just as accurately as could German shore stations. Thus there was a severe problem of overloading the 'airship special wavelength', as each vessel had to make several calls for each bearing. Nor was this all: other problems arose, for although the German Navy enjoyed a healthy reputation for its competent medical department in most areas, it failed to keep pace with the rapid progress in aviation medicine. Flight crews received a rigorous physical examination on their entry into the service but no subsequent check-ups were made – a surprisingly casual approach that could prove fatal, as witness the tragedy of *L49*'s elevator man who during an altitude test flight on 7 August dropped dead in the control car with an undetected heart disease.

While the human body is capable of compensating for a small decrease in oxygen tension, at over 12,000ft 'altitude sickness' occurs, and as the operational heights of the Zeppelins increased so did the discomfort of the crews. In an attempt to combat the problem, individual bottles of oxygen were issued, though for many months airship crews scorned them as a sign of weakness until far-sighted commanders ordered their use above 16,000ft. The compressed oxygen was often impure, with unpleasant side effects resulting in severe stomach pains at worst or cracked lips at best. Only later were the bottles replaced by Dewar flasks of liquid air.[5]

Hand in glove with the increased altitude was extreme bitter cold, causing stiff joints and often frostbite; no on-board heating was available, and the only way long-suffering crews might alleviate their numbness was to pile on extra clothing, fur-lined flying suits and helmets replacing standard naval garb. But not only crews suffered, for in the cold rarefield air standard airship motors could lose up to 50 per cent of their efficiency, dramatically reducing speed; moreover, although each piston stroke took in the same volume of air, it was so lacking in oxygen that the amount of fuel had to be reduced. The Zeppelin crews had to make do until November, when at long last the high-compression altitude motors began to be installed.

Strasser, filled with fresh confidence in his improved airships, pressed the Navy Minister for increased airship production, indicating his heavy requirements for scouting and bombing operations, but it was not until 16 March that the 'Height-Climbers' made their operational debut over England with an ineffectual attack involving *L35*, *L39*, *L40*, *L41* and *L42*. London was the target, but none of the raiders made it that far, unexpected storms blowing the Zeppelins off course. Strasser was aboard *L42*, which failed to reach England altogether owing to a forward engine breakdown and a loss of radio bearings. Having been carried south and within sight of the Ostend lighthouse, Dietrich next steered due north, but with only four motors operative *L42* was driven southwards, tail-first. At 23.47hrs Dietrich headed back for Nordholz but, hampered by fog, was unable to locate the base, and with petrol running low steered eastwards, landing at Jüterbog with one hour's fuel aboard.[6]

London was once more the target on 23 May, when Strasser despatched *L40*, *L42*, *L43*, *L44*, *L45* and *L47*, the Leader of Airships participating again by joining the complement of *L44*. Kraushaar in *L43* claimed an attack on the capital, yet his 38 bombs were traced between East Wrentham and Great Ryburgh where they damaged several cottages and killed one man. With the unofficial 'Jonah' aboard, *L44* suffered two engine breakdowns over Harwich and another soon afterwards, at which point *Kapitänleutnant* Franz Stabbert gave up all thoughts of reaching London and

> ...turned back, all bombs dropped at 1.40 am over Harwich when ship fell again. No unusual results seen due to overcast. Immediately after attack last two engines failed one after the other. Ship continued to descend and after slipping six fuel tanks, dropping water, radiator water, spare parts and most of the ship's equipment she was held at 3900 metres.[7]

The drastic but necessary act of dumping all spare radiator water forced Stabbert to limp home with one of his motors at full speed and another at half. On only two engines *L44* made slow progress: the airship finally arrived over Nordholz at 17.00hrs, having been escorted by *L23* for three hours, the latter earlier despatched from Tondern with orders to assist.

Through hail, winds and cloud, *L42* battled towards the English coast, Dietrich making his landfall south of the Naze, proceeding inland to Braintree and then moving

'Height-Climber aces': *Hauptmann* Kuno Manger (left), killed on 10 May 1918 when *L62* exploded in mid-air over Heligoland; *Kapitänleutnant der Reserve* Franz George Eichler (centre) killed in *L48*; and *Kapitänleutnant* Hans-Karl Gayer (*L49*) captured on 20 October 1917 when he forced-landed at Bourbonne-les-Baines, France, following the abortive 'Silent Raid'. Eichler was born at Giebichenstein on 28 October 1877, his father, Ignatz, and mother living at Halle an der Salle. Young Franz joined the Naval Reserve in the Hamburg reserve district on 2 April 1895 and attained his ultimate rank on 8 February 1908. Nine years later, almost to the day, Eichler was in command of *L36* when it was destroyed in an operational accident.
By courtesy of R Frey

L48 (builder's number LZ95) was constructed at Friedrichshafen's Factory Shed 1, made its first flight on 22 May 1917 and was commissioned the following day when *Kapitänleutnant der Reserve* Eichler took the vessel over.
Luftschiffbau Zeppelin

northwards to Norfolk and going out at Sheringham. Several bombs distributed between Mildenhall and East Dereham caused no damaged as *L42* pointed its nose homewards. On the return journey Dietrich encountered a ferocious thunderstorm, his ship being struck at least three times by lightning; on landing, scorched areas were found on the port aft propeller.

Kapitänleutnant der Reserve Richard Wolff, in the newly commissioned *L47*, did not even reach England, despite that commander's claim of having done so. *L40* and *L45* did manage to cross East Anglia, and both commanders were to claim having bombed Norwich, but only three missiles from these ships were traced on land and the total amount of damage the raiders caused was worth only £599.[8]

If the latest assault caused the English defences few headaches, the same could not be said for the German airship crews. Flying for several hours at heights over 16,000ft caused severe head pains, stomach disorders, nausea and vomiting – even mild exertion left men exhausted and gasping for air. More alarming were the adverse effects which high altitude had on the Zeppelins themselves. Radiator water evaporated rapidly due to reduced atmospheric pressure and a lowered boiling point, while metals expanded and contracted at extreme changes of height. For instance, engine telegraph wires and rudder and elevator control cables could slacken off, the latter often as much as 4in at –25° Fahrenheit, sufficient for them to jump out of their guide sheaves, although they took up again at lower levels. Despite these problems, a raid in each 'attack period' was scheduled, and mid-June saw Strasser sending his ships out once again.

June 16
With the shortest night of the year less than a week away, *L42*, *L44*, *L45*, *L46*, *L47* and *L48* were assigned to attack the English capital, and to many it seemed an almost suicidal mission. Surviving airship personnel remain incredulous that Strasser should have despatched a force that would find a mere three hours of semi-darkness over London. In later years Dietrich was to recall that his chief would never admit to the effectiveness of English defences and often simply refused to believe his subordinates whenever they related heart-stopping mid-air encounters with aircraft.

L48 was to lead the attack, and sharing the control gondola with *Kapitänleutnant der Reserve* Franz George Eichler was *Korvettenkäpitan* Viktor Schütze, who on 9 December 1916 had relinquished command of the ill-starred *L36* to succeed Strasser as head of the Naval Airship Division. As the newly commissioned Zeppelin was walked out of the *Normann* shed, the Nordholz station band swung into 'Admiral of the Air', and, halfway through, 'the midday heat cracked the skin of the big drum'.[9] To many it seemed an omen of sorts. Supervising the withdrawal of *L48* was Executive Officer Otto Mieth:

> As soon as I boarded the ship our mooring lines were loosened, propellers began to whirl, and the L48 rose quickly but majestically in the air. A last wave of the hand, a shout of 'Back tomorrow!' and the North Sea rolled beneath us.
>
> Our course lay due west. We were in the best of spirits, and though our sailors are superstitious, no one recalled the fact that this was our thirteenth raid. Our sealed orders were opened. They read briefly: 'Attack South England – if possible, London'. Wilhelmshaven appeared on our port side. The vessels of our High Seas Fleet, lying on watch at Schillig Reede, signalled, 'A successful trip'.
>
> The North Friesland islands came into sight and disappeared behind us. We pushed steadily onward. Slowly the homeland sank into the misty distance, and over Terschelling we found ourselves already in the enemy zone of operations. Only a few days before, the British had surprised and destroyed two of our reconnaissance airships at this point. We rose to the 3000-metre level, scanning the air anxiously in all directions, but discovered no sign of the enemy.
>
> On and on. Our motors hummed rhythmically, our propellers whistled. It gradually became darker. The last rays of the sun gilded the waves, and a light mist spread like a thin veil over the earth, making it difficult to pick up our bearings. We had gradually risen to 5000 metres, and were close to the south-eastern coast of England. But it was still too light for our purpose, so we were forced to bear away from land and wait for darkness. Suddenly a heavy thunderstorm swept over England. Flashes of lightning a kilometre long rent the clouds. This wonderful scene lasted but a few minutes and then passed on, but when we resumed our course we discovered that there had been a violent atmospheric disturbance, and that the direction of the wind had suddenly changed and we were bucking a strong south-west gale that impeded our progress.[10]

Stiff crosswinds had confined both *L46* and *L47* to their sheds, and with *L44* and *L45* returning due to engine trouble the only other ship actually to reach English shores was Dietrich's *L42*. By 19.30hrs this ship was 40 miles from Southwold, the commander prudently staying his hand as the thunderstorm raged. Three hours later came a radio message from *L48* to the effect that the weather was clearing further inland and an attack on London was to proceed. Thus Dietrich made his landfall between Dungeness and Dover, but at midnight, when he fancied he observed lights from the latter town, the wind had increased and, with storms still raging westwards, the commander went for Dover, leaving London until later if conditions improved.

At least two hours had elapsed before *L42* was in an ideal attacking position, and even as the first bomb whistled down 14 searchlights snapped on. Several anti-aircraft guns opened fire and at least one aeroplane was seen, but the black camouflage hindered the searchlight crews, who were unable to locate the raider. *L42*'s bombs struck Ramsgate, not Dover and Deal as Dietrich believed, his third 660pdr hitting a naval ammunition depot near the Clock Tower. A series of explosions followed, rocking the depot and practically destroying the entire naval base; three civilians were killed and 14 injured, and also hurt were two servicemen, in blasts that caused over £28,159 worth of damage. Over the next few days, newspapers reported in some detail how the Ramsgate fatalities occurred:

> One [bomb] fell in the common garden attached to a cluster of houses in the poorer quarter of the town. Several of these were smashed, and the wreckage began to burn. A man and his wife and a lodger were sleeping in two of the upstairs rooms of one little house. The rooms and everything in them fell through to the ground floor, burying the man and his wife. Half an hour afterwards the man was dug out of the wreckage, dead; two hours later his wife was taken out alive. The floor joists of the bedroom had fallen across her, screening her head and shoulders. But her body and limbs were crushed, and this afternoon she died in hospital.
>
> The only other fatal case was that of a man in an adjoining house – the sole occupant. The whole place 'crumpled up' around him, and hours later his mangled body was dug out of the ruins. In the next house a woman and her four children were sleeping when the first crash came. The mother hurried her infants out into the street. They were hardly outside when a bomb fell clean through the children's bed and wrecked the house.[11]

By this time it was too late for Dietrich to risk a London

A trial flight photo of L48 over Friedrichshafen in May 1917. L48 was the first of the 'u' type class and had an envelope capacity of 1,970,300 cu ft; it was also the first Zeppelin to carry a streamlined control gondola. Luftschiffbau Zeppelin

attack, so he swung his ship on a north-easterly course towards the coast. Both *L42* and *L48* had already been tracked by ground observers and the coastal defence units alerted accordingly. From the Great Yarmouth Air Station at least 12 aircraft rose, three of which attempted to attack *L42* on its way out.

First to encounter the Zeppelin was Flight Lieutenant Walker in BE2c 8629, who pursued Dietrich eastwards for 30 miles but was unable to overtake his quarry and returned to Burgh Castle, landing at 04.30hrs. Flight Lieutenant George Henry Bittles, in Blackburn-built Sopwith Baby N1064, sighted *L42* east of Lowestoft at 11,000ft. Closing to within 30yds of the airship, Bittles emptied a full drum of incendiary ammunition, but whilst he was engaged in reloading *L42* rose 4000ft, well out of range. Unable to do anything other than watch the airship make good its escape, Bittles flew back to Great Yarmouth, alighting there at 05.05hrs. The third of the station's airmen to take up the challenge was Egbert Cadbury, flying Sopwith Pup 9904:

> I chased one of them for about 20 minutes at 15,500 feet but could not catch up with it. It was about 16,000 feet and still 15 miles away. The new Zeppelin must be very fast, as I was flying at about 80 to 90 miles an hour and could not catch him up. I was forced to give up the chase, for when about 20 miles out, a petrol pipe fractured and started letting all my petrol out. However, by keeping my finger over the end of the broken pipe, I stemmed the flow a little and just made the coast of Yarmouth, soaked in petrol.[12]

Other airmen who pursued *L42* equally fruitlessly were Gerard Fane in Sopwith Pup 9905, Flight Sub-Lieutenant H B Brenton in Sopwith Baby N1108 and the crew of Curtiss H12 8666. Commanded by Vincent Nicholl, piloted by 'Bob' Leckie and crewed by Leading Mechanics W Fairnie and A Grant, the flying boat left Great Yarmouth at 03.05hrs. Less than half an hour later its crew sighted *L42* at about 8000ft and gave chase, Nicholl climbing to 12,000ft. For one and a half hours 8666 pursued the Zeppelin to a position ten miles north of Ameland, but, unable to close the gap, Nicholl gave up at 05.15hrs and turned back for Great Yarmouth.

L42, its crew seemingly unaware of the various aeroplane pilots endeavouring to burn them alive, eventually landed safely at Nordholz after a 39-hour flight, 14 hours of which had been spent at 13,000ft and 11 at 16,500ft. Dietrich and his crew had acquitted themselves well; however, they were hardly in the mood for celebration, since they had witnessed a chilling spectacle. They were 70 miles away when disaster overtook their comrades and Dietrich, for one, never forgot it:

> At 3.35, two points abaft the port beam, a red ball of fire suddenly appeared, which quickly grew bigger and in falling, showed the shape of a Zeppelin airship. The burning ship was at the same altitude as L42, therefore 4000–4500 metres. Some 500 metres higher a plane was clearly visible, which twice fired a bright white light.[13]

Dietrich radioed the tragic news ahead of him, and when he brought *L42* back to Nordholz his chief was already out on the field to greet him. Clambering aboard the control gondola, a shocked Strasser demanded details, initially refusing to accept that *L48* could possibly have been destroyed by aircraft. But the commander of *L42* was insistent, and, as one of the most experienced officers, had to be believed. Strasser climbed out of *L42* thoroughly despondent and remained in his quarters for several days afterwards.

The first that English defences were aware of *L48* was at 22.34hrs when the Zeppelin was seen lying 40 miles northeast of Harwich:

> By this time it was bitterly cold, the temperature having fallen 72° since we left Germany, and we shivered even in our heavy clothing. At our high altitude, moreover, we breathed with great difficulty, and in spite of our oxygen flasks several members of the crew became unconscious. Nevertheless we pushed on steadily against the south-west wind, driving our machines at their full power. But June nights are short in England, and our chances of reaching London grew constantly less. Suddenly a starboard propeller stopped, and an engineer reported that the motor had broken down.
>
> As our forward motor was also knocking badly, we had to

FE2b B401 flown by Holder and Ashby against *L48* on 16 June 1917. This was the first machine built by Ransomes, Sims and Jefferies of Ipswich, being passed by the Air Department in April 1917. Initially it was sent to Martlesham Heath before it flew to Orfordness. Subsequent to its combat against *L48*, B401 was fitted with a bowsprit and wire fenders and piloted by Captain Roderick Hill for balloon deflection experiments.
Aeromodeller

BE12 C3237, built by The Daimler Co Ltd of Coventry, seen at Orfordness in 1917; an Armstrong Whitworth FK3 lies beyond. It was in a machine of the former type, 6610 (also built by Daimler), that Watkins was flying when he attacked *L48*.
Aeromodeller

give up London. Thereupon one bit of bad luck followed another. Our compass froze and we had great difficulty in keeping our bearings. At length we decided to attack Harwich, which lay diagonally ahead of us wrapped in a light stratum of fog. So we made for the leeward of the town in order to cross over quickly with the wind behind us. It was 2am and our altitude was 5600 metres.[16]

L48 made landfall south of Orfordness, where the motors were shut down and the Zeppelin drifted over the RFC Experimental Station for 15 minutes whilst mechanics laboured over the engines. Yet the station had heard the Zeppelin's approach at 01.45hrs, and Major P C Cooper, commandant of the unit, despatched two aircraft. Second Lieutenant E D Clarke, in BE2c 8896, took off at 01.50hrs, closely followed by Second Lieutenant F D Holder in FE2b B401 with Sergeant Sydney Ashby manning the guns:

Our two machines were then gaining height in the direction in which the Zeppelin was drifting, and after about 20 minutes the airship was lost sight of. A little later the Harwich guns became very active (we did not hear any guns firing north of Orfordness).
At 1.48am the position of the Zeppelin was reported to AA Harwich and at 1.51am I telephoned the same message to No 37 Squadron and suggested that they should send up machines flying North along the coast. Similar information was again transmitted to AA Harwich at 1.55am and to No 37 Squadron at 2am.[17]

Ten minutes later the first of Eichler's bombs, whistled down, not on Harwich but harmlessly on open fields at Kirton five miles further north, the Zeppelin coming under heavy gunfire during its attack. In all, 13 bombs were traced at Kirton, official records indicating nine more at Falkenham and a further three at Martlesham. Following the bomb run, *L48* dropped to 13,000ft, clearly visible as it moved slowly across a bright starlit sky:

It was half-past two, and from our altitude the pale glow of England's midsummer dawn was already visible. So it was high time to get back over the open sea, for once there our principal danger would be over. But our frozen compass was our undoing. Instead of steering to the east, we inadvertently headed towards the north, and before we discovered our error, we had lost valuable time. Added to that our forward motor also failed us, so that our speed was sensibly diminished.[18]

At this point Eichler radioed the stations in the German Bight for bearings. With them came notification of useful tailwinds at 11,000ft, and, acting on this information, the commander reduced altitude accordingly. As *L48* moved across East Anglia, ground observers made regular reports to local military units:

About 2.45am the Zeppelin was again sighted at a lower altitude steering due North and the engines could be distinctly heard. Information was immediately transmitted to No 37 Squadron, and No 51 Squadron were asked to send machines Southward as I then feared that our own machines had lost touch with the HA [hostile aircraft]. I then instructed Capt R H M S Saundby to ascend in DH2 A5058 and he left the ground at 2.55am.[19]

Motorcycling along the Sizewell Road towards Leiston that morning was Captain J M Dimmock, who dismounted and shut off his engine when a level crossing impeded his progress. On hearing gunfire he climbed to higher ground in order to gain a better view of the action, and at 03.05hrs observed an aircraft, presumably Saundby's, passing overhead at 'about 300/400 feet with the tail drooping'. The machine appeared to follow the Aldeburgh–Saxmundham railway line and Dimmock subsequently lost sight of it. Ten minutes later he observed a Zeppelin travelling in the same direction, its movements suggesting it was in some difficulty:

The engines of the airship were only just audible and from the way it swung gently from side to side it would seem that only a portion of her engine power was working and that corrections had to be made with the rudder to keep the ship on a comparatively straight course. By this time dawn had begun to break and the movements of the airship could quite clearly be distinguished against the reddish tint of the sky.[20]

As *L48* headed towards Saxmundham it treated local village residents to an unexpected thrill as it sailed slowly over their upturned faces. One impressionable 14-year-old living at Waldringham followed the course of the raider as it proceeded in a north-easterly direction:

We were watching it for some hours turning in the sky sometimes broadside to us, sometimes end-on but clearly visible in the early light of that morning. Then at long last we heard the sound of a plane going from Martlesham aerodrome which was only about two and a half miles from where we were.
After a short time we saw a flash of light from the plane to the airship and in no time at all it was on fire from end to end.[21]

George Foster was another teenager with a grandstand view of Eichler's *L48* as it passed directly over his parent's home:

> With my brother and sister, my parents took us out of the house to open ground where we were able to observe that the Zeppelin appeared to be in trouble (knocking could be heard coming from the airship) and was drifting towards the North Sea. After an interval of some 15 minutes a plane could be heard coming from a nearby airfield, and as it was by then getting daylight, could be seen quite clearly. It passed the Zeppelin, made a turn and when in line could be seen to fire a couple of short bursts from a machine gun.[22]

When Major Cooper had transmitted instructions to 37 HDS at Goldhanger, that unit's commander, Major W B Hargrave, sent up his pilots. Between 01.54 and 03.22hrs two airmen from Rochford and four from Goldhanger took to the skies, first away being Captain William Sowrey in RE7 2232. The brother of Peterson's conqueror suffered engine trouble which forced his return to Goldhanger within 20 minutes. As Sowrey brought his aircraft down, Second Lieutenant Loudon Pierce Watkins was preparing to take off.

Canadian-born Watkins was one of four sons: Edward, Harry, John and himself, 'Don', of Edward J Watkins, who lived at 95 Breadalbane Street, Toronto. All the boys went into uniform as war broke out, John as a sapper in France with divisional signallers of the Engineers and Harry subsequently becoming a cadet at Burwash Hall, RAF Canada. Edward and 'Don' attended the Toronto Curtiss School together and were taken on strength by the RFC in Canada on 7 December 1915. Within 16 days 'Don' Watkins was in England, and following further training his rank of Second Lieutenant was confirmed on 18 May 1916. He served in France, first with 7 Squadron between May and June, then with 21 Squadron at Fienvillers which undertook offensive and defensive patrols, escort work and bombing. Watkins saw some action, albeit indecisive, with three enemy aircraft on 16 September, and on 30 November left the squadron and returned to England for home defence duty. He reported to 37 HDS on 11 December.

It was Watkins, Saundby and Holder who simultaneously caught up with and attacked *L48* on the fateful morning of 17 June. Not at any time were all three machines in sight of each other as they blazed away with their guns at the target, and thus it is difficult, but perhaps irrelevant after 67 years, to decide to whom the destruction of the airship can be accredited. To Holder, *L48* appeared to be just inland of Aldeburgh as he closed in:

> We opened fire with both guns firing obliquely but my gun jammed and Ashby was unable to correct the fault. As the airship continued to lose height, and [with] only the observer's gun firing, I altered course so that Ashby could use the easiest aim, firing straight ahead, without deflection and approaching the airship's starboard rear, still slightly below. Ashby, with a clear view of the target, fired three drums, the last at a range of 300 yards, at which point we were aware of tracer bullets coming from the direction of the enemy. I started to take evasive action, but as we did so we saw flames appear at the point at which we were aiming. The time was 3.25am.[23]

Enter Saundby:

> When I reached 14,000 feet I judged that I was less than 1000 feet beneath it and I raised my gun to an angle of 45° and let fly at about 300 yards range with a double drum of incendiary bullets. I aimed at the nose of the ship hoping to keep on hitting it in the same place somewhere further aft. When I

An unidentified DH2 flies over an FE2b and an NE1 at Orfordness during 1917. It was in a machine of this type that Saundby flew when he joined in the attack on *L48*.
Aeromodeller

> fired they saw my tracer bullets and shot back with a heavy slow-firing machine gun but I had time to get off a double drum before it was necessary to jink out of the way.[24]

Watkins was flying over Harwich at 11,000ft when he first sighted *L48* 2000ft above him. Pulling back the control stick of BE12 6610, he climbed laboriously to 11,500ft, at which stage he loosed off one drum of incendiary bullets into the Zeppelin's swaying tail. Observing no apparent effect, the pilot climbed another 500ft and repeated the performance. Watkins then decided to get in very close for his next attack and when within 500ft fired three short bursts of about seven rounds and then the remainder of the drum. To his brief combat report, Watkins later appended:

> About ten minutes after I first saw the Zeppelin I saw another machine come up from the north and fire a short burst at the Zeppelin from the side. I then lost sight of the other machine until just before my last drum when I saw him going from north to south across the bow of the Zeppelin which was heading east when she caught fire.[25]

L48, rocked by an explosion and rapidly wreathed in flames, sank stern-first at a 60° angle for about three minutes, before crashing in a field near Holly Tree Farm,

Viktor Schütze, in the control car of *L11*, 5/6 March 1916. Schütze was later killed when *L48* fell in flames at Theberton, Suffolk, in 1917. When Strasser was promoted to 'Leader of Airships' on 23 November 1916, *Korvettenkäpitan* Schütze gave up command of *L36* to become commander of the Naval Airship Division.
By courtesy of P Amesbury

An unusual aerial view of *L48* down at Theberton, Suffolk. Two cordons of troops surround the wreck and picket fences have been set up beyond them in an effort to keep sightseers at a respectable distance. On 18 June Second Lieutenant F D Holder and Captain Walden Hammond, the latter the photographic officer at the Orfordness-based Experimental Station, flew over *L48* to secure a series of overhead photographs.
Aeromodeller

The battered control car of *L48*, from where watch officer Otto Mieth was dragged out alive by police and civilians who were the first upon the scene.
Sir Victor Goddard

Engineers of the Admiralty's Constructional Department arrived at Theberton on 18 June. As they dismantled *L48* they carefully measured and detailed all the major components.
Sir Victor Goddard

One of the engine cars of *L48* with its Maybach embedded almost vertically in the ground. One of the tubular exhaust pipes (one to each gondola) is seen at right.
Sir Victor Goddard

Sorting through the remains. On the left, the floor of the upper gun platform can be seen. The task of dismantling the wreckage took several weeks and eventually the remains left East Anglia by rail.
Sir Victor Goddard

Flight Lieutenant Victor Goddard RNAS, who officially took charge of the *L48* wreck on behalf of the Admiralty, poses with Army officers at Theberton in June 1917.
Sir Victor Goddard

The nose of *L48*, supported by scaffolding to prevent premature collapse. Tattered shreds of fabric covering flutter from the girders. The remainder of the structure telescoped beneath the bows as the tail struck the ground.
Sir Victor Goddard

Another view of the wrecked *L48*. Incredibly, three crew members survived as the blazing airship struck the ground.
Aeromodeller

Zeppelin!

Theberton, land owned by Mr H Staulkey. As the Zeppelin caught fire, Saundby was very close:

> She broke into a 'V' shape and fell slowly past me, the flames roaring so loudly that I could hear them above the sound of my engine. I followed her down as she sank earthwards and she took a long time to fall. She struck the ground at the bottom of the V, forcing out the remaining gas in a huge tower of flame, then crumpled and lay still in a pathetic skeleton of metal girders.[26]

On observation duty at Sizewell was Sergeant J Marriot:

> At 3.27am smoke appeared on top of the nose of the envelope and immediately flame ran along her back and the Zeppelin nose-dived [sic] and struck a ploughed field near Theberton Hall Farm at 3.30am. A bright white light appeared in the sky near where the Zepp had been, apparently from [an] aeroplane, but none of our machines were visible to me until 15 to 20 minutes later when one appeared flying low over [the] spot where the Zeppelin fell.[27]

The 1st/6th Suffolk Cyclists were encamped on The Layers, a parkland situated to the south of Saxmundham, and their medical officer Dr Kenneth Kier, of Wickham Market, was lodging with the Orford family at their home in Fairfield Road. A E Orford, a youngster at the time, recalls:

> For some reason we were all awake; I suppose everybody left their beds when Zeppelins were in the vicinity. I can well remember my mother sitting me on the window sill as we watched a bright glow which slowly drifted across the sky and then plummeted to earth.
> Dr Kier hurriedly dressed, jumped on his motorcycle and dashed off to find the scene of the crash. My father took me to see the wreckage next day seated on a cushion strapped on the crossbar of his bicycle.[28]

'Zeppelin Field'

When the blazing wreckage of *L48* struck the ground, midsummer dawn was already breaking and the flaming hydrogen showed pale against the lightening eastern sky. Schütze, Eichler and 12 of the ship's crew either jumped out or were burnt to death. That *L48*'s bow survived intact endorses reports that the ship fell slowly to earth and the rear took up the impact, absorbing the shock. One of three survivors was Otto Mieth, who was later to relate chilling scenes in the control gondola when the incendiary bullets took effect:

> I had just returned to my station after despatching a radiogram reporting the success of our raid, and was talking with Captain Schütze, when a bright light flooded our gondola, as if another searchlight had picked us up. Assuming that we were over the sea, I imagined for a minute that it must come from an enemy war vessel, but when I glanced up from my position, six or eight feet below the body of the ship, I saw that she was on fire. Almost instantly our 600 feet of hydrogen was ablaze. Dancing, lambent flames licked ravenously at her quickly bared skeleton, which seemed to grin jeeringly at us from the sea of light. So it was all over. I could hardly credit it for an instant. I threw off my overcoat, and shouted to Captain Schütze to do the same, thinking that if we fell into the sea we might save ourselves by swimming. It was a silly idea, of course, for we had no chance of surviving. Captain Schütze realised this. Standing calm and motionless, he fixed his eyes for a moment upon the flames above, staring death steadfastly in the face. Then, as if bidding me farewell he turned and said 'It's all over'.

Farmer Staulkey looks on as Army and Navy officers discuss matters by the side of a Crossley tender. *Sir Victor Goddard*

> After that absolute silence reigned in the gondola. Only the roar of the flames was audible. Not a man had left his post. Everyone stood waiting for the great experience – the end. This lasted several seconds. The vessel still kept on an even keel. We had time to think over our situation. The quickest death would be the best; to be burned alive was horrible. So I sprang to one of the side windows of the gondola to jump out. Just at that moment a frightful shudder shot through the burning skeleton and the ship gave a convulsion like the bound of a horse when shot. The gondola struts broke with a snap, and the skeleton collapsed with a series of crashes like the smashing of a huge window. As our gondola swung over we fell backwards and somewhat away from the flames. I found myself projected into a corner with others on top of me. The gondola was now grinding against the skeleton, which had assumed a vertical position and was falling like a projectile towards the earth. Flames and gas poured over us as we lay there in a heap. It grew fearfully hot. I felt flames against my face, and heard groans. I wrapped my arms about my head to protect it from scorching flames, hoping the end would come quickly. That was the last I remember.
> Our vessel fell perpendicularly, descending like a mighty column of fire through the darkness, and striking stern first. There was a tremendous concussion when we hit the earth. It must have shocked me back to consciousness for a moment for I remember a thrill of horror as I opened my eyes and saw myself surrounded by a sea of flames and red-hot metal beams and braces that seemed about to crush me. Then I lost consciousness a second time and did not recover until the sun was already high in the heavens.[29]

Local civilians and police were among the first on the scene but were soon joined by members of the RAMC and the 1st/6th Suffolk Cyclists from Saxmundham. Even as *L48* began its death-plunge Captain R R Powell of the 319th Field Ambulance Division at Yoxford RAMC bundled five stretcher-bearers into an ambulance and tore off towards Holly Tree Farm. On his arrival, a dazed Mieth had already been dragged clear of the forward gondola, and Powell lost little time in examining his patient before placing him on a stretcher and thence to the ambulance. *L48*'s executive officer began slowly to regain his senses:

> I half raised myself painfully, and saw that my legs were in thick, bloody bandages. I could hardly move them, for they were broken. Then I made a new discovery: my head and legs were covered with burns; my hands were lacerated; when I breathed I felt as if a knife were thrust into me.
> I thought to myself, 'Am I dreaming or awake?' Just then a human voice interrupted my groping thoughts: 'Do you want a cigarette?' and a Tommy stuck a cigarette-case under my nose with a friendly grin. So it was no dream. I was a prisoner.[30]

As all the hospitals in the area had long been overcrowded with British wounded from France, Mieth was transported to nearby Ranelagh Road School in Leiston which had been temporarily converted into a field hospital:

> My mother who worked part time at the hospital as a VAD told me that the Matron was terribly worried about the admission of the German officer and the effect that it would have upon the British soldiers. When the latter heard of this admission there was, at first, a very strong feeling of resentment, quite naturally. But during the many weeks he was in the hospital, his personality, charm and friendliness won over both staff and patients alike. So much so that then the time came for him to be discharged to a prisoner of war camp all the staff and as many of the British wounded who were mobile, gathered at the hospital entrance to see him off and wave farewell.[31]

Another survivor was Machinist's Mate Wilhelm Uecker, who was hauled from the crumpled starboard gondola by civilians and borne to a stretcher. Captain Powell offered him water as his bearers made the injured German as comfortable as possible. Later, Powell had both Mieth and Uecker searched and the contents of their uniforms handed, via a quartermaster, to a staff officer of the Northern Army. The badly burnt Uecker had received severe internal injuries and would never again see his native Germany, for on Armistice Day 1918 he died.

Heinrich Ellerkamm had escaped by forcing his way out of the red-hot cage of girders with his bare hands. On extricating himself from the duralumin prison, his first encounter was with a herd of frightened horses who galloped away from the blaze, tails held high in the air. Home on leave from the Royal Navy that week was Chief Petty Officer F W Bird, whose house at Eastbridge lay about 1000yds from where L48 fell. Bird sprinted over to the crash site and was within 20yds from the wreck when he saw Ellerkamm wandering dazedly about the field:

> He appeared to be totally unhurt and I beckoned him towards me as I ran. He looked very confused and helpless, and, could not or would not speak English. By signs I asked him for any papers he might be carrying, and, not being reassured by his actions, I made him put his hands above his head and then searched him. He had a purse containing various coins, some of them English, a railway ticket and a knife. The latter I took from him.
>
> From now onwards I confined all my attention to my prisoner in view of the possibility of obtaining valuable information from him. On a policeman coming up I placed him in charge of the wreck and the wounded therein, and seeing many people running towards us took my prisoner to a safer and less warm spot. Later I took him to an adjoining cottage.
>
> About an hour after the Zeppelin came to earth two Junior Army Officers came to the cottage, but as these seemed rather undecided as to what course to adopt I kept him in my charge until later when two Senior Officers arrived, to whom I handed over my prisoner. He was then marched away under the escort of two sergeants.[32]

Ellerkamm was taken to Darsham station under guard, thenceforth to a prisoner-of-war camp where he was interrogated but revealed nothing. Both Uecker and Mieth were also to come under the attention of Military Intelligence, even though hospitalized. Whilst L48's executive officer was recovering at Ranelagh, a German prisoner was introduced into his room, suffering from shell-shock. Understandably suspicious, Mieth made his new companion join in the singing of Teutonic nursery and student songs, and after a while was convinced, finally accepting the man as a fellow-countryman. It says a lot for the training of British Intelligence personnel that Mieth's new-found friend was in fact an MI5 Colonel who, after ten days, admitted that nothing useful had been extracted from the Zeppelin officer:

> He seemed to realise that it was indiscreet to discuss, even with a 'brother officer', many of the subjects that were touched on...
>
> He is convinced that Germany started the war and he violently blames her diplomatists for their continual clumsiness... He has not the slightest doubt that Germany will be the loser and he seriously contemplates that his occupation as a Naval Officer will disappear as the Allies will probably seize and divide the German Fleet.[33]

Following the crash of L48, it did not take long for the military to throw up stiff cordons around it, local police helping to keep civilians away from the immediate area. Their main task was to prevent further pilfering from the wreck, as several foraging locals had already managed to get clear with sections of girder and other artifacts before the military came on the scene. Officers and men of the 2nd/5th Cheshire Regiment were amongst the first to turn up, managing the hold the rapidly growing crowds at a respectable distance. At 04.10hrs the 1st/6th Suffolk Cyclists arrived and put up a barricade of two fences around the wreck, a task that occupied them for at least two hours; 20 minutes later Major Ennion RAMC reported to Colonel Churcher of the Cheshires:

> I was informed that five bodies were lying out in the field. I was instructed to bring the bodies into the enclosure.
>
> I marked spots where bodies were found. The civil police accompanied me. They had previously searched the bodies. In the first case visited the police handed the identity disc to me. This I replaced on the body. The bodies were carried in by stretcher bearer parties. I went to each body in turn. All property which police had were [sic] put back on body securely and brought in on them. Police stated that some valuables had been taken from Kapt Eichler. They were wrapt [sic] up in a handkerchief, which I did not examine. It was then put back in his tunic. I reported when all bodies had been collected.[34]

Next to arrive was Colonel Gilbertson-Smith, commanding 500 men of the 2nd/25th London Cyclists, who established his headquarters at the entrance to the inner cordon. Having had his men clear the nearby lane of civilian vehicles, Gilbertson-Smith posted two picket lines and had the field cleared of all remaining spectators. At 06.00hrs three members of Admiralty Intelligence rolled up and instructed that the bodies be searched and that bags be brought up in which to secure all watches, rings and papers:

> I sent to Camp for bags and ordered Capt. Keir, RAMC Suffolk MO, to search bodies. He did so. Articles found, including log of ship, were placed in bags and taken possession of by Lt Col de Watteville... then stated he wanted men to remove some burning bodies near forward engine as there were papers underneath them. Four officers removed the bodies and brought out some half-burnt maps. These were placed in a box fetched from a motor car, and subsequently the party left for Yoxford to interrogate two Germans who had been taken there. Before leaving, Lt Col de Watteville gave me instructions to turn out the pockets most carefully of other corpses still in [the] wreckage and to send all rings, watches, papers and marks on clothing to the Intelligence Department, Admiralty.[35]

Among the papers recovered from the demolished control gondola were three vital code-word lists and the general

Zeppelin!

The open-air inquest for *L48*'s dead was chaired by the Ipswich Coroner, Bernard Pretty. At this stage several members of the crew had yet to be removed, but it was decided that the burial of the fourteen already recovered should proceed without further delay.
Author's Collection

cypher table for the naval signal book. For British Admiralty Intelligence it was quite a scoop, but for their opposite numbers in the German Navy it came as a shock since *L48* should never have carried such important documents in the first place. On 22 June Admiral Scheer wrote to the Chief of the Naval Staff, requesting that the now compromised codes be changed.

The day following *L48*'s destruction was a busy one, hundreds of sightseers making their various ways to Theberton whilst the military continued the search for bodies. During the morning several staff officers clutching the precious 'red passes' arrived, and they later left with portions of the wreckage.[36]

Constructor-Lieutenant Coles from the Admiralty's Constructional Department was the next to make an appearance, his first task being to supervise Gilbertson-Smith's men in an attempt to recover three bodies pinned under the wreckage of the rear gondola. Despite vigorous efforts, only one body, by a process of elimination believed to be that of either Heinrich Ahrens or Michael Neunzig, was pulled clear; soon afterwards Coles left for Lowestoft to obtain a rigging party and the scaffolding required to shore up the towering nose of *L48*, preserving it long enough for photographs to be taken. In Cole's absence a thunderstorm threatened to demolish the frail structure, but a fatigue party was able to secure the quivering framework with ropes.

Flight-Lieutenant Victor Goddard RNAS[37] appeared on the following day and officially took charge of the wreckage on behalf of the Admiralty. Later, Constructor-Commander C I R Campbell was expected to arrive to take over from Coles, when the long task of dismantling the airship would begin. Gradually the team of naval constructors measured and drew up the entire ship, telescoped and battered though it was. Their findings led to design improvements in such subsequent British rigids as the *R35, R36, R37* and *R38*.[38]

The burial of 14 bodies that had so far been recovered from the wreckage took place during the afternoon of 20 June at the tiny parish church of St Peter, Theberton. Earlier, an open-air inquest had been held at an adjacent farmhouse, chaired by the Ipswich coroner, Bernard Pretty:

> [I] understand that the charred remains of five other members of the crew are still amongst the debris of the Zeppelin but it was impossible to recover them in time for the inquest today, and owing to the state of the bodies it was not practicable to leave over the inquest longer...
>
> Under these circumstances and in view of the fact that the

Theberton, 20 June 1917: the crew of *L48* are buried in the grounds of St Peters in a ceremony that is well attended.
Author's Collection

The RFC erected this fitting epitaph over *L48*'s dead. Their other contribution to the funeral was a wreath; they were severely criticised in several quarters for this gesture.
P Amesbury

L48, 17 June 1917

The wreck of *L48*, once the experts and technicians were finished with it, was chopped up and carted off to the Leiston railway station by RNAS trucks. Here the remains are being loaded on to railway wagons.
Author's Collection

holding of the inquest in such a case as this involves the presence of a number of military and police officials I hardly think it seems necessary to hold an inquest on the remaining five victims and if you agree I propose to authorise the burial without a further inquest.[39]

The actual funeral was a well-attended yet simple affair, with a procession consisting of four gun carriages and three military wagons accompanied by an officer and a squad of cyclists. The rector of the parish, a brigade chaplain and a Roman Catholic clergyman officiated in front of a large number of sightseers from hundreds that had come to gaze at the scorched skeleton in Farmer Staulkey's field. Eichler's coffin was carried separately, and upon it was the only wreath, from the Experimental Station at Orfordness, with an inscription that read 'To a very brave enemy from the RFC officers'.[40] Within the next 48 hours sufficient wreckage had been removed to enable the two remaining bodies from the rear gondola to be extricated, *Obermaschinistenmaat* Karl Milich positively identified from documents in his tunic. Both were buried alongside their comrades on 23 June, and there in a communal plot they remained for 49 years.[41] The Germans are no longer at Theberton, but a framed record of the event and a portion of girder remain at St Peter, and one of *L48*'s machine guns was displayed in the VC plot in the churchyard for several years until some light-fingered individual appropriated it.

Dismantling the pathetic remains of *L48* continued for many weeks, the wreckage being chopped up by Admiralty technicians and RNAS personnel who carted it by truck to Leiston railway station. Many trips were undertaken between 'Zeppelin Field' and the station goods terminal. Opportunist souvenir hunters were able to retrieve fragments which fell off the back of lorries as they plied the East Anglian lanes.

There remains a sequel. On Thursday 5 July, PC 176 Arthur Kiddle was on duty in Theberton when he spotted two young women cycling towards Leiston, one of them clutching a 3ft section of girder. Kiddle halted the pair and relieved 20-year-old munitions worker Kathleen Levett of her prize, much to the young lady's distress. Kiddle dutifully reported the affair to his superintendent, and the whole matter may have been neatly settled had not Miss Levett claimed that one of the men dismantling the airship had salved the girder for her.

Memos flew in all directions on receipt of this and other reports that several soldiers had been observed handing out fragments of metal to civilians. Each of the respective unit commanders denied that any man of their battalions had been responsible for such misconduct. Nevertheless, Lieutenant-Colonel W A J O'Meara of the Northern Army desired to make an example of Kathleen Levett:

> It should be noted, however, that as the piece of Zeppelin was given to her, she has not technically committed an offence under Regn 35B, therefore any prosecution against her would have to be under Regn 49 for not having notified the CMA that the soldier had committed an offence under Regn 35B.[42]

Colonel W Graydon Carter, Competent Military Authority in receipt of O'Meara's memo, decided against taking any action over the Levett affair although he was less lenient towards Harry Whatling Junior, a Theberton farmer's assistant. During the first week of September, a Saxmundham court heard of Whatling's offence,

> ... that he having found certain articles, to wit, one brown handbag, a cigarette case, a table knife, a battery for an electric hand-lamp, a small phial of whisky, and three papers, which he had reasonable grounds for believing or suspecting to have formed part of the personal effects of the crew of an aircraft of the enemy, without lawful authority or excuse, did neglect forthwith, after finding the same, to communicate the fact to a military post or to a police-constable in the neighbourhood, contrary to Regulation 35B of the Defence of the Realm Regulations, etc.[43]

The defendant admitted having failed to report the items,

As the lorries travelled to and from Leiston, several fragments of duralumin fell by the wayside and were quickly appropriated by civilians. The relics were made into napkin rings, paper knives, airship-shaped brooches, medallions and ashtrays. Usually stamped with the date and the Zeppelin's number, they enjoyed vigorous sales.
Author

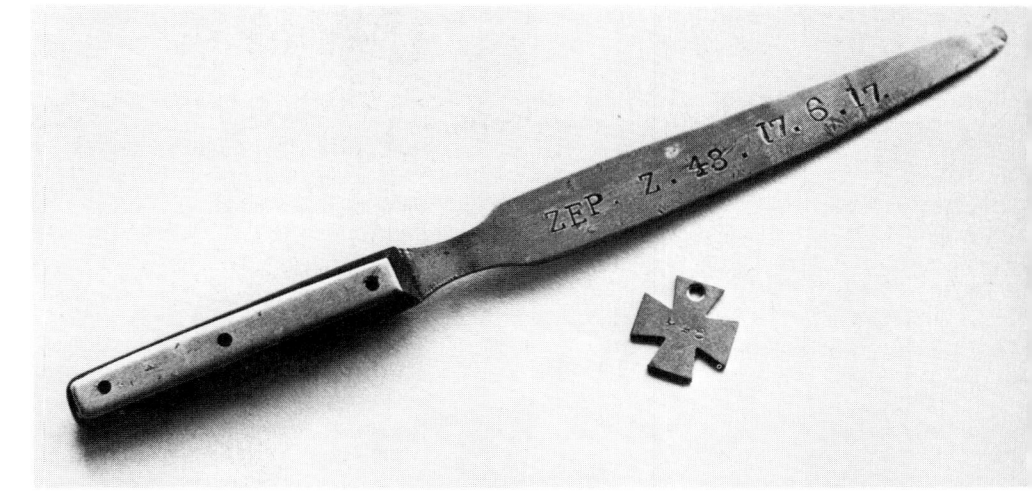

Watkins (left) with officers of 50 Home Defence Squadron. In the background stands one of the unit's BE2c night-fighters, wearing B Flight's somewhat macabre (and unofficial) insignia on the fuselage. Watkins gained Aero Club Certificate 2532 on 12 February 1916.
D Whetton

Temporary Lieutenant Frank Douglas Holder, photographed at Orfordness RFC on 26 January 1916. Holder completed his training with 9 Reserve Squadron at Mousehold in Norfolk.
Aeromodeller

Sergeant Sydney Ashby in the cockpit of an SE5a, presumably at Orfordness, in 1917. Ashby, who manned the gun of FE2b B401 when Holder attacked *L48*, was fated to die in a flying accident during 1918.
Aeromodeller

and he denied knowing that it was his duty to do so despite the posters put up throughout the parish. Mr Gotelee, for the prosecution, after lengthy cross examination, proved Whatling to be guilty, and the bench fined him 40 shillings.

For his part in the destruction of *L48*, Second Lieutenant Holder was awarded the Military Cross on 7 August 1917, in 'recognition of conspicuous gallantry and determination in connection with the destruction of an enemy airship'. Frank Douglas Holder was born in London on 26 June 1897 and was subsequently educated at Felsted School and Sandhurst, where he became a prize cadet. On 26 January 1916 Holder was granted a commission as a Second Lieutenant in the RFC, having unsuccessfully applied to join the Machine Gun Corps. His initial posting was to 1 Reserve Squadron at Farnborough, and from there he went to 9 Reserve Squadron at Mousehold, Norfolk, during the first week of April. He continued his training in Maurice Farman Longhorns and Shorthorns and obtained a well earned 'brevet' on 27 May.

December 31 saw Holder posted to the new experimental station at Orfordness where, on 5 May, he was promoted to Temporary Lieutenant.[44] He remained at the station until the summer of 1919 when it ceased to become operational, and Holder found himself as the only pilot and senior officer left. Resigning his commission on 14 February 1920 with the rank of Captain, Holder moved to Chelmsford and in 1932 began devoting much of his spare time to the Prisoners' Aid Society. He was also co-opted on to Chelmsford Town Council, where he subsequently rose to serve as Deputy Mayor prior to becoming an Alderman.

When war came again, Holder offered his services to the RAF, and on 31 March 1941 he was granted a commission as Acting Pilot Officer with the ATC, the appointment being confirmed six months later. He continued working with the Corps committee after the war, and resigned his commission on 26 January 1948. Holder served for many years as a JP, and for a time was chairman of the Chelmsford Magistrates Bench as well as holding a similar position on the Chelmsford High School board of governors. In 1978, at the age of 81, Frank Douglas Holder OBE MC JP DL died at his home in Maldon Road, Danbury, Essex.

Robert Henry Magnus Spencer Saundby was born in Birmingham on 26 April 1896 and educated at St Edward's School. His lengthy service career began on 15 June 1914, when as a second lieutenant he entered service in the 5th Battalion of the Royal Warwickshire Regiment, Territorial Force, being promoted to Lieutenant on 3 June the following year. Saundby was graded and seconded as a flying officer in the RFC on 17 June and was to serve with the famous 24 Squadron. This unit, the very first single-seat fighter squadron to go to any battle front, was formed

L48, 17 June 1917

Flight Commander Robert Henry Magnus Spencer Saundby was in command of C Flight at Orfordness when he took part in the action against *L48*. He entered the RFC on 17 June 1915 and after the Armistice remained in the RAF and went on to enjoy a long and distinguished career in that service.
Lady Saundby

Second Lieutenant Loudon Pierce Watkins, seated in the cockpit of a Sopwith 1½ Strutter at Goldhanger sometime in 1916. Canadian-born 'Don' Watkins served in France with both 7 and 21 Squadrons before joining the strength of 37 HDS in England on 11 December 1916.
Canadian Forces Photo RE 64-470

at Hounslow on 1 September 1915 and was initially commanded by Major Lanoe George Hawker VC. Saundby, flying DH2 5925, formed part of the four-machine patrol that took place on 23 November and ended with the death of Hawker at the hands of Manfred von Richthofen after a protracted duel.[45]

Saundby was promoted to Flight Commander (Temporary Captain) on 2 February 1917 and went on to command C Flight at the Orfordness experimental unit. For his involvement in the *L48* affair, Saundby was awarded the Military Cross on 5 July 1917, and his log-book entry for 17 June simply records a 'Night flight after Zeps – during which Holder and I brought one down in flames near Middleton.'[46] Certainly in Saundby's eyes there was no mystery surrounding the destruction of Strasser's ship.

Robert Saundby relinquished his Territorial Force Commission on 1 August 1919, retaining his captaincy on appointment to a permanent commission in the RAF as a flight lieutenant. He continued his career in the Air Ministry, then at Netheravon, and then in Aden, where he was awarded the DFC on 21 January 1926, after which he became the commander of a training school in Egypt. Following a spell at the Staff College, Saundby went on to the Wessex Bomber Area Staff and thence to the Air Ministry, where by 1939 he had risen to being Director of Operational Requirements.

Later Saundby was appointed Assistant Chief of the Air Staff, and in November 1940 had joined Bomber Command as Senior Air Staff Officer under Sir Richard Pierse, staying on with his successor, Sir Arthur Harris, and eventually being appointed C-in-C in 1943. Saundby was knighted the following year, promoted to the rank of Air Marshal in 1945 and was finally placed on the retired list on 23 March 1946. Stress of the wartime years had caused a general deterioration of Saundby's health, which led to the discovery of a spinal injury (of which he was ignorant), the result of a forced landing in a field when serving in France with the RFC during 1916. Sir Robert continued his love of aviation during his retirement, writing books and contributing to aeronautical journals up until 1971, when he died at his home in Burghclere, Berkshire.

Tragically, Watkins would not live to see the end of the war. On 8 August 1917 he was promoted to Temporary Captain (Flight Commander), and in the following month he joined the strength of 38 Home Defence Squadron. It was the Canadian's final stint in a UK-based unit, for his next posting would return him to France.

No 148 Squadron was formed at Andover, Hampshire, on 10 February 1918 under the command of Major I T Lloyd and initially formed part of Lieutenant-Colonel R Lorraine's 36th Wing. On 1 March the squadron moved to Ford Junction when it was transferred to the 18th Wing under the jurisdiction of Lieutenant-Colonel R G Small. No 148's ground personnel were shipped overseas on 20 April and were followed five days later by the 12 FE2b night bombers that made up the squadron. All the machines landed without mishap at Anchel aerodrome, and among the pilots was Captain L P Watkins MC.

On 3 May German artillery shelled 148 from its base and the unit moved to Sains Les Pernes, from where it continued to bomb enemy aerodromes, billets and railheads by

Zeppelin!

night, as well as undertaking nocturnal reconnaissances, supporting tanks and making machine-gun runs over roads and general enemy positions. One notable exploit took place on 20 May when 148's FE2bs made a low bombing attack on Rumbeeke aerodrome, home of *Jasta* 3, in which five direct hits were made on the hangars there.

On 1 July Watkins and other members of 148 were making preparations for another night-bombing mission. With observer Lieutenant C W Wridgway aboard, Watkins took off at 00.30hrs in FE2d A6599.[47] The 'Fee's bomb load that night comprised two 20lb bombs and a single 112pdr, and at each wingtip was fitted the standard Michelin Flare navigation light. Within 50 minutes of leaving the aerodrome, the machine lay on its back in a field of standing corn near Ostreville. According to the official casualty report, the forced landing was caused by engine failure, a broken rocker arm on No 3 cylinder being pinpointed as the culprit. An injured Wridgway clambered out of the wreckage, but Watkins was dead. The 'Fee' was severely damaged, interplane struts, upper wing sections, tail booms, propeller, nacelle, Lewis gun and wireless set all suffering in the smash, yet not sufficiently enough to prevent the aircraft being transferred to a depot for repair.[48]

Watkins was the fourth, and last, 'giant killer' to end his career in a flying accident.

Captain Loudon Pierce Watkins MC. Watkins returned to overseas duty on 20 April 1918 with 148 Squadron, and it was whilst taking part in a night bombing attack on 1 July that his FE2b suffered engine failure. Watkins lost his life in the resulting crash. *Canadian Forces Photo RE 64–453*

THE BUSINESS OF THE MOMENT.

JOHN BULL. "I'VE LEARNED HOW TO DEAL WITH YOUR ZEPP BROTHER, AND NOW I'M GOING TO ATTEND TO YOU."

A *Punch* cartoon of 18 July 1917 reflects the new confidence of Britain's aerial defences. However, with the airship menace diminishing, the RFC and RNAS now had to combat German Gotha bombers. *Punch*

CHAPTER 14

L23, 21 August 1917

'A loud knock on the door, "Hullo-o-o-o-o" I called. "Half past two, sir", came the answer. I rolled over thinking what an awful war it was to get one up at that ungodly hour, and silently cursing the Huns in general and Count Zeppelin in particular...'

Sub-Lieutenant B A Smart, August 1917

It was at 04.50hrs on 21 August that Zeppelin *L23* rose from its Tondern base to embark on a routine patrol. Ten minutes later, the airship's commander, *Oberleutnant zur See* Bernhard Dinter, was to report sighting four *Aurora* class cruisers and 15 destroyers steaming some 30 miles west of Bovbjerg. The British vessels belonged to the Third Light Cruiser Squadron of the British Grand Fleet, which was making one of its customary sweeps beyond the coast of Jutland. Electing to shadow them, Dinter followed the fleet out to sea, using clouds to conceal his presence, the very last thing he expected to encounter being a British fighter aeroplane.

Shipboard Fighter
Bernard Arthur Smart was born on 24 December 1891 to Mr and Mrs Charles Smart of Charlton House, London Road, Luton, Bedfordshire.[1] He was educated locally at Luton Modern School, and the years leading up to 1914 found him engaged in the hat trade 'on his own account'. When war came, Smart expressed a desire to join up and entered the RNAS, being attached to the Scott Machine Gun Section. This unit subsequently went out to the Dardanelles, Smart serving in the trenches throughout the Suvla Bay campaign. Two weeks before the traumatic evacuation of Gallipoli, Smart contracted malaria and was hospitalised at Lemnos before being returned to England. Once home he applied for pilot training, and it was at Chingford aerodrome in Essex that Smart soloed in a Maurice Farman Shorthorn after less than four hours' tuition under his instructor, Ben Travers. At Chingford, a home defence aerodrome, Smart flew a number of types, including the BE2c, Sopwith 1½ Strutter and Pup. As with the majority of service pilots who flew the Pup, Smart instantly took to the small Sopwith:

> It was a wonderful aeroplane, so light that you could use it as a glider. If you got up to 15,000 feet and turned the engine off with not a sound in the air, you could glide it back to the aerodrome even if it was 15 miles away.[2]

During 1916 and 1917 Smart was attached to several small aerodromes and largely engaged upon experimental flying preparatory to landing on decks of suitably modified warships. The aircraft he flew were fitted with wooden skids and wheels, the latter being discarded in mid-air so that trial landings on skids only could be made.

It was the redoubtable Flight Commander Frederick

The light cruiser HMS *Yarmouth*, her Sopwith Pup lashed to the platform over the forward turret. It was Flight Commander F J Rutland whose initiative saw the Pup become a shipboard fighter for use against patrolling airships.
IWM SP1388

193

Squadron Commander Rutland successfully flies a Sopwith Pup (serial number unknown) off the special 20ft platform over *Yarmouth*'s forward turret, June 1917. Orders despatched on 17 August stated that each light cruiser squadron would have one of its ships fitted with a 'flying-off platform'; five days later Flight Sub-Lieutenant B A Smart repeated Rutland's feat and in addition destroyed a Zeppelin.
IWM Q65578

Joseph Rutland who was mainly responsible for getting the Sopwith Pup accepted as a shipboard fighter early in 1917. *Campania, Furious* and *Manxman* – all aircraft carriers – were equipped with Pups, but there were other experiments involving the use of 'flying-off platforms' mounted on light cruisers. HMS *Yarmouth* was typical. A *Weymouth* class vessel, *Yarmouth* had been completed by London and Glasgow shipbuilders in 1912. With a complement of between 475 and 540 officers and men, the ship was 453ft long, 48½ft in beam, displaced 5250 tons, carried eight 6in guns, one 3in gun and two 21in torpedo tubes, and turbines driving two screws delivered 23,500hp for a speed of 25.5kts. By June, Rutland had successfully flown a Pup from a wooden platform mounted over *Yarmouth*'s forward gun turret, and the idea showed such promise that on the 17th it was decided to equip one vessel in every light cruiser squadron with the new decks. Pups flown off these platforms were fitted with Mark One Emergency Flotation Bags as pilots had no option but to ditch their machines in the sea after each sortie. So it was on 21 August, when HMS *Yarmouth* sailed with the 3rd Light Cruiser Squadron, complete with Sopwith Pup N6430 lashed to its platform, to patrol the North Sea. The regular pilot, Lieutenant P G Williams, was on leave for a fortnight, and transferred from HMS *Manxman* to take his place was Flight Sub-Lieutenant B A Smart.

When *L23* was finally spotted by alert lookouts, Smart was in his cabin, snatching some rest while waiting for a call for action. When that call came, he was not slow to respond, and he set down subsequent events in a letter to his mother a few days later:

Once again comes the knock and 'Zeppelin sighted on the port quarter, sir!' 'What?' say I and rush up as hard as I can go, with a nasty schoolboy, 'now-I've-got-to-go-through-it' sort of feeling and wondering why I hadn't entered the submarine portion of the Navy. The Zepp had just disappeared behind a cloud and presently the Captain points out a light, cigar-shaped object in the dim distance and converging towards us. 'That's good enough,' I say with a sinking feeling which I must try to put down to hunger. Anyway I yell out to mechanics to take all lashings from the machine except the quick-release gear and then the plainness of those great big red, white and blue circles and colourings strike [sic] me very forcibly. 'Go and get me some grey paint and brushes at the double,' I call to one of the seamen looking on and in a few

L23 (builder's number LZ66) was constructed at Potsdam, hence the purely rectangular control surfaces; on ships built elsewhere the inner edges of these followed the line of the tail cone. *L23* made its first flight on 8 April 1916 and was initially commanded by von Schubert, then Ganzel, Stabbert and Bockholt, Dinter taking over on 14 June 1917. This 'q' type Zeppelin made 101 flights, of which eight were raids on England. The vessel is seen here landing at Nordholz.
F Moch

minutes the distinguishing marks are toned down and although still discernible at short distance did not talk quite so loudly as before. 'That'll give them a chance to take me for a friend,' I thought and reported to the Captain that everything was ready. The Zepp was considerably nearer now and through a telescope the enormous size could be realised. She came in until a matter of seven or eight miles distance and then altered course parallel to ours. Wireless was being continually heard, as she was evidently reporting all she could see from that distance. when it was obvious she was coming no nearer, Captain Grace signalled to Commodore of Squadron for permission to turn ship into wind. The answer came back and I put on my goggles and helmet etc and took my place in the machine and strapped myself in. I had a flask of brandy and a couple of lifebelts which I thought would be handy in case of a bath.

There was a moderate wind and as the ship moved into it a slight singing in the wires of the plane could already be heard, but nothing showed on my air-speed indicator, so I called out to the Captain on the bridge 'Can you let me have a bit more speed, sir?' The ship almost immediately leaped forward and I signalled the mechanic to proceed.

Curiously enough, although I had a bad attack of 'cold feet' when the Zepp was first reported, by this time I was perfectly calm and collected, greatly to my own surprise and probably to the others – anyway I was glad to yell out orders as though I meant them and the very fact of hustling everyone gave me confidence.

The Commander lay down under the machine to work the release gear and, after the usual preliminaries, the engine was running satisfactorily and I moved my hand to signal 'Ready'. The Captain in turn signalled the Commander who pulled the release cord and the lively little plane rose like a bird without using even the 16-foot run of the platform. It was a glorious morning, not a 'bump' anywhere and, under other circumstances, would have been ideal for a joy ride. I observed some friendly clouds to starboard and made straight for their protection climbing hard as possible. The Zepp was also dodging about in some clouds so I took a careful compass bearing to use in case I temporarily lost sight of her. The perfect toned roar of the engine was music to my ears and I watched the altimeter needle slowly creep up, one, two, three, until I finally emerged out of a fleecy cloud with it pointing at nine, which represented about two miles high. The Zepp had turned tail and was making for Germany and I had been climbing so hard that my forward speed had been hardly 60mph, and I had gained very little ground. I could now see however that I was considerably higher than Fritz, and the joystick was pushed slightly forward when the pointer of the airspeed indicator immediately left the 60mph mark and was up to the 110 mark where I kept it steady. The difference was very marked and every time the aluminium coloured monster grew in size. I turned to have a look for the ships but nothing but sea, sky and slight haze to be seen. I had been slowly descending with full engine and my height was now 8000; I kept the same speed and was obviously able to out-manoeuvre the Zepp to a standstill – each time she made the slightest turn I swerved round to keep absolutely end-on, in which position the men in the gondola underneath were unable either to see or attack me. I could see the head of a man and an object unpleasantly like a machine gun on the top of the envelope and I now realised that the time had come. I was now at 7000 feet and the Zepp 1000 feet below at an angle of 45 degrees and I was still heading straight for her stern. I pushed forward the control stick and dived. The speed indicator went with a rush up to 150mph and I was aiming to cut under the Zepp a few yards astern of her. The roar of the engine had increased to a shrill scream while the wires were whistling and screeching in an awful manner. I completely lost my head – the earth vanished, the sky vanished, the sea was no more, my universe consisted of that great round silvery object, myself and space. Everything then happened automatically: 250 yards astern and same height as Zepp I flattened out slightly and pulled the lever which works the fixed machine gun. I had misjudged the angle at which this was mounted on plane and saw the white stream of my incendiary bullets going too high. In a flash I had nosed down again, flattened out and pressed down the machine gun operating lever again and held it there. The gun spat out and although the machine was wobbling on account of the extreme sensitiveness of my controls due to the enormous speed, I had just time to see about half a dozen (bullets) enter the blunt end of the Zepp and a spurt of flame, before my very soul froze with the thought that in my eagerness to aim [the] gun, I had waited too long and couldn't avoid a collision. Spasmodically I jammed the joystick hard forward and my heart seemed to come into my mouth in the absolute vertical nose dive which followed.

The End of L23
Smart continued:

Automatically again I found myself straightened out 5000 feet lower and turned to see what happened. The after end of Zepp was now a mass of flame, and had dropped so that the nose was pointing to the sky at an angle of 45 degrees while the flames were fast licking up towards [the] nose. It is extraordinary the tricks nature plays on one's impressions at a time like this: I know what struck me more than anything was that the engines were still turning away merrily with the Zepp enveloped in flames and pointing up at that ridiculous angle. It struck me as the funniest thing I had seen in my life and I laughed like an idiot. An object was adrift from the forward end of the Zepp and which I first took to be some part of the fabric fallen off but on looking again discovered it to be a man descending in a parachute. He was the only one and as he floated down, he and I seemed to be alone in space. I turned until my compass was in opposite direction from that when chasing the Zepp and then turned back to have a last look at the blaze. The wreck had just hit the sea, only the very tip still being intact; it was still burning away merrily and continued to burn on the water for three or four minutes, the smoke having changed to a much blacker colour probably due to an oil tank bursting and mixing with the flame. I was now a considerable way off, and as the flame finally died out, the smoke in spite of the wind hung over the sea in a tremendous column reaching an apparently enormous height and reminding me of my childish interpretation of the way 'genis' [sic] used to appear in a 'tower of smoke reaching to the sky' from a brass bottle.

Dresden Navigation School, 1915: (left to right) *Segelmacher* May, *Kapitänleutnant* Bottermann (*Truppenführer*), *Oberleutnant* Richard Frey, unknown, *Hauptmann* August Stelling (Parseval PL19, PL25, L9 and L21), unknown army officer, *Kapitänleutnant* Erich Blew (later Flight Instructor at Nordholz), *Ober Arzt* Nonhoff (Medical Officer) and *Kapitänleutnant* Wilhelm Ganzel (L9, L23). Sitting are *Kapitänleutnant* Waldemar Kölle who commanded SL9, SL12 and L45, and (right) *Oberleutnant* Bernhard Dinter, commander of L23.
P Amesbury

Zeppelin!

I began by this time to look anxiously for the squadron which I knew I should meet on the starboard side as I had been edging to port so as to be sure of getting them between myself and the sun, thinking the sheen on the water would make them show up at a much greater distance. I had been going about 45 minutes and knew that I should sight them by this time, but although I peered as far as I could in every direction nothing could be seen and I had almost made up my mind for a trip to Denmark when I caught sight of them seven or eight miles distant on my port beam. I was simply delighted and made for them as hard as I could go. It appears they had taken the smoke from the Zepp for the German fleet and had altered course to get position so that in edging to the left as I had done, I had done the one thing that could enable me to spot them.

I was now over the squadron and selecting two destroyers near together turned off my engine and planed down so as to be a couple of hundred yards ahead. This was my first attempt at coming down on the sea in a land machine, but instinct told me that at all costs I must hit with practically no forward way on whatever to avoid turning head over heels and possibly getting pinned underneath. I undid my strap and put a plug in the tube which acts as a valve to the air bags in tail and when within about 15 feet of the surface pulled back the stick gradually, keeping at that height while the machine was getting slower and slower until I had finally got the stick back as far as possible, the machine lost all flying speed and I dropped like a stone, hitting the water with a nasty jerk which would probably have meant broken bones had it been on mother earth. The destroyers' boats were alongside in a short time but not before the nose of machine had sunk and left me just hanging on to the tail. I was soon safely aboard and giving [a] short report to be signalled to the Commodore. The officers aboard were very relieved to hear no Germans were in sight owing to the smallness of the squadron.

After a few questions by signal from the flagship I had the satisfaction of receiving congratulations of 'Captain and crew of the *Yarmouth*', and the following signal from the Commodore:

'Commodore, HMS *Caledon* to Flight Sub-Lieutenant Smart, HMS *Prince*. You have done most splendidly and I am sure your reward will be prompt.'[3]

The crew of HMS *Prince* salvaged the Pup's engine and machine gun and the squadron eventually steered back for port. From the outset the destruction of *L23* was classified; Smart's award of the DSO was subsequently reported in newspapers on 4 October as being for 'a specially brilliant feat', and that was all the public got.

After the last radio message from *L23*, 'Am pursued by enemy forces', nothing else was heard and several German seaplanes were despatched to make a sweep over the Zeppelin's last reported position.[4] Towards the evening one of the pilots spotted a large, scummy patch of oil and petrol 25 miles south-west of Bovbjerg. Alighting on the water, the pilot taxied his aircraft to the slick and with the help of his observer managed to fish out some small wooden fragments and a charred part of propeller blade. Such pathetic remnants were all that remained of *L23*, its 17-man crew and their 28-year-old commander Bernhard Dinter. Dinter, born on 10 January 1889 at Kaindorf, was a former *Wachoffizier* to *Kapitänleutnant* Waldenmar Kölle and one of very few executive officers to be specifically trained as a commander. *L23* had been his first and last command.

That the Germans were unaware of the exact manner in which their airship had been destroyed – they believed gunfire to be the culprit – suited the British very well, and the secret of the attack was carefully guarded, even the victorious pilot being told little. As late as 1919 Smart sent a letter to Naval Intelligence requesting some information on the Zeppelin that he had destroyed many months earlier. The reply went direct to Captain Nicholson of the carrier HMS *Furious* on which Smart was serving at the time:

> If you consider it desirable to do so, this officer may be given the following information, which need not be considered confidential.
>
> The Zeppelin brought down on 21 August 1917, was L23. She was built at Friedrichshafen and was completed about March 1916, and was similar to L14, details of which will be found in CB01386 [*sic*].
>
> In August, 1917, she was based at Tondern and at the time of her destruction was commanded by *Oberleutnant zur See* (Lieutenant) Bernhard Dinter, Iron Cross, who was lost with his ship.
>
> It is presumed that this officer (Smart) will understand that this information must not be communicated to the press without permission.
>
> It is suggested that he should be informed that in future all communications with the Admiralty should be passed through the proper service channels.[5]

The day after Smart was invested with his DSO at Buckingham Palace on 7 November 1917, the French Government honoured the pilot with the *Croix de Guerre* (bronze palm), the medal and certificate arriving at his parent's home in Luton soon afterwards. A bar to the DSO was awarded in 1918 when Smart led the first ever successful carrier strike, on Tondern, where *L54* and *L60* were destroyed.[6] He left the RAF after the war ('I got so bored with the idea of just doing nothing but having a little flight now and again'[7]) and was formerly placed on that service's unemployed list on 4 June 1919 before going back into his father's business of importing hemp and braid in which he worked until 1928. During the 1920s he became noted as a tennis player in Luton and in 1921 married Miss Cicely Ella Keens, only daughter of Mr Thomas Keens, MP for Mid-Buckinghamshire, and Mrs Keens, of Warden House, New Bedford Road, Luton.

Smart moved to Norfolk in 1928, where he helped found a company called Jentique Ltd, and during World War II he was helping to supply 'large quantities of wooden containers' to the Air Ministry. At the close of hostilities, the wood and metal organisation which Smart had built up was used for furniture and electric clock manufacture, and he was both designer and inventor of Metamec clocks, the firm developing into a public company employing 1100 workers and enjoying good business.

On 5 May 1979 Bernard Arthur Smart, the last surviving 'giant killer', died peacefully at his Dereham home, aged 87.

Sub-Lieutenant Bernard Arthur Smart joined the RNAS in 1915 and learnt to fly at Chingford, gaining Aero Club Certificate 3262 on 24 July 1916. His instructor was Ben Travers, later to become the successful writer of farce. Smart was awarded the DSO for his part in the destruction of *L23* and gained a bar to that award in 1918 following his involvement with a bombing attack on the Tondern airship base.
B A Smart

CHAPTER 15

Carrying the Fight

'...The bomb or bombs dropped on shed 'A' ignited L54 and L60. The shed had both doors open at one end which allowed the heat gases to expand freely, and consequently, the structure was little damaged. The shed is now completely repaired, except that some of the roof boards have not yet been covered with tarred felt...'

Inspection of Naval Airship Station, Tondern, 10 December 1918

During World War II, the aircraft carrier played a leading role in the war at sea, the British attack on Taranto, Pearl Harbor's pounding by a Japanese task force and the Battle of Midway serving to underline the value of combined operations. But the origins of carrier warfare can be traced back even further, for in 1918 came the first successful operation of shipborne aircraft against a land objective. Tondern was the target, and when a small force of Sopwith Camels appeared over the airship base, they took the Germans completely by surprise: as the last of the aircraft disappeared from view two Zeppelins were blazing furiously in their shed.

The 'Silent Raid'

On 21 August 1917 Strasser mounted a raid on the Midlands with *L35*, *L41*, *L42*, *L44*, *L45*, *L46*, *L47* and *L51*, the Leader of Airships aboard *L46*. The raid could hardly be considered successful from the German point of view as only *L41* was traced over England, this ship coming in over Tunstall. Its bombs fell east of Hull, demolishing two chapels and damaging a YMCA hut.[1] One civilian was injured as a result of *L41*'s attack, and the Zeppelin left the coast unscathed, despite 19 aircraft going up after it. Only one managed to get anywhere near the raider: Lieutenant H P Soloman, from 33 HDS at Scampton, was flying over Beverley at 15,000ft when he first sighted *L41*. Soloman immediately gave chase, pursuing the Zeppelin for at least 20 miles out to sea before abandoning his intended prey and returning. Several airship commanders claimed to have flown inland and attacked Grimsby, Lincoln and Louth, but if they did they went unseen, for the depletion of ground observers and the airships' extreme height rendered the raiders virtually undetectable:

> At 20,000 feet the Zeppelins had nothing to fear from the night-flying aeroplanes with which the defence squadrons were equipped, none of which could get near this 'ceiling'. Nor did the airships' commanders need to concern themselves overmuch with the searchlights or gun defences.[2]

As usual extreme altitude bedevilled the airship crews, with men suffering the debilitating effects of compressed oxygen and instrument failure occurring frequently. In *L46*, Heinrich Hollender had taken in great lungfuls of the glycerin-contaminated oxygen and became violently ill as a result.

Dazed, he was led to the radio room by executive officer Richard Frey, who in later years was to recall Strasser's frustration with the incapacitated commander:

> 'What's wrong with you? Why are you standing there with your hands in your pockets?' When he could not arouse him, Strasser ordered me to take command, and I had to remove the binoculars from around Hollender's neck. Later, when Hollender regained partial consciousness, he was angry at me for taking over the ship.[3]

'Attack Middle or North' were Strasser's orders for 24 September, and *L35*, *L41*, *L42*, *L44*, *L45*, *L46*, *L47*, *L51*, *L52*, *L53* and *L55* were sent out. Contrary to expectations, this impressive force returned with negligible results: Ehrlich went furthest inland in the old *L35*, making landfall at Mablethorpe. At 02.55hrs, the commander observed several lights over to the south, lights that served to betray the position of the Parkgate Steel Works and Silverwood Colliery near Rotherham. Neither establishment received an air raid warning until *L35* was almost overhead, but the lights flicked out just in time. With an invisible target, Ehrlich bombed blind and his missiles missed completely, breaking some windows and demolishing a wall.

Another of the raiders reached Hull, dropping 11 bombs on the city centre, where only minimal damage resulted and three women were slightly injured. A total of 37 aircraft went aloft that night after the Zeppelin, but very few made contact and, to make matters even worse, there were tragedies. Second Lieutenant C Pinnock of 33 HDS left Elsham in an FE2b and after a fruitless patrol struck a tree when landing, the crash killing observer Lieutenant J A Menzies. From 36 HDS at Seaton Carew an FE2d crewed by Second Lieutenants H J Thornton and C A Moore failed to return and was presumably lost out to sea. Just five airships were traced over the country, and they left only £2210 worth of damage in their wake.[4]

On the morning of 19 October, commanders at Ahlhorn, Nordholz, Tondern and Wittmundhaven received orders to 'Attack Middle England, industrial region of Sheffield, Manchester, Liverpool, etc.' Thirteen Zeppelins were to take part – *L41*, *L42*, *L44*, *L45*, *L46*, *L47*, *L49*, *L50*, *L51*, *L52*,

197

Zeppelin!

L53, *L54* and *L55* – and from this impressive number five were destined never to return, as unpredicted gales in the upper regions blew all the ships far astray, back from England and ultimately over France in broad daylight. One exception was von Buttlar in *L54*, who, recognising the early signs of an impending storm, abandoned the intended targets of Sheffield or Manchester, bombed Derby and Nottingham instead, wasted little time in heading back for Tondern, and despite being blown north set down safely at the base with 205 gallons of fuel unused.

Of the other airships that had set out so confidently, *L55* was wrecked by a forced landing at Tiefenort, and *L44*, *L45*, *L49* and *L50* were total losses; only Waldemar Kölle in *L45* managed to achieve a measure of success. Having been driven backwards he found himself over the capital at 22.30hrs, less than an hour after *L45* had bombed Northampton where its 23 missiles killed one woman and two children. As the gale swept the Zeppelin over London, Kölle managed to release a salvo of bombs: three 660pdrs fell in the Administrative County and one near Piccadilly Circus, where store fronts were blown in and a large crater made in the road outside Swann and Edgar's. Seven people were killed here and 13 injured, while in Camberwell another bomb smashed two houses and killed a further 12 people. At Hither Green one 660pdr wrecked four homes and damaged a further 26 in the immediate vicinity, with 14 people killed and nine more injured as a result.

Driven further eastwards, *L45* was south of the Medway when Lieutenant T B Pritchard in a BE2c from 39 HDS opened fire on the Zeppelin at a range of 2000ft. Kölle turned south to run before the gale, and with a sick crew and an engine failure eventually made a forced landing at Sisteron, France, crew members managing to fire their ship before being taken prisoner.

L44 was shot down by anti-aircraft fire at 06.45hrs over St Clement, all 18 members of the crew perishing as the Zeppelin fell blazing to earth. *L49*, commanded by *Kapitänleutnant* Hans-Karl Gayer, was also borne over France by the gales, with only two of its engines running and the radio out of commission. Having already witnessed the sickening demise of *L44*, the crews of the crippled *L49* and *L50* had another shock as Nieuport scouts of *Escadrille* N152 ('The Crocodiles') pounced:

> Arriving at a height of 5300 metres, the patrol found themselves higher than the Zepps – we dived for them. Sub-Lt Lefargue now attacked the L49, which was the beginning of the fight. The other aviators immediately followed the example. The Zepp, fearing the attack, seemed to ascend. At this moment, I counted my machines – we were five, as Cpl Vandendorpe had rejoined us. While the Zepps pointed down, we followed them without shooting. But, as soon as they tried to straighten themselves, immediately, two machines would dive simultaneously, and as soon as the L49 heard the guns, she dived again. After a sudden dive, she started to go up almost straight. At that moment we dived down, and the Zeppelin did not insist. To make her dive without her catching fire, we continued to shoot a few cartridges at her side. Arriving in the neighbourhood of 1000 metres, the Zepp hoisted the white flag, signalling her surrender. We continued to make circles around her.[5]

Gayer force-landed in woods on the slopes of the River Apance near Bourbonne-les-Bains. Owing to a faulty Very pistol, Gayer was unable to set *L49* afire before he and his 18-strong crew were disarmed by local farmers, hunters and four of the Nieuport pilots who had landed in adjacent fields.[6]

Eventually *Kapitänleutnant* Roderich Schwonder's *L50* appeared over the grounded *L49* and 'The Crocodiles' prepared to take off again; one of them, however, was still airborne:

> Cpl Denis gave chase to the second Zepp (the L50). Arriving at an altitude of 5600 metres, he entered a lively fight, continuing to 800 metres.
>
> He was caught under a violent fire of their guns, throwing explosive bullets. Having run out of gas, he landed at Chetives (10 kilometres from Neuf Chateau) at 9.20.[7]

Thus ended an inconclusive engagement between aeroplane and airship and one of very few involving French airmen.[8] Having escaped destruction by the Nieuport pilot, Schwonder pressed on, but with three engines out of commission the commander realised he could never reach Germany and he deliberately drove *L50* nose-first towards the ground. This attempt at self-destruction almost came off, but as the Zeppelin struck the ground at Dammartin, its descent had levelled off and only succeeded in ripping off the control gondola. Most of the crew leapt out of the ship as it struck and bounced away, drifting at an angle of 45° with four men still aboard. During the day *L50* swung on its tail at 23,000ft, well out of range of several French aircraft who were trying to blast it out of the sky. *L50* eventually drifted out to sea, and as night fell disappeared entirely from view. The ship and the four men stranded on board were never seen again.[9]

To this day, the October 1917 attack is remembered as the 'Silent Raid', for at their high ceiling the airship engines went unheard and anti-aircraft guns were muzzled lest they betray London's position.[10] For the officers and men of the Naval Airship Division it was just another in a long run of recent disasters, yet the official British air historian did not consider it much of a victory for the defenders either, for

> ...although the Germans had little to show for their appreciable losses, it should be realised that things might have gone very differently. The defence system did not have much to do with the disastrous ending to the night's attack. The searchlights and guns were of small use, and not one of the 73 pilots who went up in England was equipped with an aeroplane capable of reaching the 'ceiling' heights of the Zeppelins.[11]

Yet more disasters were to follow. On 27 December, in circumstances which even now have not been fully

One of the Great War's most remarkable photographs: Zeppelin L49, brought down intact at Bourbonne-les-Baines, France, in October 1917 following the abortive 'Silent Raid'. The commander of L49, Kapitänleutnant Hans Karl Gayer, and his 18-man crew were captured.
US National Archives, by courtesy of D H Robinson

The battered control gondola of *L49*, believed to be on display in the courtyard of Les Invalides following recovery by French forces. A section of *L49*'s fabric bearing its service number serves to identify the 'relic'.
US National Archives, by courtesy of D H Robinson

resolved, four hangars at Ahlhorn exploded without warning, destroying *L46*, *L47*, *L51*, *L58* and *SL20*. Adding to the dreadful calamity were the deaths of 14 men; a further 134 were injured, including Hollender, who broke a leg and never flew again.[12]

Strasser opened the 1918 campaign on 12 March when in *L62* he led a force including *L53*, *L54*, *L61* and the new *L63* in an attack on the Midlands industrial area. Again the effort was negated by the results, with material damage limited to £3474 and one civilian killed. Weather conditions hampered both attackers and defenders: only ten aircraft were sent aloft, and all of them returned with nothing to report.

The following night the Zeppelins came again, but in less impressive numbers, just *L52*, *L56* and Martin Dietrich's *L42* taking part. At 18.13hrs Strasser recalled the ships on the strength of a forecast of veering westerly winds, but for Dietrich, lying off Northumberland when the order came through, the temptation was much too great. Ignoring Strasser's command, he kept going, fully aware of the consequences should the fates conspire against him. In fact for Dietrich it all turned out rather well, as West Hartlepool was quite unprepared for the airship's 21 bombs which destroyed £14,280 worth of buildings, killed eight people and injured 29 more. Whilst over the town *L42* came under fire from an FE2d of 36 HDS crewed by Second Lieutenants E C Morris and R D Linford, who pursued Dietrich for 40 miles out to sea until the mist swallowed up their quarry. Up from Hylton in an FE2b from the same unit was Sergeant A J Joyce, who was killed in landing at Pontop Pike after a 90-minute patrol.

On his return to Nordholz, Dietrich wondered what kind of reception he was likely to receive, and the fact that Strasser was not on the field to greet him was significant. In the afternoon Dietrich, with some trepidation, reported to his superior,

> ... who was very cool at first, and said hardly anything, but presently he smiled and remarked, 'In honour of your successful attack, I name you "Count of Hartlepool"'. Of course he couldn't report to a higher authority that I had disobeyed orders. The raid was described as 'additional to a scouting mission'.[13]

On 12 April another attempt on the Midlands was made, with *L60*, *L61*, *L62*, *L63* and *L64* participating. Only two Zeppelins managed to make successful forays inland. Kuno Manger's *L62* made landfall at Norfolk, dropped a trio of bombs on the Tydd St Mary night-flying ground and the remainder of his load south of Coventry, Hallgreen and Shirley, to the accompaniment of heavy gunfire. It was during this raid that some accounts record a British aircraft being brought down by gunfire from Manger's crew, but an official report subsequently filed by Major C Wigram of 38 HDS, Melton Mowbray, does little to substantiate the claim:

> Lieut C H Noble Campbell (at present in Messrs White and Poppe's private hospital Coventry) ascended at 23.25 from B Flight, Buckminster on [*sic*] FE2b A5707.
>
> This officer states that whilst patrolling between Grantham and Peterborough he noticed a Zeppelin at about 00.15 [*sic*] he thinks over Peterborough, but he could not identify any landmarks – it was very thick, the Zeppelin was at about 17,500 [feet] and some 1500 above him. Two searchlights were converging, but below the Zeppelin. Efforts to overtake the HA proved hopeless and Lieutenant Noble Campbell fired on it at about 1500 feet. It disappeared into a bank of cloud and he followed until 01.15 when he was hit in the head, the propeller smashed and the controls affected. He made to land, not knowing where he was. Holt flares showed him trees and a tall chimney, and he crashed at 01.30, almost against a wall of White and Poppe's Filling Factory.[14]

Apparently Noble Campbell suffered a scalp wound and was left rather shaken by his experiences. Major Wigram concluded his report by holding a firm belief that his pilot had been struck by a nearby shellburst, and Manger's report made no mention of the FE2b. Nevertheless *L62* did go out over Norfolk under heavy gunfire, and on the return leg to Nordholz, which was reached at 23.30hrs, it was noted that cell 9 had been pierced, presumably by shrapnel.[15]

Ehrlich, in *L61*, came in over Withernsea and was fired at by coastal batteries as he flew on. Unknowingly, the commander was heading directly for Liverpool, which had always been a prime target, but within ten miles of the city *L61* turned north, dropping all its bombs on Wigan. Fifteen missiles killed seven, injured 12 and caused £11,673 worth of damage, the last bombs falling in open fields near Aspull, where some cottages were damaged and four civilians injured.

Twenty aircraft took off to intercept the airships but only one, F2a N4283, crewed by Captains G E Livock and 'Bob' Leckie from Great Yarmouth, sighted *L61*. However, Ehrlich took advantage of some providential cloud and managed to elude them. Egbert Cadbury was also aloft that night:

> I went off in my DH9 about three-quarters of an hour before it began to get light. I have never flown a machine of this type at night before let alone on a filthy night like last night, and have no wish to do so again. I went through 4000 feet of clouds, to emerge in clear stratum between two cloud levels, went through the next lot to 8000 feet, but found more clouds – enough to hide thousands of Zeppelins.[16]

Thus ended the penultimate raid on England by Zeppelins, and the last, which took place in August, was to sound the death knell not only of the German Naval Airship Division itself but of its revered commander as well.

The Bombers Bombed

While this chronicle is concerned mainly with *aerial* combats involving aircraft and airships, some mention must be made of attacks on the airship bases, several of which were undertaken with great success. It was the RNAS that mounted the first such operation – as early as 22 September 1914, when four machines of Samson's Eastchurch Squadron from Antwerp took off to attack the sheds at Düsseldorf and Cologne. Only Flight Lieutenant C H Collett found the target, although his bombs fell short of the shed at Düsseldorf.

More positive results were obtained on 8 October, during the Antwerp evacuation, when Squadron Commander Spenser D Grey and Flight Lieutenant Reginald Lennox George Marix in Sopwith Tabloids 167 and 168 took off at 13.20 and 13.30hrs respectively. Spenser Grey's target was the Cologne airship base, which thick mist prevented him from locating; choosing Cologne's railway station instead, he unloaded his bombs. Marix, however, managed to reach his objective, and from 600ft dropped his bombs on the Düsseldorf shed, resulting in a massive explosion. Inside, the Army Zeppelin *ZIX*, which had made its first flight on 29 August, was totally destroyed. Damaged by ground fire, the Tabloid took Marix to within 20 miles of Antwerp before the pilot was compelled to make a forced landing. Borrowing a bicycle from a peasant, he eventually rejoined his unit, and together with Spenser Grey, who had landed at 16.45hrs, made his way to Ostend.[17]

On 21 November 1914 came the dramatic attack on the Zeppelin sheds at the Friedrichshafen base, Lake Constance, by four pilots of the RNAS. A month previously, Noel Pemberton Billing RNVR arrived in Belfort to make preparations for the attack, and on 28 October, when he had completed his task, he returned to England in order to collect the aircraft and pilots required for the mission. A flight of four Avro 504 biplanes had formed at Manchester under Squadron Commander P Shepherd, the pilots being Squadron Commander Edward Featherstone Briggs, Flight Commander J T Babington, Flight Lieutenant Sidney Vincent Sippe (a famous prewar pilot) and Flight Sub-Lieutenant R P Cannon. The force arrived at Belfort with 11 air mechanics on the night of 13 November; soon afterwards Shepherd was taken sick, and bad weather postponed the attack for a week.

Conditions were considered ideal on 21 November, and the brand-new Avros were brought out for engine tests. The raid was to be their maiden flights although their 80hp Gnome rotary engines were older than the airframes. Each machine was armed with four 20lb high explosive Hales bombs mounted on rudimentary fuselage racks.

At five-minute intervals the Avros left the ground, Briggs in 874 leading the small formation which was depleted at an early stage when Cannon's machine broke its tailskid and was unable to take off. Briggs pressed on with Babington and Sippe, reaching the extreme end of Lake Constance at 11.30hrs. Once over the target the machines managed to drop only two bombs on the airship base, one from Briggs falling between two sheds and another from Sippe blowing out the window of *L7*'s shed. Despite claims by the British to the contrary, damage was slight, yet the pilots' courage greatly impressed the German personnel on the base. Briggs ran a veritable gauntlet of machine-gun and rifle fire as he made his bomb run, a head wound, a riddled petrol tank and ten bullet holes in his Avro compelling him to land, whereupon he was attacked by locals but rescued, almost fainting, by German soldiers. Both Sippe and Babington were fired upon vigorously as they made their individual attacks:

> By descending almost vertically with the engine on at what I judge as approximately 200 feet per second, I was enabled to

The former large light cruiser HMS *Furious* in 1918, modified to true aircraft carrier configuration: the starboard battery of 5.5in guns is visible, as is the crash netting aft of the funnel. *Furious* carried a total of ten 5.5in guns, plus four 3in weapons for use against aircraft.
Conway Picture Library

keep the shrapnel bursts almost above the machine, except for a pause at some seconds in the fire, after which the shells were noticeably closer, and momentarily unpleasant.

Below 300 feet at close range the regular discharge of the Maxims and the rapid irregular fire of the rifles could be distinctly heard: it is impossible, however, to give any clear account of the shooting except that for the many hundreds of rounds expended the number of hits scored was negligible.[18]

Despite the fact that the Germans got off extremely lightly, the results of the attack, whilst encouraging, did not persuade the RNAS to give a repeat performance. Switzerland later complained to the British Government that the aircraft had violated Swiss neutrality by flying over their territory. In reply the British Foreign Office stated that instructions had been given to the pilots not to fly over Switzerland and was confident that they had not.[19]

Another attempt to raid an airship base took place on 25 December when aircraft were lowered from the seaplane carriers *Empress*, *Engadine* and *Riviera* as part of a special combined operation. The attack was unsuccessful, for the seaplanes failed to find Nordholz and returned to their ships lying off Heligoland pursued by German naval aircraft.[20] No more attacks were made on an airship base for another four years, but when the last attack was made it proved to be by far the most destructive.

Carrier Strike!
In the middle of 1918 it was decided to mount an air strike against the airship sheds at Tondern, this base being selected 'because with its command of the northern approaches to the German Bight, its Zeppelins were particularly well placed to watch the Grand Fleet'.[21] Thus were two specially trained flights of RAF Sopwith 2F1 Camels despatched to the carrier HMS *Furious*, and on June 29 this vessel, along with the 1st Light Cruiser Squadron and accompanying destroyers, was steaming off the Danish coast. Unfavourable weather resulted in the cancellation of the operation, and the force returned to port. Then on 16 July Admiral David Beatty reissued the orders for 'Operation F7' from the flagship, HMS *Queen Elizabeth*. The instructions, to be destroyed when complied with, were:

1 OBJECT
To attack the Zeppelin sheds at Tondern with bombs and to attack any enemy airships sighted.
2 FORCES EMPLOYED
Force 'A' – *Furious* and 3 destroyers of 13th Flotilla, 1st Light Cruiser Squadron and 5 destroyers of 13th Flotilla.
Force 'B' – 1st division of 1st Battle Squadron under Admiral, Second in Command, and 8 destroyers detailed by Commodore (F). 7th Light Cruiser Squadron...
...5 MOVEMENTS
Force 'A' is to leave Rosyth on the night of 16th/17th July and proceed to position 'A' – 237° 14 miles from Lodbierg Light – lat: 56. 49N., long: 8. 16E. and thence to position 'C' – 56. 03N., 7. 36E., arriving about 0300 on 18th July.
Machines for attacking Tondern are to be flown from position 'C' and force is then to cruise as ordered by Admiral Commanding Aircraft.
After the return of all machines as ordered by the Admiral Commanding Aircraft, force is to return to Rosyth.[22]

The memorandum went on to provide special orders that if weather conditions prevented a fly-off, the operation could be put off for 24 hours or the force return to Rosyth. In the event the weather did force a postponement, but the

Zeppelin!

ships did not return to port, and on the morning of 19 July, as *Furious* lay off the Schleswig coast, the seven Camels finally embarked on their historic flight.

First away was the leader of the first flight, Captain W D Jackson, whose aircraft cleared *Furious'* deck at 03.14hrs, closely followed by Captain W F Dickson and Lieutenant N E Williams. Just over an hour later the Camels were all over the Zeppelin sheds, and from a height of 100ft three bombs fell on the double *Toska* shed housing *L54* and *L60*. Instantly the Zeppelins were ablaze and a thick banner of smoke issued from the shattered hangar roof. Another bomb struck the *Tobias* shed, splinters shredding the captive balloon within, and despite spirited ground fire the three Camels sped westwards unscathed. To Dickson, the 80-mile flight was well worth it:

> Captain Jackson dived right onto the northernmost shed and dropped two bombs, one a direct hit in the middle and the other slightly to the side of the shed. I then dropped my one remaining bomb and Williams two more. Hits were observed. The shed then burst into flames and [an] enormous conflagration took place rising to at least 1000 feet and the whole of the shed being completely engulfed.[23]

Close on the heels of Williams as he took off was *L23*'s destroyer, Captain Bernard Arthur Smart DSO, leader of the second flight which comprised Captain T K Thyne and Lieutenants S Dawson and W A Yeulett. The flights left *Furious* in succession with no interval between them, the first forming up to starboard of the carrier and the second to port, Yeulett, the last man away, taking off at 03.20hrs. Although the flights departed together, Smart's section arrived over Tondern ten minutes after Jackson's had left. Smart explained the reason for this to his mother a few days later in a letter that remains a detailed and unique record of the Tondern raid:

> ...as soon as the others were in V formation behind me, I set off on the course which was to take me to [the] Tondern Zepp base. The wind was higher than allowed for with the result that we struck the coast of Denmark 20 miles north of the spot we should have done, so we followed it down to Blaavand Point. Here my best man (Capt Thyne) dropped out of formation and I saw him descending through the clouds with engine trouble – I went dead slow to give him a chance if it picked up but could not wait as the whole show was a fight against time and fuel consumption. We were now only three – two Subs and myself and for some unearthly reason I could not get them to open out their engines and go full speed – every time I opened mine I left them miles behind. What they were lagging for I cannot conceive as they made no attempt to come closer – I intended asking them about it when we got back but unfortunately they are both missing though I think there is every reason to assume they got to Denmark. Anyway it was very annoying as it left us further and further behind the other flight and every minute [of] delay meant more time of warning for the Germans and consequently a hotter reception for the second flight when it arrived.
>
> However, the only thing to do was grin and bear it, though my state of mind was somewhat lurid and the things I called the others simply unprintable, so we crawled along at a miserable 60 knots with my absolutely priceless engine begging and praying to be opened out to 90 or more!
>
> We were at about 8000 feet until this but now the holes in the clouds got fewer and smaller and I finally lost my bearings and decided to come below them. I dived through a hole and sighted the little island which showed me we were on the

A clutch of Camels mustered on the deck of HMS *Furious* prior to the Tondern raid of 19 July 1918. The over-painted roundels were probably Smart's idea. In the foreground can be seen the lift hatch through which aircraft stowed beneath decks could be pulled up; the hoisting cable can be seen on the upper wing centre-section of each machine. *IWM Q20627*

boundary line between Denmark and Germany. My feelings at seeing for the first time this land, the very name of which we have all got to hate so thoroughly, were simply beyond description. I gloated over every detail of my machine, the engine with its perfect even healthy roar which only *my* engine (in my estimation) could give, the controls trued up to a nicety till the machine would practically fly itself, my own patent windscreen with a hole for the telescopic sight, for my guns, in the middle, and every other patent gadget of mine which I had spent interesting weeks in fitting all over the machine to suit my own little fads, and lastly the two little messages for Germany which I carried on the bomb frames below.

In the excitement I bunged open the throttle in the vain hope the others would hang on – the machine leapt forward but they soon got far adrift and I had to slow up again. I now followed the railway for a bit to get a careful compass course and then climbed up through the clouds again to avoid observation. After 15 minutes on this course which I calculated should have brought me to a point some 2 or 3 miles north of Tondern, I dived the formation through the clouds again and looked around. I couldn't find my bearings for a bit but finally, by carefully comparing the map, discovered Tondern some 10 miles to the SW the wind having driven me eastwards. I turned W and as I neared the N side of Tondern began to look around for Zepp sheds. Hardly had I formed this idea in my mind when – 'boom', 'boom' – 'woof', 'woof' went the guns and two black round puffs of smoke appeared in the sky on my left – then a number of other batteries opened out on us and the flashes of three close together attracted my attention – close to these I saw the three Zepp sheds, two large double ones and one small. One of the large ones had a large hole in the roof and was literally belching out thick black smoke from every crack and crevice in the building. I gave the signal and dived on the other big shed at full speed, the 150 kn registered on the indicator giving me a sense of security against the wretched archies, which, although not particularly well ranged, were properly 'putting the wind up me'! Down and down I came until only 800 feet at which height I dropped the bombs in succession and swerved away. I had just a glimpse of one falling short and the other landing in the middle of the shed after which my whole attention was taken up in saving my skin! The aerodrome I now saw to be absolutely thick with men running wildly in all directions and over the roar of the engine I heard the crackle of numerous rifles and several machine guns – it sounded just like a little infantry attack, that irregular crackle which I had learned so well out east. My 'wind up' was now nothing short of 'kollosal' [sic] and I nosed the bus down with full engine till the wires simply shrieked. At 50 feet from the ground I flattened out and skimmed over the ground in a zig zag course at a terrific speed which made it an almost impossible target. I had vague impressions of men rushing about and waving, horses tearing round in mad fright and frightened cattle leaping in all directions to escape the unusual noise of my 150hp – then I felt I was clear of the guns and began to look around for the other members of my flight and incidentally for Hun planes, but nothing was in sight.[24]

Smart had already anticipated such a situation and prior to the flight had arranged a rendezvous point with his colleagues ten miles up the railway line at Brede. Smart circled the town, saw no sign of the other Camels, and as a glance at his watch revealed he had but one hour of fuel aboard, his chances of returning to *Furious* were getting slimmer by the second. Torn between waiting for his flight, for whom he was of course responsible, and getting back to his ship, he chose the latter course, thinking that to 'return ignominiously without my flight was better than not returning at all'.[25] Still 20 miles within enemy territory, Smart decided to 'turn off' the engine and hedge-hop for the return journey. On emerging from clouds at 700ft he was dismayed that when on opening the throttle nothing happened. After a few frantic minutes, two cylinders started firing as the Camel sank lower, until at 20ft, when Smart thought it was all over, 'another cylinder or two chipped in' and within ten minutes had resumed full power:

The reason must have been that she oiled up the plugs in my descent through the clouds so I cut out any chances of a repetition of this by skimming along at 500 feet. I kept a look out for Huns but saw nothing. I was over Denmark now and began to feel easier as internment was the worst [that] could happen to me. I had plenty of petrol but the oil had ceased to show in the pulsator glass, which might mean the end of the oil supply or not – anyway I had only ¼ hour more to make up the 3 hours and was still not in sight of the landmark which would tell me the position of the ships. I studied the map which showed I had still 30 miles to go. 15 minutes fuel and 30 miles to go – would she do it? My eyes were glued on the watch fascinated by that crawling minute hand which was slowly creeping to the time when I could expect my engine to konk out [sic].

...The 15 minutes was up when I sighted the landmark. The clouds had lifted but a thin haze made it difficult to spot ships. My engine was going perfectly still, but I dare not get out of gliding distance of the land as the three hours had gone, so I climbed as hard as I could go, each 1000 feet enabling me to go another mile or more out to sea, without leaving gliding distance of land. At 6000 feet and about seven miles out I saw a little white speck through the haze. I looked hard – yes, it was moving. I turned straight for it and as I got nearer it showed

Captain Bernard Arthur Smart poses in front of the Sopwith 2F1 Camel with which he participated in the Tondern raid. Smart had the metal panels of his machine painted in ultramarine and white squares for recognition purposes.
B A Smart

plainly the wake of a ship though [I] was still unable to distinguish the latter. It presently turned out to be one of our destroyers and I thankfully turned off my engine and landed ahead of her.

My troubles were not yet over however as the destroyer had barely finished picking up Capt Dickson... and was not ready for me. She came alongside, by which time I was sitting on the tail with much difficulty owing to the rough sea. They threw a line which I stretched to catch when a big wave caught me on the chest and into the ditch I went. I had had two belts on but the one which blew up with [the] compressed air bottle had got caught in the machine and [I] had taken it off – the other was one of the type you blow up with your mouth. I regained the tail and held on by one wire at the same time trying to blow up the belt. I was too far gone for this though as [I] had swallowed buckets ;of sea water and simply hadn't the necessary wind! Could only hang on to the tail wire with both hands.

The waves, which were from 10 to 15 feet, kept first lifting the machine bodily during which time my head and everything was totally under water, then as the wave subsided I was left hanging with my whole weight on the wire. By the time they had lowered a boat and got alongside I was completely done to the wide and don't think could have held on more than another minute or two. I hadn't the strength to make an effort to get into the boat but three sturdy ABs clutched hold of any suitable part of my clothes and hauled me inboard like a sack of flour. I luckily got rid of a few gals of seawater I had swallowed and when alongside just had enough strength to climb the rope ladder and stagger aboard. They had a hot bath for me but I was not cold and my only wish was to lie down and die in peace. I went to the captain's cabin where they pulled off my sodden clothes and I flopped in between the blankets of his bunk and lay there for the rest of the day.[26]

When Smart awoke, it was confirmed that four of the seven pilots had failed to return, their loss attributed to low cloud giving poor visibility and thus causing the pilots to lose their way and run out of fuel, the margin for which was small. Later, a summary of operations gave an indication of what befell the missing airmen:

Capt Jackson... Failed to return. Landed near Ebsjerg in Denmark owing to petrol supply failing. He destroyed his machine. Scored 1 hit on a second large shed.
Lieut Williams... Failed to return. Dropped two bombs on large Zeppelin shed. Landed near Scallinger in Denmark owing to petrol supply failing. Machine not destroyed.
Lieut Dawson... Failed to return. Landed near Rinkjobing in Denmark. Machine not destroyed.
Lieut Yeulett... Failed to return. One report states he was seen to land near Tondern, but a later report says a machine was salved from the sea near Hoyer. No definite news of this pilot.[27]

Tondern's defences were meagre, being restricted to small arms shouldered by the ground troops, and on 6 March five Albatros DIII fighters had been withdrawn while the levelling of a landing ground was taking place – their absence was probably known to British Intelligence. Four men were injured as a result of the Camels' attack, and whilst *L54* and *L60* were destroyed they had not exploded and the big *Toska* shed was soon repaired. The raid revealed how exposed Tondern really was, and the base was thereafter maintained only as an emergency landing ground. As for Smart, further ordeals were in store:

On the way back the Admiral sent congratulations and we visited Beatty next morning. He remembered me from last time and seemed very pleased. Since then have been very busy seeing the nobs or celebrating...

The *Toska* shed on the morning of 20 July 1918, smoke still pouring from its roof. The attack by the RAF Camels took the Germans completely by surprise and subsequently, fearing further attacks, they maintained Tondern as an emergency landing ground only.
Luftschiffbau Zeppelin

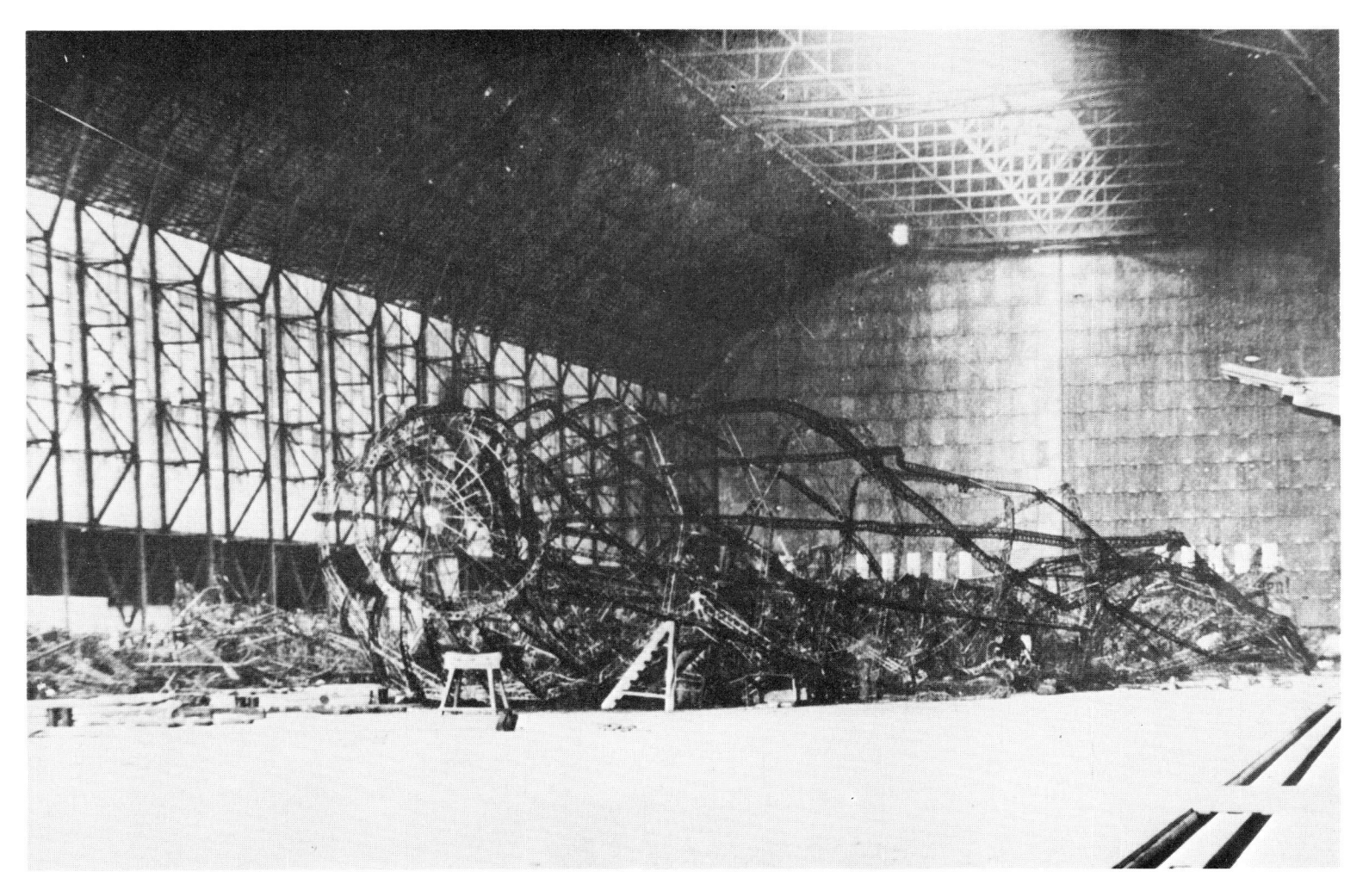

The King happened to be coming up for his annual Fleet inspection yesterday and [we] were very surprised at having orders to go aboard the *Queen Elizabeth* with the Admiral. Imagine our still greater surprise when aboard to find that Dickson was having a DSO and I a bar to mine and the King was presenting it that morning!

My old Commodore, Cowan, sent for me and patted me on the back, seeming as pleased as if it had been his own son. Several Vice-Admirals and Rear-Admirals whom I had met last time also congratulated me and really the fuss made was altogether out of proportion to the stunt. At the investiture Dickson and I were saved till last when the battery of cameras and cinematographs made us absolutely quake! As the senior I went up first and to my surprise did everything correctly, coming to a halt three paces from him, smartly saluting and advancing without falling over the steps to the dais!

The King seemed awfully pleased and knew practically every detail. He talked to me for nearly ten minutes and wanted to know all about the show. His questions were really very sensible and to the point, and his speech is very dignified and gentlemanly. Having given me the bar he shook hands, after which I saluted and walked off when Dickson had to go through the mill.[28]

Lieutenant-Colonel R Davies, commanding the RAF unit of HMS *Furious*, subsequently despatched a report to the ship's captain summing up the operation:

The failure of Lieuts Dawson and Yeulett to return is very probably due to insufficient oil, as Capt Smart in the same flight was in the air for three hours 15 minutes and the oil carried in the Camels is sufficient only for from 3–3½ hours flight. Capt Dickson was in the air for two hours 41 mins. It is therefore surprising that the other machines in the first flight did not return. But in view of the thick clouds and poor visibility it is possible they went out of their way, and so ran short of oil.[29]

While the loss of two Zeppelins was yet another blow to Strasser, he comforted himself with the development of a new class of high-climbing, seven-engined Zeppelin capable of great speed. First off the stocks was *L70*, which made its maiden flight on 1 July 1918 and was basically a 'Height-Climber' of the *L53* class with an additional 15-metre gas cell fitted amidships. With a length of 693ft 11in, a capacity of 2,195,800 cu ft and seven Maybach MBIVa 'altitude motors', the sleek monster attained 19,700ft statically and 23,000ft dynamically on its flight trials with ease. *L70* was the fastest airship built up to that time and could reach 81mph with a useful lift of 97,130lb, and an 8000lb bomb load was planned for raids on England. Strasser appointed an inexperienced officer to command the new wonder ship, one *Kapitänleutnant* Johann von Lossnitzer. It would prove to be a fateful choice.

The burnt-out wreck of *L54* in the *Toska* hangar at Tondern following the strike from HMS *Furious*; beyond lie the crumpled remains of *L60*. The fact that there were no explosions prevented the total destruction of the shed; it was soon repaired.
Archiv: Marine-Luftschiffer-Kameradschaft

CHAPTER 16

L70, 5 August 1918

> '... If the English should succeed in convincing us that the airship attacks had little value and thereby cause us to give them up, they would be rid of a severe problem and would be laughing at us in triumph behind our backs ...'
>
> Letter, Fregattenkäpitan Peter Strasser, 23 June 1917

Attack on south or middle (London only at order of Leader of Airships.) Bombs: four of 300, eight of 100, 12 of 50kg. For L70, eight of 300, eight of 100, eight of 50kg. Take-off for L56, 3pm; the others at 2pm. Approach along 54th parallel as far as four degrees east. Participants: L53, L56, L63, L65, L70. Blankenberghe wind measurements at 2, 5pm, 5am. Wind measurements from German Bight as required. Afternoon weather map will be wirelessed, night map will not. Preserve careful wireless discipline. Airship special wavelength. Leader of Airships aboard L70. Direction from Nordholz on Leader of Airships' instructions.

Leader of Airships[1]

Final Assault

Strasser's brand new flagship, the seven-engined *L70*, was placed in commission on 8 July 1918 by von Lossnitzer, who that same day flew the vessel to Nordholz. Once there, *L70* was to be berthed overnight in the *Nordstern* hangar, but severe cross-winds compelled von Lossnitzer to place his charge in the 645ft revolving hangar instead, with 40ft of *L70*'s tail exposed to the elements. Next morning the Zeppelin was transferred to the designated shed, where rough weather confined it until 1 August, on which day its commander embarked on a scouting patrol.

In company with two other airships, *L70* embarked on its maiden reconnaissance flight over the Dogger Bank, where its commander caught ships of the Harwich Force completely by surprise by aiming several bombs at Commodore Tyrwhitt's cruisers and coastal motor boats. This unsuccessful attack, 'made by an overbold newcomer, in a hurry to make his reputation',[2] certainly caught Tyrwhitt unawares and persuaded him to comment that the airship commanders 'were losing their sense of caution and that it would be worth while, next time, to take a fighting aeroplane'.[3] With the benefit of hindsight it could be argued that had von Lossnitzer stayed his hand, the destruction of *L53* a fortnight later by a Sopwith Camel of the Harwich Force might have been avoided.[4]

With the issue of his final attack orders on 5 August, *Fregattenkäpitan* Peter Strasser not only unwittingly sealed his own fate but also that of the German Naval Airship Division as an effective offensive weapon. On that fateful day, Strasser boarded *L70* to lead in person four ships against England – a seemingly suicidal final gesture. It is generally conceded that Strasser's unshakable confidence in his beloved airships tended to cloud his judgement; indeed, his contempt for the English defences was no secret.[5] That the Leader of Airships decided to head the first raid in four months was mainly in order to keep a paternal eye on von Lossnitzer, for however much faith Strasser placed in his subordinate he was hardly in a position to let the inexperienced commander loose over England without supervision. But the combination of Strasser, blindly confident, and von Lossnitzer, untried and anxious to prove himself, was a deadly one: 'neither man would be a restraining influence on the other.'[6]

L70, 5 August 1918

The ill-starred L70 being walked into Friedrichshafen Factory Shed II where it was built. This photograph was taken in July 1918.
Luftschiffbau Zeppelin

Peter Strasser received his *Pour le Mérite* award from Admiral Scheer at Ahlhorn on 4 September 1917. This photograph, believed to have been taken that day, shows Strasser posing proudly on the steps of the Ahlhorn *Kasino*. Leader of Airships from October 1913 until his death aboard *L70* in August 1918, Strasser was greatly respected by his subordinates, a respect that for former comrades has not diminished over seven decades.
F Moch

From Ahlhorn, where two new hangars had already risen, Phoenix-like, to replace those destroyed in the January explosions, *L63* departed at 13.47hrs under the command of *Kapitänleutnant* Michael von Freudenreich, and, from Nordholz, *L53*, *L65* and *L70*. *Kapitänleutnant* Walter Zaeschmar was last away, *L56* lifting off from Wittmundhaven at 15.12hrs to join the other ships out to sea.

Weather conditions could not be considered ideal for the raid. The ground temperature at Nordholz was 75°F, the humidity 85 per cent, and the barometer showed a reading of 29.77in; never before had a raid been attempted with barometric pressure so low. In standard atmospheric conditions *L65* could boast a useful lift of 86,215lb, but on 5 August the airship was only able to manage 72,315. Such adverse conditions would cost *Kapitänleutnant* Walter Dose dearly, hundreds of feet of precious altitude being lost despite the dumping of most of *L65*'s water ballast. Once over the North Sea and at 16,400 ft, Strasser's fleet encountered the familiar low cloud base beneath them. More unsettling was the fact that, despite freshening winds having been forecast in the upper regions, the westerly wind actually decreased in strength as the airships climbed. At 18.30hrs the Nordholz ships were some 60 nautical miles from English shores and it was still daylight. Dose, in *L65*, had been unable attain a safe attack altitude even though 43,000lb of ballast had been released, and when 2200lb ;of unfused bombs were jettisoned as a last resort the Zeppelin managed to reach 17,000ft. At 21.00hrs Strasser imprudently wirelessed his final orders to the Zeppelin commanders:

To all airships. Attack according to plan Karl 727. Wind at 5000 metres [16,400ft] west south-west 3 doms [13½mph].
Leader of Airships[7]

Actually Strasser had already passed through Karl 727 some two hours prior to despatching this signal, and it can be considered likely that both Strasser and von Lossnitzer had been misled by inaccurate radio bearings. We have already seen that, in the war's earlier stages, British radio operators had been able to plot the Zeppelins' positions as they requested bearings, but now the raiders maintained strict radio silence, taking their own bearings on signals transmitted at 30-minute intervals from stations at Cleve and Tondern. Bearings plotted during the night of 5/6 August proved to be wildly in error, placing the ships 40 to 60 miles west of their actual positions. By transmitting his attack orders, Strasser betrayed his presence to English defences (or so many of his former comrades have attested), yet *L53*, *L65* and *L70* had already been sighted.

As early as 21.00hrs the crew of the Leman Tail lightship, moored 30 miles off the Norfolk coast, had observed Zeppelins ten miles to the north and seen them climbing steadily and eventually deploying into vee formation:

I beg to report that on August 5 at 8.10pm BST three Zeppelins were sighted from this vessel bearing East eight miles steering WNW and flying slow. Two of them passing this vessel six miles north steering WNW at 9.0pm BST.

207

The port after engine gondola of *L70* shows the exhaust side of the 6-cylinder Maybach MB IVa 'altitude motor' directly coupled to the 10ft diameter wooden propeller. The MB IVa answered the need for a more efficient power unit for high-altitude operation. With its oversize cylinders and a compression ratio increased to 6.08:1, it could not be fully opened up until a height of 5900ft had been reached, and up to that limit delivered a constant 245hp. At 19,700ft the MB IVa could still attain 142hp, and a later version with aluminium pistons and a compression ratio of 6.07:1 produced 162hp at this altitude.
Luftschiffbau Zeppelin

The third Zeppelin passing two miles north at 9.25pm BST, steering WNW. Last seen 9.40pm BST. Also at 9.25pm BST a fourth Zeppelin sighted ESE eight miles SW, this one disappeared in the clouds.

At 10.5pm BST saw a large red flame descending through the clouds which lasted 30 seconds bearing west and a long way from this station.

All Zeppelins were at a great height.[8]

Tragedy had been a foregone conclusion. From an early stage both Dose in *L65* and Prölss in *L53* were uncomfortably conscious of the real danger into which their chief was leading them, and the commanders hesitated to follow the flagship, its short exhaust stacks emitting telltale sparks as it flew westwards into the still-lightened sky.

'The Bank Holiday Raid'

The glorious summer weather had lured thousands of sun-seeking visitors to Great Yarmouth over the Bank Holiday weekend. Indeed, it was reported that not since 1911 had the popular east coast resort been so heavily patronised:

> It was known in advance that many were coming, but the reality has far surpassed all expectations. Despite the restrictions imposed by rationing, our welcome guests have had their reasonable wants remarkably well supplied. They have found plenty of excellent entertainments, and, best of all, they have enjoyed glorious holiday weather. Yarmouth has just now something like its appearance in the good old times before the war.[9]

There was certainly no shortage of entertainment that day: visitors were able to forget the war for a while and either simply bask in the sunshine or attend any one of a large number of holiday events. During the afternoon thousands flocked to a 'Grand Fete' organised by the Royal Navy in aid of the Missions to Seamen. A well-supported sports programme and a whist drive was followed by concerts in the pavilion which went on well into the evening. If concerts did not appeal there was always the theatre or the cinema. At the Theatre Royal, E Hamilton Jordan played Horace Parker in *A Message From Mars*, and at the Regent the Myra Forbes Trio performed a 'refined musical, vocal and dancing act' and were ably supported by Irene Rose's character studies and Jack Cunard and sister, 'novelty dancing entertainers'. The Empire was screening *My Lady's Dress* starring Gladys Cooper, together with *My Four Years in Germany*, and at the Coliseum the ever-popular Charlie Chaplin film *A Dog's Life* was being shown.

The warning of an impending air raid reached Great Yarmouth's civilian populace just after 21.00hrs, when at all places of entertainment the King's message, 'Hold Fast', was being read out to audiences. Cinema- and theatre-goers responded by remaining in their seats and only dispersing when the performances had come to an end. As they filed out of the exit doors, local defence units were already at work.

When Commodore Ellison at Lowestoft had received the sighting report from the Leman lightship crew, the airships' positions were rapidly transmitted to Major Robert Leckie, then commanding 228 Squadron (Boat Flight) at the Great

Yarmouth air station. Leckie telephoned for Lieutenant-Colonel Vincent Nicholl and Major Egbert Cadbury, commanding 212 Squadron (Land Flight), to report immediately for duty. Then Leckie placed every available aircraft at Burgh Castle, Covehithe and Great Yarmouth on standby, and within 20 minutes seven aircraft had taken off. After another quarter of an hour a further eight machines had left their respective landing grounds, one of the first away being DH4 A8032, piloted by Cadbury, who had previously been enjoying his wife's singing at the Wellington Pier pavilion:

> It all happened very quickly, and very terribly. Mary was singing at a concert across the road in aid of some charity – and singing very well, too. I was enjoying the music, and war and rumours of war were far away from my thoughts. Nita – a cousin of Mary's staying with us – and I were enjoying a particularly fine piece of music when a cross-eyed RAF orderly struck me with his diverging vision.
>
> I guessed I was wanted and hastened to join him. He informed me that Nicholl wanted me at HQ. I dashed along the front, and, to my intense surprise, saw an airship in the dim distance silhouetted against an extremely bright, clear, northerly evening light. That was about 8.45pm.
>
> I learnt at HQ that three Zeppelins were at a point about 50 miles NE of here, well to seaward. Knowing that there was only one machine available that had the necessary speed and climb – its twin having already gone – I saw that the race was to the nimblest, to the pilot who could get into the waiting seat.[10]

Cadbury leapt into his Ford and tore off in the direction of the station airfield, once there grabbing only scarf, goggles, helmet and jacket as he raced Captain C B Sproatt to the cockpit of A8032. Cadbury got there first, barely noticing 'Bob' Leckie clambering into the rear cockpit. As the pilot was convinced that the three Zeppelins heralded the start of a major German naval assault, he ordered the pair of 110lb bombs under the DH4's wings to be left in place. Shortly after Cadbury had left the ground at 21.05hrs, he was followed by Captain C S Iron and Lieutenant H G Owen in D5793, one of the station's underpowered and decidedly unpopular DH9s; soon afterwards Captain B G Jardine and Lieutenant E R Munday took off in DH9 D5802.

Having climbed through clouds at 10,000ft, Cadbury and Leckie were afforded an excellent view of the three Zeppelins starkly revealed against the slowly fading twilight. The British airmen flew away from the airships and endeavoured to gain extra height, yet despite engaging the bomb release and thus lightening the aircraft, the DH4 still seemed strangely heavy on the controls. By 22.20hrs Cadbury and Leckie were at 16,400ft and approaching the leading Zeppelin head-on but slightly to its port side, in order to 'avoid any hanging obstructions.'[11] In the rear cockpit, Leckie swung his single Lewis gun to bear. It carried no sights and the first rounds missed their target, keeping alight for several hundred feet beyond. A small correction and it was all over:

> The ZPT was seen to blow a great hole in the fabric and a fire started which quickly ran along the entire length of [the] Zeppelin. The Zeppelin raised her bows as if in effort to escape, then plunged seaward, a blazing mass. The airship was completely consumed in about ¾ of a minute. A large petrol tank was seen to become detached from the framework and fell blazing into a heavy layer of clouds at about 7000 feet below.[12]

Strasser had gambled and lost. He paid the price of underestimating his opponents and took 21 of his comrades with him; neither the superbly improved design of *L70* nor the much-vaunted 20mm Becker cannon had prevented disaster. The dream of conquest by Zeppelin finally ended with the blazing skeleton of *L70* smashing into the sea five miles north-west of the Blakeney Overfalls bell buoy. The remains fell close to the schooner *Amethyst*, Mate Benjamin Browne later providing a vivid impression of Strasser's last moments. A national newspaper reported:

> [*Amethyst*] was about 40 miles off the east coast when the sound of engines was heard, and two Zeppelins appeared over the trawler [*sic*]. One of them remained stationary while the other continued on its course. The first airship started to move again, but before it had gone far it burst into flames and dropped its bombs. It kept a fairly even keel as it dropped through the air. Alighting on the sea, it lay a burning mass for nearly an hour. Directly afterwards the mate heard the noise of aeroplanes. One descended close to the trawler, and the pilot shouted out something which the mate could not catch. For a long time the aeroplane circled around the burning Zeppelin and then made for home. Browne added that he looked through his glasses but could see no sign of survivors.[13]

Horrified at the catastrophe, the commanders of *L53* and *L65* hurriedly dumped water ballast, altering course eastwards as they climbed rapidly away and out of firing range. Dose, nearest to the flagship when disaster struck, later recorded the fall of *L70*:

L70 in flight. With a length of 693ft 11in, this 'x' class Zeppelin had a volume of 2,195,800 cu ft and boasted a useful lift of 97,100lb. The seven altitude motors delivered a total horsepower of 1715, giving *L70* a maximum speed of 81mph. *Luftschiffbau Zeppelin*

Beneath the airships was a complete layer of clouds, through which L65 was repeatedly hit between 11.0 and 11.15am. At about 11.10pm L70 was port astern about 3000 metres from L65.

Suddenly we saw a small light on the otherwise quite dark ship which rapidly spread, and shortly afterwards the whole ship was in flames. She started to fall with running engines, first slowly, then faster and faster, and was broken to pieces shortly before she entered the above-mentioned cloud screen. We could not see if any of the crew jumped out in parachutes.[14]

Even as *L65* began to rise, Cadbury made for the Zeppelin, but almost immediately his engine cut out, owing to a temporary block in the petrol system. However, he managed to get it going again, heading directly for the nearest airship as Leckie let fly with the Lewis gun. After a few rounds, a light was observed in the Zeppelin's port midships gondola: the ship was seemingly on fire, yet the glare was rapidly extinguished, and then came frustration for the Great Yarmouth airmen. Only in later years would Walter Dose realise how close he had come to sharing Strasser's fate, for a double feed jammed Leckie's gun and he was unable to rectify the problem:

Had I had *two* guns the result might have been different for L65 and L53 or if I had gloves to wear and/or a coat I might have been able to clear the jamb [*sic*]. I have been outdoors in Canada both before and after that eventful night, in temperatures down to –60°, but never in my life have I been so cold as I was that night, and the rear cockpit of the DH4 sure was draughty![15]

Dose and his crew made good their escape, turning north to avoid the DH4. Still, some damage had been done:

Later, bullet holes – 340 in all – were found in the after gas cells. There was no fire of course. The mechanic in the port midships gondola lifted the black window-curtain without turning out the light, producing the illusion of a fire inside.[16]

Only a few of the bullet holes, if any, could be attributed to Leckie, since he only managed a short burst before his gun jammed. Both he and Cadbury were in agreement that Jardine and Munday in their DH9 had inflicted the major proportion of damage to *L65*, which, losing gas from four cells, faced a perilous return journey to Nordholz.

When Leckie's gun failed, Cadbury had vainly tried to raise the nose of the DH4 in order to bring the two forward-firing Vickers guns to bear, but the machine's absolute ceiling had been reached. When it stalled and fell back Cadbury gave up, and in later years he expressed no regrets at his failure, an opinion shared by Leckie:

I cannot but rejoice that the ships' company of L65 and L53 escaped to live normal and useful lives after the war. The destruction of these fine ships would have been an 'overkill'. We accomplished our object in that the shooting down of L70 put an end to the Zeppelin raiding of England. The lesson of the airships is plain for all to read. The Germans had in their possession the most effective vehicle for fleet reconnaissance in any power's hands at that time. It was, at the same time, just about the world's worst strike aircraft![17]

Cadbury's return flight was a nightmare for he became completely lost and was later to confess that flying through 12,000ft of cloud in inky blackness 'on a machine that I had been told could not land at night, even if I ever made land again',[18] was the most terrible half-hour he ever experienced. It appears that no orders to light runway flares had been issued to East Anglian landing grounds that night,

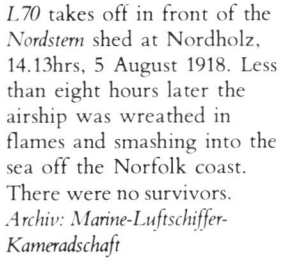

L70 takes off in front of the *Nordstern* shed at Nordholz, 14.13hrs, 5 August 1918. Less than eight hours later the airship was wreathed in flames and smashing into the sea off the Norfolk coast. There were no survivors. *Archiv: Marine-Luftschiffer-Kameradschaft*

and Cadbury was compelled to fly blindly on over the darkened countryside. Eventually the pilot made out two rows of lights inland from Hunstanton, thanks to the initiative of a watch officer as the flares at Sedgeford had been lit. Yet for Cadbury, a few more shocks were in store:

> [After] I made Sedgeford and landed safely, missing another machine that was circling round the aerodrome by inches, it suddenly loomed up in the blackness.
> To my horror I discovered that my bombs had failed to release, and that I had landed in a machine which I thought was certain to crash and catch fire with two 100-pound bombs on board; also that my life-saving belt had been eaten through by acid from an accumulator.[19]

Dose, having escaped destruction by Cadbury and Leckie, next came under fire from guns which he believed belonged to King's Lynn, and he duly retaliated by dropping 3750lb of bombs. It was of little consequence, for the bombs fell harmlessly in the sea – the inaccurate radio bearings had deceived *L65*'s commander, who was actually 65 miles east of his supposed position. On the long haul back to Nordholz the Zeppelin lost a quantity of gas from the peppered cells: in cell VII there was a hole the size of a fist, and with the 'Height-Climber's fragile hull threatening to break up, two aft engines were throttled back to half speed. After 16 hours 20 minutes in the air, Dose gingerly brought *L65* safely back to its hangar where the ship was laid up for 18 days whilst repairs were carried out.

Prölss had originally planned to attack either Nottingham or Sheffield, but, having witnessed *L70*'s destruction, he climbed to 19,400ft, beyond the range of British aircraft. As *L53* rose, several bombs were aimed at Boston, although they actually fell into the sea 65 miles off Cromer, as if to underline the folly of bombing purely by radio bearings. Neither did von Freudenreich in *L63* or Walter Zaeschmar of *L56* enjoy any measure of revenge for the loss of the flagship. No bombs from either Zeppelin were traced on land, despite claims by both commanders on their return. Whilst most of Great Yarmouth's airmen had sighted the Zeppelins, only a few came within range. From Burgh Castle, Lieutenants G F Hodson and Tompkins, led by Captain Gerard Fane, took off in Sopwith Camels,[20] Fane leaping into B5706, the nearest available machine, since his own was hangared. As Fane had acted upon reports of hostile *aeroplanes* he was not unduly worried that the Camel's guns were loaded with standard ammunition rather than incendiary – at least not until he saw three Zeppelins:

> However, I proceeded towards them knowing that Hodson was all right with a Lewis gun and plenty of ammunition, and also a DH4 from Yarmouth was not far behind me. I unfortunately found that an oil pipe had come unscrewed just where I could not reach it, so I was forced to return, and I landed at Yarmouth after dark to find that a Zeppelin had been shot down off Cromer by Cadbury. If *only* the telephone operator had said airships instead of aeroplanes, I should have gone in my own Camel and probably have been there about ten minutes before Cadbury.[21]

Jardine and Munday's DH9 failed to return, neither were Hodson or Camel N6620 ever seen again, and it was thought that the airmen mistook the burning fuel from *L70* for landing flares, crashed into the sea and were drowned. Munday's body was found a few days later by a patrolling minesweeper but there was never any trace of his comrades or their aircraft. Another of the defence's fatalities that

L65, under the command of *Kapitänleutnant* Walter Dose, takes off in front of the *Nordstern* shed at Nordholz, 14.35hrs, 5 August 1918. *L65* was built at Löwenthal and made a total of 28 flights before it was decommissioned on 9 November 1918.
Archiv: Marine-Luftschiffer-Kameradschaft

Zeppelin!

night was Lieutenant F A Benitz of 33 HDS, who had left Scampton at around 22.30hrs, ending his patrol within 20 minutes owing to engine trouble. Within a quarter of an hour he was aloft again and flew a fruitless 105-minute patrol before coming in at Atwick, crashing Bristol F2B Fighter C4698 in the process. Benitz did not survive the accident and his observer, Second Lieutenant H L Williams, was seriously injured.

Various home defence units sent up a total of 19 aircraft, none of which made contact with the raiders. Pilots from 33, 38, 51, 75 and 76 Home Defence Squadrons made patrols along their allotted sectors, poor weather and a lack of positive sighting reports adding to their frustrations. Second Lieutenant A J Marsden, in command of 38 HDS's A Flight at Leadenham, filed a report that can be considered typical:

> I reached 6000 feet over the Aerodrome and then proceeded to climb towards Grantham, which town I was apparently over at 10.25.
>
> The weather did not permit of my being able to see the Town or the ground. I then proceeded North for 20 miles when I should have been over Lincoln. I was then at 12,000 feet. The same weather conditions prevailed, preventing me from seeing the ground. It was also raining.
>
> I then turned south for 10 minutes and then proceeded east. I turned south again after reaching 14,800 feet.
>
> The weather then becoming so bad, the visibility to the ground being nil, I decided to land, particularly as the rain was increasing. I landed on my own aerodrome at 11.45pm.[22]

Marsden, in FE2b C9806, got down safely. During his 286-minute flight the pilot had seen no searchlights nor any sign of anti-aircraft guns being in action.

In retrospect, Peter Strasser can be justifiably criticised for his foolhardiness in approaching the English coast at such an early hour, low speed and height. His contemporaries on both sides evinced incredulity at these actions, but in later years Leckie considered that Strasser's low opinion of English defences was not entirely to blame for the disaster:

> ... Following an almost perfect day with sky unusually clear of clouds, a heavy bank of nimbus spread from the *West* and *before* the attack, had covered the East coast and sea to the East to 10/10ths. I feel it is more probable that Strasser was assured by his Met organisation that he could count on clear weather in the Bight of Heligoland and vicinity of the Dutch Islands (making for easy and accurate navigation) and a thick cloud cover during the last 100-150 miles to his objective. We know the cloud cover did arrive but probably about two hours late.[23]

Leckie did admit that Strasser had exercised poor judgement in persisting with the attack without waiting for this cloud cover, and as far as Martin Dietrich was concerned L70 had been recklessly handled. The veteran commander went on to attest that had he been in command of the flagship he would have steered an easterly course to await the arrival of darkness.[24]

Salvage

The captain of the *Amethyst* had lost precious little time in reporting L70's fiery descent to the Naval Commander-in-Chief of the East Coast, Admiral E Charlton, stationed at

Majors Robert Leckie and Egbert Cadbury flank an unidentified companion at Great Yarmouth shortly after the destruction of L70 on 5 August 1918. Both airmen later enjoyed long and distinguished careers in their respective air forces. *Peter Cadbury*

A photograph reputed to show DH4 A8032, in which Cadbury and Leckie destroyed L70. The aircraft is finished in the standard PC10 khaki for upper surfaces, with the forward fuselage in light grey and the undersides left in clear doped finish. Two vertical white stripes are visible on the rear fuselage. *The Aeroplane*

Immingham. Charlton was determined to recover as much of Strasser's ship as possible, for it promised to yield a great deal of useful information, perhaps even classified documents and code-books. Within 48 hours HMT *Scomber* was anchored over where *L70* lay and the crew had buoyed the wreck.

From 7 August to 22 September, the trawlers *Bullfrog*, *Driver*, *Peking*, *Star of Britain* and *Topaz*, under the command of Lieutenant-Commander John Pitts aboard *Scomber*, worked over the wreck. The trawlers operated mainly in pairs, and dragging sweep chains between them managed to bring a large amount of debris to the surface. Major portions of the framework, most of the gondolas complete with their Maybach engines, propellers and radiators, gas valves, shreds of gas cells, pieces of outer fabric covering and even a complete tail fin were subsequently dumped on the quay at Immingham. Locals managed to sneak off with some of the smaller fragments, but it was Cadbury and Leckie who were to have the lion's share. On 3 September, in Felixstowe F2a N4304, the two airmen set off to view the remains of their victim:

> We started off at about 11.45 and reached Killingholme at about 2.15. It is about 120 miles. Killingholme used to be a large RNAS Station, and was handed over in its entirety to the US Navy. They were awfully decent to us and gave us a terrific lunch – rations are unknown in the US Services! Real pure white bread and tons of butter were among some of the delights. They gave us a magnificent car and we drove in state to the Admiral's Headquarters. Charlton was our Admiral in *Sagitta*, and incidentally got me my commission.
>
> He is an absolute topper and full out for Leckie and myself, giving leave to take anything we liked. 'It is your Zeppelin, so you are entitled to first choice; go and see if we have anything you want, and take it. If I get anything good I will send it to you.'
>
> They have got a mass of wreckage but all the best bits had been already hot-stuffed. We afterwards went and had tea with him (Charlton). He had got a large piece of the track [*sic*] along the keel. He insisted on sending for a carpenter and cutting it in half, and is sending me half.
>
> He also promised to send the enormous framework of the rudder, about eight feet high, down by a Drifter, for a Mess Trophy.[25]

Cadbury had picked out a number of pieces from the wreckage strewn over the quayside, including pieces of the framework, one of the propellers and a few air valves, which were subsequently placed on board a destroyer by Charlton and sent down to Great Yarmouth.[26]

The salvage operation afforded the Admiralty Intelligence Division staff an almost complete picture of the advanced design and operational capabilities of the latest Zeppelin class. Many of *L70*'s performance details were gleaned from the contents of a personal notebook found on von Lossnitzer's body. Also apparently recovered from the battered control gondola was *L70*'s war diary, plus a package of papers which contained weather codes, along with 'Name List 1090 Volume Two' and cipher key 1373 for 31 July to 15 August 1918.[27] *Korvettenkäpitan* Paul Werther, Strasser's successor, had assumed these vital records to be destroyed, their secrets denied to the enemy, yet *Topaz*'s mate had witnessed an officer retrieving 'a despatch case of papers' which was promptly rushed ashore by a fast naval pinnace.[28]

Admiral Charlton later confided to Cadbury that a search of Strasser's body had yielded not only 'all the German codes' but also a complete history of the other German airship raids as well.[29] Naval Intelligence obtained much useful material from the study of *L70*'s remains and especially the various papers they had so fortuituously recovered. They learnt a lot about the Maybach 'altitude motor' – its power output at different heights, its fuel and oil consumption and its physical dimensions – from von Lossnitzer's notebook. Probably from the same source were extracted details such as the dynamic rate of climb at various nose-up inclinations and bomb loadings – 2200lb for North Sea patrols, 6600 for raids on London and up to 10,580 for other targets. A figure of 8800lb of bombs for the fateful 5 August mission came apparently from the ballast sheet and deck log found amongst the papers in the control car:

> ... For a normal raid on England with 4000kg of bombs, the airship was intended to rise statically to 19,400 feet, with an additional climb dynamically to 19,700 feet. After the discharge of the bombs at this height she would rise to 21,000 feet and would have enough fuel left for the return journey.[30]

L70's rough war diary revealed that von Lossnitzer had apparently intended to use all seven of the Zeppelin's engines on the outward journey but only five for the return. Perhaps if the opposite course had been adopted *L70* would have arrived much later and history might have taken quite a different course. A close scrutiny of the Zeppelin's remains revealed that the girders were even lighter than these found in *L48*, and several other drastic modifications to reduce weight were noted, such as the silk rather than cotton gas cell fabric.

A study of the ship's ballast sheet indicated that 154lb of ammunition was aboard *L70*, and in the control gondola the naval men found a sturdy mounting which they presumed to have been designed for 'some kind of small quick-firing gun, possibly a one pounder'.[31] No trace of Becker Cannon was ever found, but Cadbury was certain that he came under fire and so it has to be assumed that the guns fell out during *L70*'s death-plunge and ultimately eluded the sweep nets of the trawlers.

Of the 21 members of Strasser's crew, several leapt to their deaths when the Zeppelin caught fire, but the majority rode the burning ship right down to the sea. Five bodies were found amongst the debris brought abroad *Topaz*, and having

The three individuals that contributed most to the development of rigid airships: Dr Hugo Eckener, Count Ferdinand von Zeppelin, and Strasser. Eckener, later to command the famous *Graf Zeppelin*, one of history's most successful airships, first collaborated with von Zeppelin in the prewar years and was the airship's most energetic campaigner. Eckener later enrolled in the Navy as a volunteer airship pilot to direct the training of naval crews, of which some 50 followed through the principles of theoretical knowledge and expert airmanship evolved by Eckener and Strasser throughout their five-year association. Von Zeppelin died on 8 March 1917 and had lived long enough to see his invention assume full military potential, yet, in the knowledge that women and children were being killed by Zeppelin bombs, he accepted no responsibility for such occurrences. As he once remarked to an American reporter: 'No one regrets more deeply than I do that non-combatants have been killed, but they have been killed by other weapons of war too'.
Archiv: Marine-Luftschiffer-Kameradschaft

been searched for papers and a few badges appropriated for souvenirs they were weighted with furnace bars and unceremoniously committed to the sea:

> An interesting feature of the whole operation was that all the bodies were recovered intact, and that of Captain Strasser was completely untouched and his death was due either to drowning or the shock of the impact with the water – I am not sure which – but he showed no disfigurement or burns or injuries of any kind.[32]

Subsequent days saw six or seven further bodies washed up on a Lincolnshire beach, along with some pieces of wreckage. Local parishioners refused to allow the Germans to be buried in their churchyard. Thus were the bodies sewn up in sacking, and under sealed orders HMT *Venus* took them aboard and subsequently committed the Germans to the sea. The same fate befell the wreckage of *L70* after the Admiralty's Intelligence officers had finished with it, although locals managed to make off with further fragments before the ships carried the debris out to sea and dumped it.

Only one body from *L70* was laid to rest on English soil, that supposed to be of 23-year-old *Leutnant zur See* Kurt Krüger, who was buried in Weybourne Cemetery near Holt on Norfolk's northern coast. His body was washed ashore on 6 October, this date being inscribed upon the plain headstone which also bore the legend 'Airman Unknown'. On 8 July 1966 Krüger's body was re-interred at the German War Graves in Cannock Chase.[33]

The loss of *L70* – and of *L53* less than a week afterwards – marked the end of Germany's Naval Airship Division. The Leader of Airships had totally believed in the Zeppelin as a war-winning weapon, had shared his subordinates' dangers, tragedies and triumphs by joining them on raids, had assisted designers in improving and perfecting the airships, and finally, by falling in action with his comrades, had earned unflinching loyalty from those that survived him:

> The airship, which was created by the inventive genius and stubborn perseverence of Count Zeppelin, was developed by Captain Peter Strasser, as Senior Airship Officer, with untiring zeal, and in spite of every obstacle, into a formidable weapon of attack. The spirit with which he succeeded in inspiring his particular arm on many an air raid he has crowned by his heroic death over England. As Count Zeppelin will live for ever in the greatful memory of the German people, so also will Captain Strasser, who led our airships to victory.[34]

Two days after *L70*'s destruction, the *Kölnische Zeitung* published a brief obituary:

> If the hypothesis of his death proves correct we have lost in *Korvettenkäpitan* Peter Strasser one of our most successful airship commanders whose brilliant achievements had been recognised by the grant of the order Pour le Mérite. He entered the Navy on 16 April 1894 and became *Korvettenkäpitan* on 14 April 1911. At the outbreak of war he commanded the Fuhlsbüttel naval airship section at Hamburg. Previously he had been in the Admiralty in the department in charge of naval artillery. As a *Kapitänleutnant*, to which rank he was promoted on 21 March 1905, he was artillery officer on the battleship *Westfalen*. Previously he was artillery officer of the *Mecklenburg*. Among other decorations received before the war he had the life saving medal. He received the order Pour le Mérite in September 1917. Strasser always endeavoured to maintain this offensive spirit in his men and in spite of all the increased defensives [sic] to develop the airship arm so that it could continue to attack...[35]

'Aces' Back to Back

For their dual role in the destruction of *L70*, both Cadbury and Leckie were awarded the DFC, gazetted on 21 August, as was Lieutenant R E Keys who had claimed the destruction of a Schütte Lanz airship on that same night. Nicholl had put Cadbury's name forward for the VC, but this recommendation was not approved, even though the authorities took into account his courage in 'flying in a land machine with no flotation gear 30 to 40 miles out to sea in bad weather'.[36] Several days prior to the notifications of the DFC (an award he did not personally welcome) the modest Cadbury had been enjoying some evening tennis:

> I left my car at Burgh Castle Air Station on my way back. I managed to intimidate its young Commander – Fane – to overhaul it before I go on leave. He is engaged to a young lady of the name of Bacon. Pa Bacon is an extraordinarily wealthy man and owns a quarter of Norfolk. Packe – another friend of mine and Fane's – owns another quarter, Loame, also a friend of ours, owns a further quarter, and also we know well the headkeeper of Earl Grey and Montagu's estates in Norfolk – in which lie Hickling Broad and Hornsea Mere: the best duck and wild fowl in England – so I have warned Fane that unless he arranges three days shooting a week during the season, I will wring his neck.[37]

Shooting was just one of a number of leisure pursuits that Cadbury enjoyed throughout his long and successful life. Following his transfer to the Unemployed List on 15 April 1919, Cadbury joined his father's associate company, J S Fry and Sons Ltd, becoming managing director within two years. Subsequent appointments saw him on the boards of Lloyds Bank and The Daily News Ltd, amongst others, and during World War II he served as an Air Commodore for the City of Bristol Squadron and as Regional Controller of fuel and power.

In 1957 Cadbury received a knighthood for his public services, which covered a great number of organisations, mostly in the Bristol area where he lived at Abbots Leigh. His many posts included treasurer of the Bristol Royal Infirmary, as well as chairman of the Boys' Clubs, the local

Fregattenkapitän Peter Strasser, Leader of Airships: born 1 April 1876, killed in action 5 August 1918.
Archiv: Marine-Luftschiffer-Kameradschaft

gliding school and the Bristol wing of the Air Training Corps. The Cadburys had two sons, Patrick, who was tragically killed in a flying accident during 1941, and Peter, who at the age of 15 was taught to fly by his father. Today Peter Cadbury, one time chairman of Westward Television, still flies his own aeroplanes and helicopters. His famous father, who played a particularly outstanding role in the defeat of the Zeppelin menace, ended an active working career in 1962 when he retired as vice-chairman of the Cadbury chocolate empire, a post which he had held for four years. In 1967, on 12 January, Sir Egbert Cadbury died peacefully at his Bristol home.

'Bob' Leckie continued to serve with distinction up to the Armistice, after which he was assigned to command 1 Canadian Wing of the RAF on 2 April 1919. That same year he returned to Canada, assuming a civilian post as director of flying operations for the Air Board, in which he played a vital role developing Canadian civil aviation, participating in the first trans-Canada flight. The year 1919 also saw Leckie accepting a permanent commission in the RAF as a wing commander seconded to the Canadian Air Board, and in 1922 he returned to England to serve at the Naval Staff College and Coastal Command headquarters. Later, Leckie married Bernice, an American girl whom he had met on board ship. There were two sons, Robert and John, the former (and elder) being christened in a font made from a ship's bell from HMS *Courageous*. Leckie had served on board this aircraft carrier between 1927 and 1929 as commander of its squadrons, having already undertaken the same role on HMS *Hermes* between 1925 and 1927.

Back in England during 1929, Leckie took over command of a bomber station at Bircham Newton, then in 1931 of the Marine Aircraft Experimental Establishment at Felixstowe, and that same year he returned to his first love, commanding a flying boat squadron, 210, at Pembroke Dock. Between 1933 and 1935 he commanded the RAF station at Hendon, and on leaving this post he was made Superintendent RAF Reserve and in charge of Elementary

Egbert in later years. He was knighted in 1957 for his public services and retired as vice-chairman of the Cadbury chocolate empire five years later.
Peter Cadbury

The birthplace of the Royal Canadian Air Force: the station at Rockcliffe, circa 1920. This DH9A belongs to the Air Board and at the extreme left (in the 'boater') is Bob Leckie.
Royal Canadian Forces Photo RE 12606

Zeppelin!

Civil Flying schools, responsible for training many airmen later to fight in the Battle of Britain. During 1938 and 1939 Leckie was commanding the RAF in the Mediterranean with his headquarters in Malta, later regretting having missed all the action which subsequently took place there, for in 1940 he was back in Canada. It was during February that he returned to his uncle's homeland as senior ranking officer of an RAF party comprising some 271 officers and men selected to co-operate with Canadians in establishing flying schools.

Leckie was made a Member of the Air Council for training on 8 November 1940 and promoted to the rank of Air Vice-Marshal in the following year. Then in 1942 he transferred to the RCAF, and in 1944, when Air Marshal L S Breadner CB DSC went to England as Air Officer, Commander-in-Chief of the RCAF overseas, Air Marshal Leckie took over as Chief of the Air Staff on 1 January. Leckie retained this office until 1 September 1947 when he retired, but he continued to serve as special consultant to the Air Cadet League. On 1 April 1975 Robert Leckie died in the Canadian Forces Hospital, Ottawa, at the age of 84.

'Bob' Leckie in later years a an Air Marshal, a rank he attained on 1 January 1944, taking over as Chief of the Air Staff of the Royal Canadian Air Force.
Canadian Forces Photo PL117672

CHAPTER 17

L53, 11 August 1918

> '... If on days when the weather conditions are good, a Destroyer could tow a Lighter with a Camel aboard, arriving at the South Doggerbank Light Vessel at dawn, and remain cruising in the vicinity, sending up the Camel when the Zeppelin was sighted, it is certain that the Zeppelin will not see the Camel until the Zeppelin has got within 10 miles of the Destroyer...'
>
> *Colonel Charles Rumney Samson, 2 August 1918*[1]

Early morning, 11 August 1918. The British destroyer HMS *Redoubt* was steaming with four light cruisers and 12 destroyers of the Harwich Light Cruiser Force on special operations in the Heligoland Bight. Behind her, *Redoubt* towed a large floating platform which bore a Sopwith 2F1 Camel fighter manned by a determined 22-year-old RAF Lieutenant. At 08.30hrs, alert lookouts observed a sole patrolling Zeppelin and the Camel pilot, making a successful take-off, climbed away to engage the enemy. Eventually he closed with his quarry and emptied two full drums of incendiary bullets into the black-doped airship. The bullets found their mark, the Zeppelin burst into flames and disappeared into the sea well before the victorious pilot had ditched his aeroplane and been safely hoisted back aboard *Redoubt*. It was only then that Rear Admiral R Y Tyrwhitt from the flagship *Curacoa* sent a unique signal: 'Flag – general – Your attention is called to hymn number 224, verse 7'. Uncomprehending, mystified sailors flicked through their hymn books and, on finding the quoted passage, read it and understood.

Camels at Sea

Stuart Douglas Culley was born in Omaha, Nebraska, on 23 August 1895, the son of an English father and a Canadian-born mother. From an early age Culley considered himself an Englishman and not 'in any way American or Canadian' – with good reason, since his mother was the daughter of a famous Yorkshireman. Robert Stother had emigrated to Canada during the 1860s and became, amongst other things, the most famous salmon fisher in the Maritime Provinces before moving to Quebec. It was there that the young Culley spent his annual summer holidays from 1906 onwards until he contracted typhoid and was taken to Santa Monica, California, where the climate was considered more favourable. During 1910 and 1911 the Culleys resided in Vancouver, but 1913 saw them living in England up to the outbreak of war, when they sailed back to Canada, setting up home in Montreal.

Young Culley's first real job was as a government munitions inspector, a post which he held for several years before deciding to enter military service. Recruiting for the RNAS was very strong in Canada, and after six months on a waiting list of 250, Culley and 49 other hopefuls were finally accepted as candidates on 10 March 1917. Joining the RNAS as Probationary Flying Officers, the new intake were to be the last sent to England for preliminary training, subsequent applicants joining RFC and RNAS schools in both Canada and the USA which had just entered the war. On 3 May, Culley and his fellow-officers sailed from Halifax on the troopship SS *Metagama*, Liverpool-bound. Subsequently spending a week in London where uniforms and kit were acquired, the latest RNAS recruits eventually reported to Manston on May 21, joining the training school under Squadron Commander R Hilton Jones. Culley soloed on 25 May and then reported to Cranwell for further training and examinations. He went on to 'intense scout flying' next. This was mostly on Sopwith Pups, practising 'deck flying' from large wooden platforms laid out on the aerodrome, and by 12 September Culley had been appointed to the rank of Flight Sub-Lieutenant.

In December there came a posting to Calshot for a seaplane and flying boat course, it being felt advantageous that fleet pilots become accustomed to handling such aircraft. January 1918 saw Culley completing his training at Calshot and joining HMS *Nairana*, a ship originally laid down as a passenger steamer but completed as a makeshift aircraft carrier. Culley continued his deck-flying training from that ship, and after a month joined the crew of HMS *Cassandra* in the 6th Light Cruiser Squadron of the Grand Fleet.

Cassandra boasted one aeroplane, an example of the disappointing Beardmore SB3D, a development of the Sopwith Pup complete with folding wings and flotation bags. There was no flying-off platform on *Cassandra*'s forecastle; instead, the aircraft was launched in the same manner as practised by Culley at Cranwell:

> Aircraft were flown from this deck by means of a quick-release gear which consisted of a trestle to hold the tail in flying position, on top of the trestle there being a groove to guide the tail skid. The pilot opened the engine of the aircraft full out and pulled a toggle in the cockpit which operated an ordinary bomb release anchored to the deck at one end and engaged with a cable attached to the aircraft. The aircraft, on being released, accelerated quickly and left the deck with a shorter run than with the normal method of taking off.[1]

During the two months that Culley was aboard *Cassandra*

Zeppelin!

A series of photographs that illustrates the first attempt to fly a Sopwith Camel off a lighter towed by a destroyer. The date: 30 May 1918; the aircraft: 2F1 Camel N6623; the pilot: Colonel Charles Rumney Samson. Here the aircraft is seen on its lighter at the jetty at Felixstowe. Samson eschewed wheels in lieu of skids in troughs which (he attested) would give him a straight run.
Sir Egbert Cadbury

Truculent clears Harwich with lighter *H3* in tow. With his back to the cameraman is Egbert Cadbury talking to Samson, who is facing the Camel on the port side of the lighter.
Sir Egbert Cadbury

Samson just about to take off. The trestle has gone, and the smoke from the destroyer shows *Truculent* steaming out of wind. Cadbury and the crew of the lighter could not get the Camel's tail into the correct flying attitude until Cadbury lifted the rear of the aircraft with his feet!
Sir Egbert Cadbury

218

L53, 11 August 1918

N6623 aboard the lighter with its tail supported by the trestle, the premature jettisoning of which caused problems for the pilot when he prepared to take off.
Sir Egbert Cadbury

Disaster! The Camel veers to port and, without sufficient flying speed and with the ship not dead into the wind, pitches straight into the water. Samson emerged unscathed and was later persuaded by Cadbury to let one of his men make the next attempt with a modified lighter and in an aircraft fitted with wheels.
Sir Egbert Cadbury

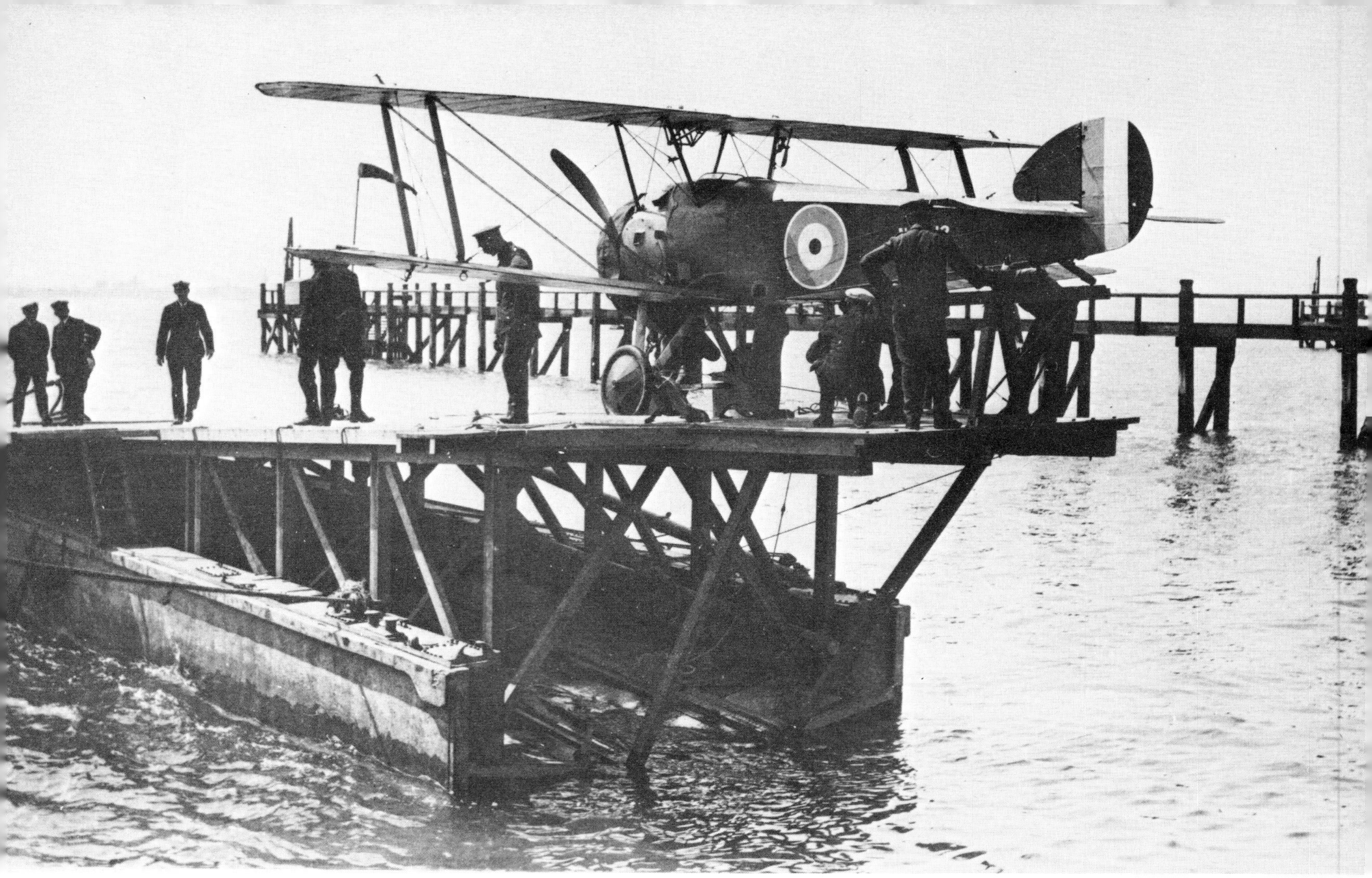

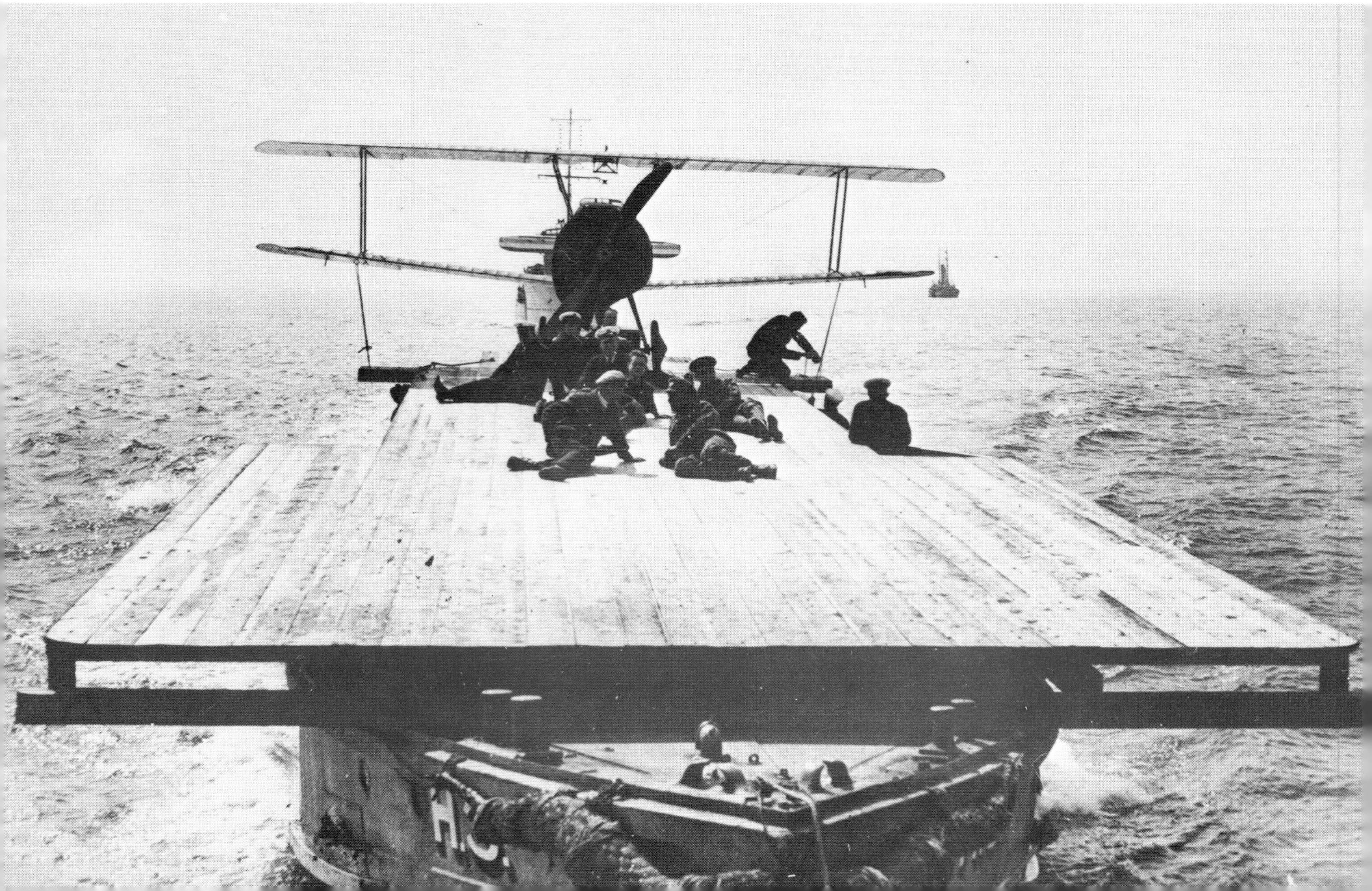

On 31 July 1918 a second attempt was made to fly off a modified lighter. Here Sopwith 2F1 Camel N6812 is seen at Felixstowe, being prepared for transfer to the floating take-off platform. *PRO Air 1/643*

The lighter *H3* towed by HMS *Truculent* for the second, and successful, attempt to take off from a floating platform. The pilot was Culley, who can be seen bare-headed amidst the group of officers. Camel N6812 was unarmed for the attempt. *PRO Air 1/643*

L53, the last airship to be destroyed by British forces, was built at Friedrichshafen, made its first flight on 18 August 1917, and was commissioned into service three days later. *L53* undertook four raids and made a total of 19 scouting flights before Culley brought its career to a fiery end. *Luftschiffbau Zeppelin*

he only once obtained permission to fly the Beardmore off. As a result he found himself becoming 'gradually less qualified as a pilot and more qualified as a Naval Officer',[2] required to act as Officer of the Watch and assisting the Navigating Officer as the situation demanded. On 25 March Culley was sent to Great Yarmouth, detailed to fly Sopwith 2F1 Camels defending flying boats and seaplanes engaged upon anti-submarine patrols. Constantly harassed by Hansa Brandenburg seaplanes of superior performance, the pilots of the slower aircraft welcomed their Camel escorts, which, however, were seldom used in anger: their very presence was deterrent enough.

For several months the large flying boats operating out of Felixstowe had been transported into enemy waters by lighters, special floating platforms towed by destroyers. Thus could the aircraft enjoy a great radius of action by not having to consume the greater part of their fuel flying to the centre of operations. Sound though the idea was, the slow-climbing boats with their ceiling of 11–12,000ft were failing to engage the scouting Zeppelins that patrolled the Heligoland Bight. Obviously an alternative had to be sought.

The man with the answer was the irrepressible Samson, then commander of No 4 Group, South East Area, and stationed at Felixstowe. Samson, whose war record had already made him a legend in the service, proposed that the lighters be modified to carry a Sopwith Camel fighter and, confident the scheme was sound, he elected to try the first experiment personally. On 30 May 1918 HMTBD *Truculent* could be found steaming off Orfordness towing a lighter bearing Sopwith 2F1 Camel N6623, Samson and several other RAF officers, including Egbert Cadbury:

> In spite of advice from those concerned, Samson would insist on fitting skids instead of wheels to the undercarriage of the Camel. These skids fitted into grooves which ran along the whole length of the lighter on a specially rigged-up stage. Samson's idea with regard to the skids was to keep the machine straight and prevent it toppling over the side of the lighter before it gained sufficient flying speed.[3]

At 32 knots Samson took off, and as Cadbury and other officers had predicted, the Camel's skids jumped from the grooves and the aircraft pitched over the bows of the lighter. Before the horrified gaze of Lieutenant-Colonel E D M Robertson, Commanding Officer of the Felixstowe Air Station, Cadbury and the crew of *Truculent*, the lighter ran over the Camel, the remains of which bobbed up 300yds astern. Cadbury could not believe that Samson might survive the tragedy, yet survive he did:

> Suddenly up bobbed a little white flying cap, and all heaved a sigh of relief. An escorting destroyer had got a whaler away in about 30 seconds and picked him up. He was unhurt, but had had a nasty time under the water disentangling himself from the wires of the wreck. The first thing he said as he ran nimbly up the side of the destroyer was, 'Well! Robertson, I think it well worth trying again...'[4]

There were several reasons why the experiment failed. *Truculent* was steaming slightly out of wind because her captain was forced to alter course to avoid sandbanks, thus taking longer to work up to the desired 35kts. Cadbury would later record another problem, that of getting the Camel's tail up into flying position after the support trestle had been jettisoned. Cadbury had to crawl along the staging to lay flat on his back and with his feet push the Camel's tail into the correct attitude:

> I think one of the reasons why Samson could not get the tail of his machine up was the fact that the lighter was not sufficiently far astern of the destroyer and he was, therefore, in a certain amount of down draught... Samson had the heart of a lion but was not by our standards a very good pilot though he had done a tremendous amount of flying, and I had implored him that either I or someone else should be allowed to make this experiment but he was quite adamant that he and he alone, would carry it out.[5]

It was also discovered that the lighter rode decidedly stern-down when the destroyer was at speed, and when the lighter was fitted with its 30ft flying-off deck it was arranged to slope towards the bows thus giving a horizontal platform under tow. Following the 'inquest' with his fellow officers on board *Truculent*, Samson at last listened to reason: he agreed that the lighter should be boarded over and that another pilot flying a Camel with a conventional undercarriage make the second attempt. It was Culley who volunteered, his previous experience of 'deck flying' making him an obvious candidate for the task.

On 31 July *Truculent* was again at sea towing the standard 56ft lighter with its newly designed deck. The rear half of the new platform was just over 13ft wide, the forward half 21ft, thus allowing for any 'accidental swerve' of the aeroplane. Camel N6812 was secured in flying attitude by chocks that held the machine's axle. Fitted to the tailskid was a ball to run in a slotted tube supported on the trestle, giving slight negative attitude and preventing premature rising of the aeroplane whilst stationary under tow. The Camel was held in the chocks and tail guide by a 'wire span' on the axle, gripped by a quick-release clip to a horizontal cable attached to the aft deck, the clip to be released by Culley via a trip line. In order to prevent the engineer rating who swung the airscrew from being thrown into it, a safety belt secured by a length of cable to the deck was installed. Stowed beneath the platform was a portable derrick capable of recovering the Camel from the sea and back on to the deck.

Zeppelin!

Truculent, escorted by her sister-ship *Thisbe*, left Felixstowe harbour at 14.00hrs and worked up to 28kts; off Orfordness the course shifted to bring the vessel and its lighter directly into wind. Culley boarded the Camel, the engine was started and the aircraft was warmed up for two minutes. Then, with the throttle flat out, the Camel was 'slipped', running about 36ft before it rose. The tail dropped some 2ft as the skid cleared its guide tube and the aircraft slewed to port, Culley immediately correcting the swing to climb safely away, subsequently flying shorewards and touching down at Martlesham Heath. The practicability of the scheme had been proven dramatically, and it only remained for it to be used operationally, an opportunity that was not long in coming.

Combined Operations

The Harwich Light Cruiser Force had been continually hampered in its operations by shadowing Zeppelins which, at their 20,000ft altitude, were safe from anti-aircraft fire and the flying boats with their limited ceiling. When the Force next put to sea on the evening of 10 August, Culley and his Camel went with it. Three destroyers towed lighters carrying flying boats, and HMS *Redoubt* towed Culley, his Camel now armed with two Lewis machine guns fixed to a special mounting above the upper wing. In support, three or more Curtiss H12 flying boats flew from Great Yarmouth to accompany the fleet, these under the command of the redoubtable Major Robert Leckie.

The cruisers each carried two coastal motor boats, the idea being to lower these into the sea when they were within striking distance, whereupon they would enter the Bight to torpedo any enemy ships they encountered. It was 05.30hrs when the cruisers arrived off Terschelling, and an hour passed before the CMBs were 'slipped' and in a moderate sea made their way to the mouth of the River Ems. Meanwhile the Curtiss boats were being floated off their lighters, but owing to a long, smooth swell, a lack of wind and an increased load of fuel and ammunition, they were unable to take off and had to return to the floating platforms. Four German seaplanes appeared as the CMBs started off and shadowed the Force for a while, but they had gone by the time Major Leckie and his Curtiss boats arrived. Leckie was immediately ordered to locate the six CMBs, which were slow in returning to the British ships. This was Leckie's first surprise, for he had no indication that CMBs were to be used on the operation. Flying towards Terschelling, one of his consorts sighted a Zeppelin way above them and commenced sending a visual message to the commander. Barely had he received the start of the signal when he too spotted the airship hovering at around 15,000ft to the north-east.

Leckie made a rapid assessment of the situation. The flying boats could not possibly reach and engage the Zeppelin, and knowing Culley and his Camel to be with the Fleet he returned, sending a visual signal that an airship was in the area. Leckie received an acknowledgement: the Camel was to be launched, and then came the second surprise, a signal ordering him to return to base. Leckie was mystified, but nevertheless obeyed, and it later transpired the order had been despatched in error.

L53 – for that was the Zeppelin – had been sighted at 08.30hrs, and in turn the Harwich Force had been spotted by a flotilla of German torpedo-boats, which were quick to alert their seaplane stations in the Bight. Thus was the stage set for a battle royal. Rear Admiral Tyrwhitt ordered his ships out to sea, a deliberate attempt to draw the Zeppelin away from the coast and, ultimately, the range of protective seaplanes. Smoke screens completed the illusion.

The commander of *L53*, *Korvettenkäpitan der Reserve* Eduard Prölss, who as one of Strasser's most senior officers had spent 19 years in the Navy, enlisting on 1 October 1889. A reservist, Prölss had previously been employed as the fire chief of the city of Magdeburg; thus, unlike most of the reserve naval men, he was not a merchant marine officer, and initially was less familiar with the sea than were his colleagues. He was commissioned into the rank of *Korvettenkapitän* on 14 October 1917, almost two months after assuming command of *L53*.
Archiv: Marine-Luftschiffer-Kameradschaft

Commanding *L53* was Eduard Prölss, who had previously participated on at least two raids over England in this ship. Prölss, born in Brandenburg on 10 February 1867, had been a reserve officer since 1889 and unlike most of his fellow officers was not a professional seafarer; in the years before the war he had been the Chief of the Fire Department in the city of Magdeburg. Now Prölss was shadowing the Harwich Force for the second time in his career. On 19 August 1916, during the abortive 'Sunderland Operation', scouting for Admiral Scheer who planned to shell that town, Prölss in *L13* had come under heavy fire from Tyrwhitt's ships. The 50-year-old commander and his crew had been fortunate to escape destruction that time, the luck of Mathy's *L13* holding yet again.

Culley took off safely from *Redoubt*'s lighter (No *H5*) at 08.58hrs, only running 5ft before the 30kt speed of the destroyer gave sufficient headwind for the Camel to be borne aloft. Immediately climbing towards the airship, Culley took care to keep the low sun behind him, thus hoping to avoid detection until the last moment. Just over half an hour later the Camel was at 18,000ft, with *L53* another 1000ft beyond. The gap was closing – but slowly. A further 28 minutes, and Culley was 200ft below *L53*, but he had reached the Camel's operational ceiling and the aircraft became difficult to control, its propeller mushing in the thin air. There was only one way that he was going to get his guns to bear; pulling the control column into the pit of his stomach, the Camel almost at the brink of a stall, he let fly.

The port Lewis gun fired just seven rounds before it jammed, but the other continued to operate until the double drum had emptied. All the while Culley was firing he could see the incendiary bullets striking the black flanks of the airship, which showed no sign of igniting. Falling out of the stall he glanced back over his shoulder in time to see flickers of flame dancing along the hull of the Zeppelin. A few seconds later came the explosion.

In a matter of minutes *L53* was ablaze and sinking slowly seawards, bow first. Bombs and gondolas, then the bow itself, broke away; standing on end, the remains of the doomed Zeppelin plunged down, blazing furiously. The gaunt, scorched framework had been stripped of all its covering well before it struck the water and sank, a patch of oil and a greasy column of smoke the only tangible evidence of the Zeppelin's existence. Although well over three miles above the sea when the ship was set alight, several crewmen had jumped from the gondolas. Culley himself was amazed to see a man, his clothes ablaze, deliberately leap from the wreck.[6] He did not survive the long fall, nor did any of the 20-man crew, the last airship men to be killed by aerial action in World War I.

Culley's subsequent report of the action was typically brief:

08.58 hours, flew from lighter to attack Zeppelin from 300 feet below. Fired seven rounds from No 1 gun which jammed and a double charge from No 2. Zeppelin burst into flames and was destroyed.[7]

After seeing what was left of *L53* disappear, Culley flew towards the Dutch coast, turning south, then to the pre-arranged 'rendezvous point' over Terschelling. He became concerned when at 6000ft, amongst cloud, he was unable to locate the Force. At that juncture his pressure tank ran dry

L53 at Friedrichshafen in August 1917, with its forward upper gun platform barely visible. The stippled demarcation line of the black camouflage dope is noteworthy.
Luftschiffbau Zeppelin

Zeppelin!

L53 being walked into the building shed at Friedrichshafen in 1917; the naval ensign hangs from the stern post. *L53* initiated a major change in Zeppelin hull structure with its nine largest frames spaced 15m, rather than 10m, apart. The airship's useful lift was 89,523lb (62.7 per cent of the total) and it attained 20,700ft on its maiden raid. Not surprisingly *L53* and its sister craft of the 'v' class remained the standard type over the North Sea for almost a year.
Luftschiffbau Zeppelin

and he switched immediately to the gravity tank, the contents of which would be sufficient to keep him airborne for less than half an hour; reaching the coast now was out of the question.

Flying lower, Culley spotted a Dutch fishing boat and was preparing to ditch alongside when at last he saw two British destroyers and then the rest of the Fleet. His relief can best be imagined, and he reportedly indulged in a few mild aerobatics before picking out *Redoubt* and setting the Camel down near her bows:

In landing the aircraft was very little damaged as my fuel was completely used up and it sat on the water at almost no forward movement. It was hoisted out of the water by a special jig very quickly. Only one bottom plane was somewhat damaged.[8]

It was only when he knew that Culley was safely back aboard *Redoubt* that Rear Admiral Tyrwhitt sent that famous signal. And hymn number 244, verse 7? It read:

> Oh happy band of pilgrims,
> Look upward to the skies,
> Where such a light affliction,
> Shall win so great a prize.

Indeed, so delighted was the Admiral at the destruction of

Sopwith 2F1 Camel N6812 at Felixstowe, 1918. The Beardmore-built machine is seen in the configuration it adopted when Culley attacked *L53*. The offset Vickers gun has been removed from the forward fuselage and twin Lewis guns are mounted over the upper wing instead of the standard single fitting. Underneath the axle can be seen the 'wire span' with its quick-release clip which, hooked to a horizontal cable attached to the lighter, held the aircraft on its chocks and in its tail guide. The latter took the form of a slotted tube mounted on a trestle, a ball being attached to the tail skid (another feature readily apparent in this photograph).
IWM Q69932

224

Lieutenant Stuart Douglas Culley, in naval uniform, photographed at Felixstowe in 1919. Behind the group is a Sopwith 2F1 Camel fitted with twin Vickers guns – an untypical installation as the majority of 2F1 variants carried a single offset Vickers and a single Lewis mounted above the upper wing.
IWM Q69934

L53 that Culley was persuaded to stand atop one of *Redoubt*'s gun turrets while the rest of the Force sailed by, the ship's officers and men cheering the young pilot to the hilt. Yet there remains a less satisfactory sequel to Culley's success that deserves to be recorded.

The six coastal motor boats that had set out with good intentions prior to Culley's historic flight were later attacked by ten German Hansa Brandenburg seaplanes out from their Borkum and Norderney bases. With the loss of only two aircraft the Germans were to mete out heavy punishment to the British sailors. At 08.40hrs all the boats were just outside Dutch territorial waters, two vessels having broken down, their guns out of action. After destroying these boats, the crews took to the water, striking out for shore, but before reaching it they were picked up by Dutch torpedo-boat destroyers.

> Number 47 was on fire with two of crew badly wounded, so steamed within half mile of shore and was then blown up. Captain swam ashore and crew were rescued by Dutch sailors who swam out from shore. Number 41 steamed ashore but crew were prevented from destroying their boat by Dutch authorities who fired on them.[9]

If this were not enough, a solitary German seaplane machine-gunned boat 41 for over 15 minutes after it had been beached. Boat 48 was disabled, its smoke tank punctured, and, abandoning ship, the crew were taken aboard boat 44, which soon had its own engine shot up by the German seaplanes. Drifting inside territorial waters, the CMB was approached by Dutch destroyers, the English captain requesting permission to destroy the boat before boarding the Dutch vessel. His request was refused; instead, the neutral captain took possession of boat 44 and the drifting 48, towing them both to port, the British and their boats, to face internment.

The successful German seaplane crews later observed the end of *L53* and also two British flying boats in the distance before returning to their bases. The coastal motor boat operation was a complete failure, for not one German ship had been torpedoed from the time the six CMBs left the Harwich Force until the time the German aircraft pounced. Only later did it transpire that during the planning of the whole operation the Great Yarmouth pilots were convinced that sending the boats unescorted into the Bight could only end one way – complete destruction by enemy airmen. Events were to show how right their fears had been. It was a pity that their warnings went unheeded; the matter only served to show the continued lack of really close co-operation between the higher échelons of England's oldest and youngest forces.

Later, Tyrwhitt put Culley's name forward for a Victoria Cross, and received the official reply to that recommendation from the Director of the Air Division:

> The report of the operations has not been seen in this Division. If you concur that the action of Lieutenant Culley on this occasion is worthy of the award of the Victoria Cross, the matter will be referred to the Air Ministry for consideration. In a former similar case, however, Flt Sub-Lt B A Smart who flew off the forecastle of HMS *Yarmouth* and destroyed a Zeppelin was awarded the DSO.[10]

And it was the DSO that was awarded to Stuart Douglas Culley on 2 November, for a 'most difficult undertaking'. Culley continued to serve with distinction in the RAF until the Armistice, and in March 1919 was posted to Leuchars, then to Finland, joining HMS *Vindictive*, operating with the Baltic Fleet under Rear Admiral Sir Walter Cowan. Mentioned in Despatches on 31 March 1920 for his Baltic service, Culley went on to serve in 6 and in 14 Squadrons – both overseas – and returned to England in 1924. Serving in various capacities before World War II, he became the Senior Air Staff Officer of the RAF headquarters in Palestine on 3 September 1940 and, rising to the rank of Wing Commander, retired from the service on 9 December 1945, retaining the rank of Group Captain. In his later years he lived in Italy with his wife Marguerite and it was at Villa

Stuart Douglas Culley as a
Wing Commander during
World War II
Mrs S D Culley

Culley's famous Camel, as
displayed in the Imperial
War Museum at Lambeth,
London. A repaint after
World War Two destroyed
the original finish and
structural alterations were
also made which further
altered its appearance.
R Cranham

Stuart in Salo, Lago di Garda, that Stuart Douglas Culley passed away peacefully on 10 June 1975 at the age of 80.

Today the Sopwith Camel Culley flew to destroy *L53* is preserved in the Imperial War Museum as one of its most historic and highly coveted exhibits. N6812 was initially stored, together with various other machines, at the RAF South East Area Equipment and Personal Department, Chingford Aerodrome, on 24 July 1919, and during October it was moved to the IWM, then at Crystal Palace. During the latter stages of World War II the aircraft was in storage at Cardington, and before being returned for exhibition was 'restored' by the RAF who saw fit to bring the naval Camel to F1 configuration. The original fabric was replaced, the airframe recovered, markings incorrectly re-applied and the steel centre-section struts, peculiar to the 2F1 version, replaced with wooden ones. Visitors to the museum today should also be aware that Culley's Camel originally bore pale blue doped undersurfaces and not the clear fabric finish it now presents. This timeless relic of the Great War stands as a mute and fitting tribute to the men of the RFC, RNAS and RAF who strove to defeat the airship menace, for *L53* was the last Zeppelin to be destroyed in combat in World War I, and brought the curtain down on a never-to-be-repeated battle campaign.

Per Ardua Ad Astra

CHAPTER 18

Zeppelin Swansong

'...Considering what these airships faced on every one of their later raids – what their commanders and crews must have known were the odds against them after the night when the destruction of the first Zeppelin [sic] over Cuffley in September, 1916, proved that the British had effectually solved the problem of igniting the hydrogen of the inner ballonettes – one cannot but conclude that the morale of the whole personnel must have been very high...'

Lewis Freeman, 1919

Korvettenkäpitan Paul Werther, former head of the ground troop and airship schools at Nordholz, was appointed Leader of Airships following Strasser's death, yet there was little opportunity for Werther to emulate his predecessor's achievements, for the recent airship losses and the advent of large, long-range Dornier flying boats persuaded the Navy to restrict severely scouting and reconnaissance patrols.[1] With reservations, raids on England could still be mounted, and efforts to improve airship performance were encouraged by an Admiralty conference on 7 September 1918. However, further proposals to lengthen existing ships or to build the 3,813,480 cu ft *L100* went unrealised. As World War I drew to its close, an acute shortage of materials and men, changes of policy, and a downgrading of the airship's role resulted in the cancellation of the new airships. Sheds were to be dismantled, and flights restricted: for the German Naval Airship Division, future prospects were anything but bright.

Scapa Flow – Airship Style

On 28 October, sailors of the German High Seas Fleet mutinied and the blight quickly spread. Soldiers' and Sailors' Councils assumed control throughout Germany, and at Nordholz Werther's ground troop took over the base in a bloodless *coup*. Other stations fell to the Soldiers' Soviet, officers were arrested, detained and later packed off home, Zeppelins were hung up in their sheds and their gas cells drained, and looting was rife. Airship bases became prime targets for pillaging by the naval revolutionaries, vast quantities of petrol, oil and Maybach powerplants, along with parachutes and boxes of spare parts, gradually finding their way to Sweden in exchange for millions of marks.

In December, the *Colossus* class battleship HMS *Hercules* took an inter-allied commission to Kiel and other German naval bases in order that the victors could ensure that Armistice disarmament terms were being respected. Between 7 and 10 December, E A D Masterman led a party of mixed journalists on a tour of the airship bases.[2] Amongst the group was one Lieutenant Lewis Freeman RNVR:

> The inspection of an airship to see if it had been properly disarmed according to the provisions of the Armistice was, as may be imagined, rather more of a job than a similar inspection of even a 'giant' seaplane. In a Zeppelin that is more or less the same size as the *Mauretania* the distances are magnificent, and while most of the inspection was confined to the cars, that of the wireless, with a search for possible concealed machine gun mountings, involved not a little climbing and clambering. One's first sight of a deflated [ship] – in an inflated one the bulging ballonettes obstruct the view considerably – is quite as impressive in its way as the premier survey of it from the outside. No 'tween decks prospect in the largest ship afloat, cut down as it is by bulkheads, offers a fifth of the unbroken sweep of vision that one finds opened before him as he climbs up inside the tail of a modern airship.[3]

On 21 June 1919 the German Navy infuriated the Allies by scuttling its fleet of surrendered warships at Scapa Flow in the southern Orkneys. The fleet consisted of ten battleships, six battlecruisers, eight light cruisers and 50 destroyers, all under the command of Rear Admiral von Reuter, upon whose orders the ships were sunk. All the capital ships went to the bottom with the exception of the battleship *Baden*. Five light cruisers went down, the remainder being beached, along with 18 destroyers; of the latter, four remained afloat but the rest were successfully sunk. It was the only gesture left to the defeated fleet, and airship men still loyal to the old regime were not slow to emulate their comrades' actions.[4]

Two days after Scapa Flow, von Buttlar and other 'loyalists' pulled away the timber shores supporting the hulls of the deflated Zeppelins and loosened suspension tackles with irreversible results. Like a group of beached whales, *L14*, *L41*, *L42*, *L63* and *L65* lay smashed on the floors of their Nordholz sheds, at Wittmundhaven a similar scene was enacted, and *L52* and *L56* were completely wrecked.[5]

At Ahlhorn, the Sailors' Soviet discovered the plot and was able to prevent the destruction of *L64* and *L71*. The reluctant saboteurs were sworn to secrecy and claimed that their actions were not so much to deny their precious airships to the Allies, rather to prevent them from 'falling into the hands of those damned Communists in Berlin!'[6]

Not surprisingly, the Inter-Allied Commission took a dim view of these events and quickly outlined reprisals. The remaining 'Front' ships, *L61*, *L64* and *L71*, were to be

Zeppelin!

'The Scapa Flow of the German Airships': *Kapitänleutnant* Gerhold Ratz's *L63* and *L42* (latterly in use as an advanced training ship), lie wrecked at Nordholz on 23 June 1919 having been sabotaged by loyalists.
F Moch

Nordholz in the summer of 1918 as it would have appeared when the inter-allied commission paid its visit after the war. The giant *Nogat* and *Nordstern* sheds are in the foreground, the small *Nora* and *Norbert* sheds in right distance, and the large *Normann* shed in the middle distance, with the revolving shed *Nobel* seen at far left, end-on.
Archiv: Marine-Luftschiffer-Kameradschaft

surrendered immediately, together with the obsolete *L30*, *L37*, *LZ113* and *LZ120* and, despite protests, the newly completed *L72*, which, the Germans argued, was the private property of the Zeppelin Company. This made no impression whatsoever, and the vessel was seized along with the small commercial airships *Bodensee* and *Nordstern*. If this were not bad enough, the Allies ordered the factory at Friedrichshafen to be completely demolished; clearly they were determined to abide by Article 202 of the Versailles Treaty and destroy Germany's airship industry once and for all.

To France went *L72*, *LZ113* and *Nordstern*; to Italy, *L61*, *LZ120* and *Bodensee*; and to the Belgians *L30* which, because the new owners had nowhere to put it, was broken up at Seerappen.[7] The same fate befell *L37*, which went to the Japanese, whilst *SL22* was dismantled at Jüterbog, portions of its wooden structure being distributed to the Allies. Yet the airships themselves were not enough; the victorious powers wanted sheds as well. Jüterbog's double hangar was taken down, later to reappear at Kasumigaura in Japan, whilst German contractors were ordered to destroy many other sheds. Even so the Germans had the last laugh, for the Allies were to enjoy scant success with their valuable prizes. Britain's share of the spoils included *L64* and *L71*, both these airships arriving at Pulham airship station on 21 July and 1 July 1920 respectively. One of the many officers who witnessed the arrival of the latter, under the command of former *Delag* Captain Anton Heinen, was Gerard Fane:

...I don't think I ever saw such an exhibition of airmanship and complete control as the crew of the ship gave. I was simply astounded at the way the Commander brought the ship to the hangar screens; he had his hands on the telegraphs to the various parts of the ship and his head out of the window, and he manoeuvred the ship practically into the shed before he dropped a single landing rope.[8]

And therein lay the problem. Designed for bombing at great altitudes, the lightly built 'Height-Climbers' could only be handled by experienced crews and commanders like Anton Heinen. Even had German airship men been prepared to pass on their hard-won experience to their former enemies (which they were not), after two years the airships had deteriorated badly, gas cells in particular suffering the ravages of time and neglect. Thus by the end of 1921 most of the surrendered Zeppelins had been scrapped, having spent their remaining days in hangars; rarely were they flown.[9]

With the benefit of hindsight, it can be said, with some conviction, that as strategic bombers the airships were a dismal failure. In 51 raids on England just over 196 tons of bombs were dropped. They killed 557 people and injured 1358 more, and the total material damaged amounted to £1,527,585, which would have paid for nine Zeppelins of the 'Height-Climber' class; it is worth noting that the Germans lost a total of 17 airships and their crews; in addition *L7* and *L48* were destroyed with great loss of life.[10] The year 1915

Torn down in 1968 along with Strasser's HQ building, the former radio station at Nordholz was still standing, albeit abandoned, in 1964.
D H Robinson

The officers' *Kasino* at Nordholz, as it appeared in 1964. The officer is *Kapitänleutnant* Steindorf of *Marinefliegergeschwader* 3 'Graf Zeppelin', a NATO unit flying Breguet Atlantics from the former airship station.
D H Robinson

was the most effective for the raiders; 1916 saw the improved defences getting the measure of the airships, forcing new designs to operate at higher altitudes for the remainder of the war; and the sporadic raids of 1917–18 only really served to tie down British defences. The last, while a justifiable situation, nevertheless had little overall effect on the war in the long-term scheme of things. If the many defence units, their men and machines had not been required and fought overseas, the war just possibly might have ended a few months earlier.

Towards mid-1918 there were 15 home defence squadrons based in England with 166 aircraft on strength. Bristol Fighters, SE5as and Sopwith Camels flew with success against the Gotha and 'Giant' Staaken bombing aeroplanes that took over the Zeppelins' offensive role in 1917. And here an interesting comparison can be made. German aircraft made a total of 52 raids, they dropped fewer bombs than the airships (2772) yet they killed more (857) and injured more (2058), although the estimated monetary damage was less, the balance hovering around the £9000

Zeppelin!

Following a dedication by the late *Kapitänleutnant* Richard Frey, last commander of *L64*, the Peter Strasser memorial at Nordholz is unveiled during a special ceremony held on 3 August 1968. The propeller in the background is supposed to be from the wreck of *L10* but of course this is not so, although the gear drive probably comes from Wenke's ill-fated ship. The entire assembly was found in the 1960s on a nearby farm, the farmer having fabricated the metal propeller to use the device as a windmill!
D H Robinson

The large farmhouse at Hainault Farm is all that remains of the former home of C Flight, 39 HDS. All traces of the airfield itself have long since vanished.
J R Barfoot

One of the most heavily-patronised restaurants in the area, the 'Leefe Robinson' at Harrow Weald in Middlesex stands at the other side of the Uxbridge Road opposite the small graveyard of All Saints' Church. Perhaps not the most fitting memorial to the VC airman, it is nevertheless in the establishment's contract that flowers be placed regularly on the grave. *Author*

mark. Doubtless Mathy's two most successful attacks on London, which caused £660,787 worth of damage, helped to bump up the airship total.[11]

Yet mere cold statistics made more than six decades later fail to convey the courage and self-sacrifice that was shown by these pioneer aerial combatants over England in 'The Great War'. To fly over enemy territory in slow-moving giants filled with highly volatile gas – literally flying bombs – at the mercy of the elements demanded a rare kind of bravery; to fly underpowered and obsolete biplanes fitted with rudimentary lighting equipment and armed initially with a variety of questionable gadgets demanded another. It was inevitable, of course, that the aeroplane would prove its superiority over the airship, a lead which it has never lost and perhaps never will, although ambitious plans to reintroduce the dirigible for world commerce are currently well in hand.

Today, scant material evidence remains to remind people of World War I's unique aeroplane v airship campaign. Only two aircraft involved with the destruction of airships still exist, no restored Zeppelins are to be found and few museums can offer more than sections of propellers, fragments of duralumin and pieces of fabric and gas cell material.[12] Yet for those interested in seeking it out, tangible evidence of this bygone age can still be found. At Nordholz, for example, there are reminders of its past association with Strasser's Zeppelins. In 1919, when it was visited by the inter-allied commission, the station presented an awe-inspiring spectacle:

> Scarcely less impressive than the immensity of the sheds and the broad conception of the general plan of the station was the solidity of the construction. Everything, from the quarters of the men and the officers to the hangars themselves, seemed built for all time and to play its part in the fulfilment of some far-reaching plan. Costly and scarce as asphalt must have been in Germany, the many miles of roads connecting the various sheds were laid deep with it, and as I had a chance to see where repairs were going on, on a heavy base of concrete. The sheds were steel-framed, concrete-floored, and with pressed asbestos sheet figuring extensively in their sides. All

Zeppelin Swansong

A section of Schütte Lanz plywood girder, a 'temperature-controlled switch' and a control wheel, all relics in the hands of the author and allegedly from *SL11* destroyed over Cuffley. While the remnants in the foreground are thought to be authentic, some doubt still exists over the wheel, which does not conform to usual SL design. The author would welcome confirmation of its origin from any reliable source.
Author

For valour: Robinson's Victoria Cross, bearing the date of the action for which it was awarded. The medal is currently in the family's possession.
Author

The cup that was presented to Robinson at Grey Towers on 14 October 1916 and retained by St Bees School in Cumbria. The school itself is in the background.
St Bees School

the daylight admitted (as we saw presently) filtered through great panes of yellow glass in the roof, shutting out the ultra-violet rays of the sun, which had been found to cause the airships' fabric to deteriorate properly.

The barracks of the men were of brick and concrete, and were built with no less regard for appearance than utility. So, too, the officers' quarters and the Casino [*sic*] and the large and comfortable-looking houses for married officers... All had been recently built, many in the by no means uneffective 'Bew Art' style, to the simple solidity of which the Germans seemed to have turned in reaction from the Gothic. Beyond all doubt, Germany was planning years ahead with Nordholz, both as to war and peace service.[13]

Nordholz today is very different. As part of the West German *Bundesmarine* it is still a naval air station operating the anti-submarine *Marine Geschwader* 3, *Graf Zeppelin*, flying Breguet Atlantics as part of its contribution to NATO. Despite Lieutenant Freeman's belief that the airship base

Even in the 1980s Zeppelins were hitting the headlines. This rope-bound incendiary bomb, thought to be from either *L13* which bombed Lincoln on 28 July 1916 or *L16* which raided the city on 31 July, was found in a garage at Lord Brownlow's Belton House in Grantham on 22 February 1980. The bomb was subsequently defused by Army experts and later placed in a museum.
T Bailey, Foreman Ltd, D460

231

would last forever, there is now little evidence to show that it ever existed. The Allies were thorough. As well as destroying the sheds themselves, German contractors tore up the foundations then filled them in, all traces being obliterated completely. Later, in World War II, the *Luftwaffe* used Nordholz as a fighter station, and after the war the Allies dynamited the runways.

Despite the ravages of war and time a few original buildings still stood at Nordholz as late as 1968. But Strasser's headquarters at the main gate, the radio station building, the three-storey *Kasino* and, along the entrance road, several concrete-built barracks with tiled roofs were then torn down, and now only an assorted number of broken concrete slabs remain to show the outline of the foundations upon which the giant sheds were built. On 3 August 1968 the station was host to a moving and unique anniversary that was attended by a select group of ex-airship men, their families and their associates. They were there to attend the unveiling of a memorial erected to the memory of *Korvettenkäpitan* Peter Strasser who, 50 years earlier almost to the day, was killed in *L70*. The stone and its inscribed bronze tablet, a preserved gear drive from *L10* and a small museum of relics remain as a mute memorial to a lost age.[14]

The old airfield at Suttons Farm has long disappeared under council development, and at the time of writing all that really remains of 39 Home Defence Squadron is the large house at Hainault Farm where some of the pilots were billeted. At Cuffley, just past The Plough on top of the hill, is a memorial built close to the site where *SL11* crashed to earth. In Essex, the fields and surrounding countryside of Little Wigborough and Great Burstead have changed little since *L33* and *L32* fell there, whilst at Theberton, where *L48* crashed, 'Zeppelin Field' is still to be found.

Visitors to Harrow Weald can seek out Robinson's grave. Opposite the tiny cemetery lays the Berni Inn that proudly bears his name, the staff of which regularly place flowers on the airman's final resting place. The restaurant has a wall where snapshots of young pilots jostle with a case of metal fragments, a few of which may originate with *SL11* but more likely come from Mathy's *L31* which wrapped itself around an oak at Potters Bar. And a trip to Staffordshire will reward the visitor with the sight of the four suitably inscribed sarcophagi at the entrance to the Cannock Chase German war graves under which lie the crews of four airships brought down over England.

The Last Airship Raid of All
Midnight, Wednesday 2 August, and the Zeppelin slipped its moorings, rose majestically into the night air and headed for the North Sea. The vessel's commander had orders to patrol off the coast of England but to venture no further than 15 miles from the shore; fighter aircraft could be abroad and caution had to be exercised. Poor weather and low clouds enabled the airship to remain undetected, and during the next morning it cruised unmolested towards Bawdsey, turning north for the Wash.

It was not until 15.00hrs that ground observers finally spotted the airship as it pushed on northwards towards Scapa Flow; coastguards at Collieston, Aberdeenshire, sighted the airship 30 minutes later, and two aircraft from Dyce took off and identified the airship. The huge vessel was last seen at Girdleness and it sailed over Scapa, where several British warships were anchored, before turning back to Germany. But the airship was not one of Strasser's, nor did its belly carry bombs.

The year was 1939 and the recently commissioned *Graf Zeppelin*[15] was carrying high-frequency receivers under its main gondola. *LZ130*'s crew were trying to discover if British radar was operational, suspicions having been aroused when the Germans noticed that 350ft tall masts had appeared along the south and east coasts of England. The *Graf* made a total of nine 'ferret' flights, but its detection gear was unreliable and failed to bring the results that General Wolfgang Martini, chief of the *Luftwaffe* signals organisation, required.[16] Had definite returns been recorded and the existence of the British radar system proven, perhaps the *Luftwaffe*'s tactics in 1940 would have been very different and altered the outcome of the Battle of Britain.

But that's another story.

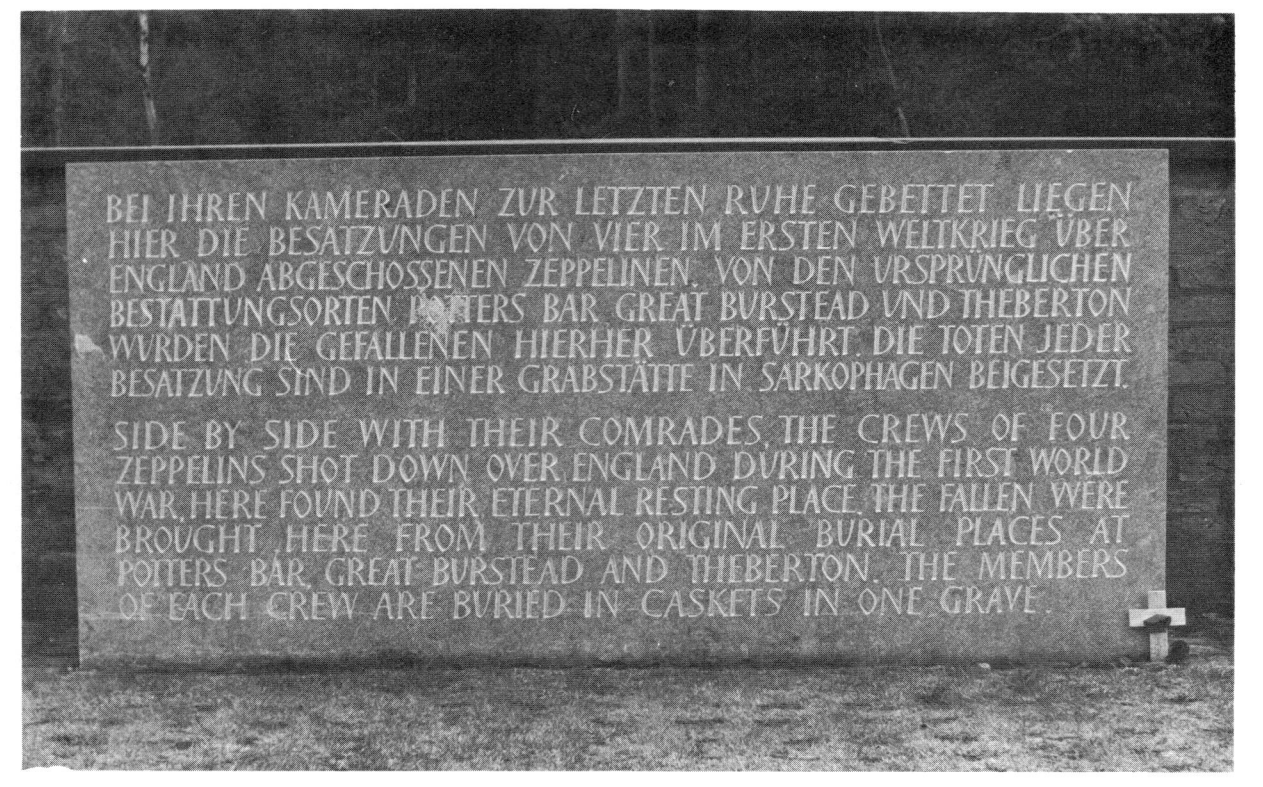

The commemorative stone at the German war grave site in Cannock Chase, Staffordshire, marks the final resting place of the crews from *SL11*, *L31*, *L32* and *L48*. The airship crews are laid in a large plot near the entrance. All were transferred here in 1966 from their original burial places at Potters Bar, Great Burstead and Theberton. Five crew members from *L34* and one from *L70* are also to be found in this cemetery.
I R Stair

APPENDICES

APPENDIX I
GERMAN AIRSHIPS DESTROYED BY AIRCRAFT IN WORLD WAR I

Builder's no	Service use	Service no	Date destroyed	Remarks
Schütte-Lanz (Luftschiffbau Schütte-Lanz GmbH)				
SL11	Army	SL11	3.9.16	Shot down in flames by Lt W L Robinson in BE2c 2693 from 39 HDS (B Flight), Suttons Farm, Hornchurch, Essex. Crashed on 'Plough Hill', Cuffley, Herts. All 16 crew members killed.
Zeppelins (Luftschiffbau Zeppelin GmbH)				
LZ25	Army	ZIX	8.10.14	Bombed in Düsseldorf shed by Flt Lt R L G Marix in Sopwith Tabloid 168 from 2 Aeroplane Squadron RNAS, Antwerp.
LZ37	Army	LZ37	7.6.15	Bombed in mid-air by Sub-Lt R A J Warneford in Morane Saulnier L 3253 from 1 Squadron RNAS, Dunkirk. Crashed on convent at Ghent, Belgium. Nine killed, one survivor.
LZ38	Army	LZ38	7.6.15	Bombed in Brussels-Evère shed by Flt Lt J P Wilson and Flt Sub-Lt J S Mills in two Henry Farmans (3999 and ?) from 1 Squadron RNAS, Dunkirk.
LZ61	Navy	L21	28.11.16	Shot down in flames by Flt Lt E Cadbury in BE2c 8625 from Great Yarmouth, Norfolk. Disappeared into sea 10 miles E of Lowestoft. All 17 crew members killed.
LZ64	Navy	L22	14.5.17	Shot down in flames by Flt Lt Galpin from front cockpit of Curtiss H12 8666 flown by Flt Sub-Lt R Leckie from RN Air Station, Great Yarmouth, Norfolk. Disappeared into sea 18 miles NNW of Texel Island. All 21 crew members killed.
LZ66	Navy	L23	21.8.17	Shot down in flames by Flt Sub-Lt B A Smart in Sopwith Pup N6430 from HMS *Yarmouth*. Disappeared into sea. All 21 crew members killed.
LZ72	Navy	L31	2.10.16	Shot down in flames by Lt W J Tempest in BE2c 4577 from 39 HDS (B Flight), Suttons Farm, Hornchurch, Essex. Crashed on Oakmere Farm, Potters Bar, Herts. All 19 crew crew members killed.
LZ74	Navy	L32	24.9.16	Shot down in flames by Lt F Sowrey in BE2c 4112 from 39 HDS (B Flight), Suttons Farm, Hornchurch, Essex. Crashed on Snail's Hall Farm, near Great Burstead, Essex. All 22 crew members killed.
LZ78	Navy	L34	28.11.16	Shot down in flames by 2nd Lt I V Pyott in BE2c 2738 from 36 HDS, Seaton Carew, Teeside. Disappeared beneath sea at mouth of Tees off West Hartlepool. All 20 crew members killed.
LZ92	Navy	L43	14.6.17	Shot down in flames by Sub-Lt R F L Dickey from front cockpit of 'Large America' 8677 flown by Flt Sub-Lt B D Hobbs from RN Air Station, Great Yarmouth, Disappeared into sea off Vlieland. All 24 crew members killed.
LZ95	Navy	L48	17.6.17	Shot down in flames by Lt L P Watkins (?) in BE12 6610 from 37 HDS, Blackwater Estuary, Goldhanger, Suffolk. Crashed on Holly Tree Farm, near Theberton, Suffolk. Fourteen crew members killed, three survivors.
LZ99	Navy	L54	19.7.18	Bombed in *Toska* shed, Tondern, by three Sopwith 2F1 Camels (serials not confirmed) flown by Capts W D Jackson and W F Dickson and Lt N E Williams from HMS *Furious* lying off Danish coast.
LZ100	Navy	L53	11.8.18	Shot down in flames by Lt S D Culley in Sopwith 2F1 Camel N6812 from lighter towed by HMS *Redoubt* in waters N of Terschelling. Disappeared into sea. All 19 crew members killed.
LZ108	Navy	L60	19.7.18	Bombed in *Toska* shed, Tondern, by three Sopwith 2F1 Camels (serials not confirmed) flown by Capts W D Jackson and W F Dickson and Lt N E Williams from HMS *Furious* lying off Danish Coast.
LZ112	Navy	L70	5.8.18	Shot down in flames by Capt R Leckie from rear cockpit of DH4 A8032 flown by Maj E Cadbury from RN Air Station, Great Yarmouth. Disappeared into sea off Cromer. All 22 crew members killed.

APPENDIX II
HOME DEFENCE SQUADRONS UP TO 1916

Squadron	Date of formation	Commanding Officer	HQ	Flight stations
33	12.1.1916	Major A A B Thompson MC	Gainsborough	Brattleby (Scampton), Kirton Lindsey
36	1.2.1916	Major A C E Marsh	Newcastle	Ashrington, Hylton, Seaton Carew
37	15.8.1916	Major W B Hargrave	Woodham Mortimer	Goldhanger, Rochford, Stow Maries
38	14.7.1916	Major the Hon L J E Twistleton-Wykeham-Fiennes	Melton Mowbray	Buckminster, Leadenham, Stamford
39	15.4.1916	Major A H Morton	Woodford	Hainault (Ilford) North Weald Bassett, Suttons Farm (Hornchurch)
50	15.5.1916	Major M G Christie MC	Harrietsham	Bekesbourne (Canterbury), Dover, Throwley (Faversham)
51	15.5.1916	Major H Wyllie	Hingham	Harling Road (Roudham), Marham, Mattishall
75	1.10.1916	Major H Petre MC	Goldington (Bedford)	Old Weston (Thrapston), Therfield (Baldock), Yelling (St Neots)
76	15.9.1916	Major E M Murray MC	Ripon	Catterick, Copmanthorpe, Helperby
77	1.10.1916	Major M Milne MC	Edinburgh	New Haggerston (Berwick-on-Tweed) Turnhouse (Edinburgh), Whiteburn (Grant's House)
78	1.11.1916	Major H A Van-Ryneveld MC	Hove	Chiddingstone Causeway (Tonbridge), Gosport, Telscombe Cliffs (Newhaven)
II Reserve HD Training Squadron	1.11.1915	Major B F Moore	Northolt	

APPENDIX III
TECHNICAL DATA: THE AIRSHIPS

Builder's no	Type	Where built*	Service no	Length (ft–in)	Diameter (ft–in)	Gas cells	Useful lift (lb)	Power-plant	Trial speed (mph)	Cars	Propellers	Raids	Total flights
German Army Airship Division													
LZ37	'm'	Potsdam	LZ37	518–2	48–6	18	20,250	3M C-X	50.9	2	4	?	?
SL11	'e'	Leipzig	SL11	570–10	65–11	19	47,400	4M HSLu	58.8	5	5	1	?
German Naval Airship Division													
LZ74	'r'	Factory Shed 11, Friedrichshafen	L32	649–7	78–5	19	64,900	6M HSLu	62.6	4	6	3	13
LZ72	'r'	Löwenthal	L31	649–7	78–5	19	62,500	6M HSLu	63.8	4	6	8	19
LZ61	'q'	Löwenthal	L21	585–5	61–4	18	38,800	4M HSLu	57.5	2	5	13	70
LZ78	'r'	Löwenthal	L34	644–8	78–5	19	68,600	6M HSLu	64.0	4	6	2	11
LZ64	'q'	Löwenthal	L22	585–5	61–4	18	38,600	4M HSLu	59.0	2	5	11	81
LZ92	's'	Factory Shed 1, Friedrichshafen	L43	644–8	78–5	18	80,300	5M HSLu	62.0	4	4	1	14
LZ95	'u'	Factory Shed 1, Friedrichshafen	L48	644–8	78–5	18	85,800	5M HSLu	66.9	4	4	1	?
LZ66	'q'	Potsdam	L23	585–5	61–4	18	40,700	4M HSLu	57.3	2	5	8	101
LZ112	'x'	Factory Shed 11, Friedrichshafen	L70	693–11	78–5	15	97,100	7M Mb IVa	81.0	6	6	1	?7
LZ100	'v'	Factory Shed 1, Friedrichshafen	L53	644–8	78–5	14	89,200	5M Mb IVa†	66.0	4	4	4	?53

*SL11 was built by Luftschiffbau Schütte-Lanz GmbH, the rest by Luftschiffbau Zeppelin GmbH. †After 16–23.4.18.

APPENDIX IV
TECHNICAL DATA: THE AIRCRAFT

Aircraft	Serial no	Constructor	Powerplant	Armament
Morane Saulnier L	3253	Aéroplanes Morane Saulnier, Villacoublay, France	1 × 80hp Le Rhône 7cyl rotary	6 × 20lb Hales bombs
RAF BE2c	2693	Ruston Proctor & Co Ltd, Lincoln, England	1 × 90hp RAF 1a 8cyl air-cooled	1 × 0.303 Lewis MG (incendiary ammunition)
RAF BE2c	4112	The British & Colonial Aeroplane Co Ltd, Bristol, England	1 × 90hp RAF 1a 8cyl air-cooled	1 × 0.303 Lewis MG (incendiary ammunition)
RAF BE2c	4577	Group-built under G & J Weir Ltd, Glasgow, Scotland	1 × 90hp RAF 1a 8cyl air-cooled	1 × 0.303 Lewis MG (incendiary ammunition)
RAF BE2c	8625	The Blackburn Aeroplane & Motor Co Ltd, Leeds, Yorkshire, England	1 × 90hp RAF 1a 8cyl air-cooled	1 × 0.303 Lewis MG (incendiary ammunition), 4 × 20lb bombs
RAF BE2c	8626	The Blackburn Aeroplane & Motor Co Ltd, Leeds, Yorkshire, England	1 × 90hp RAF 1a 8cyl air-cooled	1 × 0.303 Lewis MG (incendiary ammunition), 4 × 20lb bombs
RAF BE2c	8421	Hewlett & Blondeau Ltd, Leagrave, Bedfordshire, England	1 × 90hp RAF 1a 8cyl air-cooled	1 × 0.303 Lewis MG (incendiary ammunition), 4 × 20lb bombs
RAF BE2c	2738	Ruston Proctor & Co Ltd, Lincoln, England	1 × 90hp RAF 1a 8cyl air-cooled	1 × 0.303 Lewis MG (incendiary ammunition)
Curtiss H12 convert	8666	Curtiss Aeroplane & Motor Corporation, Hammondsport, New York, USA	2 × 250hp Rolls-Royce Eagle 12cyl air-cooled	3 × 0.303 Lewis MG (incendiary ammunition), 4 × 65lb bombs
Curtiss H12	8677	Curtiss Aeroplane & Motor Corporation, Hammondsport, New York, USA	2 × 250hp Rolls-Royce Eagle 12cyl air-cooled	3 × 0.303 Lewis MG (incendiary ammunition), 4 × 65lb bombs
RAF BE12	6610	The Daimler Co Ltd, Coventry, Warwickshire, England	1 × 150hp RAF 4a 12cyl air-cooled	2 × 0.303 Lewis MG (incendiary ammunition)
De Havilland DH2	A5058	Aircraft Manufacturing Co Ltd, Hendon, Middlesex, England	1 × 100hp Gnome Monosoupapé rotary	1 × 0.303 Lewis MG (incendiary ammunition)
RAF FE2b	B401	First aircraft built by Ransome, Sims & Jeffries, Ipswich, Suffolk, England	1 × 160hp Beardmore 6cyl water-cooled	2 × 0.303 Lewis MG (incendiary ammunition)
Sopwith Pup (Admiralty type 9901)	N6430	William Beardmore & Co Ltd, Dalmuir, Dumbartonshire, Scotland	1 × 80hp Gnome 7cyl rotary	1 × 0.303 Lewis MG (incendiary ammunition)
De Havilland DH4	A8032	Aircraft Manufacturing Co Ltd, Hendon, Middlesex, England	1 × 375hp Rolls-Royce Eagle VIII 12cyl air-cooled	1 × 0.303 Lewis MG, 1 × 0.303 Vickers MG (incendiary ammunition), 2 × 100lb bombs or depth charges
Sopwith 2F1 Camel	N6812	William Beardmore & Co Ltd, Dalmuir, Dumbartonshire, Scotland	1 × 750hp Bentley BR1 9cyl rotary	2 × 0.303 Lewis MG (incendiary ammunition)

*Standard BE2c. †Approximate figure. ‡Maximum figure.

Span (ft–in)	Length (ft–in)	Height (ft–in)	Max Speed (mph)/at (ft)	Endurance (hrs)	Fuel (gal)	Fate
36–9	22–6¾	12–10⅝	72/6560	2½	?	Selected for preservation but presumed scrapped 1922.
37–0	27–3	11–1½	72/6500*	3¾†	32¾*	Destroyed in take-off accident 16.9.16.
37–0	27–3	11–1½	72/6500*	3¾†	32¾*	Preserved; now part of Canadian Aeronautical Collection, Ottawa
37–0	27–3	11–1½	72/6500*	3¾†	32¾*	Wrecked on landing at 12.10hrs, 2.10.16
37–0	27–3	11–1½	72/6500*	3¾†	32¾*	?
37–0	27–3	11–1½	72/6500*	3¾†	32¾*	?
37–0	27–3	11–1½	72/6500*	3¾†	32¾*	?
37–0	27–3	11–1½	72/6500*	3¾†	32¾*	Arrived at East Fortune from Penston (part of 77 HDS) 19.10.17, flown by Capt Williams with 2nd Lt Thom as passenger; subsequent fate unknown
93–0	46–0	16–9	93/2000	6	218	?
93–0	46–0	16–9	93/2000	6	218	Shot down in flames 25.4.18 by *Oberleutnant* d R Christiansen
37–0	27–3	11–1½	102/ground level	3	57	Crashed and struck off charge at Woodham Mortimer 12.12.18
28–3	25–2½	9–6½	93/ground level	2¾	26¼	Still on strength of School of Aerial Fighting at Turnberry Jan 1919; flown by Capt C B Ridley 21.8.19
47–9	32–3	12–7½	91/ground level	3†	50	?
26–6	19–3¾	9–5	110†/ground level	3†	19¼†	Engine and gun salvaged, remainder dumped at sea 21.8.17
42–4⅝	30–8	11–0	143/ground level	6¾‡	65¾	?
26–11	18–8	9–1	122/10,000	3†	37	Preserved; now in Imperial War Museum, Lambeth, London

APPENDIX V
THE ROLL OF HONOUR: BRITISH AND CANADIAN PILOTS

Ultimate rank	Name	British awards	Nationality	Birthplace	Born	Died
Sub-Lieutenant	Reginald Alexander John Warneford	VC	British	Bengal, India	15.10.1891	17.6.1915
Captain	William Leefe Robinson	VC	British	South Coorg, India	14.7.1895	31.12.1918
Group Captain	Frederick Sowrey	DSO, MC, AFC	British	Gloucester, England	25.8.1893	21.10.1968
Major	Wulstan Joseph Tempest	DSO, MC, AFC	British	Yorkshire, England	22.1.1891	20.12.1966
Captain	Gerard William Reginald Fane	DSO	British	London, England	7.8.1898	13.5.1979
Major	Egbert Cadbury	DSO	British	Birmingham, England	20.4.1893	12.1.1961
Flight Sub-Lieutenant	Edward Laston Pulling	DSO	British	Kent, England	22.7.1890	2.3.1917
Captain	Ian Vernon Pyott	DSO	British	Dundee, Scotland	31.8.1895	23.7.1972
Air Marshal	Robert Leckie	CB, DSO, DSC, DFC	British	Glasgow, Scotland	16.4.1890	1.4.1975
Captain	Christopher John Galpin	DSO	British	Essex, England	13.7.1892	Unconfirmed
Group Captain	Basil Deacon Hobbs	DSO, OBE, DSC, Bar, CVSM and Clasp	Canadian	Reading, England	20.12.1894	27.11.1965
Captain	Robert Frederick Lea Dickey	DSC	British	Londonderry, Northern Ireland	30.7.1895	Unconfirmed
Lieutenant (Temporary Captain)	Loudon Pierce Watkins	MC	Canadian	Toronto, Canada	26.3.1897	1.7.1918
Air Marshal	Robert Henry Magnus Spencer Saundby	KCB, KBE, MC, DFC, AFC, DC	British	Birmingham, England	26.4.1896	25.9.1971
Squadron Leader	Frank Douglas Holder	OBE, MC, JP, DL	British	London, England	26.6.1897	24.10.1978
Captain	Bernard Arthur Smart	DSO	British	Bedfordshire, England	24.12.1891	5.5.1979
Group Captain	Stuart Douglas Culley	DSO	British	Nebraska, USA	23.8.1895	10.6.1975

APPENDIX VI
THE ROLL OF HONOUR: GERMAN AIRSHIP CREWS

Rank	Name	Born	Birthplace
Crew of LZ37, KIA 7 June 1915			
Oberleutnant	Kurt Ackermann	14.5.1886	Berlin
Maschinist	Carl Claus	31.3.1886	Mettingen
†Oberleutnant	Otto von der Haegen	23.5.1887	Creuzthal
MG-Schütze Sergeant	Hermann Kirchner	3.5.1893	Berlin
Fahringenieur Feldwebelleutnant	Karl Mahr	30.6.1881	Leipzig
Maschinist Unteroffizier	Wilhelm Müller	9.1.1887	Bonn
Maschinist	Gustav Ruske	17.7.1880	Soldin
Untersteuermann	Otto Schwarz	5.4.1890	Harburg
Crew of SL11, KIA 3 September 1916			
Obermaschinist	Jakob Baumann	3.7.1887	Nordach
Leutnant	Hans Geitel	6.6.1892	Berlin
Vizefeldwebel	Rudolf Goltz	24.7.1881	Koschmin
Feldwebel Leutnant	Paul Hassenmüller	5.7.1887	St Johann
Gefreiter	Bernard Jeziorski	3.5.1892	Schlesien
Untermaschinist	Fritz Jourdan	9.5.1892	Pforzheim
Untermaschinist	Karl Kächele	24.2.1894	Blaubeuren
Obersteuermann	Fritz Kopischke	2.7.1891	Prenzlau
Obermaschinist	Friedrich Mödinger	24.7.1886	Strümpfelbach
Obermaschinist	Reinhold Porath	5.9.1892	Randow
Unteroffizier	Heinrich Schlichting	26.5.1891	Bielefeld
†Hauptmann	Wilhelm Schramm	11.12.1885	London
Obersteuermann	Rudolf Sendzick	8.3.1891	Berlin
Unteroffizier	Anton Tristam	28.1.1889	Witzenhausen
Oberleutnant der Reserve	Wilhelm Vohdin	8.7.1882	Widdern
Untermaschinist	Hans Winkler	28.5.1892	Calau
Crew of L32, KIA 24 September 1916			
Obersignalmaat	Adolf Bley	1.10.1886	Magdeburg
Obermaschinistenmaat	Albin Bocksch	5.4.1886	Bautzen
Funkentelegrafieobermaat	Karl Bortscheller	10.6.1889	Frankenthal
Oberheizer	Wilhelm Brockhaus	5.11.1888	Giebichenstein
Leutnant zur See	Karl Brodrück	26.1.1891	Diedenhofen
Maschinistenmaat	Paul Dorfmüller	22.10.1889	Vienenburg
Obermaschinistenmaat	Richard Fankhänel	16.3.1882	Hermsdorf
Obermaschinistenmaat	Georg Hagedorn	28.9.1887	Effelder
Oberbootsmannsmaat	Friedrich Heider	18.8.1888	Niedermauck
Funkentelegrafieobergast	Robert Klisch	28.2.1893	Wurbitz
Obermaschinist	Hermann Maegdefrau	31.9.1878	Berlin
Obersegelmachersgast	Bernhard Mohr	1.10.1894	Barmstedt
Matrose	August Müller	7.1.1888	Duisburg
Bootsmannsmaat	Friedrich Pasche	28.9.1889	Schiedlow
Obermaschinistenmaat	Karl Paust	29.11.1889	Hörde
†Oberleutnant zur See	Werner Peterson	24.7.1887	Minden
Obersignalmaat	Ewald Picard	30.3.1887	Düsseldorf
Maschinistenmaat	Walter Prüss	31.12.1894	Hamburg
Obermatrose	Paul Schiering	22.8.1885	Eisleben

238

Appendices

Rank	Name	Born	Birthplace
Steuermann	Bernhard Schreibmüller	18.10.1882	Hof
Obermaschinistenmaat	Karl Völker	7.6.1889	Flensburg
Oberbootsmannsmaat	Alfred Zöpel	11.1.1889	Finsterwalde

Crew of L31, KIA 2 October 1916

Rank	Name	Born	Birthplace
Maschinistenmaat	Eugen Boudange	27.9.1890	Ars an der Mosel
Bootsmannsmaat	Arthur Budwitz	30.12.1888	Porsfunden
Obermatrose	Karl Dornbusch	16.4.1890	Allner
Maschinistenmaat	Nikolaus Hemmerling	13.2.1886	Quebach
Obermaschinistenmaat	Karl Hiort	18.6.1893	Wiesbaden
Segelmachersmaat	Ernst Kaiser	14.9.1892	Fuchshöfen
Funkentelegrafieobergast	Ernst Klee	9.5.1890	Steinkirchen
Steuermann	Siegfried Körber	10.5.1885	Wolferstedt
Signalmaat	Gustav Kunisch	2.2.1892	Brietschütz
†*Kapitänleutnant*	Heinrich Mathy	4.4.1883	Mannheim
Maschinistenmaat	Karl Mensing	25.9.1884	Unna (Westphalia)
Obersteuermannsmaat	Friedrich Peters	8.3.1889	Epenwordenfeld
Obermatrose	Heinrich Phillip	22.3.1889	Eistrawischken
Maschinistenmaat	Friedrich Rohr	25.1.1889	Strasburg
Maschinistenmaat	Hubert Stender	24.12.1892	Heimbach
Maschinist	Joseph Wegener	19.12.1878	Mülheim (Ruhr)
Bootsmannsmaat	Heinrich Witthöft	21.5.1888	Cologne
Obermaschinistenmaat	Viktor Wöllert	2.11.1881	Jakobshausen
Leutnant zur See	Jochen Werner	3.11.1894	Rastenburg (East Prussia)

Crew of L34, KIA 28 November 1916

Rank	Name	Born	Birthplace
Maschinistenmaat	Johannes Blunk	28.8.1885	Guben
†*Kapitänleutnant*	Max Dietrich	27.11.1870	Angermünde
Maschinistenmaat	Ernst Doering	5.5.1885	Strasburg (Uckermark)
Obermatrose	Otto Ehlers	1.6.1879	Eutin
Obermaschinistenmaat	Alexander Keller	8.3.1887	Dermbach
Segelmachersmaat	Wilhelm Koberg	15.9.1889	Stolzenau
Oberleutnant	Christian von Nathusius	22.8.1889	Hoffstädt
Funkentelegrafiemaat	Paul Nettlau	19.8.1890	Merseburg
Obermaschinistenmaat	Heinrich Oelbrich	11.10.1874	Hamburg
Signalmaat	Julius Petitjean	2.2.1890	Prenzlau
Obermaschinistenmaat	Wihelm Pfirrmann	11.3.1889	Munich
Signalmaat	Heinrich Predel	28.5.1888	Garz
Bootsmannsmaat	Hermann Pufahl	30.3.1887	Stargard (Pomerania)
Maschinistenmaat	Alfred Rüger	12.8.1890	Löbau
Maschinistenmaat	Josef Schydlo	8.4.1892	Sakrau
Obermaschinist	Franz Seemann	10.5.1875	Hohenwicheln
Maat der LA	Friedrich Siegel	14.6.1880	Altenwalde
Maat	Adam Smieskol	22.12.1887	Zawatzki
Bootsmannsmaat	Bernhard Wewer	14.7.1885	Dülmen
Obersteuermannsmaat	Hans Würst	24.10.1885	Mülheim

Crew of L21, KIA 28 November 1916

Rank	Name	Born	Birthplace
Obermaschinistenmaat	Alfred Brieger	4.3.1889	Kohlfurt
Obersignalmaat	Albert Carlsen	6.10.1888	Neumünster
†*Oberleutnant zur See*	Kurt Frankenberg	30.4.1887	Kassel
Oberbootsmannsmaat	Otto Grass	20.3.1888	Delitzsch
Obermaschinistenmaat	Hans Hintzer	17.1.1886	Culmisch
Steuermann	Christian Jensen	26.6.1883	Amrum
Obermatrose	Theophil Kaczikowski	30.4.1890	Zuckau
Obermaschinistenmaat	Wilhelm Kiel	1.12.1884	Elende
Maschinistenmaat	Walter Klann	7.10.1880	Elbing
Obermatrose	Wilhelm Metzger	25.5.1893	Tuttlingen
Funkentelegrafiemaat	Paul Petznick	12.9.1889	Bromberg
Obersignalmaat	Otto Prinke	22.7.1888	Wrist
Maschinist	Anton Reischel	5.3.1892	Hirschfeld
Obermaschinistenmaat	Theodor Schmidt	30.9.1887	Danzig
Maschinistenmaat	Alfred Schwarz	15.3.1891	Rostock
Leutnant zur See	Hans Werner Salzbrunn	21.12.1892	Berlin
Bootsmansmaat der Reserve	Wilhelm Wittkugel	18.1.1890	Stadthagen

Crew of L22, KIA 14 May 1917

Rank	Name	Born	Birthplace
Obermaschinistenmaat	Ludwig Bader	17.9.1883	Cologne
Funkentelegrafieobergast	Paul Böttger	16.11.1889	Eisenach
Funkentelegrafieoberanwärter	Friedrich Bruns	24.4.1894	Bockenem
Segelmachersmaat	Willi Friedenreich	12.1.1888	Wanzleben
Matrose	Friedrich Grislawski	29.1.1894	Essen
Maschinistenmaat	Georg Hasemeier	30.1.1889	Neuwied
Obersignalmaat	Wilhelm Hellmer	22.6.1892	Eutin
Obermaschinistenmaat	Kurt Hildebrandt	8.8.1883	Magdeburg
Obersignalmaat	Martin Hoepfner	22.8.1890	Allenstein
Steuermann	Reinhard Ketzmarik	16.9.1883	Sandow
Leutnant zur See	Hans Ewald von Knobelsdorf	1.9.1892	Oldenburg
Obermaschinistenmaat	Gustav Kocher	25.11.1880	Stuttgart
†*Kapitänleutnant*	Ulrich Lehmann	11.3.1889	Köslin
Maschinistenmaat	Wilhelm Maack	18.3.1895	Winsen
Maschinistenmaat	Hans Nielsen	26.8.1876	Altona
Maschinistenmaat	Heinrich Richter	6.3.1896	Dillenburg
Maschinistenmaat	Otto Siggelkow	5.7.1895	Stendal
Obermatrose d LA	Johannes Sihr	25.5.1895	Altona
Obermaschinistenmaat	Otto Überschär	20.9.1886	Herne
Obermatrose	Hermann Weber	30.11.1887	Bönstadt
Maschinist	Johannes Zimmermann	26.11.1884	Perleberg

Crew of L43, KIA 14 June 1917

Rank	Name	Born	Birthplace
Obermaschinistenmaat	Gustav Alex	29.12.1882	Rosslau
Maschinistenmat	Maximilian Attenberger	12.10.1890	Salzdorf
Maat	Emil Baer	8.11.1890	Wanne
Obermaschinistenmaat	Heinrich Bertram	12.7.1884	Bigge
Funkentelegrafieobergast	Albert Beurich	21.2.1892	Coswig
Obermatrose	Gerhard Brings	18.8.1885	Bergheim
Segelmachersmaat	Johann Dahl	26.9.1888	Danzig
Obermaschinistenmaat	Karl Dauner	16.2.1884	Salzburg
Signalmaat	Johann Haupt	1.1.1889	Weisenau
Maschinistenmaat	Heinrich Helling	21.1.1887	Fuleram
Obermaschinist	Hermann Hellwig	11.2.1876	Gnevsdort
Maschinistenmaat	Hans Johannsen	2.12.1890	Hamburg
Obermatrose	Heinrich Junker	9.2.1894	Bremen
Maschinistenmaat	Peter Kaiser	19.12.1890	Thüringen-bei-Mayen
Matrose	Anton Klein	20.2.1895	Cologne
†*Kapitänleutnant*	Hermann Kraushaar	23.5.1881	Haus Ahr Voerde
Funkentelegrafiegast	Hermann Kruppke	16.12.1896	Dorstfeld
Obermatrose	Friedrich Lacks	12.12.1890	Mönchengladbach
Maschinistenmaat	Erich Lipinski	13.11.1883	Berlin
Obersignalmaat	Paul Lorenz	8.12.1880	Berlin
Obermaschinistenmaat	Johannes Vetter	25.1.1890	Stettin
Bootsmann der Reserve	Wilhelm Wallas	27.11.1889	Trier
Maschinistenmaat	Paul Weber	10.3.1895	Halle
Steuermann	Rudolf Wegener	17.1.1884	Hamburg

Zeppelin!

Rank	Name	Born	Birthplace
Leutnant zur See	Ernst Zimmermann	2.2.1891	Görlitz

Crew of L48, KIA 17 June 1917‡
Rank	Name	Born	Birthplace
Obermaschinistenmaat	Heinrich Ahrens	22.2.1880	Bremerhaven
Maat	Wilhelm Betz	4.3.1892	Thalheim
Obersignalmaat	Walter Dippmann	13.9.1880	Frankenberg
†*Kapitänleutnant*	Franz Eichler	29.10.1877	Giebichenstein
Obermaschinistenmaat	Wilhelm Glöckel	21.9.1881	Nürnberg
Bootsmannsmaat	Paul Hannemann	21.8.1886	Grube Jlse
Signalmaat	Heinrich Herbst	10.7.1892	Grohn-Blumenthal
Bootsmannsmaat	Franz König	9.9.1892	Magdeburg
Funkeltelegrafiemaat	Wilhelm Meier	25.9.1894	Meitzendorf
Obermaschinistenmaat	Karl Milich	18.8.1880	Striegau
Obermaschinistenmaat	Michael Neunzig	21.1.1882	Cologne
Obermatrose	Karl Plöger	9.10.1880	Hiddesen
Korvettenkapitän	Viktor Schütze	6.3.1878	Hanover
Obermaschinistenmaat	Hermann von Stockum	4.1.1894	Duisburg
Obermatrose	Paul Suchlich	11.5.1888	Niedersalzbrunn
Steuermann der Reserve	Paul Westphal	4.5.1887	Insterburg

Crew of L23, KIA 21 August 1917
Rank	Name	Born	Birthplace
Maschinistenmaat	Johannes Buhr	21.9.1894	Berlin
Obersteuermannsmaat	William Deglau	3.8.1882	Hamburg
†*Oberleutnant zur See*	Bernhard Dinter	10.1.1889	Kaindorf
Obermatrose	Ernst Dittmer	2.12.1889	Potsdam
Obermaschinistenmaat	Konrad Grebenstein	3.1.1885	Allendorf
Leutnant zur See	Otto Hamann	6.4.1891	Kottbus
Signalmaat	Otto Hamer	29.10.1893	Schuby
Funkentelegrafiemaat	Jakob Harnecker	25.8.1894	Sarmsheim
Funkentelegrafieanwärter	Johannes Lege	15.10.1896	Lübeck
Maschinist	Hermann Jaax	2.5.1884	Düsseldorf
Maschinistenmaat	Hans Klughardt	26.3.1891	Bayreuth
Maschinistenmaat	Georg Messerschmidt	12.9.1896	Fambach
Obermatrose	Walter Rohde	6.4.1894	Potsdam
Segelmachersmaat	Johann Schüttrap	2.11.1888	Westerende
Maschinistenmaat	Christoph Strohmeyer	7.2.1892	Geestemünde
Obermaschnistenmaat	Georg Tiedt	11.1.1891	Marmerow
Signalmaat	Adolf Till	22.9.1894	Braunschweig
Bootsmansmaat	Hermann Zetzsche	12.8.1890	Grosser Schocher

Crew of L70, KIA 5 August 1918
Rank	Name	Born	Birthplace
Maat	Adam Anstatt	3.6.1890	Weisenau
Obersignalmaat	Hermann Barnick	27.11.1884	Stettin
Funkentelegrafiemaat	Paul Berndt	12.7.1892	Forst Bukowitz
Maschinistenmaat	Wilhelm Bernt	2.8.1895	Flensburg
Maschinistenmaat	Karl Blöcker	26.10.1892	Neumünster
Bootsmannsmaat	Adolf Grube	19.8.1892	Tettens
Maschinistenmaat	Georg Hartmann	3.6.1896	Kempten
Maat	Hugo Hellmich	1.7.1886	Radevormwald
Steuermann	Max Hormann	5.6.1887	Kiel
Bootsmannsmaat	Ernst Hoynk	1.4.1887	Dortmund
Leutnant zur See	Kurt Krüger	2.1.1895	Koblenz
Ober-Segelmachersmaat	Brunno Kuhnt	10.11.1888	Schweidnitz
Maschinistenmaat	Deflet Kähler	12.3.1892	Meggerkoog
Signalmaat	Peter Lorch	22.12.1889	Bad Reichenhall
†*Kapitänleutnant*	Johannes von Lossnitzer	13.2.1889	Riesa
Maschinistenmaat	Heinrich Meyer	19.5.1892	Hemelingen
Maschinistenmaat	Hans Nagat	15.4.1895	Thorn
Maschinistenmaat	Ludwig Schäfers	14.7.1893	Gronenberg
Maschinist	Lüggo Schmidt	27.4.1883	Oldersam
Obermaschinistenmaat	Robert Schulte	15.11.1886	Frankenhausen
Fregattenkapitän	Peter Strasser	1.4.1876	Hanover
Maschinistenmaat	Karl Wendelborg	5.8.1885	Rüstringen

Crew of L53, KIA 11 August 1918
Rank	Name	Born	Birthplace
Obersteuermannsmaat	Erich Beutel	30.6.1889	Stepenitz
Obermaschinistenmaat	Konrad Borchers	21.2.1893	Neustadt (Rübg)
Steuermann	Wilhelm Brahde	7.6.1884	Forst (Lausitz)
Maschinistenmaat	Georg Bremer	11.4.1894	Lübeck
Funkentelegrafiemaat	Heinrich Düren	31.7.1889	Duisburg
Funkentelegrafieoberanwärter	Günther Giller	18.6.1898	Crossen
Obermatrose der Matrosen-Artillerie	Paul Gillet	19.3.1892	Kriescht
Maschinistenmaat	Paul Golgert	16.10.1893	Steenrade
Maschinist	Karl Grape	14.8.1884	Oldenburg
Obermaschinistenmaat	Otto Hey	10.9.1890	Roitzsch
Maat	Karl Heyman	18.3.1889	Köppelsdorf
Obersignalmaat	Max Holve	12.4.1888	Niederhemer
Obermatrose	Walter Müller	11.5.1894	Chemnitz
Obermaschinistenmaat	Artur Niemann	24.6.1887	Swinemünde
Leutnant zur See	Karl von Pröck	24.10.1887	Obilow
†*Korvettenkapitän*	Eduard Prölss	10.2.1867	Brandenburg
Obersegelmachersgast	Wilhelm Reuter	27.11.1885	Emden
Maschinistenmaat	Gustav Richters	16.12.1893	Neukloster
Obermaschinistenmaat	Friedrich Rose	4.11.1891	Einbeck
Obersegelmachersmaat	Ludwig Schneider	27.2.1894	Darmstadt
Maschinistenmaat	Artur Stüven	4.3.1893	Harburg

*One survivor: *Obersteuermann* Alfred Mühler
†Airship Commander
‡There were three survivors from L48: *Maschinistenmaat* Heinrich Ellerkamm, d 4.8.1963 at Heidelberg, Germany; *Leutnant zur See* Otto Mieth, d 30.4.1956 at Iranga, Tanganyika; and *Maschinistenmaat* Wilhelm Uecker, d 11.11.1918 in England.

APPENDIX VII
CAMOUFLAGE AND MARKINGS

Airships
As has been described in Chapter 2, Zeppelins such as *L33* and its brethren adopted an overall light greyish-blue colour with fabric-covered gondola areas painted to match the surrounding duralumin structure. On earlier ships, such as *L14* and *L15*, the fabric covering the hull was seen as a natural cream shade without the printed dots and lines and giving a more pleasing overall aspect. To date, research has only revealed one Zeppelin upon which the Germans experimented with disruptive camouflage patterns. A handful of photographs show that *L11* was at one stage painted in irregular patches of two, possibly three, shades of colour. Just what these colours were is now anybody's guess since no records have survived to verify them.

During 1917 most Zeppelins and Schütte Lanz vessels were doped in black on their undersides and flanks, leaving the upper third of the envelope in natural finish. The 'colour' extended to the control cars, struts and all flying surfaces, the overall finish appearing slightly glossy. Contrary to popular belief, wartime German rigids were *not* aluminium-doped, although a clear-doped Zeppelin would resemble a shimmering bar if caught by searchlights – hence eyewitness descriptions of a 'silvery cigar', 'polished steel bar', etc.

Markings were kept simple. The ship's number appeared on either side of the bows in large black figures, or in white if the ship was black-doped. On Army ships, numerals were rarely seen for security reasons, and most carried simply 'LZ' for Zeppelins and 'SL' for Schütte Lanz ships. The Cross Patée national insignia (*Eisernes Kreuz*) appeared under the extreme bow on the centreline and low on either side amidships. Sometimes the crosses appeared on the centreline forward of the upper fins, but this was not common. On clear-doped vessels, white outlines to the national markings were rare: normally the crosses were bordered by a black outlined version around the main one with the resultant space between left natural. On black ships, white outlines were sufficient to produce the desired effect.

In March 1918 came the official directive that all aircraft carrying the *Eisernes Kreuz* be re-marked with the straight-sided *Balkenkreuz*. Photographs of the big rigids towards the end of the war show the latter form of marking, which was retained until the Armistice.

Aircraft

Most of the aircraft which fall within the parameters of this history enjoyed standard colours and markings of the period. There were no bright colours, few individual pilots' markings and no 'jazzy' camouflage patterns. Aircraft like Warneford's Morane and the BE2cs of the home defence units were clear-doped, leaving the overall warm cream colour that linen thus treated tended to adopt. National markings, roundels and fin stripes were of three shades, Ultramarine (Methuen 21C8) white and Vermillion (9A8) – quite different from the shades employed on current RAF aircraft.

In the early period of the war, RNAS roundels adopted the French pattern, with a red outer ring and a blue centre. On Warneford's Morane, supplied by France, the roundels and rudder stripes were naturally in that nation's shades of blue (23D4) and red (10D8), and the RNAS applied fuselage roundels in the slightly darker national shades used by the British. It is thought that 3253 bore these roundels with the blue ring outermost.

The BE2c machines used by Robinson, Sowrey, Cadbury *et al* were mostly clear-doped overall, although in late 1916 the well-known camouflage PC10 khaki (4F8-4F2) was introduced and began to be applied to uppersurfaces and then overall for night camouflage. Some units went even further, 50 HDS for example. On 17 August 1916 this unit had six BE2e aircraft painted black overall, 'partly for the sake of invisibility but mainly to prevent the pilot becoming blinded by the glare of his wing tip flares which he ignites when close to the ground'. Relieving this sombre scheme were simple white rings usually to the same dimensions as the Ultramarine circles. Serials were in white, or outlined in white, and some machines carried a small skull-and-crossbones motif on the fuselage sides and sometimes under the outer sections of the upper wing.

Colours for British aircraft on home defence and North Sea duties changed little throughout the war. Aircraft like Culley's Camel and Cadbury's DH4 were doped PC10 on their uppersurfaces, with metal panels and cowlings in Battleship Grey (B1-C1). Wooden struts and airscrews were usually varnished and polished, and many machines adopted a glossy finish when new which soon dulled in service.

Further reading

Kornerup, A and Wanscher, J H: *Methuen Handbook of Colour*, Methuen & Co Ltd (London 1963). This book, vital for any student of colours, contains several hundred printed 'chips' showing all variation of colour tones along with detailed annotations and reference numbers (as quoted above).

Munson, Kenneth: *Fighters 1914–1919: Attack and Training Aircraft*, Blandford Press (Dorset 1968) contains a detailed treatise on World War I colour sources and application by I D Huntley AMR AeS.

Notes

The following notes are designed to aid the reader in locating contemporary records and as a guide towards further sources of reference. For those consulting original documents it should be noted that both belligerents initiated Summer Time in 1916 *viz*:
1916: Summer Time began 21 May; ended 1 October.
1917: Summer Time began 8 April; ended 17 September.
1918: Summer Time began 24 March; ended 30 September.
During these periods Greenwich Mean Time was advanced by one hour; there was no 'Double Summer Time'. Times quoted throughout the text have not necessarily been converted from GMT to Central European Standard Time.

Chapter 1
1 *L15* made its maiden flight on 9 September 1915 and was commissioned three days later at Nordholz, berthed in the *Nora* shed. The airship was on its third raid when brought down by British defences.
2 See Chapter 6.
3 Robinson, D H: *The Zeppelin in Combat*, p136.
4 Breithaupt, J: ' I Bombed London', *RAF Flying Review*, Dec 1956, p50.
5 On 6 April 1916 HMT *Seamew* located and buoyed the *L15* wreck, bringing up 30ft of tail section and the two rudders. Over the ensuing weeks other vessels had joined *Seamew* and retrieved more debris, towing much of it shorewards to Margate Sand:
'Up to the 8th June, numerous parts had been sent in, including 5 canvas bags and 1 metal case of charts, 2 propellers with shaft and gear boxes, 1 machine gun, bomb dropping machines [*sic*], instruments and control and steering gear. The body of a German was also found and after a short service was buried. A purse containing an identification disc, a 5 mark note and 5 coins were found in his coat pocket...'
Strong winds, heavy seas and shifting sands prevented any further recovery of *L15*'s remains, and at the close of the salvage operations Chief Gunner W A Austin of HMT *Seamew* submitted his final report. See PRO (Public Records Office) file, Air 1, 645.
6 *The Daily Telegraph*, Monday 3 April 1916, p9.
7 *ibid*.
8 Douglas Robinson interviewed *General der Luftwaffe* Otto Kühne in Hamburg on 7 July 1962:
'[Kühne] said Breithaupt had been hit on the head getting out of the control car and was somewhat confused. Kühne did not believe his commander had been taken ashore naked although two crew members were forced to strip before being picked up by one of the destroyers. Kühne and the *Steuermann* were the last off; later at Chatham the executive officer was confined to a cell, and, believing he would be tried for murder and hanged, threatened reprisals to his captors if such a sentence was carried out. He confirmed his sister had married an Englishman and was living in England yet denied trying to telephone her after L15 was brought down, but his interrogators knew all about his visit to her in 1910!'
Interrogation of *L15*'s crew resulted in a wealth of information on early Zeppelin operations, although surviving records should be viewed with caution since obvious attempts to deceive their captors were made by the airship men. See PRO Air 1, 537/16/13/1 and Air 1, 539/16/15/1.
9 Interview: G H Cooper with author, 5 October 1978.

Chapter 2
1 The story of Count Ferdinand von Zeppelin's rival, Professor Johann Schütte, who developed the wooden-hulled rigid airship, is beyond the scope of this work. Readers are referred to Robinson, D H: *Giants in the Sky*; Schütte, J (ed): *Der Luftschiffbau Schütte Lanz, 1909–1925*; and Hardesty, F S: *Key to the Development of the Super Airship: Luftfahrzeugbau Schütte Lanz, Mannheim-Rheinau, Germany, 1909–30*.
2 Admiralty, War Staff, Intelligence Division, CB1265: 'German Rigid Airships'. (Confidential). Ordnance Survey, February 1917, p17.
3 A Schütte Lanz patent, the axial cable was introduced with *L30*.
4 On ships built in 1917–18, the catwalk was made of light plywood strips, 'grating' style, and often smashed by crewmen running on it.
5 Douglas Robinson suggests that the cells were actually cut by the cables when they lifted or shifted.
6 CB 1265, p48.
7 This is the cell numbering system (running from the nose) as followed in the British airship service and adopted by the compilers of CB1265. In proper German fashion (from the stern), manoeuvring valves were found on cells 5, 6, 8, 9, 12, 13, 14, 15 and 18, none of which was situated over gondola positions. German sources confirm nine cells with manoeuvring valves in '*L30* class' Zeppelins.
8 CB1265, p22.
9 *ibid*, p50.
10 *ibid*, p21.
11 *ibid*, *loc cit*.
12 See Kornerup, A and Wanscher, J H: *The Methuen Handbook of Colour*, Appendix VII.
13 As described in Chapter 13, the gun platforms were omitted on the first of the much-lightened 'Height-Climbers'.
14 Recollections of August Siem, from Marben, R (ed): *Zeppelin Adventures*, p92.
15 A statascope (not the same as a variometer) could be set by the elevator man at any ordered attitude and would show even slight variations up or down.

242

16 Possibly an additional speaking tube to the crew space in the keel was also carried.
17 Robinson, D H: *The Zeppelin in Combat*, p154.
18 The rear gondola was also the duty station of the *Warrant Maschinist*.
19 Marben, *loc cit*. Small measures of rum or brandy were distributed amongst the crews of naval airships but not on a widespread scale – there were more 'dry' ships than 'wet' ones!
20 See Chapter 3.
21 Robinson, *op cit*, p355.
22 On 17 April 1916 *L22* struck the *Toska* shed doors, demolishing the bows and necessitating lengthy repairs. Several months later, on December 28, *L24* came to grief at the same Tondern hangar when wind gusts flung the ship against the doors, breaking its back. Flaring up immediately, *L24* was completely destroyed, along with its hangar-mate *L17*.
23 Robinson, *op cit*, p356.
24 For a full and detailed account of Zeppelin operation and handling, see Robinson, D H: 'Flying the Zeppelin Bomber', *Cross and Cockade Journal* (US), Vol 2 No 3 (1961), pp199–207.
25 For a full appraisal of the use and development of hydrogen and the wartime airships, see Robinson, D H: 'Hydrogen for German Airships in World War One', *Cross and Cockade Journal* (US), Vol 7 No 4 (1966), pp389–94.

Chapter 3
1 Jones, H A: *The War in the Air*, Vol III, p69.
2 *ibid*, p70.
3 *ibid*, *loc cit*.
4 Vickers received the contract for 'HM Airship No 9' as early as 1913 but Great Britain's second rigid was not completed until June 1916, the maiden flight taking place on 27 November that year. The ship was a disappointment (barely 200 flying hours were recorded) and was dismantled at Pulham during 1918.
5 Robinson, D H: *The Zeppelin in Combat*, p56.
6 Letter: R Nouchton to author, 2 September 1978.
7 Private information.
8 One eyewitness to Böcker's attack was a young Egbert Cadbury:
'I was serving as an AB in HMS *Sagitta* on April 15, 1915 when L5 bombed Lowestoft and the *Sagitta* was lying alongside the quay when the Zeppelin appeared. It was a most extraordinary sight to see this huge airship, the first I had ever seen, flying low over us in broad daylight and just circling round the town without any interference whatsoever except from .303 rifles, revolvers etc which we all fired off from the deck as there were no anti-aircraft guns at all and the L5 could do exactly as she wanted. She came down the harbour dropping her bombs and incendiaries and set fire to a timber yard on the quay alongside us, and we had to move our ship across the harbour to the other side in order to avoid being engulfed in the flames of the yard'. (Letter: Major E Cadbury to D H Robinson, 29 January 1962.)
9 *Southend Standard*, 11 May 1915.
10 Some accounts have Linnarz signing this message personally, though contemporary newspapers published photographs of this alleged calling card signed simply 'German'.
11 Redford Henry Mulock (born in Canada on 11 August 1884) joined the RNAS at Eastchurch, taking his 'ticket' in a Short biplane on 9 March 1915 (Aero Club Certificate 1103). On 28 September, whilst serving with 1 Wing at Dunkirk, Mulock carried out a raid on the Zeppelin sheds at Brussels in daylight and under heavy fire: his bombs dropped from 600ft, missing their target. Mulock was awarded the DSO on 22 June 1916 and a bar on 26 April the following year, and ended the war with the rank of Colonel in command of the 27th Group.
12 Morison, F: *War on Great Cities*, p47.
13 Linnarz, Major, E: 'I Was London's First Zepp Raider', *I Was There*, December 1938, p450.
14 'Air Raid by Hostile Aircraft', 2 June 1916. PRO, MEPO 2, 1650.
15 Pankhurst, S: 'I was in London's First Air Raid', *I Was There*, December 1938, p466.
16 Ben Travers was later to become universally acclaimed for his theatrical farces. He learnt to fly at Hendon, obtaining Aero Club Certificate 1170 on 12 April 1915.
17 'Air Raid by Hostile Aircraft'.
18 Letter: W Morgan to author, 2 October 1978.
19 Groos, O: *Der Krieg in der Nordsee*, Vol IV, p174.
20 See Chapter 5.
21 Robinson, *op cit*, p96.
22 2 Wing's report, 10 August 1915. PRO Air 1, 629/17/122/15.
23 *ibid*.
24 *ibid*.
25 Morison, *op cit*, p64.
26 *ibid*, p75.
27 *ibid*.
28 Robinson, *op cit*, p107.
29 Breithaupt, J: 'How We Bombed London', *Living Age*, January 1928.
30 Wickham, J: 'Grisly Death Over the Gaiety', *I Was There*, December 1938, p454.
31 Robinson, *loc cit*.
32 Slessor's personal account of his 'duel' with *L15* can be found in his biography *The Central Blue*, pp12–14.
33 See von Buttlar-Brandenfels, *Freiherr* Treusch: *Zeppelins over England*, p166. The *King Stephen* was sunk by *G41*, the leader of the 6th Torpedo-Boat Flotilla, on 25 April 1916. Despite denials that they were the crew responsible for leaving Loewe and his men to their fate, the steam trawler's complement were taken back to Germany as POWs.
34 Groos, Volume V, pp63–4.
35 'Air Raid by Hostile Aircraft'.
36 Letter: H D Raine to author, 19 October 1978.
37 Kemball's report, 25 April 1916. PRO Air 1, 147/15/74.
38 In later years, sightings of the fabled 'Nessie' were once explained away as a wrecked Zeppelin!
39 See Robinson, *op cit*, pp142–5.
40 Freeman later submitted his report to the CO of HMS *Vindex*:
'I was taken on board and treated with great courtesy and kindness by the Captain of the ship. My engine was rescued, but due to the salt water etc it was sufficiently damaged to be practically useless. The remainder of the machine was smashed.
'The steamer arrived at the Hook of Holland about 5.0am, and I was taken off in the Examination Service tug and removed under guard to the fort. After one day's detention, I was advised by the British Consul, although dressed in the clothes supplied to me by the Captain of the *Anvers*, to make a true report of my status and rank. I was then allowed to sign a temporary form of parole and on Sunday was permitted to proceed to Rotterdam, where I interviewed the British Consul General and The Admiral. On Sunday I was permitted to leave the Country and returned in SS *Cromer*, arriving at Tilbury at 7.0pm the same day...' (From Freeman's report, 7 August 1916. PRO Air 1, 657.)
41 Mathy reported that 'the ship fell very hard, because she had become heavy due to an extraordinary load of rain, and no more emergency ballast was at hand. The radiator water of the three engines not needed for the landing was dropped beforehand also. The ship needs a new after gondola, otherwise she has sustained no significant damage'. Curiously, Mathy failed to mention the quite substantial hull damage that kept *L31* hangared for a long period.

Chapter 4
1 Jones, H A: *The War in the Air*, Vol III, p161.
2 *ibid*, p73.
3 *ibid*, *loc cit*.
4 *ibid*, p75.
5 *ibid*, p81.
6 *ibid*, p84.
7 *ibid*, p106. Jones added a footnote: 'Night flying at this time entailed so many casualties that the Admiralty considered the necessity, in view of the small chances of success that night attacks offered, of prohibiting flying by night altogether.'
8 See Sutton, H D: *Raiders Approach!*, p12.
9 *ibid*, p13.
10 Higgins' biography. PRO Air 1, 2393/230/1.
11 'Anti-Aircraft Summary'. PRO Air 1, 2393/230/1.
12 PRO Air 1, 148/15/89.
13 *ibid*.

14 *ibid.*
15 *ibid.*
16 Jones, *op cit*, p172.
17 *ibid*, p174.
18 *ibid*, p175.
19 *ibid*, p179.
20 *ibid*, p181.

Chapter 5
1 Letter: E Cranmer to author, 3 May 1979.
2 Martin Courtenay was later to spend 33 years in the RAF as a pilot and served in India, Burma, the Middle East and Europe, whilst Terence served for many years with the Royal Tank Regiment and the Commandos in North Africa, Europe and in Cyprus. (Information from letter: M P C Corkery to author, 11 October 1979).
3 Gibson, M: *Warneford VC*, p52.
4 *ibid*, p55.
5 *ibid, loc cit*.
6 *Daily Express*, Saturday 19 June 1915, p6.
7 Gibson, *op cit*, p60.
8 See Longmore, A M: *From Sea to Sky*, p45.
9 See Longmore, *op cit*, p46.
10 Gibson, *op cit*, p66.
11 See Longmore, *op cit*, p47.
12 Gibson, *op cit*, p67.
13 Longmore's report, 13 June 1915. PRO Air 1, 1259/204/9/3.
14 According to the official air historian, *LZ39* made a rough but safe landing on its return:
 'A dead officer and some wounded men were taken from one of the gondolas, and an inspection of the airship revealed 5 damaged gasbags and the loss of the starboard after propeller'. (Jones, H A: *The War in the Air*, Vol II, p350.
15 Longmore's report.
16 Gibson, *op cit*, p68.
17 See Longmore, *op cit*, p47.
18 Mühler, A: 'Mit LZ37 aus 2000m Brennend Abgestürzt', *Kyffhaüser*, Nr 19, 8 May 1938.
19 *ibid*.
20 *ibid. Oberleutnant* Kurt Ackermann is in error here for no bombs were traced on English soil during this raid.
21 *ibid*.
22 Warneford's report, 8 June 1915. IWM file 'Pilots' Reports Relating to Destruction of Zeppelins'.
23 *Kyffhaüser*, Nr 19.
24 *ibid*.
25 *ibid*.
26 Gibson, *op cit*, p95.
27 Wilson's report, 8 June 1915. IWM file 'Pilots' Reports Relating to Destruction of Zeppelins'.
28 Mills' report, 8 June 1915. IWM file 'Pilots' Reports Relating to Destruction of Zeppelins'.
29 J P Wilson learnt to fly at the Brooklands-based Vickers School and was awarded his pilot's certificate (810) on 8 June 1914. Born in York in 1889, Wilson had been a Yorkshire county cricketer prewar and was commissioned into the RNAS in August 1914. After the war he became a notable steeplechaser and in 1925 he won the Grand National riding Double Chance. Wilson died in 1959.
 Mills, born in 1888, trained at Hendon with the famous Grahame White School, taking his certificate (1049) on 26 January 1915.
30 *The Times*, Wednesday 9 June 1915, p8.
31 Gibson, *op cit*, p99.
32 *ibid*, p110.
33 Other accounts indicate that the mortally injured Warneford was conveyed to Versailles in the Baroness's own car.
34 Gibson, *op cit*, p116.
35 *ibid*, p117.
36 From the files of D Whetton.
37 *Daily Express*, Monday 21 June 1915, p6.
38 *The Times*, Wednesday 23 June 1915, p11.

39 D Whetton.
40 The Highworth connection with the Warneford family is fully explained in Chapter 9 of *Warneford VC*, pp57–60.

Chapter 6
1 By tradition, training schools placed pupils in the front, one reason being that in the event of a crash the more valuable instructor stood a better chance of survival. Nevertheless, some trainer aircraft (such as the Maurice Farman MF7 and MF11) reversed the positions in order that pupils could observe their tutor's movements and reach over his shoulders as necessary. Furthermore, prior to the war it was commonplace for the passenger to sit in front; in many cases he was the mechanic of the 'gentleman' pilot.
2 A complete set of flares for one BE2c machine cost exactly £6 10s 0d. (From Holt Pilot Light, List P, Catalogue, Yorkshire Steel Co Ltd, 1916.)
3 This was not the first time such a scheme had been mooted. As early as 1911 Clement Ader proposed the trailing of a grenade on a wire from an aircraft in order to combat others.
4 'Aerial Torpedoes'. PRO Air 1, 612/16/15/297.
5 The airborne searchlight was anticipated by Igor Sikorsky who first made such an installation to the nose balcony of his 'Le Grand' four-engined aeroplane in 1913.
6 See Bruce, J M: *British Aeroplanes 1914–1918*, pp643–4.
7 See Bruce, J M: *War Planes of the First World War: Fighters*, Vol 1, p200.
8 Usborne's memo: 'Anti Zeppelin Defence', 18 October 1915. PRO Air 1, 2633.
9 For details of other 'radio-controlled flying bombs' see *British Aeroplanes*, pp459–60.
10 Interview: G W R Fane with author, 10 October 1978.
11 Information from RNAS Gunnery Memorandum No 92: 'Rocket Gear', 16 December 1916.
12 'RAF Fiery Grapnel, Mark II'. PRO Air 1, 863/204/5/491.
13 *ibid*.
14 *ibid*.
15 Edwards, A: 'Anti Zeppelin Weapons', *Cross and Cockade Journal* (GB), Vol 5 No 2 (1974), pp78–80.
16 For anti-airship use, two types of *flèchette* were developed. One, a small incendiary version in use during early 1915, consisted of a body in two parts. The upper portion opened out into a cross when released; as the dart struck the airship's covering the cruciform prevented entry while the lower, heavier portion detached itself and pierced the gas bags. The resultant air and hydrogen mix was ignited by a small charge contained in the upper portion still fixed to the covering, this automatically exploding as the lower half detached. The Ranken Anti-Aircraft Dart was merely a development of this, although the idea of a dart with hooks and an incendiary charge was proposed and designed in 1914 by a Frenchman called Guerve, who dropped prototype missiles from the Eiffel Tower. It should be noted that the original plain *flèchettes* were not intended for, or ever used against, Zeppelins.
17 Interview: G W R Fane with author. There were also grenades, adapted from the Hales rifle grenade, which were issued for use against Zeppelins especially by the RNAS. A rack was designed to allow them to drop singly or in salvo, the idea being for the aircraft to fly over the Zeppelin dropping the missiles across its back in a straddle. For further details of the Hales bomb see PRO Air 1, 704/27/703 and 'Improvements in or pertaining to Explosive Shells or similar Bodies', 16 November 1914. (Patents Office Files, Class 9 (i) 22602).
18 Gerard Fane recalled one of the problems with the Ranken Dart:
 'In practice, when you went up at night it was very cold, and considerable condensation was experienced (thus the darts were unusable) since in effect you were really trying to strike a dead match.'
For further details see 'Ranken Anti-Aircraft Dart' (PRO Air 1, 1583/204/82/14) and 'Improvements in and in the Manufacture of Small Darts or Projectiles', 2 December 1914 (Patents Office files, Class 9 (i) 23398).
19 See 'The Buckingham Incendiary Bullet' (PRO Air 1, 719/35/8) and 'Improvements in Incendiary Bullets, Shells and the like', 29 August 1916 (Patents Office files, Class 9 (i), 125593).
20 For further details of both Brock and Pomeroy bullets, see PRO Air 1, 658/17/122/597 and 673/17/153/3.

21 See also 'Summary of the War Development of Tracer, Incendiary and Explosive Ammunition' (Jones, Vol III, Appendix V).

Chapter 7

1 Ernest was educated at Dover College and the RMC, Sandhurst, before being commissioned into the 1st Lincolnshire Regiment, Bangalore, on 19 January 1902. He entered the Indian Army in 1903 and with the 75th Carnatic Infantry served in Mauritius, Ceylon, Aden and various parts of India. As a recruiting officer for three years he was largely responsible for the enormous expansion of the Army with men of India's southern races. A lifetime in the Army ended with Major Robinson appointed as curator of Aldershot's RASC Museum until the late 1950s. Retiring to Sands near Farnham, Surrey, Ernest died in 1963 at the age of 80.
2 Letter: Mrs D Barclay to author, 12 August 1978.
3 Letter: WLR to Irene and Ruth, 11 August 1907.
4 At St Bees School Chapel on 18 June 1932 a tablet was unveiled to commemorate the valour of William Leefe Robinson VC, John Fox-Russell VC MC and Richard William Leslie Wain VC. Captain Russell was killed in action on 6 November 1917 in Palestine. The official citation, announcing his VC award, describes his 'most conspicuous bravery'. Until he was killed by a German marksman, Fox Russell 'repeatedly went out to attend the wounded under murderous fire from snipers and machine guns, and in many cases, when no other means were at hand, carried them in himself, although almost exhausted'.

Captain Wain of the Tank Corps was killed on 20 November 1917:

'During an attack the tank in which he was, was disabled by a direct hit, near an enemy strongpoint which was holding up the attack. Captain Wain and one man, both seriously wounded, were the only survivors. Though bleeding profusely from his wounds, he refused the attention of stretcher bearers, rushed from behind the tank with a Lewis gun, and captured the strongpoint, taking about half the garrison prisoners. Although his wounds were very serious, he picked up a rifle and continued to fire at the retreating enemy until he received a fatal wound in the head. It was due to the valour displayed by Captain Wain that the infantry were able to advance.'

5 Letter: WLR to his mother, undated.
6 Letter: WLR to his mother, undated.
7 Letter: WLR to his mother, September 1912.
8 Letter: WLR to Irene, 25 September 1912.
9 Letter: WLR to his father, 10 January 1913.
10 Letter: WLR to his mother, 23 January 1913.
11 Letter: C S Cay to author, 13 May 1976.
12 Letter: C S Cay to author, 24 June 1976.
13 *ibid.*
14 Letter: WLR to his mother, 1915.
15 *ibid.*
16 Letter: WLR to his mother, 19 April 1915.
17 Letter: WLR to Ruth, 10 May 1915.
18 Letter: WLR to his mother, 11 November 1915.
19 Letter: WLR to his mother, 10 December 1915.
20 Letter: WLR to his mother, 1 January 1916.
21 Letter: WLR to his mother, 6 February 1916. At Croydon, Robinson officially joined the strength of 17 Reserve Squadron on 24 January just prior to his Suttons Farm posting.
22 *ibid.*
23 *ibid.*
24 Written notes: Ruth Irwin, March 1967.
25 Conversation: Mrs Vera Tate with author, 19 August 1979.
26 Letter: WLR to Grace, April 1916.
27 Neuman, G P (ed): *The German Air Force in the Great War*, p119.
28 Superintendent William Fitt's report, 26 April 1916. PRO Air 1, 578/16/15/168, Part 1.
29 WLR's report, 26 April 1916. PRO Air 1, 578/16/15/168, Part 1.
30 Harris's report, 26 April 1916. PRO Air 1, 578/16/15/168, Part 1.
31 *ibid.*
32 Neuman, *op cit*, p121.
33 Higgins' report, 26 April 1916. PRO Air 1, 578/16/15/168, Part 1.
34 Poolman, K: *Zeppelins over England*, p158.
35 The sub-cloud car (*Spähkorb*) was invented by Ernst Lehmann and his executive officer in ZXII, *Freiherr* von Gemmingen, and was used extensively by the Army airship service but shunned by the Navy. LZ90's car is currently on display at the Imperial War Museum in London.
36 Russell Mallinson, P: 'Scareships!', *The London Magazine*, date unknown (via P Amesbury.)
37 Letter: H Tuttle to author, 1976.
38 Letter: WLR to his parents, 22 October 1916.
39 Letter: W Ash to author, 25 September 1976.
40 Letter: W J Clark to author, 31 May 1976.
41 Private information.
42 L32 War Diary. PRO Air 1, 2585, p9.
43 Robinson, D H: *The Zeppelin in Combat*, p176.
44 Letter: A J Gogh to author, 15 July 1976.
45 Letter: L A Aves to author, 14 September 1976.
46 Letter: WLR to his parents.
47 Gran T: '39HDS history', PRO Air 1, 691/21/20/39, p23. The official chronicler of 39 HDS, Captain Tryggve Gran (a native Norwegian) served with the RFC and later the RAF having already made a name for himself prior to the war. Gran had been the skiing expert to Captain Robert Scott's ill-fated 1912 Antarctic expedition and a member of the relief party which found the bodies of Scott and his companions. Flying a Blériot monoplane, Gran also made the first flight across the North Sea, on 30 July 1914.
48 Sutton, H D: *Raiders Approach!*, p28.
49 Letter: A J Gogh to author.
50 Conversation: A Hatt with author, 6 June 1976.
51 Letter: Mrs D Barclay to author.
52 Inquest report, Sergeant F Buttler, 'Y' Division, Metropolitan Police. PRO MEPO 2/1652.
53 *ibid.*
54 *ibid.*
55 *ibid.*
56 *ibid.*
57 This inaccurate reference to 'L21' was perpetuated on Robinson's graveside epitaph, on souvenir cards, in contemporary records and, until comparatively recently, on the memorial at Cuffley – why this was so is difficult to understand. Perhaps Douglas Robinson, the 'elder statesman of rigid airship history', has the answer. In July 1937 he visited the Air Ministry Library and discussed the question with J C Nerney, the Chief Librarian:

'He called for all the original documents on the September 2/3 raid; here were track charts of the ships over England and messages from tracking stations, as well as radio intercepts. L21 was clearly shown both reaching England and departing the coast. I am not sure if SL11 was correctly identified by radio intercepts, though she surely was identified by examining the wreckage. (Army ships were identified by the first three letters of the CO's last name, so SL11 should have been 'SCH'). There was absolutely no doubt in the minds of either of us that L21 was correctly identified, and we concluded that the 'L21' number had been pulled out of the air for no particular reason, as the public would have been severely disappointed if they had learned that the night's victim was *not* a Zeppelin.'

58 *The Barnet Press*, 16 September 1916, p3.
59 *The Barnet Press*, 6 September 1916, p5.
60 *The Barnet Press*, 16 September 1916, p5.
61 *The Daily Graphic*, Monday 4 September 1916. The contravention of Section 35B could result in heavy penalties for souvenir hunters. Police and military forces spared no efforts in tracking down likely suspects; several men and women were taken before the courts and subsequently fined.
62 Holt's report, 3 September 1916. PRO, FO 371, 12069.
63 PRO, FO 371, 12069.
64 *ibid.*
65 Letter: Lieutenant G H Lewis to his father, 17 September 1916. From Lewis, G H: *Wings over the Somme*. In another letter, dated 25 September, he recorded another aside referring to an RNAS pilot who 'must have been a very good fellow, and even in these days when half the fellows in the corps earn a VC every other day...'
66 Letter: WLR to his parents.
67 *ibid.*
68 The actor Ronald Adam, quoted in letter from P G Cooksley to author, 10 January 1976.

69 Conversation: Mrs Vera Tate with author. At least one ex-39HDS fitter confirmed the actresses' visits to Suttons Farm.
70 *ibid.*
71 Perfect, C T: *Hornchurch in the Great War*, p126.
72 Russell Mallinson, *op cit*, p266.
73 Letter: Nancie Vera Nicholson to Frederick Sowrey, 3 November 1916.
74 Gran, *op cit*.
75 *ibid.*
76 '48 Squadron Mobilisation'. PRO Air 1, 128/15/40/167
77 *ibid.*
78 *ibid.*
79 Letter: Captain E N Griffith (ex-48 Squadron) to author, 3 October 1978.
80 Information via D Whetton.
81 Von Richthofen, Manfred: '*Der Rote Kampfflieger*', 1918.
82 Letter: WLR to his parents, 21 July 1917.
83 Second Lieutenants Arthur A Baerlin and J V Wischer of 16 Squadron were brought down in BE2g A2745 on 28 April 1917 as Kurt Wolff's 23rd victory.
84 Second Lieutenant H E Hervey, 60 Squadron, flying Nieuport 17 A311, was brought down by anti-aircraft fire on 8 April; Macintosh, of 1 Squadron, force-landed on 26 May in Nieuport 17 B1685 following a one-sided duel with four Albatros scouts.
85 Hervey, H E: *Cage Birds*, pp26–7.
86 Robinson's fellow escaper was brought down on 28 April 1917 in Sopwith 1½ Strutter A993, Reece's observer being Second Air Mechanic A Moult. It must be recorded that Robinson's many escape attempts earned him a mention in despatches, for 'valuable service while in captivity'. The citation was awarded on 16 December 1918.
87 Hervey, *op cit*, pp43–4.
88 Hockstra, G: 'Trial of Captain Robinson and Lieutenant Baerlin', (MS) 16 October 1917.
89 *ibid.*
90 Later Sir William Stephenson, a key figure in British espionage during World War II. Code-named 'Intrepid', Stephenson was reputedly the man upon whom James Bond creator Ian Fleming based his character 'M'.
91 Letter: O Weightman to WLR, 1918.
92 Quoted in letter from P G Cooksley to author, 17 January 1976.
93 Durnford, H G: 'The Tunnellers of Holzminden'.
94 Private information.
95 This was WLR's sister Katherine, who had married Baron Heyking on 14 July 1917.
96 *The Harrow Observer*, Friday 3 January 1919.
97 *ibid.*
98 For a detailed account of the Niemeyer twins and their exploits see Winchester, B: *Beyond the Tumult*.
99 Yet again the 'L21' legend reared its head. At the time of writing there appear to be no plans to have the error corrected on the stone.

Chapter 8
1 Robinson, D H: *The Zeppelin in Combat*, p183.
2 For a full account of Admiralty Intelligence operations in World War I see James, Admiral Sir W: *The Code Breakers of Room 40*.
3 Brandon's report, 24 September 1916. IWM file 'Pilots' Reports Relating to Destruction of Zeppelins'.
4 Böcker's report from Joachim Breithaupt's unfinished MS: '*Marine-Luftschiffe im 1 Weltkrieg*, 4 December 1917.
5 It should not be surprising that Böcker and his officers would be able to speak good English. The commander was a merchant marine officer, as indeed were most of the German Navy's reserve officers; as a matter of course they would have learnt English since this was the language of the predominant sea power and mercantile fleet of the world at that time.
6 *The Daily Mirror*, Monday 25 September 1916.
7 Nicholas' statement in J H Harris' report, 24 September 1916. Essex Records Office.
8 Smith's report, 25 September 1916. Essex Records Office.
9 Unett's letter, 2 October 1916. Essex Records Office.
10 Smith's report.
11 Robinson, D H: 'Zeppelin Intelligence', *Aerospace Historian*, March 1974, p5. In 1962 Douglas Robinson interviewed *Vizeadmiral* Ernst-Wilhelm Schirlitz, executive officer of *L33*:
'In connection with the loss of L33, he said he doubted that a shell had exploded inside a cell, but believed major gas loss was caused by shells going right through the ship. All motors were run at full power to keep the ship in the air nose up, but [she] rapidly became so heavy that she eventually came to the ground in a nose up attitude. L33 was not over the sea at any time, and did not go out to sea and turn back as stated by the British. Schirlitz wished to believe that nothing of value was retrieved from the wreck after it had burned. He stated he too was threatened with a trial for murder, held prisoner and interrogated for some time by English Intelligence. He remembered Trench when I mentioned the name, and previously had remembered him as a Marine Officer.'
12 *Steuermann* Emmerlich and five fellow crew members of *L33* broke out of Stobbs on 22 August 1917 and for 13 days roamed the hills until reaching the coast and finding an old boat. The Germans rigged up a rudimentary sail from their overcoats and put to sea. For three days and nights the crew sailed on, encountering English patrol boats on several occasions but managing either to avoid them or to 'bluff it out' with their crews. But luck was against them when a British destroyer hove-to: 'But they did not believe us. We were taken on board, and our hopes of seeing home again sank to zero'. See Marben, R (ed): *Zeppelin Adventures*, pp156–160.
13 *The Listener*, 7 February 1974, p178.
14 Thompson, J O: 'Dr Salter of Tolleshunt D'Arcy'. From Dr Salter's diary, 23 September 1916.
15 'Yesterday's Witness', BBC2, 31 January 1974.
16 Interview: Mrs D Buck with author, 17 October 1976.
17 Cowell's report, 31 March 1917. Essex Records Office.
18 Unett's letter, 8 April 1917. Essex Records Office.
19 Account via Mrs D Buck. We can be certain that the 'coracle' to which the correspondent referred was not one of two lifeboats that some airships then carried but one of the bumpers that were strapped to the underside of both main gondolas. See Chapter 2.
20 'Yesterday's Witness'.
21 Private information.
22 Russell Mallinson, P: 'Scareships!', *The London Magazine*, date unknown, p266. (via P Amesbury.)
23 *ibid.*
24 Brandon's report.
25 Statement. Major F Sowrey, 143 Squadron, 11 April 1919. PRO Air 1 608/16/15/264.
26 Letter: L Goddard to author, 17 October 1978.
27 Letter: L D Jarvis to author, 12 September 1978.
28 Russell Mallinson, *op cit*.
29 This German Navy signal book was one of the biggest intelligence *coups* of the war since *Magdeburg* had been replaced by the Germans in August 1916. As a result, Admiral Hall's cryptographers were having the greatest difficulty in deciphering German signals, but *L32*'s book effectively solved the problem; furthermore, the Germans were totally unaware of the scoop.
30 L32 War Diary. PRO Air 1, 2585.
31 Perfect, C T: *Hornchurch in the Great War*, p130.
32 Conversation: Miss Mary Sowrey with author, 14 December 1979.
33 Conversation: Mrs Vera Tate with author, 19 August 1979.
34 *Daily Express*, Thursday 5 October 1916.
35 Letter: Mrs Susan Sowrey to Frederick Sowrey, 7 September 1916.
36 Letter: E M Jewell to John Sowrey, 6 October 1916.
37 Letter: J Grinling to Frederick Sowrey, October 1916.
38 Conversation: Mrs Vera Tate with author.
39 Ellis's report, 28 September 1916. Essex Records Office.
40 Myddleton Gavey's report, 30 September 1916. PRO Air 1, 608/16/15/264.
41 The foundations of the old 'High Barn' can still be seen.
42 Letter: F Green to D Whetton, 7 October 1963.
43 Ellis's report.
44 Mrs Eales's statement, 27 September 1916. Essex Records Office.
45 Major Cyril F Fleming's report, 27 September 1916. PRO Air 1, 608/16/15/264.
46 Macdonagh, M: 'I Saw the Doom of L32', *I Was There*, February 1939, pp867–8.

47 Walters, E W: *Heroic Airmen and their Exploits*, pp81–2.
48 Macdonagh, *loc cit*.
49 Local girl Gwendoline Stuff can still recall Kraushaar's attack on Nottingham, how the streets were littered with glass and how the flames of the iron works furnaces were banked down with ash and earth to reduce the glare. The ore was taken on lifts to the chimney tops, dropped and then fired from beneath until the required temperature was reached. The glow of the resultant flames could be seen in the sky from the coast and was easily visible to Zeppelin commanders.
50 On 14 June 1917 Captain Frederick Sowrey joined the strength of 19 Squadron as a Flight Commander. Between then and mid-October he brought down several enemy aircraft and shared 'kills' with other officers. The log of 19 Squadron records Sowrey as having participated in at least 15 successful air combats, although only three of his victories were confirmed. On 17 August, flying Spad VII B3620, Sowrey shot down a two-seater over Ypres for his first confirmed victory. The second was a Fokker east of Gheluvelt on 7 October (Sowrey in Spad B6777) and the third a black and white Albatros north-east of Moorslede six days later, Sowrey flying Spad A6709. See Kilduff, P: *That's My Bloody Plane: The World War Experiences of Major Cecil Montgomery-Moore* DFC, The Pequot Press, Ct, USA, 1975.
51 Now Air Marshal Sir Frederick Sowrey KCB CBE AFC.
52 As this book goes to press, 4112 is currently undergoing a full restoration, which will result in this historic aircraft appearing in its original 1916 colour scheme.

Chapter 9

1 Undoubtedly Mathy's greatest achievement by his own admission was the attack on London of 8 September 1915, as fully described in Chapter 3.
2 *LZ4* was completed in June 1908 and on 4 August Count Ferdinand von Zeppelin embarked on a 24-hour test flight for the German Army. A motor failed him 11 hours into the flight, but after repairs *LZ4* remained airborne until the next day when a recurrence of the problem compelled von Zeppelin to land at Echterdingen near Stuttgart. During repairs, a sudden thunderstorm swept the Zeppelin into the air and it caught fire and fell half a mile further on, totally wrecked. The accident was the turning point in von Zeppelin's fortunes, for his stubborn determination to continue with his airships made him a national hero. A tide of patriotic fervour resulted in sufficient public subscriptions to enable the Count to build a replacement ship.
3 Jones, H A: *The War in the Air*, Vol III, p 238.
4 Robinson, D H: *The Zeppelin in Combat*, p11.
5 *ibid*, pp193–4.
6 *ibid*.
7 Major Charles Lloyd's report to GHQ Home Forces, 4 October 1916. PRO Air 1, 585/16/15/185.
8 Police Superintendent W A Jenkins' report, 2 October 1916. PRO MEPO 2, 1654.
9 Personal account: Squadron Commander W J Tempest RAF DSO MC, 15 August 1920.
10 *ibid*.
11 *ibid*.
12 Wulstan's godparents were Mr Frank Clifford and a Mrs Gurner.
13 *The Stonyhurst Magazine*, Vol XIII (Part 2), No 208, October 1916, p1694.
14 Edmund would eventually enjoy a successful career in the RFC and serve with 64 Squadron in France, scoring 14 confirmed victories. He joined that unit on 15 October 1917 at Izel-le-Hameau, initially flying DH5s, which were replaced by SE5as in early 1918. On 17 March Captain E R Tempest led a patrol over the lines and dived on a flight of five German machines, shooting one down in flames over Douai. Five minutes later, together with Second Lieutenants J Barrett and C B Stringer and Lieutenants K S P Hendrie and C A Bisonette, he sent a Pfalz DIII down out of control over Baiche. (See combat report in PRO Air 1, 1255/204/5/2634.) Tempest's fifth victory took place the following day over Cambrai when he sent an Albatros down out of control. On 24 March Tempest was awarded the MC and on 30 August he was posted to Home Establishment, the second highest scoring pilot of 64 Squadron. He was awarded the DFC for service in France and was killed in a DH9 in Mesopotamia during 1919, the victim of a flying accident.

15 *The Stonyhurst Magazine, loc cit*.
16 Conversation: Mrs Vera Tate with author, 19 August 1979.
17 Major Wilfred Norman Tempest, born on 8 June 1887, served with the KOYLI and was in command of a battalion in this regiment when he was killed during the Battle of the Somme on 25 September 1916. A fellow officer wrote to Tempest Senior:
'The Colonel was ill, but I knew that the battalion was certain to be well and wisely commanded by your son. He was shot through the head and heart, so death was quite instantaneous. He was such a good soldier that I am sure it was the death he would have preferred.' (*The Stonyhurst Magazine*, Vol XIII (Part 2), No 208, October 1916, p1708.)
18 Letter: Wilfred Francis Tempest to his wife, 7 October 1916. The term 'Archies' was period slang for anti-aircraft fire.
19 *London Gazette*, 13 October 1916.
20 Burge, Major C G: *The Annals of 100 Squadron*, p70.
21 *London Gazette*, 7 March 1918.
22 The son, Norman Edmund, once took his father to the aircraft collection at Rockcliffe, Ontario; naturally, Sowrey's preserved BE2c 4112 was the highlight of the visit, and Major Tempest was deeply moved as 'he had flown it many times'.
23 Letter: R G Hollies Smith to author, 28 April 1979.
24 Lieutenant Harry Carter's report to OCT, POW Camp, Alexandra Palace, 2 October 1916. PRO Air 1, 585/16/15/185.
25 Walters: *Heroic Airmen*, pp99–100.
26 *Daily Express*, Tuesday 3 October 1916.
27 *Daily Mail*, Wednesday 4 October 1916, p5.
28 Letter: C J Cole to author, 17 August 1978.
29 *The Times*, Thursday 5 October 1916, p3.
30 *The Barnet Press*, 7 October 1916, p6.
31 Bahn, Heinrich. 'In a German Airship over England', *Journal of the Royal United States Services Institution*, February 1926, p106.
32 Robinson, *op cit*, p196.
33 *The Barnet Press*, 21 October 1916, p3.
34 It was on 20 July 1938 that Mr J Berwick Thompson, official receiver of 'Standard Properties (Potters Bar) Ltd', wrote to Mr T T Thorpe of the Potters Bar UDC:
'... In regard to the plot of land at Potters Bar on which the Zeppelin Tree stands, I have recently had a letter from Mr E Parker of 7 Tempest Avenue, Potters Bar, complaining that the Zeppelin tree is in a dangerous condition and having regard to its proximity to the road, may do some damage unless it is taken down.'
The precise date on which the famous oak fell to the woodman's axe has eluded the author thus far, but it was probably during World War II that the council took action.

Chapter 10

1 Robinson, D H: *The Zeppelin in Combat*, p197.
2 Letter: E Cadbury to his mother, 13 June 1915.
3 Letter: E Cadbury to his mother, 4 June 1915.
4 Letter: E Cadbury to his mother, 19 September 1915.
5 Letter: E Cadbury to his mother, 6 August 1916.
6 Letter: E Cadbury to his mother, 24 September 1916.
7 Snowden Gamble, C F: *The Story of a North Sea Air Station*, p190.
8 Letter: E Cadbury to his mother, 20 October 1916.
9 Hollender, *Korvettenkäpitan* H: *Marineluftschiffe, Die Deutschen Luftstreitkräft in Weltkrieg*, p395.
10 Robinson, *op cit*, p197.
11 Letter: W H Bell to author, 18 August 1978.
12 Pyott related his experiences to fellow 20 Squadron member Stanley Walters, a native South African. Colonel Walters provided these details to the author via letter, 28 August 1979.
13 Letter: S Thompson to author, 27 August 1978.
14 Robinson, *op cit*, p199 (Ehrlich's report).
15 *ibid*, p200 (Hollender's report).
16 Ellison's report, 28 November 1916. IWM file 'Pilots' Reports Relating to Destruction of Zeppelins'.
17 Letter: G H Unwin, South African Merchants, to IVP, 7 April 1916.
18 Letter: E Charteris to IVP, 5 April 1916.
19 *The Courier*, 16 December 1916, p4.

20 Ellison's report.
21 Interview: G W R Fane with author, 10 October 1978.
22 Interview: G W R Fane with author.
23 Pulling's report, 28 November 1916. IWM file 'Pilots' Reports Relating to Destruction of Zeppelins'.
24 *The Yarmouth Independent*, 2 December 1916.
25 *ibid*.
26 *The Daily Telegraph*, 4 December 1916.
27 Ellison's report, 6 August 1916. PRO Air 1, 147/15/74.
28 Letter: E Cadbury to his mother, 4 March 1917.
29 Letter: E Cadbury to his mother, 11 March 1917.
30 Snowden Gamble, *op cit*, p283.
31 *ibid*, p402.
32 Lieutenant A E Whiting's report to Intelligence Section, GHQ Home Forces, 7 December 1916. PRO Air 1, 614/16/15/315.
33 *The Daily Graphic*, 29 December 1916, p2.

Chapter 11
1 Snowden Gamble, C F: *The Story of a North Sea Air Station*, p28.
2 *ibid*, p30.
3 *The Yarmouth Independent*, 17 June 1913.
4 Snowden Gamble, *op cit*, p102.
5 For further data on wartime flying boats see Robinson, Austin: 'The Recognition of First World War Flying Boats', *Cross and Cockade Journal* (GB), Vol 11 No 1 (1980), pp21–28.
6 Aircraft 8666 enjoyed a long and successful career at Great Yarmouth, earning it the title of 'the most famous flying boat in the service'. Even today the memory of 'Old eighty-six sixty-six' is kept alive by members of an air historical society in the Great Yarmouth area. 'The 8666 Group' is formed of a small but dedicated band of friends drawn together by their common interest in aeronautical subjects in general, aircraft modelling and antique and modern firearms.
7 Leckie's biographical data from Official Canadian Air Force historical records.
8 Galpin's report, 14 May 1917. IWM file 'Pilots' Reports Relating to Destruction of Zeppelins'.
9 Leckie's report 14 May 1917. IWM file 'Pilots' Reports Relating to Destruction of Zeppelins'.
10 Galpin's report.
11 Cadbury's report, 14 May 1917. PRO Air 1, 637/17/122/153.
12 Scheer, R: *Germany's High Seas Fleet in the World War*, pp283–4.
13 For a full account of the 'Height-Climbers', see Chapter 13.
14 Galpin's report, 24 May 1917. Snowden Gamble, *op cit*, p242.
15 Sommerfeldt's report. See Robinson, D H: *The Zeppelin in Combat*, p238.
16 See Chapter 16.

Chapter 12
1 Robinson, D H: *The Zeppelin in Combat*, p238.
2 This date is quoted in RAF records although Hobbs' service record, held by the Directorate of History, National Defence Headquarters, Ottawa, gives it as 1895.
3 Hallam, Squadron Leader T D: *The Spider Web*, pp17–18.
4 *ibid*, p113.
5 *ibid*, pp42–3.
6 In the afternoon of 5 September 1917, H12 8666, with Leckie and Nicholl aboard, in company with a DH4 crewed by Flight Lieutenant A H H Gilligan and Observer Lieutenant G S Trewin, engaged *L44* some 30 miles from Terschelling. Both *L44* and its consort *L46* were well out of range, and German light cruisers below opened fire, scoring hits on both British aircraft. The DH4 ditched and Leckie came down alongside to rescue the crew, but 8666 refused to take off from the rough sea and as Leckie taxied the leaking boat towards England, messenger pigeons were released; two out of four released made it back to Great Yarmouth. But it was not until 9 September that HMS *Halcyon* found the boat and retrieved its totally exhausted crew. Fuller accounts of this remarkable story can be found in Snowden Gamble, C F: *The Story of a North Sea Air Station*, pp259–71, and B V Cousens: 'A Pigeon and Prayer', *Aeroplane Monthly*, October 1974, pp922–7.
7 The weighted boots were vital: at several stations where there was a strong running tide, waders without these boots had been literally swept off their feet and drowned.
8 Hallam, *op cit*, pp47–8.
9 *ibid*, p114.
10 Hobbs' and Dickey's joint report, 14 June 1917. IWM file 'Pilots' Reports Relating to Destruction of Zeppelins'.
11 *ibid*.
12 Hallam, *op cit*, p121.
13 *The Daily Telegraph*, Monday 18 June 1917, p7.
14 Snowden Gamble, *op cit*, p246.
15 Snowden Gamble, *loc cit*.
16 Hollender's report. Robinson, *op cit*, p240.
17 Snowden Gamble, *op cit*, p254.
18 Recollections of *Oberleutnant* Richard Frey. Snowden Gamble, *op cit* pp255–6. Kraushaar was 35 when he was killed and curiously his was the only body ever found, washed up on the shoreline at Hage. He was buried in the Hage churchyard, and when his English-born wife died in 1974 she was buried by her husband's side. Current travellers on the *Prinz Hamlet* en route from Hamburg to Harwich will pass within a mile or two of where *L43* struck the water.
19 See note 6, also Robinson, *op cit*, pp245–6.
20 See Chapter 17.
21 For a fuller account, see Snowden Gamble, *op cit*, pp394–400.
22 Hallam, *op cit*, p421.

Chapter 13
1 Robinson, D H: *The Zeppelin in Combat*, p232. Ellerkamm gives an earlier and different account of his ordeal in Marben, R (ed): *Zeppelin Adventures*, pp52–60.
2 Gladisch, W: *Der Krieg in der Nordsee*, Vol VI, p290.
3 Jones, H A: *The War in the Air*, Vol III, p243.
4 *L36* was later destroyed in an operational accident on 6 February 1917 during a scouting mission; its commander, *Kapitänleutnant der Reserve* Franz Georg Eichler, was exonerated by Strasser at the subsequent court of enquiry. See Robinson, D H: 'The Loss of the Zeppelin L36', *Cross and Cockade Journal* (US), Vol 2, No 3, (1961), pp351–9.
5 See von Buttlar-Brandenfels, *Freiherr* Treusch: *Zeppelins over England*.
6 For a full and detailed account, see Robinson, *op cit*, pp216–20.
7 Stabbert's report. Robinson, *op cit*, pp223–4.
8 For a fuller account, see Robinson, *op cit*, pp222–7.
9 Marben, *op cit*, p52.
10 Mieth, O: 'Shot Down by the British – A Zeppelin Officer's Story', *Frankfurter Zeitung Illustriertes Blatt*, 28 February 1926. Mieth is in error in referring to 'two . . . reconnaissance airships' for only one was destroyed – see Chapter 12.
11 *Daily Mail*, Monday 18 June 1917, p5.
12 Letter: E Cadbury to his mother, 10 June 1917.
13 Dietrich's report. Robinson, *op cit*, p230.
14 Mieth, *op cit*.
15 Cooper's report: 'Air Raid Action Taken on June 16–17, 1917'. PRO Air 1 589/16/15/200.
16 Mieth, *op cit*.
17 Cooper's report.
18 J M Dimmock's report, 23 June 1917. PRO Air 1, 589/16/15/200.
19 Letter: A E Tuckwell to author, 6 November 1978.
20 Letter: G E Foster to author, 7 September 1978.
21 Holder, Squadron Leader F D: 'The Destruction of the L48', *Cross and Cockade Journal* (GB), Vol 7 No3 (1976), p104.
22 'Saundby Papers'. Accession AC72/12, RAF Museum Aviation Records Department.
23 Watkins' report, 18 June 1917. PRO Air 1, 589/16/15/200.
24 'Saundby Papers'.
25 Marriot's report, 18 June 1917. PRO Air 1, 589/16/15/200.
26 Letter: A E Orford to author, 21 August 1978.
27 Mieth, *op cit*.
28 *ibid*.
29 Private information.
30 Bird's report, 19 July 1917. PRO Air 1, 589/16/15/200.
31 Robinson, D H: 'Zeppelin Intelligence', *Aerospace Historian*, March 1974, p6.

32 Ennion's report: 'Information as to Action of Guard', undated. PRO Air 1, 589/16/15/200. The first body was thought to be that of *Obermaschinistenmaat* Hermann von Stockum by his identity disc, 1138 MLA 1843.
33 Gilbertson-Smith's report: 'Information as to Action of Guard' undated. PRO Air 1, 589/16/15/200.
34 Passes were of two kinds: a special pass (white with red band) printed in red gave access to wrecks permitting the 'bearer to perform special duties mentioned thereon'; an ordinary pass (white printed in black) only permitted bearers to view wreckage from beyond the inner cordon. See 'Instructions for the Disposal of Enemy Aircraft brought to earth in the United Kingdom', 20 October 1916. PRO Air 1, 1269/204/9/86.
35 Later Sir Victor Goddard KCB CBE MA.
36 *R38* was lost on 24 August 1921 when it broke up in mid-air over Hull and caught fire, killing 44 people; among the dead was Campbell himself. For the full story of *R38* see Robinson, D H: *Giants in the Sky*.
37 Pretty's letter to Home Office, 20 June 1917. In quoting five bodies, Pretty would seem to have mistakenly included the three survivors in the tally. See PRO Air 1, 615/16/15/320.
38 According to Holder's account (note 22), the placing of this wreath met with some criticism from certain circles. Quoting further: 'It was, however, normal to do this in France as we had respect for our fellow fliers and it was impossible not to admire their courage'. Over the communal grave the RFC later erected a long wooden board with a poignant inscription that reflected the general feeling: 'Who art thou that judges another man's servant? To his own master, he standeth or falleth' (Romans 14:4).
39 In earlier years, stone memorial tablets had been sent from Germany by sea to Southampton, to Leiston by rail and thence by horse-drawn cart to the little churchyard, the last operation under the supervision of James Coate, landlord of The Red Lion. The crew are no longer at Theberton, having been reinterred at Cannock Chase, but a framed record of the *L48* event and a portion of girder remains on view at St Peter.
40 O'Meara's report to No 9 Area EC, Warley, 30 July 1917. PRO Air 1, 589/16/15/200.
41 *East Anglian Daily Times*, 7 September 1917.
42 For a full appraisal of Holder's Orfordness service, see *Cross and Cockade Journal* (GB), Vol 8 No 1 (1977), pp49–61.
43 Hawker had gained the VC as a result of consistent gallantry over almost a year of operational flying and fighting, the award gazetted on 24 August 1915. He earns a place in this chronicle, for on 18 April 1915 in BE2c 1780 he single-handedly attacked the Gontrode airship base. Scoring two hits on the shed that usually housed *LZ35*, he was robbed of a claim since this Zeppelin had been damaged by AA fire and wrecked in a forced landing near Ypres just five days previously. For this officer's full biography see *Hawker VC* by Colonel Tyrrell M Hawker, Mitre Press, 1965. Lovers of trivia will note that Hawker attended Captain E N Clifton's wedding on 8 November 1916, being driven to the ceremony with Fred Sowrey and Joan Whipple with 'Billy' Robinson at the wheel of his Vauxhall. Clifton had served as Hawker's observer-gunner in France with 6 Squadron during 1915.
44 Saundby's logbook. RAF Museum file, Accession AC72/12.
45 This, the serial number quoted in the official casualty report, confirms A6599 as one of 250 FE2ds built by Boulton and Paul Ltd.
46 Casualty report, 1 July 1918. PRO Air 1, 857/204/5/412.

Chapter 14
1 There was a brother, Charles, who served with 5 Squadron RFC during the war. For a full and detailed account of his wartime experiences, see *Cross and Cockade Journal* (USA), Vol 10 No 1 (1969), pp1–33.
2 Interview: B A Smart with author, 18 September 1978.
3 Letter: B A Smart to his mother, August 1917.
4 This aircraft, Friedrichshafen FF23 1098, was operating from the seaplane station at List and crewed by *Leutnant der Reserve der Marine-Artillerie* Gottsauer and *Flugmaat* Steindmüller.
5 Letter: Director of Naval Intelligence to CO, HMS *Furious*, 27 January 1919.
6 See Chapter 15.
7 Interview: B A Smart with author.

Chapter 15
1 See Morris, Joseph: *The German Air Raids on Great Britain*, p174.
2 Jones, H A: *The War in the Air*, Vol V, p56.
3 Robinson, D H: *The Zeppelin in Combat*, p264.
4 For a fuller account, see Robinson, *op cit*, p265.
5 Lefevre's report: *Cross and Cockade Journal* (USA), Vol 4 No 3 (1963), pp278–9.
6 The pilots included Lefevre, to whom Gayer surrendered.
7 Lefevre's report.
8 During the raid on Paris, 29 January 1916, *LZ79* was damaged by anti-aircraft fire, resulting in the airship crash-landing short of its base at Namur. While over the French capital, *LZ79* was attacked by Maurice Farman MF7 1187, crewed by *Sergeant* Denneboude and *Corporal* Louis Vallin. The latter described what happened:
'...I opened fire with an 1874 model Gras carbine, sending about 30 Desvignes incendiary bullets one by one, several of which hit the target. The response was immediate. We were met with several bursts of machine gun fire, which to our great good fortune passed us by.
'According to reports of the time, Zeppelin L79 [*sic*] released a quantity of water ballast as soon as it realised it was under attack, allowing the ship to gain altitude. We needed to climb, and banked away, losing sight of the Zeppelin'. ('Icare', *Revue de l'Aviation Française*', No 46, Autumn 1968, p80.)
9 Presumably the derelict and its hapless passengers went down in the Mediterranean.
10 For fuller accounts see Robinson, *op cit*, Ch XVIII and *id*: 'World Power or Downfall – The Story of the "Silent Raid"', *Cross and Cockade Journal* (USA), Vol 4 No 1 (1963), pp1–17.
11 Jones, *op cit*, p101.
12 Robinson, D H: *The Zeppelin in Combat*, Ch XXI.
13 Robinson, *op cit*, p308.
14 Wigram's report, 13 April 1918. PRO Air 1, 602/16/15/232.
15 *L62* was later destroyed in an operational 'accident' at around 10.05hrs on 10 May 1918, while on the same day a British flying-boat crew attacked *L56*. Surviving naval airship personnel believe sabotage was the cause of *L62*'s loss, while the official history *War in the Air* credits its destruction to Killingholme Air Station officers. At 13.20hrs F2a flying boat N4291 took off with Captain T C Pattinson as first pilot, Captain Albert H Munday, a Canadian, as second pilot and engineer H R Stubbington and a radio man. Fifty miles from the Borkum Reef lightship, at 16.30hrs, the boat crew observed an airship and an attack ensued. The vessel was *L56*, commanded by *Kapitänleutnant* Walter Zaeschmar, and the British airmen forced it to break off its patrol prematurely. Although in his subsequent report Munday observed the Zeppelin heading 'for Holstein in a crabwise fashion emitting much smoke', *neither he nor Pattinson officially claimed to have destroyed it.*
For fuller accounts see Munday and Pattinson's reports, 10 May 1918. IWM file 'Pilots' Reports Relating to Destruction of Zeppelins'. Also Robinson, D H: 'History Corrected', *American Aviation Historical Society Journal*, Vol 4 No 1 (Spring 1959), pp50–53.
16 Letter: E Cadbury to his mother, 13 April 1917.
17 Raleigh, Sir W: *The War in the Air*, Vol 1, pp389–90.
18 Babington's report, 22 November 1914: memo by the Director of Air Department, Admiralty. PRO Air 1, 361/15/228/37.
19 Raleigh, *op cit*, pp401–2.
20 *ibid*, pp402–5.
21 Robinson, *op cit*, p319.
22 'Report on Attack on Zeppelin sheds at Tondern by Aeroplanes from HMS *Furious*, 19th July 1918'. PRO Air 1, 344/15/226/287.
23 Dickson's report, 29 July 1918. IWM file 'Pilots' Reports Relating to Destruction of Zeppelins'.
24 Letter: B A Smart to his mother, 21 July 1918. Thyne returned safely to the fleet at 05.30hrs and after ditching his machine was picked up by one of the ships.
25 *ibid*.
26 *ibid*.
27 'Summary of Bombing Attack on Tondern', 20 July 1918. PRO Air 1, 344/15/226/287.
28 Letter: B A Smart to his mother.
29 *ibid*.

Chapter 16

1 Robinson, D H: *The Zeppelin in Combat*, p328.
2 *ibid*, p327.
3 *ibid, loc cit*.
4 See Chapter 17.
5 As evidence of this, note Strasser's reaction on learning the news of *L48*'s destruction from Dietrich. See Chapter 13.
6 Robinson, *op cit*, p329.
7 *ibid, loc cit*.
8 W Gouge's report to Superintendent, Trinity Store, Great Yarmouth. PRO Air 1, 603/16/15/234.
9 *The Yarmouth Independent*, 10 August 1918, p5.
10 Letter: Major E Cadbury to his father, 6 August 1918. The 'twin' referred to was DH4 A8039, crewed by Lieutenant R E Keys and Private A T Harman, Gunlayer ON 210675, who left Great Yarmouth at 20.55hrs. Keys was later to claim the destruction of a Schütte Lanz airship during his patrol but this was never substantiated. The claim always puzzled Cadbury. Nita Blackstock, mentioned in the first paragraph, had joined the Cadburys on 2 August.
11 Robinson, D H: 'The Loss of L70', *Cross and Cockade Journal* (USA), Vol 4 No 4 (1963).
12 Cadbury's report, 6 August 1918. IWM file 'Pilots' Reports Relating to Destruction of Airships'.
13 *The Times*, Thursday 8 August 1918.
14 Snowden Gamble, C F: *The Story of a North Sea Air Station*, pp410–11.
15 Letter: R Leckie to E Cadbury, February 1962.
16 Snowden Gamble, *loc cit*.
17 Letter: R Leckie to E Cadbury.
18 Letter: Major E Cadbury to his father.
19 *ibid*.
20 Lieutenant Tomkins' Camel was N6624.
21 Snowden Gamble, *op cit*, p413.
22 Marsden's report, 5 August 1918. PRO Air 1, 619/16/15/355.
23 Letter: R Leckie to E Cadbury.
24 Dietrich made this comment to Douglas Robinson during an interview in the early 1960s. Dietrich was probably jealous that the command of *L70* had gone to von Lossnitzer, but it is doubtful that Strasser considered experience when making his selection. Former airship officers have gone on record to state how the Leader of Airships was unduly impressed by titles of nobility.
25 Letter: E Cadbury to his mother, 3 September 1918.
26 Some of these relics are now in the custody of the Fleet Air Arm Museum at Yeovilton and include portions of girder and a valve cover.
27 Admiralty Intelligence certainly obtained their first copy of the new squared position chart of the North Sea introduced on 15 July 1918, and von Lossnitzer's notebook apparently recorded results of trial flights in Friedrichshafen. One can only wonder at the commander's carelessness.
28 Robinson, D H: *The Zeppelin in Combat*, p337.
29 *ibid, loc cit*.
30 *ibid*, p336.
31 Robinson, D H: 'The Loss of L70'.
32 Letter: E Cadbury to D H Robinson, 28 January 1962.
33 Aside from the complete crews of *SL11*, *L31*, *L32* and *L48*, only four other airship casualties are at Cannock Chase: there are three from *L34*, plus 'Krüger'.
34 Telegram: Admiral Scheer to the Naval Airship Division, August 1918.
35 *Kölnische Zeitung*, 7 August 1918. PRO Air 1, 603/16/15/234.
36 Snowden Gamble, *op cit*, p414.
37 Letter: E Cadbury to his mother, 9 August 1918.

Chapter 17

1 Culley's autobiographical notes, May 1930. PRO Air 1, 2391/228/11/153.
2 *ibid*.
3 Snowden Gamble, C F: *The Story of a North Sea Air Station*, p393.
4 *ibid, loc cit*.
5 Robinson, D H: 'A Land Based Fighter Taking off at Sea', *Cross and Cockade Journal* (USA), Vol 4 No 1 (1963), pp28–30.
6 Some accounts have this survivor later being picked up unharmed by the crew of a Dutch fishing vessel, yet the author has found nothing to substantiate this claim.
7 Culley's report, 5 August 1918. IWM file 'Pilots' Reports Relating to Destruction of Zeppelins'.
8 Letter: S D Culley to R V Dodds, 1 June 1963.
9 Lieutenant Commander A Coke's reports of action, 16 August 1918. PRO Air 1, 343/15/74.
10 Memo: Director of Air Division to Rear Admiral Tyrwhitt, 18 August 1918. PRO Air 1, 343/15/74.

Chapter 18

1 It was on 19 February 1918 that the *Zeppelin Werke Lindau* had delivered the first all-metal Dornier RS III to the seaplane station at Norderney. For further details of these fascinating aircraft see Haddow, G H and Grosz, P M: *The German Giants*, Putnam (1962).
2 Masterman was one of England's true airship pioneers: he supervised the inflation of the ill-starred *Mayfly*, developed a mooring mast for non-rigids in 1916 and collaborated with Barnes Wallis in the development of Vickers-built rigids. See Morpurgo, J E: *Barnes Wallis*.
3 Freeman, Lewis: *To Kiel in the Hercules*.
4 See von Buttlar: *Zeppelins over England*.
5 *L61* was not destroyed; instead the airship was inflated with hydrogen for film use and flown by von Schiller. On 30 August 1920, *L61* was surrendered to the Italians and in 1921 was wrecked at Ciampino.
6 Interview: *Maschinistenmaat* Ernst Weiss with D H Robinson, 1957.
7 Since the USA had not ratified the Versailles Treaty none of the Zeppelins was allocated for American use, although *L14* and *L65* had been previously assigned for this purpose.
8 Snowden Gamble, C F: *The Story of a North Sea Air Station*, p428.
9 With the exception of *L72* and the small commercial ships *Bodensee* and *Nordstern*.
10 Air raid statistics from Jones, H A: *The War in the Air*, Appendix XLIV, p164.
11 See Chapter 3.
12 The control gondola from *LZ113* is preserved at the Musée de l'Air in Paris. Visitors to Friedrichshafen should take in the Zeppelin Museum housed in the Municipal Offices building (*Stadtverwaltungs-Gebäude*), part of the Bodensee Museum. Models and engines form the bulk of the exhibits, while there is also a postal service for postcards, books and photographs.
13 Freeman, *op cit*.
14 For the full story see Robinson, D H: 'Peter Strasser, The Leader of Airships, Honoured 50 Years Later at Nordholz'. *Cross and Cockade Journal* (USA), Vol 11 No 1 (1970), pp85–8.
15 This was not the famous and most successful of all Zeppelins, but the second ship to bear the name, *LZ130*, unofficially named *Graf Zeppelin II*. This, the last Zeppelin to be built, first flew on 14 September 1938, was over 803ft in length, possessed a volume of 7,062,100 cu ft, boasted a speed of just over 80mph and was luxuriously appointed. After its unsuccessful 'ferret' missions *LZ130* was laid up at Frankfurt, and on 29 February 1940 its destruction (along with the original *Graf*) was ordered by Hermann Goering and both ships were broken up soon afterwards. For further details see Robinson, D H: *Giants in the Sky*, pp295–6.
16 See Wood & Dempster: *The Narrow Margin*, pp1–2.

Bibliography

Official Documents

Air Historical Branch and Admiralty records in class AIR 1, held at the Public Records Office, Ruskin Avenue, Kew, Richmond, Surrey, England.
CB1265: 'German Rigid Airships', published by the Ordnance Survey, 1917, compiled by the Intelligence Division of the Admiralty War Staff.
Various pilots' personal records held at the RAF Museum, The Hyde, Hendon, London, England.
Police records of air raids and the destruction of airships L32 and L33, held by the Essex Record Office, County Hall, Chelmsford, Essex, England.
Armament patents in Class 9 (i) 'Ammunition', held by The Patent Office, 25 Southampton Buildings, London, England.
'Pilots' Reports Relating to Destruction of Zeppelins' and maps of air raids held by the Imperial War Museum, Lambeth, London, England.
Contemporary newspapers, held by The British Library's Newspaper Library, Colindale Avenue, London, England.

Books

Bacon, Sir Reginald: *The Dover Patrol 1915–1917* (2 volumes), Hutchinson (London, 1923).
Bowyer, Chaz: *For Valour – The Air VCs*, William Kimber (London, 1978).
Bowyer, Chaz: *Sopwith Camel – King of Combat*, Glasney Press (Falmouth, 1978).
Bruce, J M: *British Aeroplanes 1914–1918*, Putnam (London, 1957).
Bruce, J M: *The Aeroplanes of the Royal Flying Corps (Military Wing)*, Putnam (London, 1982).
Bruce, J M: *Warplanes of the First World War – Fighters* (3 volumes), MacDonald & Co (Publishers) Ltd (London, 1968 & 1970).
Burge, Major C Gordon: *The Annals of 100 Squadron*, Herbert Reiach (London, 1919).
Bushby, John R: *Air Defence of Great Britain*, Ian Allan (London, 1973).
Collier, Basil: *The Airship – A History*, Hart-Davis, MacGibbon (London, 1974).
Durnford, H G: *The Tunnellers of Holzminden*, Cambridge University Press (London, 1920).
Elliot, Christopher: *Aeronauts and Aviators*, Terence Dalton (Suffolk, 1971).
Gibson, Mary: *Warneford VC*, Friends of the Fleet Air Arm Museum (Somerset, 1979).
Groos, Otto and Gladisch, Walter: *Der Krieg in der Nordsee* (6 volumes), E S Mittler u Sohn (1920–27 & 1936).
Guttery, Wing Commander T E: *Zeppelin – An Illustrated Life of Count Ferdinand von Zeppelin, 1838–1917*, Shire Publications (Buckinghamshire, 1973).
Haddow, G W, and Grosz, P M: *The German Giants – The Story of the R-Planes, 1914–1919*, Putnam (London, 1962).
Hallam, Squadron Leader T M: *The Spider Web*, William Blackwood & Sons (Edinburgh and London, 1919).
Hervey, H E: *Cage Birds*, Penguin Books (London, 1940).
Higham, Dr Robin: *The British Rigid Airship 1908–31*, G T Foulis & Co Ltd (London, 1961).
James, Admiral Sir William: *The Code Breakers of Room 40*, St Martins Press (New York, 1956).
Jane, Fred T: *Jane's All The World's Aircraft 1917*, Sampson Low, Marston & Co Ltd (London & Edinburgh, 1917).
Jones, H A: *The War in the Air*, Vols II, III, IV and V, Oxford University Press (London, 1928–31).
Lewis, Freeman R: *To Kiel in the Hercules*, John Murray (London, 1919).
Livock, G E: *To the Ends of the Air*, HMSO (London, 1973).
Longmore, Sir Arthur M: *From Sea to Sky 1910–1945*, Geoffrey Bles (London, 1946).
Marben, Rolf (ed): *Zeppelin Adventures* (trans Claud W Sykes), John Hamilton Ltd (London, 1931).
MacDonagh, Michael: *In London During the Great War*, Eyre & Spottiswoode (London, 1935).
Mason, F K: *Battle over Britain*, McWhirter Twins (London, 1970).
Merriam, F Warren: *First Through the Clouds*, Batsford (London, 1954).
Morison, Frank (Ross, Albert H): *War on Great Cities*, Faber & Faber (London, 1937).
Morpurgo, J E: *Barnes Wallis*, Longman (London, 1972).
Morris, Joseph: *The German Air Raids on Great Britain*, Sampson, Low, Marston & Co Ltd (London, 1925).
Neuman, G P (ed): *The German Air Force in the Great War* (trans J E Gurdon), Hodder & Stoughton (London, 1921).
Perfect, Charles Thomas: *Hornchurch During the Great War*, Benham (Colchester, 1920).
Poolman, Kenneth: *Zeppelins Over England*, Evans Brothers Ltd (London, 1960).
Purnell's History of the First World War (8 volumes), Phoebus Publishing Co (London, 1969).
Raleigh, Sir Walter A: *The War in the Air* Vol I, Oxford University Press (London, 1922).
Ramsey, Winston (ed): *The Battle of Britain – Then and Now*, Battle of Britain Prints International Ltd (London, 1980).
Rawlinson, Sir Alfred: *The Defence of London, 1915–1918*, Andrew Melrose (London, 1923).
Robertson, Bruce: *British Military Aircraft Serials 1912–1969*, Ian Allan (London, 1969).

Robinson, Douglas Hill: *The Zeppelin in Combat*, G T Foulis & Co Ltd (London, 1962).
Robinson, Douglas Hill: *Giants in the Sky*, G T Foulis & Co Ltd (London, 1973).
Robinson, Douglas Hill: *LZ129 'Hindenburg'*, Morgan-Dallas (Texas, 1964).
Roskill, S W (ed): *Documents Relating to the Naval Air Service* Vol 1, 1908–1918, Navy Records Office (London, 1969).
Scheer, Reinhard: *Germany's High Seas Fleet in the World War*, Cassell & Co Ltd (London, 1920).
Scott, Admiral Sir Percy: *Fifty Years in the Royal Navy*, George H Doran Co (New York, 1919).
Slessor, Sir John: *The Central Blue*, Cassell & Co Ltd (London, 1956).
Snowden Gamble, C F: *The Story of a North Sea Air Station*, Oxford University Press (London, 1928).
Staunton, G S: *Report on Police Observation Work in Connection with Raids by Hostile Aircraft and Men-of-War on the County of East Suffolk*, W S Cowell (Suffolk, 1919).
Sueter, Rear-Admiral Sir Murray: *Airmen or Noahs*, Sir Isaac Pitman & Sons Ltd (London, 1928).
Sutton, Squadron Leader H T: *Raiders Approach!*, Gale & Polden Ltd (Aldershot, 1956).
Thetford, Owen: *British Naval Aircraft, 1912–1958*, Putnam & Co Ltd (London, 1958).
Thompson, J O: *Dr Salter of Tolleshunt D'Arcy*, John Lane, The Bodley Head (London, 1933).
Travers, B: *A-sitting on a Gate*, W H Allen (London, 1979).
Von Buttlar-Brandenfels, *Freiherr* Treusch: *Zeppelins over England* (trans Huntley Patterson), G G Harrap (London, 1931).
Von Richthofen, *Freiherr* Manfred: *The Red Air Fighter*, 'The Aeroplane' & General Publishing Co (London, 1918).
Walter, E W: *Heroic Airmen and their Exploits*, Kelly (London, 1917).
Wilson, Herbert Wrigley: *The Great War* (13 volumes), Amalgamated Press (London, 1914–19).
Whitehouse, Arch: *The Zeppelin Fighters*, Robert Hale Ltd (London, 1966).
Winchester, Barry: *Beyond the Tumult*, Alison and Busby (London, 1970).
Wollard, Commander Claude L A: *With the Harwich Naval Forces, 1914–18*, George Kohler (Belgium) (Antwerp, date unknown).
Wood, Derek, with Dempster, Derek: *The Narrow Margin*, Hutchinson & Co (London, 1961).
Wright, C E: *The Fate of Zeppelin L32*, Chanticleer Publications (Essex, 1977).

Periodicals (additional to those appended in chapter notes)
Dodds, R V: 'The Canadian Zepp Killers', *Cross and Cockade Journal* (USA), Vol 6 No 3 (1965).
Dwelle, D C: 'The Davis Gun', *Cross and Cockade Journal* (USA), Vol 6 No 1 (1965).
Iron, C S: 'The Last of the Zeppelins', *Blackwoods*, January 1936.
Lloyd, T A ('Icarus'): 'No 39 Squadron', *The Army, Navy and Air Force Gazette*, Vol LXIX (1928).
Lloyd, T A ('Icarus'): 'Reminiscences of No 39 HD Squadron, RAF', *Air*, August–December 1929.
Lloyd, T A ('Icarus'): 'Memorial to No 39 (HD) Squadron', *Flight*, Vol XXIV (1932).
Lloyd, T A ('Icarus'): 'The Zepp Strafers', *Popular Flying*, Vol 11 No 8 (1933).
Miller, Major E: 'The Zeppelin Dropped Like a Gigantic Roman Candle into the North Sea', *East Anglia Monthly*, April 1981.
Outhwaite, C: 'The Sea and the Air', *Blackwoods*, November 1927.
Roskill, Captain S W: 'The Destruction of Zeppelin L53', *US Naval Institute Proceedings*, August 1960.
Rimell, R L: 'Reginald Alexander John Warneford', *Battle*, September 1975.
Rimell, R L: 'William Leefe Robinson', *Battle*, November 1975.
Rimell, R L: 'Frederick Sowrey', *Battle*, January 1976.
Rimell, R L: 'Egbert Cadbury and Robert Leckie', *Battle*, March 1976.
Rimell, R L: 'Stuart Douglas Culley', *Battle*, May 1976.
Rimell, R L: 'Zeppelmania', *Cross and Cockade Journal* (GB), Vol 12 No 2, 1981.
Rimell, R L: 'Death of a Zeppelin', *Flypast*, August 1982.
Rimell, R L: 'Warneford VC - Giant Killer', *Flypast*, September 1983.
Saunders, H A St G: 'Air Raids and Bombardments – Section 1, Airship Raids January 19, 1915–April 13, 1918', *Flight*, Vol XI (1919).
'The Strafing of LZ76 [L53]', *Blackwood's*, February 1922.

Index

A
Aachen (Germany), 129
Ackermann, *Leutnant* (*LZ37*), 68.
  Killed, 69.
Adams, Lieutenant A T (RFC), 111.
Ahrens, Heinrich (*L48*), 188.
Aircraft (American)
  Curtiss H4 'Small America', 167.
  Curtiss H8, 171.
  Curtiss H12 (Large America), 162, 165, 167–176, 181, 222.
  Curtiss H16, 171.
Aircraft (British)
  AD Scout, 76, 78.
  Armstrong Whitworth FK3, 90.
  Avro 504 (various), 36, 65, 152, 159, 200.
  Beardmore SB3D, 217, 221.
  BE2c, 14, 15, 39, 44, 52, 56–58, 82, 87–91, 94, 96, 98, 99, 107, 108, 119, 126, 138, 143, 153, 154, 156, 159, 160, 181, 182, 193, 198.
    Technical description of, 75f.
  BE2d, 75.
  BE8, 88, 89.
  BE8A, 89.
  BE12, 94, 110, 182, 183.
  Blackburn Triplane, 76.
  Bristol Fighter (F2A), 110, 111.
    (F2B), 138, 212, 229.
  Bristol Scout, 39, 52.
  de Havilland DH2, 111, 182, 183, 191.
  de Havilland DH4, 159, 162, 176, 209–211.
  de Havilland DH9, 159, 199, 209, 211.
  de Havilland Humming Bird, 126.
  Fane F1/40, 162.
  FE2b, 111, 182, 191, 192, 197, 199, 212.
  FE2d, 192, 197, 199.
  Felixstowe F1, 167.
  Felixstowe F2a, 167, 176, 199, 213.
  Felixstowe F3, 171.
  Felixstowe F5, 167, 171.
  Felixstowe Fury Triplane, 167.
  Gloster Grebe, 126.
  Handley Page O/100, 159.
  Martinsyde S1, 89, 159.
  NE 1, 78, 79.
  Parnall Scout, 79.
  Port Victoria PV2, 76.
  RE7, 110, 183.
  Robey Peters Davis Gun Carrier, (RRF 25 Mk II), 76–78.
  SE4a, 57.
  SE5a, 138, 229.
  Short 184, 169.
  Sopwith Baby, 59, 181.
  Sopwith 2F1 Camel, 138, 197, 201–205, 211, 217–226, 229.
  Sopwith Pup, 181, 193, 194, 196, 217.
  Sopwith Schneider, 153.
  Sopwith 1½ Strutter, 194.
  Sopwith Tabloid, 200.
  Sopwith Two-Seater Scout, 152.
  Supermarine 'Nighthawk,' 77, 78.
  Vickers FB 25, 79.
Aircraft (French)
  Blériot Monoplane, 31, 37, 56.
  Breguet Atlantic, 231.
  Caudron, 56, 152.
  Henry Farman, 65, 70–72.
  Maurice Farman, 88, 152, 159, 165, 190, 193.
  Morane Saulnier 'L', 65, 69, 70, 72.
  Nieuport, 65, 198.
  Voison, 64.
Aircraft (German)
  Albatros DIII 111, 204.
  Albatros Seaplane, 31.
  DFW biplane, 166.
  Dornier Flying Boat, 227.
  Fokker 'Eindecker', 15, 58, 75.
  Gotha, 138, 177, 229.
  Hansa Brandenburg Seaplane, 176, 221, 225.
  LVG CII, 164.
  Zeppelin Staaken, 177, 229.
Airships (British)
  HMA No 1, *Mayfly*, 30.
  HMA No 9, 25.
  R33, 125, 126.
  R34, 125.
  R35, 188.
  R36, 188.
  R37, 188.
  R38, 188.
Airships (German)
  LZ4, 139.
  ZI, 94.
  ZII, 94.
Airships (German Army)
  LZ37, 38, 65–67, 72.
    Destroyed, 68f.
  LZ38, 35–38.
    Destroyed, 70.
  LZ39, 38, 65, 67, 75, 93, 94.
  LZ74, 41, 42, 94.
  LZ77, 41, 42, 94.
  LZ79, 94.
  LZ87, 50.
  LZ88, 47–49, 50.
  LZ90, 47–49, 93, 95.
  LZ93, 47, 48, 50, 94.
  LZ97, 50, 52, 92–94.
  LZ98, 50, 51, 93, 96.
  LZ107, 169.
  LZ113, 229.
  LZ120, 229.
Parseval PIII, 94.
SL2, 41, 94.
SL3, 37.
SL9, 52, 53.
SL11, 93–96, 100–104, 107, 109, 114, 117, 131, 149, 153, 231, 232.
  Destroyed at Cuffley, 97f.
SL13, 95–97.
ZIX, 200.
ZX11, 94.
Airships (German Navy)
  L1, 139.
  L2, 139.
  L3, 33, 34.
  L4, 33, 34.
  L5, 35.
  L6, 33, 35.
  L7, 35, 155, 200, 229.
  L8, 34.
  L9, 13, 34, 35, 38, 39, 40, 41, 140.
  L10, 20, 21, 37–40, 56.
    Destroyed, 41.
  L11, 13, 38–43, 45, 47–52, 93, 99.
  L12, 38, 39.
    Destroyed, 40.
  L13, 13, 38–45, 47–52, 93, 99, 117, 137, 140, 142, 154, 156, 223.
  L14, 40–52, 93, 99, 117, 122, 137, 141, 142, 154, 156.
    Sabotaged, 227.
  L15, 43–45, 47–53, 93, 99, 102, 117, 141, 142, 154, 156, 158.
  L17, 45, 48, 49, 50–52, 93, 94, 117, 137, 142.
  L18, 155.
  L19, 25, 45.
    Destroyed, 46f.
  L20, 45, 46, 49, 50.
    Destroyed, 51.
  L21, 45, 49–53, 93, 99, 117, 137, 141, 142, 152, 154–158, 161, 162.
    Destroyed, 159f.
  L22, 47, 48, 51, 93, 99, 117, 137, 141, 142, 152, 155, 156, 165, 167, 168.
    Destroyed, 169f.
  L23, 49–52, 93, 99, 117, 137, 138, 141, 142, 168, 171, 179, 193, 194, 202.
    Destroyed, 195f.
  L24, 51, 52, 93, 99, 117, 142, 154, 156.
  L30, 51, 52, 93, 99, 117, 141, 142, 154, 229.
  L31, 25, 51–53, 117, 126, 138–142, 145–149, 151, 232.
    Destroyed, 143f.
  L32, 21–23, 52, 53, 93, 99, 117, 126, 132–140, 232.
    Destroyed, 127f.
L33, 117–119, 122–126, 139, 232.
  Crash lands at Little Wigborough (Essex), 120f.
  Technical description of, 18–28.
L34, 142, 152, 154, 159, 162.
  Destroyed, 155f.
L35, 154, 156, 167, 178, 179, 197.
L36, 154, 156, 178.
L37, 229.
L39, 167, 178, 179.
L40, 169, 170, 178–180.
L41, 169, 179, 197.
  Sabotaged, 227.
L42, 169, 171, 178–181, 197, 199.
  Sabotaged, 227, 228.
L43, 169, 171, 173, 176, 179.
  Destroyed, 174f.
L44, 169, 175, 176, 179, 180, 197.
  Destroyed, 198.
L45, 169, 175, 179, 180, 197.
  Captured, 198.
L46, 170, 173, 175, 176, 197.
  Destroyed, 199.
L47, 169, 179, 180, 197.
  Destroyed, 199.
L48, 162, 171, 173, 177, 179–185, 188–191, 213, 229, 232.
  Destroyed, 186f.
L49, 179, 197.
  Captured, 198, 199.
L50, 197.
  Destroyed, 198.
L51, 197.
  Destroyed, 199.
L52, 197, 199.
  Sabotaged, 227.
L53, 178, 197, 199, 205–211, 214, 217, 221, 222, 225, 226.
  Destroyed, 223f.
L54, 197–199, 204, 205.
  Destroyed, 202f.
L55, 197.
  Wrecked, 198.
L56, 199, 206, 207, 211.
  Sabotaged, 227.
L58, destroyed, 199.
L60, 197, 199, 204, 205.
  Destroyed, 202f.
L61, 199, 227.
L62, 199.
L63, 199, 206, 207, 211.
  Sabotaged, 227, 228.
L64, 199, 227.
L65, 20, 206, 208, 209, 210, 211.
  Sabotaged, 227.
L70, 205–208, 211–214.
  Destroyed, 209f.
L71, 229.
L72, 229.
L100, 227.
Airships (German, non-military)
  SL8, 52, 53, 93, 99.
  SL20, destroyed, 199.
  SL22, 229.
  Bodensee, 229.
  Nordstern, 229.
  LZ130, *Graf Zeppelin*, 232.
Airship Bases (German Army)
  Brussels-Etterbeek (Belgium), 67.
  Brussels-Evère (Belgium), 35, 36, 38, 65, 69, 70.
  Düsseldorf (Germany), 34.
  Gontrode, (Belgium), 34.
Airship Bases (Germany Navy)
  Ahlhorn (Germany), 129, 140, 173, 197, 199, 207, 227.
  Fuhlsbüttel (Germany), 33, 34, 139, 214.
  Hage (Germany), 12, 34, 40, 43, 45, 46, 47, 52, 140, 156.
  Jüterbog (Germany), 179, 229.
  Kiel (Germany), 139, 227.
  Nordholz (Germany) 27, 37, 38, 40, 42, 43, 45, 46, 48, 53, 99, 138, 173, 178–181, 197, 199, 206, 207, 210, 227, 228, 230–232.
  Seerappen (Germany), 229.
  Tondern (Germany), 45, 137, 179, 193, 196, 197, 201, 205, 207.
    Bombed by RAF, 202f.
  Wittmundhaven (Germany), 29, 197, 207, 227.
Airship Commanders (German Army)
  Boemack, *Kapitänleutnant* Fritz, 37.
  Falck, *Hauptmann*, 49.
  George, *Hauptmann* Fritz, 41, 42.
  Haegen, *Oberleutnant* Otto von der, 65, 67.
    Killed, 69.
  Horn, *Hauptman* Alfred, 41, 42.
  Lehmann, *Oberleutnant zur See der Reserve* Ernst, 49, 51, 95.
  Linnarz, *Hauptmann* Erich, 35–38, 50, 52, 56, 92, 93.
  Schramm, *Hauptmann* Wilhelm Emil Eugen, 50, 93–97.
    Killed, 99f.
  Wobeser, *Hauptmann von IGA*, 41, 94.
Airship Commanders (Germany Navy)
  Beelitz, *Kapitänleutnant* Helmut, 34.
  Böcker, *Kapitänleutnant der Reserve* Aloys, 18, 35, 40–44, 46–49, 51, 117–120, 125, 126, 140.
    Captured, 121f.
  Breithaupt, *Kapitänleutnant* Joachim, 12–17, 43, 44, 46, 47, 119.
  Buttlar-Brandenfels, *Kapitänleutnant* Horst Freiherr Treusch, 33, 35, 38, 39,

253

40, 42, 43, 45, 99, 117, 141, 142, 154, 198, 227.
Dietrich, *Kapitänleutnant* Martin, 47, 48, 99, 137, 178, 179, 180, 181, 212.
Dietrich, *Kapitänleutnant* Max Konrad Johannes, 45, 51, 142, 152, 154, 155.
  Killed, 156.
Dinter, *Oberleutnant zur See* Bernhard, 193.
  Killed, 195, 196.
Dose, *Kapitänleutnant* Walter, 207–211.
Ehrlich, *Kapitänleutnant* Herbert, 45, 48, 49, 50, 52, 156, 197, 199.
Eichler, *Kapitänleutnant der Reserve* Franz George, 179, 180, 182, 183, 186, 187, 189.
  Killed, 186.
Frankenberg, *Oberleutnant zur See*, 53, 99, 141, 152, 156, 158.
  Killed, 159f.
Freudenreich, *Kapitänleutnant* Michael von, 203, 211.
Friemel, *Oberleutnant zur See* Kurt, 156.
Fritz, *Kapitänleutnant* Hans, 33.
Ganzel, *Kapitänleutnant* Wilhelm, 99, 137, 141, 195.
Gayer, *Kapitänleutnant* Hans-Karl, 179, 198.
Hirsch, *Kapitänleutnant* Klaus, 37, 38, 40, 56.
  Killed, 41.
Hollender, *Kapitänleutnant* Heinrich, 156, 170, 175, 176, 197, 199.
Koch, *Kapitänleutnant* Robert, 51, 52, 93, 99, 142.
  Killed, 169.
Kölle, *Kapitänleutnant* Waldemar, 195, 196, 198.
Kraushaar, *Kapitänleutnant* Herman, 117, 137, 175, 176, 178.
  Killed, 174.
Lehmann, *Kapitänleutnant* Ulrich, 168.
Loewe, *Kapitänleutnant* Odo, 39, 40, 41.
  Drowned, 46f.
Lossnitzer, *Kapitänleutnant* Johann von, 205, 206, 207, 213.
  Killed, 209f.
Manger, *Hauptmann* Kuno, 52, 99, 156, 179, 199.
Mathy, *Kapitänleutnant* Heinrich, 13, 34, 35, 38–45, 47–49, 51–53, 56, 117, 126, 138, 142, 148–150, 154, 223, 230, 232.
  Early career, 139f.
  Killed in *L31*, 143f.
Peterson, *Oberleutnant zur See* Werner, 35, 39, 40, 44, 45, 48–51, 53, 99, 117, 126, 133, 136, 137, 140, 276.
  Killed in *L32*, 127f.
Platen-Hallermann *Kapitänleutnant* Magnus Graf von, 33, 34.
Prölss, *Kapitänleutnant der Reserve* Eduard, 49, 51, 52, 99, 208, 211, 222.
  Killed, 223.
Schubert, *Kapitänleutnant* Otto von, 50.
Schütze, *Korvettenkäpitan* Viktor, 47–50, 52, 99, 154, 156, 180, 183.
  Killed, 186f.
Schwonder, *Kapitänleutnant* Roderick, 198.
Sommerfeldt, *Kapitänleutnant* Erich, 99, 102, 169, 170.
Stabbert, *Kapitänleutnant* Franz, 45, 51, 179.
Stelling, *Hauptmann* August, 52, 160, 195.
Wenke, *Oberleutnant zur See* Friedrich, 38, 39, 40.
Wolff, *Kapitänleutnant* Guido, 99.
Wolf, *Kapitänleutnant der Reserve* Richard, 180.
Zaeschmar, *Kapitänleutnant* Walter, 207, 211.
Aldeburgh (Suffolk), 35, 40, 47, 182, 183.
Alderton (Suffolk).
  Bombed, 49.
Alford (Lincolnshire).
  Bombed, 50.
Ameland, Island (Holland), 46, 174, 181.
Anderby, (Lincolnshire).
  Bombed, 50.
Anchel (France), 191.
Annsley, Captain James (RFC), 131.
Arnstein, Dr Karl, 24.

Ashby, Sergeant Sydney (RFC), 182, 183, 190.
Ashby Woulds (Derby).
  Bombed, 46.
Ashford (Kent).
  Bombed, 40.
Aspull (Manchester).
  Bombed, 199.
Atwick (Humberside), 156, 212.

B
Babington, Flight Commander J T (RNAS), 200.
Bachman, *Admiral*, 38.
Bacton (Norfolk), 34, 93, 99, 138, 158, 159.
  Bombed, 50.
Badlesmere (Kent),
  Bombed, 40.
Baerlin, Second Lieutenant Arthur A, (RFC), 112, 113.
Balfour, Lord, 51.
Ball, Captain Albert, VC (RFC), 104.
Barker, Captain, (RAF), 176.
Barkingside (London).
  Bombed, 50, 92.
Barnby Moor (Humberside).
  Bombed, 156.
Barnes, Flight Lieutenant D M, (RNAS), 37.
Barnsley (South Yorkshire), 156, 158.
Barwise, Mechanic H B (RFC), 138.
Bass, Captain E C, 166.
Bayfield (Norfolk).
  Bombed, 45.
Bealings (Suffolk).
  Bombed, 53.
Beatty, Admiral David (RN), 201, 205.
Behncke, *Konteradmiral* Paul, 31.
Benitz, Lieutenant F A (RAF), 212.
Bennersley (Leicester).
  Bombed, 45.
Bentley, Captain J M (DADAE), 110.
Bentley, Lieutenant W O, 125.
Berlin (Germany) 140, 173, 227.
Berwick (on Tweed) (Northumberland) 52.
  Bombed, 48.
Besson, Flight Lieutenant (RNAS), 39, 40.
V Bethman-Hollweg, Theobald, Chancellor, 31.
Bettingham, Flight Lieutenant (RNAS), 40.
Beverley (Humberside), 49, 58, 98, 138, 197.
  Bombed, 47.
Bigsworth, Flight Commander A W (RNAS), 64, 65.
Billericay (Essex), 36, 129, 132–136.
Bird, Chief Petty Officer F W (RN), 187.
Birley, Lieutenant George H (RFC), 92.
Birmingham (West Midlands), 45, 46, 58, 89, 90, 190.
Bittles, Flight Lieutenant G H (RNAS), 181.
Black, Second Lieutenant C T (RFC), 92.
Blackheath (London).
  Bombed, 52.
Blackmore (Essex).
  Bombed, 48.
Boelcke, *Hauptmann* Oswald, 75.
Boldison, Second Lieutenant A (RFC), 111.
Bolton (Manchester).
  Bombed, 141.
Borkum Island (Germany), 39, 46, 169, 225.
Boswell, Sub Lieutenant H G (RNAS), 165.
Bow (London).
  Bombed, 119.
Bowers, Captain (RFC), 129.
Braintree (Essex), 179.
  Bombed, 48.
Brandenburg (Germany), 223.
Brandon, Second Lieutenant Albert de Bathe (RFC), 12, 15, 17, 48, 90, 92, 94, 119, 127.
Brandt, *Deck Offizier* Paul, 164.
Brenton, Flight Sub-Lieutenant H B (RNAS), 181.

Brentwood (Essex), 15, 36, 48, 117, 124, 127.
Briggs, Squadron Commander Edward Featherstone (RNAS), 200.
Brixton (London).
  Bombed, 126.
Brock, Lieutenant C C G (RFC), 90, 129.
Brock, Commander Frederick Arthur, 83.
Brock Bullet, 83, 119, 127, 168, 170, 174, 175.
Brock Immediate Rocket, 80.
Bromley-by-Bow (London).
  Bombed, 119.
Broomhill (Northumberland).
  Bombed, 49.
Brotton (Cleveland), 50.
  Bombed, 48.
Buckingham, James Francis, 82.
Buckingham Mk VII Bullet, 82, 83.
Bulls Cross (London).
  Bombed, 96.
Bungay (Suffolk).
  Bombed, 99.
Burge, Major C G (RFC), 145.
Burgh Castle (Norfolk), 52, 154, 158, 159, 160, 162, 181, 209, 211, 214.
Burnham-on-Crouch (Essex), 15, 36, 37.
Burton-upon-Trent (Staffordshire).
  Bombed, 45, 46.
Bury St Edmunds (Suffolk).
  Bombed, 35.
Buss, Flight Lieutenant (RNAS), 40.
Byland (Norfolk).
  Bombed, 42.

C
Cadbury, Major Egbert, DSO, 152, 161, 162, 168, 169, 181, 199, 211–215.
  Destroys *L21*, 159f.
  Attacks *L70*, 209f.
Caister (Norfolk), 49, 165.
Calais (France), 68, 169.
Calshot (Hampshire), 142, 217.
Cambridge, 42, 48, 97, 152.
Campbell, Captain, DSO, 62.
Campbell, Commander C I R (RCNC), 124, 125, 188.
Camberwell (London).
  Bombed, 198.
Cannock Chase (Staffordshire), 137, 151, 164, 214, 232.
Cannon, Flight Sub-Lieutenant R P (RNAS), 200.
Carlin How (Cleveland).
  Bombed, 50.
Carter, Lieutenant Harry (RDC), 148.
Castle Bromwich (West Midlands), 58, 59, 89, 90.
Central Flying School, Upavon (Wiltshire), 64, 79, 81, 88, 90.
Charles, Colonel Louis, 55.
Charlton, Admiral E (RN), 212, 213.
Chatham (Kent), 16, 17.
Chelmsford (Essex), 40, 47, 55, 119, 142, 190.
Cheshunt (Hertfordshire), 100, 102.
  Bombed, 41, 143.
Chesterton (Staffordshire).
  Bombed, 158.
Chingford (Essex), 55, 58, 152, 168, 193, 226.
Chislet Marshes (Kent).
  Bombed, 50.
Churcher, Colonel, 187.
Churchill, Winston, 54–56.
Clacton (Essex), 36, 41, 49, 55.
Clarke, Second Lieutenant E D (RFC), 183.
Clayhill (London).
  Bombed, 96.
Cleethorpes (Humberside).
  Bombed, 47.
Cliffe Station (Kent), 31, 35.
Clifton, Captain Edward Noel (RFC), 115, 193.
Colchester (Essex), 12, 42, 44, 95, 121, 122–124.
Coles, Constructor Lieutenant, 188.
Collett, Lieutenant C H (RNAS), 200.
Coltishall (Norfolk).
  Bombed, 43.

Cooper, Sergeant George H (RRA), 14, 17.
Cooper, Lieutenant H A (RFC), 111.
Cooper, Major P C (RFC), 182, 183.
Corkery, Captain Martin Percy (RAMC), 62.
Corkery, Patrick Courtenay, 63.
Corkery, Terance Reginald, 63.
Courtney, Lieutenant C L (RNAS), 165.
Covehithe (Suffolk), 47, 138, 162, 166, 209.
Coventry (West Midlands), 57, 58, 82, 199.
Cowan, Rear Admiral Sir Walter (RN), 205, 225.
Cowen, Colonel Joseph, 107.
Cramlington (Northumberland), 35, 49.
  Bombed, 49.
Cresswell, Lieutenant T S (RMLI), 165.
Cromer (Suffolk), 34, 45, 46, 49, 51, 138, 211.
  Bombed, 51.
Croydon (Kent), 44, 58, 90, 126.
Cuffley (Hertfordshire) 100–104, 108, 116, 232.
Culley, Group Captain Stuart, DSO, 217, 221, 222, 224–226.
  Destroys *L53*, 223f.
Curtiss, Glenn, 166.

D
D'Albiac, Second Lieutenant John H (RNAS), 64.
Danby High Moor (Yorkshire).
  Bombed, 50.
Davies, Wireless Operator H M (RNAS), 174.
Davies, Lieutenant-Colonel R (RAF), 205.
Davis Gun, 76, 77.
Denis, Corporal (French Air Service), 198.
Deptford (London).
  Bombed, 41, 52, 94.
Derby, 59, 214.
  Bombed, 61, 295.
Derby, Lord, 74.
Dickey, Captain Frederick Lea, DSC, 173, 174, 176.
Dickey, Robert Henry Frederick, 173.
Dickson, Captain William F (RAF), 202, 204.
Dilham (Norfolk).
  Bombed, 50.
Dimmock, Captain J M, 182.
Doddinghurst (Essex).
  Bombed, 46.
Dodworth (South Yorkshire).
  Bombed, 158.
Dog Kennel Hill (London), 50, 92.
Dörr, Dr, 177, 178.
Doughty, Lieutenant-Colonel Arthur, 138.
Dover (Kent), 52, 53, 55, 58, 59, 64, 68, 74, 99, 129, 180.
  Bombed, 31.
Drage, Dr Lovell, 101, 102.
Dringhouses (North Yorkshire).
  Bombed, 51.
Drydale, Captain G, 110.
Dudley (West Midlands).
  Bombed, 46.
Duncan, Captain (RE), 124.
Dungeness, (Kent), 95, 126, 129, 180.
Dunkirk (France), 39, 64, 65, 69, 159.
Dürr, Dr E H L, 20, 23, 177, 178.
Durnford, H G (RFA), 114.
Durston, Lieutenant C C (RFC), 90, 105, 129.

E
Easington (Northumberland).
  Bombed, 50.
Eastchurch (Kent), 31, 54, 55, 64, 138, 161, 200.
  Bombed, 39.
East Dereham (Norfolk), 158.
  Bombed 42, 180.
East Halton (Humberside).
  Bombed, 51.
East Retford (Nottingham).
  Bombed, 99.
Eckener, Dr Hugo, 25, 213.

Edinburgh (Scotland), 45, 108, 156, 159.
  Bombed, 49.
Edmonton (London).
  Bombed, 96.
Ellerkamm, *Maschinistenmaat* Heinrich (*L48*), 177, 187.
Ellison, Commander A (RNAS), 158, 160, 208.
Ellison, Major General G F, 76.
Eltham (London).
  Bombed, 52.
Ely (Cambridge).
  Bombed, 52.
Enfield (London), 102.
  Bombed, 96.
Engberding, *Marine Schiffbaumeister*, 177.
Ennion, Major (RAMC), 187.
Erith (Kent), 14, 31, 52.
Escadrille N152, 198.
Essendon (Hertfordshire), 103.
  Bombed, 102.
Evans, Captain (RAF), 116.
Everwood (Durham).
  Bombed, 49.
Ewood Bridge (Lancashire).
  Bombed, 141.

F
Fairnie, Leading Mechanic W (RNAS), 181.
Fane, Captain Gerard William Reginald, DSO, 50, 161, 162, 181, 211, 214, 219.
  Attacks *L21*, 159f.
Farnborough (Kent), 54, 55, 81, 88, 89, 145, 190.
Felixstowe (Suffolk), 35, 56, 165, 166, 168, 171, 174, 176, 215, 221, 222.
  Bombed, 52.
Festner, *Vizefeldwebel* Sebastian, 111.
Fiery Grapnel, RAF Mk II, 80, 81.
Finsbury (London), 44, 96.
Fisher, Lord (RN), 56.
Fiskerton (Nottingham).
  Bombed, 51.
Fitzgibbon, Lieutenant Robert Francis (RN), 72.
Flamborough Head (Humberside), 37, 39, 47, 48, 156.
Flèchette, 81.
Folkestone (Kent), 53, 74, 129.
Forth, Firth of (Scotland), 48, 49, 51, 59, 171.
Fraser, Second Lieutenant (RFC), 99.
Freeman, Flight Lieutenant Charles Teverill (RNAS), 52.
Freeman, Lieutenant Lewis (RNVR), 227.
Freiburg-in-Breisgau (Germany), 111, 112, 113, 115.
French, Field Marshal Lord, 58, 59, 104, 124, 125.
Frey, *Oberleutnant zur See* Richard, 152, 195, 197, 230.
Fridaythorpe (Humberside).
  Bombed, 51.
Friedrichshafen (Germany), 18, 122, 178, 196.
  Bombed, 200f.
Fyfield (Essex), 50.
  Bombed, 92.

G
Galpin, Captain Christopher John, DSO, 52, 165, 168–170, 175, 176.
Gaynor, Lieutenant W R (RNAS), 158.
George, Second Lieutenant H D K (RFC), 111.
Gerrard, Squadron Commander Eugene (RNAS), 64.
Ghent (Belgium), 65, 68, 69, 92.
Gilbertson-Smith, Colonel, 187, 188.
Goddard, Flight Lieutenant Victor (RNAS), 186.
Goldenhill (Stafford).
  Bombed, 158.
Goody, Engineer A W (RNAS), 174.
Grace, Captain (RN), 195.
Gran, Leading Mechanic Tryggve (RFC7), 108.
Grant, Leading Mechanic A (RNAS), 181.
Gray's Inn (London).
  Bombed, 44.
Graydon Carter, Colonel W, 189.

Gravesend (Kent), 117.
 Bombed, 37.
Great Burstead (Essex), 132, 134, 136, 232.
Great Hautbois (Norfolk).
 Bombed, 43.
Great Oakley (Northampton).
 Bombed, 53.
Great Yarmouth (Norfolk), 33, 35, 40, 42, 45, 49, 50, 52, 55, 99, 126, 138, 152–154, 158–162, 167–170, 175, 176, 181, 199, 208–213, 221, 225.
 Establishment of Air Station, 165f.
Greenwich (London).
 Bombed, 52, 94.
Gregory, Lieutenant R (RN), 165.
Grey, Squadron Commander Spenser D A (RNAS), 65.
Grey Towers (Essex), 63, 114, 149, 231.
Grimsby (Humberside), 46, 47, 137, 197.
Groves, Commander 'Crasher,' 63.

H
Hackenjors, *Unteroffizier*, 113.
Hackney (London), 74, 142.
 Bombed, 36.
Hainault Farm (Essex), 15, 17, 44, 50, 55, 57–59, 90, 92–94, 96, 98, 99, 119, 230, 232.
Hales bomb, 39, 65, 80, 81, 200.
Hall, Rear Admiral Sir Reginald, 59, 93, 117, 129, 168.
Hallam Fields (Derbyshire).
 Bombed, 45.
Hallgreen (West Midlands).
 Bombed, 199.
Hamburg (Germany), 178, 214.
Hamming, Captain (RAF), 116.
Hargrave, Major W B (RFC), 183.
Harris, Captain Arthur Travers (RFC), 50, 92, 191.
Harrow (Middlesex), 74, 89.
Harrow Weald (Middlesex), 108, 115, 116, 232.
Hartlepool (Cleveland), 49.
 Bombed, 199.
Harwich (Essex), 37, 39, 41, 49, 50, 52, 171, 179, 181–183.
 Bombed, 40.
Haughley (Suffolk), 47.
 Bombed, 99.
Hawker, Major Lanoe George (RFC) 191.
Heinen, Captain Anton, 229.
Hendon (London), 55, 58, 63, 152, 158, 166, 215.
Henham Hall (Essex).
 Bombed, 35.
Henderson, Sir David, 54, 104.
Henry, Sir Edward, 55.
Hervey, Second Lieutenant Hamilton E (RFC), 112–114.
Hertford (Hertfordshire), 143.
 Bombed, 44.
Hetton Downs (West Midlands).
 Bombed, 48.
Higgins, Major T C R (RFC), 58, 59, 90, 92, 93, 116, 131.
Hilliard, Flight Sub-Lieutenant G W (RNAS), 42.
Hilton-Jones, Squadron Commander R (RNAS), 217.
Hipper, *Käpitan zur See* Franz von, 139.
Hitchin (Hertfordshire) 96, 99.
 Bombed, 142.
Hither Green (London).
 Bombed, 198.
Hobbs, Group Captain Basil Deacon, DSO, OBE, DSC Bar, CVSM and Clasp, 131–173, 176.
 Attacks, *L43*, 174f.
Hodson, Lieutenant G F (RAF), 211.
Hodson, Captain John (RAF), 176.
Holborn (London).
 Bombed, 44.
Holcombe (Lancashire).
 Bombed, 141.
Holcombe Brook (Lancashire).
 Bombed, 141.
Holder, Squadron Leader Frank Douglas, OBE, MC, JP, DL, 182–184, 190.
Hollesley (Suffolk).
 Bombed, 49.
Holme, Lieutenant R C L (RFC), 92, 98.

Holt (Norfolk), 45, 158, 214.
Holt, Lieutenant-Colonel F V, 59, 90, 100, 104, 108.
Holt landing light, 15, 77.
Holt, Lieutenant Colonel Harold Edward Sherwin, 76.
Holzminden (Germany) 114, 115.
Honingham (Norfolk).
 Bombed, 50.
Honing Hill (Norfolk).
 Bombed, 50.
Hornchurch (Essex), 57, 63, 90, 100, 114, 128.
Horstead (Norfolk).
 Bombed, 43.
Houghton-le-Spring (Tyne and Wear).
 Bombed, 48.
Hounslow (Middlesex), 50, 58, 90, 92, 116, 131, 191.
Hucks, Second Lieutenant Benjamin C (RFC), 31.
Hull (Humberside), 14, 60, 122, 156, 197.
 Bombed, 38, 39, 47, 49, 52, 197.
Humber, River, (England), 33, 34, 38, 45, ,47, 49, 51, 52, 55, 56, 98, 99, 137, 142, 175.
Humberstone (Leicestershire).
 Bombed, 47.
Hunstanton (Norfolk), 45, 51, 211.
Hunt, Second Lieutenant B H (RFC), 96, 98, 99.

I
Ilges, *Leutnant* Walther, 164.
Immelmann, *Oberleutnant* Max, 75.
Immingham (Humberside), 45, 141, 166, 213.
 Bombed, 51.
Incendiary ammunition.
 See Brock, Buckingham, Pomeroy.
Ipswich (Suffolk), 12, 35, 40, 47, 49, 53, 188.
Ireland, Flight Commander C W P (RNAS), 35.
Iron, Captain C S (RAF), 208.

J
Jackson, Captain WD (RAF), 202, 204.
Jagdstaffel 3, 192.
Jagdstaffel 11, 111.
Jardine, Captain B G (RAF), 208, 210, 211.
Jarrow (Tyne and Wear).
 Bombed, 38.
Jenkins, Lieutenant (RFC), 57.
Johnston, Flight Lieutenant D K (RNAS), 39.
Jones, Captain H A, 140.
Joyce Green (Kent), 14, 44, 48, 55, 58, 89, 94, 98.
Joyce, Sergeant A J (RFC), 199.

K
Kemball, Flight Sub-Lieutenant Stanley (RNAS), 50.
Keys, Lieutenant R E (RAE), 214.
Kidsgrove (Stafford).
 Bombed, 158.
Killingholme (Lincolnshire), 47, 51, 55, 213.
Kilner, Flight Sub Lieutenant (RNAS), 65.
King George V, HM, 31, 106.
King's Lynn (Norfolk), 41, 211.
 Bombed, 34.
Kingsway (London).
 Bombed, 43.
Kirchner, *MG-Schutze Sergeant* Hermann (*LZ37*), 67.
Kirton (Lincolnshire).
 Bombed, 52, 182.
Kitchener, Lord Earl, 54, 58.
Knipton (Leicester).
 Bombed, 46.
Krüger, *Leutnant zur See* Kurt (*L70*), 214.
Kühne, *Oberleutnant* Otto (*L15*), 17.

L
Lampel, *Oberleutnant* (*LZ97*), 92.
Laroche, Baroness Raymonde de, 71, 72.
Laycock, Air Mechanic O R (RNAS), 168, 169.
Lealholm (North Yorkshire).
 Bombed, 50.

Leckie, Air Marshall Robert CB, DSO, DSC, DFC, 165, 168–170, 175, 176, 181, 208, 211–215.
 Destroys *L70*, 209f.
Leckler, Second Lieutenant Arthur Norman (RFC), 111.
Lefargue, Sub-Lieutenant (French Air Service), 198.
Leiston (Suffolk), 182, 187, 189.
Le Prieur, Lieutenant, 80.
 Rocket, 76, 79, 80.
Letheringsett (Norfolk).
 Bombed, 45.
Lincoln, 47, 51, 59, 117, 137, 141, 197.
Linford, Second Lieutenant R D (RFC), 199.
Little Heath (Hertfordshire).
 Bombed, 96.
Little Wigborough (Essex), 18, 120, 122–126, 232.
Liverpool (Merseyside), 45, 46, 197, 199, 217.
Livock, Captain G E (RNAS), 200.
Lloyd, Major Charles, 149.
Lloyd, Major I T (RFC), 191.
London, 12, 40, 45, 47–50, 52, 53, 71, 79, 84, 92–95, 99, 100, 101, 104, 107, 108, 126, 127, 138, 139, 142, 143, 169, 177, 179, 180, 182, 190, 198, 217.
 Air defence of, 55–88.
 Bombed, 50, 52, 92, 95f, 198.
 First aeroplane raid on, 164.
 First Army airship raid on, 36.
 First Naval airship raid on, 40.
 First squadron raid on, 41f.
London Colney (Hertfordshire).
 Bombed, 96.
Longcroft, Major L A H (RFC), 87.
Longmore, Wing Commander Arthur M (RNAS), 64, 65, 70, 71.
Loos (France), 130, 131.
Lorraine, Lieutenant-Colonel R (RFC), 191.
Loughborough (Leicestershire).
 Bombed, 45.
Low, Major C F G, 76.
Lower Bradley (West Midlands).
 Bombed, 45.
Lowestoft (Suffolk), 39, 40, 45, 49, 50, 51, 99, 142, 152, 158, 160, 181, 188, 208.
 Bombed, 35.

M
Mackay, Second Lieutenant J I (RFC), 96, 98.
Mackintosh, Second Lieutenant Robert R (RFC), 112, 114.
Mackintosh, Lieutenant WR (RN), 16.
Mallinson, Lieutenant P R (RFC), 90, 129.
Malone, Lieutenant L'Estrange (RN), 165.
Mansfield, Major W C H (RFC), 90.
Mappleton (Humberside).
 Bombed, 156.
Margate (Kent), 36, 39, 42, 50.
Marix, Flight Lieutenant Reginald Lennox George (RNAS), 200.
Marsden, Flight Lieutenant A J (RAF), 212.
Marsden, Flight Lieutenant Michael S (RNAS), 71, 72.
Martlesham Heath (Suffolk), 79, 162, 182, 222.
 Bombed, 182.
Martini, General Wolfgang, 232.
Masterman, Brigadier E A D, 227.
Maud, Lieutenant-Colonel Philip, 59, 60.
Meddis, Leading Mechanic G E (RNAS), 64, 65, 75.
Melton Mowbray (Leicestershire), 59, 199.
Menzies, Lieutenant J A (RFC), 197.
Merriam, Flight Lieutenant Warren (RNAS), 63.
Metzing, *Korvettenkäpitan* Friedrich, 139.
Michelham, Lord, 106, 132.
Middlesborough (Cleveland), 51.
 Bombed, 48.
Mieth, *Leutnant zur See* Otto (*L48*), 180, 186, 187.
Milich, *Obermaschistenmaat* Karl (*L48*), 189.

Millfield (Essex).
 Bombed, 48.
Mills, Flight Lieutenant John Stanley (RNAS), 38, 65, 71.
Millwall (London).
 Bombed, 94.
Millwall Docks (London).
 Bombed, 41.
Moore, Second Lieutenant C A (RAF), 197.
Moorsholm (Cleveland).
 Bombed, 50.
Morris, Second Lieutenant E C (RAF), 199.
Morrison, Flight Sub-Lieutenant C D (RNAS), 40.
Morton, Major A H (RFC), 90, 102, 129.
Mousehold (Norfolk), 43, 190.
Muhler, *Obersteuermann Alfred*, 67, 68, 69.
Mulock, Flight Sub-Lieutenant Redford Henry (RNAS), 36.
Munday, Lieutenant ER (RAF), 209, 211.
Mundesley (Norfolk), 45, 50.
 Bombed, 99.
Murdoch, General Burn, 132, 134.
Murrell, Sergeant Major (RAF), 116.
Myddleton-Gavey, Major H (RAMC), 133.

N
Needham, Henry Beech, 71, 72.
Neunzig, Michael (*L48*), 189.
Newbury Park (Essex).
 Bombed, 50.
Newchurch (Lancashire).
 Bombed, 141.
New Cross Gate (London).
 Bombed, 41.
Newmarket (Suffolk).
 Bombed, 50.
Nichol, Captain J, 49.
Nicholl, Flight Commander Vincent (RNAS), 160, 181, 208, 214.
Nicholson, Captain US (RN), 196.
Niemeyer, Camp Commandant Heinrich, 114.
Niemeyer, Camp Commandant Karl, 114, 115.
Noble-Campbell, Lieutenant C H (RFC), 199.
Norris, Captain (RN), 135.
Northolt (Middlesex), 57, 58, 88, 116.
Northrop, Flight Sub-Lieutenant John C (RNAS), 160.
North Weald Bassett (Essex), 90, 96, 98, 143.
 Bombed, 42.
Norwich (Norfolk), 34, 47, 48, 49, 52, 58, 59, 99, 142, 180.
Nottingham, 45, 46, 52, 99, 198, 211.
 Bombed, 137.

O
Oevee, Colonel, 122.
O'Malley, Second Lieutenant H MacD (RFC), 57.
Old Newton (Suffolk).
 Bombed, 50.
O'Meara, Lieutenant-Colonel W A J, 189.
Ongar (Essex).
 Bombed, 45, 92.
Ontario (Canada), 168, 171.
Orfordness (Suffolk), 35, 40, 42, 49, 182, 189, 190, 221, 222.
Ostend (Belgium), 15, 39, 64, 65, 68, 179, 200.
Ottawa (Canada), 168, 171, 176, 216.
Overseal (Derbyshire).
 Bombed, 46.
Owen, Lieutenant H G (RAF), 208.
Oxney (Kent).
 Bombed, 36.

P
Parker, Major L (RFC), 110.
Parkeston (Essex).
 Bombed, 40.
Payne, Lieutenant (RFC), 89.
Peldon (Essex), 120, 121, 124.
Pemberton Billing, Noel (RNVR), 75, 77, 200.

Penn Gaskell, Major L da C (RFC), 47.
Peterborough (Cambridgeshire), 158, 199.
Peters, *Obersteuermannsmaat* Friedrich (*L31*), 142.
Pinnock, Second Lieutenant C (RFC), 197.
Pitts, Lieutenant Commander John (RN), 213.
Plumstead (London), 14.
 Bombed, 52.
Pohl, Admiral Hugo von, 31, 44.
Police Officers
 Bead, Special Constable Henry, 122.
 Cowell, Police Superintendent, 124.
 Crack, Acting Sergeant, 149.
 Croxon, Sergeant, 149.
 Edwards, Sergeant, 120–122.
 Ellis, Inspector Allen, 132, 133.
 Fairhead, Special Constable, 122.
 Gollin, Commander, 103.
 Green, Constable, 100.
 Hyam, Special Constable Clement, 122.
 Kiddle, PC176 Arthur, 189.
 King, Special Constable Charles, 122.
 Lane, Sub Divisional Inspector, 149.
 Leakey, Constable, 100.
 Magor, Superintendent, 133.
 Marriot, Sergeant J, 186.
 May, Special Constable Joseph, 122.
 Meade, Special Constable Horace Charles, 122.
 Moore, Special Constable, 100.
 Nicholas, Special Constable Edgar, 121, 122.
 Ogden, Police Sergeant Thomas, 103.
 Palmer, PC John, 42.
 Sands, Sergeant Albert, 116.
 Smith, PC 354 Charles, 121, 122, 124.
 Sparkes, PC 186, 134.
 Traylor, Special Constable Elijah, 122.
 Unett, Captain, 122.
 White, Acting Sergeant Jesse, 100.
Pomeroy, John, 83.
Pomeroy Bullet (PSA and PSA MkII), 83, 119, 127, 168, 170, 174, 175.
Ponders End (London).
 Bombed, 96.
Porte, Lieutenant John Cyril (RN), 166, 167, 168.
Portsmouth (Hampshire), 55.
 Bombed, 139, 142.
Potters Bar (Hertfordshire), 96, 99, 100, 102, 103, 145–151, 232.
Powell, Captain R R (RAMC), 186, 187.
Powell, Lieutenant (RFC), 92.
Preston (Kent).
 Bombed, 50.
Pritchard, Lieutenant T B (RFC), 198.
Prondzynsk *Leutnant* von, 31.
Pulling, Flight Sub-Lieutenant Edward Laston, DSO, 52, 159–161, 164.
Pulling, George Perriam, 160.
Purfleet (Essex), 14, 15, 41, 54, 56, 93.
Pyott, Captain Ian Vernon, DSO, 155, 158, 159.
 Destroys *L34*, 156f.

Q
Queen Mary, HM, 31.

R
Ramsbottom (Lancashire).
 Bombed, 141.
Ramsgate (Kent), 39, 52, 55, 142.
 Bombed, 36, 180.
Ramsholt (Suffolk).
 Bombed, 49.
Ranken, Engineer Lieutenant Commander Francis (RN), 82.
Ranken Explosive Darts, 15, 81, 82, 83.
Raveningham Hall (Norfolk), 162.
Rawlinson, Commander W (RN), 44, 56, 93.
Rawtenstall (Lancashire).
 Bombed, 141.
Redcar (Cleveland), 52, 56, 164.
Reece, Second Lieutenant C M (RFC), 113.
Reeves, Flight Sub-Lieutenant F (RMAS), 50.
Reid, Private (RAF), 176.

255

Appendices

Rennie, Chief Technical Officer Lieutenant J D, 166.
Rentes, Rear Admiral von, 227.
Richthofen, *Leutnant* Manfred *Freiherr* von, 111, 115, 191.
Ridley, Second Lieutenant Claude Alward (RFC), 14, 48.
Robb, Squadron Leader JM, (RAF), 162.
Robertson, Flight Lieutenant A W (RNAS), 37.
Robertson, Lieutenant Colonel EDM (RAF), 221.
Robinson, Katherine (Baroness Heyking), 84–86, 102, 115, 116.
Robinson, Captain William Leefe VC, 84–86, 94, 100, 101, 107–109, 125–128, 131, 132, 145, 153, 232.
  Attacks LZ97, 92.
  Awarded VC, 104f.
  Destroys SL11, 96f.
  Dies, 115f.
  Enters RFC, 87–90.
  Joins 48 Sqn, 110f.
  POW 111–114.
Rodwell, Captain R M (RFC), 89.
Roeper, Flight Lieutenant B P H de (RFC), 52.
Rolls, Air Mechanic (RNAS), 165.
Rose, Sub-Lieutenant (RNAS), 65.
Ross, Captain L S (RFC7, 90.
Ross, Lieutenant (RFC), 94, 99.
Royal Aircraft Factory (Farnborough), 75, 79.
Royal Air Force Units
  6 Squadron, 225.
  14 Squadron, 225.
  210 Squadron, 25.
  212 Squadron, 209.
  228, Squadron, 208.
  231 Squadron, 176.
Royal Flying Corps Units
  1 Reserve Squadron, 190.
  4 Squadron, 87.
  5 Reserve Squadron, 58.
  7 Squadron, 183.
  8 Squadron, 75.
  9 Reserve Squadron, 190.
  10 Reserve Squadron, 89.
  12 Reserve Squadron, 131.
  14 Squadron, 57; as RAF, 225.
  16 Squadron, 112.
  19 Reserve Squadron, 59, 89, 90, 130.
  21 Squadron, 110, 183.
  23 Squadron, 57.
  24 Squadron, 111, 190.
  27 Squadron, 159.
  33 Home Defence Squadron (HDS), 59, 138, 197, 212.
  34 HDS, 58.
  36 HDS, 59, 156, 159, 197, 199.
  37 HDS, 58, 138, 182, 183.
  38 HDS, 59, 191, 212.
  39 HDS, 17, 59, 90, 92, 95, 96, 101, 108, 119, 131, 138, 143, 144, 198, 232.
  43 Squadron, 113.
  47 Squadron, 58.
  48 Squadron, 110f.
  50 HDS, 59, 99, 138.
  51 HDS, 59, 183, 212.
  55 Squadron, 159.
  73 Squadron, 115.
  75 HDS, 212.
  76 HDS, 212.
  100 Squadron, 145.
  141 Squadron, 138.
  143 Squadron, 138.
  148 Squadron, 191.
Royal Naval Air Service Units
  1 Squadron, 65.
  2 Squadron, 65.
  7 Squadron, 159.
Rutland, Flight Commander Frederick Joseph (RNAS), 194.

S

St Pol, (France), 65, 70, 71.
Salmond, Lieutenant Colonel W G, 57.
Salter, Dr J H, 123, 124.
Samson, Commander Charles Rumney (RNAS), 65, 200, 217–219, 221.
Sandringham (Norfolk), 34.
  Bombed, 99.
Sarigny, Captain Rene de (RFC), 101, 102, 135.

Sarre (Kent).
  Bombed, 50.
Saundby, Air Marshal Robert Henry Magnus Spencer, KCB, KBE, MC, DFC, AFC, DC, 183, 190, 191.
  Attacks L48, 183f.
Saxmundham (Suffolk), 38, 183, 186, 189.
Scapa Flow (Orkneys), 227, 228, 232.
Scarborough (North Yorkshire), 49, 51, 52, 56, 156.
Scarning (Norfolk).
  Bombed, 42.
Scheer, *Vizeadmiral* Reinhard, 44.
Schirlitz, *Leutnant zur See* Ernst Wilhelm (L33), 122.
Schultze *Maschinistenmaat* Adolf (L33), 122.
Schütte Lanz, see Airships (German).
Scott, Admiral Sir Percy, 57.
Scunthorpe (Humberside).
  Bombed, 45.
Seamer (North Yorkshire).
  Bombed, 51.
Seaton Carew (Cleveland), 156, 158, 159, 164, 197.
Selwyn, Captain (RAF), 116.
Shalford, Surrey.
  Bombed, 44.
Sharlston (West Yorkshire).
  Bombed, 158.
Shaw, Major General W, 104.
Sheffield (South Yorkshire), 55, 90, 137, 197, 211.
  Bombed, 141.
Shepherd, Squadron Commander P (RNAS), 200.
Sheringham (Norfolk), 34, 45, 46, 49, 142, 180.
Ships (Belgian).
  SS *Albertville*, 52.
Ships (British).
  HMT *Active*, 162.
  HMS *Adventure*, 38.
  Amethyst, 209, 212.
  Argus, 50.
  HMS *Brilliant*, 38.
  HMS *Bullfrog*, 213.
  HMS *Caledon*, 196.
  HMS *Campania*, 194.
  HMS *Canterbury*, 52.
  HMS *Carysfoot*, 52.
  HMS *Cassandra*, 217.
  Conway, 41.
  HMS *Conquest*, 52.
  HMS *Courageous*, 215.
  HMS *Curacao*, 217.
  HMT *Driver*, 213.
  HMS *Empress*, 201.
  Empress (steamer), 64, 70.
  HMS *Engadine*, 59, 201.
  HMS *Furious*, 194, 196, 200–202, 205.
  Hastaway, 41.
  HMS *Hercules*, 227.
  HMS *Hermes*, 215.
  HMT *Itonian*, 52.
  John Evelyn, 41.
  King Stephen, 46, 47.
  Louise, 41.
  SS *Lusitania*, 14, 160.
  HMS *Manxman*, 194.
  SS *Mauretania*, 227.
  Miranda II, 52.
  Manx Queen, 41.
  SS *Metagama*, 217.
  Mina Brea, 63.
  HMS *Nairana*, 217.
  SS *Orsova*, 217.
  HMT *Olivine*, 16.
  HMT *Peking*, 213.
  Poppy, 49.
  HMS *Prince*, 196.
  HMS *Queen Elizabeth*, 201, 205.
  HMS *Redoubt*, 217, 222–224.
  HMS *Riviera*, 201.
  SS *Royal Edward*, 35.
  Sagitta, 152, 213.
  HMT *Scomber*, 213.
  SS *Somali*, 63.
  HMT *Star of Britain*, 213.
  HMS *Thisbe*, 222.
  HMT *Topaz*, 213.
  HMS *Truculent*, 218, 221.
  HMT *Venus*, 214.
  HMS *Vindex*, 52, 59.

HMS *Vindictive*, 225.
HMS *Vulture*, 16.
Worcester, 144.
HMS *Yarmouth*, 193, 194, 195.
Zarefa, 152.
Ships (German).
  Baden, 227.
  Brandenburg, 151.
  Friedrich Karl, 139.
  Gneisenau, 139.
  Grosser Kurfürst, 155.
  Herzogin Cecilie, 155.
  Kolberg, 141.
  Mainz, 59.
  Magdeburg, 59.
  Mecklenburg, 214.
  S177 (T177), 140.
  Sigmaringen, 155.
  UC-6, 176.
  Westfalen, 214.
Shirley (West Midlands).
  Bombed, 199.
Shoeburyness (Essex), 36, 47, 53.
Shoreditch (London).
  Bombed, 37.
Simon, *Leutnant* George, 111.
Singer, Rear-Admiral Morgan (RN), 55.
Sippe, Flight Lieutenant Sidney Vincent (RNAS), 200.
Sitwell, Squadron Commander (RNAS), 63.
Skinningrove (Yorkshire) 52.
  Bombed, 41, 49, 50.
Sleaford (Lincolnshire).
  Bombed, 138.
Slessor, Second Lieutenant John (RFC), 44, 57.
Small, Lieutenant-Colonel R G (RFC), 191.
Smart, Captain Bernard, DSO, 193, 194, 204, 205, 225.
  Destroys L23, 195f.
  Attacks sheds at Tondern, 202f.
Smith, Lieutenant (RRA), 14, 17.
Smith, Flight Lieutenant Chichester (RNAS), 153.
Smyth-Pigott, Flight Commander J R W (RNAS), 39.
Soloman, Flight Lieutenant H P (RFC), 197.
South Bermondsey (London).
  Bombed, 44.
South Denes (Norfolk), 33, 40, 152, 153, 160, 165.
South Farningham (Kent), 15, 58, 89, 90, 98.
South Mimms (Hertfordshire).
  Bombed, 96.
Southminster (Essex), 15, 36, 37.
Southend (Essex).
  Bombed, 35.
Southwold (Suffolk), 35, 47, 49, 160, 175, 180.
Sowrey, Group Captain Frederick, DSO, MC, AFC, 90, 98, 100, 107, 108, 118, 126, 132–134, 136, 138, 145.
  Destroys L32, 127f.
  Service career, 129f.
Spenser Grey, Squadron Commander D A (RNAS), 200.
SPK MK II (Sparklet), Incendiary bullet, 82.
Springfield (Essex).
  Bombed, 48.
Sproatt, Captain C B (RAF), 209.
Sproxton (Leicestershire).
  Bombed, 47.
Stammers, Captain Robert Sidney (RFC), 90, 107, 129, 131, 132.
Stanford-le-Hope (Essex).
  Bombed, 48.
Starke, *Admiral*, 177.
Stephenson, Captain W S (RFC 7, 114.
Stewart, Lieutenant D J (RFC), 111.
Stewart, Lieutenant M S (RFC), 92.
Stoke Newington (London), 142.
  Bombed, 36.
Stoke-on-Trent (West Midlands).
  Bombed, 45.
Stowmarket (Suffolk), 137.
  Bombed, 47.
Strasser, *Fregattenkäpitan* Peter, Chief of German Naval Airship Division, 33, 35, 39–41, 45, 47, 48, 52,

117, 138–140, 142, 150, 152, 154, 164, 168, 169, 171, 175, 177–181, 191, 197, 199, 205–207, 212–214, 227, 230, 232.
  Killed aboard L70, 209f.
Stratford (London).
  Bombed, 119.
Streatham (London).
  Bombed, 126.
Sudbury (Suffolk).
  Bombed, 48.
Sueter, Captain Murray (RN), 54–56, 65.
Suttons Farm (Essex), 44, 50, 57–59, 88–90, 92–94, 100, 104, 107, 119, 126, 129–131, 138, 232.
Swadlincote, (Derbyshire).
  Bombed, 46.
Swaffham (Norfolk), 158.
  Bombed, 45.
Square, Sub-Lieutenant H H (RNAS), 40.

T

Tempest, Major Wulstan Joseph, DSO, MC, AFC, 90, 105, 114, 131, 148, 149.
  Destroys L31, 143f.
Terschelling Island (Holland), 34, 47, 168, 169, 170, 176, 180, 224.
Thames, River (England), 12, 15, 31, 33, 39, 44, 47, 50, 52, 55, 92, 120, 126.
  Estuary, 48, 54, 117.
Theberton (Suffolk), 184, 186, 188, 189, 232.
Thetford (Norfolk), 58, 131, 138.
  Bombed, 52.
Thistleton (Leicestershire).
  Bombed, 47.
Thompson, Leading Mechanic (RNAS) 175.
Thornton, Second Lieutenant H J (RFC), 197.
Thrapston (Northampton).
  Bombed, 45.
Thurston, Flight Lieutenant (RNAS), 73.
Thyne, Captain T K (RAF), 202.
Tipton (West Midlands).
  Bombed, 45, 46.
Tinsley, Sergeant H, (104).
Todmorden (Lancashire).
  Bombed, 141.
Tomkins, Lieutenant (RAF), 211.
Townsend, General, 92.
Travers, Flight Lieutenant Ben (RFC), 37, 193.
Trench, Major R M, 17, 122.
Trenchard, Major General Hugh, 110.
Trentham (Stafford).
  Bombed, 158.
Trimley (Suffolk).
  Bombed, 52.
Trowley (Leicestershire).
  Bombed, 45.
Tydd St Mary (Lincolnshire).
  Bombed, 199.
Tudor, Rear-Admiral (RN), 55.
Turner, Lieutenant E E (RFC), 128.
Tunstall (Humberside), 47, 48, 197.
Tunstall (Staffordshire).
  Bombed, 158.
Tyrwhitt, Commodore Reginald (RN), 206, 217, 222, 224, 225.

U

Uecker, *Maschinistenmaat* Wilhelm, (L48), 187.
Unwin, Major E F (RFC), 47.
Usborne, Wing Commander N, 79.

V

Vancouver (Canada), 217.
Vandenthorpe, Corporal (French Air Service), 198.
Vaughn Lee, Rear Admiral (RN), 56, 58.
Vickers Crayford Rocket Gun, 79.

W

Wakefield, Sir Charles, Mayor of London, 17.
Walker, Captain, 134, 135.
Walker, Flight Lieutenant (RNAS), 181.
Walmer (Kent), 50.
  Bombed, 153.

Walsall (West Midlands), 45.
  Bombed, 46.
Wallsend (Tyne and Wear).
  Bombed, 35.
Waltham Abbey (Essex), 41, 49, 55.
Walthamstow (London), 103.
  Bombed, 40, 96.
Walton (Suffolk).
  Bombed, 52.
Wangford (Suffolk).
  Bombed, 47.
Warburton, Lieutenant Edward Darien (RFC), 111.
Ware (Hertfordshire), 143.
  Bombed, 99.
Warneford, Sub-Lieutenant Reginald Alexander John, VC, 62, 63, 65, 66, 70–75.
  Destroys LZ37, 68f.
Watkins, Lieutenant (Temporary Captain), Loudon Pierce, MC, 190–192.
  Attacks L48, 183f.
Watteville, Lieutenant Colonel de, 187.
Wednesbury (West Midlands).
  Bombed, 45, 46.
Werther, *Korvetten Käpitanleutnant* Paul, 227.
West Hartlepool (Cleveland), 156, 162, 164.
  Bombed, 155, 199.
Whatling, Chief Petty Officer V F (RNAS), 168, 169.
Whipple, Captain Herbert Connell, 108.
Whipple, Joan, see Uppleby Stapylton-Smith, 108, 109, 115, 116.
Whitby (North Yorkshire), 51, 52.
Whitley Bay (Tyne and Wear).
  Bombed, 52.
Wickelhausen, Hertha, 140.
Wigan (Manchester).
  Bombed, 199.
Wigram, Major C (RFC), 199.
Wilhelm II, *Kaiser*, 31, 38, 42.
Wilkens, Captain (RAF), 116.
Wilkinson, Flight Commander Allan Machin (RFC), 111.
William, Second Lieutenant H L (RAF), 212.
Williams, Lieutenant, N E (RAF), 202, 204.
Williams, Lieutenant P G (RNAS), 194.
Williamson, Captain (RFC), 90.
Willington (Tyne and Wear).
  Bombed, 38.
Wilson, Flight Lieutenant John Phillip (RNAS), 38, 65, 71.
Windmill Hill (London).
  Bombed, 49.
Winterton (Humberside), 33, 34, 43, 46.
Wisbech (Cambridge).
  Bombed, 46.
Witham (Essex), 120, 123, 124, 170.
Witton (Norfolk).
  Bombed, 50.
Woodbridge (Suffolk), 42, 53.
  Bombed, 40.
Woodhouse, Captain W J (RFC), 53, 99.
Woodridden Farm (London).
  Bombed, 49.
Woolwich (London), 14, 17, 63, 92.
  Bombed, 45.
Wridgeway, Lieutenant C W (RFC), 192.

Y

Yates, Second Lieutenant R (RFC), 57.
Yewlett, Lieutenant W A (RAF), 202, 204.
York (North Yorkshire) 51, 90.
  Bombed, 141, 156.

Z

Zeppelins, see Airships (German)
Zeppelin, Count Ferdinand von, 18, 155, 213.

256